Cognition

Cognition

Margaret Matlin

State University of New York at Geneseo

Holt, Rinehart and Winston
New York Chicago San Francisco Philadelphia
Montreal Toronto London Sydney Tokyo
Mexico City Rio de Janeiro Madrid

Publisher: John L. Michel
Acquisitions Editor: Marie Schappert
Senior Project Editor: Arlene Katz
Production Manager: Annette Mayeski
Art Director: Gloria Gentile
Managing Editor: Jeanette Ninas Johnson
Text Design: Caliber Design Planning, Inc.
Cover Design: Gloria Gentile

Library of Congress Cataloging in Publication Data

Matlin, Margaret W.
  Cognition.

  Bibliography: p. 383
  Includes index.
  1. Cognition.   I. Title.
BF311.M426   1983   153   82-9333
                             AACR2

ISBN 0-03-057461-7

Copyright © 1983 by CBS COLLEGE PUBLISHING
Address correspondence to:
383 Madison Avenue
New York, N.Y. 10017

Printed in the United States of America
Published simultaneously in Canada

4 5 6   038   9 8 7 6 5 4 3 2 1

CBS COLLEGE PUBLISHING
Holt, Rinehart and Winston
The Dryden Press
Saunders College Publishing

Copyright Acknowledgments

Demonstration 2.4, p. 24. Eleanor J. Gibson, PRINCIPLES OF PERCEPTUAL LEARNING AND
    DEVELOPMENT, © 1969, p. 88, Fig. 5.5. Reprinted by permission of Prentice-Hall, Inc.,
    Englewood Cliffs, N.J.

Figure 3.1, p. 50. R. C. Atkinson and R. M. Shiffrin. Human memory: A proposed system and its control processes. In K. W. Spence & J. T. Spence (Eds.), *The psychology of learning and motivation: Advances in research and theory* (Vol. 2). Copyright 1968 by Academic Press. Reprinted by permission.

Figure 3.5, p. 65. D. D. Wickens, R. E. Dalezman, and F. T. Eggemeier, Multiple encodings of word attributes in memory. *Memory and Cognition, 1976, 4,* 307–310. Reprinted by permission of the Psychonomic Society.

Figure 3.7, p. 83. E. E. Smith, Theories of semantic memory. In W. K. Estes (Ed.), *Handbook of learning and cognitive processes* (Vol. 6: *Linguistic functions in cognitive theory*). Copyright 1978 by Lawrence Erlbaum Associates. Reprinted by permission.

Figure 3.9, p. 91. G. H. Bower and M. C. Clark. Narrative stories as mediators for serial learning. *Psychonomic Science,* 1969, *14,* 181–182. Reprinted by permission of the Psychonomic Society.

Demonstration 4.1, p. 99. R. N. Shepard and J. Metzler. Mental rotation of three-dimensional objects, *Science,* 1971, *171,* 701–703. Copyright 1971 by the American Association for the Advancement of Science. Reprinted by permission.

Figure 4.1, p. 100. R. N. Shepard and J. Metzler. Mental rotation of three-dimensional objects, *Science,* 1971, *171,* 701–703. Copyright 1971 by the American Association for the Advancement of Science. Reprinted by permission.

Figure 4.3, p. '105. A. Paivio, Comparison of mental clocks. *Journal of Experimental Psychology: Human Perception and Performance.* 1978, *4,* 61–71. Copyright 1978 by the American Psychological Association. Reprinted by permission of the publisher and author.

Figure 4.4, p. 107. R. N. Shepard and S. Chipman, Second-order isomorphism of internal representations: Shape of states. *Cognitive Psychology,* 1970, *1,* 1–17. Reprinted by permission of Academic Press.

Figure 4.6, p. 119. K. A. Wollen, A. Weber, and D. H. Lowry, Bizarreness versus interaction of mental images as determinants of learning. *Cognitive Psychology,* 1972, *3,* 518-523. Reprinted by permission of Academic Press.

Demonstration 5.7, p. 160–161. J. J. Jenkins, Remember that old theory of memory? Well, forget it. *American Psychologist,* 1974, *29,* 785-795. Copyright 1974 by the American Psychological Association. Reprinted by permission of the publisher and author.

Figure 6.2, p. 193. P. Winston, Learning to identify toy block structures. In CONTEMPORARY ISSUES IN COGNITIVE PSYCHOLOGY: THE LOYOLA SYMPOSIUM, edited by Robert L. Solso. Copyright 1973 by V. H. Winston & Sons; reprinted by permission of Hemisphere Publishing Corporation, present holder of the copyright.

Demonstration 6.6, p. 196. J. S. Bruner, J. J. Goodnow, and G. A. Austin, *A study of thinking.* Copyright 1956 by John Wiley & Sons, Inc. Reprinted by permission.

Figure 6.4, p. 202. E. H. Rosch, Natural categories. *Cognitive Psychology,* 1973, *4,* 328–350. Reprinted by permission of Academic Press.

Figure 6.5, p. 203. E. H. Rosch, Natural categories. *Cognitive Psychology,* 1973, *4,* 328–350. Reprinted by permission of Academic Press.

Table 6.2, p. 207. E. Rosch and C. B. Mervis, Family resemblances: Studies in the internal structure of categories. *Cognitive Psychology,* 1975, *7,* 573–605. Reprinted by permission of Academic Press.

Figure 6.7, p. 214. E. L. Newport and U. Bellugi, Linguistic expression of category levels in a visual-gestural language: A flower is a flower is a flower. In E. Rosch & B. Lloyd (Eds.). *Cognition and categorization.* Copyright 1978 by Lawrence Erlbaum Associates. Copyright, Ursula Bellugi. Reprinted by permission.

Figure 7.1, p. 222. Instruction manual: Double insulated 13" and 16" lawn trimmers, p. 2. Assembly instructions compliments of Allegretti & Company, Chatsworth, CA 91311—Service Department.

Figure 8.3, p. 281. D. E. Rumelhart and A. A. Abrahamson, A model for analogical reasoning. *Cognitive Psychology,* 1973, *5,* 1–28. Reprinted by permission of Academic Press.

Figure 9.1, p. 298. M. Manis, I. Dovalina, N. E. Avis, and S. Cardoze, Base rates can affect individual predictions. *Journal of Personality and Social Psychology,* 1980, *38,* 231–248. Copyright 1980 by the American Psychological Association. Reprinted by permission of the publisher and author.

This book is dedicated to

**Helen and Donald White
and
Clare and Harry Matlin**

Preface

For the past two years, I've been sitting in the upstate New York woods, communing with my Smith-Corona. The product of these communings is *Cognition*. Some instructors may wonder why another book on this topic is necessary. Their students could provide a partial answer: previous textbooks were typically written for instructors, rather than students. Consequently, they were often either difficult or boring, and they usually did not employ any learning aids.

Cognition is student-oriented for the following reasons:

- The writing style is clear and interesting.
- The text stresses how cognition is relevant in our everyday, real-world experiences.
- Numerous, easy-to-perform demonstrations illustrate important experiments in cognition and clarify central concepts.
- The text frequently examines the applications of cognition in other disciplines, such as education, clinical psychology, law, and the arts.
- Each new term is introduced in **boldface print** and is accompanied by a concise definition in the same sentence.
- Pronunciation guides are included for new terms that are difficult to pronounce.
- Chapters are introduced with an outline and a preview.
- There are summaries within each chapter at the end of each major section. Students can review and consolidate material before moving to the next section, rather than waiting until the chapter's end for a single, long summary.
- A list of review questions and new terms concludes each chapter.

In addition, instructors will find the following features appealing:

- *Cognition* offers a comprehensive overview of the field. There are chapters on perception, memory, imagery, language, concept formation, problem solving and creativity, reasoning, and decision making.
- Two additional chapters examine cognitive development throughout the lifespan, and individual differences in cognition. Each of these chapters

has separate sections on memory, language, and concept formation/ problem solving. As a result, instructors have additional flexibility. For example, they may wish to assign Chapter 3 on memory, then the section on the development of memory in Chapter 10, and then the section on individual differences in memory in Chapter 11.

- Each chapter can stand by itself. For example, a new term such as *heuristics* is defined in each chapter in which it is discussed. This feature allows instructors considerable flexibility in the sequence of coverage.
- The bibliography includes more than 600 references.

I have many individuals to thank for their impressive efforts related to this book. First, I would like to praise the people at Holt, Rinehart and Winston. Marie Schappert, Psychology Editor, has been an ideal collaborator on this project. Her expertise, planning skills, encouragement, and sensitivity are invaluable! Arlene Katz, Senior Project Editor, has been spectacular in managing the production end of *Cognition*. Her editorial skills, carefulness, and sense of humor make even the copyediting experience pleasurable! Others who deserve special thanks include Ray Ashton, John Michel, Fran Beaumont, Joan Green, Gloria Gentile, George Bergquist, and Annette Mayeski.

During my undergraduate and graduate training, many professors kindled my enthusiasm for the growing area of cognition. I would like to thank Gordon Bower, Albert Hastorf, Leonard Horowitz, and Eleanor Maccoby of Stanford University, and Edwin Martin, Arthur Melton, Richard Pew, and Robert Zajonc of University of Michigan.

Many others have contributed in important ways to this book. Anthony DelBove deserves high praise for his skill in finding and duplicating references, checking the bibliography, proofreading the manuscript and compiling the name index. Jean Amidon, super-typist, was exceptionally speedy and professional. Thanks are also due to Connie Ellis and Mary Lou Perry for their numerous services that allowed me to devote more energy to writing.

Many colleagues provided information that I used throughout the book. In particular, I would like to thank Jacques Chevalier, Zelda Chevalier, Jerome Meyer, Susan Whitbourne O'Brien, and George Rebok. The students in my course in Cognitive Psychology also gave me valuable feedback on many occasions.

I would also like to express my appreciation to the reviewers. Richard Kasschau (University of Houston) deserves special thanks for reading the entire manuscript twice and maintaining his enthusiasm and encouragement throughout. Mark Ashcraft (Cleveland State), Randolph Easton (Boston College), Barbara Goldman (University of Michigan—Dearborn), Harold Hawkins (University of Oregon), Joseph Hellige (University of Southern California), Richard High (Lehigh University), James Juola (University of Kansas), and R. A. Kinchla (Princeton University) also made superb suggestions for improving factual, organizational, and syntactic aspects of the manuscript.

The State University of New York deserves acknowledgment for granting me a sabbatical leave. A major part of this book was written during that period.

The final words of gratitude belong to various family members. My husband, Arnie, and my daughters, Beth and Sally, deserve thanks for their help, enthusiasm, and appreciation; their pride in my accomplishments helps enormously. Last, I want to thank four important people in my life, my parents by birth and my parents by marriage: Helen and Donald White, and Clare and Harry Matlin.

M. Matlin
May 1982

Contents

8 Reasoning   258

9 Decision Making   288

10 *Cognitive Development*   **321**

Cognition

1

Introduction

This book is about **cognition,** or mental activities. Cognition involves how we acquire, store, retrieve, and use knowledge. If we use cognition every time we acquire a bit of information, place it in storage, bring it out of storage, or use that information in some way, then cognition *must* include a wide range of mental processes. We will be investigating eight kinds of mental processes in this book: perception, memory, imagery, language, concept formation, problem solving, reasoning, and decision making.

You may have seen a related term, cognitive psychology. **Cognitive psychology** has two meanings; sometimes it is a synonym for cognition, and sometimes it refers to a particular approach to psychology. The cognitive approach is often contrasted with two other current perspectives: the behaviorist perspective, which emphasizes behaviors that are observable, and the psychoanalytic perspective, which focuses upon emotions and feelings.

Why should you study cognition? First of all, cognition is a major portion of the study of human psychology. Think about what you have been doing in the past hour; there are probably few activities that did not somehow involve perception, memory, language, or some other higher mental processes. In fact, you are even using cognition to think about what you have been doing!

A second reason for studying cognition is that the cognitive psychology outlook has widespread influence on other areas of psychology. For instance, social psychology has been deeply affected by cognitive psychology (e.g., Hendrick, 1977; Nisbett & Ross, 1980; Sampson, 1981). Moreover, the area of personality is frequently examined from the cognitive view (e.g., Forgus & Shulman, 1979). In addition, a cognitive approach to educational psychology is popular (e.g., Reid & Hrensko, 1981). The cognitive psychology of Jean Piaget—which we shall briefly examine in Chapter 10—dominates much of developmental psychology. Cognitive psychology has even penetrated the study of animal learning and behavior (e.g., Bolles, 1975; Hulse, Fowler, & Honig, 1978). Thus an appreciation of cognitive psychology will be helpful in other areas in psychology.

The final reason for the study of cognition is more personal. You own an impressive piece of equipment—your own mind—and you use this equipment every minute of every day. When you buy a new car, you often receive a booklet that describes how it works. However, no one issued you an owner's manual when you were born. In a sense this book is an owner's manual, describing what we know about how your mind works. In many cases, you will also find hints on how to improve performance. (Unfortunately, however, there is no five-year warranty or list of service representatives in the back of the book!)

We have four areas to cover in the remainder of this introductory chapter: a brief history of cognitive psychology, an overview of the chapters in the book, discussion of several common themes that occur throughout the book, and hints on how to use the book.

A Brief History

The history of cognitive psychology begins about 100 years ago, although even the early Greek philosophers had wondered about how humans acquire knowledge (Boring, 1950). The year 1879 is usually celebrated as the birthday of scientific psychology because it was then that Wilhelm Wundt (pronounced "Voont") opened his laboratory in a small lecture room in Leipzig, Germany. Thus, psychology emerged as a new discipline that was separate from philosophy and physiology. Within several years, students flocked from around the world to study with Wundt, who eventually sponsored 186 Ph.D. dissertations in psychology (Hearst, 1979).

Wundt and his students most often examined psychological issues with the **introspection technique,** a method in which carefully trained subjects described what they were thinking as they worked on a task. In many ways, Wundt's rigorous methods were similar to modern-day cognitive research. Wundt specifically wrote, however, that higher mental processes such as thinking, language, and problem solving could not be investigated with the introspective technique. As we will see in our discussion of consciousness in Chapter 2, psychologists are still arguing about whether we can have reliable insights into our own higher mental processes.

Although introspection was alive and well in Europe at the end of the nineteenth century, Americans were only lukewarm about this intense, structured method. William James was the most prominent American psychologist at that time. James preferred a more informal approach, and his book *Principles of Psychology* (1890) gives detailed descriptions about the stream of human experience. His most significant contributions to the field of cognitive psychology were his theories on memory. His proposals about two kinds of memory and his distinction between memory structure and memory process were very close to the memory models proposed about 80 years later.

Around 1900, behaviorism developed as laboratory psychologists began to attack the introspective technique. An American named John Watson was one of the strongest supporters of **behaviorism,** an approach that relied only on objective, observable reactions. The behaviorists believed that introspection was unscientific and consciousness was far too vague to be investigated properly. In fact, any terms referring to mental events, such as *image, idea,* or *thought,* were rejected. Thinking was simply classified as subvocal speech. In other words, if you are thinking as you read this sentence, early behavioral theory says that you are really just talking to yourself, but so quietly that you cannot be heard.

Although it is unfortunate that behaviorists refused to study mental activity, behaviorism still contributed a great deal to the methods of current cognitive psychology. Behaviorists stressed that concepts should be carefully and precisely defined. For example, *performance* might be defined as the number of trials that a rat required to complete a maze without error. Similarly, research in cognitive psychology stresses precise definitions. Furthermore, behaviorists mainly used laboratory experiments in their research. Although some cognitive psychologists (for example, Neisser, 1976, 1978), have argued that research should be more concerned with the mental activities that occur in everyday life, the laboratory experiment is still the most popular kind of research.

While behaviorism thrived in the United States, a different approach arose in Europe. **Gestalt psychology** (pronounced "Geh-*shtahlt*") emphasizes that the whole is greater than the sum of its parts and that humans have basic tendencies to organize what they see. The Gestalt psychologists strongly objected to the introspective technique of analyzing experiences into separate components because they stressed that the whole experience is greater than the sum of these separate components. For example, a picture of a square is more than the sum of four straight lines of equal length. Gestalt psychologists also emphasized the importance of insight in problem solving; initially the parts of a problem seem unrelated to each other, but suddenly the parts fit together into a solution. Most of the early research in problem solving was conducted by Gestalt psychologists. Their work represents an important contribution to cognitive psychology, even though Gestalt theory itself has little current support.

In the late 1950s and early 1960s interest in cognitive processes began to emerge. In fact, the increasing enthusiasm for the cognitive approach in preference to the behaviorist approach has sometimes been called the "cognitive revolution." Although behaviorism still has its strong supporters in some areas, many psychologists currently favor cognitive perspectives.

Several factors contributed to the dramatic rise in popularity of cognitive psychology:

1. Psychologists were becoming increasingly disappointed with the behaviorist outlook that dominated American psychology. It was difficult to explain complex human behavior using only the terms and concepts from learning theory.
2. Information processing was developed from origins in computer science and in the communication sciences, and this view was appealing to many psychologists. This approach is currently the major perspective within cognitive psychology. According to the **information processing approach,** information is handled by a sequence of stages; each stage performs a specified function, and then the information proceeds to the next stage for a different kind of processing. Thus our sensory receptors receive information, which is changed during one stage and passed on through a sequence of stages until we either respond or store the information in memory. One extremely influential information processing model, for example, proposed that information passes through three kinds of memory processing stages—sensory memory, short-term memory, and long-term memory. This particular model, outlined by Atkinson and Shiffrin (1968), will be discussed in more detail in Chapters 2 and 3.

    The information processing approach is partly based on a computer analogy; humans resemble computers that take in information, process it, and produce a response. Information processing models are often expressed in terms of a **flowchart,** or diagram with arrows connecting a series of boxes, each box representing one kind of processing. Figure 3-1 is one example of a flowchart.
3. Linguists, such as Noam Chomsky (1957), rejected the behaviorist approach to language acquisition and emphasized psychological processes necessary for language use. Specifically, the linguists proposed that the structure of language was too complex to be explained in behaviorist terms. Many linguists suggested that humans have the inborn ability to master language, an idea that clearly contradicted the behaviorist approach.
4. Memory research began to blossom at the end of the 1950s. Researchers explored the possibility of different kinds of memory, examined how memory

was organized, and proposed models of memory. Behavioral terms were of limited usefulness in this area.

5. Piaget, whose theory had been a major force in developmental psychology, stressed the importance of cognitive growth. His theory, which emphasizes the coordination between the individual and the environment, will be summarized later in the book.

In summary, the growth of cognitive psychology was encouraged by a disillusionment with the behaviorist approach and the emergence of an attractive alternative, the information processing approach. Some encouragement for the cognitive psychology approach came from outside psychology—from computer science, communication sciences, and linguistics—but other encouragement came from within the discipline—from researchers in human memory and developmental psychology.

An Overview of the Book

This textbook covers many different kinds of mental processes. We begin with perception and memory, two processes that are involved in virtually every other aspect of cognition. Then we consider imagery, a topic that is critical in discussing how knowledge is stored in the brain. It is also particularly relevant to topics such as memory, problem solving, and reasoning. The next chapter concerns language, an essential feature of human mental processes. The four chapters after that represent "higher-order" cognition because they depend on the more basic cognitive processes discussed in the first part of the book. These four topics are: concepts and categories; problem solving and creativity; reasoning; and decision making.

The final two chapters assess how people differ from one another in their cognitive processes. Chapter 10 concerns the development of cognition; is cognition in a 5-year-old different from cognition in a 20-year-old or an 80-year-old? Chapter 11 concerns other potential sources of individual differences in cognition, such as sex differences and cross-cultural differences. In general, we will see in these last two chapters that the similarities are frequently more noteworthy than the differences. Let us now preview these ten chapters, illustrating each with examples from everyday life.

Perceptual processes (Chapter 2) involve the use of previous knowledge in order to interpret the stimuli that are registered by our senses. Have you ever heard a clock chiming out the time when you were not really paying attention? Sometimes, the chimes seem to be still ringing in your head after the physical stimulus has stopped. You can "listen" to the chimes in your sensory memory— bong, bong, bong, bong—and conclude that it is four o'clock. Another kind of perceptual process is pattern recognition, the activity that allows you to recognize the letters on this page. Another perceptual process is attention. You have probably noticed the limits of attention if you have ever daydreamed while reading an assignment. You could not simultaneously attend to both your daydreams and your reading, and you may not recall a single fact from the page of text.

Memory (Chapter 3) involves maintaining information over time. You use memory whether that information is maintained for less than a second or for an entire lifetime. Thus, memory is necessary when you listen to a lecture and store the beginning of a sentence long enough to combine it with the end of the sentence. Memory is also involved when you try to remember the name of your kindergarten teacher or when you remember that a nasturtium is a kind of flower.

Imagery (Chapter 4) is a mental representation of something that is not physically present. You use mental imagery when you try to find out the time by looking at a friend's upside-down watch; you mentally rotate the image in order to decipher the time. You may also use mental imagery to aid your memory. For example, you might remember that *separate* is spelled with two *a*'s rather than *seperate* by thinking of a vivid mental image of two *a*'s quarreling and a strong, authoritarian *r* being invited in to *separate* them. In addition, mental imagery is necessary when we make mental maps—for example, when someone asks you to describe how to get to the nearest gas station.

Language (Chapter 5) is the expression of thoughts in order to communicate. Language is an essential part of almost every human activity. We must understand language in order to know what time breakfast is served, whether the weather forecast predicts rain, and whether the statistics test will be on Monday or Wednesday. We must produce language in order to tell others that we want fried eggs, rather than scrambled, that Greta Garbo was the star of *Camille,* and that cognition focuses on the acquisition, storage, retrieval, and use of information. Language is also involved in remembering. For example, how well do you remember the word-for-word definition for memory?

Concepts and categories (Chapter 6) are systems for organizing items into groups so that the members of each group share one or more characteristics. You use concepts when you organize the clothes in your dresser (socks in one place, shirts in another). The books in your college library are also organized according to concepts; *Wuthering Heights* is housed near other English novels, some distance away from Russian novels, and even farther away from *Human Experimental Psychology.* The concepts we use in everyday life are not based on a list of characteristics; instead, these natural categories seem to be organized in terms of a best example, or prototype. For instance, a robin might be a prototype for the category *bird* and a clinical psychologist might be a prototype for the category *psychologist*.

Problem solving (Chapter 7) involves finding a satisfactory method of reaching a goal when that goal is not readily available, and **creativity** means finding a solution that is both unusual and useful. Some problem-solving situations are clear-cut, such as calculating the standard deviation on a set of numbers in your statistics textbook or figuring out how to get your laboratory assignment to the professor before the deadline. Other problem-solving situations are less defined, such as an assignment to draw a picture of a tree or write an essay about good and evil.

Reasoning (Chapter 8) involves drawing conclusions from several known facts. You use reasoning, for example, when you hear your psychology professor say, "Performance in the Repetition Condition was better than performance in the

Control Condition, but performance in the Imagery Condition was even better than performance in the Repetition Condition," and you conclude, "Imagery—best; Repetition—intermediate; Control—worst." You also use reasoning when you detect the flaws in people's arguments.

Decision making (Chapter 9) is concerned with choices about the likelihood of uncertain events. You make a decision, for example, when you decide to leave your seat belt unbuckled—because you heard that a friend would have been killed in an accident if she had used her seat belt—even though you recently read a fact-filled article about how the use of seat belts could reduce traffic fatalities. You also use decision making when you make predictions about what will happen in the future.

Cognitive development (Chapter 10) examines differences in cognitive processes that are related to a person's age. For example, you might worry about trusting your 4-year-old nephew when he says that he remembers seeing your missing book in the garage. You might also wonder about whether your 75-year-old grandmother's ability to solve everyday problems has declined in recent years.

Individual differences in cognition (Chapter 11) involve the examination of certain factors that could be systematically related to cognitive processes. You might wonder, for example, whether females and males differ in their ability to memorize course material. You might also be curious about other kinds of differences, such as whether test results of people who finish their multiple-choice examinations quickly differ consistently from those of people who finish slowly.

Themes in the Book

Throughout the book we will stress certain themes or consistencies in cognitive processing. It will be helpful to keep these points in mind in later chapters.

1. The cognitive processes are all interrelated with one another, rather than existing in isolation. In this as well as other introductions to cognition, a separate chapter is devoted to each topic. However, you should not conclude that each process can function by itself without input from other processes. For example, consider concept formation. Perhaps the task requires people to respond "yes" to all circles and "no" to all squares. Perceptual processes are necessary to identify the figures and to attend to the shape, rather than the color and size of the figure. Memory is essential in order to recall the responses from previous trials, and imagery may be useful in aiding memory. Language is necessary to provide the labels *circle* and *square* as well as the responses "yes" and "no." Depending upon the particular concept formation task, other cognitive processes—such as problem solving, reasoning, and decision making—may also be involved. Keep in mind, then, that there are complex interactions and coordinations among the various components of cognition.

2. The cognitive processes are active, rather than passive. According to the behaviorist approach, humans were viewed as passive organisms. They waited for a stimulus from the environment, and then they responded. The cognitive

approach is quite different. According to this view, people are eager to acquire information; they continually search for knowledge and new developments. Information from earlier activities is vitally important in guiding this search and in influencing what people remember. In summary, your mind is not a sponge that passively absorbs information leaking out from the environment. Instead, you continually search for interesting and important items.

3. The cognitive processes are remarkably efficient and accurate. The development of language, for example, is an astounding accomplishment because of the large number of new words and complex language structures. The amount of material in your memory is awesome. Naturally, humans make mistakes, but these mistakes can often be traced to the use of a strategy that is quite rational. For example, people frequently base their decisions on the ease with which examples spring to mind. This strategy often leads to a correct decision, but it can occasionally produce an error. Furthermore, many of the limitations in human information processing may actually be advantageous. For instance, we may sometimes regret that we are unable to keep information in our memories for more than a few seconds. However, if we retained all information forever, our memories would be hopelessly cluttered with facts that are no longer useful.

4. The cognitive processes handle positive information better than negative information. We understand sentences better if they are worded in the affirmative (e.g., ''John is honest'') rather than in the negative (e.g., ''John is not dishonest), and we also remember positive information more accurately. We perform better on concept formation tasks if we know what figures are examples of a concept than if we know what figures are *not* examples of the concept. Reasoning tasks are also easier with positive than with negative information. We also tend to perform better on a variety of different tasks if the information is pleasant (emotionally positive) rather than unpleasant (emotionally negative). We also remember a word better if we can form a mental image of the word. Furthermore, children can often solve a problem when objects are present, though they may fail when objects are absent. In short, our cognitive processes seem to be designed to handle *what is,* rather than *what is not.*

5. The cognitive processes are generally not directly observable. You can't learn much from watching someone remember a fact, solve a prolem, or make a decision. As a result, it is often difficult to explain how the cognitive processes operate. For example, the information we gather about cognitive processes frequently allows us to eliminate several explanations for a particular mental activity, but two or three remaining explanations may seem equally likely. In many places throughout the book, you will find that two or more alternate theories are proposed to explain a particular process. In these cases, experiments have yielded results that are compatible with several theories. Thus, the nature of cognitive processes makes it difficult to select one theory and reject all others.

Because cognitive processes are generally not directly observable, researchers must be particularly clever when they design experiments. The measures must be carefully devised so that subjects' thoughts and mental processes can be translated into observable responses. In this book, for example, you will read about experiments that test whether forgetting is caused by decay of a memory or interference from other items, whether we react to mental images the same way we react to real objects, and whether babies can tell the difference between *bah* and *pah*. Even the most clever cognitive psychologist could not watch a baby listening to two sounds and determine whether the baby knows that they are different sounds, and so an experiment must provide for a way to translate the baby's knowledge into measurable responses. In this case, incidentally, researchers designed an experiment in which sucking was the measurable response.

The unobservable nature of mental activities makes it difficult to choose among alternate explanations and makes it difficult to conduct research. We definitely do not have all the answers. However, it is this difficulty that makes the examination of cognitive processes intriguing, challenging, and exciting.

How To Use the Book

Your textbook has several features designed to help you understand and remember the material. The purpose of this section is to describe how you can use each of these features most effectively.

Notice that each of the chapters begins with an outline. When you begin to read a new chapter, first examine the outline so that you can appreciate the general structure of a topic. For example, notice that there are three major sections in Chapter 2 (Perceptual Processes): Sensory Memory, Pattern Recognition, and Attention.

Another feature in the next ten chapters is a chapter preview, a short description of the material to be covered. The preview builds upon the framework provided in the outline and introduces some important new terms.

As you read the chapters themselves, notice that there are numerous descriptions of applications. In many cases, research in cognition has important applications in professions such as education, clinical psychology, and advertising. The purpose of these examples is to show you concrete illustrations of psychological principles. I have also included numerous applications of cognition in everyday life, and I will frequently ask you to think of illustrations from your own experience. As you will see in Chapter 3, people recall material better if they try to see whether it applies to themselves. A third kind of application you will find in this book is the informal experiments, or "Demonstrations." Each demonstration requires very little equipment and time, and you can perform most demonstrations by yourself. My students have reported that these demonstrations help to make the material more concrete; again, relating the material to your own experiences makes it more memorable. Incidentally, more tips on improving memory will be discussed in Chapter 3 (the "Improving Memory" section) and Chapter 4 (the "Applications of Imagery in Memory" section). You may want to read these sections before you begin Chapter 2.

Notice, also, that a new term appears in boldface type (for example, **cognition**) when it is first discussed. The definition is presented in the same sentence, so you do not need to search through an entire paragraph to discover the term's meaning. In some cases a phonetic pronunciation for a new word is provided, with the accented syllable in italics. It can be embarrassing if you know what a word means, but you do not know how to pronounce it! Also, there are some important terms that appear in several chapters. I will define these terms each time they occur, to remind you of their meaning. This approach will also allow you to read the chapters in any order you want because you will not need to depend upon vocabulary learned in previous chapters.

Instead of a summary at the end of each chapter, this book has a Section Summary at the end of each of the major sections in a chapter. For example, Chapter 2 has three Section Summaries. This feature allows you to review the material more frequently and to master small, manageable "chunks" before you move on to new material. When you reach the end of a section, test yourself to see whether you can remember the important points. Next read the section summary and notice what items you omitted or remembered incorrectly. Then test yourself again, and recheck your accuracy. You may also find that you learn the material more efficiently if you read only one section, rather than an entire chapter, at a time.

A set of review questions and a list of new terms appear at the end of each chapter. Many review questions ask you to apply your knowledge to a practical problem. Other review questions encourage you to integrate information from several parts of a chapter. Notice that the new terms are listed in their order of appearance in the chapter. Check whether you can supply a definition and an example for each new term. If you are unsure, you can find the definition by checking the subject index at the end of the book.

One unusual aspect of cognition is that you are actually using cognition in order to learn about cognition! I hope that these suggestions can help you use your cognitive processes even more efficiently.

Chapter Review Questions

1. What are cognition and cognitive psychology? Think about the future career that you have selected and suggest several ways in which cognitive psychology may be relevant in that discipline.

2. Compare (a) Wundt's introspective technique, (b) the William James approach, (c) behaviorism, (d) Gestalt psychology, and (e) the cognitive approach; mention whenever possible the area of their investigation and the rigor of their technique.

3. List several reasons for the increased interest in cognitive processes. Figure out a memory device (perhaps using the first letter of a key word in each reason) that will help you remember these reasons.

4. Go back over the description of Chapters 2–9 and think of something that you have done in the past few hours or days that could qualify as an example of each topic.

5. The higher-order cognitive processes depend upon the more basic cognitive processes. Think about a problem you have solved recently and point out how the solution to that problem depended upon perceptual processes, memory, language, and possible other cognitive processes.

6. One theme in the book is the efficiency and accuracy of cognitive processes. We often tend to downplay our accuracy and emphasize our errors. Think about the occasions on which you have recently forgotten something, and contrast that with the numerous occasions when you accurately recall material, such as the names of people in your high school, the names of vegetables, the names of countries, and the names of psychologists.

7. What aspects of the behavioral approach are still important for cognitive psychologists, and how are these aspects important to the fifth theme of the book, the unobservable nature of cognitive processes?

New Terms

cognition	flowchart	creativity
cognitive psychology	perceptual processes	reasoning
introspection technique	memory	decision making
behaviorism	imagery	cognitive development
Gestalt psychology	language	individual differences in
information processing	concepts and categories	cognition
approach	problem solving	

Perceptual Processes

Preview

Perception involves the use of our previous knowledge in order to interpret the stimuli that our senses register. Three aspects of perception are most relevant for cognition: sensory memory, pattern recognition, and attention.

Stimuli that are registered by our senses first enter sensory memory. Sensory memory holds information in an unprocessed form for a very brief period. Each of the senses can be represented in sensory memory, but only iconic (visual) memory and echoic (auditory) memory have been examined in detail.

Pattern recognition involves the identification of a complex arrangement of sensory stimuli, such as a letter of the alphabet or a human face. Several theories of pattern recognition have been proposed, and we will examine three of them. Pattern recognition is influenced by the context in which the pattern appears.

Attention is a word with many different meanings; the general definition we will use is that attention is a concentration of mental activity. Studies have demonstrated that performance usually suffers if attention must be divided between two or more tasks; however, practice may help. When we selectively attend to one task, we recall very little about other, irrelevant tasks. Several models of attention are discussed in this chapter as well as an applied area, Attention Deficit Disorder. Finally, we will consider the topic of consciousness and its relation to cognition.

What is perception? Definitions for this term vary, but one general definition is that **perception** involves the use of previous knowledge in order to interpret the stimuli that are registered by our senses. Thus you use perception to interpret each of the letters on this page. You combine the information that is registered by your eye about a particular stimulus—say the letter A—together with your previous knowledge about the letters of the alphabet in order to interpret that letter as being an A. Notice that perception combines aspects of both the outside world (the stimuli) and your own inner world (your previous knowledge).

The topic of perception is extensive enough to occupy an entire course in most colleges. Obviously, we cannot do justice to this topic in a single chapter; more details are available elsewhere (e.g., Goldstein, 1980; Haber & Hershenson, 1980; Matlin, in press). We will confine our discussion of perceptual processes to three topics that are most relevant to cognition: sensory memory, pattern recognition, and attention. These three processes are important in cognition because they are involved in preparing the "raw" sensory information so that we can use this information in more complex mental processes, to be discussed in the other chapters of this book. Sensory memory holds information in a raw form for a short period of time until pattern recognition can take place. A third process, attention, is responsible for our further processing of some information and our neglecting other information.

Sensory Memory

Let us first examine sensory memory, which has also been called **sensory storage** or the **sensory register**. **Sensory memory** holds information in relatively raw, unprocessed form for a short period of time until it can be interpreted further. Thus, sensory memory permits some trace of a stimulus to remain after the stimulus itself has vanished. Try Demonstration 2.1 so that you can become aware of several examples of sensory memory. A few studies have explored sensory memory in the "minor" senses—such as touch, smell, and taste (e.g., Hill & Bliss, 1968). However, the vast majority of information about sensory memory concerns vision and hearing. Therefore, we will look only at visual sensory memory (iconic memory) and auditory sensory memory (echoic memory).

Demonstration 2.1   *Examples of Sensory Memory.*

Visual Sensory Memory.   Take a flashlight into a dark room and turn it on. Swing your wrist around in a circular motion, shining the flashlight onto a distant wall. If your motion is quick enough, you will see a complete circle. Your visual sensory memory stores the beginning of the circle while you examine the end of the circle.

Auditory Sensory Memory.   Take your hands and beat a quick rhythm on the desk. Can you still hear the echo after the beating is finished?

Tactile (Touch) Sensory Memory.   Take the palms of your hands and quickly rub them along a horizontal edge of your desk, moving your hands so that the heel touches first and the fingertips touch last. Can you still feel the sharp edge, even after your hand is off the desk?

Why do we need sensory memory? Sensory memory is generally viewed as necessary for two major reasons. First, the stimuli that bombard your senses are constantly changing at a rapid rate. For example, consider what happens when you read the sentence "Why do we need sensory memory?" aloud to a friend. The *wh* sound from the *why* is long gone by the time you speak the *y* sound of the word *memory*. Still, a listener needs to retain information about the pitch of your voice at the beginning of the sentence and compare it with similar information at the end of the sentence. The rising pitch in your voice allows the listener to decide that this sentence was a question. Listeners also need to retain an entire sentence so that they can determine which word in the sentence is stressed. Notice, for example, how the meaning of the sentence

I wouldn't buy tickets to hear him sing

changes, depending upon whether you stress the *I*, the *buy*, the *him*, or the *sing*.

A second reason why we need sensory memory is that we need to keep an accurate record of the sensory stimulation for a brief period of time while we select the most important stimuli for further processing. For example, think about the rich variety of stimuli that are now entertaining your senses. You can see the words on the page in front of you and other details of the surrounding area in which you are reading. Maybe you hear the squeak of your marker as it underlines an important point, and you may also hear faint music in the background. You can feel the pressure of your chair against your back and can also sense information about room temperature. Perhaps you can barely taste the toothpaste you used several hours ago or smell the distant aroma of cookies baking. It would be overwhelming to notice all the information from all of your senses all the time. Instead, the sensory memory keeps a record of all the stimuli for a few moments, and the stimuli are quickly examined to determine which ones will receive further processing.

In the next chapter we will consider other memory systems: short-term memory and long-term memory. Sensory memory differs from these systems in several respects. First, items in sensory memory remain there for about a second or less, so the sensory memory process is extremely short-lived. Second, it is much larger in storage capacity than short-term memory but smaller than long-term memory. Third, information in sensory memory is raw and unprocessed. The information in the other memory systems has already been recognized, coded, and categorized. Fourth, the information in sensory memory is a rather accurate representation of the stimuli, whereas the information in the other memory stores may be distorted and inaccurate.

Iconic Memory

Neisser (pronounced "*Nice*-ur") used the term **iconic memory** to describe visual sensory memory, or the brief persistence of visual impressions that "makes them briefly available for processing even after the stimulus has terminated" (Neisser, 1967, p. 15). Iconic memory (pronounced "eye-conn-ick") refers to the memory process, and the term **icon** (pronounced "*eye*-conn") refers to a particular visual impression, such as your impression of the letter A. You may have heard of the words *icon* and *iconography* in an art class, referring to figures and the art of representing figures.

Sperling (1960) conducted one of the first demonstrations of iconic memory. His experiment cannot be demonstrated without the use of special equipment, but Demonstration 2.2 shows how experiments prior to Sperling's might have measured the size of iconic memory. It is likely that you recalled only four or five letters.

Demonstration 2.2   *The Whole-Report Technique.*

DO NOT GLANCE DOWN AT THE LETTERS UNTIL THE INSTRUCTIONS INDICATE TO DO SO! Below is a display of letters. As soon as you have finished reading these instructions, close your eyes. Then open your eyes for the briefest moment and quickly close them again. Try to recall as many of the letters as possible. OK, begin.

H	B	S	T
A	H	M	G
E	L	W	J

However, you believe that you *saw* more than what you were able to report. It may seem that you saw about ten items rather than four or five, but many of these items faded during the time it took you to report the earlier items. Sperling's objective was to measure the true size of iconic memory.

Sperling showed his subjects a display of letters similar to the one in Demonstration 2.2. This display was presented for 50 milliseconds, or 1/20 of a second. Rather than asking subjects to report everything they saw, however, he asked them for partial report. The **whole-report technique,** which you tried in Demonstration 2.2, asks subjects to report everything they saw. The **partial-report technique,** on the other hand, requires subjects to report only a specified portion of the display. Subjects discovered which portion of the display they were to report by listening to a tone that was presented just after the stimulus display disappeared. For example, a high tone would indicate that the listener should report the top row, a middle tone indicated the middle row, and a low tone indicated the bottom row.

Suppose you were a subject in Sperling's experiment. You would see the display flashed on briefly. Then a middle tone might sound, indicating that you should report as much as possible from the line with the letters *A H M G*. Notice that you would have no clue to the relevant line in the display until after it was gone. Therefore we can assume that if you reported three of the letters from *A H M G*, you would have been able to report three letters from either the top or the bottom line if they had been requested instead of the middle line. Thus the number of items correct on any one line can be multiplied by three to obtain an estimate of the number of items the subject saw in the entire display. Sperling found that people recalled slightly more than three items from one line when the partial-report technique was used. Therefore, he estimated that people actually saw between nine and ten items out of the 12 possible items. However, the image of these nine or ten items fades so rapidly that a person can only report about four of them before the remainder have disappeared from iconic memory.

Sperling also varied the amount of delay between the disappearance of the stimulus display and the sounding of the tone that indicated which line was to be recalled. If this partial-report tone sounded just as soon as the display disappeared, then people saw an estimated nine to ten items in the display. However, if the partial-report tone was delayed as little as half a second (500 milliseconds), then people saw only an estimated four to five items. In other words, the iconic memory fades so rapidly that it is gone in half a second, and recall performance deteriorates to the same unspectacular level as in the whole-report technique.

Many other studies have been conducted to verify Sperling's findings. In general, these studies have confirmed the existence of a very brief, relatively large-capacity iconic memory. For example, Averbach and Coriell (1961) modified Sperling's experiment so that it had a visual instead of auditory cue to indicate partial report. That is, people saw a display of 16 letters. After the display disappeared, a small vertical bar appeared in a position previously occupied by one of the letters. Subjects were instructed to report which letter the bar replaced. The estimates obtained by Averbach and Coriell with this somewhat different method agreed quite well with Sperling's results. Specifically, they estimated that people saw about 12 letters out of the 16 possible letters when the cue appeared just as soon as the visual display disappeared. Furthermore, they estimated that iconic memory lasted only one-quarter of a second (250 milliseconds).

Recently there has been some debate about the location of iconic memory. Specifically, Sakitt (1976) has argued that the icon is stored in the visual receptors in the eye rather than in some more central part of the brain. Her research found evidence that the icon is stored in the **rods,** the light receptors that are sensitive to black-and-white stimuli but not to colored stimuli. (You may recall rods and cones from other psychology or biology courses—**cones** are the light receptors that are sensitive to colored stimuli.) However, Banks and Barber (1977) demonstrated that color information is available in iconic memory, and so cones—as well as rods—must be involved in iconic memory. They argued that the location of iconic memory is still unclear. At present, then, we do not know whether iconic memory occurs as soon as the stimuli are registered on the visual receptors in the eyes or whether iconic memory occurs at a higher, more central level in the information processing system.

Echoic Memory

Neisser coined the phrase *echoic memory* to be the auditory equivalent of iconic memory. **Echoic memory** (pronouned "eh-*koe*-ick") refers to the brief auditory impressions that persist after the sound itself has disappeared. A particular auditory impression is called an **echo,** because of its similarity to the echo that sometimes persists after a sound disappears. The name "echoic memory" seems particularly suitable at times. Have you ever noticed how you can "hear" a loud crash echoing inside your head after the sound has really stopped? You may also have noticed that when your professor has been lecturing, his or her words will "echo" in your head for a few moments after they have been spoken—fortunately just long enough for you to write them down.

One of the most important demonstrations of echoic memory was a study that was modeled on Sperling's partial-report technique. You will recall that Sperling presented a visual display to his subjects and used an auditory signal to indicate which part of the display was to be reported. Darwin, Turvey, and Crowder (1972) neatly reversed Sperling's study by presenting an auditory display and using a visual signal to cue the partial report. These authors used special headphones to present three different auditory messages to their subjects. Figure 2.1 illustrates how this was done. Thus, one group of items (*J 4 T*) was presented to a person's right ear. A second group of items (*A 5 2*) was presented to the left ear. A third group of items (*3 M Z*) was prepared by recording the list on both the right and left channels; this list was presented in such a way that it seemed to come from in between the right and the left ear—in other words, right in the middle. All three sequences were presented at the same time. After hearing the sequences, the subjects were shown a visual cue on a screen that indicated which of the three sequences they should report. Specifically, a bar on the left meant that the subject should report the sequence from the left ear, a bar in the middle indicated the middle sequence, and a bar on the right indicated the sequence from the right ear.

Darwin and his coauthors found that the partial-report technique allowed

---

Figure 2.1   *A Person Participating in an Echoic Memory Study.*

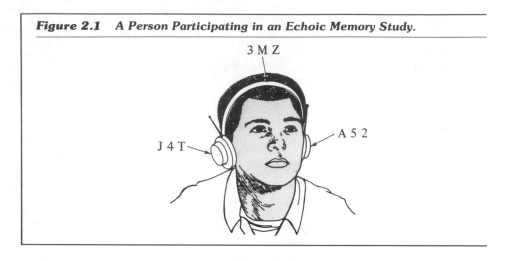

people to report an estimated larger number of items than with the whole-report technique, in which people tried to report all nine items. These results are similar to the results for iconic memory. Thus sensory memory stores items for a brief period of time—so brief that this memory is gone before people can list all the items in their sensory memory. However, this study also pointed out some potential differences between the two kinds of sensory memory. Specifically, the maximum number of items that were correctly recalled in echoic memory was estimated to be about five items, which is substantially less than the nine to ten items in iconic memory. Darwin and his coauthors speculate that the reason that echoic memory was relatively small was that the subjects had difficulty separating the three different input channels. Another difference between echoic memory and iconic memory was their apparent duration. This study of echoic memory estimated that echoic memory could last as long as 2 seconds, in contrast to the fraction of a second that iconic memories last.

Other researchers have used different methods to measure the length of echoic memory. For example, Massaro (1970) used a technique called **masking** in which one tone is presented and another tone is then presented less than a second later; the second tone often masks or prevents the perception of the first tone. With the masking technique, Massaro concluded that echoic memory lasts about ¼ second. Other researchers, Kubovy and Howard (1976), used a complex method that involved detecting whether one tone sounded separate, or segregated, from other tones. With their method, five subjects had echoic memories that lasted about 1 second. However, a sixth subject, who had absolute pitch, seemed to have an echoic memory that lasted about 10 seconds. Thus, there may be large individual differences in the duration of echoic memory.

How, then, does the evidence for echoic memory compare with the evidence for iconic memory? Crowder (1978) reviews the two systems and discusses the differences between them. Crowder feels, for example, that there is stronger support for the existence of iconic memory than for the existence of echoic memory. He notes that the evidence for echoic memory is weaker because much of the research (which we have not discussed here) relies on finding methods that destroy echoic memory rather than methods that demonstrate its existence. Crowder also reports that estimates of the duration of iconic memory show agreement; it lasts approximately ¼ second. In contrast, estimates of the duration of echoic memory have varied from ¼ second to several seconds, depending upon the method of measurement. In summary, there is evidence for both kinds of sensory memory, but we have more reliable information on iconic memory than on echoic memory.

SECTION SUMMARY: *Sensory Memory*

1. Perception involves the use of previous knowledge in order to interpret the stimuli that are registered by our senses.
2. Sensory memory holds information in relatively unprocessed form for a brief period until it can be interpreted further.
3. Sensory memory is necessary because we must retain some trace of a part of a stimulus in order to interpret the entire stimulus and because we need to keep an accurate record of the sensory stimulation long enough to select which stimuli need further processing.
4. Iconic memory, or visual sensory memory, has been demonstrated by Sperling's partial-report technique.
5. Iconic memory can hold about ten items and lasts less than half a second.
6. Some psychologists believe that the icon is stored in the visual receptors of the eye, but others believe that iconic memory occurs at higher levels in the information processing system.
7. Echoic memory, or auditory sensory memory, has been demonstrated with a technique similar to Sperling's partial-report technique.
8. Echoic memory can hold about five items and lasts ¼ second to several seconds, depending upon the method of measurement.

Pattern Recognition

We have mentioned that sensory memory stores information from the senses in a raw and unprocessed form. Pattern recognition is the process that transforms and organizes this raw information. More specifically, **pattern recognition** is the identification of a complex arrangement of sensory stimuli. Pattern recognition involves comparing the sensory stimuli with information in other memory storages. In some cases, pattern recognition involves applying a label to a particular arrangement of stimuli. For example, you recognize the letter *Z*, you recognize your Aunt Matilda, and you recognize Beethoven's Fifth Symphony. In each case, you match a particular set of stimuli with a label you have stored in long-term memory. In other cases, pattern recognition involves the realization that you have seen a particular pattern before. For example, you may notice a supporting actor in a movie. You recognize his face, even though you cannot attach a name or a label.

Our examination of pattern recognition has two parts. First, we will discuss three theories of pattern recognition. Then we will talk about the influence of context on pattern recognition. This chapter will be limited to visual pattern recognition; auditory pattern recognition is covered in the chapter on language (Chapter 5).

Theories of Pattern Recognition

Many different theories of pattern recognition have been proposed, but we will look at only three of them. The first theory, template matching, is now generally acknowledged to be inadequate, and most psychologists favor some variation of a prototype model or a distinctive features model. Nonetheless, we will begin this section with an examination of the template-matching theory because it was the first modern theory; the other theories represent more sophisticated developments of this template theory.

Template-Matching Theory.   You look at a letter *Z* and you immediately recognize it. According to the **template-matching theory,** we compare a stimulus to a set of **templates**—specific patterns that we have stored in memory. After comparing the stimulus to a number of templates, we note the template that matches most closely. You've probably had this experience of trying to find a piece of a jigsaw puzzle that will complete part of the puzzle. The piece must fit precisely, or else it won't work. Similarly, the stimulus must fit the template precisely. Thus, the letter *Q* will not fit the template for the letter *O* because of the extra line on the bottom.

Some nonhuman pattern recognition systems are based on templates. For example, if you have a checking account, take out one of your checks and look at it. Notice the numbers at the bottom of the check, which are specially designed to be recognized by check-sorting computers. Each of the numbers has a constant, standardized shape. Furthermore, each of the numbers is distinctly different from one another. Humans sometimes write a number *4* that looks like a *9.* The *4* on your check, however, looks very different from the *9,* so the computer will not make errors in pattern recognition when the patterns are compared with the templates.

A template system may work well for computers that must recognize a standardized set of numbers. However, it is totally inadequate for explaining the complex process of pattern recognition in humans. One problem with the template-matching theory is that it is extremely inflexible. For example, if a letter differs from the appropriate template even slightly, the pattern would not be recognized. However, every day we succeed in recognizing letters that differ substantially from the classic version of a letter. Notice, for example, how all of the *Z*'s in Figure 2.2 differ from each other. The print types vary and the sizes vary. Some *Z*'s are fragmented, blurry, or rotated. Still, all of these patterns are recognizable *Z*'s. Our pattern recognition procedure must therefore involve a more flexible system than matching a pattern against a specific template.

A second problem with the template system is that we would need to have an infinite number of templates in order to recognize all the possible variations found among letters and numbers—let alone faces and other shapes. It is difficult to

---

Figure 2.2   Various Versions of the Letter Z.

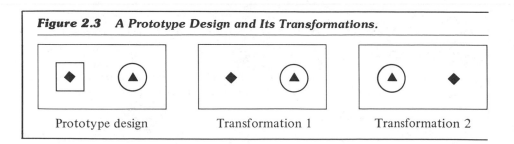

---

imagine how all of this information could be efficiently stored. A final problem with the template system is that the procedure would require too much time. Each time we tried to recognize a letter, we would need to compare this letter with a large number of templates. We could not possibly read at a rate of at least 200 words per minute if each letter in each of the 200 words required comparison with dozens of templates!

Prototype Models.   Prototype models are more flexible versions of template-matching theories. According to **prototype models** (pronounced "*proe*-toe-tipe"), we store prototypes—which are abstract, idealized patterns—in memory. When we see a stimulus, we compare it with a prototype. The match does not need to be exact; minor variations are allowed. If the match is close enough, we recognize the stimulus. If the match is inadequate, we compare the stimulus with other prototypes until we locate a match.

For example, think about the prototype you have developed for your best friend. This abstract, idealized pattern includes certain characteristic facial features, body build, and height. It does not include a specific set of clothing or a specific facial expression. After all, you have stored a prototype in memory, not a template. Thus you can recognize your friend even when the stimulus pattern and the prototype differ on certain features, such as hair length, the presence or absence of glasses, and clothing style.

A number of studies have demonstrated the usefulness of prototypes. For example, Franks and Bransford (1971) constructed a prototype design using geometric figures. Figure 2.3 shows a typical prototype design. Then this prototype design was systematically distorted or transformed. For example, in Figure 2.3, transformation 1 differs from the prototype because the square around the diamond has been removed. Transformation 2 differs more drastically from the

---

Figure 2.3   A Prototype Design and Its Transformations.

Prototype design	Transformation 1	Transformation 2

prototype; the square around the diamond has been removed, and the two sides have been reversed.

People in Franks and Bransford's study examined each figure and then drew it. Later, they were shown more figures, including some that they had already seen. People were much more confident that they had previously seen the designs that closely resembled the prototypes (such as transformation 1) in comparison with designs that differed greatly from the prototypes (such as transformation 2). Furthermore, they were confident that they had seen the prototypes before, even when they had never been presented. These results suggest that experience with variations of a pattern is sufficient to develop a prototype for that pattern, even when the prototype itself is never seen. Similarly, you may have developed a prototype for your best friend, even though your friend may never have looked exactly like this prototype.

Other researchers have demonstrated the importance of prototypes in recognizing letters as well as geometric figures (Posner, Goldsmith, & Welton, 1967). A study by Reed (1972) demonstrates how prototype models can also be applied to the recognition of faces. Demonstration 2.3 is a modification of Reed's experiment. Participants in this experiment saw two categories of faces. As in Demonstration 2.3, there was no single feature that reliably distinguished between the two categories of faces. For example, in Demonstration 2.3 the faces in category 1 tend to have round heads, whereas the faces in category 2 tend to have oval heads. However, there are exceptions in each category. Furthermore, the faces in category 1 tend to have high mouths, whereas the faces in category 2 tend to have low mouths—but again there are exceptions. Other features, the shape of the nose and the shading of the eyes, are randomly distributed across the two categories.

Demonstration 2.3   *Forming Prototypes of Faces.*

Examine the faces below, which belong to two different categories.
Category 1:

Category 2:

Now look at each of the faces below and figure out whether it belongs to category 1 or category 2. (Cover up the above pictures.)

After studying the faces for two minutes, Reed's subjects were asked to classify 25 new faces as belonging either to category 1 or category 2. The model that best predicted the subjects' choices was a prototype model. In other words, the predominant strategy was for subjects to abstract a prototype representing each category. They then compared the novel patterns with each of the prototypes, emphasizing those features that best discriminated between the two categories. Thus, if you used a prototype approach in Demonstration 2.3, you first formed abstract prototypes for faces in category 1 and category 2. Then you compared each new picture with those two prototypes, paying particular attention to head shape and mouth position.

We will return to prototypes in Chapter 6, in which we will focus on the research of Eleanor Rosch and her colleagues. We will see that real-life categories—such as birds or tools or vehicles—are organized in terms of a prototype or best example.

Distinctive-Features Models.   The **distinctive-features models** state that we make discriminations among letters on the basis of a small number of characteristics. These characteristics that differentiate one letter from another are called **distinctive features** or **critical features.** According to the prototype models that we just discussed, people store an abstract, idealized version of each letter in their memory. In contrast, the distinctive-features models suggest that we store a list of feature components for each letter of the alphabet. For example, the letter G has a curved component and a horizontal line in the middle. When we see a new letter, we compare that letter with the lists of distinctive features that we have stored in memory.

Try Demonstration 2.4, which is based on a chart developed by Eleanor Gibson (1969). Distinctive-features models propose that these distinctive features remain constant, whether the letter is handwritten, printed, or typed.

Estes (1978) remarks that distinctive-features models are clearly the most popular type of model for research focusing on letter recognition. One advantage of distinctive-features models is that they are compatible with some physiological evidence. For example, Hubel and Wiesel (1968) presented simple line patterns to animals that had tiny electrodes implanted in their brains. They found that some nerve cells in the brain showed electrical activity only when a vertical line was shown. Other nerve cells responded only when a horizontal line was shown. Still other cells in another area of the brain responded only to certain kinds of angles. Thus, the visual system seems to have specialized feature detectors "wired in" that facilitate the recognition of certain features of letters and patterns.

Gibson and her colleagues proposed a distinctive-features model after their research showed that people required a relatively long time to decide whether some letters, such as P and R, were different from each other. Notice that P and R are similar to each other on a large number of critical features. In contrast, people decided relatively quickly whether other letters, such as G and M, were different from each other. Notice that G and M differ from each other in terms of critical features.

Gibson's results have been supported by more recent research by Garner (1979), who presented people with a one-letter target. They next saw a display that

---

Demonstration 2.4   A Distinctive-Features Approach. (From Gibson, 1969.)

Eleanor Gibson proposed that letters differ from each other with respect to their distinctive features. She proposed the table that is reproduced below. Notice the top three kinds of features—straight, curve, and intersection. Notice that *P* and *R* share many features. However, *Z* and *O* have none of these kinds of features in common. Compare the following pairs of letters: (1) *E* and *F*; (2) *K* and *M*; (3) *Z* and *B;* (4) *N* and *M*.

Features	A	E	F	H	I	L	T	K	M	N	V	W	X	Y	Z	B	C	D	G	J	O	P	R	Q	S	U
Straight																										
horizontal	+	+	+	+		+	+								+				+							
vertical		+	+	+	+	+	+	+	+	+	+				+		+		+			+	+			
diagonal /	+							+	+	+	+	+	+	+	+											
diagonal \	+							+	+	+	+	+	+	+	+									+	+	
Curve																										
closed																+		+			+	+	+	+		
open V														+												+
open H												+					+	+					+			
Intersection	+	+	+	+		+	+						+			+						+	+	+		
Redundancy																										
cyclic change		+						+	+						+										+	
symmetry	+	+		+	+		+	+	+		+	+	+	+		+	+	+			+					+
Discontinuity																										
vertical	+		+	+	+	+	+	+	+					+								+	+			
horizontal		+	+			+	+								+											

---

showed one letter at a time. They pressed one key if the letter in the display was the same as the target, and they pressed another key if it was different. People made 50 to 75 of these letter judgments before moving on to the next target. All 26 letters were used in the study. Garner's results were very similar to Gibson's despite the differences in procedure. For example, people required a long time to make decisions about several pairs that shared many distinctive features, such as *M* and *W* or *O* and *Q*.

Let us now compare the distinctive-features model with the other two theories. The distinctive-features model proposes that we try to match a particular component of a new letter with a similar component in memory. In contrast, the template theory proposes that we try to match the entire shape of a new letter with a similar entire letter in memory. Furthermore, the prototype model suggests that we store an abstraction of an entire letter, whereas the distinctive-features model suggests that we store lists of features.

Klatzky (1980) proposes that the two major theories, the prototype model and the distinctive-features model, may actually be compatible. For example, Klatzky notes that a prototype may consist of the features common to all or most instances of a pattern. To see how this explanation works, look back at Demonstration 2.3. Your prototype for the faces in category 1 may have two features, round heads and high mouths. Your prototype for the faces in category 2 may have two different features, oval heads and low mouths. The two prototypes may be similar with respect to other features, such as absence of eyebrows and lack of hair. Thus, the prototype for category 1 faces is both different from and similar to the prototype for category 2 because they share only a moderate number of features. Similarly, the prototype for the letter *O* is both different from and similar to the prototype for the letter *C*.

Context and Pattern Recognition

In this section of the chapter, we will see how context can influence the perception of a pattern. First, try Demonstration 2.5. Notice how the same shape, an ambiguous letter, is sometimes perceived as an *H* and sometimes as an *A*. Read the sentence below. Then go back to the beginning of the sentence and identify each of the letters in the sentence.

Demonstration 2.5   Context and Pattern Recognition.

THE MAN RAN

So far we have examined only isolated patterns. A letter, for example, is stored in iconic memory until pattern recognition allows us to identify the letter. Notice that the process of pattern recognition that we have been discussing begins with the stimulus in the outside world, such as the letter *A* on a page of text. However, it is clear that this process represents only part of the story. We must also consider the fact that context and expectations aid pattern recognition.

Let's see why a theory of pattern recognition based completely on stimulus information is inadequate. For example, suppose that we do identify each letter in terms of its distinctive features. Suppose further that each letter contains four distinctive features, a conservative guess. This would mean that a typical reader would need to make about 5,000 feature detections each minute, an outlandishly high estimate. Furthermore, does it seem to you that you see each letter of each word that you read in this sentence? You probably could read most sentences fairly well even if only half of the letters were present. F−r −x−−pl−, −t's a br−−z− t− r−−d t−−s s−−t−n−−.

Psychologists make a distinction between two kinds of processing. In the previous sections on pattern recognition, we stressed data-driven processing. **Data-driven processing** (also known as **"bottom-up" processing**) stresses the importance of the stimulus in pattern recognition. Data arrive from the sensory receptors (from the bottom level in processing). The arrival of the data sets the pattern recognition process into motion. The combination of simple, bottom-level features permits us to recognize more complex, whole patterns.

An opposing approach to perception is called **conceptually driven processing** or **"top-down" processing;** this approach stresses the influence of a person's concepts and higher-level processes in shaping pattern recognition. According to this approach, our knowledge about how the world is organized helps us identify patterns. We expect certain shapes to be found in certain locations, and these expectations help us make rapid pattern recognitions. We begin by recognizing a whole, complex pattern, and our knowledge of the whole helps us identify a fragment of the pattern. For example, we identified the whole word *THE* in Demonstration 2.5, and our knowledge of that whole word helped us identify the second letter as an *H*.

Which is the better explanation, data-driven processing or conceptually driven processing? Actually, both kinds of processing occur and both are necessary to explain the complexities of pattern recognition. Palmer (1975a) notes that it is impossible to believe *only* in data-driven processing or *only* in conceptually driven processing:

> . . . which happens first: interpreting the whole or interpreting the parts? How can someone recognize a face until he has first recognized the eyes, nose, mouth, and ears? Then again, how can someone recognize the eyes, nose, mouth, and ears until he knows that they are part of a face? This is often called the parsing paradox. It concerns the difficulties encountered with either a pure "bottom-up" (part-to-whole) or a pure "top-down" (whole-to-part) strategy in interpretive processing. (p. 295)

Thus we have a puzzling problem. We cannot recognize the whole face without recognizing the component parts, yet we cannot recognize the component parts without recognizing the whole face. Palmer suggests that pattern recognition occurs simultaneously in both the bottom-up direction and the top-down direction. This simultaneous processing in both directions must occur in order to let us recognize patterns quickly and accurately. Notice, for example, how the parsing paradox operates when you recognize the face on the Halloween pumpkin in Figure 2.4. The triangles, the circle, and the jagged line by themselves are unrecognizable as eyes, nose, and mouth. When each shape is placed in the context of a face, it becomes recognizable because of conceptually-driven processing. Similarly, data-driven processing forces us to combine the component features into a perception of a face.

Figure 2.4   The Simultaneous Operation of Bottom-Up and Top-Down Processing.

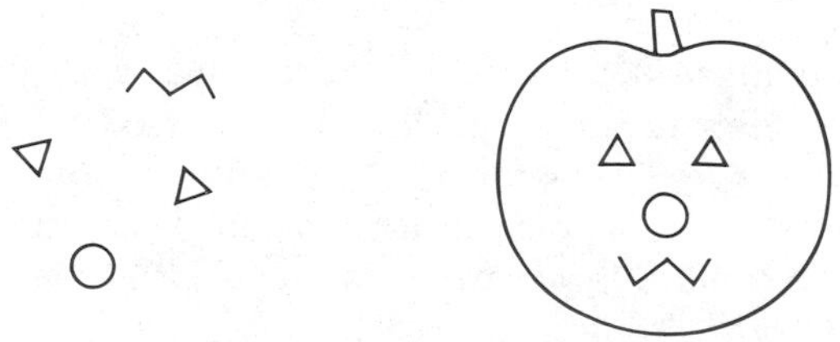

We've considered some informal evidence for the influence of context and expectations on pattern recognition. Let's now look at some of the research. For example, Palmer (1975b) found that people were more likely to recognize a figure when it was in an appropriate context. Thus in a kitchen scene, a loaf of bread was recognized more readily than a mailbox.

In another study, Biederman (1972) examined the identification of objects in real-world scenes. Try Demonstration 2.6, which is an adaptation of Biederman's study. Biederman constructed two versions of several different scenes. Each scene was then cut into six pieces. One version of the scene was assembled in the normal, coherent fashion, as in picture A of Demonstration 2.6. The other version of the scene was rearranged so that the natural spatial relations were destroyed, as in picture B. Note, however, that one of the six pieces remained in its normal position.

Subjects in Biederman's experiment looked briefly at a slide. Then the slide disappeared and an arrow appeared, pointing to a position in which a critical object had been located. Subjects then saw pictures of four objects, and they selected the object that they thought had been located in the position indicated by the arrow. The results showed that people were much more likely to identify the object correctly in the normal pictures than in the jumbled pictures.

Thus, our knowledge about how the world is organized helps us identify patterns. A meaningful picture creates an appropriate context for objects and so we recognize them readily. A jumbled picture deprives us of context, and it makes top-down processing either difficult or impossible.

Other researchers have demonstrated that lines, as well as objects, are easier to recognize in a meaningful context. For example, Weisstein and her colleagues have shown that a portion of a line is recognized better when it is part of a meaningful drawing, a phenomenon that they call the **object superiority effect** (Weisstein & Harris, 1974; Williams & Weisstein, 1978).

Context also helps us identify letters and words. Several studies have shown that we can identify a single letter more accurately when it appears in a word than when it appears by itself or in a random string of letters (for example, Reicher, 1969; Wheeler, 1970). The phenomenon—identifying a letter more accurately when it appears in a word than when it does not—has been called the **word superiority effect.** Unfortunately, however, several appealing explanations for the word superiority effect have not received experimental support.

Let us examine a study by Solman, May, and Schwartz (1981) that failed to support two possible explanations. Solman and his coauthors speculated that iconic memory might last longer for words than for nonwords, and so their study varied the amount of time that the stimulus would be stored in iconic memory. They made use of iconic memory by first presenting a set of four fragments of letters, then waiting 0 to 150 milliseconds, and then presenting the missing fragments. They tested three kinds of stimuli: nonwords, low-constraint words (words in which many other letters could be substituted for the critical letter and still form a word; for example, the S in *RISE* could be replaced by the letters C, D, F, L, P, and T), and high-constraint words (words in which few other letters could be substituted; for example, no other letter could replace the S in *WISH*). Figure 2.5 illustrates the three kinds of stimuli.

Demonstration 2.6　The Identification of Objects in Real-World Scenes.

Locate two friends to participate in this demonstration. The first friend will work with picture A. Cover up everything except picture A with one sheet of paper. Cover up picture A with a second sheet of paper. Instruct your friend that you will briefly expose a picture, which must be quickly examined. Now remove the paper from picture A for less than one second and cover it again quickly. Shift your two pieces of paper so that the four objects in the center are exposed. Ask your friend which object appeared in the lower left-hand corner.

　Now repeat the process with your second friend, using picture B. Compare your friends' accuracy and the latency of their responses.

Picture A:

Picture B:

Figure 2.5   *The Word Superiority Effect: Setup for Solman, May, and Schwartz (1981) Study.*

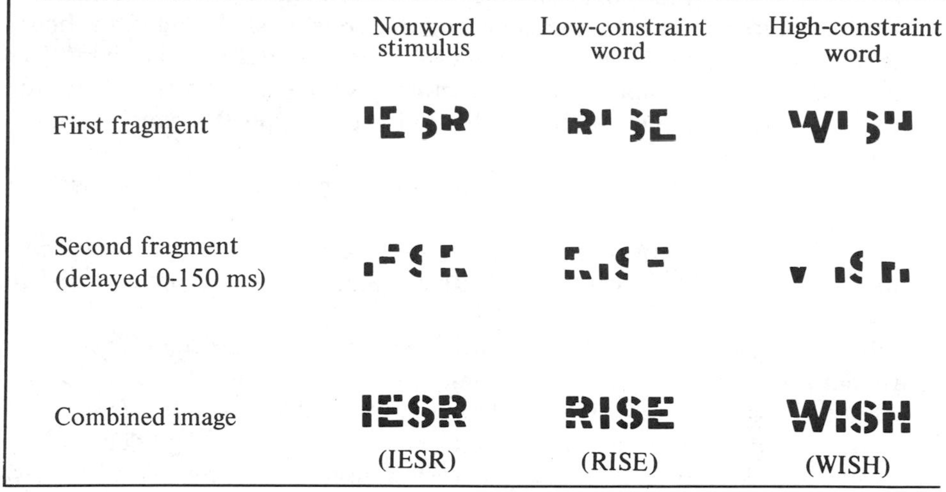

	Nonword stimulus	Low-constraint word	High-constraint word
First fragment	**'L 3R**	**R' 3L**	**W' 3'**
Second fragment (delayed 0-150 ms)	**'´ S L**	**R,S ´**	**v ,S r**
Combined image	**IESR** (IESR)	**RISE** (RISE)	**WISH** (WISH)

The results showed that letters were recognized more accurately when they appeared in words than when they appeared in nonwords. However, there was no difference between the low-constraint and the high-constraint words. This particular finding ruled out one explanation for the word superiority effect, that people perform a kind of sophisticated guessing on these tasks. Previous researchers had suggested that people achieve accuracy because of clever guesses, but this explanation would have predicted better accuracy for the *S* in *WISH* than for the *S* in *RISE,* where so many guesses would have been incorrect. The second potential explanation, differential iconic storage, was also ruled out; the word superiority effect was found to be unrelated to the delay period prior to presenting the missing fragments. In short, the word superiority effect is quite robust. At present, though, we have no explanations that can thoroughly account for this phenomenon. In particular, we know that guessing and iconic storage are unlikely explanations.

Think how the word superiority effect influences the speed of reading. The previous letters in a word help you identify the remaining letters more quickly. Consequently, you can read a word relatively fast. Furthermore, as we will note in Chapter 5, the previous words in a sentence help you identify the remaining words more quickly. Consequently, you can read the sentence relatively fast. Without context to help you read quickly, you might still be reading the beginning of this chapter!

SECTION SUMMARY: *Pattern Recognition*

1. **Pattern recognition is the identification of a complex arrangement of sensory stimuli.**
2. **Three theories of pattern recognition have been proposed; template-**

matching theory is less favored than prototype models or distinctive-features models.

3. According to template-matching theory, we compare a stimulus to a set of specific patterns and select the one that matches most closely. This theory is too inflexible and bulky to account for human pattern recognition.

4. According to prototype models, we store prototypes—abstract, idealized patterns—and compare each stimulus with a prototype; the matches do not need to be exact.

5. Experiments have demonstrated that people can form prototypes based on similar, but not identical, examples.

6. According to distinctive-features models, we recognize patterns by comparing a pattern with a list of distinctive features that we have stored in memory.

7. Distinctive-features models are the most popular models for pattern recognition; supporting research demonstrates that people require more time to make decisions about letters that share distinctive features.

8. In data-driven processing, the stimulus sets the pattern recognition process in motion; conceptually driven processing emphasizes the role of context and expectations in identifying patterns.

9. Research with figures, real-world scenes, line segments, and letters in words has demonstrated that context and expectations facilitate pattern recognition.

Attention

Attention is a word we use frequently in everyday speech. You have probably used this word to refer to several different kinds of mental activity. Psychologists also use the word in many different contexts. Attention can refer to the kind of concentration on a mental task in which people try to exclude other interfering stimuli—for example, when taking an examination. It can refer to being prepared for further information—for example, when someone tells you to pay attention to an important announcement. It also refers to receiving several messages at once and ignoring all but one—for example, when you focus on one conversation at a noisy party. Moray (1969) has pointed out several additional interpretations of attention. We will use a general definition of attention that applies to all these interpretations. **Attention** is a concentration of mental activity.

Attention is relevant in many other chapters of this book. For example, attention is an important factor in concept formation (Chapter 6), because people must pay attention to the relevant attributes in order to form a concept. For example, a child learning the concept *bird* must pay attention to some attributes—such as wings—and ignore other attributes—such as color. Furthermore, attention is critical in problem solving. In Chapter 7 you will see that when people read a description of a problem, they read certain important sentences several times and disregard other sentences that seem to be trivial. Chapter 9 explains why attention is important in decision making.

Our discussion of attention in this chapter has six components: divided attention, selective attention, models of attention, attention and practice, application, and consciousness. Other sources can be consulted for information about factors that attract our attention, such as novelty, change, and informativeness (Dember & Warm, 1979; Matlin, in press).

Divided Attention

In a scene from an "I Love Lucy" episode, Lucille Ball tries to divide her attention among three tasks. She polishes a shoe with one hand, types with another hand, and speaks into the phone that is wedged between her head and her shoulder. Of course, she cannot manage all three at the same time. Although we often can do two things at once, in many cases it is impossible to divide our attention between two or more tasks that must be performed simultaneously. Try Demonstration 2.7 to convince yourself of the difficulty of divided attention.

Demonstration 2.7   The Difficulty of Divided Attention.

The purpose of this demonstration is to illustrate the problems involved in spreading attention across several tasks. Turn on the radio or the record player and find a fast song with lyrics. Copy down the lyrics to that song as you recite the Pledge of Allegiance. With the hand that you are not using to record lyrics, rub your stomach twice and then pat your stomach twice, alternating between the two activities. If you can manage these activities simultaneously, invent another activity to do with your feet!

Neisser and Becklen (1975) conducted an experiment to demonstrate how performance suffers in divided-attention tasks. Two games were simultaneously projected onto one television screen. Subjects were instructed to press a switch whenever a significant event occurred in either game. One game involved bouncing a ball, and subjects pressed a switch whenever the ball was thrown from one player to another. The other game was a hand game you may have played when you were young. Subjects pressed a switch whenever one of the players managed to remove his hands quickly and slap the other player's hands.

People were easily able to follow one game at a time, even with the other game superimposed. However, their performance was extremely poor when they were instructed to follow both games simultaneously. According to one measure, the error rate for following two games was about eight times as high as the error rate for following a single game. According to Neisser and Becklen, there is a structured flow of information involved in the perception of events. If we are following one particular flow of information, it is impossible to follow another, unrelated flow of information.

Neisser and Becklen's study offers a pessimistic outlook on the possibility of successfully performing two tasks at once. However, the section on attention and practice offers a glimmer of optimism: with practice, people can sometimes do two tasks simultaneously.

Selective Attention

Selective attention is closely related to divided attention. In divided attention, people are instructed to pay equal attention to several tasks. In **selective attention,** people are instructed to pay attention to only one task. Selective-attention studies show that they notice very little about the other tasks. We talked about one example of selective attention at the beginning of this section: If you pay close attention to one conversation at a noisy party, you'll be unaware of the content of other conversations. You have also experienced selective attention when picking up two stations on your radio. If you listen closely to one program, you notice only the superficial characteristics of the other program.

At times, you might wish that attention were *not* so selective. Wouldn't it be wonderful to participate in one conversation, yet notice the details of all the other conversations going on around you? On the other hand, think how confusing this would be. Perhaps you would start talking about baseball, the topic of a neighboring conversation, when you had originally been talking about a friend's new job prospect. Furthermore, imagine the chaos you would experience if you simultaneously paid attention to all the information in your sensory register. You would notice hundreds of sights, sounds, smells, tastes, and touch sensations. It would be extremely difficult to focus your mental activity enough to respond appropriately to just a few of these sensations. Consequently, it is fortunate that selective attention can simplify our lives. As we will see throughout this book, our cognitive apparatus is impressively well designed. Such features as selective attention, which may initially appear to be drawbacks, are really beneficial.

A classic study in selective attention was performed by Cherry (1953), who used the shadowing technique. In the **shadowing technique** a person must listen to a series of words and repeat them after the speaker. A shadow is something that follows closely behind you, and a person performing a shadowing task must follow the speaker equally closely. Cherry asked people to wear earphones. They were told to shadow the message presented to one ear. Meanwhile, a second message—recorded by the same speaker—was presented to the other ear.

Cherry's results showed that people noticed very little about the second message. For example, Cherry sometimes changed the unattended, second message from English words to German words. People reported that they assumed that this unattended message was in English. In other words, their attention was so concentrated upon the attended message that they failed to notice the switch to a foreign language! People did notice, however, when the voice of the unattended message was switched from male to female. Thus, some characteristics of the unattended message can be detected.

People can notice the gender of the speaker—or more likely, the pitch of the speaker's voice. What else do they notice? Moray (1959) found that people notice their own name if it is inserted in the unattended message. You have probably noticed this phenomenon. Even if you are paying close attention to one conversation at a party, you easily notice when your name is mentioned in a nearby conversation. Furthermore, in some cases they can follow meaning in the unattended ear. For example, Treisman (1960) presented two messages to her subjects. As Figure 2.6 illustrates, people were instructed to shadow one message

---

Figure 2.6   An Illustration of Treisman's (1960) Shadowing Study.

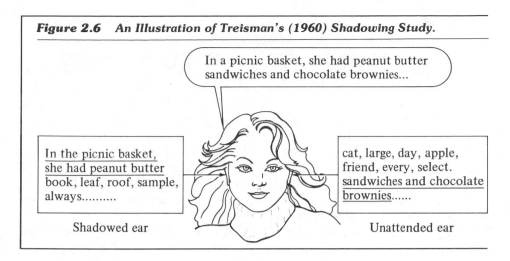

In a picnic basket, she had peanut butter sandwiches and chocolate brownies...

In the picnic basket, she had peanut butter book, leaf, roof, sample, always..........

Shadowed ear

cat, large, day, apple, friend, every, select. sandwiches and chocolate brownies......

Unattended ear

---

and to leave the other message unattended. However, after a few words, the meaningful sentence in the to-be-shadowed ear was suddenly interrupted by a string of unrelated words. Simultaneously, that same sentence continued in the "unattended" ear. Triesman found that people sometimes followed the meaningful sentence and began to shadow the message in the ear that they were supposed to ignore. Thus, they might say, "In the picnic basket, she had peanut butter sandwiches and chocolate brownies."

There is a controversy about the extent to which people notice the meaning of the unattended message. Several experiments in this area involve the **galvanic skin response,** which is a change in the electrical responsivity of the skin that occurs when sweat is produced. One standard way to produce a galvanic skin response is to deliver a mild electric shock every time a particular word is spoken. After the word has been associated with the shock, subjects respond with a galvanic skin response whenever they hear the word—even if the shock is no longer delivered.

How can the galvanic skin response be used in connection with selective attention? Several researchers, including Corteen and Wood (1972), found that words that had been associated with the electric shock continued to produce galvanic skin responses when they were presented in the unattended message. For example, Corteen and Wood delivered a mild shock to people every time they heard three city names. In a second task, these same people shadowed a prose passage; shock was no longer delivered. Meanwhile, other words were presented in the unattended ear. Included among these words were the same three city names plus three additional city names. Corteen and Wood reported that the three familiar city names frequently continued to produce a galvanic skin response. Even more surprising, the three additional city names produced a galvanic skin response rather frequently in comparison to control words. Psychologists interested in attention were particularly impressed by these findings on the additional city names because it indicated that people must be noticing the meaning of the unattended message.

That is, people must have been following the unattended message enough to be able to categorize the new words as city names.

However, attempts to replicate this experiment have sometimes been unsuccessful. For example, Wardlaw and Kroll (1976) followed Corteen and Wood's procedure carefully. Nonetheless, they found no difference in galvanic skin responses for control words versus city names. Thus neither the city names that had originally been associated with shock nor the new city names produced galvanic skin responses beyond the level produced by irrelevant control words. According to Wardlaw and Kroll's research, then, people fail to recognize familiar words in the unattended ear, and they also show no evidence of noticing the meaning of the unattended words. It is not clear why the same procedure led to two such different results. People may notice the meaning of the unattended message some of the time but certainly not all of the time.

In summary, we have seen that people sometimes notice some of the characteristics of the unattended message, such as the gender of the speaker, whether their own name is mentioned, and the meaning of the message. On the other hand, they are often unaware of the meaning of the message and may even be unaware whether this message is in English or in a foreign language. Clearly, knowledge of the unattended message is far from complete.

Models of Attention

Several different models of attention have been proposed. We shall look at three of them.

Bottleneck Theories.   A bottleneck is a narrow opening—so narrow that it restricts the flow from one area to another. You are familiar with a bottleneck on a bottle and with a bottleneck, perhaps caused by a stalled car, that restricts the flow of traffic along a busy highway. **Bottleneck theories** propose that there is a similar narrow passageway in human information processing, and this bottleneck limits the quantity of information to which we can pay attention. If one piece of information is currently flowing through the bottleneck, then other pieces of information must be left behind. This limitation on the amount of information that can be processed is another example of one of the themes we discussed in Chapter 1: Many of the limitations in human information processing may actually be advantageous. In this case, a bottleneck regulates the flow of information. Restricting the amount of information that receives further processing is vital because it prevents information overload.

Many variations of the bottleneck theory have been proposed (for example, Broadbent, 1958; Treisman, 1964). Broadbent's early, influential model, for instance, suggested that there is a bottleneck that occurs early in information processing, just after the sense organs have recorded the information. The purpose of this bottleneck is to limit input and to keep us from being overwhelmed by too much information. Notice in Figure 2.7 that when the message from the right ear is receiving attention, the barrier blocks the message from the left ear. On another occasion, the position of the barrier could be shifted to block the message from the right ear. How is the position of the barrier determined? According to Broadbent,

Figure 2.7 *An Example of a Bottleneck Model.*

the physical characteristics of the message allow us to select one message and ignore the other. For example, we may pay attention to a high-pitched voice and ignore a low-pitched voice.

Broadbent's model explains why so many characteristics of the unattended message are not noticed; that is, they simply cannot get through the barrier. However, it does not explain why we notice other characteristics. For example, how can you notice your own name in an unattended message if it is blocked by a barrier?

Other kinds of bottleneck models suggested that the bottleneck occurs much later in information processing. For example, a theory proposed by Deutsch and Deutsch (1963) suggests that all stimuli are perceptually analyzed. However, the bottleneck occurs between pattern recognition and the choice of a response. Thus, we simultaneously analyze all the information that is recorded by the sense organs. The bottleneck simply prevents us from responding to more than one kind of information.

Kahneman (1973) contrasts the two kinds of bottleneck models by using a concrete illustration. Imagine that a person at a cocktail party is actively participating in one of many loud conversations in the room. The two theories differ with respect to the fate of the unattended message. According to Broadbent's theory, the other conversations are never perceptually analyzed. In fact, they are not really "heard." According to Deutsch and Deutsch's theory, however, all the conversations are heard, but the person responds to only one of them. Both of these theories propose some kind of barrier that limits the flow of information, but they differ in the location of the proposed barrier. More recent theories, however, have dispensed with the notion of a barrier.

Norman and Bobrow's Model.   Norman and Bobrow (1975) approach attention from a different perspective. They propose that the limits of attention are related to the limited amount of mental effort that we can spend on a task. They reject the proposal of a bottleneck that limits the flow of information. Instead, they argue that the deterioration of performance that occurs when we divide our attention is a result of several processes competing for the same limited resources.

Norman and Bobrow make a distinction between data-limited tasks and resource-limited tasks. In a **data-limited task** performance is restricted either by our limited memory ability or by the quality of the stimulus. An example of a task involving a poor-quality stimulus would be if you were asked to hear a pin dropping while a marching band was playing "Stars and Stripes Forever" in the next room. No matter how much attention you focused on this task, you would do poorly. A data-limited task, as the name implies, is limited by the quality of the data (or information) rather than by the limits of attention.

In contrast, a **resource-limited task** is a task in which performance can be improved if more resources are supplied to the task. In other words, performance is faster or more accurate in a resource-limited task if you devote a greater proportion of your processing capacity to the task. An example of a resource-limited task would be doing arithmetic problems while singing "We Shall Overcome." You would probably solve the problems very slowly and make many errors on them. However, your performance would improve if you could devote all your attention to the arithmetic task.

According to Norman and Bobrow, there is a fixed upper limit on the amount of resources that are available for processing. There is no interference among activities as long as this limit is greater than the total processing resources required by the tasks you are performing. For example, you can chew gum and listen to a conversation at the same time because the total processing resources required for these two tasks is clearly lower than your fixed upper limit. However, there would be interference if you wanted to perform mental long division and listen to a conversation. The total processing resources would be much higher than your fixed upper limit. Therefore, performance on one or both tasks would suffer.

Neisser's Viewpoint. Ulric Neisser (1976) disagrees with the argument that there must be an overall limit to our capacity for information. In contrast to the limited capacity proposed by bottleneck theories or by Norman and Bobrow's model, Neisser writes, "... there is no physiologically or mathematically established limit on how much information we can pick up at once" (p. 99).

Neisser discusses the predominant view that there are set limits to the amount of information to which we can pay attention. The limited-capacity idea has led neurophysiologists to search for filtering mechanisms located in the nervous system, and it has led sociologists to lament the information overload experienced by inhabitants of our society.

Neisser argues, however, that the concept of limited capacity may be appropriate for a passive container into which things can be placed, but it is less appropriate for active, developing structures such as those in the human brain. The brain contains millions of neurons, which are related to each other in extremely subtle ways. The potential capacity is enormous. Neisser points out that there are probably no limits on the size of long-term memory, our memory for information and events that we stored more than a few seconds ago. We can keep on meeting new people, learning new languages, and exploring new places for as long as we wish. Similarly, Neisser argues, there should be no fixed capacity to the amount of information we can gather at one time.

Neisser acknowledges that in everyday life we do become inefficient if we try to do several things at once. However, with practice, many pairs of activities can be successfully combined. For instance, after years of practice, you can take notes while you listen to a lecturer. We will see that Neisser's viewpoint that there is no set limit to our attention capacity is relevant to the topic of attention and practice.

Attention and Practice

So far we have seen that people have great difficulty performing two tasks at the same time. Furthermore, if they pay attention to one task, they notice very little about other tasks. However, you can point out many situations in which you can do two things at once. You can drive and talk at the same time, walk and eat, knit and watch television, listen to a lecture and take notes. In each of these cases of divided attention, though, the skills are ones that have been extensively practiced. When you were first learning a skill, divided attention would have been much more difficult. For example, when you were first learning to drive, you were so busy concentrating on turning the key in the ignition, moving the gear shift, steering, and using the brakes that you certainly could not carry on an intelligent conversation about a topic unrelated to driving.

Several studies have demonstrated that people can learn to do two complicated activities simultaneously. For example, Spelke, Hirst, and Neisser (1976) trained college students to read stories silently at the same time that they copied down irrelevant words dictated by the experimenter. After a semester of practice, they could even categorize the dictated word (for example, write *fruit* when they heard the word *apple*) without any decline in their reading rate.

A study by Shaffer also illustrates the benefits of practice. In this experiment, Shaffer (1975) found that a particular professional typist was able to type successfully at a high speed while she simultaneously performed another verbal task. For example, she was able to type while shadowing a prose passage. She was also able to type while reciting nursery rhymes. Try Demonstration 2.8 to illustrate the difficulty of dividing attention between typing and reciting nursery rhymes. However, if you practice long hours, you, too, may be able to type term papers while reciting "Jack Be Nimble"!

Demonstration 2.8   *Reduced Efficiency with Divided Attention, Prior to Practice.*

Select a long paragraph from this textbook and locate a watch with a second hand. Type this paragraph as quickly as you can and measure the number of seconds it takes to type it. Now type the same paragraph over again while reciting the following nursery rhymes: "Jack Be Nimble," "Mary Had a Little Lamb," "Little Boy Blue," and "Hickory, Dickory Dock" (repeating them if necessary). Again, measure the number of seconds it takes to type it. Compare the times you have recorded and the number of errors made in each condition.

LaBerge and Samuels (1974) have demonstrated how the relationship between attention and practice has important implications for the area of reading skills, a topic that we will explore more thoroughly in Chapter 5. These authors point out that reading is a complex skill, involving many different components, such as eye movements, coding features into letters, combining letters into words, consulting semantic memory, and using linguistic knowledge. If each of the components involved in reading were to require attention, then it would be impossible to read quickly. Attention could not be adequately divided among all the components, and the limits of attention would be exceeded. Skilled readers, according to LaBerge and Samuels, are able to process some of the components automatically. Thus the demands on attention are within the acceptable limits, and skilled readers can read quite rapidly.

LaBerge and Samuels argue that a skill becomes an **automatic skill** when that skill can be completed while attention is directed toward another activity. For example, if you have known how to drive for several years, driving is now an automatic skill. You can drive while you direct your attention toward the music on the radio, a conversation with a passenger, or your daydreams.

Let us see how automatic skills are relevant in reading. As we discussed in the section on pattern recognition, many theorists believe that one component of reading is the coding of features into letters. Beginning readers must pay close attention to this coding process. However, skilled readers can code a letter's features automatically, and attention can be directed toward other components of the reading process. For example, they can pay attention to combining letters into words. (Incidentally, however, a recent article by Paap and Ogden, 1981, questions LaBerge and Samuels' theory.)

Schneider and Shiffrin (1977) have further developed the concept of automatic processing in relation to practice. In one of their studies subjects performed *consistent* search tasks. For example, they were instructed to look for numbers that were located in a list of letters. Sometimes they were instructed to search for a single target, for example, the number 7. Other times they were instructed to search for as many as four targets simultaneously, for example, the numbers 4, 7, 8, and 1. After many practice trials, people were able to search for the four targets almost as quickly as they searched for a single target. In other words, attention shared among four targets was just as efficient as attention devoted to one target.

In other sessions, the same subjects performed *varied* search tasks. For example, they were instructed to look for particular letters that were located in a list of other letters. Furthermore, a target letter on one trial might appear as a nontarget letter on another trial. As in the consistent search tasks, subjects sometimes searched for a single target and sometimes searched for up to four different targets simultaneously. After more than 2000 trials on this varied search task, however, people still required much more time to search for four targets than to search for one target.

Schneider and Shiffrin's study shows that in some conditions a practiced subject can spread attention across four targets without substantial reduction in efficiency. In other conditions even a large amount of practice is useless in eliminating the handicap produced by divided attention.

Schneider and Shiffrin argue that people who have been trained on consistent search tasks use **automatic detection**. For them, search is activated automatically, without the necessity of active attention or control by the subject. Similarly, when you are driving and see a red traffic light, you automatically place your foot on the brakes. A large amount of consistent training is required to develop an automatic process, whether the task is searching for numbers or braking at a red light.

In contrast, Schneider and Shiffrin point out that people who work on varied search tasks must still use **controlled search,** which involves processes that require the control and attention of the subject, no matter how extensive the practice. Controlled processes require so much active attention that only one activity may be controlled at any given time. When we try to perform two or more controlled processes at once, interference occurs and performance suffers. Furthermore, you will remember that even people who had practiced for 2000 trials had difficulty performing several tasks simultaneously. Some tasks, it seems, cannot be combined, despite Neisser's argument that there should be no fixed capacity to the amount of information we can gather at one time. Humans may be less limited than we had originally thought, but there still seem to be some built-in capacities for attention.

Application: Attention Deficit Disorder
Attention Deficit Disorder is a condition in which the primary problem is failure to pay attention or to concentrate. We discussed the topic of selective attention at the beginning of this chapter. For example, we talked about focusing on only one conversation at a noisy party. A child with Attention Deficit Disorder finds selective

attention extremely difficult because the disorder does not allow him or her to screen out the irrelevant messages.

In the United States, Attention Deficit Disorder occurs in about 3 percent of preadolescent children (American Psychiatric Association, 1980). Thus a typical elementary school teacher is likely to find one child with Attention Deficit Disorder in a class of 30−35 students. This disorder has been known by a variety of names in the past, such as Hyperactive Child Syndrome and Minimal Brain Dysfunction.

Children with Attention Deficit Disorder can be classified in two categories: Attention Deficit Disorder with Hyperactivity and Attention Deficit Disorder without Hyperactivity. **Hyperactivity** means excess motor activity; children who are hyperactive are constantly running and have difficulty sitting still. Furthermore, their motor behavior is haphazard, poorly organized, and not goal-directed. Thus children who have Attention Deficit Disorder with Hyperactivity may be more noticeable than the children with Attention Deficit Disorder without Hyperactivity. For both groups of children, however, inattention is the major problem.

In the classroom, children with both kinds of Attention Deficit Disorder have difficulty organizing and completing their work. Furthermore, they are easily distracted, and they frequently do not wait their turn. They often do not listen to the teacher. Their work is typically sloppy, and they may leave out some portions or add inappropriate material. These children have particular difficulty in a group situation, such as the classroom, where the teacher expects sustained attention.

What kind of person is likely to have Attention Deficit Disorder? Attention Deficit Disorder is about ten times more common in boys than in girls. Contrary to what you might expect, however, it is not related to intelligence. Some of the symptoms of Attention Deficit Disorder disappear when children reach adolescence, but others may persist into adulthood.

What can be done to help children with Attention Deficit Disorder? The three most common treatments are: drug therapy, behavior modification, and diet control. Gittelman-Klein, Klein, Abikoff, Katz, Gloisten, and Kates (1976) examined the relative effectiveness of drug therapy and behavior modification. In their study, children between the ages of 6 and 12 were randomly assigned to one of three experimental conditions. One group of children received Ritalin (methylphenidate), a stimulant that is often used in treating Attention Deficit Disorder; Ritalin seems to stimulate the part of the brain that controls attention. Another group of children received behavior modification treatment both at home and at school; they were rewarded for good behavior, such as completing the work, cooperating, and not interrupting. A third group of children received both Ritalin and behavior modification treatment.

All of the children were evaluated after an eight-week period. Children in all three conditions showed significantly fewer behavior problems than they showed prior to treatment. However, the two groups that had received the Ritalin showed the most improvement, and they did not differ from each other. Thus, these authors concluded that Ritalin treatment is superior to behavior modification treatment that is not supplemented by drug therapy. However, behavior modification treatment is clearly better than no treatment at all.

You may have heard reports that children with Attention Deficit Disorder seem to improve if they eat a special diet. Feingold (1973), for example, claimed that behavior improved for these children if artificial food colors and flavors and other chemicals were removed from their diet. The influence of diet on Attention Deficit Disorder was recently examined by Williams, Cram, Tausig, and Webster (1978). The results showed that about 20 percent of the children seemed to improve on some measures when their diet was controlled. However, drug therapy was clearly found to be more effective. Other research by Conners (1980) concludes that the Feingold program can help some children, but the effect is small and inconsistent.

In summary, we can conclude that drug therapy appears to be the most effective form of treatment for children with Attention Deficit Disorder. Behavior modification is also useful. Diet control, the third alternative, may help some children.

Educators and physicians have been concerned about Attention Deficit Disorder for many years, but there has been little effort made to integrate the research on Attention Deficit Disorder with the research and theory that psychologists have developed for normal attention patterns. This issue was recently discussed by Koppel (1979). Koppel points out that there are several alternate models to explain why attention patterns are different in people who have Attention Deficit Disorder. One possibility is that these people have the ability to attend to task-relevant information, rather than task-irrelevant information, but they are *less likely* to do so than normal people. Another possibility is that people with Attention Deficit Disorder differ from normal people in the quality of their attention rather than the probability of their attention. According to this model, people with Attention Deficit Disorder continuously process task-irrelevant information together with task-relevant information; they are not appropriately selective. A third possibility is that people with Attention Deficit Disorder simply have less processing capacity to devote to any task. Notice that this third possibility fits nicely with Norman and Bobrow's (1975) idea of resource-limited tasks. It is obviously too early to decide which of these three models or others discussed by Koppel most accurately predicts the behavior of people with Attention Deficit Disorder.

Consciousness

Our final topic in this chapter is a controversial one: consciousness. We will use the word **consciousness** to mean awareness. Consciousness is a term that is closely related to attention, but the terms are not identical. After all, we are not aware or conscious of tasks we are performing with the automatic processing kind of attention. For example, you may use automatic processing to put your foot on the brake in response to a red light. However, you may not be at all *conscious* that you put your foot on the brake.

In fact, Jaynes (1976) argues that we are typically conscious of very little in our everyday activitites. He mentions playing the piano as one example:

> . . . Here a complex array of various tasks is accomplished all at once with scarcely any consciousness of them whatever: two different lines of near hieroglyphics to be read at once, the right hand guided to one and the left to the other; ten fingers assigned to

various tasks, the fingering solving various motor problems without any awareness, and the mind interpreting sharps and flats and naturals into black and white keys, obeying the timing of whole or quarter or sixteenth notes and rests and trills, one hand perhaps in three beats to a measure while the other plays four, while the feet are softening or slurring or holding various other notes. (p. 25)

For many years, as we noted in Chapter 1, topics such as consciousness were considered inappropriate for scientific study. However, experimental psychologists now frequently discuss consciousness. In fact, the topic of consciousness is now important in so many areas of academic psychology that *Annual Review of Psychology* recently included an essay called "Consciousness in Contemporary Psychology" (Hilgard, 1980).

Hilgard distinguishes between two basic kinds of consciousness, the passive mode and the active mode. The **passive mode of consciousness** includes an awareness of the environment, the relaxed enjoyment of our own fantasies and daydreams, and aesthetic enjoyments in which we are the receivers rather than the performers. The passive mode of consciousness is involved when you relax and listen to music, for example. The fringe movements in psychology, including groups who are interested in Eastern religions, are particularly interested in this passive mode of consciousness. Furthermore, they often discuss **altered states of consciousness,** which they describe as a kind of awareness that differs from our usual, everyday kind of awareness; altered states of consciousness are produced by drugs, meditation, dreaming, and hypnosis. Hilgard, however, questions whether the term is a useful one because the difference between our ordinary state of consciousness and an altered state of consciousness may not be great. He proposes that there is a gradual change between states, rather than a clear-cut difference. Further discussion of altered states of consciousness is beyond the scope of this chapter, but McConnell (1980) discusses it in more detail.

The **active mode of consciousness** involves the need to plan, to make decisions, and to act upon these decisions. The active mode of consciousness is the major part of our mental life, because we are continually planning. Sometimes the planning is long range ("Should I become a school psychologist?") and sometimes it is short range ("Should I reread the definition for 'active mode of conscious-ness'?"). Our focus throughout this book will be on the active mode of conscious-ness, rather than the passive mode.

An interesting question of concern to cognitive psychologists is the extent to which we are conscious of our own higher mental processes. For example, what is your mother's maiden name? Now think about how you arrived at that answer. As Miller (1962) pointed out, the answer appears swiftly in your consciousness and you probably cannot explain your thought processes. Your answer was probably a vague statement such as, "I have no idea how I thought of the name—it just popped out."

Nisbett and Wilson (1977a) argue that we have little or no direct access to our thought processes. We may be full conscious of the *products* of our thought processes, but we are not usually conscious of the way in which we created these products. Nisbett and Wilson cite evidence that we may be unaware of the existence of a stimulus that had an important influence on a response. We may also be unaware of the existence of the response. Finally, we may be unaware of the relationship between the stimulus and the response.

Most of Nisbett and Wilson's discussion involves social psychology examples. However, they also consider problem solving, an important topic in cognitive psychology. Many creative people have noted that their problems appear to be solved spontaneously, without conscious effort. For example, a mathematician reported that:

> . . .on being very abruptly awakened by an external noise, a solution long searched for appeared to me at once without the slightest instant of reflection on my part . . . and in a quite different direction from any of those I previously tried to follow. (Ghiselin, 1952, p. 15)

Thus, the product of our thought processes appears withour our knowing how it arrived.

Other evidence for our lack of awareness of our thought processes in problem solving comes from classic research by Maier (1931). In this study two cords hung down from a ceiling, and the subject was told to tie the two ends of the cord together. (The cords were so far apart that the subject could not hold one and reach for the other simultaneously.) The correct solution was to swing one cord like a pendulum. When Maier casually swung a cord during the study, people typically reached the solution in less than a minute. However, when asked how they solved the problem, they typically provided answers that showed no consciousness of the process. They might respond, "It just dawned on me," or "It was the only other possibility."

In summary, Nisbett and Wilson propose that people's reports of how they think are unreliable. (For other aspects of this argument, you can consult articles by Nisbett & Wilson, 1977b; Smith & Miller, 1978; and Wilson & Nisbett, 1978.) Unfortunately, this inaccuracy makes the task of cognitive psychologists much more difficult. It would be wonderful if we could trust every human introspection. Then we could simply conduct interviews and have immediate answers to how we perceive (Chapter 2), remember (Chapter 3), form images (Chapter 4), speak and understand language (Chapter 5), form concepts and categories (Chapter 6), solve problems (Chapter 7), reason (Chapter 8), and make decisions (Chapter 9). With appropriate samples of people, we would also have all the answers about the development of cognition (Chapter 10) and individual differences in cognition (Chapter 11).

However, as Nisbett and Wilson argue, we cannot trust verbal reports. Furthermore, we cannot usually observe thought processes directly. Therefore, we typically obtain our understanding of thought processes by conducting experiments that are designed to answer specific questions. As we discussed in Chapter 1, thought processes are hidden. Thus, it is quite a challenge to design an experiment to measure these covert, private thoughts. Sometimes experiments yield different results, and sometimes different interpretations of a group of experiments yield different models. We saw, for example, that some psychologists prefer prototype models of pattern recognition, whereas others prefer distinctive-features models. This controversy exists because we cannot ask people how they recognize patterns and we cannot directly observe people recognizing patterns. Instead, we must examine the experiments that have been conducted and decide which explanations offer the most evidence. In this chapter on perception and in the chapters that will follow, we examine some topics in which there are rival explanations or insufficient explanations. This uncertainty is an inevitable result in an area as complex, covert, and inaccessible as human cognition.

SECTION SUMMARY: *Attention*

1. *Attention* is a word with many different meanings; a general definition is that attention is a concentration of mental activity.
2. When attention is divided between two or more activitites, performance may suffer.
3. Selective attention studies show that people notice very little about irrelevant messages. They can notice some physical characteristics of the irrelevant message, but it is unclear whether they notice its meaning.
4. Bottleneck theories of attention propose that there is a bottleneck that limits the quantity of information to which we attend.
5. Norman and Bobrow's model of attention proposes that poor performance on divided-attention tasks results from limited resources that are available for processing.
6. Neisser argues that there is no set limit to our attention capacity.
7. With extensive practice, some complicated activities can be performed simultaneously.
8. LaBerge and Samuels propose that skilled readers can perform many components of reading simultaneously because some of the components have become automatic.
9. Schneider and Shiffrin found that consistent search tasks could be performed simultaneously. However, varied search tasks could not be efficiently performed at the same time, even with extensive practice.
10. In Attention Deficit Disorder the major problem is failure to pay attention and concentrate; it is sometimes accompanied by hyperactivity, or excess motor activity.
11. The three most common kinds of treatment for Attention Deficit Disorder are (in decreasing order of effectiveness): drug therapy, behavior modification, and diet control.
12. Consciousness, or awareness, was originally a popular topic in psychology. It disappeared during the emphasis on behaviorism and revived with the increased interest in cognitive psychology.
13. Cognition is more concerned with the active mode of consciousness than the passive mode of consciousness.
14. According to Nisbett and Wilson, we are not usually aware of our thought processes. We may, for example, solve a problem without being conscious of the exact steps involved in the solution.
15. The inaccessibility of our cognitions creates uncertainty rather than firm conclusions about our thought processes.

Chapter Review Questions

1. We discussed sensory memory for sights and sounds. Sperling's method of testing iconic memory was applied to test echoic memory; describe these studies. How could the method be adapted to test memory for the sense of touch?

2. Explain why sensory memory is necessary in both vision and hearing, giving examples from everyday activities.

3. How is sensory memory related to attention? If we have sensory memory, why is selective attention necessary?

4. You are trying to read a blurry number in a friend's notes, and you conclude that it is an *8*. Explain how you identified that number, using each of the three theories of pattern recognition that we discussed.

5. Compare the three theories of pattern recognition, mentioning (a) whether an entire letter or a part of a letter is stored in memory, (b) whether the match must be exact or rough, and (c) the number of items that must be stored in memory to enable pattern recognition.

6. Distinguish between data-driven processing and conceptually driven processing. Explain how conceptually driven processing can aid the recognition of visual patterns, citing relevant studies. Give examples of how conceptually driven processing could help you recognize sounds, tastes, odors, and touch sensations.

7. What are divided attention and selective attention? Summarize the studies concerning the effects of practice on divided attention. As people practice a selective attention task, what would you guess might happen to the amount of information recalled about the irrelevant tasks?

8. Read over the sections on divided attention and selective attention and explain how a child with Attention Deficit Disorder would perform on each of the tasks described in those sections.

9. Imagine that you are trying to carry on a conversation with a friend at the same time you are reading an interesting article in a magazine. Describe how the three models of attention would explain your performance. Also mention why sensory memory might be useful in this situation.

10. Discuss Nisbett and Wilson's argument that we do not typically have access to our thought processes. Think of an example of each of the following tasks in which you can arrive at an answer without being conscious of the thought process: (a) speaking a sentence, (b) remembering information about a word's meaning, (c) deciding what category an object belongs to.

New Terms

perception	rods	prototype models
sensory storage	cones	distinctive-features models
sensory register	echoic memory	distinctive features
sensory memory	echo	critical features
iconic memory	masking	data-driven processing
icon	pattern recognition	"bottom-up" processing
whole-report technique	template-matching theory	conceptually driven
partial-report technique	templates	processing

"top-down" processing
object superiority effect
word superiority effect
attention
selective attention
shadowing technique
galvanic skin response
bottleneck theories

data-limited task
resource-limited task
automatic skill
automatic detection
controlled search
Attention Deficit Disorder
hyperactivity
consciousness

passive mode of
    consciousness
altered states of
    consciousness
active mode of
    consciousness

Memory

Preview

Since memory is involved whenever we maintain information over time, it is a critical part of all cognitive processes. Other chapters in this book—those on imagery, language, and concepts—consider the relationship between memory and each of these areas. In this chapter we will explore four topics: Models of Memory; Short-Term Memory; Long-Term Memory; and Improving Memory.

In the section on models of memory, we look at two important approaches to memory. The Atkinson-Shiffrin model views memory as consisting of three memory stores: sensory memory, short-term memory, and long-term memory. The levels-of-processing approach proposes that the way we process material influences how well we recall it. Both approaches, and their variants, have supporters.

Short-term memory, which refers to the information we are currently using, is relatively fragile. Furthermore, there is a clear limit to the amount of information we can hold in short-term memory at one time. Usually we store items in short-term memory in terms of the way they sound. In this section of the chapter we will also look at rehearsal and forgetting in short-term memory.

Long-term memory is a relatively permanent kind of memory, and the accuracy of long-term memory can be quite impressive. In this section we will look at two kinds of long-term memory, the kind of memory concerned with when certain events occurred (episodic memory) and the more general kind of basic knowledge about words and their meanings (semantic memory). Our discussion of episodic memory will emphasize how items are retrieved from memory, the relation between motivation and memory, and forgetting. Less is known about semantic memory, but we will examine the tip-of-the-tongue phenomenon and two major theories of semantic memory.

The section on improving memory points out how the research on memory can be applied in order to improve memory. Chunking is a grouping strategy used in short-term memory, whereas organization is a comparable but more thorough strategy that is used in long-term memory. Another technique, mediation, involves adding extra material in order to make items more memorable. Several additional memory techniques are also discussed.

Suppose that your memory were to suddenly disappear, right in the middle of the next sentence. You couldn't continue to read this paragraph because you would be unable to recognize any letters or know the meaning of any words. In fact, you wouldn't even be able to remember why the book was lying in front of you. You wouldn't know your name or your age, let alone the name of your cousin's girlfriend. Your roommate would look like a complete stranger. Furthermore, you wouldn't even be able to recall what you were thinking about a minute ago!

Memory is so central to our cognitive processes that it influences virtually every aspect of every topic in this book. Attention and pattern recognition, two topics from the previous chapter, are clearly affected by the strategies we remember and by our memory for stimuli, and sensory memory is itself a form of memory. In Chapter 4, we will discuss the ways in which images are stored in memory. Chapter 5, on language, has a section on memory for sentences and other prose material. Half of Chapter 6 is concerned with the way concepts are categorized in memory. Thus, memory is a major part of three other chapters in this book. Furthermore, without memory, we couldn't speak, form concepts, solve problems, reason, or make decisions.

Memory is a word we use frequently. Ask a friend to define the word *memory*. He or she will probably give a definition of memory that is more narrow than the definition used by cognitive psychologists. **Memory** involves maintaining information over time (Lachman, Lachman, & Butterfield, 1979). The duration for which information is maintained can be less than a second or as long as a lifetime. For example, memory is involved when you must store the beginning of a word in your memory until you hear the end of the word. Memory is also involved in your recalling your own first name, which you probably learned when you were a year old.

Our memory abilities sometimes amaze us and sometimes depress us. For example, think about the names of the children in your third-grade class. Isn't it astounding that you can remember any of them, when you have not thought about most of them for years? On the other hand, you can easily think of occasions when you forgot someone's name a few seconds after being introduced.

Lachman and his coauthors make an interesting observation: We are more likely to notice our memories when we forget than when we remember. We become flustered when we cannot remember something trivial. However, we take for granted the fact that our memories are functioning accurately to help us with mundane operations as well as impressive feats of recall.

The purpose of this chapter is to make you aware of what you remember and how you remember it. We will begin with theoretical approaches to memory and end with practical advice derived from memory research. In between those two sections, we will examine short-term memory for the material we are currently processing and long-term memory for the material that is not currently being used.

Models of Memory

Many different theoretical explanations of memory have been proposed throughout the history of psychology. In this section we will discuss two influential models in some detail: a model proposed by Atkinson and Shiffrin (1968) and a levels-of-processing approach.

The Atkinson-Shiffrin Model
In 1968, Atkinson and Shiffrin proposed a model of memory that influenced many researchers in the area of human memory, who frequently proposed their own models of memory. The Atkinson and Shiffrin model adopted an **information processing approach,** in which humans are similar to computers; they put

information into storage, keep it there, and take it out at a later time. Information processing approaches typically represent their models in terms of flowcharts to indicate that information is transferred from one storage area to another.

Description of the Atkinson-Shiffrin Model. Figure 3.1 shows Atkinson and Shiffrin's model. The sensory register is the same as the sensory memory we discussed in the last chapter. **Sensory memory** is a large-capacity storage system that accurately records information from the senses; memories decay rapidly in sensory memory.

The two other memory stores, short-term memory and long-term memory, will be examined extensively in the second and third sections of this chapter. (Note that the model calls them "stores" rather than "memories.") **Short-term memory** (abbreviated STM) contains only the small amount of information that we are actively using. Memories in STM are fragile, and they can be lost from memory within 30 seconds unless they are somehow repeated. **Long-term memory** (abbreviated LTM), in contrast, has a large capacity and contains memories that are

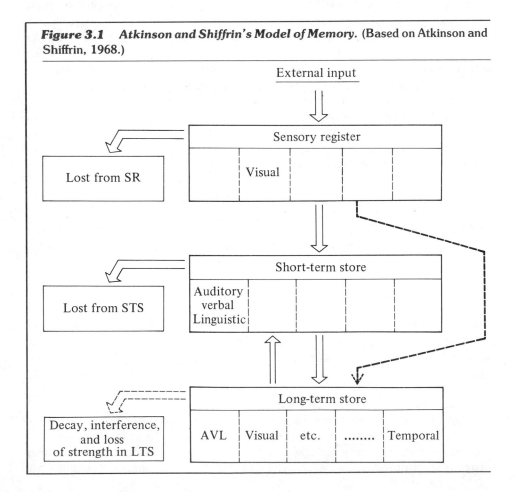

Figure 3.1 *Atkinson and Shiffrin's Model of Memory.* (Based on Atkinson and Shiffrin, 1968.)

many years old in addition to memories that have arrived relatively recently. Memories in LTM are relatively permanent, and they are not likely to be lost.

According to the Atkinson-Shiffrin model, information first arrives in sensory memory. Most of that information is lost from sensory memory, but some of it is transferred to short-term memory. It is also possible for information to be transferred directly from short-term memory to long-term memory. Information in short-term memory has two options: It can be lost, or forgotten, or it can be passed on to long-term memory. The information in long-term memory can be transferred back to short-term memory, or it can be lost from memory.

For example, suppose that you see this sentence:

The East African whimpersnuff typically has three nostrils.

That sentence would be registered in your sensory memory, specifically in the visual store. The sentence can next be transferred to short-term memory. Given the proper processing, it can then be transferred on to long-term memory. If someone later asks you what you know about the East African whimpersnuff, you can retrieve that information from long-term memory and bring it back into short-term memory in order to answer the question.

So far we have examined the model's **structural features,** the stable sequences that are used for all memories. Atkinson and Shiffrin also proposed **control processes,** which are strategies that people use flexibly and voluntarily, depending upon the nature of the material and personal preferences. One kind of control process that we will examine later in the chapter is **rehearsal,** or "the cycling of information through the memory store" (Klatzky, 1980, p. 112). For example, you may silently repeat some information to yourself in order to remember it later. Rehearsal is important in the Atkinson-Shiffrin model because it keeps information "alive" in short-term memory and because it helps transfer information from short-term memory to long-term memory (Rundus & Atkinson, 1970).

Is There a Difference between STM and LTM?   The most controversial aspect of the Atkinson-Shiffrin model and other similar models was the suggestion that there were two types of nonsensory memory: short-term memory and long-term memory. This question has been debated in many publications (for example, Craik & Levy, 1976; Matlin, 1979; and Wickelgren, 1973). In general, the consensus is that there is some reason to believe that short-term memory really is different from long-term memory, but the evidence is not overwhelmingly strong. Wickelgren, for example, reviews a number of studies and concludes that there are several phenomena that justify the distinction between short- and long-term memory. However, he concludes that the remainder of studies would be compatible with the view that there is really only one kind of memory.

The issue, then, is whether we have enough evidence to support a model with two separate memory storages, a short-term memory that stores information for about 30 seconds or less and a long-term memory that stores material for long periods of time. In general, psychologists prefer simple models, if these models can explain all of the data. However, suppose that we can demonstrate that certain factors have one kind of effect on material that is in short-term memory and another kind of effect on material that is in long-term memory. Then it is worthwhile to support a **duplex model,** or a model in which there are two separate kinds of memory.

Let's examine one representative study that investigated the duplex model. In this study, Kintsch and Buschke (1969) asked people to learn 16 English words in order. They proposed that the words from the beginning of the list would be in LTM when recall was requested because so much time had passed since they were presented. On the other hand, the most recent items should still be in STM. Their study focused upon one distinction that duplex theorists had proposed: material in STM is coded in terms of its **acoustic** or sound characteristics, whereas material in LTM is coded in terms of its **semantic** or meaning characteristics. The first study examined whether items at the beginning of the list—which were presumably in LTM—would be influenced by semantic factors. The second study examined whether items at the end of the list—which were presumably in STM—would be influenced by acoustic factors. Table 3.1 shows lists that are similar to the ones used in Kintsch and Buschke's two studies.

Notice that the first list contains pairs of synonyms, which are words that are similar to each other in *meaning.* This list is similar to Kintsch and Buschke's semantically similar list. After the subjects had learned the list, the experimenters presented one word from the list, for example, *pleased.* The subjects were requested to supply the next word in the list. The correct answer would be *forest.* However, suppose that a person confuses the word *pleased* with its synonym *happy.* Then this person might supply the word *rug* as the answer, because *rug* follows *happy.* Kintsch and Buschke measured the number of instances of this kind of semantic confusion that occurred for items in each part of the list. They found that items at the beginning of the list produced a relatively greater number of semantic confusions than items at the end of the list. This result suggests that items at the beginning of the list, which should be in LTM, are coded in terms of their meaning.

TABLE 3.1   Two Lists Similar to Those Used by Kintsch and Buschke (1969)

List 1 (Semantically Similar)	List 2 (Acoustically Similar)
angry	tacks
pleased	so
forest	buy
sofa	owe
ocean	tied
woods	sew
carpet	their
sea	tax
happy	by
rug	there
mad	oh
couch	tide

The second list contains pairs of homonyms, which are words that are similar to each other in *sound*. This second list is comparable to Kintsch and Buschke's acoustically similar list. If a person confuses two words that sound the same, then he or she might see the word *so* and respond *their*, because *so* was confused with *sew*. Kintsch and Buschke found that acoustic confusions were relatively more likely at the end of the list than at the beginning of the list. This result suggests that items at the end of the list, which should be in STM, are coded in terms of their sound.

In psychology it often happens that distinctions seem crisp when they are first proposed. As more research and theory are produced, however, the distinctions seem to blur. For example, one crisp distinction used to be that short-term memory was acoustically coded, whereas long-term memory was semantically coded. We saw how this was demonstrated in the study by Kintsch and Buschke. However, more recent research has demonstrated that items in short-term memory can also be coded in terms of their meaning, a topic we will soon discuss in detail. In addition, people pointed out that we often have a clear representation of the sound of an item in long-term memory. STM seems to be *primarily* acoustic, and LTM seems to be *primarily* semantic, but the distinction is fuzzy. Other attributes that were supposed to be different for STM and LTM were also called into question. Furthermore, even if STM and LTM are actually different from one another, they are highly interdependent. Rehearsals in STM lead to memories in LTM, and LTM is necessary for STM encoding (Klatzky, 1980).

Just when many researchers were growing dissatisfied with the duplex model proposed by Atkinson and Shiffrin, other psychologists proposed a new theory. In this new levels-of-processing theory, other concepts were stressed, and the distinction between STM and LTM was not emphasized.

Levels-of-Processing Approach

Try Demonstration 3.1, which is a modification of a study examining levels of processing (Craik & Tulving, 1975). Which kind of task produced the best recall, the task in which you judged the physical appearance, rhyming, or the suitability in a sentence?

Demonstration 3.1   Levels of Processing.

Read each of the following questions and answer "yes" or "no" with respect to the word that follows.

1. Is the word in capital letters?   BOOK
2. Would the word fit the sentence:
   "I saw a _____ in a pond"?   duck
3. Does the word rhyme with BLUE?   safe
4. Would the word fit the sentence:
   "The girl walked down the _____ "?   house
5. Does the word rhyme with FREIGHT?   WEIGHT
6. Is the word in small letters?   snow
7. Would the word fit the sentence:
   "The _____ was reading a book"?   STUDENT

8. Does the word rhyme with TYPE?   color
9. Is the word in capital letters?   flower
10. Would the word fit the sentence:
    "Last spring we saw a _____ "?   robin
11. Does the word rhyme with SMALL?   HALL
12. Is the word in small letters?   TREE
13. Would the word fit the sentence:
    "My _____ is six feet tall"?   TEXTBOOK
14. Does the word rhyme with BOOK?   look
15. Is the word in capital letters?   FOX

Now, without looking back over the words, try to remember as many of them as you can. Count the number correct for each of the three kinds of tasks: physical appearance, rhyming, and meaning.

The **levels-of-processing approach** proposes that we can analyze information in many different ways, from the shallow, sensory kind of processing involved in judgments about the appearance of letters in the word, to the deeper, more complex kind of processing involved in judgments about whether a word's meaning is appropriate for a particular sentence. Furthermore, deeper processing of material leads to more permanent retention of that material. Because of its emphasis on the depth of processing, levels-of-processing theory is often called **depth-of-processing theory.**

The levels-of-processing theory was proposed by Craik and Lockhart in 1972. This paper was one of the most influential papers on human memory that has ever been written. In fact, Roediger (1980) pointed out that it had been quoted at least 700 times prior to 1980!

The Atkinson-Shiffrin model emphasized the structure of memory—specifically, the division of memory into three components. In contrast to this emphasis on fixed structures, levels-of-processing theory stresses the flexibility that humans can use in processing information.

Let us examine the levels-of-processing theory in more detail. Craik and Lockhart propose that perception involves the analysis of stimuli at a number of different levels. The early levels involve analysis in terms of physical or sensory characteristics, such as brightness or pitch. The later levels involve analysis in terms of meaning. When you analyze for meaning, you may think of other, related associations, images, and past experiences related to the stimulus.

The by-product of all this analysis is a memory trace. If the stimulus is analyzed at a very shallow level (perhaps in terms of whether it had capital letters or whether it was printed in red), then that memory trace will be fragile and may be quickly forgotten. However, if the stimulus is analyzed at a very deep level (perhaps in terms of its semantic appropriateness in a sentence or in terms of the meaning category to which it belongs), then that memory trace will be durable; it will be remembered.

Craik and Lockhart also discuss rehearsal, the process of cycling information through memory, which we discussed in connection with the Atkinson-Shiffrin model. Craik and Lockhart propose that there are two kinds of rehearsal. **Maintenance rehearsal** (also called **Type I rehearsal**) merely repeats the kind of analysis that has already been carried out. **Elaborative rehearsal** (also called **Type II rehearsal**) involves a deeper, meaningful analysis of the stimulus. Thus, if you see the word *book,* you could use maintenance rehearsal and simply repeat the sound of that word to yourself. On the other hand, you could use elaborative rehearsal by thinking of an image of a book or by relating the word *book* to another word on the list.

What will happen if you spend more time rehearsing? Craik and Lockhart predict that the answer to this question depends upon the kind of rehearsal you are using. If you are using shallow maintenance rehearsal, then increasing rehearsal time will not influence later recall. Simply repeating the word *book* five more times will not make it any more memorable. However, if you are using deep elaborative rehearsal, then an increase in rehearsal time *will* be helpful. During that time, you can dig out all kinds of extra images, associations, and memories to enrich the stimulus, and later recall will be more accurate. We will examine the issue of maintenance rehearsal and rehearsal time in another section of this chapter.

The major hypothesis that emerged from Craik and Lockhart's paper was that deeper levels of processing should produce better recall. This hypothesis has been widely tested. For example, Craik and Tulving (1975) found that people were about three times as likely to recall a word if they had originally answered questions about its meaning than if they had originally answered questions about the word's physical appearance.

An even more effective "deep-processing" task is self-reference. Self-reference is encouraged by questions such as "Does this word describe you?" In addition to groups of subjects who had the standard physical, acoustic (sound), and semantic meaning kinds of tasks, Rogers, Kuiper, and Kirker (1977) asked another group to answer whether a particular word could be applied to themselves.

As you can see from Figure 3.2, the self-reference task is the clear winner. Apparently, when we think about a word in connection with ourselves, we develop a particularly rich, detailed coding for that word. For example, the most effective way to remember the word *greedy* would be to contemplate whether it applies to you. You might think about the time you contemplated snatching a chocolate bar from a 2-year-old—yes, greedy does apply. Your rich, elaborate encoding for *greedy* should make the word particularly memorable.

Craik and Lockhart's original description of levels-of-processing theory emphasized **encoding,** or how items are placed into memory. It did not mention details about **retrieval,** or how we recover items from memory. In a later paper, Craik and another colleague proposed that retrieval conditions should duplicate encoding conditions in order for deep processing to be highly effective (Moscovitch & Craik, 1976).

Other researchers have placed even more emphasis on retrieval. For example, Bransford, Franks, Morris, and Stein (1979) stress the importance of the similarity between encoding and retrieval conditions. Suppose that you performed the various encoding tasks in Demonstration 3.1. Imagine, however, that you were then given a rhyming test, rather than a free-recall test. For example, a question

Figure 3.2   Number of Words Recalled as a Function of Level of Processing.

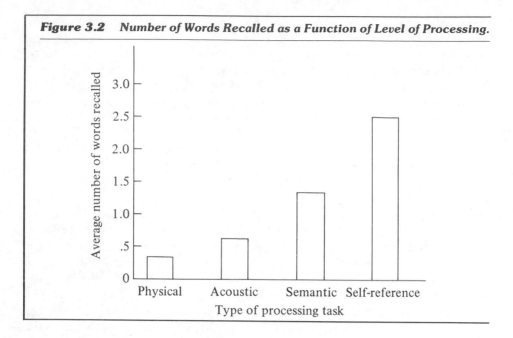

might ask, "Was there a word on the list that rhymed with *toy*?" Bransford and his colleagues found that performance on this rhyming test was better for those who had performed the rhyming encoding task than for those who had performed the sentence encoding task. Thus, the "shallow" acoustic task produced greater recall than the "deep" semantic test. Their research demonstrates that deep semantic processing may not be ideal if the retrieval task emphasizes some other aspect of words, such as their sound or their appearance.

Recently, Craik and other researchers have been trying to specify *why* deep processing produces better recall. Craik (1979) proposes that when a stimulus is processed at a deep level, for a long period of time, this stimulus becomes distinctive. **Distinctiveness** describes the extent to which a stimulus is different from the other memory traces in the system. For example, suppose that you want to remember the word *egg*. If you perform deep, elaborate processing on that word, you may come up with an encoding that features a hen laying an egg on your head, which cracks and dribbles down your face into a frying pan. That encoding is probably very distinctive, because it is different from any other memory trace in your system. Your recall for the word *egg* should be excellent!

The strongest criticism of levels-of-processing theory comes from Baddeley (1978). He points out, for example, that it is difficult to conduct research about levels of processing because there is no independent, objective measure of processing depth. It seems intuitive that we can define physical encoding as "shallow" and semantic encoding as "deep." However, psychologists have been trained to base their definitions on measurable characteristics, instead of intuitions. Furthermore, we cannot define depth in terms of recall (for example, if people recall many words, then recall must have been deep), because that would be circular.

Although the levels-of-processing theory has been well received so far, its future success may depend upon finding a way to measure the critical feature, depth of processing.

At present, there is no one, dominant model of memory that is widely accepted by all. Some researchers support the current version of the levels-of-processing theory. Others support one of the recent variations of the Atkinson-Shiffrin model, and still others have rejected both models.

The debate about theoretical matters produces a very practical problem: how should a textbook chapter on memory be organized? Most authors find it convenient for organizational purposes to preserve the distinction between STM and LTM, even though the difference is sometimes fuzzy. This approach seems reasonable. Therefore, we will first discuss short-term memory, the limited set of items that are currently being used. After that, we will concentrate on long-term memory, that vast quantity of currently inactive material.

SECTION SUMMARY: *Models of Memory*

1. Memory involves maintaining information over time.
2. Two influential models are the Atkinson-Shiffrin and the levels-of-processing approach.
3. Atkinson and Shiffrin's model consists of three memory stores: sensory memory, which records information from the senses; short-term memory, which contains the information we are actively using; and long-term memory, which stores information in a more permanent form.
4. In the Atkinson-Shiffrin model, control processes supplement the structural features. An example of a control process is rehearsal.
5. There has been an enormous volume of research about whether short-term memory (STM) is different from long-term memory (LTM). One study showed, for example, that material in STM is coded in terms of its sound and material in LTM is coded in terms of its meaning. However, other studies have indicated that there may be only one kind of memory.
6. Craik and Lockhart proposed a levels-of-processing theory, which states that deeper processing of material leads to more permanent retention. An increase in the amount of shallow, maintenance rehearsal will not aid later recall. However, additional deep, elaborative rehearsal will be helpful.
7. Levels-of-processing theory has been further developed to reflect the importance of method of testing. Furthermore, current theory suggests that deep processing is effective because it produces stimulus distinctiveness.

Short-Term Memory

You have probably had an experience like this in recent weeks. You are standing at a pay telephone, looking up a telephone number. You find the number, repeat it to yourself, and close the phone book. You take out the coins, insert them, and raise your finger to dial the number. To your dismay, you can't remember the number!

The first digits were *586,* and there was a *4* somewhere else in the number, but you have no idea what the other numbers are!

When you are trying to remember a number for several seconds, you are using short-term memory. Short-term memory refers to the small amount of information that we keep in an active state for a brief period of time. It involves the information that we are currently using—the information that we are currently attending to, processing, and repeating to ourselves. Some theorists argue that short-term memory applies to all the information of which we are consciously aware. (Recall our discussion in Chapter 2 about the limited amount of information in consciousness.)

Incidentally, you may find other terms that are similar to short-term memory. Three of these terms, **working memory, active memory,** and **immediate memory,** emphasize the idea that STM consists of the information we are currently processing (Craik & Levy, 1976; Lewis, 1979). Another term that is frequently used is **primary memory.** This term points out that short-term memory comes first, before secondary memory, which is a synonym for long-term memory (Klatzky, 1980). A fourth term, **short-term store,** emphasizes the physical storage of items in short-term memory. A comparison of different terms for short-term memory is included in a chapter by Craik and Levy (1976).

What can short-term memory do for us? Craik and Levy point out how STM is essential for listening to speech. Think about what happens when you listen to a sentence. You must hold several words in memory until the end of a phrase in order to interpret the phrase. For example, a sentence that begins "A bank . . ." is ambiguous until the remainder of the phrase informs you whether the speaker refers to a river bank, a piggy bank, or a bank building. Thus, we hold a few words in STM while we work on them, consulting our knowledge in LTM to help us understand the meaning and the structure of the phrase. You may sometimes be aware of the limits of STM in language processing when a sentence is too long and too complex. Suppose, for example, that you heard this sentence:

> *The girl who asked about the boy that the woman with the large income hired never came back again.*

Did you have the sensation that items were slipping away? We will return to the role of memory in language in Chapter 5.

Baddeley (1976) discusses the importance of STM in other mental processes. For example, STM is critical for reading and for reasoning. As you read the remaining chapters in this book, try to imagine how you could form images, speak and understand language, identify concepts, solve problems, reason, and make decisions *without* STM.

We have been discussing the usefulness of short-term memory. One feature of STM might strike you as particularly *useless*, however. You may wish that STM information could be more permanent, rather than being so fragile. The temporary nature of STM is actually an advantage. It is quite desirable for STM to purge itself of information that we do not need any longer. Do you really want that telephone number that you dialed last week to be cluttering up the information you are currently processing? Think how chaotic your short-term memory would be if it retained information about every meal you ever ate, every odor you ever sniffed, every song you ever heard, every pain you ever felt, and every sight you ever saw! The loss of information from our short-term memories is necessary, rather than undesirable, because we want to be able to attend to the current task. As we have discussed before in this book—and will discuss throughout the book—our cognitive apparatus is impressively well adapted to the tasks it must accomplish.

What methods have been used to determine the characteristics of short-term memory? Demonstration 3.2 shows a modified version of the Brown-Peterson technique, one method that is frequently used. John Brown (1958), a British psychologist, and Peterson and Peterson (1959), two American psychologists, independently demonstrated that material held in memory for less than a minute could be forgotten. The technique therefore bears the names of both research groups.

Demonstration 3.2   *A Modified Version of the Brown-Peterson Technique.*

Take out five index cards. On one side of each card write a group of three words, one underneath another. On the opposite side write the three-digit number. Randomize the order of the cards and set them aside for a few minutes. Then show yourself the first card, with the side containing the words toward you, for about 2 seconds. Then immediately turn over the card and count backward by threes from the three-digit number. Go as fast as possible for 15−20 seconds. (If you can, convince a friend to time you.) Then write down as many of the three words as you can remember. Continue this process with the remaining four cards.

1. appeal
   temper
   burden
	687		4. flower
			   classic
			   predict
				573

2. sober
   persuade
   content
	254		5. silken
			   idle
			   butcher
				433

3. descend
   neglect
   elsewhere
	869			

Peterson and Peterson, for example, asked people to study three letters. Then the subjects counted backward by threes for a short period of time and tried to recall the letters they had originally seen. Although it sounds like a very easy task, recall was alarmingly poor after just 18 seconds of counting backwards. Figure 3.3 shows some typical results with the Brown-Peterson technique. People forgot about half of what they had studied after a mere 5-second delay!

This demonstration of astounding forgetting after a few seconds' delay had an important impact on memory research. Psychologists who had previously asked their subjects to learn long lists of words and recall them after long delays now began to investigate recall after just a few seconds' delay. In general, their research

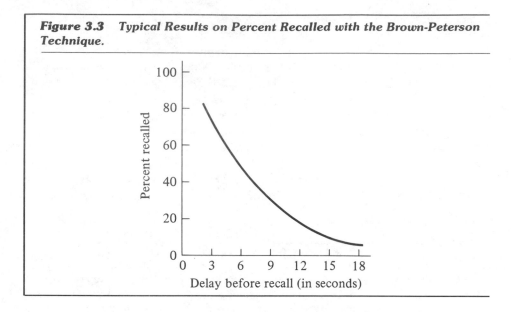

Figure 3.3   *Typical Results on Percent Recalled with the Brown-Peterson Technique.*

focused on four areas: (1) the size of STM, (2) the code in STM, (3) rehearsal, and (4) forgetting. Klatzky's (1980) book can be consulted for information on other issues in short-term memory.

The Size of Short-Term Memory

Suppose that a friend told you his age—19. You would have no trouble remembering that. You would have little trouble remembering a four-digit street address, such as 2614. However, a standard seven-digit phone number is more challenging—346-3421. If you added on an area code to make the phone number 212-346-3421, it is unlikely that you would remember the number correctly.

There are two ways to measure the size of short-term memory. One way is to ask people to look at a long list of items, perhaps 20 to 25 words long, and to recall as many of these words as possible. Then you graph the relationship between the position in which a word was presented (first, second, third, and so on) and the likelihood of recalling the word. Typically, the results look like Figure 3.4. This relationship between a word's position and its recall is called a **serial position curve;** the curve usually shows accurate recall at the beginning and end of the list and inaccurate recall in the middle. Many researchers in short-term memory believe that the relatively accurate recall of words at the end of the list can be attributed to the fact that these items were still in STM at the time of recall. Thus, we can measure the size of short-term memory by determining the number of items at the end of the list that are accurately recalled. Typically, the size of short-term memory is estimated to be two to five items when the serial-position curve method is used.

More often, short-term memory size is measured in terms of **memory span,** or the number of items in a row that can be correctly recalled. Your ability to remember phone numbers is therefore a test of memory span. Several intelligence tests, such as the Wechsler Adult Intelligence Scale, include a test of memory span.

Figure 3.4 **A Typical Serial Position Curve.**

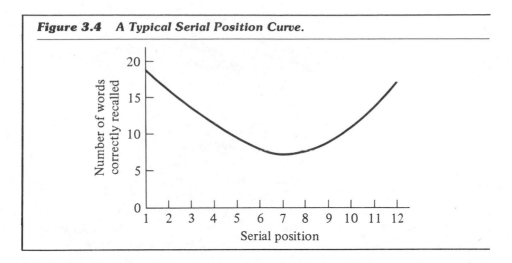

Researchers have been interested in the size of the memory span for about 100 years. However, memory span research gained particular importance in 1956 when George Miller wrote his famous article titled "The Magical Number Seven, Plus or Minus Two: Some Limits on Our Capacity for Processing Information." Miller proposed that humans cannot keep many items in short-term memory at one time. In particular, he suggested that people can remember about seven items (give or take two), or between five and nine items.

Miller used the term **chunk** to describe the basic unit in short-term memory. Thus we can say that short-term memory holds about seven chunks. A chunk can be a single digit or a single letter, because people can remember about seven digits or letters if they are in random order. However, those digits and letters can be organized into larger units. For example, you may know that your area code is 212 and that all of the phone numbers at your college begin with the same digits, 346. If 212 is one chunk and 346 is another chunk, then the phone number 212-346-3421 really has only six chunks. It may be within your memory span. Loudon and Della Bitta (1979) mention in their book on consumer psychology that radio advertisers should take advantage of chunking if they plan to include a phone number in their ad. The number should be announced in chunked form to facilitate memory.

Although Miller's article received major attention, many people complained that the *chunk* was not a well-defined concept. For example, Simon (1974) complained that the problem with the term *chunk* was that it was defined in a circular fashion. That is, a chunk is what there are seven of in short-term memory! In order for a chunk to be a more meaningful term, it should have some relationship to another psychological task, in addition to short-term memory. Simon chose to examine performance on long-term memory tasks. He reasoned that if the chunk is a real, legitimate concept, then the amount of time required for long-term memory learning should be related to the number of chunks in memory. In fact, Simon did find this kind of relationship. Thus, the chunk is a legitimate concept. It is not simply an arbitrary term describing the seven units in memory, because it is so closely related to learning time.

There is some argument about whether the number of chunks in short-term memory is seven or whether the actual number is smaller (Broadbent, 1975). However, there is strong agreement that the capacity is indeed limited. You cannot easily fit an entire shopping list of 27 items into your short-term memory unless you use special organizational techniques, such as those described in the last section of this chapter.

I want you to remember this number—*639721*—while you are reading the next few sentences. How are you doing? Don't you feel your comprehension failing as you try to slip in one more silent repetition of the number? Alternately, that number may be floating away as you try to read this sentence. Since the capacity of short-term memory is limited, you cannot remember and work at the same time. This point was demonstrated by Baddeley and Hitch (1974) in their article on working memory. They found that when people were asked to hold a list of items in memory, their performance on other tasks suffered. For example, some people were given a six-digit number and were asked to respond "true" or "false" to statements such as "*A* is not preceded by *B*—*AB*." Now this reasoning task would be simple if no additional memory tasks were required, but people took much longer when they had to remember a string of digits. Language comprehension and free recall also suffered when there was an additional memory load.

Baddeley and Hitch's work has a very practical implication. Do not try to remember something if you want to perform on another task. You cannot carry on a decent conversation if you are trying to remember the mileage on your car's odometer! As we discussed in Chapter 2, performance often suffers when attention is divided among two or more tasks, and memory is a task that requires attention.

The Code in Short-Term Memory

Suppose that you have just called the post office to find out the zip code for a friend in Altadena, California. The clerk tells you "91001." How do you keep *91001* in your short-term memory until you can write it down? Do you store it in terms of the way it sounds, the way it looks, or some aspect of its meaning? In other words, how are items coded in short-term memory?

Most likely, you will answer that you would code *91001* in terms of its sound. In fact, you might claim that you can almost "hear" yourself repeating *91001* over and over to yourself. You would even be likely to code in terms of sound if you looked at a visual version of the zip code, located on a page of a zip code directory. As you will see, the evidence strongly favors an **acoustic code**—that is, storage in terms of the sound of an item. (You may recall our discussion of acoustic coding in short-term memory from the first section of the chapter.) However, as Postman (1975) warns us, the acoustic code is certainly not the only code used in short-term memory. An item can also be coded in terms of a **semantic code**, involving the meaning of the item, or in terms of a **visual code**, involving the physical appearance of the item.

Acoustic Coding in STM.   Numerous experiments have demonstrated the importance of acoustic coding in short-term memory (for example, Conrad, 1964). The study by Kintsch and Buschke that we discussed in connection with the

Atkinson-Shiffrin model also supports acoustic coding. We will look at one other representative study, performed by Wickelgren (1965). On each trial, Wickelgren presented a tape recording of an eight-item list, consisting of four letters and four digits in random order. Thus, a typical item might be *4NF9G27Z*. As soon as the list was finished, people tried to recall it. Wickelgren was particularly interested in the kinds of substitutions people made. For example, if they did not correctly recall the *Z* at the end of the list, what did they recall in its place? He found that people tended to substitute an item that was acoustically similar. For example, instead of the last *Z*, they might substitute a *B, C, D, E, G, P, T,* or *V*, all letters with the "ee" sound. Furthermore, if they substituted a number for *Z*, it would most likely be the similar-sounding number *3*.

Semantic Coding in STM.   There is also substantial evidence that items in short-term memory can be coded in terms of their meaning (Shulman, 1971). For example, Shulman (1972) found that people tended to confuse words that had similar meanings, just as Wickelgren found that people tended to confuse items that had similar sounds.

Wickens, Dalezman, and Eggemeier (1976) used a different technique to demonstrate the importance of meaning in short-term memory. Their technique is based on a concept from verbal learning called proactive inhibition. **Proactive inhibition** (abbreviated PI) means that people have trouble learning new material because previously learned material keeps getting in the way of new learning. Thus, if you previously had to remember the items *XCE, HBR,* and *TVY* in a Brown-Peterson test of short-term memory, you will have trouble remembering a fourth item, *KRI*, because the three previous items keep interfering. However, if the experimenter shifts the nature of the items from letters to, say, numbers, there will be a **release from proactive inhibition**; performance on the new, different item (say, *529*) will be amost as high as it was on the first item, *XCE*.

Many experiments have demonstrated release from PI when the class of items is shifted, as from letters to numbers. However, Wickens and his coauthors demonstrated that release from PI could be obtained when the semantic class of items is shifted. They gave people three trials on the Brown-Peterson test, with each trial consisting of three names of fruits, as outlined in Table 3.2. Thus, on Trial 1 a person might see *banana, peach,* and *apple,* followed by the three-digit number *259*. After counting backward by threes from this number for 18 seconds, they tried to recall the three words.

Everyone received the same three trials concerning fruits, but there were five different kinds of material presented on the fourth trial: fruits, vegetables, flowers, meats, and professions. We would expect the buildup of PI to be the greatest for the people who had to remember fruits on the fourth trial; their performance should be poor. After all, their memories should be full of other fruits that would be interfering with the new fruits! However, if meaning is important in short-term memory, performance in the other four conditions should depend upon the semantic similarity between these items and fruit. For example, people who received vegetables on the fourth trial should do rather poorly, since fruits and vegetables are similar—they are both edible and grow in the ground. People who received

TABLE 3.2   The Setup for Experiments on Release from PI

Condition	Trial 1	Trial 2	Trial 3	Trial 4
Fruits (Control)	banana	plum	melon	orange
	peach	apricot	lemon	cherry
	apple	lime	grape	pineapple
Vegetables	banana	plum	melon	onion
	peach	apricot	lemon	radish
	apple	lime	grape	potato
Flowers	banana	plum	melon	daisies
	peach	apricot	lemon	violet
	apple	lime	grape	tulip
Meats	banana	plum	melon	salami
	peach	apricot	lemon	bacon
	apple	lime	grape	hamburger
Professions	banana	plum	melon	doctor
	peach	apricot	lemon	teacher
	apple	lime	grape	lawyer

flowers and meats should do somewhat better, since flowers and meats share only one attribute with fruits. However, people who received professions should do the best of all, since professions are not edible and do not grow in the ground.

Figure 3.5 is an example of the kind of results every researcher hopes to find. Note that the results are exactly as predicted. In summary, meaning is important in short-term memory because old words interfere with the recall of new words that are similar in meaning. Furthermore, the degree of semantic similarity is related to the amount of interference.

Visual Coding in STM.   Items can also be coded in short-term memory in terms of their visual characteristics. We will talk about visual images in memory in the next chapter, and the experiments by Shepard and Metzler (1971), Brooks (1968), and Segal and Fusella (1970) are among those that demonstrate that the physical appearance of items can be coded in short-term memory.

A study by Posner and Keele (1967) also shows that we can store an item in terms of the way it looks. In their experiment, people saw pairs of letters such as A-A, A-a, A-B, and A-b. Sometimes the two letters were presented at the same time, but other times there was a brief delay between the two letters. In each case, people were requested to answer whether the letters had identical names or not. Posner and Keele were particularly interested to see whether people took longer to respond "yes" to A-a pairs than to A-A pairs. After all, if items are stored merely in terms of their *sounds*, then the response to A-a should be as fast as the response to A-A. However, if items are stored in terms of the way they look, then A-a pairs should take longer because the visual symbols must be translated into the appropriate names. A-A pairs, in contrast, would require no translation.

Posner and Keele found that when the delay between the two letters was less

Figure 3.5   Release from PI, as a Function of Semantic Similarity. (Based on Wickens, Dalezman, and Eggemeier, 1976.)

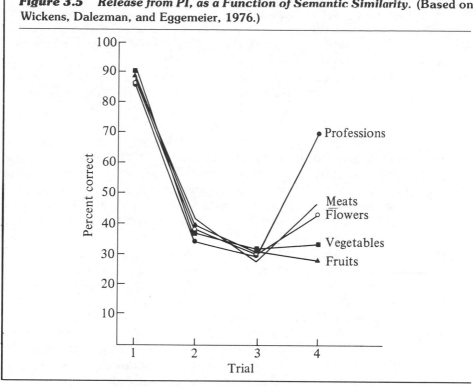

than 1.5 seconds, *A-a* pairs did indeed take longer than *A-A* pairs. However, when the delay was longer than 1.5 seconds, *A-a* pairs and *A-A* pairs took the same amount of time. The pair *A-a* was therefore initially coded in terms of the physical appearance of the letters, but after 1.5 seconds the letters were coded in terms of the identical letter name, "Ay." Thus, a visual code can be stored in short-term memory for very brief periods of time. However, this visual code seems to be quite fragile, because it is soon replaced by an auditory code.

In this section, we have explored the various ways in which information is stored in short-term memory. In general, an auditory code is used. However, in some experimental situations, people can use either semantic or visual codes. (Incidentally, what was the number I asked you to remember several pages ago?)

Rehearsal in Short-Term Memory

You've just been introduced to Abigail Jones at a party, and you want to remember her name. You might find yourself repeating "Abigail Jones, Abigail Jones, Abigail Jones . . ." in an attempt to keep that name in your memory. You are using rehearsal, the cycling of information through memory that we mentioned earlier.

Rehearsal is one of the kinds of jobs that short-term memory performs. You may recall that Atkinson and Shiffrin's (1968) model proposed that rehearsal is necessary in order to keep information in short-term memory. Without rehearsal, an item could be forgotten. In fact, remember that the Brown-Peterson technique specified that people must count backward by threes during the interval between the presentation of an item and its recall. This counting-backward task was included in order to prevent rehearsal. After all, if people simply saw three letters, such as *XLU*, and were allowed to do anything they wanted for the next 18 seconds, they would industriously mutter to themselves "*XLU, XLU, XLU,* . . ." for the entire 18 seconds. However, the counting backward task effectively prevented rehearsal, and so only a small fraction of the unrehearsed material was recalled after an 18-second delay.

Although rehearsal may sound like an innocent topic, a small battle has raged among psychologists interested in memory. This battle concerns the nature and the function of rehearsal. Atkinson and Shiffrin had originally suggested not only that rehearsal maintained information in short-term memory, but that it also was vitally important for information to be transferred to long-term memory. That is, items that received more rehearsal in STM were more likely to be stored in LTM.

However, several researchers found that the amount of rehearsal in short-term memory was *not* always related to the probability of recall from LTM (for example, Craik & Watkins, 1973; Woodward, Bjork, & Jongeward, 1973). Craik and Watkins, for example, emphasized that there are two different kinds of rehearsal. One kind of rehearsal, maintenance rehearsal, simply maintains an item in short-term memory; it cannot influence LTM. In contrast, the other kind of rehearsal, elaborative rehearsal, enriches and supplements the item with extra meaning, making it more likely to be stored in LTM. (You will recall that we discussed this issue in our examination of the levels-of-processing theory proposed by Craik and Lockhart.) Thus, if people simply use maintenance rehearsal and repeat an item over and over to themselves, this shallow kind of rehearsal would provide no advantage in transferring that item to LTM. As a practical suggestion, then, repeating Abigail Jones' name over and over to yourself will not force the name into LTM.

More recent evidence suggests that the maintenance rehearsal issue may not be that simple. A study by Glenberg, Smith, and Green (1977) examined the influence of maintenance rehearsal on both recall and recognition. **Recall** is typically the more difficult task, because it requires a person to supply an appropriate answer, with no hints given. In contrast, **recognition** simply requires a person to identify whether or not an item has been seen before. Thus, if I ask you who wrote the short story, "The Yellow Wallpaper," I am requesting recall. However, if I ask you whether you have seen the name "Renoir" in the previous pages of this book, I am requesting recognition. At any rate, Glenberg and his colleagues found that maintenance rehearsal did help people *recognize* the rehearsed items. However, it was not useful in helping people *recall* the items. Further discussion of the topic of rehearsal and memory appears in an article by Baddeley (1978).

Forgetting in Short-Term Memory

Think about the occasions in the past few weeks in which you forgot something in short-term memory. You may have forgotten a phone number or a person's name that you had just heard. You may have been pondering an idea, and then something briefly distracted you. When you wanted to return to the original idea, it floated away mysteriously.

Why do we forget things from short-term memory? Two of the most popular theories of forgetting in short-term memory are interference theory and decay theory. **Interference theory** states that forgetting occurs because other items get in the way of the information we want to remember; that is, these other items cause interference. We discussed one source of interference, proactive inhibition, when we talked about the study by Wickens and his colleagues. You'll recall that people who had to remember a list of fruits had trouble by the fourth trial because all the other fruits kept getting in the way. In proactive inhibition, the *old* memories interfere with the *new* memories. *Pro*active, like *pro*gress, means that memories work in a *forward* direction to harm the new memories.

Another source of interference in forgetting is **retroactive inhibition** in which the *new* memories interfere with the *old* memories. Thus, if you are trying to remember Abigail Jones' name, a new name like Priscilla Brown will cause retroactive inhibition. Similarly, have you noticed how the two kinds of inhibition operate if you borrow someone else's car? At first you experience proactive inhibition; all the characteristics of the car you usually drive interfere with learning the characteristics of this new car. If you drive this car long enough, however, the experience will lead to retroactive inhibition. That is, the new learning will interfere with the old, and you will forget certain characteristics that you once knew well. In short, proactive inhibition and retroactive inhibition both provide interference.

Decay theory states that a memory trace decays or fades as time passes, unless you repeat or rehearse the item. Imagine that you have written a word in water on a hot summer sidewalk. The "trace" becomes fainter and fainter as the water evaporates. Eventually, you can no longer identify the word. People who support decay theory believe that time passage alone is sufficient for forgetting, and that interference from old and new items is not necessary.

Now it may seem that it would be easy to perform an experiment to determine, once and for all, whether forgetting in short-term memory is due to interference or decay. We could present a word and ask the subjects to do absolutely nothing for perhaps 18 seconds. Specifically, they must not think about other words because this would cause interference, and they must not rehearse this word. After 18 seconds, we ask for recall. If recall is perfect, the interference theorists win because there was no interference and consequently no decline in memory. If recall is poor, the decay theorists win because the mere passage of time was sufficient to cause forgetting. However, as you can imagine, subjects are extremely uncooperative on this task—they refuse to do nothing!

After several false starts at trying to answer the interference-decay question, one well-designed experiment produced an interesting answer: *both* decay and interference seem to cause forgetting in short-term memory. Judith Reitman (1974) tried to find a task that would prevent people from rehearsing but would cause minimal interference. For example, she rejected the Brown-Peterson technique of having people count backward because saying the names of the numbers probably causes interference. She decided to use a tone detection task, in which people tried to listen for a pure tone against a noisy background. Thus, people saw some words, then listened for the tones, then recalled the original words.

Now it would be tempting to cheat on this task and rehearse surreptitiously. You might listen for a few seconds, then sneak in a rehearsal of one word, listen a bit longer, rehearse once more, and so on. In fact, most of Reitman's subjects did rehearse. She used a clever method to identify the people who rehearsed. As another part of the experiment, she included a tone detection session in which subjects were not required to remember any words. Thus, Reitman could compare people's performance on the tone detection task for the two conditions, the memory condition and the no-memory condition. Reitman found that 42 of her 52 subjects performed more poorly in the memory condition. In other words, these people missed some of the tones because they were surreptitiously rehearsing.

Let us examine the remaining ten subjects—those who could not have been rehearsing because their performance was equivalent for the two conditions. Reitman found that these nonrehearsing subjects forgot 33 percent of the material. The title of her article summarizes this conclusion: "Without Surreptitious Rehearsal, Information in Short-Term Memory Decays."

Reitman found evidence for interference as well as decay, however. Some other subjects detected syllables, rather than tones, as their rehearsal prevention task. Syllables are quite similar to the words in memory, whereas tones are quite different. Interference theorists maintain that similar items cause greater interference. How did the syllable condition compare with the tone condition? They forgot much more of the material, because increased interference caused greater forgetting. Reitman's experiment thus demonstrated that both decay and interference cause forgetting. When you cannot remember someone's name 20 seconds after you have been introduced, you can therefore blame *both* decay and interference!

SECTION SUMMARY: Short-Term Memory

1. **Short-term memory (STM) refers to the small amount of information that we keep in an active state for a short period of time.**
2. **Short-term memory is essential in the understanding of speech and in other mental processes.**
3. **A large proportion of material is forgotten in STM after a few seconds' delay.**
4. **The amount of information in STM is clearly limited, but estimates of the amount range between two and nine items.**
5. **Information in STM is usually stored in terms of an auditory code, but semantic and visual codes can also be used.**
6. **In general, maintenance rehearsal does not aid the recall of items from long-term memory, although it does aid recognition.**
7. **Items are forgotten from STM because of both interference and decay.**

Long-Term Memory

Let us now turn our attention to long-term memory, the huge, relatively permanent kind of memory. Think for a moment about the enormous capacity of long-term memory and the wide variety of information it contains. It contains terms such as *belly button* and *Constantinople*. It contains facts such as *Baltic Avenue is not prime property in the game of Monopoly* and *My sister's child is named Jerome*. It contains information about the world such as *What goes up most come down* and *Blue crayon plus yellow crayon equals green.* It contains spatial information such as *To get to the Crêpe restaurant, turn left at the gas station and go about one mile* and *The number 9 is to the left of 3 on the face of a clock.* Think about other kinds of information you have in your long-term memory, such as knowledge of social behavior, motor skills, and perceptual skills. Concentrate on identifying several additional far-flung facts that you have stored somewhere in your long-term memory.

You may recall that we discussed several alternate names for short-term memory. There are also some alternate names for long-term memory. Some people use the name permanent memory, although we shall see that this name is misleading. Another name, **secondary memory,** emphasizes that information must first pass through another store before reaching this second storage area. The phrase **long-term store** emphasizes the physical storage of items in long-term memory. Finally, the name **inactive memory** emphasizes the information we are not currently using.

We have six topics to consider in our discussion of long-term memory: (1) the accuracy of long-term memory, (2) the distinction between episodic memory and semantic memory, (3) retrieval from long-term memory, (4) motivational factors and long-term memory, (5) forgetting in long-term memory, and (6) semantic memory.

The Accuracy of Long-Term Memory

When you were contemplating the contents of your long-term memory, you may have amazed yourself by uncovering some topic you hadn't thought about in years. Researchers have recently become interested in demonstrating some spectacular memory accomplishments. The subjects in these studies are ordinary humans, typically college students, rather than "memory specialists."

One of the first of these studies was performed by Shepard (1967). He presented 540 English words to people and then tested their recognition memory by asking them to identify which number of a pair had been previously exposed. They correctly identified an average of 88 percent of the words. Furthermore, another group of people were 89 percent accurate on a series of 612 short English sentences. Thus, people are quite accurate in identifying whether or not they have previously seen semantic material.

People are even more impressive, however, when the material is visual. Shepard also tested recognition memory for pictures, primarily magazine advertisements. Two hours after seeing the picture, people correctly recognized 99.7 percent of the pictures! Standing (1973) found impressive recognition for people who had seen *10,000* pictures. In fact, from one set of pictures, he estimated that if people were shown 1 million pictures, they would retain 731,400 of them two days later.

Our recall of pictures is astounding in terms of accuracy and quantity, but it is also equally impressive in terms of time. Standing, Conezio, and Haber (1970) found that people were 63 percent accurate a *year* after viewing 2560 pictures. Keep in mind that these pictures are seen only once, and for just a few seconds, yet people are substantially better than chance in recognizing them a year later.

How will people perform on visual stimuli to which they have been exposed for longer periods of time? Bahrick, Bahrick, and Wittlinger (1975) answered this question using an ingenious kind of material—high school yearbook pictures. They tested people who had graduated from high school as recently as two weeks ago and as long ago as 57 years. One of the most impressive facts was that, 15 years after graduation, people could still match names with pictures for 90 percent of their classmates' faces. Furthermore, people who were in their 50s and 60s could still recognize 75 percent of their classmates' faces!

So far we have examined words, sentences, and pictures. How accurate are people in recognizing other sensory material? Lawrence and Banks (1973) tested memory for 194 sounds such as a baby sneezing, horses neighing, and a tap-dancing routine. Recognition for these sounds was about 87 percent correct. Memory for smells is also impressive. Engen and Ross (1973) found that recognition of smells three months after exposure was almost as accurate as it had been after a delay of three seconds. Think about your own long-term recall of tactile and taste sensations. Do your jeans feel scratchier than when they last came out of the wash? Could you recognize the lemon ice at Sal's pizzeria, even though you were last there three years ago?

Incidentally, this information about long-term memory for different kinds of information tells us something about the coding mechanics used in long-term memory. You will recall that we concluded that coding in short-term memory was primarily acoustic, but that other kinds of coding could also be used. In long-term memory, it is clear that multiple codings can also be used. We can code an Italian sausage in terms of the meaning of the words, the visual image, the spicy smell, the peppery taste, the hot juices, and the sound our teeth make as they puncture the crisp skin. In general, semantic and visual codes would probably be the most important codes. As we will see in the next chapter, there is an argument about the relative importance of these two codes.

Episodic versus Semantic Memory

In 1972, Tulving introduced an important distinction between two kinds of memory: episodic memory and semantic memory. Let us examine how these two kinds of memory differ from each other.

Episodic memory (pronounced "ehp-ih-*sah*-dick") stores information about *when* events happened. Here are some examples of episodic memory: (a) The telephone rang a short while ago, followed by a thump as snow fell off the roof; (b) At Christmas time, I saw a Santa Claus whose beard was falling off; (c) I have a dentist appointment at 3:30 tomorrow; (d) The word *dulcimer* was on the first of the lists I learned in this experiment; and (e) I know that *jump* was paired with the number *378* on this list of items. Notice that each of these statements refers to personal experience, and each experience is remembered in relation to other experiences.

Semantic memory is the organized knowledge about words and symbols. This knowledge includes their meaning, the relationship among the words and symbols, and the rules for manipulating them. Here are some examples of semantic memory: (a) I know that *pi* equals 3.1416; (b) I know that velvet is soft; (c) I know that the shortest day of the year is in December; (d) I remember that the chemical formula for water is H_2O; and (e) I know that the meaning of the word *semantic* is closer to the meaning of the word *vocabulary* then it is to the word *huckleberry*. In each case, these statements do not refer to unique episodes that I have experienced. Instead, they refer to general concepts and the way these concepts are related.

The episodic and semantic memory systems differ in other ways, according to Tulving. For example, forgetting is much more likely in episodic than in semantic memory. You can retrieve information from episodic memory only if you have the right kind of cues about when the event occurred. However, information in semantic memory is usually encoded into a rich structure of concepts, and this rich structure probably protects the stored information from interference.

Is episodic memory really very different from semantic memory? A study conducted by Underwood, Boruch, and Malmi (1978) suggests that it is. These researchers managed to find 200 college students who agreed to be tested on 28 different measures of episodic memory and 5 different measures of semantic memory. The episodic memory tests included free recall, paired-associate learning, and serial learning, which are outlined in Demonstration 3.3, as well as other less common measures. The semantic memory tests mainly emphasized vocabulary.

Demonstration 3.3 *Free Recall, Paired-Associate Learning, and Serial Learning.*

Three common tasks in long-term memory are free recall, paired-associate learning, and serial learning. **Free-recall** tasks present a list of words, and then subjects recall the words in any order they wish. **Paired-associate learning** requires the subjects to associate two members of a pair. Later, the experimenter presents the first member of the pair and requires the subjects to supply the second member. **Serial learning** tasks require the subjects to supply a list of words in exactly the same order in which they were presented. Try an example of each of these tasks.

Free Recall. Study this list of words. Then close your book and recall the words in any order you wish.

> safe wait student house color duck owe idea fable
> bench pencil window card flowers blouses

Paired-Associate Learning. Study this list of pairs. After you are done, cover up the pairs and look at the list of items below. These are the first members of each pair. In each case, supply the second member.

tall – bone	nose – leaf	grew – few	pear – rain	print – kiss
plan – flea	park – fight	rabbit – cook	mess – crowd	smoke – hand

park – ?	grow – ?	rabbit – ?	smoke – ?	plan – ?
tall – ?	nose – ?	pear – ?	mess – ?	print – ?

Serial Learning. Study this list of words. Then close your book and recall the words in exactly the same order as they appear here.

> cat lawn just news race mint nest tan movie tree

In general, people's scores on the episodic memory tests were not closely related to their scores on the semantic memory tests. For example, a person who recalled a large number of words on a free-recall test was *not* especially likely to have a magnificent vocabulary. Thus, this study points out that episodic and semantic memory are different. Our discussion of long-term memory will emphasize episodic memory. However, the last part of this section examines semantic memory.

Retrieval from Long-Term Memory

Two issues concerning retrieval from long-term memory have been of particular interest to memory psychologists. One issue is whether people who have been asked to retrieve some information simply locate the material in memory and recover the material directly or whether they reconstruct the information on the basis of certain major characteristics. This issue will be discussed in the section on Remembering Language in Chapter 5.

The other issue is the relationship between recall and recognition. Is there a difference between recall and recognition, or are they really similar processes? Indeed, we measure them in different ways. When we measure recall, we require people to produce an answer. When we measure recognition, we merely ask them to decide whether they have previously seen a particular item.

If recall and recognition are similar processes, then we would expect to find that they are influenced in the same way by the same variables. However, if a variable has one effect on recall and a different effect on recognition, then we would suspect that recall and recognition are different processes.

Let us discuss some variables that have different effects on recall and recognition. First of all, there is **word frequency,** or the number of times a word appears in the English language. Many studies have demonstrated that high-frequency words, such as *door* and *spoon* are recalled better than low-frequency words, such as *lemur* and *catarrh*. However, Shepard (1967) found that recognition was much more accurate for those low-frequency words. After all, you know you haven't seen *catarrh* in this book prior to this paragraph, but you are uncertain about *door*. Second, list organization has different influences on recall and recognition. Kintsch (1968) found that recall was better for lists in which words were highly associated with category names than it was for lists in which the associations were weak. However, recognition performance did not differ on the two kinds of lists. Third, you will recall that maintenance rehearsal has different influences on recall and recognition, as discussed in the section on rehearsal.

In summary, there is some evidence that recall and recognition are different processes. A book edited by John Brown (1976) and an article by Rabinowitz, Mandler, and Patterson (1977) discuss other aspects of this argument.

Motivation and Long-term Memory

Zajonc (pronounced, "*Zeye*-unce" to rhyme with "science") has complained that contemporary cognitive psychology has ignored aspects of motivation, such as affect, emotion, and feeling (Zajonc, 1980). However, there are some areas of research on long-term memory in which we do have information about motivation and memory. These areas include the relationship between arousal and memory and the relationship between affect and memory.

Arousal and Memory. You have probably had this experience before. You nervously look over the questions on an examination, and you draw a complete blank on some of them. You may recall learning the material, but you cannot remember enough information to answer the questions. After you leave the exam, however, the answers immediately jump out! The high arousal—or elevated state of bodily function—produced by the examination blocked the retrieval of difficult information.

Eysenck (1976a) has summarized a number of studies on the relationship between arousal and memory. Eysenck hypothesizes that high arousal at the time of recall can either improve or decrease recall, depending upon the nature of the task. High arousal biases people's search processes so that they choose responses that are accessibly stored. In contrast, they cannot retrieve the responses that are inaccessibly stored. If you are working on an easy task, such as taking an examination on material that you know well, then high arousal will lead to easier retrieval of these accessibly stored items. However, if you are working on a difficult task, then high arousal will lead to difficulty in retrieving those inaccessibly stored items.

What is the moral to be drawn from Eysenck's paper? If you know the material well, you will do better if you can give yourself a pep talk beforehand so that you are more aroused and motivated. If you do not know the material well, however, try to relax and calm down so that you can retrieve those answers that are buried in memory.

Brown and Kulik (1977) have examined a particularly vivid kind of memory we occasionally have when we are aroused, which they call flashbulb memories. **Flashbulb memories** are memories for the situation in which we first learned of a very surprising and emotionally arousing event. Try Demonstration 3.4 to see whether you can find examples of flashbulb memories.

Demonstration 3.4   Flashbulb Memory.

Ask several friends whether they can identify any memories for situations in which they first learned about a very surprising, emotional event. Tell them, for example, that many people can recall in vivid detail the circumstances in which they learned about the death of President Kennedy or John Lennon or the circumstances in which they learned of a personally important event. Ask them to write a paragraph describing the flashbulb memory.

My clearest flashbulb memory, like many of my generation, is of learning that John Kennedy had been shot. I was a sophomore at Stanford University, just ready for a mid-day class in German. I had entered the classroom from the right, and I was just about to sit down at a long table on the right-hand side of the classroom. The sun was streaming in from the left. There was only one other person seated in the classroom, a blond fellow named Dewey. He turned around and said, "Did you hear that President Kennedy has been shot?" I also recall my reaction and the reactions of others as they entered the class. Kennedy was shot about 20 years ago, yet trivial details of that incident are stunningly clear today. You can probably think of personal events in your own life that triggered flashbulb memories—the death of a relative, a piece of important good news, or an amazing surprise.

Brown and Kulik point out that these flashbulb memories are clearly not as accurate as a photograph in which a true flashbulb has been fired. For example, I don't remember what books I was carrying or what Dewey was wearing. Nonetheless, they do include details that would be missing from a neutral memory of comparable age.

To examine flashbulb memories, Brown and Kulik questioned people to see whether various national events triggered these memories. Six kinds of information were most likely to be listed in these flashbulb memories, the place, the ongoing event that was interrupted by the news, the person who gave them the news, their own feelings, the emotions in others, and the aftermath. Check the responses to Demonstration 3.4 to see if these items were included in the recall.

Brown and Kulik concluded that the two main determinants of flashbulb memory were a high level of surprise and a high level of emotional arousal or perceived importance. These authors also proposed that these surprising, arousing events were more likely to be rehearsed, either silently or in conversation. Consequently, the memory of these events is more elaborated than that of more ordinary daily events.

Affect and Memory.   Zajonc delivered a Distinguished Scientific Contribution Award address to the American Psychological Association entitled "Feeling and Thinking: Preferences Need No Inferences" (Zajonc, 1980). In this address, Zajonc considers the relationship between feeling, or **affect** (pronounced "*aff*-ekt"), and cognition. Zajonc's basic point is that we often have affective reactions to stimuli before we have cognitive reactions. Thus, when you taste a new soup, you are likely to make an affective reaction, such as "This is absolutely loathsome," before you make a cognitive reaction, such as "The cabbage is the soup tastes burned."

Zajonc also points out that affective reactions can be remembered, even if cognitive reactions have been forgotten. Maybe you've had this kind of experience. Someone mentions a movie or a book, and you draw a complete blank on the plot. However, you remember quite clearly that you liked it very much. For example, think of some books you read between the ages of 10 and 15. Are there some that you recall loving or hating, yet you cannot summarize beyond the content suggested by the title? Similarly, you may remember that you dislike someone intensely yet have no recall for the cause of the conflict.

An early study by Yavuz and Bousfield (1959) offers experimental support for Zajonc's point about affect and memory. These authors asked people to learn a list of paired associates, in which the stimulus was a nonsense word and the response was an English word that was pleasant, neutral, or unpleasant. Even when people couldn't remember the exact response, they were highly accurate in recalling whether it was pleasant or unpleasant. For example, if they couldn't remember the response "trouble," they still recalled that the response was something unpleasant.

One aspect of affect and memory that has been extensively researched is recall for items and events that differ in pleasantness. Before you read further, try Demonstration 3.5. We saw in the discussion of flashbulb memories that people have very distinct recall for intensely tragic events. Intensely happy events—though it is more difficult to think of intensely happy events at the national level—are also distinctly recalled. If we match for intensity, however, do people recall pleasant and unpleasant items equally well? In a book called *The Pollyanna Principle: Selectivity in Language, Memory, and Thought* (Matlin & Stang, 1978), we found that pleasant items are recalled better than either negative or neutral items.

Demonstration 3.5   Lists of Items.

Take out a piece of paper and make three columns of numbers from 1 to 10. For the first set of numbers, list 10 vegetables, in any order you wish. For the next set, list 10 fruits. For the last set, list 10 professors that you have taken courses from.

Now, arrange each of the three lists in alphabetical order on a separate piece of paper, and set the original lists aside. Rank each item with respect to the other members of the list. For example, give your favorite vegetable a rank of 1 and your least favorite vegetable a rank of 10. Finally, transfer each of the ranks back to the original list. Thus, each of the ten items on each of the three lists should now have a rank next to it.

The **Pollyanna Principle** states that pleasant items are usually processed more efficiently and more accurately than less pleasant items. This principle holds true for a wide variety of phenomena in perception, language, and decision making, but it has been most widely documented in memory. We located 52 long-term memory studies in which people were asked to recall items or events that varied in pleasantness. In 39 of the studies, pleasant items were recalled significantly more accurately than unpleasant items.

Furthermore, pleasant items are remembered *before* less pleasant items. Now look at your responses for Demonstration 3.5. Did you list vegetables you like (those with ranks of 1, 2, and 3) before the vegetables you detest (those with ranks of 8, 9, and 10)? Are your favorite professors first on the list? Matlin, Stang, Gawron, Freedman, and Derby (1979) found that when people made lists of fruits, vegetables, and professors, pleasant items "tumbled out" of memory prior to neutral or unpleasant items. Matlin and Stang (1978) propose that pleasant items may be stored more accessibly in memory. As a result, they can be recalled quickly and accurately. The Pollyanna Principle is consistent with a theme we discussed in Chapter 1: Positive information is easier to process accurately than negative information.

Forgetting in Long-Term Memory

The topic of forgetting in long-term memory is an enormous one. Aspects of this subject will be covered in Chapter 5 when we discuss the kinds of errors people make when they are trying to recall language material. Right now, however, we will examine two topics: the permanence of memory and theories of forgetting.

The Permanence of Memory.   Try Demonstration 3.6. What answers did your friends give? What is your own response to the question? Loftus and Loftus (1980) informally asked this question to a number of people, some of whom were psychologists and some of whom had other occupations, such as lawyers, taxicab drivers, and philosophers. They found that 84 percent of the psychologists and 69 percent of the nonpsychologists favored answer 1. In other words, there is a widespread belief that the information we learn is permanently stored somewhere in memory, even if we cannot always recover it.

Demonstration 3.6   The Permanence of Memory.

Ask several friends the following question:

> **Which of these statements best reflects your view on how human memory works?**

1. Everything we learn is permanently stored in the mind, although sometimes particular details are not accessible. With hypnosis, or other special techniques, these inaccessible details could eventually be recovered.
2. Some details that we learn may be permanently lost from memory. Such details would never be able to be recovered by hypnosis, or any other special technique, because these details are simply no longer there.

> Please elaborate briefly or give any reasons you may have for your view.

(Loftus and Loftus, 1980, p. 410.)

Loftus and Loftus review the kinds of evidence that people use in support of the permanence of memory, and they conclude that the evidence offers no support for the permanent-memory idea. Their article covers several techniques that presumably recover inaccessible ideas: hypnosis, psychoanalysis, and brain stimulation.

Many people believe that hypnosis can be used to reactivate memories. In fact, various law agencies have used hypnosis to try to solve criminal cases. However, Loftus and Loftus criticize this technique because there is no evidence that recall under hypnosis is any more accurate or complete than recall under normal waking conditions. It is more difficult to assess the usefulness of psychoanalysis because researchers usually cannot obtain independent judgments of accuracy. For example, suppose that a man recalls in a therapy session that he was scared by a snake when he was a child—a "memory" that he had not previously recalled. How can we know whether that really happened or whether it was a fantasy? However, both hypnosis and psychoanalysis may help a person relax, and people may be more willing to report *some* memories when they are relaxed. (As you recall, arousal influences memory.) Still, this does not imply that *all* memories are potentially retrievable.

When the psychologists in the Loftus and Loftus survey provided a rationale for the permanent-memory idea, they most often cited the studies conducted by

Wilder Penfield. You may have seen movies or otherwise learned about his brain stimulation research (e.g., Penfield, 1969). Penfield worked with patients undergoing brain surgery, and he stimulated various areas of the surfaces of the brain with a weak electric current. Sometimes, a stimulation caused a patient to report a specific, vivid memory, typically a memory that had not been recalled in years. This work led Penfield to believe that our memories are highly stable, complete records of all our past experiences. However, Loftus and Loftus reexamined Penfield's studies and found that the reports of vivid experiences were relatively rare. In fact, only 3 percent of the patients recalled these vivid memories. Moreover, Loftus and Loftus argue that many of these memories may not have been accurate. Thus, brain stimulation research does not provide compelling evidence for the permanence of memory.

Loftus and Loftus offer other evidence against the permanence of all items in memory. Elizabeth Loftus' own research on eyewitness testimony suggests quite strongly that, in some cases, a memory trace can be wiped out completely. For example, in a study by Loftus, Miller, and Burns (1978), people watched a series of slides about an automobile accident. In one condition, subjects saw slides of a Datsun near a stop sign. One of the questions that followed was, "Did another car pass the red Datsun while it was stopped at the yield sign?" Finally, subjects were asked to identify which of two slides they had previously seen. The critical pair of slides consisted of one slide with a Datsun at a stop sign and another slide with a Datsun at a yield sign. The subjects overwhelmingly chose the pictures with the yield sign. Thus, they relied on the information from the misleading question rather than from the original slide that they had seen.

This study points out how we should be suspicious of eyewitness accounts in courtroom trials. (Other aspects of eyewitness accounts are covered in books by Loftus, 1979, and Yarmey, 1979.) However, the study also has implications for the permanent-memory idea. Specifically, it seems that the information about the yield sign actually substituted for the information about the stop sign; that is, the stop sign was completely lost from memory. Loftus and Loftus describe other attempts they made to see whether the stop sign information could be recovered, but these attempts were not successful. For example, when people were offered a $25 reward for accurate recall, they still rejected the correct "stop sign" answer and chose the "yield sign" alternative. Loftus and Loftus conclude that when new information replaces old information, the old information can be completely lost from memory. Thus we should reject the idea that everything we learn is permanently stored in memory.

Theories of Forgetting in LTM. We discussed one theory of forgetting, interference theory, in connection with short-term memory. Interference theory states that forgetting is caused by proactive inhibition, in which old memories interfere with new memories, and by retroactive inhibition, in which new memories interfere with old memories. Interference theorists proposed that the same kind of interference causes forgetting for all memories, whether they were in storage for a few seconds or for many years. Details on interference theory and alternative explanations for its effects can be found in Postman and Underwood (1973) and Klatzky (1980).

In recent years, however, more attention has been directed toward another theory of forgetting, proposed by Tulving. Tulving proposed the **encoding specificity principle,** which states that the encoding operations which you perform at the time you are encoding an item will determine which retrieval cues will be helpful at the time of recall (Tulving & Thomson, 1973; Flexser & Tulving, 1978). Stated more simply, context is important. In order to recall an item, the context in which we encoded the item must be similar to the context at the time of recall. Forgetting occurs when the two contexts do not match. Incidentally, you may recall that we already briefly mentioned the match between encoding and retrieval in our discussion of levels-of-processing theory.

You can probably think of many examples of the encoding specificity principle. For example, you might be in your bedroom and realize that you need something from the kitchen. Once you are in the kitchen, however, your mind is completely blank. Without the context in which you encoded the item, you cannot retrieve it! You return to the bedroom, filled with context cues, and you immediately remember what you wanted. Similarly, an isolated question on a test may look completely unfamiliar, although you would have remembered the material in the right context.

A classic study of encoding specificity was performed by Tulving and Pearlstone (1966). People learned a list of items that were grouped together in categories and accompanied by the category names. During recall, some people received the category names, but others received none of the cues that were present at the time of encoding. As expected, those who had received the category names performed better.

The encoding specificity principle has been applied in many areas of memory. For example, Bjork (1978) has been concerned with how we update our memories to keep information current. For instance, you need to know where you left your car today and you need to know where you last put your sweater.

You also need to remember where you currently live, and even this very basic bit of information may be forgotten if the context cues are not appropriate. Bjork describes a professional couple who used to work at their office until 2 A.M. and then drive home to their apartment. After their child was born, however, they moved into a house and adopted more standard hours. One night the husband was forced to work until 2 A.M. When he left the building, he drove straight to his old apartment. The problem was that the context cues at the time of retrieval (when he was leaving the building) matched the context cues that were connected with an old memory.

The encoding specificity principle predicts that recall will be greatest when testing conditions duplicate learning conditions. Smith, Glenberg, and Bjork (1978) showed that environmental factors are a critical part of the testing conditions. In one experiment they asked people to learn material in two very different settings. On one day they learned words in a windowless room with a large blackboard and no cabinets, and the experimenter was formally dressed in a coat and tie. On another day they learned a different set of words in a tiny room with two windows, located in a different section of the campus, and the experimenter was dressed in a flannel shirt and jeans. On the third day, they were tested on both word lists. Half took the test in the windowless room with the formal experimenter and half took it in the room with windows with the informal experimenter. The results showed that performance was better for material that had originally been learned in the same setting. Thus, if *coat* had been learned in the windowless room, it was recalled better in that room than in the room with windows.

The encoding specificity principle has some practical applications. Your performance on tests should be better if the testing situation duplicates the learning situation as closely as possible. A student once came to my office to take a make-up examination, and she hesitantly asked me whether she could take the exam in the regular classroom rather than in my office. When I asked her why, she said that things in the classroom might help her remember the answers. Informally, she must have been aware of the value of encoding specificity!

Semantic Memory

Try Demonstration 3.7 to see whether any of the definitions encourage you into a tip-of-the-tongue experience. The **tip-of-the-tongue** (TOT) experience refers to the sensation we have when we are confident that we know the word for which we are searching, yet we cannot recall the precise word. Brown and McNeill's (1966) study on the tip-of-the-tongue phenomenon is one of the classics in semantic memory.

Demonstration 3.7   The Tip-of-the-Tongue Phenomenon.

Look at each of the definitions below. Supply the appropriate word for the definitions, if you know it. Indicate "Don't know" for those that you are certain you don't know. Mark TOT next to those for which you are reasonably certain you know the word, though you can't recall it now. For these words, supply at least one word that sounds similar to the target word. The answers appear later in the text.

1. An absolute ruler, a tyrant.
2. A stone having a cavity lined with crystals.
3. A great circle of the earth passing through the geographic poles and any given point on the earth's surface.
4. Worthy of respect or reverence by reason of age and dignity.
5. Shedding leaves each year, as opposed to evergreen.
6. A person appointed to act as a substitute for another.
7. Five offspring born at a single birth.
8. A special quality of leadership that captures the popular imagination and inspires unswerving allegiance.
9. The red coloring matter of the red blood corpuscles.
10. Flying reptiles that were extinct at the end of the Mesozoic Era.
11. A spring from which hot water, steam, or mud gushes out at intervals, found in Yellowstone National Park.
12. The second stomach of a bird, which has thick, muscular walls.
13. The green coloring matter found in plants.
14. The long-haired wild ox of central Asia, often domesticated as a beast of burden.
15. The art of speaking in such a way that the voice seems to come from another place.

Brown and McNeill's description of a person "seized" by a TOT state might capture the torment you may feel when you fail to snatch a word from the tip of your tongue:

> The signs of it were unmistakable; he would appear to be in mild torment, something like the brink of a sneeze, and if he found the word his relief was considerable. (p. 326)

The similarity between "the brink of a sneeze" and the irritation of the tip-of-the-tongue experience is amazing! Don't you wish you had a substance similar to pepper that could coax the missing word out of memory?

At any rate, Brown and McNeill produced the TOT state by giving people the definition for an uncommon English word, such as *cloaca, ambergris,* and *nepotism.* Sometimes people supplied the appropriate word immediately, and other times they were confident that they did not know the word. However, in some cases, the definition produced a TOT state. In these cases, the experimenter asked people to provide words that resembled the target word in terms of sound, but not meaning. For example, when the target word was *sampan,* people provided these similar-sounding words: *Saipan, Siam, Cheyenne, sarong, sanching,* and *symphoon.* The experimenter also asked for words that resembled the target word in terms of meaning, but not sound. For *sampan,* people provided words like *barge, houseboat,* and *junk.*

Brown and McNeill's results showed that the similar-sounding words were indeed very similar to the target words. The similar-sounding words matched the target's first letter 49 percent of the time, and they matched the target's number of syllables 48 percent of the time. Check back at your responses on Demonstration 3.7. The target words were:

1. despot	6. surrogate	11. geyser
2. geode	7. quintuplets	12. gizzard
3. meridian	8. charisma	13. chlorophyll
4. venerable	9. hemoglobin	14. yak
5. deciduous	10. pterodactyl	15. ventriloquism

Do your similar-sounding words resemble the targets?

Brown and McNeill proposed that our long-term memory for words and definitions is like a dictionary. However, our mental dictionaries are much more flexible than the alphabetized version you have on your bookshelf. We can recover words from memory by either their meaning or their sound, and we need not examine the entries in alphabetical order.

Brown and McNeill's paper was concerned with the words we store in long-term memory and how we retrieve the word that belongs to a particular definition. More recent research has focused on the organizational structure of the information in semantic memory. A wide variety of theories has been proposed. We will look at two of the most widely accepted theories: the network model developed by Collins and Loftus (1975) and the feature comparison model suggested by Smith, Shoben, and Rips (1974).

Network Model.   Think for a moment about the meaning of the word *apple.* How can we find an effective way to represent the different aspects of meaning for *apple* that are stored in long-term memory? Collins and Loftus developed a theory based on earlier models (e.g., Collins & Quillian, 1969) in which meaning can be represented by networks. The word *network* was originally applied to an arrangement of threads in a netlike structure, with many connections among them. Similarly a **network model** of semantic memory proposes that there is a netlike organization of concepts in memory, with many interconnections. The meaning of a particular concept, such as *apple,* depends upon the concepts to which it is connected.

Each concept can be represented as a **node,** or location in a network. There are links or associations that connect a particular node with other concept nodes. Figure 3.6 shows a small portion of the network that might surround the concept *apples.* Keep in mind that each of the other concepts in this figure has its own individual network structures. Imagine networks surrounding each concept in Figure 3.6 and then add a few more concepts to your mental picture. You can appreciate the richness and complexity of semantic memory!

The semantic network theory proposes that there are different kinds of links between concepts. Two kinds of links that are shown in Figure 3.6 are a superordinate link and a modifier link. A **superordinate link,** represented by the label ISA to represent the words ''is a'' shows that one concept is a member of a larger class. For example, the concept *McIntosh* has a superordinate link to the concept *apple.* A **modifier link,** represented by the label M, shows the properties of a concept. For example, the property *red* is connected to *apple* via a modifier link.

We have examined the structure of semantic networks. How do they work? When the name of a concept is mentioned, the node representing that concept is activated. The activation expands or spreads from that node to other nodes with which it is connected, a process called **spread of activation.** The activation spreads first to all the nodes linked to the original node, and then spreads to more remote nodes. As activation spreads, it grows weaker at the more remote nodes.

Figure 3.6   **An Example of a Network Structure for the Word Apple.**

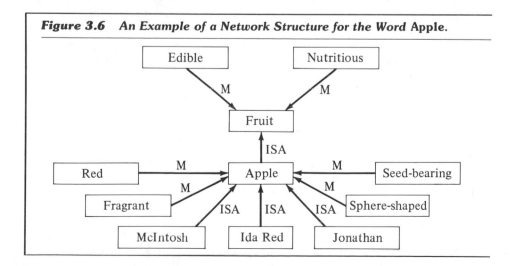

When a node has been activated, an activation tag is left behind along with information about the nature of the activation.

A frequent task in semantic memory experiments requires people to respond "yes" or "no" to statements such as "A McIntosh is a fruit." If you hear this sentence, network models propose that the nodes *McIntosh* and *fruit* will be activated. The activation at each of these nodes will spread, and the node *apple* will receive some of this spreading activation from each of two sources. An **intersection** occurs when spreading activation from two different sources arrives at the same node. Thus *apple* represents an intersection. When a search of memory produces an intersection, we then evaluate the information on the activation tags. "A McIntosh is a fruit" therefore deserves a "yes" answer on the basis of information in the activation tags.

We have been discussing cases in which an intersection can be found. Consider the sentence, "An apple is a mammal." In this case, activation would spread from both *apple* and *mammal,* and no intersection would be found. You can't get there from here!

The Collins and Loftus article summarizes some research findings that are consistent with their theory of spreading activation and semantic networks. For example, one study asked people to produce a member of a category that begins with a specified letter. Think what your response would be for "vegetable—B." Then, after several unrelated items, people were asked to produce another member of that category, for example, "vegetable—C." Responses were much faster on the second try. Here is why these results support the theory. According to the theory, when an item is processed, other nearby items are activated. Thus when you search vegetables for one that begins with B, other vegetable-related nodes are activated. Other findings also support the Collins-Loftus model. However, E.E. Smith (1978) points out some areas of semantic memory research that produce problems for network models, and so many researchers favor other models.

Feature Comparison Model.   Smith, Shoben, and Rips (1974) did not believe that any variations of the network models were adequate for describing semantic memory. They therefore proposed a **feature comparison model,** in which concepts are stored in memory in terms of a list of features or attributes. A two-stage decision process is necessary in order to make judgments about these concepts. We will first look at the structure they propose for semantic memory and then examine the decision process.

Consider the concept *cat* for a moment. We could make up a list of features that are often relevant to cats:

> has fur
> dislikes water
> has four legs
> meows
> has a tail
> chases mice

The decision process that Smith and his coauthors describe becomes relevant when people must answer a question such as "Is a cat an animal?" In the first stage in the decision process, people compare all the features of the subject of the sentence, *cat,* and the predicate, *animal.* Figure 3.7 shows an outline of the model.

Three decisions are possible at stage 1. First of all, the subject term and the predicate term may show low similarity, and so the person quickly replies "false" to the question. For example, the question "Is a robin a pencil?" has such little similarity between the two terms that you would immediately answer "false." However, the subject and the predicate terms may show high similarity, leading to a quick "true" answer. "Is a cat an animal?" leads to an immediate "true." Note, however, that a stage 2 comparison is required if there is intermediate similarity between the subject and the predicate; these decisions should take longer.

The article by Smith, Shoben, and Rips summarizes some experimental support for the model. These studies demonstrated that **latencies** (reaction times) are faster for statements that can be answered with only the first stage than for statements that require both stages. For example, consider a phenomenon known as the typicality effect. According to the **typicality effect,** decisions should be made quickly if an item is a typical or representative member of a class. In contrast, decisions about unusual or atypical members take longer. Now, the robin is an example of a typical bird, and so there is high similarity between the features of robins and birds. People quickly answered the question "Is a robin a bird?" because they only required the first stage. However, the chicken is an example of an atypical bird. People took much longer to answer the question "Is a chicken a bird?" because they required both stages.

We have examined two dominant theories of semantic memory, the Collins and Loftus network model with spreading activation, and the Smith, Shoben, and Rips feature comparison model. Smith (1978) summarizes other theories. For example, Meyer's set theory model claims that the best way to describe semantic memory is in terms of a set, or group, of attributes (Meyer, 1970). We decide

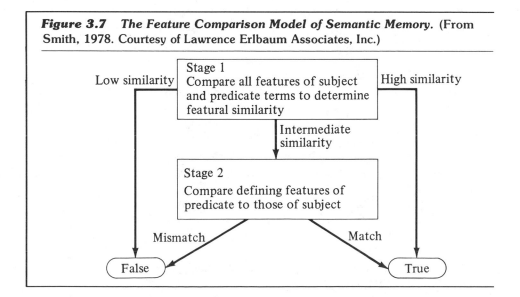

Figure 3.7   *The Feature Comparison Model of Semantic Memory.* (From Smith, 1978. Courtesy of Lawrence Erlbaum Associates, Inc.)

whether a sentence is true or not by figuring out whether the sets described in the sentence overlap appropriately. Thus, we would say that the sentence "Some students are Democrats" is true because the sets for *students* and *Democrats* can overlap. Another model, called the ACT model (Anderson, 1976), deals with language understanding and problem solving as well as semantic memory. ACT is a complex extension of the network model. Finally, in Chapter 6 we will examine Eleanor Rosch's theories about natural concepts; her theory has implications for semantic memory.

SECTION SUMMARY: Long-Term Memory

1. The accuracy of long-term memory is very high, particularly for visual material.
2. Tulving made a distinction between episodic memory, which stores *when* items happened, and semantic memory, which is the organized knowledge about words and symbols.
3. There is an argument about whether recall and recognition involve different processes. Although there is some evidence that they are similar, several variables have one kind of influence on recall and a different influence on recognition. Thus we tentatively conclude that they are different.
4. High arousal causes people to choose responses that are accessibly stored. Arousal aids retrieval for easy material and hinders retrieval for difficult material.
5. Flashbulb memories are memories for the situation in which we first learned about a surprising, emotionally arousing event.
6. Affective reactions can be remembered, even when cognitive reactions have been forgotten. Furthermore, pleasant items are recalled more accurately—and prior to—less pleasant items.
7. When we forget an item from LTM, it is sometimes stored in memory even though it is temporarily inaccessible. However, there is evidence that some memory traces can be wiped out completely, so LTM is not entirely permanent.
8. Two theories for forgetting in LTM are interference theory, in which other items interfere with recall, and the encoding specificity principle, in which forgetting occurs when encoding context and retrieval context do not match.
9. The tip-of-the-tongue experience occurs when we know the word we are trying to locate, yet we are unable to retrieve it. We can identify information about the word's sound and meaning, even if we cannot recall the exact word.
10. The Collins-Loftus network model of semantic memory proposes that concepts are interconnected in a netlike organization. When we hear a word representing a particular concept, activation spreads to nearby concepts.
11. Smith, Shoben, and Rips' feature comparison model proposes that

concepts are stored in terms of a list of features. Some decisions about semantic memory can be made rapidly, but other decisions require two stages.

Improving Memory

In our discussion of memory we have already uncovered two very important suggestions for improving memory performance. First of all, the levels-of-processing literature shows that recall is superior if it is processed at a "deep" level. As you learn material, you should concentrate on its meaning and try to develop rich, elaborate encodings. Whenever possible, try to relate the material to your own experiences because, as shown in study by Rogers, Kuiper, and Kirker (1977), self-reference is the best way to learn material. You will notice throughout the book that you are asked to think about experiences in your life that are similar to the experimental results that you are reading about. If you can relate a concept to yourself, you will be more likely to recall it.

The second suggestion for improving memory comes from our examination of the encoding specificity principle. You will recall that performance is better if the context at recall matches the context at encoding. Try to figure out ways to make the encoding conditions similar to the conditions at the time of testing. For example, a popular study technique suggests that you make up questions about each section of the material you are learning. Later in the study period, you try to answer the questions (Thomas & Robinson, 1972). This question-and-answer format is similar to the format in which you will be tested, so recall on the test should be improved.

Many of the methods for improving memory involve using **imagery,** or mental picture representations for things that are not physically present. Chapter 4, which is devoted to the topic of imagery, contains material on the applications of imagery in memory. However, there are many other memory aids that do not specifically involve imagery. We will examine them in the remainder of this chapter. A word that we will use often throughout this section is mnemonics. **Mnemonics** (pronounced with a silent *m*, "ni-*mon*-icks") is the use of a strategy or learned technique to help memory. Mnemonic devices are sometimes referred to as "memory tricks," an appropriate reference unless the word *tricks* conjures up visions of unsavory villains with waxed mustaches who perform in sideshows.

Some people criticize mnemonics, arguing that they are simply "memory crutches." However, Higbee (1978) notes that material that is initially learned with the aid of a mnemonic and is then used frequently can become so well learned that the mnemonic is no longer neccessary. Mnemonics need not be crutches. Our discussion of methods of improving memory will include four techniques: chunking, organization, mediation, and a miscellaneous category called *other mnemonic techniques*.

Chunking

Earlier we used the word *chunk* to refer to the basic unit in short-term memory (Miller, 1956). Miller used the word **chunking** to mean the process of combining several small units into larger units. For example, rather than remembering nine individual letters, m-n-e-m-o-n-i-c-s, we can combine those letters into a single word, *mnemonics.* Instead of nine small chunks, we have one large chunk.

Chunking is a term that is usually applied to short-term memory. We use chunking when we want to remember items in a specified order for a short period of time. Thus, chunking is ideal for a phone number that you want to remember just long enough to find a pencil. Short-term memory has limited capacity in terms of the number of chunks it can hold. Thus we can combine some small units into larger chunks. The more we can fit into each chunk, the larger will be the total amount stored in memory.

Try Demonstration 3.8, which is a modification of a study by Bower and Springston (1970). These researchers found much better recall when a string of letters was grouped according to meaningful, familiar units, rather than arbitrary groups of three. In the second list, you could store the string in terms of six chunks. The first list was arbitrarily grouped, however. Although you may have made chunks out of some of the groups of three, some letters probably refused to form chunks with neighboring letters that were unrelated. Consequently, the first list may have contained about 12–15 chunks, far beyond your memory span.

Demonstration 3.8   Chunking.

Read this list of letters and then cover them up. Try to recall them as accurately as possible.

   YMC   AJF   KER   AIW   WLS   DTV

Now read this list of letters and then cover them up. Try to recall them as accurately as possible.

   AMA   PHD   TWA   FBI   XKE   NOW

Finally, read this list of letters and then cover them up. Try to recall them as accurately as possible.

   NZKLEQBNPIJWUYHRTM

Frequently, however, it is useful to break a string of items into groups, even though the items in the group are not related to each other. Thus, you probably recalled the first list better than a list of uninterrupted letters, such as the third list. When items are presented rhythmically, they are recalled better than when they are presented at an even rate (Bower & Winzenz, 1969). Children probably learn the alphabet song

   ABCD–EFG–HIJK–LMNOP–QRS–TUV–WX–YZ

quickly because of the grouping. (However, that song may lead to strange chunks. When you were a child, did you think there was a letter called "elimeno"?)

Lists that are difficult to group are difficult to learn. American zip codes, such as 94305, are easier to learn than Canadian postal codes. It's difficult to form M4K1E6 into two neat rhythmic groups! (And speaking of zip codes, it is interesting that the American public has not responded favorably to the post office's implementation of nine-digit zip codes, whose length is at the very upper limit of our short-term memory.)

Organization

Whereas *chunking* is a term that is generally used for short-term memory, *organization* is a term used for long-term memory. **Organization** is the attempt to bring order and pattern to the material we learn. Typically, organization is used in connection with large amounts of information that can be recalled in any order and is learned over several trials (Klatzky, 1980). In contrast, remember that chunking occurs with relatively short lists that must be recalled in a specified order after one trial.

Organization, like chunking, may save space in memory, but long-term memory is so large that space-saving is not a prime goal. The problem with items in long-term memory, however, is that they are often difficult to retrieve. Cermak (1976) points out in his book *Improving Your Memory* that organization is the key to easier retrieval of information from memory, just as it is the key to finding items in your purse, your briefcase, or your knapsack. Thus, the time spent in organization when items are placed into memory (or a knapsack) pays off when you want to locate them later. Try Demonstration 3.9 before you read any further.

Demonstration 3.9   Organization in Memory.

Read the first list of words, cover it up, and try to recall these words in any order you wish. Then repeat the process on the second list of words. (Note that the words are the same in the second list; they are simply rearranged.)

List 1	List 2
limpet	maltase
nosegay	acupuncture
sylvan	muffler
griffin	neuron
maltase	bookstall
neuron	griffin
osprey	harpoon
doorplate	osprey
causeway	sylvan
dotage	gazette
gazette	doorplate
harpoon	horsefly
acupuncture	causeway
bookstall	nosegay
horsefly	dotage
muffler	limpet

Psychologists interested in memory have been examining organization for several decades. In general, the studies have shown that people spontaneously organize items, even when they have not specifically been instructed to do so. In one classic study, for example, Bousfield (1953) presented people with a list of 60 nouns. There were 15 nouns from each of four categories: animals, names, professions, and vegetables. Even though the words were presented in random order, people tended to group them into categories when the words were recalled.

However, people even tend to organize material in which the items are essentially unrelated to each other. Tulving (1962) constructed lists of words like those in Demonstration 3.9. From the experimenter's point of view, there was no organization. However, Tulving found evidence for **subjective organization;** subjects tended to impose their own, individual organization on a list of words. Check your recall order in Demonstration 3.9. Did some words seem to "belong" together, and did they appear near each other on both recall trials? Tulving asked for recall of the same list on 16 trials, and he found that people showed increasing subjective organization as the trials progressed.

Most of the studies on organization in recall examine words that are learned in one session in the laboratory. Do people show the same kind of organized recall for items that are learned gradually through everyday experiences? Rubin and Olson (1980) asked a number of undergraduates who were in their last semester at Lawrence University to list the names of faculty members. Sure enough, the names were clustered according to departments—psychology professors were more likely to be listed next to other psychology professors than they were to be listed near Slavic language professors.

Organizational tendencies are so strong that many researchers find it difficult to disrupt people's organizational patterns (Peterson, 1977). Furthermore, stable organization is related to the amount of material people recall. In contrast, the number of times people see or sort various words is less important than the stability of the organization (Mandler, 1979). Thus, if you have found a good way to organize some material, keep it! Shifting to a new organizational strategy will only reduce your recall.

One of the most effective ways to organize material is to construct a hierarchy. A **hierarchy** (pronounced "high-ur-*are*-key") is a system in which items are arranged in a series of classes, from the most general classes to the most specific. For example, Figure 3.8 presents part of a hierarchy for animals.

Bower, Clark, Lesgold, and Winzenz (1969) asked people to learn words that belonged to four hierarchies similar to the one in Figure 3.8. Some people learned the words in an organized fashion, and the words were presented in the format of the upside-down trees you see in Figure 3.8. Other people saw the same words, but they were randomly scattered throughout the different positions in each tree. Thus, there was no pattern for the words. The group who had learned the organized structure performed much better. For instance, on the first trial, the organized-structure group recalled an average of 73 words, in comparison to only 21 for the random-structure group. Other studies (for example, Wittrock, 1974) have shown that hierarchical organization is useful even for recalling words chosen at random from a dictionary. Structure clearly aids recall.

A hierarchy is a form of an outline. The value of an outline, therefore, is to provide organization and structure for concepts that you learn in a particular discipline. Naturally, the material is usually not as simple as a list of individual words, but the ideas can still be arranged into a series of classes. For example, this

Figure 3.8   An Example of a Hierarchy.

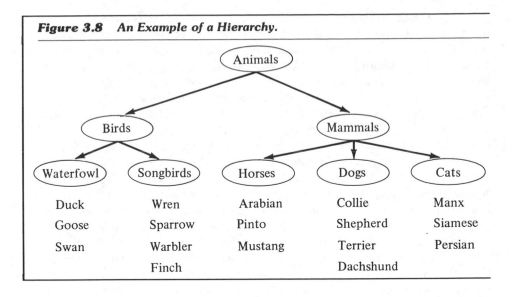

chapter is divided into four general ideas: models of memory, short-term memory, long-term memory, and improving memory. See if you can construct an upside-down tree diagram that includes more specific classes for this chapter. Check back with the more standard outline at the beginning of the chapter to see whether you left anything out. If you study the outline of each chapter, you will have an organized structure that can help your recall on an examination.

Mediation

Suppose that you decided that it would be a good idea to memorize your license plate number, MIJ967. After some searching, you realize that MIJ is like the name of your friend Midge and 967 can represent the year 1967, the year in which your brother was born. These internal codes that you use—in between seeing the stimulus and supplying the response—are known as **mediators.** The term *mediator* is used for a wide variety of codes in which extra words or images are added to the material in order to make it more memorable.

An important study on mediation was performed by Prytulak (1971), who examined how people decode mediators. He gave them a list of nonsense words and asked them to write down an English-word mediator for each nonsense word. When they were finished, Prytulak gave them their mediators and asked them to recall the nonsense words. He found that people were very likely to recall the nonsense word if the mediator used the same letters in the same order. When the mediator did not use all of the letters, or when the order of the letters was rearranged, people were much less likely to recall the nonsense word correctly. Thus, if you remember the nonsense word *XYL* with the word *XYLOPHONE*, you will be likely to recall it. However, if you remember the nonsense word *PXT* with the word *TYPEWRITER,* you will forget it! So, one lesson to be learned from Prytulak's research is to find a mediator that uses as many of the letters as possible and also maintains their original order.

One popular kind of mediator, called the **first-letter technique,** involves taking the first letter of each word that you want to remember and composing a word or a sentence from these letters. Maybe you learned the colors of the rainbow by using the mediator *ROY G. BIV* to recall Red, Orange, Yellow, Green, Blue, Indigo, and Violet. My daughter told me about another mediator, "My Very Earnest Mother Just Showed Us Nine Planets," a mnemonic used to remember the order of the planets. Can you think of others that you have heard or developed yourself?

Gruneberg (1978) reports that first-letter mediators are frequently used. In one group of medical students, for example, more than half used this technique at least sometimes in preparing for anatomy examinations. However, the effectiveness of this method has not been carefully tested. Morris (1978) reports that the technique helps recall if the order of the items is important. On the other hand, it is not useful when you need to remember unrelated items. Fortunately, though, when you need to memorize a list of words for an examination, they are almost always related to each other. Try this technique and see whether you find it helpful.

Try Demonstration 3.10. By now it may have been difficult for you to simply learn the first list without the use of mnemonics. Still, compare your performance on the two lists. Bower and Clark (1969) performed a more elaborate version of this demonstration. One group of people used the **narrative technique;** they made up narrative stories to link the words together. They were allowed to spend as long as they wanted making up the story. Different people—the control group—spent the same amount of time learning the words, but they were simply told to study and learn each list. Immediately after learning a list, both groups of people recalled almost all of the words. However, Bower and Clark presented a total of 12 lists. After all the lists had been presented, they asked for recall from all 12 lists. Figure 3.9 shows the impressive results. As you can see, there is absolutely no overlap in the performance of the two groups. Clearly, the narrative technique aids memory for words that must be recalled after a delay.

Demonstration 3.10   Mnemonics.

First, study and learn the following list of words by simply repeating the words over and over. Try *not* to use any mnemonic technique in learning these words. Later, you will recall them in order.

   yellow   stamp   paper   women   pay   water   grade   part   stay   tree

Now, study and learn this second list of words by making up a story that links the words together in order. Later, you will recall them in order.

   fact   ship   says   pencil   problem   job   study   trip   idea   friend

Now, wait about 24 hours and try to recall both lists of words in order.

We have seen that mediators involve adding more material to the items we want to remember. If we add more, ironically, the items are easier to recall. In particular, effective mediators can involve composing a word or a sentence with the first-letter technique or making up a story with the narrative technique.

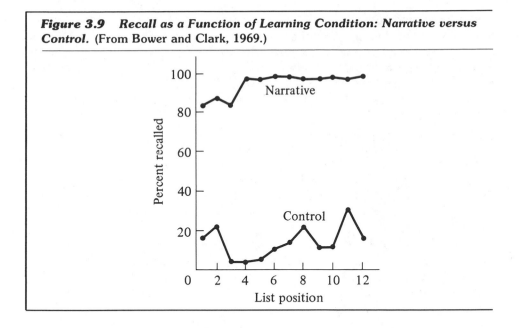

Figure 3.9 *Recall as a Function of Learning Condition: Narrative versus Control.* (From Bower and Clark, 1969.)

Other Mnemonic Techniques

A variety of other mnemonic techniques have been proposed, although the value of many of them has not been tested experimentally. Some examples of other techniques include substitutions, rhymes, ad hoc mnemonics, and external memory aids.

In the substitution method, one kind of symbol is substituted for another symbol in the items you want to remember. Suppose that you want to remember a number, and the methods of chunking, organization, and mediation simply cannot be applied. Some mnemonic experts have devised a system of substitution in which a letter is substituted for each number; for example, a *T* is substituted for a *1*, an *N* for a *2*, and so forth (the method is discussed by Young and Gibson, 1974). The resulting letters can then be used to make up words or sentences as mediators.

On a simpler level, I have sometimes used the substitution method to translate a difficult phone number into letters. Look at a telephone dial and notice that letters accompany each number. Choose one letter to represent each number, selecting letters that make a pronounceable nonsense word. For example, an unmemorable phone number, 548-7376, becomes JITPEPO. Alternatively, you could substitute a word for each number, with the rule that the number of letters in each word must equal the number for which it is substituting. For example, the word "Susan" could substitute for 5 because "Susan" has 5 letters. By this rule, 548-7376 can become "Susan eats buttered carrots and broiled steaks." Obviously, decoding the mnemonic will be time-consuming, but you probably will not forget it!

Rhymes are also useful. When you are struggling to remember whether you want to write about a *friend* or *freind,* do you find yourself repeating the rhyme that describes the general rule of thumb, "*i* before *e* except after *c* . . ."? When you are trying to figure out in late December whether next Tuesday will be January 4th or 5th, do you silently chant, "Thirty days have September . . ." in order to recall the number of days in December? More information on mnemonic techniques using rhymes can be found in a book by Higbee (1977).

Finally, we have all used **ad hoc mnemonics,** or memory aids developed to learn some particular thing (Hunter, 1977). Right-handed children learn which side is called "right" and which is called "left" by using an ad hoc mnemonic, "You write with your right hand, and the hand that is left over is left." Ad hoc mnemonics are useful in spelling: the princi*pal* is your pal, you use a pe*n* to write on statio*n*ery, and they might take atten*dance* if you atten*d* a *dance*. Also, as Hunter reminds us, Britain has only one *t* because Bri*t*ishers poli*t*ely take only one cup of *t*ea. Ad hoc mnemonics are each devised to help us remember a single rule, and they need not be applicable to other occasions.

Harris (1978) points out that in everyday life people typically make little use of the kinds of mnemonics we have been discussing. (However, our discussion should encourage you to try some!) On the other hand, people frequently use external memory aids. In a survey, Harris found that people frequently use external memory aids—such as shopping lists, notes on calendars, and cooking timers—to remind them of items. Harris notes that cues may vary in their effectiveness. For example, a reminder on a calendar will be useless if you forget to look at the calendar, and a knot in your handkerchief may only remind you to remember *something*—even if you are not certain what you must remember. Although we frequently use these external memory aids, their usefulness is limited. After all, how often are you permitted to take examinations using any external aids?

SECTION SUMMARY: *Improving Memory*

1. **Recall is superior if it is processed at a "deep" level, in terms of its meaning or in terms of self-reference.**
2. **Recall is superior if the context at recall matches the context at encoding.**
3. **Recall is superior when people use imagery, a topic to be considered in the next chapter.**
4. **Chunking, or combining small units into larger units, is usually applied to short-term memory. Grouping in terms of meaningful units or rhythmic patterns aids recall.**
5. **Organization is a term that is usually reserved for long-term memory. People spontaneously organize items in memory. Constructing a hierarchy is a particularly effective way to organize material.**
6. **Mediation is an internal code in which extra material is added to items to make them more memorable. Two effective mediators include (a) composing a word or a sentence based on the first letter of each item, and (b) making up a story based on the items.**
7. **Other mnemonic techniques include substituting one kind of symbol for another kind of symbol; rhymes; ad hoc mnemonics created to recall a particular item; and external memory aids such as lists, notes, and timers.**

Chapter Review Questions

1. What is rehearsal, and how do the Atkinson-Shiffrin and levels-of-processing theories view rehearsal's role? What do the studies on rehearsal show?

2. Some theorists stress the difference between structure and process. Compare the Atkinson-Shiffrin and levels-of-processing theories in terms of their emphasis on structure and process.

3. A fourth-grade teacher asks his class to read a paragraph about mealtimes in the Bedouin culture. With respect to levels-of-processing theory, what kinds of instructions should he use to encourage the greatest retention of the material, and what kind of instructions would be least effective?

4. Compare short-term memory and long-term memory in terms of their size and their ability to retain material. Cite experimental evidence wherever possible.

5. What is a chunk and what is chunking? Imagine that you have to search a list to see whether it includes three particular items. Why would it be helpful to use chunking before beginning the search process?

6. We discussed coding in memory in several places. Discuss the implications of each of the following areas for the nature of coding: (a) Kintsch and Buschke's experiment on semantically similar and acoustically similar lists; (b) Wickens' study on release from PI; (c) Posner and Keele's study on pairs of letters; (d) the studies on the accuracy of LTM; and (e) the tip-of-the-tongue phenomenon.

7. A true-false question on an examination reads: "Acoustic coding refers to meaning." Describe how you would process that question in terms of the Collins-Loftus model of semantic memory and in terms of the feature comparison model.

8. Summarize what you know about arousal and memory and about affect and memory. How does this information help you understand why it is difficult to remember an average meal—neither outstandingly good nor terrible— that you had a year ago?

9. Discuss as many mnemonic techniques as possible that you learned in this chapter, and describe how you can use each one to memorize some fact from this chapter for your next cognition examination.

10. Some theorists have argued that mnemonic techniques work becuase they encourage deeper encoding of the material. Review the mnemonic techniques and show how most of them focus on deeper processing, rather than processing in terms of a shallow attribute such as a word's physical characteristics.

New Terms

memory	control processes	maintenance rehearsal
information processing	rehearsal	Type I rehearsal
approach	duplex model	elaborative rehearsal
sensory memory	acoustic	Type II rehearsal
short-term memory	semantic	encoding
long-term memory	levels-of-processing approach	retrieval
structural features	depth-of-processing theory	distinctiveness

working memory

active memory

immediate memory

primary memory

short-term store

serial position curve

memory span

chunk

acoustic code

semantic code

visual code

proactive inhibition

release from proactive
  inhibition

recall

recognition

interference theory

retroactive inhibition

decay theory

secondary memory

long-term store

inactive memory

episodic memory

semantic memory

free recall

paired-associate learning

serial learning

word frequency

arousal

flashbulb memories

affect

Pollyanna Principle

encoding specificity principle

tip-of-the-tongue

network model

node

superordinate link

modifier link

spread of activation

intersection

feature comparison model

latencies

typicality effect

imagery

mnemonics

chunking

organization

subjective organization

hierarchy

mediators

first-letter technique

narrative technique

ad hoc mnemonics

Imagery

Preview

An image is a mental representation of something that is not physically present. In this chapter we look at three aspects of mental images: (1) the characteristics of mental images; (2) imagery and memory; and (3) cognitive maps.

In the first section, on the characteristics of mental images, we examine various operations and judgments that people can perform on mental images. We discover, for example, that people can rotate mental images and can make judgments about their size, angle, and shape. In many ways, mental images and perceptual reactions to real objects are similar.

In the second section, on imagery and memory, we see that imagery is an aid to memory. English words that produce images are remembered better than low-imagery words. Furthermore, memory improves if people are encouraged to make vivid images of the words they must remember.

We consider cognitive maps in the third section. People have definite images of both cities and college campuses, and their estimates of distances are reasonably accurate. Chimpanzees, too, seem to have cognitive maps.

Imagine a yellow school bus. Imagine wings sprouting out of each side of the bus. Now imagine the wings lifting the bus off the ground and conveying the bus to Washington, D.C., depositing the bus on the dome of the Capitol Building. It is obvious that you never saw this happen, but the event was probably fairly easy to construct using imagery. In this book we will use **imagery** to refer to mental representations of things that are not physically present. We can have mental images of events, such as walking into a classroom, or objects, such as the cover on a favorite record. Mental images can represent events and objects that we have actually experienced, and they can represent events and objects that we purely imagine.

Most people report having imagery. McKellar (1972) found in a survey of 500 adults that 97 percent reported visual imagery, 93 percent auditory imagery (for example, imagine you hear a horn), 74 percent motor imagery (imagine yourself lifting your leg), 70 percent tactile (imagine touching a marshmallow), 67 percent gustatory (imagine eating strawberry ice cream), and 66 percent olfactory (imagine smelling vinegar).

Despite the frequency with which people experience imagery, psychologists have been reluctant to examine images. Roger Shepard, a prominent researcher in the area of imagery, explains why imagery had been avoided until recently:

> Cognitive psychology has long been preoccupied with processes that are verbal or at least readily verbalizable. I attribute the origin of this preoccupation to the former ascendance of behaviorism, with its preference for responses that are overt. . . . (Shepard, 1978, p. 12)

As we have discussed before, cognitive processes are hidden and covert, which makes them extremely difficult to examine. In recent years, however, the study of imagery has begun to flourish. Cognitive psychologists have become very interested in the description and use of mental images, and they have devised clever methods for examining these hidden processes. According to a recent book about mental imagery (Kosslyn, 1980), there are four major reasons for examining mental images:

1. In many ways, a mental image is similar to a perception, and many research projects have examined this similarity. As we will see throughout the first section, for example, we handle a visual image in much the same fashion as we handle a visual perception.
2. People have many introspections about the structure of mental images, and research projects have tried to quantify these introspections. You will recall that one theme that reoccurs throughout this book is that the cognitive processes are generally unobservable; this is particularly true of mental images. As Kosslyn remarks,

   > . . . researchers have tried to externalize mental events (often in terms of performance time) of internal processing. If a given introspection is not spurious, then there ought to be externally observable consequences of the observed internal state or event. (p. 4)

   For example, we will see in the first section that Shepard and Metzler (1971) introspected that mental images rotate, just like physical objects rotate, and their study was an attempt to demonstrate that some external measure (in this case, performance time) reflected this mental rotation. The third section, on cognitive maps, examines other aspects of the structure of mental images.
3. Most research has focused upon the effects of the use of imagery on people's ability to perform various tasks, most often involving memory. Generally, this research focuses upon performance on the other task and de-emphasizes the examination of images for their own value. We will discuss the effect of imagery on memory in the second section of this chapter.
4. The final reason for examining mental images is to discover tasks in which people spontaneously use mental imagery. We will investigate this aspect of mental images in other chapters throughout the book. We will see, for example, that people seem to use mental imagery when they solve problems and when they perform reasoning tasks. This particular point is an example of one of our major themes, that cognitive processes are interrelated with one another.

The first section of this chapter examines the nature of mental images; it stresses the similarity between mental images and perception (Kosslyn's first point) and the structure of mental images (Kosslyn's second point). The second section explores the relationship between imagery and memory (Kosslyn's third point). The final section discusses the structure of a particular kind of mental image, cognitive maps (Kosslyn's second point). Clearly, we now know quite a lot about these unobservable cognitive processes called mental images now that they are no longer forbidden topics for research.

The Characteristics of Mental Images

What are the characteristics of mental images? In this section, we will examine the qualities of mental images that have been discovered in recent research. In particular, we will see that numerous experiments demonstrate that mental images resemble perceptual experiences. Does that mean that we store information about objects in terms of "pictures in our heads"? There is excited debate about this question, and the answer is not clear. Many people, such as Shepard (1978), claim that information is stored in analog codes. An **analog code** is a representation that closely resembles the physical object. (If you haven't already formed your own mnemonic, remember the word *analog* by thinking about an *analogy* between the real object and the mental picture.) Other people, for example, Pylyshyn (1973, 1978), argue that we store information in terms of abstract descriptions of objects or **propositions;** storage is verbal rather tthan visual or spatial. When we think of an object, however, we can recreate a mental image out of the verbal description. Although there is good evidence for an analog code, the issue is not resolved.

Some of the characteristics of mental images that we will examine are the fact that they can be rotated, the preservation of relative size in mental images, and the preservation of shape in mental images. Thus, physical objects and mental images are similar. We will note, for example, the following ways in which mental images are similar to the physical objects they represent:

1. When a real object is rotated in space, it takes longer to rotate the object 160° than to rotate it 30°. Similarly, it takes longer to rotate a mental object 160° than to rotate it 30°.
2. A real elephant is bigger than a real fly. Similarly, the mental image of an elephant is bigger than a mental image of a fly.
3. We judge the pictures of Colorado and Oregon to be similar in shape. When the pictures are absent and we must rely on our mental images, we also judge Colorado and Oregon to be similar.

After examining the characteristics of mental images, we will return to the discussion of the way in which information is stored. It will be useful as you read the following pages to decide which studies support the "visual image storage" hypothesis and which support the "verbal description storage" hypothesis. At the end of this section on the characteristics of mental images we will look at some applications of mental imagery in clinical psychology and in other disciplines.

Imagery and Rotation

Try the experiment in Demonstration 4.1, which is based on a study by Shepard and Metzler (1971). Notice that in the top pair the left-hand figure can be changed into the right-hand figure by keeping the figure flat on the page and rotating it clockwise. Suddenly, the two figures match up, and you reply "same." The middle pair, however, require a rotation in a third dimension. You may, for example, take the two-block "arm" that is jutting out toward you and push it over to the left and away from you. Suddenly, again, the figures match up, and you reply "same." In the case of the bottom figure, all attempts to rotate the figure are unsuccessful, and you conclude "different."

Demonstration 4.1   Mental Rotation. Which of these pairs of objects are the same, and which are different? (From Shepard and Metzler, 1971.)

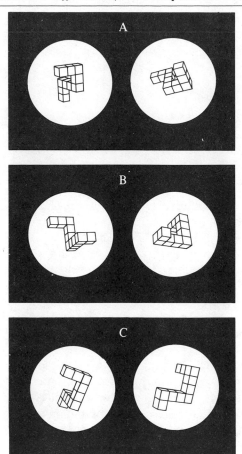

Shepard and Metzler asked eight brave subjects to judge 1600 pairs of line drawings like these. Subjects pulled a lever with their right hand if they judged the figures to be the same, and they pulled another lever with their left hand if they judged the figures to be different. In each case, the experimenters measured the amount of time required for a decision.

Does it take longer to rotate pairs in depth, as in the middle pair, than to rotate them in the picture-plane, as in the top pair? Figure 4.1 shows the results for the two kinds of pairs. Notice that there is no difference for the two tasks. However, the angle of rotation has a strong influence on decision time. It takes much longer to rotate a figure 180° than to rotate it a mere 20°.

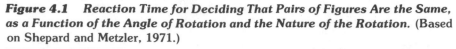

Figure 4.1 *Reaction Time for Deciding That Pairs of Figures Are the Same, as a Function of the Angle of Rotation and the Nature of the Rotation.* (Based on Shepard and Metzler, 1971.)

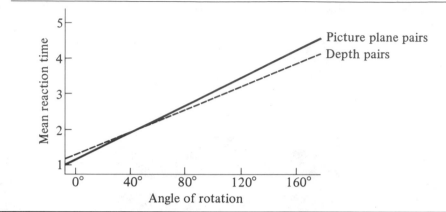

The Shepard and Metzler study is an excellent demonstration that the operations we perform on objects in our mind are similar to the operations we would perform on the actual physical objects. If you were holding two figures in your hands, trying to decide whether they were the same, you would find that rotating a figure in depth would be no more difficult than rotating it while holding it flat. However, it would take longer to rotate a figure 180° than to rotate it 20°.

Cooper and Shepard (1973) also demonstrated that the amount of rotation influences decision time when people must make decisions about letters of the alphabet. In this study, people saw rotated figures such as ↻. Is this a normal letter, or is it backwards? In other words, is this a normal *R* or a mirror image of an *R*, if the figure were upright? Cooper and Shepard found that people took longer to make a decision (normal versus mirror image) for letters that required extensive rotation (for example, ß) than for letters that required very little rotation (for example, ϟ). Whether the objects are three-dimensional figures or alphabet letters, mental operations resemble physical operations.

Kosslyn and Pomerantz (1977) have commented on these mental rotation experiments:

> One explanation posits that it may be optimal to transform available images a portion at a time to minimize the amount of effort expended any given moment. If images are transformed a part at a time, only relatively small transformations could be used or the image would seem to bend, warp, or fragment. Thus, "rotation" may consist of a series of stepwise transformations, each so small as to appear continuous. More time is required to rotate further distances because more intervening small transformations are performed. (p. 68)

Does that description match your experiences with Demonstration 4.1? Did it seem that you had to rotate the figures quite slowly to keep them from breaking in the middle and leaving a fragment behind, unrotated?

When people perform a mental rotation task, is it necessary for the information to be represented in a *visual* image? Carpenter and Eisenberg (1978) thought of a good way to examine this issue: They studied mental rotation in blind people: People who have been blind from birth presumably do not have visual representations for objects. Carpenter and Eisenberg used rotated letters, like Cooper and Shepard (1973). The letters *P* and *F,* either normal or reversed, were 1 cm thick, and subjects felt the letters and then reported whether they were normal or reversed. Both blind and sighted people (who wore blindfolds) showed the same trend as Cooper and Shepard found for their sighted subjects; people take longer to make decisions for letters that require extensive rotation than for letters that require little rotation.

Carpenter and Eisenberg concluded that mental rotation can be represented in terms of *spatial* information, rather than just visual information, or else blind people would not be able to perform the task. They concluded that blindfolded, sighted people judge orientation by using the position of their hand to code the orientation of the letter. Then they may either translate this hand position code into a visual image, or they may use some kind of spatial representation that is not visual.

Imagery and Size

The previous section discussed how we treat mental images like physical objects when we rotate them in space. In this section we will examine how mental images resemble physical objects when we make judgments involving size. First, try Demonstration 4.2.

Demonstration 4.2   *Imagery and Size.*

A. Imagine an elephant standing next to a rabbit. Now answer this question: *Does a rabbit have a beak?*
B. Imagine a fly standing next to a rabbit. Now answer this question: *Does a rabbit have an eyebrow?*

In which picture was the rabbit largest, A or B? Which picture seemed to have more detail in the area you were examining for the beak or the eyebrow, A or B?

Questions like this were part of a carefully planned series of experiments by Kosslyn (1975), who wanted to discover whether it would take longer to judge small images than to judge large images. But how can we control the size of someone's mental image? Kosslyn figured that a mental image of an elephant next to a rabbit would force people to imagine a relatively small rabbit. In contrast, a mental image of a fly next to a rabbit would produce a relatively large rabbit.

When you see *real-life* pictures of animals, you can see all the details quite clearly on a large picture. On the other hand, details are squeezed in so close together on a small picture that it is difficult to make judgments about them. If this same rule for real-life pictures also holds true for pictures in our heads, then people should make judgments more quickly with a large mental image (as in a rabbit next to a fly) than with a small mental image (as in a rabbit next to an elephant). In the experiment, people made judgments about objects, for example, whether a rabbit had legs. Kosslyn's results support his prediction; judgments were 0.21 second faster with a large mental image than with a small mental image.

Kosslyn was concerned, however, that critics might argue that the results might be due to some aspect of elephants and flies other than their relative size. For example, people might find elephants so fascinating that the rabbit part of the elephant-rabbit mental image is relatively undeveloped. In a second experiment, therefore, Kosslyn (1975) asked subjects to imagine various animals next to either a monstrous fly (one that was as big as an elephant) or next to a minuscule elephant (one that was as small as a fly). The results showed that judgments were 0.29 second faster with a large mental image (that is, when the animal is next to the minuscule elephant) than with a small mental image (that is, when the animal is next to the monstrous fly). In other words, these two experiments demonstrate that characteristics are easier to "see" when the mental image is large, and the effect cannot be explained by another factor, the relative interest of the competing figure.

Kosslyn anticipated yet another argument that his critics might make. Perhaps people take longer to create a small mental image than to create a large mental image. Perhaps, then, these small mental images are relatively incomplete at the time of the test, when subjects are asked to make judgments about the images, and consequently the judgments take longer. In a final experiment Kosslyn (1975) asked people to imagine an animal and to make the mental image of the animal into a "picture" of specified dimensions. When an image was clearly in mind, the subjects gave a signal. The results of this study showed that it took much longer to create *large* mental images. Kosslyn therefore answered another potential criticism of his study, and at the same time provided further proof for the analogy between physical objects and mental images. After all, it takes longer to fill in all the detail on a large painting than on a small painting. Similarly, it takes longer to "paint" a large mental image than a small one.

Psychologists other than Kosslyn have been concerned about the correspondence between relative size of objects in our mental images and the relative sizes of physical objects. Moyer (1973), for example, used a principle from **psychophysics,** the area of psychology that measures people's reactions to perceptual stimuli. In psychophysics, we know that when people are asked to judge which of two lines is longer, they take longer to make a decision if the lines are almost equal. If the lines are clearly different from one another, the decision is much easier.

Moyer searched for evidence of an **internal psychophysics,** one that operates on images stored inside the head, rather than images on paper. He proposed that people should take longer to decide which was larger, a moth or a flea, than to decide which was larger, a moose or a roach. This prediction, remember, was based on the longer decision times for physical objects when the two choices are similar in size.

Subjects in Moyer's experiment saw many different pairs of names for animals, with the animals ranging in size from a flea to a whale. Moyer measured how long it took subjects to decide which member of the pair was larger. Then subjects assigned a number to each animal name, estimating that animal's size. The results showed evidence of an internal psychophysics. There was a **symbolic**

distance effect; that is, the smaller the difference in size between the two animals, the longer was the decision time (Moyer & Dumais, 1978). Thus it took longer to decide whether an ant (whose size was ranked 1) was larger than a bee (size ranking of 2) than it took to compare an ant with an elk (size rankings of 1 and 7). Moyer argued that subjects convert the animal names into mental images that preserve the sizes of the animals. Decisions regarding relative size take a long time if two objects are similar, whether the objects are in our minds or physically in front of us.

Imagery and Angle

Try Demonstration 4.3, which is similar to a study by Paivio. In solving these problems you probably consulted two pictures that you created in your head. Therefore, the task required visual imagery rather than verbal reasoning.

Demonstration 4.3   Imagery and Angles.

For each item below, imagine two standard, nondigital clocks. Each clock represents one of the specified times. Compare those two mental clocks and decide which clock has the smaller angle between the hour hand and the minute hand. Notice which two items were the most difficult.

1. 4:10 and 9:23
2. 3:20 and 7:25
3. 2:45 and 1:05
4. 3:15 and 5:30

Paivio (1978a) (pronounced "*Pay*-vih-oh") decided to work with angles on "mental clocks" because these angles could be measured more precisely and consistently than the size of imagined objects and animals. Paivio measured decision times for these mental angle comparisons because he wanted to see whether decision time was related to the size of the difference between the angles. If the hands in the two clocks that are being compared form angles that are almost equal (for example, 3:20 and 7:25 or 3:15 and 5:30), the decision about which angle is smaller should be more difficult than if the angles are quite different (for example, 4:10 and 9:23 or 2:45 and 1:05). Figure 4.2 shows an easy decision and a difficult decision.

This argument is another example of a search for an "internal psychophysics," like the study by Moyer (1973) that we discussed in the "Imagery and Size" section. With real objects, people take longer to make a decision if two objects are similar than if there is a clear-cut difference. In the same way, subjects should take longer when the mental objects are similar to each other. Paivio therefore tested pairs of times corresponding to several angle size differences, varying from a 5-minute difference to a 25-minute difference.

Paivio included another variable, *individual differences,* which we should discuss before we look at his results. Some people are quite good at mental imagery tasks: Just mention the time 9:23 to them, and a mental picture of a clock reading 9:23 pops immediately into their heads. Other people have to struggle to make up

---

Figure 4.2   Decisions about Angles.

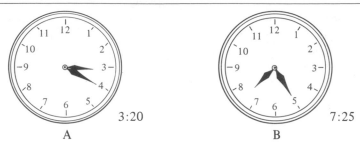

A difficult decision:
Which angle between the hands is smaller, clock A or clock B?

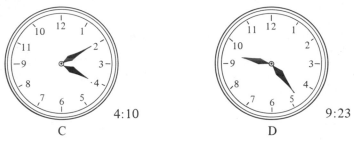

An easy decision:
Which angle between the hands is smaller, clock C or clock D?

---

an image. Slowly they picture the small hand set at the 9, then they try to keep the small hand glued there while they create a large hand pointing to the lower right-hand corner. Paivio gave his subjects several tests for mental-imagery ability, including the Block Visualization Test (Guilford, 1967). In this test he asked subjects to think of a cube with a certain size and color, which is sliced up into smaller cubes. Then he asked subjects how many of these smaller cubes have two colored surfaces, how many have three colored surfaces, and so on. Based on the results of this test and others, subjects were labeled either "high-imagery subjects" or "low-imagery subjects."

What influence did these two variables—angle difference and imagery ability—have upon reaction time, which was the time required to decide which angle was smaller? As Figure 4.3 shows, the study provided more evidence for internal psychophysics. Notice how the reaction times are much longer when the angle difference is small. Notice, also, that high-imagery subjects have consistently faster reaction times than the low-imagery subjects. Incidentally, Paivio also gave tests of *verbal* ability as well as imagery ability, but verbal ability was not related to reaction time. Paivio (1979) considers other aspects of individual differences in a recent book, *Imagery and Verbal Processes*.

Paivio believes that this study offers strong support for the idea that people use mental images rather than verbal reasoning in problems like the mental clock task. Support comes from three areas: (1) The reaction times were closely related to

Figure 4.3   *The Influence of Angle Difference on Reaction Time, for High-Imagery and Low-Imagery Subjects.* (From Paivio, 1978b.)

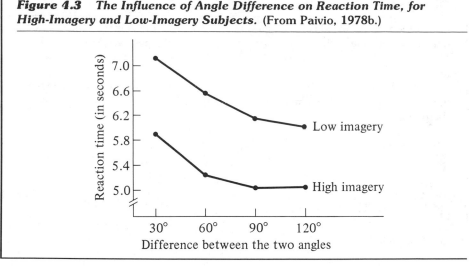

the angle differences, corresponding to the true, physical differences on "real" clocks; (2) the reaction times were related to imagery ability, rather than verbal ability; and (3) in a questionnaire that subjects filled out at the end of the experiment, they reported using mental imagery rather than other strategies.

Imagery and Shape

Look at your results from Demonstration 4.4. How similar were your two lists? Was pair B (Colorado–Oregon) near the top of both lists and pair C (Oregon–West Virginia) near the bottom?

Shepard and Chipman (1970) examined the shapes of states, because they were curious to see whether there was a correspondence between people's judgments of physical shapes and their judgments of mental shapes. Their subjects were seven extremely patient Harvard graduate students, who were given two decks of 105 cards each. One deck of cards had all possible pairs of the names of 15 different states. (You saw a fraction of them on the left-hand side of Demonstration 4.4.) They were asked to **rank** the 105 name cards according to their similarity; that is, they placed them in order from most similar to least similar. If you have ever tried to rank order as many as 12 items on a questionnaire, you can appreciate how hard it would be to rank order 105 cards. After they finished this task, they repeated the ranking with 105 cards that contained only the shapes of states, and not their names.

Shepard and Chipman found a very strong correspondence between the two list orders. States that seemed similar in the name-cards list (for example, Colorado and Oregon) also seemed similar in the shape-cards list. On the other hand, states that were judged extremely different in the name-cards list (for example, Oregon and West Virginia) were also quite different in the shape-cards list.

The authors then performed a complex statistical analysis called a multi-dimensional scaling analysis. This analysis provides a diagram in which items

---

Demonstration 4.4   The Shape of States.

Cover the right-hand side of the figure and look only at the names of the states on the left-hand side. Place the six pairs in order so that the pair whose shapes are most similar are at the top of the list. It will be easiest if you represent each pair with a letter.

Now cover the left-hand side and look only at the shape. Again, place the pairs in order according to the similarity of the shapes. Save your results; we will discuss them later.

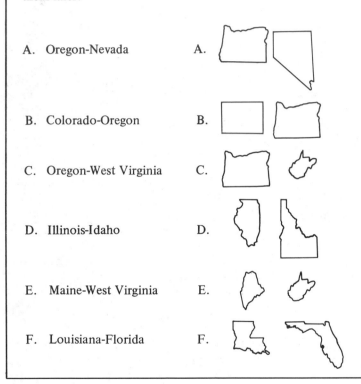

A. Oregon-Nevada   A.

B. Colorado-Oregon   B.

C. Oregon-West Virginia   C.

D. Illinois-Idaho   D.

E. Maine-West Virginia   E.

F. Louisiana-Florida   F.

---

judged similar to each other are located near each other in a diagram. Figure 4.4 shows the results. Notice the various clusters of shapes. In the upper left-hand corner are states like Illinois and Missouri; these states are perceived as similar in shape because they are all irregular and basically vertical (that is, tall and narrow). Moving clockwise, we come to Oregon and Colorado, two states that are horizontal and rectangular. Moving further clockwise, we have states with "handles" on them, such as Idaho and Florida. Down in the lower left-hand corner we have those states that Shepard and Chipman call "smallish and wiggly" (p. 13), including Maine and West Virginia.

As you looked at Figure 4.4, you probably paid the most attention to the location of the shapes of the states, whose location was represented by the dot at the tail of the arrows. The heads of the arrows represent the locations based on the name-card judgments. Notice that in most cases, the head of the arrow is not very

---

Figure 4.4   The Results of an Analysis of the Shepard and Chipman (1970) Study.

Shapes judged similar to each other appear near each other in the diagram. The points of the arrows represent the locations for the name-cards condition, and the dots (tails) represent the locations for the shape-cards condition. Note that the points are rarely far from the tails.

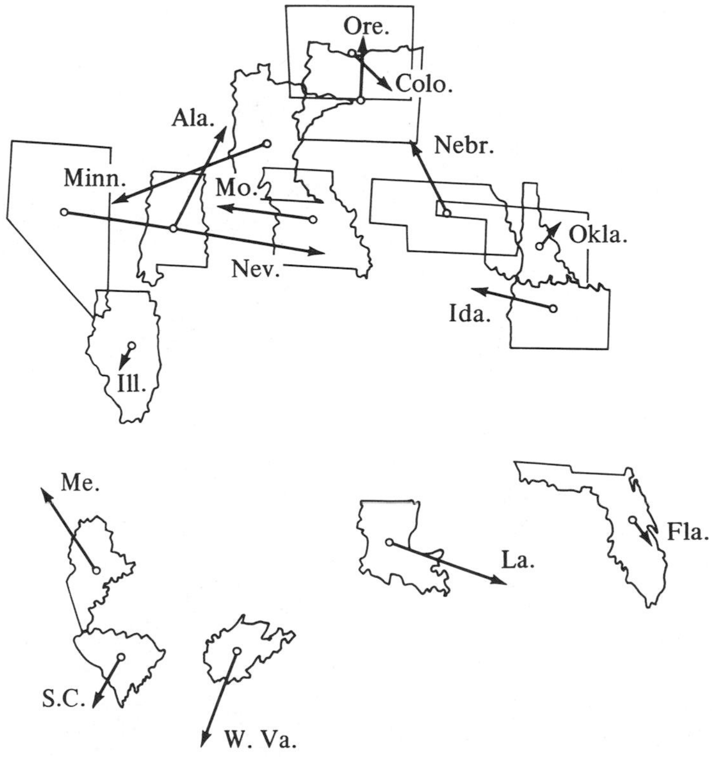

far away from the tail; people give judgments for the names that are fairly similar to the judgments for the shapes. Nevada seems to be the most glaring exception, and the inaccuracy here is probably based on the tendency for easterners to believe that most of the states out west are square.

Imagery and Part-Whole Relationships

Did the figure seen in Demonstration 4.5 contain a parallelogram? If your friend is like most people, that is a difficult question. Reed (1974) was interested in subjects' ability to decide whether a pattern was a portion of a pattern they had seen earlier. He therefore presented a series of pattern pairs, first a pattern like the Star of David in Demonstration 4.5, and then after a brief delay, a second pattern (for example, a parallelogram). In half of the cases the second pattern was truly part of the first one; in the other half of the cases it was not (for example, a rectangle).

Demonstration 4.5   *Imagery and Part-Whole Relationships.*

Cover these instructions before asking a friend to look at this figure. Then cover up the figure and ask your friend whether it contained a parallelogram.

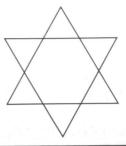

If people store mental images in their heads that correspond to the physical objects that they have seen, they should be able to produce the mental image and adjust the parallelogram into place in their mental image. However, subjects were correct only 14 percent of the time on this particular example. Overall, they were correct only 55 percent of the time, hardly better than chance. This lack of accuracy, Reed argued, suggests that people could not have been storing mental pictures. Instead, he proposed that people store pictures as descriptions. Your description of the star in Demonstration 4.5 might have been, "Two triangles, one pointing up and the other pointing down, placed on top of each other." When you were asked whether the figure contained a parallelogram, you searched through your verbal description and found only triangles, not parallelograms. Reed says,

> I have taken the view that a pattern is stored as a structural description and that it is difficult to identify a part of a pattern that is not directly coded into the structural description. This is not to say, however, that it is totally impossible to correctly identify a part that was not previously perceived. Although we do not know for sure whether a correct response is based on prior perception or a visual image, it is likely that the faster decisions are based on prior perception and the slower decisions are based on inferences from visual images. If a part is presented that was previously perceived, the S [subject] should be fairly fast in responding, whereas if a part is identified through inference, the decision should take longer. (p. 334)

Perhaps you correctly identified the parallelogram as being part of the star. If you did, you resorted to the mental image when the verbal description failed to contain the word *parallelogram,* and it probably took you a long time to come up with the answer.

Incidentally, in a later study, Reed and Johnsen (1975) established that people's difficulty with the task could not be explained by either perceptual difficulties or memory problems. In summary, then, Reed's two studies offer support for Pylyshyn's (1973, 1978) argument that we discussed earlier. Verbal descriptions are useful for storing pictures, and people have difficulty if they must rely on a mental picture.

Imagery and Interference

Try to get a mental image of a good friend's face at the same time as your eyes wander over this page. You will probably find it a difficult task, since you are trying to look at the words on the page and to look (with your "mind's eye") at your friend. You cannot look two places at once, and so you experience interference.

Brooks (1968) examined how a visual task can interfere with visual imagery. Subjects in this study saw a block letter, such as the *L* in Figure 4.5. Then, from memory, each subject was to classify each corner as to whether it was at the extreme part of the figure (either top or bottom) or whether it was not. Starting at the asterisk, for example, and moving clockwise around the figure, for example, notice that the responses should be "yes, yes, no, no, yes, yes." Now, Brooks arranged three different ways for subjects to give their answers: vocal (saying "yes" or "no"), tapping (with the left hand to indicate "yes" or the right hand to indicate "no"), and pointing (in a complex spatial arrangement of pairs of Y's and N's, subjects pointed to the correct member of each pair).

Brooks reasoned that the pointing task would require a great deal of visual activity in order to scan the display of Y's and N's. In contrast, visual activity in the vocal or tapping conditions would be minimal. Therefore, to the extent that a person's mental image of that letter is visual, people would find it diffiicult to provide responses requiring visual activity. As Brooks' results showed, subjects took about twice as long on the pointing task as on the other tasks; the visual task interfered with the visual image.

However, you might be suspicious about these results. How do we know that the pointing task is not simply a more difficult one, without considering interference? Fortunately, Brooks included another condition, in which subjects were asked to remember sentences and make judgments about the words in the sentence. This task was largely verbal or vocal, rather than spatial. The subjects in this condition responded quickly for tapping and pointing, but they experienced

Figure 4.5   An Example of a Block Diagram and an Answer Sheet for the Pointing Condition, Similar to Those Used by Brooks (1968). (A) A block letter; subjects classified each corner as to whether it was at an extreme part of the figure or not. (B) An answer sheet for the pointing condition; subjects pointed to Y or N to indicate the answer (correct answers are underlined).

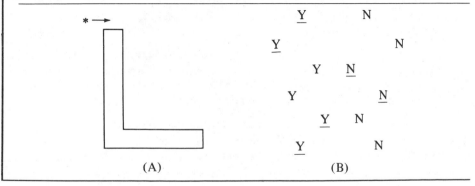

interference when the vocal response was required, and their reaction times were much longer. Thus, a visual task interferes with a visual image, and a verbal task interferes with a verbal image. This experiment thus provides evidence that we store a memory of a picture (such as a picture of the letter L) in terms of what it looks like in its arrangement in space rather than in terms of a string of verbal descriptions of its shape.

If things that we really see interfere with things we see in our mental images, will the reverse also be true? That is, can a mental image interfere when we are trying to see a physical stimulus? Segal and Fusella (1970) asked subjects to make a visual image (e.g., a volcano or a tree) or an auditory image (e.g., the sound of an oboe or a typewriter). As soon as the subject had formed the requested image, the experimenters presented either a sound on the harmonica (auditory signal), a small blue arrow (visual signal), or nothing. Subjects performed much less accurately when the image and the signal were in the same sensory mode. In other words, it was easier to see the arrow when they were imagining the sound of a typewriter than when they were imagining the shape of a tree. On the other hand, it was easier to hear the harmonica when they were imagining the shape of a tree than when they were imagining the sound of a typewriter. Once again, visual images seem to involve visual activity. Furthermore, auditory images involve auditory activity.

Marks (1977) discusses some other interesting aspects of interference and visual images. For instance, several studies have shown that people have trouble on visual perception tasks when they have taken marijuana. Marks argues that marijuana increases the number and the vividness of visual images. People may have trouble on a visual task—detecting a weak light, for example—because the vivid visual images are producing interference.

Storage of Mental Images: Pro and Con

As we examined the characteristics of mental images, we discovered many ways in which our reactions to mental images are the same as our reactions to real objects. Reviewing quickly, we have seen that mental images can be rotated like real objects; they preserve the same size, angle, and shape relationships that are present in real objects; and they produce the same interference with other tasks that real objects would produce. On the other hand, mental images cannot be examined to see if they contain hidden *parts,* to the extent that real objects could be examined.

Most cognitive theorists support some variation of the analog code hypothesis, claiming that there is an analogy between the visual image and the real object. Shepard (1978) says that the results of studies about mental imagery

> . . . indicate that mental imagery is remarkably able to substitute for actual perception: Subjects make the same judgments about objects in their absence as in their presence; subjects who imagine a particular object are uniquely fast and accurate in discriminatively responding to related external test stimuli . . . (p. 125)

Kosslyn, another major researcher in the area, has developed a computer simulation of visual mental imagery (Kosslyn & Shwartz, 1977). This simulation has a "surface representation," which is somewhat like a picture and has spatial qualities. There is also an underlying "deep representation," which stores both visual information and descriptive, verbal information. Thus both visual and verbal information are stored.

Pylyshyn (1973, 1978) has been the strongest opponent of the "picture in the head" hypotheses. He agrees that people do have mental images, but he says that these images are simply "tacked on" after the fact, after an item has been recovered from storage. People store information in terms of propositions, or abstract concepts that describe relationships between items. Pylyshyn (1973) has argued, for example, that storing information in terms of mental images would be awkward and perhaps even unworkable because a huge storage space would be required to store all the images people claim they have. (Kosslyn and Pomerantz, 1977, have responded that Pylyshyn's notion of imagery is oversimplified; their paper can be consulted for details.)

Pylyshyn (1978) has also stressed that there are differences between perceptual experiences and mental images. For example, a real picture can be reexamined and reinterpreted; however, Reed's (1974) experiment showed that a mental image cannot be reinterpreted in order to locate a hidden part that was not originally noticed. Furthermore, argues Pylyshyn, operations are possible for perceiving real objects that are impossible for mental images. For example, you can create a blurry image of a real object by partly closing your eyes, but you can't blur your mental image. Similarly, you can turn a real picture upside down and your perception will reflect that change. Create a mental image of a complex painting you like; can you turn that mental image upside down?

Despite Pylyshyn's arguments, the bulk of the experimental evidence supports the idea that mental images can be used to store information. Mental images may not preserve *all* of the qualities of perceptual experiences, but mental images and perceptions are similar on an amazingly impressive variety of characteristics. Consequently, a "pro" decision on the storage of mental images seems justified.

Applications of Mental Imagery

There is an impressive variety of ways in which imagery has been used to solve practical problems. Clinical psychologists use imagery in order to produce behavioral change. Artists, writers, and scientists also make use of imagery in their professions. You can find other applications of imagery in a very readable book called *The Mind's Eye: Imagery in Everyday Life* (Sommer, 1978).

Applications in Clinical Psychology. Traditional psychoanalysts rely heavily on imagery in their treatment of clients. Gordon (1972) discusses how their procedures depend upon the presence of imagery:

> All of them depend on the capacity to recall and to recreate persons and situations, real or fantasied, which are a part, and often a crucial part, of a person's inner world, though they are not concretely present in the therapeutic session. Only through the image can they be actualized and "animated" and so brought into relationship with each other, with the person of the therapist and with the here and now of the patient's actual life circumstances. . . . [Psychotherapy and analysis] seek to develop, to

animate, or to reanimate as wide a range of imaginal experience as is possible for any particular individual . . . the therapist draws upon dreams and waking fantasies . . . (pp. 73–74)

Gordon also discusses how the image system can change as psychotherapy proceeds. Clients become less rigid in their imagery, and they gain more control over the imagery process. Some clients may become excessive in their images, which may assume hallucinatory qualities. In those cases the therapist must help the client limit these images and encourage the client to attend to other aspects of mental life such as interpersonal relations. Other clients have the opposite problem; their imagery may be impoverished and not vivid enough. They may complain that they feel unreal or empty. If the therapist succeeds in bringing life to their image world, they often report a sense of having a unique, separate identity for the first time, and they often act more competent.

Morrison (1978) discusses how psychotherapists use imagery in the grieving process following the death of a loved one. Morrison believes that the use of imagery is ideal for dealing with a wide variety of feelings—such as affection, anger, fear, and hate—that people may feel toward the deceased person.

Whereas psychoanalysts have always incorporated imagery into the clinical process, behavior therapists resisted using imagery for a long time. After all, radical behaviorists regarded imagery as a "forbidden fruit" and "consigned it to the flames along with other cognitive concepts" (Bower, 1972, p. 51). Recently, however, imagery has been frequently used in behavior therapy. The assumption is that if a client imagines particular events in the therapist's office, then overt, outward behavior and covert, cognitive activity would change outside of the office (Cautela, 1977).

Cautela (1977) provides a description of the procedure he uses, called **covert conditioning.** The clients first learn about how reward can increase the frequency of a desired behavior. Then they are told that the same principle can operate if they *imagine* all the steps in the procedure. The imagery sequence then begins.

The therapist selects a reinforcer image, such as the following:

> You are lying on the beach on a hot summer day. Concentrate on all the details around you. Notice all the sensations. Feel the hot sun beating down on you and the warmth from the blanket. Smell the refreshing air. Watch the waves come rolling up onto the beach. Be aware of how good your body feels now that you are swimming through the water. (p. 56)

Then the therapist describes the client involved in a particular feared but desired behavior. The client signals as soon as the scene is vivid, at which point the therapist says, "reinforcement." The client then spends 10 to 15 seconds enjoying the imagery of the reinforcer. An example of a feared but desired behavior might be a woman who wishes to increase social activities but avoids them because of shyness. This person might be asked to imagine that she was sitting at home wishing she had the nerve to call a man she had recently met and ask him out for a drink. She decides to call. Reinforcement is given at this point. She dials the number, and reinforcement is given again. John accepts, and reinforcement is given again. Thus images of actions and images of reinforcements are alternated in covert conditioning.

This is one of the six covert conditioning techniques discussed in Cautela's article. Other techniques, for example, involve **covert negative reinforcement,** in which a response causes an imagined, unpleasant stimulus to stop, and **covert modeling,** in which the clients imagine watching others doing something and imagine the consequences of the behavior.

The use of imagery by behavior therapists has been discussed for a wide variety of problems. Steger (1978) describes the treatment of sexual problems, stressing that methods that require performance are more useful than imagery-based methods for many problems. Burns and Beck (1978) examine the use of imagery in treating depression and other mood disorders. Novaco (1978) shows how imagery and relaxation techniques can be combined to reduce anger.

With the public interest in "self-help" books, it is not surprising to find books that urge readers to solve life's problems without the use of a therapist. For example, Arnold Lazarus (1978) writes, "Through the proper use of mental imagery, one can achieve an immediate sense of self-confidence, develop more energy and stamina, and tap one's own mind for numerous productive purposes" (p. 3). He describes the use of imagery in building confidence, self-control, and assertiveness and in preventing suicide and psychosomatic disorders.

Cautela (1979) expresses his concern about the use of self-help techniques without the personal guidance of professional therapists. He believes, for example, that people might feel anxious and helpless if they follow the procedures and perceive no change. Also, people should be urged to find professional help if they have not successfully modified their behavior. Still, concludes Cautela, readers may benefit from some of the creative procedures suggested in the Lazarus book.

Applications outside Psychology. Professions outside psychology also make extensive use of imagery, although the processes have not been so extensively described. Gordon (1972) mentions the importance of imagery to artists. A painter, for example, tries to recreate his or her internal image on the canvas, a process that Gordon argues is the most adequate way of making images concrete. She notes, however, that art is imperfect; artists are frequently disappointed with their finished work because the work never can be the exact match of the internal image.

> This discrepancy between image and artwork ensures that there will never be a final, a last, a definitive work of art; there can be no end and no conclusion. Through the pain of the artist's travail and despair the continuity of art is assured . . . (p. 78)

Writers, as well as artists, make use of imagery in their work. For example, they may hope to describe a scene vividly enough that the description can produce an appropriate mental image for the reader. In some cases, writers are much less subtle—they directly invite us to use imagery. Shakespeare, for example, includes a chorus in his play *Henry V*. One of the primary functions of this chorus is to urge the audience to use mental imagery.

> Piece out our imperfections with your thoughts.
> Into a thousand parts divide one man, . . .

> Think, when we talk of horses, that you see them
> Printing their proud hoofs i' the receiving earth;
> For 'tis your thoughts that now must deck our kings, . . .

(Henry V, Prologue)

The chorus insists that we supplement the play with our imagery; rather than the one man on the stage in the French battlefield, we must imagine one thousand. When the play mentions horses, we must think that we see them. Later, as Henry returns to England, the chorus advises us to imagine English beaches filled with jubilant crowds.

Roger Shepard (1978), whose research on imagery has been mentioned often in this chapter, has also been concerned about the role of imagery in literature. Here, it is often a spontaneous series of images that suggests a story or a poem to an author.

The modern American novelist Judith Guest reported that her novel *Ordinary People* began as a "mental image" of the main character sitting on a bench in a garden of a mental hospital. Another character, a psychiatrist, appeared to her as a mental image in a dream (Friedman, 1977).

Shepard has also been intrigued by the way outstanding scientists have solved problems by the use of imagery. Einstein, for example, stressed that he seldom thought in words. Instead, he constructed theories by "visualizing . . . effects, consequences, and possibilities" (Holton, 1972, p. 110). Perhaps the most celebrated use of imagery in science was the case of a German chemist Friedrich Kekulé, whose insights into molecular structure came from reveries in which moving visual images showed dancing atoms hooking themselves into chainlike molecules. Kekulé practiced the production of visual images, and in one remarkable dream, the snakelike, squirming chain suddenly lept into a closed loop as if it had seized its own tail. At that moment, Kekulé discovered the answer to the problem of the structure of benzene, a problem that had plagued him for a long time. Whereas "standard" chemical molecules are long strings of atoms, the benzene molecule is a six-sided, closed ring, indeed resembling a snake that has seized its own tail.

It should be mentioned, at this point, that imagery is enormously useful in solving everyday structural problems as well as scientific ones. As I was writing this chapter, my plumber was fixing my ailing humidifier. It seemed that a particular metal part was necessary to hold a rotating rod, and the plumber described the thought processes she used in solving the problem. She visualized the size and shape and type of metal necessary for the job and then tried to visualize where she had seen such a part before. Quite suddenly, she realized that she was envisioning the small metal ring used to attach lamps to their bases. We will discuss other aspects of imagery and problem solving in Chapter 6.

SECTION SUMMARY: *The Characteristics of Mental Images*

1. **Imagery refers to mental representations of objects that are not present.**
2. **The amount of time it takes to rotate a mental image depends upon the degree of rotation required.**

3. People take longer to make judgments about characteristics of small mental images than of large mental images. Also, they take longer to decide which of two mental images is larger when the two images are similar in size than when one is clearly larger.
4. People take longer to decide which angle, of two mental images, is smaller when the two mental images are of similar angles.
5. When people are asked to judge the similarity of pairs of geographical areas such as states, using mental images stimulated by the names of the states, their judgments are similar to the ones they make using pictures of the states.
6. People have difficulty identifying a part as belonging to a whole if they have not included the part in their verbal description of the whole.
7. Visual tasks interfere with visual imagery. Furthermore, visual imagery interferes with visual tasks, and auditory imagery interferes with auditory tasks.
8. Most theorists support an analogy theory. They maintain that mental images resemble perceptual experiences, and most of the experimental evidence supports this view. Several dissenters believe that mental images are stored, instead, in terms of propositions, or abstract, verbal descriptions.
9. Imagery has numerous applications in both traditional psychoanalytic therapy and in behavior therapy. It is also useful in art, literature, and science.

Imagery and Memory

In this section we will see how imagery influences another cognitive process, memory. In the first part of the section we will explore the research on imagery and memory. Then we will briefly discuss why imagery helps memory. The last part of the section examines some practical applications of imagery in memory.

Research on Imagery and Memory

There are two different research approaches to the study of imagery and memory. The first approach, which we can call "Imagery as a Stimulus Characteristic," involves stimuli that differ in their ability to create an image. The second approach, "Mnemonics Involving Imagery," focuses upon strategies that people can use to improve memory.

Imagery as a Stimulus Characteristic.   Try Demonstration 4.6 and notice which kind of words you recalled better.

Allan Paivio is one of the important researchers who have been examining memory for stimuli that differ with respect to imagery. His early work (for example, Paivio, 1965) advanced the study of imagery by specifying a precise definition for imagery. People rated words on a five-point scale that ranged from "image aroused immediately" to "image aroused only after long delay or not at all." Paivio also observed that many studies had shown that people recalled more items when words were concrete (for example, *house* and *apple*) than when they were abstract (for example, *idea* and *truth*). In looking over the literature, Paivio (1969) drew two important conclusions. First of all, the reason that people recall more concrete words than abstract words is that concrete words encourage images. Think about the word *apple*; the image that it arouses is probably clear and well defined. Can you readily come up with an image for *truth*? Maybe, with some difficulty, you can picture a noble-looking person opening his or her mouth, with truthful sentences spilling out. However, this image would be quite fuzzy, and you would have difficulty representing the truthful nature of the sentences in a mental picture.

Demonstration 4.6   *Imagery and Memory*.

Learn the following list of pairs. Later, you will see the first member of each pair and be asked to supply the second member.

CATHEDRAL–LEMONADE
TRUTH–IDEA
KITCHEN–TOMAHAWK
SAKE–CONTEXT
BEGGAR–ORCHESTRA
QUILT–PEARL
AIM–KNOWLEDGE
UNREALITY–WORTH
RASPBERRY–SLEIGH
PARADOX–CONCEPT
SUBMARINE–ACROBAT
MEANING–PHASE

Now, here is a list of the first members of those pairs. Cover the pairs above and try to recall as many responses as possible.

1. PARADOX	————	7. QUILT	————
2. MEANING	————	8. KITCHEN	————
3. CATHEDRAL	————	9. AIM	————
4. SAKE	————	10. SUBMARINE	————
5. BEGGAR	————	11. TRUTH	————
6. RASPBERRY	————	12. UNREALITY	

Now tally up how many high-imagery pairs you recalled; these are numbers 3, 5, 6, 7, 8, and 10. Tally up the low-imagery pairs; these are numbers 1, 2, 4, 9, 11, and 12.

The second conclusion that Paivio reached was that the important factor in memory was imagery, rather than some other confounding variable that was related to imagery. As you may recall from other courses, **confounding variables** are uncontrolled factors that are present to different extents in different conditions. For example, suppose we select two groups of words, a high-imagery list and a low-imagery list. Unfortunately, the two lists will also differ in other ways. For example, Paivio (1968) found that the high-imagery words are also more familiar in the English language. The high-imagery list includes words like *car* and *tree,* which are very familiar in English, and the low-imagery list includes words like *philosophy* and *abstraction,* words which are fairly unfamiliar in English. Now if we find that the high-imagery list is recalled better than the low-imagery list, a critic of our study could reasonably point out that the variable of familiarity, rather than imagery, might have caused the difference in recall. In that study, familiarity would be a confounding variable.

At any rate, Paivio (1968, 1969) searched for other characteristics of words that might be acting as confounding variables in word imagery experiments. He concluded that there were no confounding variables that could satisfactorily account for the influence of imagery on memory. Imagery had a stronger influence on memory than any other factor, such as familiarity or word meaning. When all the other factors were equated in experiments, imagery still had a powerful effect. The most important alternative to imagery that Paivio eliminated was **meaningfulness,** which is measured in terms of the number of associations a word elicits (for example, *kitchen* is more meaningful than *tomahawk*). Paivio (1969) summarizes several well-controlled studies, however, in which imagery was found to be more closely related to recall than meaningfulness was. Incidentally, a book by Richardson (1980) summarizes the recent research on mental imagery and memory.

In this section we have seen that words high in imagery are recalled better than words low in imagery. This fact is related to one of the themes of the book that we discussed in the first chapter: Humans handle positive information better than negative information. In other words, we deal with something that exists more readily than we deal with something that does not exist. In relation to imagery, we have seen that we can remember a word better if a mental image exists for that word. In contrast, a word that does not have a mental image is more easily forgotten.

Mnemonics Involving Imagery. Try Demonstration 4.7, Which set of instructions produced the highest recall, the repetition or the imagery instructions?

This demonstration is a simplified version of a study by Bower and Winzenz (1970). They used concrete nouns in their study and tested subjects in four different conditions: (1) repetition, in which subjects repeated the pairs silently to themselves; (2) sentence reading, in which subjects read sentences devised by the experimenters, and each pair is included in one sentence; (3) sentence generation, in which subjects made up a sentence about each pair and said it aloud; and (4) imagery, in which subjects tried to construct a mental picture of the two words in vivid interaction with each other.

Demonstration 4.7   Instructions and Memory.

Learn the following list of pairs by repeating the members of each pair several times. For example, if the pair is CAT–WINDOW, say over and over to yourself, "CAT–WINDOW, CAT–WINDOW, CAT–WINDOW." Just repeat the words, and do not use any other study method. Allow yourself one minute for this list.

CUSTARD–LUMBER   IVY–MOTHER
JAIL–CLOWN   LIZARD–PAPER
ENVELOPE–SLIPPER   SCISSORS–BEAR
SHEEPSKIN–CANDLE   CANDY–MOUNTAIN
FRECKLES–APPLE   BOOK–PAINT
HAMMER–STAR   TREE–OCEAN

Now, try to recall as many responses as possible. Cover up the pairs above.

ENVELOPE   _____   JAIL   _____

FRECKLES   _____   IVY   _____

TREE   _____   SHEEPSKIN   _____

CANDY   _____   BOOK   _____

SCISSORS   _____   LIZARD   _____

CUSTARD   _____   HAMMER   _____

Learn the following list of pairs by visualizing a mental picture in which the two objects in each pair are in some kind of vivid interaction. For example, if the pair is CAT–WINDOW, you might make up a picture of a cat jumping through a closed window, with the glass shattering all about. Just make up a picture and do not use any other study method. Allow yourself one minute for this list.

SOAP–MERMAID   MIRROR–RABBIT
FOOTBALL–LAKE   HOUSE–DIAMOND
PENCIL–LETTUCE   LAMB–MOON
CAR–HONEY   BREAD–GLASS
CANDLE–DANCER   LIPS–MONKEY
DANDELION–FLEA   DOLLAR–ELEPHANT

Now, try to recall as many responses as possible. Cover up the pairs above.

CANDLE   _____   DOLLAR   _____

DANDELION   _____   CAR   _____

BREAD   _____   LIPS   _____

MIRROR   _____   PENCIL   _____

LAMB   _____   SOAP   _____

FOOTBALL   _____   HOUSE   _____

Now, count the number of correct responses on each list. Did you recall a greater number of words with the imagery instructions? Incidentally, you may have found it very difficult to *avoid* using imagery on the first list, since you have been reading a chapter about imagery. In that case, your recall scores were probably similar for the two lists. You may wish to test a friend, instead.

After learning several lists of words, subjects saw the first word of each pair and were asked to supply the second word. The results were quite remarkable. Out of a possible 15 items, subjects in the repetition condition recalled only 5.2. However, subjects in the imagery condition recalled 12.7 words, more than twice as many!

Richardson (1978) has also demonstrated that mental imagery is more effective than other memory techniques. People in his study learned paired words and were then tested for recall. Finally, they were asked to indicate how they had learned each pair of words. Specifically, had their memorizing involved imagery, verbal mediation (a mnemonic device we discussed in Chapter 3), or repetition? Richardson found that people who used mental imagery were likely to recall more items than people who had used other methods. In contrast, the use of verbal mediation was not related to the number of items recalled. Richardson's results therefore supplement the results of Bower and Winzenz in demonstrating the superiority of mental imagery as a memorizing technique.

If you have read articles about improving your memory that appear in popular magazines, the articles probably stressed the importance of concocting an unusual or bizarre image to link together the items you wish to remember. However, the experimental studies do not offer clear-cut support for this advice.

A representative study on the bizarreness of imagery was conducted by Wollen, Weber, and Lowry (1972). They controlled independently the factors of bizarreness and interaction, showing people pictures that were (1) interacting and bizarre, (2) interacting and not bizarre, (3) not interacting and bizarre, and (4) not interacting and not bizarre. Figure 4.6 illustrates these four possibilities. All of the words in the pairs were high-imagery nouns, but the relationship of the two members of each pair depended upon the condition. Interacting pictures showed the two objects interacting in either a spatial relationship, such as a cigar *on* a piano, or interacting in an active relationship, such as a piano *smoking* a cigar. In the

Figure 4.6   Sample Materials for the Four Conditions in the Experiment on Bizarreness of Imagery by Wollen, Weber, and Lowry (1972).

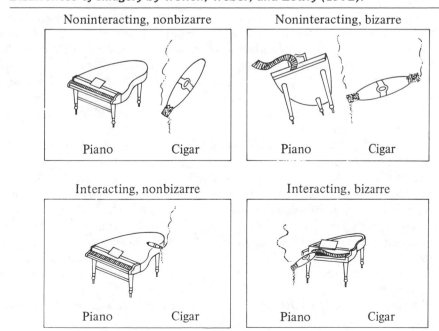

noninteracting pictures, the objects were simply drawn side by side. Bizarreness was represented by a particularly unusual relationship between two objects for the interacting pictures (for example, a piano smoking a cigar) or by a bizarre distortion of the individual objects for the noninteracting pictures (for example, a cigar burning at both ends).

The results of the study showed that people recalled the interacting pairs better than the noninteracting pairs. However, bizarreness had no effect on recall. Thus, recall was improved by showing the piano and the cigar together, and it did not matter whether their interaction was unusual or ordinary.

Although several studies support this conclusion that bizarrenesss of the image is not important, another study shows that—under some circumstances—bizarreness can improve recall. For example, Webber and Marshall (1978) found that bizarre pairs were recalled better than other pairs when recall was delayed. They concluded:

> . . . the bizarre image tends to remain stronger or more distinct from competing input which accumulates over time than does the common image. Whether such differences are due to insulation of items through the reduction of interference or to the formation of a stronger memory trace which is actively more resistant to decay remains unclear. (p. 298)

Notice that this explanation is similar to Craik's (1979) concept of distinctiveness, or a stimulus that differs from other memory traces, an idea discussed in Chapter 3.

Does bizarreness of the image make a difference? The answer is not yet clear. Bizarreness does not help in some cases, but it is useful in other cases. The answer to this question may well depend upon how we define *bizarreness* as well as other characteristics of the task.

One particular memory device that relies very heavily on imagery is the **method of loci** (loci = Latin for "places," pronounced "*low*-sigh"), a method in which people associate items to be learned with physical locations. Bower (1970) summarizes the steps in using this technique: (1) Memorize a list of locations (or "memory snapshots") arranged in a familiar order; (2) make up an image representing each of the items to be remembered; and (3) take the items in the order they are to be learned and associate them, one by one, with the corresponding location in memory.

When the Greeks used this method thousands of years ago, they used pillars and statues for their locations. Bower describes how we might use the method of loci for a familiar set of more contemporary loci, such as "driveway," "inside the garage," "front door," "coat closet," and "kitchen sink." If you need to remember a grocery shopping list, for example, hot dogs, cat food, tomatoes, bananas, and whisky, you would make up a vivid image for each item. Then imagine each item in its appropriate place. You could imagine giant *hot dogs* rolling down the *driveway*, a monstrous *cat eating food* in the *garage*, ripe *tomatoes* splattering all over the *front door*, bunches of *bananas* swinging in the *closet*, and an expensive bottle of *whisky* gurgling down the *kitchen* sink. Now you enter the supermarket and mentally walk the route from the driveway to the kitchen sink, recalling the items in order.

The method sounds a bit unlikely, but does it work? A representative

Figure 4.7 **Percentage of Words Recalled in the Correct Order, as a Function of Condition and Delay.** (Groninger, 1971.)

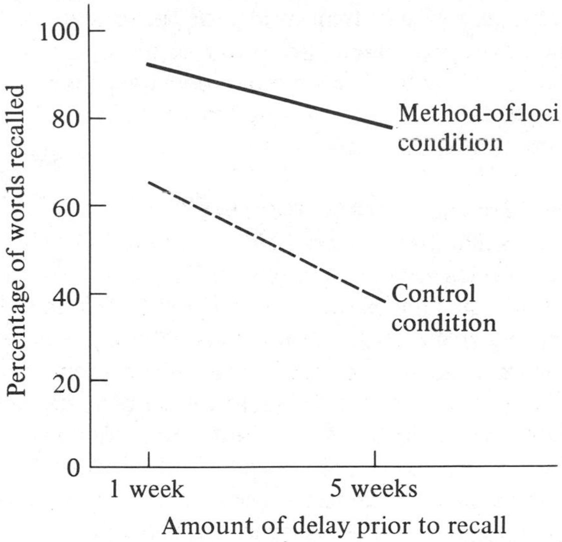

experiment is one by Groninger (1971). Subjects in one condition were told to think of 25 locations that could be placed in order. Then they mentally picture items on a 25-word list, using the method of loci. Subjects in the control condition simply learned the 25 words in order, using any method they wanted. They were instructed not to rehearse the material any further. They returned for testing one week and five weeks later, and those people who had rehearsed the material were eliminated from the study. Figure 4.7 shows the results of the study. As you can see,

---

Demonstration 4.8   **The Method of Loci.**

You will be using the method of loci to learn a list of items in order. First of all, mentally trace the route from the place you live to your classroom. Locate ten familiar, major points along the way, and spend a few minutes reviewing these locations. Now, attach the first item, chocolate ice cream, to the first location, and so on. Make a note to yourself to try to recreate this "shopping list" one month from now, and check your accuracy.

1. chocolate ice cream
2. razor blades
3. chicken noodle soup
4. one quart of milk
5. a package of salami
6. a head of lettuce
7. a can of tuna
8. a roll of paper towels
9. pork chops
10. a box of raisins

the method of loci was particularly effective when recall was measured five weeks after learning.

At this point, try Demonstration 4.8 to see how effective the method of loci can be. Once you have a list of familiar loci, or places, you might want to use that list again in the future, whenever the order of items is important. Incidentally, Bower (1970) stresses that the learner must repeat each item on the same locus. If you keep shifting the chicken noodle soup from the library steps to the dormintory doorway, you will not recall as many items!

Why Does Imagery Help Memory?

Dozens of studies testify that imagery helps memory, but only a few psychologists have developed theories about why it works. Before we consider several of these, let us look at a study by Jonides, Kahn, and Rozin (1975) that demonstrates that a theory must not rely solely on the *visual* aspects of imagery. Blind and normally sighted college students learned pairs of words, first without and then with imagery instructions. The imagery instructions, for example, suggested that the pair *locomotive – dishtowel* could be remembered by a dishtowel wrapped around a locomotive. The results showed that imagery instructions were, if anything, more helpful to the blind students than to the normally sighted students. Jonides and his coauthors support the view that imagery instructions simply promote the establishment of a meaningful relationship between two words, and therefore make them easier to remember.

Anderson (1976) expands on this view that imagery works by making the relationship more meaningful. He believes that imagery instructions encourage people to develop a richer, more detailed code for the items. After all, the typical seeing subject has had a rich lifetime of experience with the items and properties, and these properties can be put to use in memory if the instructions encourage imagery. Thus the codes for words learned under imagery conditions are so much more elaborate that recall is superior when people are encouraged to form images.

Paivio, whose work on high-imagery and low-imagery words was discussed at the beginning of the section (Paivio, 1969), favors a **dual coding hypothesis** explanation for the results of imagery studies. In this explanation, there are two independent systems. One system is the **imagery system,** which stores images that correspond to concrete objects in our world. The **verbal system,** in contrast, deals with linguistic units or words. One system deals with pictures, the other with descriptions. Although the two systems are independent, they are connected to each other and can cooperate with each other. If there is no image for a word (either because the word is too abstract to produce an image or because you have not developed an image for a word), then you must rely only on the verbal system to remember the word. On the other hand, a concrete word or an imagery strategy can create a picture, and so the word can be stored both as a memory picture and as a memory word. With two representations for the word, it is more likely that the word will be recalled. As Paivio writes, "Simply stated, two memory traces are better than one" (Paivio, 1978a, p. 116).

Do we remember better with imagery because our verbal descriptions are "fancier" than without imagery, as Anderson and Bower (1973) argue, or because we have a nonverbal representation to supplement the verbal representation, as

Paivio (1978a) maintains? The issue is not resolved. It may be that both positions are correct; the influence of imagery is so powerful that two factors, rather than one, may be responsible.

Applications of Imagery in Memory

Using imagery to improve your memory is perhaps the most obvious of all applications of imagery. In fact, I hope you have already been using imagery in memorizing, particularly after you have seen how much more effective it is than merely repeating the information.

Patten (1972) has described how he uses imagery as a physician dealing with patients whose memories have been impaired by nervous system diseases.

> For instance, suppose one wants to remember the following shopping list: bread, carrots, eggs, dog food, newspaper, bacon, and deodorant, if we know *bread* and want to remember *carrots* we picture a giant loaf of bread breaking open and carrots falling out. The instructor would pause briefly to enable the patient to form the association picture and to "see it" in his mind's eye. Similarly, eggs are connected with carrots by picturing a chicken hatching a carrot. Dog food is connected with eggs by picturing a dozen eggs running around on a leash. Newspaper was connected to dog food by seeing a dog reading a paper; bacon connected with newspaper by visualizing someone reading a bacon instead of a newspaper and deodorant was connected with bacon by picturing someone putting bacon under their arms instead of deodorant . . . (p. 547)

Patten discusses four case histories, including the case of a 37-year-old movie executive who had suffered from a virus infection of the brain and was unable to recall more than one item out of three after a delay. With the use of imagery, he increased his memory span substantially and began to add $10-25$ words to his vocabulary every day.

The applications of imagery for teaching are impressive. Atkinson and Raugh (1975) used imagery to teach Russian vocabulary. They asked students to think of an English word resembling each Russian word. For example, the Russian word *Zdanie*, meaning building, is pronounced "zdawn-yeh." The students might visualize the first rays of dawn striking a tall building. The students mastered this visualization technique quickly, and they improved their recall of vocabulary from 46 percent correct in the control condition to 72 percent correct with the visualization method.

Bull and Wittrock (1973) found that imagery helped fifth-grade children learn new vocabulary words. They asked the children to learn words like *brain, magazine, trouble,* and *truth* in three different conditions. An "imagery-discovered" group read each word and its definition, wrote them, and then drew a picture of the word and its definition. An "imagery-given" group was identical except that they *traced* a picture rather than drawing their own. A control group simply wrote the word and its definition over and over during the time period. On a multiple choice test a week later, students in the "imagery-discovered" group were best, whereas those in the control group were worst. Notice that these results are parallel to those in the Bower and Winzenz (1970) study on pairs of words; that is, people do better if they come up with their own images, rather than using the ones supplied by the experimenter. For future definitions in this book you might try producing an image for as many terms as possible.

SECTION SUMMARY: *Imagery and Memory*

1. High-imagery words are recalled better than low-imagery words. Imagery, rather than potential confounding variables, is responsible for the differences.
2. When subjects create vivid images in order to learn material, they recall far more than if they merely repeat the material.
3. Creating bizarre, unusual images may be helpful in some specified situations, but other studies have shown that bizarreness does not influence recall.
4. The method of loci, used by associating items with physical locations, is extremely helpful for remembering a list of items in order.
5. One theory of imagery claims that imagery works by making the relationship between items more meaningful. The dual coding hypothesis, on the other hand, argues that imagery works because it creates a picturelike trace to supplement the verbal trace.
6. Imagery as an aid to memory has been applied in treating patients with memory disorders and in teaching foreign-language and English vocabulary.

Cognitive Maps

Cognitive maps are mental images that let us collect, organize, store, recall, and manipulate information about the spatial environment (Downs & Stea, 1977). A cognitive map is a mental map that represents the world as you believe it to be. It might be a very detailed and accurate mental map, or it might be a rough sketch with little correspondence to reality.

Think about how you use cognitive maps. For example, if you walk across campus to the library, you are using your cognitive map. You use another cognitive map as you try to describe to a friend how to get from the dormitory to the new taco shop. Another cognitive map appears when you try to remember the layout of the house you lived in when you were in third grade. You even use a map as you open your second drawer to reach for your socks.

In this section of the chapter on imagery, we will discuss several aspects of cognitive maps: images of cities, images of college campuses, distances on cognitive maps and cognitive maps in animals. Additional aspects of cognitive maps are considered in an excellent book called *Maps in Minds: Reflections on Cognitive Mapping* (Downs & Stea, 1977), which is coauthored by a geographer and a psychologist.

Images of Cities

Think about a city you have visited recently. Try to get several mental images of that city. What kind of things do you focus upon? What favorite views pop into your mind? What landmarks do you see? What is the general shape of the city?

Kevin Lynch (1960) wrote a classic book called *The Image of the City,* in which he interviewed residents of Los Angeles, Jersey City, and Boston. He asked them to describe their own images of their environment. The residents were asked, also, to perform imaginary trips between different areas in their cities. Lynch found that people paid particular attention to certain kinds of features, such as open space, vegetation, sense of motion, and visual contrasts.

Let us look at the image that emerges of Boston:

> For almost all the persons interviewed, this Boston is a city of very distinctive districts and of crooked, confusing paths. It is a dirty city, of red-brick buildings, symbolized by the open space of the Boston Common, the State House with its gold dome, and the view across the Charles River from the Cambridge side. Most of them added that it is an old, historical place, full of worn-out buildings, yet containing some new structures among the old. Its narrow streets are congested with people and cars; there is no parking space, but there are striking contrasts between wide main streets and narrow side streets. The central city is a peninsula, surrounded by a water edge. In addition to the Common, the Charles River, and the State House, there are several other vivid elements, particularly Beacon Hill, Commonwealth Avenue, the Washington Street shopping and theater district. . . .
>
> One of the most interesting districts is one that isn't there: the triangular region between the Back Bay and the South End. This was a blank area on the map for *every* person interviewed, even the one who was born and raised there. (pp. 19–20)

If you have a map of the city you visited, check it out. Did you, like those whom Lynch interviewed, have blank areas on your map? You will probably find some clear correspondence between the "real" map and your psychological map, but there will be some important differences.

Other cities have also been examined. New York City, for example, is remembered for its downtown landmarks (Hooper, 1966). Most parts of the city have no representations on the map. However, it is interesting to contemplate individual differences in the representation of a city like New York. To me, a cognitive map of New York City is dotted with movie theaters, in the upper West Side, in the East 60s, and near Greenwich Village. Chinese, Indian, and Latin American restaurants are located on assorted streets. The Asia de Cuba restaurant is prominent, but the World Trade Center is missing. Obviously, the cognitive map of a movie fanatic who likes to eat would be different from the cognitive map of a Wall Street executive!

Images of College Campuses

Now draw a map of your college campus, and then compare it with a real map. Saarinen (1973) asked 200 students at the University of Arizona, representing 12 different departments, to make a sketch of the university area. Saarinen found wide individual differences and strong tendencies for people to expand the size and detail of the buildings most important to them. Some people had fairly complete and accurate maps, but most people forgot to record many buildings, paths, and broad areas. Sometimes people drew only a small portion of the campus, usually the area they visited most often or the area most central to the campus.

An interesting pattern emerged when the results were combined for each of the departments, because subjects showed high accuracy for the areas in which their classes were held. For students in the Women's Physical Education Department, for example, their own building, as well as the gym and the stadium, were consistently included in the sketch. These parts of the campus were often absent for other students in other departments.

Distances on Cognitive Maps

How accurate are people in judging the distances between two points on their cognitive maps? Golledge and Zannaras (1973) asked people to estimate distances between the Ohio State University campus and various locations along a major highway passing through the campus and on to the downtown area to the south of the campus. In general, there was a high correlation betweeen actual distances and estimated distances. Golledge and Zannaras also found that people who had lived in the area for a longer time were more accurate in their estimates than were relative newcomers.

In a later study in the same area near Ohio State University, Briggs (1971) confirmed something you may have wondered about: People think that a familiar location is closer than an unfamiliar location. That is, the distance from a given point to a familiar place was perceived as being shorter than the distance from that same point to an unfamiliar place. You may have found yourself lost in a strange city. Asking a resident for directions, you may learn that a particular intersection is "about a mile down the road." You may find that crossroad just as you are about to give up hope, after having traveled for what seems like three miles! Familiarity shrinks distances on a map, whereas unfamiliarity expands them. We will explore this relationship between familiarity and distance more fully in Chapter 6. Basically, we will see that some items serve as prototypes—best examples or reference points—and other items seem to be physically close to these items. A familiar place is like a prototype, and so it seems nearby. In contrast, since unfamiliar places are not prototypes, they seem distant.

One of the most complete studies of distances in cities was conducted by Canter and Tagg (1975), who questioned people in seven cities in five different countries. Subjects were asked to estimate the distance between pairs of various familiar locations in their city. Canter and Tagg, like other researchers, found a high correlation between the responses and the actual distances. However, most people overestimated distances. (See whether you, too, tend to overestimate distances, by guessing how far it may be between two points and then measuring it. Does the shopping center which you judged to be 4 miles away from your dormitory really turn out to be only 3.1 miles?) This overestimation was greater in cities that had a confusing image, sprawling rather than being confined by rivers and bays (for example, Tokyo, Japan) than in cities that could be more easily visualized (for example, Glasgow, Scotland).

Canter and Tagg also note that accuracy of cognitive maps may show strong individual differences. Most of the samples these authors studied were architecture students, and their estimates were quite accurate. However, one of the samples was pedestrians in central Glasgow, who were stopped on the street and asked to answer some questions about distance. These people were far less accurate. However, we should consider that their inaccuracy might reflect factors other than ability. How carefully would you contemplate your answer if someone stopped you on the street and asked you how far it was from Joe's Pizza to the car wash?

Some of the most recent studies on cognitive maps have been concerned with the methods of measuring cognitive maps. One experiment (Baird, Merrill, & Tannenbaum, 1979) asked students on the Dartmouth campus to locate buildings, either by constructing direct maps or by making judgments about how far apart various pairs of buildings were. These judgments were then analyzed by multidimensional scaling (which we discussed in the "shape of states" study) into a two-dimensional map. All of the subjects believed that their direct maps were more accurate. Furthermore, a group of subjects who had not participated in the experiment also agreed that the direct maps were more accurate. Isn't it refreshing to find that the easiest method of asking people about their mental maps is also the best?

As you have been reading this section on cognitive maps, you might have wondered whether "sense of direction" is related to ability to construct maps. Kozlowski and Bryant (1977) have noticed that people have clear ideas about their abilities in this area:

> Casual interviews show that (a) almost everyone readily gives an assessment of his or her own sense of direction and (b) individuals either express self-satisfaction with their orientation skills, or they disclose a series of mishaps, disorientations, and missed appointments, which they trace to a poor sense of direction. (p. 590)

Kozlowski and Bryant asked their subjects to rate their sense of direction on a seven-point scale. Then, the subjects tried several tasks to test their ability. For example, they were asked point in the direction of two large cities. People who believed they had a good sense of direction were more accurate than those who believed they had poor sense of direction; the correlation between sense of direction and pointing errors was −.49.

In another study, Kozlowski and Bryant (1977) led people with good and poor senses of direction through a section of tunnels located underneath a dormitory complex at the university. At the end of each trip, they were returned to the starting point and were asked to point to the end of the tunnel. Those with good senses of direction learned to point quite accurately after four trials; their pointing errors averaged about 25 degrees. In contrast, those with poor senses of direction remained about 60 degrees off-target for the whole study. They showed no hint of becoming more accurate as they became more familiar with the area! This study represents an initial stage in the study of sense of direction, a topic we think about in everyday life that has not been explored systematically by cognitive psychologists.

Cognitive Maps in Animals

We have seen that humans have cognitive maps that correspond to the physical world. How about animals? Menzel (1973) wondered how accurate and how efficient chimpanzees would be in locating food that they saw being hidden. The subjects in this study were six chimpanzees that had been born in the wild, and the study took place in a large enclosure in which they had lived for the last year. At the beginning of a trial, one experimenter took one animal and carried him around the field as a second experimenter walked alongside, hiding pieces of food in each of 18 places. The chimp merely watched, and was not allowed to walk along the route or to taste the food. The chimp was then returned to the cage with the other five control animals.

Next, all six animals were released at the same time. Since the other five animals had not been shown the hiding places, they served as controls. Thus, they could use cues such as food odor and unintentional cues from the experimenters, cues that were also available to the "test" chimp (who was therefore in the "experimental" condition). The experimenters recorded the search patterns of all the animals. Testing continued for 16 days, with four different animals serving as test animals. Different hiding places were used on each day.

The results showed that the test animals, who had been shown the food, found a total of 200 pieces. The animals serving as controls, however, found only a total of 17 pieces. Thus, the animals in the experimental condition found many more pieces of food than they would have found if they relied only on the cues available to the control animals. They must have had cognitive maps to repesent food locations.

Menzel describes the chimps' behavior:

> Usually, the test animal ran unerringly and in a direct line to the exact clump of grass or leaves, tree stump, or hole in the ground where a hidden food lay, grabbed the food, stopped briefly to eat, and then ran directly to the next place, no matter how distant or obscured by visual barriers that place was. His pace slowed as more and more food was obtained, and eventually he lay down for long rests; but he never wandered around the field as if conducting a general search. (pp. 943–944)

Thus chimpanzees must have mental maps to represent food locations. Also, the chimps can "read" the maps quite flexibly; they go to the nearest hiding location, rather than needing to repeat the experimenter's route. If you have a dog or a cat, you might try a simplified version of this experiment, hiding favorite foods in various locations while your animal watches. Don't forget to include control trials, in which the animal has not watched you hide the food and must rely only on smell and other incidental cues. Does Rover have a cognitive map?

SECTION SUMMARY: *Cognitive Maps*

1. Cognitive maps are mental images about the spatial environment.
2. In their mental images of cities, people pay particular attention to certain kinds of features, such as open space and visual contrasts.
3. In their cognitive maps of college campuses, people tend to expand the size and detail of areas of the campus that are important to them.
4. People are fairly accurate in estimating distances on cognitive maps, but they judge familiar locations to be closer than unfamiliar locations.
5. Chimpanzees evidently are capable of developing cognitive maps because they can recall the location of hiding places for food.

Chapter Review Questions

1. Summarize the two theories of the characteristics of mental images, the analog code and the propositions viewpoint. Describe the findings about mental rotations, size judgments, and angles, noting which theory the results support.

2. Almost all of this chapter dealt with visual imagery, because there is little available information about imagery in the other senses. How might you design a study on taste imagery that would be conceptually similiar to the Shepard and Chipman study on the shapes of states? What would you expect to find?

3. What area of research provided the strongest support for the propositional storage of information about objects? Speculate about why this area of research produced different results from the remainder of the studies we examined.

4. Why do the studies on imagery and interference support the viewpoint that visual activity is involved in visual imagery?

5. Summarize Paivio's conclusions regarding imagery and memory.

6. Imagine that you are teaching high school history. List several mnemonic tips that you might suggest to your class to help them memorize historical facts. Think of examples for each tip.

7. Describe Anderson's viewpoint about why imagery works, and contrast it with Paivio's dual coding hypothesis. Which theory is supported by the study involving imagery instructions and blind students, and why?

8. Cognitive maps sometimes correspond to reality, and sometimes they do not. Discuss this statement in relation to the studies discussed in the section on cognitive maps.

9. Are people accurate in estimating their sense of direction? Summarize what you know about individual differences in sense of direction.

10. Think about your future profession and describe two or three ways in which this information about imagery can be applied to your work. You can use the information on any of the three sections: the characteristics of images, imagery and memory, or cognitive maps.

New Terms

imagery
analog code
propositions
psychophysics
internal psychophysics
symbolic distance effect

rank
covert conditioning
covert negative
  reinforcement
covert modeling
confounding variables

meaningfulness
method of loci
dual coding hypothesis
imagery system
verbal system
cognitive maps

Language

Preview

Language is important for many cognitive processes, and it is difficult to imagine any kind of civilization in which there is no form of language. This chapter considers four aspects: (1) understanding language; (2) producing language; (3) remembering language; and (4) reading.

We look at three topics with respect to understanding language. Speech perception, which involves translating sounds into speech, has several characteristics; for example, listeners can fill in missing sounds and they can figure out boundaries between words. Listeners process language in terms of groups of words called constituents. Some kind of sentences are easier to understand than others.

In the section on producing language we discuss the social aspects of speech because they determine the format and the formality of speech. We also consider the content of speech, as in telling a story and describing a location. Speech errors and the production of speech sounds are two other important topics. We also look at the great debate about teaching champanzees to use language.

The section on remembering language supplements Chapter 3, which emphasize memory for isolated words. In this part of the chapter, we investigate laboratory studies and real-world applications of verbatim memory, memory for meaning, and memory for inferences.

The last section explores several components of the reading process. The part on perceptual processes examines the eye movements involved in reading. Then we discuss three theories of word recognition. The section on reading also considers whether speed-reading courses are effective.

Suppose, all of a sudden, language became illegal. You wouldn't be allowed to speak, to read, to write, or to use words to think or remember. What would that do to your life? You couldn't yell at your roommate about the dirty socks on the floor. You couldn't go to any lectures or read any books. In fact, you wouldn't go to school at all, because there would be no way to communicate the basic information about registration. Furthermore, you wouldn't *need* to go to school, because all professions requiring verbal communication (and it is hard to imagine any that do not) would be banned. It is difficult to imagine *even* the most primitive kind of society without language.

Some psychologists are so convinced of the importance of language that they maintain that language is the very basis of thought. The early behaviorist, John Watson (1924), believed that thought simply consisted of talking to ourselves. Few current **psycholinguists** (people who study psychological aspects of language) would agree with Watson, but most would maintain that language and thought are interrelated in many ways. As an exercise, check back through the chapters you have read so far, and notice how often the topics of language, speech, and words are mentioned. Also, as you read the rest of the book, notice how important language is to such topics as problem solving, reasoning, and decision making.

In previous years many psycholinguists concentrated their attention on the structure of language. The current emphasis has shifted to its cognitive aspects. In particular, it seems that humans are quite resourceful in using their previous knowledge to interpret language. This interpretation frequently resembles problem solving because information contained in a message must be combined with previously stored information in order to reach the goal of understanding.

Once again, we will see that humans are active information processors. Rather than passively listening to language, humans actively consult their previous knowledge, use various strategies, form expectations, and draw conclusions. For example, expectations are essential in speech perception. Furthermore, in a section on constituent structure, we will see how people interpret the language they hear by using a variety of strategies—just as they might use strategies to solve a jigsaw puzzle. Speech planning also requires strategic devices; you must guess what your listener already knows and what other facts are necessary. Studies on our memory for language demonstrate how we actively combine several sentences into a meaningful whole, rather than leaving the information fragmented. We also combine sentences with our previous knowledge about a subject so that we can reach conclusions. Thus language users must constantly remember, solve problems, and reason. Language is not an isolated system; it depends heavily on other cognitive processes.

This chapter is divided into three components: understanding language, producing language, and remembering language. We will also consider another related topic: reading.

Understanding Language

Understanding language, often called **language comprehension,** involves using permanently stored knowledge to interpret new input (Lachman, Lachman, & Butterfield, 1979). People hear a set of sounds and manage to make sense of them, using their extensive knowledge of words, language rules, and the world.

Psychologists ignored the topic of comprehension until recently. Language comprehension is another of those hidden cognitive processes that resist systematic investigation. Think about how much easier it is to examine language production—your speakers are providing you with words and sentences that you can analyze. In contrast, you cannot listen to or watch someone *comprehending*! Nevertheless, in recent years, cognitive psychologists have tackled this difficult topic.

We will discuss three areas related to understanding. First, we need to examine speech perception, which is the process of translating sounds into speech; in this section we will summarize two theories that attempt to explain how we perceive speech. Then we will look at a concept called "constituent structure," which proposes that people understand language by analyzing groups of words within a sentence. Finally we will discuss certain linguistic factors that can affect understanding.

Speech Perception

The first step in understanding spoken language is speech perception. During **speech perception** the sound vibrations that the speaker produces enter the listener's ear. The listener's auditory system then translates these vibrations into a string of sounds, which the listener perceives to be speech.

The speech perception process is extremely complex, and you can consult other books for more information (for example, Clark & Clark, 1977; Darwin, 1976; and Foss & Hakes, 1978). There are also several controversies, which Pisoni (1978) examines. To most of us, though, speech perception does not seem very complicated because we usually pay no attention to it. Instead, we usually pay attention to what the speaker is saying. We notice greetings, warnings, questions, and statements, but we do not notice the vehicle that is used to deliver this information (Darwin, 1976).

The next time you listen to the radio announcer, pay no attention to the meaning, but notice the sounds instead. Think about the string of sounds—vowels such as *a* and *e*, for which the vocal tract remains open, stop consonants such as *p* or *k*, for which the vocal tract closes completely and then quickly opens up, and other sounds such as *f* and *r*, in which the vocal tract performs other tricks. Occasionally, there are brief quiet periods in this string of sounds, but most of the words are simply run together in one continuous series.

Let us consider three facts about speech perception: (1) information about sounds is transmitted in parallel; (2) context allows listeners to fill in missing sounds; and (3) listeners can impose boundaries between words.

Parallel Transmission.   When we read the letters in a sentence, the letters follow one after another, like beads on a string. It is tempting to think of speech sounds in similar terms, with the sound of each **phoneme** (or basic unit of speech) following the sound of the previous phoneme. However, this view of speech is incorrect (Foss & Hakes, 1978). Some of the sounds in a syllable are transmitted at about the same time, rather than one at a time. The term **parallel transmission** refers to this tendency for the phonemes to be sent in parallel.

Suppose, for example, that a speaker is saying the English word *bin*, as Figure 5.1 illustrates. The first consonant, *b*, carries its sound through the first half of the word, and therefore, it influences the sound of the *i*. Since the vowel, *i*, has its influence throughout the entire word, it influences the sound of both the *b* and the *n*. The last consonant, *n*, actually begins its sound during the middle of the word, and thus it influences the sound of the *i*. Therefore, each phoneme is not pronounced in isolation, because its sound is modified by the surrounding phonemes (Liberman, 1970).

Because of parallel transmission, speech sounds flow together. This means that a small segment of speech cannot carry all the information about one phoneme, because that information is spread across several segments. Further- more, a phoneme's sound can change, depending upon which phonemes precede and follow it. Phonemes often do not have a single, constant pronunciation. For

Figure 5.1   More than One Speech Phoneme Is Transmitted at a Time.

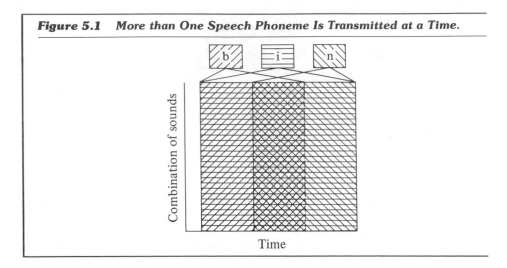

example, a *d* might sound different in a *di* combination than it sounds in a *du* combination.

From our discussion so far, you might conclude that there is no stability in the sound of a phoneme. However, Cole and Scott (1974) have argued that, in spite of the variation provided from the surrounding sounds, all consonant phonemes have some invariant features. An **invariant feature** in speech perception is a sound cue that accompanies a particular phoneme, no matter what vowels surround it. For example, the letter *s* always has a hissing sound. Furthermore, a *z* always differs from an *s* because its pitch is lower. Sometimes the invariant features are specific enough so that a person can identify the consonant. In other cases, the invariant features allow the listener to narrow down the possibilities to two or three phonemes. More details about parallel transmission and invariant features can be obtained by reading Pisoni (1978).

Context and Speech Perception.   People are active listeners. They do not passively receive speech sounds. Instead, they are able to use context as a cue to help them figure out a sound or a word.

Warren and his colleagues have demonstrated in several experiments that people can fill in sounds that are missing, using context as a cue. For example, Warren (1970) played a recording of a sentence: *The state governors met with their respective legi*latures convening in the capital city.* The *s* in the word *legislatures* was replaced with an ordinary cough lasting 0.12 seconds. Of the 20 people who heard the recording, 19 reported that there were no sounds missing from the recording! (The one remaining person reported the wrong sound as missing.) Warren noted,

> The illusory perception of the absent phoneme was in keeping with the observation of others (graduate students and staff), who, despite knowledge of the actual stimulus, still perceived the missing phoneme as distinctly as the clearly pronounced sounds actually present. (p. 392)

We are accustomed to having occasional phonemes masked by extraneous noises, and we are quite good at reconstructing the missing noises. Think about the number of times extraneous noises have interfered with your professors' lectures. People knock books off desks, cough, turn pages, and whisper. Still, you can figure out the appropriate words.

Warren and Warren (1970) showed that people are skilled at using the meaning of a sentence to select the correct word from several options. They played four sentences for their subjects:

> *It was found that the *eel was on the axle.*
> *It was found that the *eel was on the shoe.*
> *It was found that the *eel was on the orange.*
> *It was found that the *eel was on the table.*

The four sentences were identical with one exception: a different word was spliced onto the end of each sentence. As before, a cough was inserted in the location shown by the asterisk. The "word" **eel* was heard as *wheel* in the first sentence, *heel* in the second sentence, *peel* in the third, and *meal* in the fourth. In this study, then, people could not use surrounding sounds to reconstruct the word, yet they were able to reconstruct the word on the basis of a context cue that occurred four words later!

Our ability to perceive a word on the basis of context also allows us to handle sloppy pronunciations. Try Demonstration 5.1, which is a modification of a study by Cole (1973). In Cole's study, people often did not notice mispronunciations when they occurred in the context of a sentence (for example, the *gunfusion* sentence). However, they accurately distinguished syllables such as *gun* and *con* when the isolated syllables were presented.

Demonstration 5.1   *Context and Mispronunciations.*

Read the following sentences to a friend. Ask your friend to report which word in each sentence was mispronounced and to identify which sound in the word was incorrect.

1. In all the gunfusion, the mystery man escaped from the mansion.
2. When I was working pizily in the library, the fire alarm rang out.
3. The messemger ran up to the professor and handed her a proclamation.
4. It has been zuggested that students be required to preregister.
5. The president reacted vavorably to all of the committee's suggestions.

Because we are so tolerant of mispronunciations in sentences, we often fail to notice startling mispronunciations that children make. Think back about a song that you sang when you were a child in which you included totally inappropriate words. One of my students recalled singing a Christmas carol in which the shepherds washed their socks by night, rather than watching their flocks by night. A friend's version of "Rocking my soul in the bosom of Abraham" was sung "Rocking my soul in the booglia baglia." Many songs that children learn are never carefully explained to them, and so they make up versions that make sense or versions containing easier nonsense words. However, these versions sound close enough to the standard that they will not be detected. A classroom may have 25 third graders, all reciting their own variants of the "Pledge of Allegiance"!

We have seen in this section that context has an important influence on the speech we hear. You may recall a similar discussion about the effects of context in Chapter 2, when we examined the influence of context on visual pattern perception. In the context of a kitchen scene, we see a loaf of bread, rather than a mailbox. In the context of an axle, we hear a wheel, rather than a peel. Recall that the influence of context on perception is an example of conceptually driven processing or "top-down" processing. Whether we are seeing or hearing, we use our knowledge and expectations to help the recognition process. Understanding language is not merely a passive process in which the words flow into our ears, providing data for a data-driven or "bottom-up" processing. Instead, we actively use the information we know to create expectations about what we might hear. Consistent with one of the central themes in the book, humans are active information processors.

Word Boundaries.   Have you ever overheard a conversation in a language that you do not know? The words seem to run together in a continuous stream, with no boundaries between them. However, when you hear spoken *English,* you hear distinct words. When we read, we see white spaces clearly identifying the boundaries between words. When we listen, the "white spaces" seem almost as distinct.

In most cases, however, the spoken language—the actual acoustic signal—does not have clear-cut pauses to mark the boundaries (Slobin, 1979). The listener's remarkable perceptual system is responsible for the boundaries. The system relies upon stored knowledge to enable us to figure out what sounds are grouped together into words.

Children have to learn where the boundaries between words are located, and they make frequent mistakes. Dr. Eleanor Maccoby told her child psychology class at Stanford University about a child who thought that toast was called "jamonit." It seems that his mother handed him a piece of toast *every* morning and asked, "Would you like some jam on it?" Not only had the child acquired the wrong label for toast, but he had also failed to identify two boundaries. Children's mispronunciations in songs, which we discussed in the previous section, frequently involve boundary errors.

Children are not alone in boundary errors, however. Safire (1979) comments about a grandmother who had an interesting misinterpretation of "the girl with kaleidoscope eyes" from the Beatles' song "Lucy in the Sky with Diamonds." Because of her greater familiarity with illness than with psychedelic experiences, she thought that the line was "the girl with colitis goes by." We use our knowledge to interpret ambiguous phonemes and impose boundaries between words. Most of the time, this knowledge leads us to correct conclusions, but sometimes it leads us to humorous misinterpretations.

Finally, we should note that humor often relies upon ambiguous boundaries between words. Darwin (1976) in his discussion of word boundaries, notes that Shakespeare used ambiguous boundaries to create special effects. For example,

Helen of Troy in *Troilus and Cressida* is greeted by a fanfare and the shout, "The Troyans' trumpet!" Notice that if the boundary is relocated, this phrase can be heard as "The Trojan strumpet." (*Strumpet* is an old word for a prostitute.)

Demonstration 5.2   Constituent Structure.

Arrange the words in each of these sentences into natural groups. Do this by writing down the words that go together and circling that group. You may arrange the sentences into as many groups as you like, but you must use all the words.

1. Parents were assisting the advanced teenage pupils.
2. The young woman carried the heavy painting.
3. Waiters who remember well serve orders correctly.

Check to see whether your answers agree with the groupings proposed for these sentences in the discussion of constitutent structure.

Theories of Speech Perception.   Many researchers in the area of speech perception have made proposals about how we perceive speech. One popular early theory was called **analysis-by-synthesis** (Halle & Stevens, 1964). According to the theory of analysis-by-synthesis, our hearing apparatus makes up hypotheses about what the speech stimulus might be. We compare the actual speech stimulus with each of the proposed hypotheses. The one that is closest wins, and that is the message we eventually hear.

Cole and Jakimik (1980) offer an alternate interpretation of speech perception that stresses the importance of context. They believe that fluent speech is an ambiguous stimulus that can be interpreted in many different ways. Cole and Jakimik assume "that words are constrained both by their acoustic structure and the context in which they occur, and that listeners use both sources of information to recognize words from fluent speech" (p. 139). Thus, both "bottom-up" and "top-down" processes operate in speech perception.

Cole and Jakimik also suggest that as soon as we recognize a word, we can identify the beginning of the next word in the sequence. Furthermore, the recognition of a word also limits the number of possibilities that would fit the grammar and meaning of the sentence. For example, in the phrase *chocolate chip*, the recognition of the word *chocolate* alerts you that a boundary must follow. The word *chocolate* also limits the number of words that might come next.

Their theory also proposes that the initial sounds of a word are most important in word identification. Furthermore, word recognition occurs when the analysis of a word's acoustic structure has eliminated all the alternate hypotheses, and only one hypothesis remains. In summary, Cole and Jakimik suggest that we recognize speech by using both data and context to arrive at a single best guess for the message we think we hear.

Constituent Structure

How do listeners take the sounds that they perceive and understand their meaning? If your professor tells the class, "There will be an examination next Wednesday," you are able to interpret that string of sounds. Somehow you figure out the meanings of each of the words and the grammatical structure of that sentence. As if you were solving a jigsaw puzzle, you combine all this information, and then the sentence makes sense. Obviously, it must happen quickly, because you must understand this sentence before the professor begins to describe the areas that will be covered on the examination.

The Nature of Constituents.   One widely accepted view of language comprehension involves constituents. A **constituent** (pronounced "kun-*stit*-choo-ent") is a phrase or basic unit in a sentence. A constituent usually contains more than one word but less than an entire sentence. According to Clark and Clark (1977), "As a rough guide, a constituent is a group of words that can be replaced by a single word without a change in function and without doing violence to the rest of the sentence" (p. 48).

For example, suppose that we have the sentence:

> *The young woman carried the heavy painting.*

We can break this sentence down into two **immediate constituents,** the largest and highest-level parts: *the young woman* and *carried the heavy painting.* Each of those constituents can be further subdivided until we have the **ultimate constituents,** or the individual words. Figure 5.2 shows how this sentence can be repeatedly subdivided into its constituents.

Notice how Clark and Clark's replacement rule can be applied. For example, *the young woman* can be replaced by Susan, Hepzibah, or *she* without altering the structure of the rest of the sentence. Similarly, the constituent *young woman* can be replaced by a single word such as *teenager* or *student.* However, we cannot create a constituent out of *woman carried the*, because there is no single word having the same function that we can substitute.

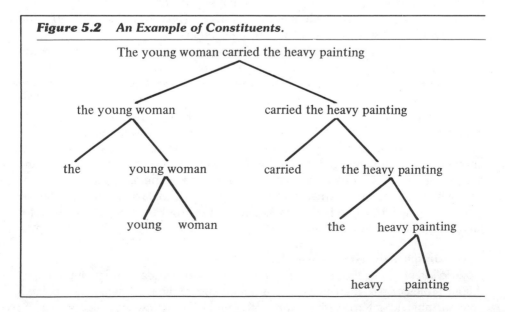

Figure 5.2   An Example of Constituents.

Why should listeners bother with constituents? Why shouldn't we simply process the words one at a time? As it turns out, we need information from the entire constituent unit in order to give us cues about the meaning of the words. For example, consider the word *painting* in the sentence we analyzed. *Painting* could be a verb or it could be a noun. However, from the context in which *painting* appears—the constituent *the heavy painting*—we know that the noun meaning is appropriate. Other words are even more ambiguous. The word *block*, for example, has many meanings in isolation, and the other words in the constituent help to identify the appropriate meaning. Thus context is helpful in figuring out the meanings of words, just as it is helpful in identifying the individual phonemes in a word.

Constituents and Understanding. Understanding a sentence involves several steps:

1. Hearing the speech sounds
2. Storing a representation of the speech sounds in short-term memory
3. Locating the meanings of the words in semantic memory
4. Organizing the representations of the speech sounds into constituents
5. Determining the meaning of the constituents
6. Combining the constituents to figure out the meaning of the whole sentence
7. Forgetting the exact wording of the constituents, retaining only the gist

Do not think of these seven steps as occurring one at a time, in a neat, orderly sequence. If you are listening to a lecture, for example, you may be hearing, storing, locating, organizing, determining, combining, and forgetting—all at the same time. Thus, you may be forgetting sentence 1 while you are performing steps 3, 4, 5, and 6 on sentence 2 and hearing and storing sentence 3.

The Psychological Reality of Constituent Structure. What evidence do we have for constituent structure? How do we know that people dissect the sentences they hear into these constituent parts? The issue of the psychological reality of constituent structure is covered in detail in other books (for example, Clark & Clark, 1977; Fodor, Bever, & Garrett, 1974). However, let us consider one example of the kind of study that demonstrates that people indeed use constituent structure in understanding sentences (Martin, 1970). An abbreviated version of this study was shown in Demonstration 5.2. Look at the answers you gave for that exercise.

Martin asked college students to draw circles around the words in a sentence that seemed to go together. As in Demonstration 5.2, they were told to make as many groups as they wished. Martin tabulated the results in terms of the number of times each word was included in the same circle as other words. He found a very strong tendency for certain words to belong together. For example, the auxiliary verb almost always appeared with the main verb; as in the phrase *were assisting*. The adjective next to the object was almost always in the same circle as the object, as in the phrase *teenage pupils*. Check to see whether you showed this same pattern. Similarly, in sentence 2, did you place *young* and *woman* together, and *heavy* and *painting* together? In sentence 3, was *who remember well* included in the same circle?

In summary, Martin's study shows that people agree about the division of a sentence. Constituents are not artificial units that linguists dreamed up from their armchairs. Instead, constituents are groups of words that language users judge as belonging together.

Strategies for Identifying Constituents.   Some researchers have tried to develop a list of strategies that listeners use when they divide sentences up into their constituents. Kimball (1973), for example, proposed a strategy that concerns function words. **Function words** are words such as prepositions and conjunctions, that are very important for the structure of a grammatical sentence. Kimball suggested that whenever listeners find a function word, they begin a new constituent. For example, in the sentence

> **Mary said that the boy went to the store.**

listeners would begin new constituents when they hear the words *that* and *to*.

Kimball also proposed that listeners develop a second strategy to accompany the first strategy. As soon as a function word indicates the beginning of a constituent, the listeners search for content words. **Content words** are words, such as nouns and verbs, that refer to persons, objects, and actions. For example, a function word such as *in* alerts the listener to search for a noun. The listener knows that a noun must come, no matter how many other words intervene. Imagine yourself listening to a sentence:

> **In the deep, dark, long-forgotten . . .**

You know that the noun must come eventually!

Clark and Clark (1977) point out other strategies, including the use of affixes. Affixes are word parts, such as *-er, -y,* and *-ly,* that indicate the part of speech of a word. Thus, *-er* words are typically nouns, *-y* words are typically adjectives, and *-ly* words are typically adverbs. (However, there are exceptions, such as the adjective *clever.*) Listeners use these word parts to identify parts of speech.

As Clark and Clark mention, we can use these three strategies to help us identify constituent structure on sentences that are almost purely nonsense. Consider the Lewis Carroll verse ''Jabberwocky'':

> **Twas brillig, and the slithy toves did gyre and gimble in the wabe; all mimsy were the borogoves, and the mome raths outgabe.**

Function words, such as *and* and *in* help us divide the sentence. When we see *in,* we know that *wabe* must be a noun. Finally, the *-y* affix tells us that *slithy* and *mimsy* are adjectives, whereas the *-s* affix tells us that *toves, borogoves,* and *raths* are all nouns.

These strategies are not foolproof, and they may lead us astray. They do not always guarantee a solution. However, they *usually* allow us to understand a sentence. Another word for strategies that are generally—but not always—helpful is ''heuristics.'' **Heuristics** (pronounced ''hyoo-*riss*-ticks'') are rules of thumb that we use to solve problems. You will see this term again in later chapters in this book.

Demonstration 5.3 Understanding Negatives.

Find a stopwatch or a watch with a second hand. Measure the number of seconds it takes you to answer Problems 1−4, 5−12, and 13−16. In each case, respond either "true" or "false." Record your answers on a sheet of paper.

Start timer.

1. star is above plus   *
                 +

2. star is below plus   *
                 +

3. plus is above star   +
                 *

4. plus is below star   +
                 *

Stop timer and record time.

Start timer.

5. star isn't above plus   +
                 *

6. star isn't below plus   +
                 *

7. plus isn't above star   *
                 +

8. plus isn't below star   *
                 +

9. star isn't above plus   *
                 +

10. star isn't below plus   *
                 +

11. plus isn't above star   +
                 *

12. plus isn't below star   +
                 *

Stop timer and record time.

Start timer.

13. star is above plus   +
                 *

14. star is below plus   +
                 *

15. plus is above star   +
                 *

16. plus is below star   +
                 *

Stop timer and record time.

Add together your solution times for Problems 1−4 and 13−16; this is the total solution time for affirmative sentences. Your solution time for Problems 5−12 is the solution time for negative sentences.

     Now check to see whether your answers are correct:

1. T; 2. F; 3. T; 4. F; 5. T; 6. F; 7. T; 8. F; 9. F; 10. T; 11. F; 12. T; 13. F; 14. T; 15. T; 16. F.

Count the number of errors on affirmative sentences (1−4, 13−16) and negative sentences (5−12).

Factors Affecting Understanding

Some sentences are easy to understand, whereas others are more difficult. We will look at four factors in this section. As you will see, sentences are more difficult to understand (1) if they contain negatives, such as *not*; (2) if they contain marked, or complex words, rather than unmarked words; (3) if they are in the passive voice rather than the active voice; and (4) if they are ambiguous.

Negatives.   Negative sentences are almost always more difficult to understand than affirmative sentences. If a sentence contains a negative word such as *no* or *not*, more time will be required for understanding.

Clark and Chase (1972) asked people to verify pictures, such as those in Demonstration 5.3. They answered the questions more quickly if the sentences were affirmative than if they contained the word *not*. Was your total solution time shorter for the affirmative questions than for the negative questions? Clark and Chase found that their subjects made very few errors on the questions; still, they did make more errors on the negative questions than on the affirmative questions. If you made any errors, were they on questions 5–12?

If it is difficult to understand a sentence with one negative, how about sentences with two or three negatives? For example, is this sentence true?

Few people strongly deny that the world is not flat. (Sherman, 1976, p. 145)

With three negatives, the sentence is almost uncomprehensible! As you might expect, understanding decreases as the number of negatives increases. Sherman (1976) found that people made no errors with affirmative sentences, but they had a 41 percent error rate when there were four negatives in the sentences. In other words, their performance was only slightly better than guessing when there were four negatives!

This discussion of negatives may have reminded you of one of the recurring themes in the book, that the cognitive processes handle positive information better than negative information. We simply find it easier to deal with something that exists than something that does not exist. It is easier to understand *He is happy* than to understand *He is not happy*.

Marking.   A linguistic phenomenon called *marking* also has an influence on understanding. We need to examine this phenomenon in some detail. Marking can be defined in several ways; let's discuss the most general definition first. **Marking** means that in any group of related words, one word is basic (or **unmarked**) and the other words are more specific (or **marked**). For example, *friend* is unmarked, whereas *friendly, unfriendly,* and *friendship* are all marked.

Sometimes marking is accomplished by adding some feature onto the basic form in order to produce a new form (Deese, 1973). In these cases the marking is easy to spot, as when we add an -*s* to a single noun to indicate the plural or we add an -*ed* to a verb to indicate the past tense. As we noted, the simple or basic form is called the unmarked form, whereas the more complex or specific form is called the marked form. Thus, *apple* and *walk* are unmarked, and *apples* and *walked* are marked. Furthermore, *happy* is unmarked, and *unhappy* is marked. Ironically, then, *unmarked* is a marked word! (It may help you remember which words are marked by thinking of a mark as an additional notation added onto a word. Thus, when you add notations such as *-s, -ed,* and *un-*, you are marking them.)

In many cases, the marking process is much more subtle and difficult to detect than this process of adding notations to the simple forms. This is particularly true of antonyms. Antonym pairs are words that are similar to each other in many ways, except that one word is marked and one word is unmarked. The unmarked word is the more basic or general of the two, whereas the marked word is the more limited term. For example, one pair of antonyms is *good* and *bad*; *good* is unmarked and *bad* is marked.

How can you decide which word is unmarked? Clark (1969a) notes that one way to tell which word is more general is to ask a question using each of the two words. The word that permits a more general reply is the unmarked one. For example, one can ask, "How good is the food?" and merely be requesting an evaluation of the food. The expected response could be "good," "average," or "bad." Thus, the expected response could come from any portion of the evaluation scale. However, notice the different implication in the question, "How bad is the food?" Here we expect a response only from the "bad" half of the evaluative scale. A person could not answer, "It's excellent!" without some kind of additional statement, such as "'. . . believe it or not!"

Thus, the question, "How good is the food?" does not necessarily imply that the food is good. Stated differently, the unmarked word, such as *good,* can be "neutralized," or used in a neutral form. The marked word, such as *bad,* cannot be neutralized.

Carpenter (1974) studied how marking influences understanding. She constructed comparative sentences using both unmarked and marked words. For example, the words *higher, faster,* and *older* are the unmarked forms of the marked words *lower, slower,* and *younger.* College students were asked to answer "true" or "false" to statements such as *Frogs are older than tadpoles* (unmarked version) and *Tadpoles are younger than frogs* (marked version). Carpenter found that people responded faster when the sentences contained the unmarked word, such as *higher, faster,* and *older.* These sentences are more basic and simple, so they can be understood more readily.

Carpenter theorizes about why the sentences with unmarked adjectives are easier to understand than sentences with marked adjectives. She partitions the comprehension task into four parts:

1. The person reads the sentence and represents it internally.
2. The person computes relevant information from another source, such as semantic memory (the world knowledge we discussed in Chapter 3). For example, knowledge about the relationship between tadpoles and frogs is relevant in the previous example.
3. The person compares the information from the sentence with the information computed from stage 2 to determine whether the two are consistent (true) or inconsistent (false).

4. The person responds "true" or "false" based on the comparison in stage 3.

Carpenter argues that unmarked adjectives have the advantage over marked adjectives in stages 2 and 3, the stages involving retrieval and comparison. She presents information from additional studies to indicate that the advantage is not due to stages 1 and 4.

Sherman (1976) found that marked words are often treated as if they were negative words. He studied trios of words, such as *happy, unhappy,* and *sad.* Notice that *happy* is unmarked, *unhappy* is marked by the obvious prefix *un-,* and *sad* is a marked word that has no obvious indications of marking. Each of these words was then placed in a sentence containing two negatives, for example:

(1) *He had just won a lot of money in a contest, and everyone doubted that he would not be happy about this.*
(2) *He had just won a lot of money in a contest, and everyone doubted that he would not be unhappy about this.*
(3) *He had just won a lot of money in a contest, and everyone doubted that he would not be sad about this.*

Sherman found that, in these sentences that already contained two negatives, the marked words acted like additional negative words. For example, sentence 1 was easier than sentences 2 and 3. Now it is easy to see why the word *unhappy* is treated like a negative word; we can readily translate *unhappy* into *not happy.* However, it is somewhat surprising that *sad* is also translated into *not happy.* It seems that people often use a complicated process in order to understand marked words, such as *sad.* We take the marked word and translate it into the unmarked, simpler form. Because this translation process takes time, it takes us longer to understand sentences that contain marked words.

The studies by Carpenter and Sherman have shown us that unmarked words can be understood more readily than marked words. Keep this in mind when you are speaking and writing. Sometimes, we must use marked words to make a particular point. However, notice how much easier it was for you to understand the first sentence in this paragraph . . . *unmarked words can be understood more readily than marked words* than if I had written *marked words can be understood less readily than unmarked words.*

Furthermore, it might be wise to try to avoid the *not un-* construction. George Orwell suggests that we should laugh the *not un-* pairing right out of existence. He proposes that we can cure ourselves of using this construction by memorizing this sentence: "A not unblack dog was chasing a not unsmall rabbit across a not ungreen field" (Orwell, 1945).

The Passive Voice. English sentences can be expressed in a variety of ways. For example, the active-voice sentence, *The students typed the papers* can be expressed in an alternate passive-voice form, *The papers were typed by the students.* The noted linguist, Noam Chomsky (1957) was one of the first to discuss how two sentences like these can have very different word orders, yet very similar meanings.

Although the active and the passive forms of sentences have similar meanings, there are important differences. For example, Anisfeld and Klenbort (1973) pointed out that the active form is unmarked, whereas the passive form is marked. Notice that something (in this case, the word *were*) has to be added to the unmarked, active form in order to create the marked, passive form. Thus, the active form is basic and the passive form is more complex.

As further evidence that the active form is more basic, notice how much more frequently we use the active voice. Svartik (1966) reported that in modern English we use the active form seven times as often as the passive form. In addition, sentences that sound normal in the active voice often sound strange in the passive. For example, consider the passive version of the first clause in the previous paragraph, *Although similar meanings are had by the active and passive forms of sentences* . . . . Finally, some verbs do not have any sensible passive forms (Anisfeld & Klenbort, 1973). What passive forms could you possibly make up for the verbs *sleep, resemble,* and *cost*?

Now that you know that the active is unmarked and the passive is marked, you can probably guess which form is easier to understand. For example, Hornby (1974) asked people to judge whether a picture correctly represented a sentence. People responded faster if the sentences were active, such as *The girl is petting the cat* than if the sentences were passive, such as *The cat is being petted by the girl*.

The passive voice used to be very popular in scientific writing. As a result, scientific writing sounded extremely pompous. Fortunately for those of us who want to understand scientific writing, the writing manuals are now recommending the active voice.

Most psychology majors are familiar with the *Publication Manual of the American Psychological Association* (American Psychological Association, 1974), which dictates the style of lab reports and journal articles. This manual comments on a particular problem: how to report first-person impressions. In previous years, style manuals prohibited the word *I*. If you wanted to say *to eliminate the alternate hypothesis, I performed the following study,* you had to write in the passive voice, *to eliminate the alternate hypothesis, the following study was performed.* The current manual states, however:

> An experienced writer can use the first person and the active voice without dominating the communication and without sacrificing the objectivity of the research. If any discipline should appreciate the value of person communication, it should be psychology. (p. 28)

Thus the active voice is preferable because it is easier to understand.

Ambiguity. Read the following sentence:

> **Time flies like an arrow,**
> **but fruit flies like a banana.**

If your reaction to this sentence was like mine, you did a double take when you came to the word *banana*. In fact, the sentence may have seemed nonsensical until you read it again and realized that the phrase *time flies* is ambiguous. A word or phrase is **ambiguous** if it has two or more meanings.

Mistler-Lachman (1975) discusses three types of ambiguity. First, there is **lexical ambiguity,** in which a word has two different meanings. The example about flies is therefore an example of lexical ambiguity. Many puns and riddles are based on lexical ambiguity. For example, a music professor once said, "We can't continue the lecture because the tape recorder is Baroque."

A second type of ambiguity involves **surface structure ambiguity,** in which words can be grouped together in more than one way. Consider the classic Groucho Marx line, "Last night I shot an elephant in my pajamas. How he got into them, I've never understood." In the first sentence, "in my pajamas" could be understood to describe either the speaker or the elephant. Have you ever insulted someone who misinterpreted a surface structure ambiguity? For example, you may have said something such as *I'm going with boring people like John and you.*

A third type of ambiguity involves **underlying structure ambiguity,** in which the essential logical relations between phrases can be interpreted in two ways. My favorite example of this kind of ambiguity is an entry that won a magazine contest in the 1970s. Contestants were asked to supply ambiguous headlines. One entry was: *Mrs. Nixon found drunk on White House lawn.* If we were to paraphrase this sentence, we would see that there are two very different kinds of logical relations between the parts of this sentence. In one case, Mrs. Nixon is the "finder"; in the other case, she was found. Two other examples that linguists frequently cite are *The shooting of the hunters was terrible* and *The lamb is too hot to eat.*

Several studies have demonstrated that ambiguous sentences are more difficult to understand. Foss (1970), for example, asked subjects to listen to ambiguous and unambiguous sentences. Meanwhile, they also performed an additional task, which involved pressing a button every time they heard the sound *b* in a sentence. People took longer to press the button if they were listening to an ambiguous sentence. Foss reasoned that ambiguous sentences are more difficult to understand, so listeners have less of their processing mechanisms available to use on other tasks.

How do we process ambiguous sentences? There has been some debate on the issue, but the favored explanation is that we retrieve all the information about the words, decide which meaning is correct, and transfer only that meaning to working memory (Cairns & Kamerman, 1975). Ambiguous sentences are more difficult to understand than unambiguous sentences because they require a decision. With reference to the Foss task, for example, people took longer to detect the *b* sound in ambiguous sentences because they were busy making a decision about the appropriate interpretation of the sentence.

SECTION SUMMARY: Understanding Language

1. Language is central to human society and thought.
2. Information about the sounds in a syllable is sent in parallel, rather than one letter at a time.
3. Listeners can fill in the missing sounds from the context of the rest of the word or other words in the sentence.

4. Listeners use their stored knowledge to figure out the boundaries between words.
5. Two theories of speech perception are analysis-by-synthesis and Cole and Jakimik's theory.
6. Listeners use the information in constituent units to figure out meaning. Constituents are groups of words that seem to belong together.
7. People develop strategies for dividing sentences up into their constituents.
8. Negative sentences are more difficult to understand than affirmative sentences. Increasing the number of negatives increase the difficulty.
9. Sentences containing marked words are more difficult to understand. Unmarked words are the basic forms of words, which are more general in their usage than marked words.
10. Passive-voice sentences are more difficult to understand than active-voice sentences.
11. Ambiguous sentences are more difficult to understand than unambiguous sentences, probably because they require a decision about which meaning is appropriate for the sentence.

Producing Language

As an adult, it seems so easy to speak! We open our mouths, and words flow out rather effortlessly. However, there are numerous subtle processes involved in the production of speech. For example, what we say depends upon many social factors, such as the knowledge of our listener and the formality of the situation. Our strategies for speaking may be different if we are telling a story rather than describing a place. The social aspects of speech and the content of speech are two topics we will consider in this section.

We also will discuss the sounds that are produced in speech. Some of these sounds are errors that have certain systematic characteristics. We will see how these errors are related to the intended words. We will also briefly consider the various speech organs and how they influence the sounds that we make.

Finally, we will look at a controversial area in the psychology of language: teaching chimpanzees to communicate. Some people claim that the symbolic language of chimpanzees is similar to human language, but others claim that it is clearly inferior. Linguists and psychologists are impressed with the complexity of language produced by humans. Many are therefore convinced that humans are the only species with the cognitive sophistication to master language.

The Social Context of Speech

We often pay so much attention to the grammatical and lexical aspects of language in formal education that we forget the social importance of language. After all, we speak so that we can influence listeners in some way or convey our emotions. We may want others to do something for us or give us information. We may want to inform, comment, or convince. Other times, the emotional nature of words is more important than their content. We choose our words so that they will be appropriate to the social situation and will accomplish our purposes.

Clark and Clark (1977) suggest that speech planning is a problem-solving task. Essentially, the speaker must solve the problem of selecting the language devices that will appropriately affect the listener. This includes guessing what the listener already knows and what additional background needs to be supplied. For example, imagine how you might describe the concept of marking to another student enrolled in your cognition course who had not yet read that section. Contrast that with the description you might give to a fourth grader who asked you what you were reading on those pages.

The Given-New Strategy.   One way in which speakers show concern for their listeners is called the "Given-New Strategy" (Haviland & Clark, 1974). According to the **Given-New Strategy,** a speaker's sentence contains some "given" information, with which the listener is already familiar, and some new information. This enables the listener to identify which information is given and which is new, and to integrate the new information into memory along with the old memory. For example, consider the sentence:

> *The story Dr. Jones told was excellent.*

The given information is that Dr. Jones told a story, whereas the new information was that the story was excellent.

Notice how the given information can be conveyed quite subtly. Thus, *Jim, too, snores at night* refers to the given information that someone else snores as well. *Julia's diamonds are real, though* (with the name *Julia* emphasized) implies that someone else's diamonds are not. Finally, *When did Tim stop drinking?* implies that Tim had been drinking previously. In order for the speaker to convey the new information successfully, however, the given information must match the information already in the listener's memory. Thus, a speaker would be more successful with this sequence,

> *We carried the books downstairs. The books were heavy.*

than with this sequence,

> *We carried the school supplies downstairs. The books were heavy.*

In the first case, the sentence *The books were heavy* is easy to interpret because it matches information that the previous sentence established in memory. In the second case, an extra step is required, as the listener must reason that the school supplies included books. Ordinarily, we converse as if speakers and listeners have unspoken contracts to obey the Given-New rule; that is, the speaker must provide the appropriate framework within which the new information can be understood.

Conversational Format.   We also have social rules about the format of our conversations. One rule is that the speakers should alternate (Schegloff, 1968). Speakers do not talk at the same time, and they do not typically leave long pauses in the middle of the conversation. Think about this rule of alternation and how it applies in different situations. In a telephone conversation, for example, alternation is required in the beginning interchanges. The answerer must speak first, but this speech segment must be brief. The answerer may say "Hello," or "Dr. Jones speaking," or "Yeah," but longer segments will not be tolerated. When I call my accountant, for example, the receptionist who answers the phone manages to condense "Kasdin, Saiger, Rossman, Elder & Gould" into something that lasts 1 second and sounds like "Kasgrsmeldrgld." The person who called must then provide identification and expect a brief acknowledgment from the answerer before proceeding with the message.

Similarly, we begin our conversations with people we meet with an alternation pattern. Notice this sequence the next time you see a friend.

There is also a specified etiquette to closing a conversation. Pay attention to this the next time you overhear a telephone conversation. It may take numerous alternations to "wind down" a conversation. Certainly, a polite adult cannot end a conversation with a simple "good-bye" flung into a random pause in the interchange. A typical ending might be this:

A. Well, I'm really glad you called, Jean.
B. I'm glad I found you home.
A. You're right, I haven't been home much. Let's get together, OK?
B. OK. And say hello to Jim.
A. Yes, and say hi to the kids.
B. See you.
A. 'Bye now.

Speech Formality.   Formality of speech is another aspect of the social context of language. Ervin-Tripp (1972) discusses three style levels: formal, colloquial, and slang. The formal style sounds either humorous or bizarre when it is used in a situation where colloquial style would be appropriate. For example, a young man in a novel by Calvin Trillin (1977) ends a letter to his father: "I shall look forward to hearing from you on this matter at your earliest convenience. With best personal wishes, I remain yours sincerely, John Ronald Sprigg IV" (p. 153). Similarly, the slang style sounds wildly inappropriate for situations calling for a formal style. Suppose your college president walked to the podium at graduation and said, "Y'know, these guys here bin reel fine." Also, imagine how you might use these three styles in greeting three types of listeners: your state senator, your parents, and your best friend.

Sloppy pronunciation is one sign of informal speech. Brown and Fraser (1979) report that another sign is the choice of words. In formal settings, we might say *dine, reside,* and *volume,* but in everyday settings we would say *eat, live,* and *book.* Also, the number of nouns we use depends upon the setting. Brown and Fraser noted that academic journal articles are "nounier" than spoken academic discourse. Furthermore, people use more nouns in academic discussions than in casual conversation.

Directives.   Ervin-Tripp (1976) has studied the social aspects of a particular kind of sentence called a directive. A **directive** is a sentence that requests someone to do something. Ervin-Tripp gathered large samples of speech in natural settings and found that there were six different kinds of directives used in American English. Each kind of directive seemed to be used in certain, well-defined circumstances. For example, one kind of directive was used to express need. It was used either by a higher-ranking person in a work setting, as when a physician says to a nurse, "I'll need an ear curette in room 3," or in families, as when a child says to a parent, "I need a drink, Daddy." Another kind of directive is very abbreviated, because the necessary action is obvious. Thus, a customer may say to a waitress, "Tea, with lemon."

Two other kinds of directives include extra words, such as *can, may,* or *would.* In some cases, they are focused upon the listener, as in "Can you shut the door?" and in other cases they are focused upon the speaker, as in "May I have that piece of paper?"

Sometimes, directives are asked in the form of indirect questions. However, the speaker does not really need information, but services. For example, a teacher might ask a class, "What are you laughing at?" The teacher is not really concerned about the source of the laughter; it is a request for silence. Finally, some directives take the form of hints. You probably know someone who says, "I wonder if there is any butter in the refrigerator," instead of the more *direct* directive, "Would you get me some butter, please." Both of these directives can easily be misinterpreted, either intentionally or unintentionally.

Selecting the Content of Speech

How do we decide what to talk about? One way to approach this question is to ask how we plan our sentences. The next time you begin a sentence, think about your planning process. Have you: (a) selected your subject, but not your verb; (b) selected both the subject and the verb; or (c) selected your subject completely but your verb only partially? Lindsley (1975) performed several experiments in which reaction time data supported the last alternative. Thus, we begin to talk once we know the subject of our statement and we have some idea of the verb. However, the exact verb choice does not have to be specified before we begin the sentence.

Other cognitive psychologists have examined the content areas of speech, such as stories and descriptions. Rumelhart (1975), for instance, sketches how people tell stories, paying particular attention to the structure of the stories. First of all, contrast the two stories in Demonstration 5.4. In both cases, there are strings of sentences. In the first case, however, the sentences seem only vaguely related to one another, whereas in the second case they form a coherent whole. Thus stories require higher levels of organization.

Demonstration 5.4   Story Structure.

Read the first story and try to understand it. Then read the second story and try to understand it.

1. Margie cried and cried. The balloon hit a branch and burst. The wind carried it into a tree. Suddenly a gust of wind caught it. Margie was holding tightly to the string of her beautiful new balloon. (Rumelhart, 1975, p. 212)

2. Margie was holding tightly to the string of her beautiful new balloon. Suddenly, a gust of wind caught it. The wind carried it into a tree. The balloon hit a branch and burst. Margie cried and cried. (p. 211)

Rumelhart lists a set of rules that describe the structure of simple stories such as the one in Demonstration 5.4. Here are some of them.

Rule 1: The *story* consists of a setting followed by an episode. The formal fairy-tale beginning, "Once upon a time, there was a . . ." is an example of a setting.

Rule 2: The *setting* equals one or more descriptions of what is happening as the story begins.

Rule 3: The *episode* consists of an event plus our hero or heroine's reaction to the event.

Rule 4: The *event* can consist of another episode—that is, an event plus a reaction—or a change of state, or an action that people carry out.

Rule 5: The *reaction* consists of an internal reaction (for example, sorrow) and an external reaction (for example, fixing a statue).

Rule 6: The *internal reaction* consists of either emotion or desire.

Rumelhart found that these basic rules for story construction explained the structure in stories such as those in *Aesop's Fables.* Ask a friend to make up a very brief story, and see whether Rumelhart's rules apply.

Description is another function of language. Linde and Labov (1975) asked New Yorkers to describe their apartments. Specifically, they requested, "Could you tell me the layout of your apartment?" The respondents were quite uniform in their descriptions . . . they began at the outside entrance, and proceeded to name each room. They also included instructions about how to reach each room. A typical description was:

> **You walked in the front door.**
> **There was a narrow hallway.**
> **To the left, the first door you came to was a tiny bedroom.**
> **Then there was a kitchen,**
> **and then bathroom,**
> **and then the main room was in the back, living room, I guess.** (p. 927)

Linde and Labov found that the "guided tour" description was most common. In contrast, people seldom described the layout in terms of a map of the apartment. Only 3 percent of their subjects presented an overview of the apartment's floor plan. You might ask friends who live in apartments to describe them. You might also ask friends who live in larger houses to describe these. They may be more likely to use a map-type description and present the general layout.

Speech Errors

Think about the number of ways in which the natural speech you hear in everyday conversation differs from perfect English. People pause in the middle of a sentence. They start a new sentence before finishing the previous one. They use extra words such as *oh, well,* and *um.* Occasionally so many extra words are included that the listener misses the point of the sentence. For example, in the early 1970s, *like* and *you know* were used to season natural speech. I recall hearing sentences such as *He's, like, you know, not the sort of person, I mean, the sort of person we want in here.*

Maclay and Osgood (1959) found that academicians are just as guilty of speech errors as everyone else. They recorded the speech of 13 professionals who attended a conference at University of Illinois. The following excerpt is representative of the kind of errors they found—with pauses represented by ellipses (. . .):

> As far as I know, no one yet has done the in a way obvious now and interesting problem of . . . doing a in a sense a structural frequency study of the alternative . . . syntactical . . . in a given language, say, like English, the alternative . . . possible structures, and how what their hierarchal . . . probability of occurrence structure is. Now, it seems to me you w-w-will need that kind of data as base line . . . (p. 25)

Researchers have been particularly interested in the kind of speech errors called slips of the tongue. **Slips of the tongue** are errors in which sounds are rearranged between two or more different words. Some of these errors are **anticipation errors,** in which a sound from the later word in a phrase arrives too early and is included in the first word. Thus, *handle of her cane* may become *candle of her cane*. Other errors are **perseverations** (pronounced "purr-seh-vurr-ai-shuns")—the reverse of anticipation errors—in which a sound from the first word remains in later words. For example, *waking rabbits* may become *waking wabbits*.

Still other errors are **reversals,** in which sounds from two words are interchanged. A speech error I made recently was to say *one swell foop* rather than *one fell swoop*. These reversals are also called spoonerisms, in honor of an Englishman, the Reverend William Spooner. Spooner is said to have uttered such wonderful reversals as *Work is the curse of the drinking classes,* rather than *Drink is the curse of the working classes,* and *You have hissed all my mystery lectures,* rather than *You have missed all my history lectures.* His most famous spoonerism, however, is *our queer old dean,* rather than *our dear old queen.* There have also been some spectacular bloopers on radio and television, such as the time a radio announcer was introducing President Hoover and said, *Ladies and gentlemen, the President of the United States, Hoobert Heever.*

One of the formal studies of speech errors has been conducted by Garrett (1975). He gathered 3400 speech errors and analyzed them to determine whether there was any systematic pattern. He drew several conclusions:

1. Segments of words exchange with or intrude into other words in the same position. For example, sounds at the beginning exchange with sounds at the beginning of other words, such as *swell foop* for *fell swoop*. Similarly, end sounds exchange for other end sounds, such as *flee fry* for *fly free*.
2. Consonants exchange with consonants, and vowels exchange with vowels. Check back through the examples mentioned above and notice how consonants never exchange with vowels.
3. The speech errors that are produced are sounds that are likely in English. For example, a speech error would be unlikely to include the sound *sg* at the beginning of a word, since that is an unlikely initial sequence in English. Notice how all the errors mentioned above produce sound combinations we frequently hear.
4. Errors occur between syllables that have equal stress. A sound from an unstressed syllable will not exchange with or intrude in a sound from a stressed syllable. Thus, *waking rabbits* produces an error, but *waking giraffes* would not,

because the first syllable in *waking* is stressed and the second syllable in *giraffes* is stressed.

Thus speech errors are not random. Instead, they obey the rules of English structure. This information on speech errors is related to one of the general themes of the book, that human information processing is impressively accurate and that our errors are typically related to our strategies. The speech errors that we make reflect our knowledge of language: our appreciation for positions within a word, consonants versus vowels, phoneme combinations, and syllable stress.

Try Demonstration 5.5 to see whether Garrett's analysis holds for your own speech sample.

Demonstration 5.5   Slips of the Tongue.

Keep a record of all the slips of the tongue you hear in the next week. Classify each slip as an anticipation error, a perseveration, a reversal, or "other." See whether any of the slips disagree with Garrett's conclusions about the patterns of slips of the tongue.

Articulation

The final stage in speech production is **articulation** (pronounced "are-tick-you-*lay*-shun"), which involves making speech sounds. The articulation process is described in detail by MacNeilage and Ladefoged (1976); here we will consider only an overview of articulation.

Stop for a moment and say something out loud, holding your hand on your throat. Notice several aspects of articulation. First of all, the source of power for almost all the speech sounds you made was the air that was pushed out of your lungs (MacNeilage & Ladefoged, 1976). In English we seldom speak by sucking air in.

Secondly, your throat vibrated when you spoke. Actually, it was your larynx that vibrated. The **larynx** (pronounced *"lare*-inks") is a structure containing the vocal cords, which are also known as vocal folds. When you have **laryngitis,** your larynx is inflamed, and you sound hoarse. Some sounds, such as *b, d,* and *v,* are called voiced sounds. For **voiced sounds,** the vocal cords are adjusted so that they are almost touching, and they vibrate. Notice how your larynx vibrates when you make the sounds *buh, duh,* and *vuh.* The vocal cords are far apart from each other and do not vibrate for **voiceless sounds,** such as *p, t,* and *f.* Again, hold your hand on your throat and notice that there is no vibration for the sounds *puh, tuh,* and *fuh.* All known languages distinguish among sounds on the basis of whether they are voiced or voiceless (MacNeilage & Ladefoged, 1976).

Third, the position of your tongue and lips determines the sound that comes out. Notice how your tongue moves to different locations when you make the consonants *th, t,* and *k.* For other consonants, however, your tongue simply lies there while the lips do all the work. Notice how your lips are important in the sounds *b, p, v,* and *f.* (Clark and Clark, 1977, can be consulted for more information on consonants.) Vowels are traditionally specified in terms of the position of the lips and the position of the highest point on the tongue (MacNeilage & Ladefoged, 1976). Pronounce the words *heed, hid, head,* and *had* and notice how the highest point of the tongue is in the front of the mouth. In contrast, pronounce *hod, hawed, hood,* and *who'd,* and notice how the tongue rises in the back of the mouth for these sounds.

The final stage in speech production is not simple. A mental representation of a sentence must somehow be translated into a motor representation. This motor representation must include muscles that move to adjust the vocal cords, the tongue, and the lips. Many different hypotheses have been suggested about how this translation occurs, and they are discussed elsewhere (for example, Foss & Hakes, 1978).

Language Production in Nonhumans

Are humans unique in their ability to use language? This question has been a particularly intriguing one for psychologists and others who are interested in language. Some researchers, for example, have developed computer programs that allow computers to "talk" by using a typewriter. One of the most famous of these programs is called ELIZA (Weizenbaum, 1966). A person types a message and ELIZA replies with a typed message. The answers resemble those that a human therapist might provide in a counseling situation. Here, for example, is a part of a conversation I had with ELIZA:

> ELIZA: How do you feel?
> Me: I feel lazy.
> ELIZA: Do you enjoy feeling lazy?
> Me: At times.
> ELIZA: Please go on.
> Me: I wish I were more ambitious today and could get motivated to get back to *Psych Abstracts.*
> ELIZA: Why do you tell me you wish you were more ambitious today and could get back to *Psych Abstracts?*
> ME: Because I felt like it.
> ELIZA: In what way?

It should be noted that ELIZA adds nothing new to a conversation. ELIZA merely rephrases what the speaker types in order to keep the conversation going.

Other, more recent uses of computers and computer models in language are discussed by Anderson (1976) and Norman and Rumelhart (1975). A more controversial issue than computers being programmed to produce language is this: Can apes really produce language?

Many people have argued very strongly that humans are the only animals that have the intellectual capacity to create language. Their statements seemed reasonable in view of previous failures to teach animals to speak. For example, Hayes (1951) tried to teach a chimpanzee to pronounce English words. The chimp could say only *cup, mama,* and *papa* after six years of continuous training.

Other researchers argued that the barrier to chimpanzee speech might be the articulation process. After all, the vocal apparatus of chimpanzees is not adapted for human sounds. In the late 1960s, therefore, people interested in teaching animals to communicate began to work with symbols rather than speech sounds. Beatrice and Allen Gardner decided to teach a chimpanzee named Washoe to use American Sign Language (Gardner & Gardner, 1975). Eventually, Washoe learned more than 100 signs, and she also combined signs into simple sentences. Washoe also made up imaginative new terms. For example, she apparently signed *water* and *bird* when she saw a swan.

Additional researchers, such as Premack, Rumbaugh, and Savage-Rumbaugh (cited in Marx, 1980) taught their chimpanzee artificial languages in which plastic chips or geometrical symbols represented words. Thus, a chimp might hold up a blue cross to indicate an apple. In general, the researchers using artificial languages were less optimistic than those who used sign language about the language capacity of chimpanzees. Nonetheless, many people questioned the viewpoint that language was limited to humans.

The controversy was opened once more, however, when Terrace (1979) published a book about his efforts to teach sign language to a chimpanzee named Nim Chimpsky (named after the linguist, Noam Chomsky). In this fascinating report of his efforts, Terrace concludes that chimpanzee language is really very different from human language. Nim was raised like a human child from the age of two weeks until he was 4 years old. Parent substitutes and teachers diapered him, dressed him, and taught him sign language. Nim developed about 125 symbols. Nonetheless, Terrace maintains that chimpanzee language is inferior to the language that humans develop as children. For example, Nim's phrases stabilized at only 1.5 signs, much shorter than the phrases used by children. Furthermore, Nim often simply imitated the signs that his teachers made rather than making up new sequences. In fact, only 12 percent of his sequences were spontaneous. Nim also failed to master basic grammatical structures.

As you might expect, other researchers reacted very strongly to Terrace's statements. Allen Gardner remarked about Terrace's work, 'It is the shoddiest piece of work I have ever seen in this area' " (cited in Marx, 1980, p. 1330). Other "pro-chimp" researchers also criticized Terrace's teaching methods and conclusions. They argued that Terrace used a sterile classroom setting, rather than a more natural setting, and that there were 60 trainers, so that Nim could not develop close relationships. Furthermore, the critics argued that many trainers were poorly trained in sign language (Marx, 1980).

However, Noam Chomsky agreed with Terrace's pessimism:

> "It's about as likely that an ape will prove to have a language ability as that there is an island somewhere with a species of flightless birds waiting for human beings to teach them to fly." (cited in "Are Those Apes Really Talking?", 1980, p. 50)

It's clear that we haven't heard the last word (or watched the last sign!) on teaching language to chimpanzees. At present, however, we cannot firmly conclude that chimpanzees can master language production. Fortunately, however, the research on chimpanzees has led to some advances in an applied area of psychology—the teaching of retarded children. Researchers at Yerkes Primate Research Center had developed a system of computerized symbols in connection with their chimpanzee training. Now the same system is being used in teaching profoundly retarded children who have not been able to learn to speak.

Previous efforts to teach these children sign language had not been successful, because of their poor motor coordination. Rock (1979) reports the case of an 18-year-old whose mental age was 2½ years, who has made startling progress since learning to communicate with symbols. A typical sentence that she can construct with three symbols is "Royce give popcorn." Furthermore, she has spontaneously begun to speak a few words and has changed from a person who resisted getting out of bed in the morning to one who "seems buoyantly happy now. She can skip to the machine, plant herself solidly in the chair and begin a lively symbolic discussion with Royce" (p. 93).

SECTION SUMMARY: Producing Language

1. Speakers have many unwritten agreements with listeners. One such agreement is the Given-New Strategy, whereby each sentence contains some given or familiar information and some new information.
2. Speakers alternate, particularly at the beginning of conversations, and several interchanges are required to end a conversation.
3. The formality level of speech is related to characteristics such as pronunciation, the choice of words, and the number of nouns.
4. The form of directives depends upon the social situation of the speaker and the listener.
5. People choose the subject of a sentence and show some verb selection before they begin a sentence.
6. People use a consistent set of rules in telling simple stories. For example, each story includes a setting and an episode.
7. People also show uniformities when they are describing places, such as their apartments.
8. Speech errors include pauses, false starts, extra words, and slips of the tongue. Slips of the tongue follow the rules of English structure.
9. Articulation—the production of speech sounds—involves the lungs, the larynx, the tongue, and the lips.
10. Several researchers have tried to teach chimpanzees to communicate. They disagree as to whether chimpanzee language is basically the same as human speech.

Remembering Language

We have talked about understanding and producing language. However, we must also discuss what happens to language when it is stored in memory. Think, for a moment, about the number of ways in which memory for language is important. It is vitally important in your college education, for example. You must store the language you hear in lectures and read in textbooks. It is important when you receive instructions. (Did the person at the gas station say "go left and then right" or "go right and then left"?) It is important when you hear some gossip and then pass the gossip on to someone else. It is important in every one of our daily conversations.

In Chapter 3 we considered many aspects of human memory. Other aspects of memory were considered in Chapter 4 when we discussed the importance of imagery in memory. However, in most cases our previous discussion has been limited to words in isolation. In this section we will be concerned with memory for **prose,** which is written or spoken language. Thus we will look at memory for sentences, paragraphs, and stories. We will look at both the research findings and at practical applications.

Our first topic will be verbatim memory. **Verbatim** (pronounced "vur-*bay*-tim") means "word for word." Thus, verbatim memory involves recalling the exact words in the exact order in which they were presented.

We will next consider memory for meaning. In general, you will see that people are fairly accurate in their memory for the meaning of written or spoken material, even if they are not accurate in their verbatim recall. They catch the gist of the message, although they may not be able to repeat the precise words or sentences.

The last topic is memory for inferences. People use their background knowledge to help them process prose. Sometimes this works to their disadvantage, and they remember—mistakenly—things that were only implied but never really said. Other times this works to their advantage because their background information helps them interpret what they hear.

Verbatim Memory

Early studies on verbatim memory for prose were primarily concerned with factors that influence accuracy. In one study, for example, people performed better on simple, active-voice, affirmative sentences than on more complex, passive-voice, negative sentences (Mehler, 1963). We saw earlier in this chapter that people understand active, affirmative sentences best, and so you probably expected to learn that memory for these sentences was also superior. Keep these findings in mind if you want your listeners to remember what you have said.

Other studies have used verbatim memory to investigate the psychological reality of constituent structure. As you may recall from the beginning of the chapter, people judge words from the same constituents as being closely related to each other. Other studies show that they also *remember* words better if they are from the constituent that is currently being processed. Jarvella (1971) presented two kinds of passages, such as:

1. *The confidence of Kofach was not unfounded.*
   To stack the meeting for McDonald,
   the union had even brought in outsiders.
2. *Kofach had been persuaded by the international*
   to stack the meeting for McDonald.
   The union had even brought in outsiders.

Notice that the third lines are indentical in both passages. The actual words in the second line are also identical in both passages. However, in the first passage, *to stack the meeting for McDonald* belongs with the third line. In contrast, in the second passage, *to stack the meeting for McDonald* belongs with the first line.

Jarvella interrupted people as they were reading passages like these and asked them to recall what they had read. As you would expect, recall in both conditions was excellent for the very most recent material, such as the line *the union had even brought in outsiders.* The interesting finding was that recall of the second line, *to stack the meeting for McDonald,* was excellent for people who saw the first passage. That line was part of a constituent that they were currently processing. In contrast, recall of that second line was poor for people who saw the second passage. For them, that line was part of a constituent that they had already completed. Consequently, they did not need to remember it verbatim. In another study, Jarvella demonstrated that people remembered the general meaning of these previous parts of the passage, even though their verbatim recall was poor.

When you read the section about directives earlier in the chapter, you might have wondered what kinds of directives are most effective. Kemper and Thissen (1980) studied verbatim memory for requests, which were either polite (for example, *Do you think you could rake the leaves?*) or impolite (for example, *Rake the leaves*). People recalled the polite requests when they were spoken by the high-status speaker, but not when they were spoken by the low-status speaker. In contrast, people recalled the impolite requests when they were spoken by the low-status speaker, but not when they were spoken by the high-status speaker. Thus social factors can have an important influence on the characteristics of verbatim memory.

What are some applications of verbatim memory? We noted at the beginning of this section that verbatim memory is generally not as important in our day-to-day life as memory for the general idea. In some classroom situations, however, verbatim memory is crucial. For example, an instructor may expect you to recall the exact definition that you heard in a class lecture three weeks ago.

What kind of lecture material do you remember best, the facts or the jokes? During a normal class period, Kintsch and Bates (1977) lectured to college students on the history of intelligence testing. Inserted in the lecture were three kinds of sentences: topic sentences, detail sentences, and irrelevant remarks, such as jokes or announcements. The students were tested several days later. Their performances on topic sentences and detail sentences were equally mediocre. Sad to say, their performance was best on the irrelevant remarks. For example, they remembered very accurately an announcement, "Oh, speaking of anxiety, that reminds me. Marcia and I will not be able to answer questions between now and next Tuesday" (p. 158). If you are a teacher who really wants students to remember something word for word, see if you can include it in a joke!

Did you ever have to memorize a historical document, a part of the Bible, or a poem in grammar school? If you did, try to remember it now. Rubin (1977) tortured undergraduates who had said they had memorized various passages by asking them to remember as much as they could from "The Preamble to the Constitution," "The 23rd Psalm," or "Hamlet's soliloquy." They were instructed to write as much as they could recall, verbatim. Notice that this study involves very-long-term memory; in fact, people had memorized these passages an average of seven years before recall.

Rubin's findings showed amazing regularity. All subjects tended to remember the same words, though some remembered more than others. Recall, of course, was best for the beginning of passages. For example, almost everyone who had been required to memorize "Hamlet's soliloquy" recalled "To be or not to be, that is the question." About 75 percent continued on with "Whether 'tis nobler," and almost everyone forgot "in the mind." About 30 percent continued on with "to suffer the slings and arrows of outrageous fortune." At that point, all but three gave up. Notice that the average student recalled only 13 words! Thus, long-term verbatim recall is limited.

Most of the research on prose memory has been concerned with memory for the general meaning of a passage. Usually we do not care whether we recall a passage word for word. Instead, we hope that we have remembered the gist of the message.

Demonstration 5.6   Memory for Meaning.

Read the following passage, and then answer the questions without looking back at the passage.

> I had some difficulty understanding how Alice could relax on a beach whose very snack bar offered eggs mimosa and *salade niçoise*. We were not, after all, on one of those Caribbean islands where the British spent a few centuries teaching the natives the art of large table settings and cool gray meat. We had served our time on those islands. Once, while we were living in a rented house on Tortola, Alice asked the storekeeper she had ordered a chicken from if he would cut it up for her, and returned to find that he had taken a frozen chicken and run it through a band saw. Alice, as I remember, said something on that occasion that sounded rather like "Blaff."
>
> How could a person who had once been handed a chicken that looked like fifteen perfectly uniform pieces of thickly sliced bologna be so casual about spending her vacation in a place that has entire books written about its cookery? (Trillin, 1978, p. 15)

Which sentence fragments did you see in the previous passage?

1. . . . the storekeeper asked Alice to cut up the chicken she had ordered from him.
2. . . . Alice asked the storekeeper who had ordered a chicken for her if he would cut it up.
3. . . . Alice asked the storekeeper she had ordered a chicken from if he would cut it up for her.

Memory for Meaning

Try Demonstration 5.6, which is similar to a classic study by Sachs (1967). Which sentence did you think you saw? You probably did *not* think you saw *the storekeeper asked Alice to cut up the chicken she had ordered from him.* However, you might think you saw *Alice asked the storekeeper who had ordered a chicken for her if he would cut it up.*

Sachs asked people to listen to a story that contained a critical sentence, and she interrupted the story shortly after they had heard that critical sentence. At this point, she asked them to judge whether they had seen a particular sentence. In some cases, she showed them a sentence that was identical to the critical sentence. In other cases, this new sentence was like the second choice in Demonstration 5.6.

In other words, it was similar in meaning to the critical sentence, but different either in its **syntax** (grammatical form) or in its arrangement of words. In still other cases, this new sentence was different in meaning, such as the first choice in Demonstration 5.6.

Sachs found that people did not pay much attention to syntax or word arrangement. They frequently thought they had seen a sentence that actually had very different word order from the original. People's verbatim memory is far from spectacular. However, performance was quite accurate for sentences with the meaning changes. People cannot be tricked into thinking, for example, that the storekeeper asked Alice to cut up the chicken. In other words, we store the meaning of prose even if we forget the exact wording.

Now try Demonstration 5.7, a simpler version of a study by Bransford and Franks (1971). How many sentences in the second half had you seen before? The answer is at the end of this section.

Demonstration 5.7   Constructive Memory.

Read each sentence, count to five, answer the question, go on to the next sentence (From Jenkins, 1974).

Sentence	Question
The girl broke the window on the porch.	Broke what?
The tree in the front yard shaded the man who was smoking his pipe.	Where?
The hill was steep.	What was?
The cat, running from the barking dog, jumped on the table.	From what?
The tree was tall.	Was what?
The old car climbed the hill.	What did?
The cat running from the dog jumped on the table.	Where?
The girl who lives next door broke the window on the porch.	Lives where?
The car pulled the trailer.	Did what?
The scared cat was running from the barking dog.	What was?
The girl lives next door.	Who does?
The tree shaded the man who was smoking his pipe.	What did?
The scared cat jumped on the table.	What did?
The girl who lives next door broke the large window.	Broke what?
The man was smoking his pipe.	Who was?
The old car climbed the steep hill.	The what?
The large window was on the porch.	Where?
The tall tree was in the front yard.	What was?
The car pulling the trailer climbed the steep hill.	Did what?
The cat jumped on the table.	Where?
The tall tree in the front yard shaded the man.	Did what?
The car pulling the trailer climbed the hill.	Which car?
The dog was barking.	Was what?
The window was large.	What was?

STOP. Cover the preceding sentences. Now read each of the following sentences and decide whether it is a sentence from the list given above.

The car climbed the hill.	(old_____, new_____)
The girl who lives next door broke the window.	(old_____, new_____)
The old man who was smoking his pipe climbed the steep hill.	(old_____, new_____)
The tree was in the front yard.	(old_____, new_____)
The scared cat, running from the barking dog, jumped on the table.	(old_____, new_____)
The window was on the porch.	(old_____, new_____)
The barking dog jumped on the old car in the front yard.	(old_____, new_____)
The tree in the front yard shaded the man.	(old_____, new_____)
The cat was running from the dog.	(old_____, new_____)
The old car pulled the trailer.	(old_____, new_____)
The tall tree in the front yard shaded the old car.	(old_____, new_____)
The tall tree shaded the man who was smoking his pipe.	(old_____, new_____)
The scared cat was running from the dog.	(old_____, new_____)
The old car, pulling the trailer, climbed the hill.	(old_____, new_____)
The girl who lives next door broke the large window on the porch.	(old_____, new_____)
The tall tree shaded the man.	(old_____, new_____)
The cat was running from the barking dog.	(old_____, new_____)
The car was old.	(old_____, new_____)
The girl broke the large window.	(old_____, new_____)
The scared cat ran from the barking dog that jumped on the table.	(old_____, new_____)
The scared cat, running from the dog, jumped on the table.	(old_____, new_____)
The old car pulling the trailer climbed the steep hill.	(old_____, new_____)
The girl broke the large window on the porch.	(old_____, new_____)
The scared cat which broke the window on the porch climbed the tree.	(old_____, new_____)
The tree shaded the man.	(old_____, new_____)
The car climbed the steep hill.	(old_____, new_____)
The girl broke the window.	(old_____, new_____)
The man who lives next door broke the large window on the porch.	(old_____, new_____)
The tall tree in the front yard shaded the man who was smoking his pipe.	(old_____, new_____)
The cat was scared.	(old_____, new_____)

STOP. Count the number of sentences judged "old." See text for answer.

Bransford and Franks asked subjects to listen to sentences that belonged to several different stories. Then they were given a recognition test that included new sentences, many of which were combinations of the earlier sentences. Nonetheless, people were convinced that they had seen them before. They were particularly certain that they had heard the complex sentences, such as *The tall tree in the front yard shaded the man who was smoking his pipe.* In contrast, they were quite confident that they had not seen simple sentences, such as *The cat was scared.* Furthermore, they did not think that they had seen sentences that violated the meaning of the earlier sentences—for example *The scared cat which broke the window on the porch climbed the tree.*

Bransford and Franks proposed a constructive model of memory for prose material. According to the **constructive model of memory,** people integrate information from individual sentences in order to construct larger ideas. People therefore think that they have already seen those complex sentences because they had combined the various facts in memory. Once sentences are fused in memory, we cannot untangle them into their original components.

These results surprised many people. The experiment has been successfully repeated in a variety of experimental situations summarized by Flagg, Potts, and Reynolds (1975). However, many psychologists criticized the Bransford and Franks results. Some suggested, for example, that people really did not understand the task instructions; perhaps they thought they were merely to choose the sentences that had the same *meaning* as the original. This alternative interpretation was dismissed by Flagg and his colleagues, however, because their research showed that people really *did* understand the instructions.

How well can people remember meaning? The studies of Sachs and Bransford and Franks have shown that people remember the general meaning of the material they hear, even though they forget the specific form of the sentences (as Sachs showed) or the specific sentences they have seen (as Bransford and Franks showed). In the laboratory, people are at a disadvantage because the nature of human memory does not allow them to recall the precise words. However, in real life this disadvantage is seldom important. Typically, we do not need to recall the original sentences exactly. Instead, we can synthesize many isolated bits of information into a well-organized whole and recall the meaning of a passage.

Notice that the constructive nature of memory emphasizes the active nature of our cognitive processes. Sentences do not passively enter memory, where each is stored separately. Instead, we try to make sense out of sentences that seem to be related to each other. We combine the sentences into a coherent story and we struggle to fit the pieces together.

In addition to the ''active cognitive processes'' theme in constructive memory, there is also a second theme. Specifically, our errors in information processing can often be traced to strategies that are generally useful. In real life, a useful heuristic is to fuse sentences together, but this heuristic can lead us astray if it is applied inappropriately. Incidentally, did you apply the constructive memory heuristic inappropriately in Demonstration 5.7? In fact, *every* one of those sentences in the test was new!

Let us look at some applications of memory for meaning. When you want people to remember the meaning of a message, word it carefully! File and Jew (1973) tested airline passengers who were waiting in the airplane terminal before boarding their planes. These passengers heard a 200-word passage about air safety—the kind you normally hear from the flight attendant once you have boarded. The passages were either active or passive, and either affirmative or negative. For example, here is part of the active affirmative passage:

Extinguish cigarettes. Remove all sharp objects from your person. When using the slides, remove your shoes, straighten your legs and place hands on knees. (p. 66)

The passive negative version of that passage is:

Cigarettes should not be left lighted. Sharp objects should not be left on your person. When using the slides, shoes should not be kept on, knees should not be bent, nor should hands be left off knees. (p. 66)

After hearing the instructions, people were asked to remember as many details as possible, not necessarily verbatim. People who were in the active affirmative condition recalled more than ten times as many statements as people in the passive negative condition. This study supplements the earlier findings about verbatim memory. People recall information better if it is stated in the active and the affirmative, and this generalization holds true for both verbatim memory and memory for important details.

Memory for Inferences

In the first part of this section on memory for prose, we discussed verbatim memory, or memory for the actual words in the presented sentences. Then we discussed memory for meaning, or memory for the messages in the sentences. Now we will consider memory for material that was never presented during the experiment! In many cases people add their own information to the material presented by the experimenter, and this information is produced during recall. Thus their recall will contain **inferences** or logical conclusions that were never part of the original stimulus material.

This area of research began with the studies of Sir Frederick Bartlett (1932), a British psychologist who emphasized the importance of previous knowledge in remembering. Much of the early work on human memory used nonsense words so that memory would not be influenced by prior associations from familiar English words (Dooling & Christiaansen, 1977). In contrast, Bartlett believed that the most interesting aspect of memory was the complex interaction between the material presented by the experimenter and the subjects' prior knowledge.

In Bartlett's most famous study, people read a North American Indian folktale called "The War of the Ghosts." Then they recalled the story several days, weeks, or years later. Bartlett found certain consistencies in the pattern of recall:

1. The recalled story was shorter than the original. In particular, place names were omitted.
2. Many phrases in the original story were worded in the subjects' own vocabulary in recall. For example, "I will not go along. I might be killed. My relatives do not know where I have gone" (p. 65) became "One of the young men excused himself on the ground of family ties" (p. 67) in the words of a British subject who recalled the story after an eight-day interval.
3. Errors appear in recall. For example, "hunting seals" in the original story might be recalled as "fishing."
4. The recalled story is more coherent and rational than the original story.

Bartlett, like Bransford and Franks nearly 40 years later, supported a constructive framework for memory. According to Bartlett, people encode information in memory in an abstract form. The main ideas of a story are then used to construct the recall. That recall will not be completely accurate; the language will be different and the details may be changed. Recall therefore represents a fusing of one's previous knowledge with the specific information presented by the experimenter. Furthermore, as time passes since hearing the original story, the recalled story borrows more heavily upon previous knowledge and less on the information in the original story (Dooling & Christiaansen, 1977).

Now try Demonstration 5.8, and see whether your friend shows the same patterns in recall that Bartlett's subjects showed.

Demonstration 5.8   Story Recall.

Read the following fable to a friend. Then ask your friend to recall the fable as accurately as possible.

A Dog and A Wolfe

> There was a hagged carrion of a wolfe, and a jolly sort of a gentile dog, with good flesh upon his back, that fell into company together upon the king's high-way. The wolfe wonderfully pleas'd with his companion, and as inquisitive to learn how he brought himself to that blessed state of body. Why, says the dog, I keep my master's house from thieves, and I have very good meat, drink, and lodging for my pains. Now if you'll go along with me, and do as I do, you may fare as I fare. The wolfe struck up the bargain, and so away they trotted together: but as they were jogging on, the wolfe spy'd a bare place about the dog's neck, where the hair was worn off. Brother (says he) how comes this I prethee? Oh, that's nothing, says the dog, but the fretting of my collar a little. Nay, says t'other, if there be a collar in the case, I know better things than to sell my liberty for a crust. (L'Estrange, 1692/1967, p. 11)

Bransford, Barclay, and Franks (1972) provided further evidence about the fusing of previous knowledge and the information in the stimulus material. They gave some subjects a sentence such as:

(1) *Three turtles rested beside a floating log, and a fish swam beneath them.*

Other subjects heard a sentence such as:

(2) *Three turtles rested on a floating log, and a fish swam beneath them.*

Notice that the only difference between these two sentences is the word *beside* or *on*.

Later, subjects received a recognition test containing sentences such as:

(3) *Three turtles rested (beside/on) a floating log, and a fish swam beneath it.*

Notice that this recognition sentence, containing *it* rather than *them*, can be derived from sentence 2. Our knowledge of spatial relations tells us that if the turtles are on the log and a fish is beneath them, then the fish must also be beneath the log. That recognition sentence is therefore a reasonable inference. Notice, however, that the recognition sentence is not necessarily an inference from sentence 1; it is ambiguous whether the fish are swimming beneath the log.

Demonstration 5.9   *Context and Recall.*

Read the following paragraph. Then close your book and recall as much of it as you can.

> The procedure is actually quite simple. First you arrange things into different groups depending on their makeup. Of course, one pile may be sufficient depending on how much there is to do. If you have to go somewhere else due to lack of facilities, that is the next step; otherwise you are pretty well set. It is important not to overdo any particular endeavor. That is, it is better to do too few things at once than too many. In the short run this may not seem important, but complications from doing too many can easily arise. A mistake can be expensive as well. The manipulation of the appropriate mechanisms should be self-explanatory, and we need not dwell on it here. At first the whole procedure will seem complicated. Soon, however, it will become just another facet of life. It is difficult to foresee any end to the necessity for this task in the immediate future, but then one never can tell.

The results of the study showed that people who had seen sentence 2 often reported that they recognized sentence 3. However, people who had seen sentence 1 were much less likely to say that they recognized sentence 3. Bransford and his coauthors explain that people who saw sentence 2 construct an idea by fusing that sentence with what they know about the world. As a result, they believe that they have seen a sentence that was never presented, even though it is a reasonable inference.

In these studies we have discussed so far, background knowledge misleads people, and they recall inferences that were not actually stated. Once more, a strategy that is typically helpful can lead us astray. In everyday life, background knowledge is often very helpful. How was your recall for Demonstration 5.9, which was adapted from a study by Bransford and Johnson (1972)? How would your recall have been if you had been told that it was a paragraph about doing laundry? Reread that paragraph, within the context of doing laundry. Once you know that it is about laundry, all your background knowledge about the washing process helps you fit the puzzling parts together into a meaningful paragraph. Bransford and Johnson found that people who knew the topic of the paragraph before reading it recalled 73 percent more material than people who did not know the topic. This kind of background knowledge improves performance because the background knowledge is consistent with the information in the paragraph.

Our background knowledge can also be helpful in helping us recall stories. Bower (1976) argues that simple stories have definite, regular structures; you will recall that we discussed Rumelhart's work on understanding story structures earlier. People become familiar with the basic structure of stories from their prior experience with stories. They use this structure in sorting out any new stories they hear. Once again, when background information is consistent with the stimulus materials, this background information is clearly helpful.

Let us now discuss some of the applications regarding memory for inferences. The research on memory for inferences shows that we think we remember hearing material that was never actually presented. When we remember the inferences, rather than the actual statements, this can present problems in several areas of everyday life. So far psychologists have looked at applications of inferential memory in three areas: advertising, medical diagnosis, and courtroom trials.

Think about some of the advertisements you have seen recently. For example, an ad might say, "Four out of five doctors recommend the ingredients in Gonif's brand medication." You might reasonably infer, therefore, that four out of five doctors would also recommend Gonif's medication itself; even though the ad never said so. Companies can be prosecuted for making false assertions about a product if the actual statements are untrue. However, can they be prosecuted for making statements that cause consumers to make false inferences, even if they never directly lie?

Harris and Monaco (1978) report that the makers of Listerine Antiseptic mouthwash were ruled against in courtroom decisions for creating a "lingering false belief," even though the actual statements contained only truthful information. Here is part of the ad:

> "Wouldn't it be great," asks the mother, "if you could make him coldproof? Well, you can't. Nothing can do that (boy sneezes). But there is something that you can do that may help. Have him gargle with Listerine Antiseptic. Listerine can't promise to keep him cold-free, but it may help him fight off colds. During the cold-catching season, have him gargle twice a day with full-strength Listerine. Watch his diet, see he gets plenty of sleep, and there's a good chance he'll have fewer colds, milder colds this year." (p. 18)

Aren't you left with the "lingering false belief" that Listerine actually prevents colds? Furthermore, aren't you likely to recall that ad as directly stating that Listerine prevents colds? Harris (1977) found that all 15 of his subjects recalled that the advertised product actually helped to prevent colds.

Harris and Monaco also report research in which subjects heard some tape-recorded mock commercials. Some commercials directly made false claims about the product. Other commercials implied false claims, but never directly stated them. For many commercials, subjects could not distinguish between what they heard and what they inferred. Try examining some advertisements to see whether they imply, but do not directly state, certain positive qualities—consumers may be remembering these inferred claims.

Harris and Monaco summarize some research on the role of inference in medical diagnosis. People who were asked, *Do you get headaches frequently; and, if so, how often?* reported an average of 2.2 headaches per week. In contrast, people who were asked, *Do you get headaches occasionally, and, if so, how often?* reported an average of only 0.7 headaches per week. The doctor's question seems to imply some extra information. That information, in turn, influences recall.

Research on the applications of inferential memory in advertising and medicine is still limited. However, applications in courtroom trials have been more thoroughly explored. Harris and Monaco point out that people on the witness stand can be accused of perjury if they lie directly. They cannot be accused of perjury if they merely *imply* a lie. For example, imagine that a prosecutor asks a man whether he stole some money. Furthermore, imagine that he had in fact stolen the money. If the witness says, "I didn't steal the money," he can be accused of perjury. However, suppose he says, "I wasn't forced into stealing the money." In this case, he implies that he didn't steal the money, but since he does not directly state it, he cannot be accused of perjury. Sneaky witnesses hope that the jury will recall the inferences of the statement, rather than the actual words, and will therefore judge them innocent.

Harris, Teske, and Ginns (1975) asked subjects to hear excerpts of mock courtroom testimonies. Some people heard a direct statement, such as *I rang the burglar alarm.* Other people heard a statement in which that action was implied, but not directly stated, such as *I ran up to the burglar alarm.* Furthermore, half of each group received specific instructions about how they were to avoid interpreting any implied information as being truly factual. Afterwards, they were asked whether they had heard statements such as *I rang the burglar alarm.* People who had heard *I ran up to the burglar alarm* were almost as likely to respond "true" as were those who had previously heard the direct statement. This was found even for those people who had been specifically told to avoid making inferences.

In connection with our discussion of memory for inferences, you might recall that we discussed related material on eyewitness testimony in Chapter 3. The study by Loftus, Miller, and Burns (1978) demonstrated that the question "Did another car pass the red Datsun while it was stopped at the yield sign?" led people to believe that they had actually seen a yield sign, when they had in fact seen a stop sign. Thus, we often remember the inferences and forget true material.

If you watch television programs or movies that include courtroom trials, analyze them for the kinds of information the witnesses imply, but do not directly state. If these dramas are realistic, the jury will be influenced by the implications as much as by direct statements.

SECTION SUMMARY: *Remembering Language*

1. Verbatim memory is better for sentences that are active and affirmative.
2. If a phrase is part of a constituent that is currently being processed, it will be recalled better than if it is part of a previous constituent.
3. Social factors influence whether people recall polite directives better than impolite directives.
4. Students remember irrelevant remarks better than factual sentences, and their verbatim recall is poor for material memorized long ago.
5. People can recall the meaning of sentences better than the exact words.
6. According to Bransford and Franks, people fuse sentences together in memory and cannot untangle them into their original components.
7. The meaning of statements is recalled better if sentences are active and affirmative.
8. Bartlett found that story recall drifts in the direction of the listener's previous knowledge.
9. Background knowledge, particularly context and an understanding of story structure, can be helpful in recalling stories.

10. People believe that they have seen sentences that have never been presented, as long as they are reasonable inferences. This is true in laboratory experiments and in applied areas.

Reading

The topic of reading has attracted considerable interest among cognitive psychologists in recent years, and a recent issue of *Journal of Experimental Psychology: Human Perception and Performance* (Vol. 7, No. 3, June 1981) was devoted to reading processes. Reading requires a wide variety of cognitive skills, as Fisher (1981) notes:

> It involves sequencing of eye movements, decoding, encoding, and utilizing linguistic awareness. It demands knowledge of orthographic regularity and irregularity. It integrates letters, words, sentences, passages with past experience. Surely reading is one of our most complex daily activities. (p. 489)

Because of the variety of cognitive skills involved in reading, we will be discussing this topic in many different parts of the book. Reading was an important part of two sections of the chapter on perceptual processes (Chapter 2); we discussed pattern recognition in connection with recognizing letters and words, and then we talked about automatic skills in reading in the section on attention. In this chapter we will emphasize linguistic aspects of reading. Then in Chapter 8 we will examine how people make analogies in order to pronounce new words.

Reading is clearly one of the most important components of education. Think about the number of hours your teachers spent in early grade school preparing you for reading, helping you pronounce the words, and encouraging you to understand what you had read. Try to imagine what your college education would be like if there were no way to communicate with written language. Naturally, you would have no textbooks, and there would be no written examinations. Furthermore, your professors would have to gather their information by the "oral tradition." They could learn only by listening to other knowledgeable people. In fact, the effects of eliminating written language would be devastating for education.

Reading is such an important topic that several books have been written about psychological aspects of reading (e.g., Gibson & Levin, 1975; LaBerge & Samuels, 1977; Resnick & Weaver, 1979). Let us consider three aspects of reading: (1) perceptual processes; (2) word recognition; and (3) speed-reading.

Perceptual Processes

For a moment, become aware of the way your eyes are moving as you are reading. Notice that your eyes make a series of little jumps as they move across the page. **Saccadic movement** refers to these very rapid movements of the eye from one spot to the next. Your eyes must make these movements in order to bring the center of the eye, where the vision is the sharpest, into position over the words you want to look at.

Good readers differ from poor readers with respect to the kind of saccadic movements their eyes make. Figure 5-3 shows how two readers might differ in their eye movements. The good reader's eyes make larger jumps. The good reader is

Figure 5.3 *Eye Movements for a Good Reader (Top Numbers) and a Poor Reader (Bottom Numbers).*

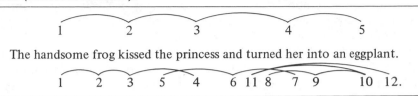

also less likely to move backward to earlier material in the sentence. Furthermore, although this cannot be seen in the diagram, the good reader pauses for a short time before making the next saccadic movement. A good reader might pause for $^1/_5$ second each time, whereas a poor reader might pause for ½ second.

People used to believe that if poor readers were taught how to make more effective saccades, their reading would improve. Unfortunately, however, this effort would not be effective because eye movement problems are a *symptom* of reading difficulty, not its *cause* (Gibson & Levin, 1975). Poor readers have difficulty understanding the material. Therefore they make more saccadic movements, pause longer, and move backward more often.

You may wish to review the section in Chapter 2 on pattern recognition, which provides information on how we recognize letters when we read. That section considered theories of pattern recognition and discussed how context aids the recognition of letters and other patterns.

Word Recognition

You just read two words in the phrase, "word recognition." Somehow, you were able to look at that pattern of letters and recognize those words. How in the world did you do it? Unfortunately, there is no simple answer, because the reading experts disagree.

Basically, there are three different hypotheses about the recognition of printed words that occurs when you read to yourself. One hypothesis, which we will call the **direct-access hypothesis,** states that the reader can recognize a word directly from the printed words. In other words, you look at the phrase, "word recognition," and the visual pattern is sufficient to let you locate information about the meaning of the word in semantic memory.

Another hypothesis, which we will call the **indirect-access hypothesis,** states that the printed words must be translated into sounds before you can locate information about meaning in semantic memory. The process is indirect because of the intermediate and necessary step of first converting the visual stimulus into a sound stimulus.

Think about whether you seem to use this intermediate step when you read. When you read, do you have a speechlike representation of the words? You probably read silently, but does it seem that you have an auditory image of what you are reading? Perhaps you are concluding that you sometimes have direct access and sometimes require the intermediate step involving the sound of a word.

The third hypothesis, called the **dual encoding hypothesis,** states that semantic memory can be reached either directly, through the visual route, or indirectly, through the sound route (Martin, 1978). Thus, there are two ways in which the visual symbols can be encoded. This hypothesis may be most likely, because there is evidence for both kinds of encoding processes.

It is worth noting that the direct-access hypothesis and the indirect-access hypothesis are parallel to the whole-word and the phonics methods of teaching reading (Doctor & Coltheart, 1980). Also you may know, some educators favor the **whole-word approach,** which maintains that readers do not stop to identify the individual letters in a word; instead, they can recognize the whole word. According to this approach, the sounds of the letters are irrelevant (F. Smith, 1971). Other educators favor the **phonics approach,** which argues that readers recognize by sounding out the individual letters in the word. If your grade school teachers told you to "sound out the word" when you stumbled on a new word, they championed the phonics approach. The phonics approach stresses that sound is a necessary intermediate step in reading. The argument between the whole-word supporters and the phonics supporters is just as feverish among educators as is the argument between direct-access supporters and indirect-access supporters among psychologists.

There are several kinds of support for the direct-access hypothesis (Bradshaw, 1975). One kind of evidence comes from homonyms, which are words that are spelled differently but sound the same. When you see the two homonyms THEIR and THERE, these two words are connected with different meanings. If each of those visual stimuli were translated into sound, as the indirect-access hypothesis claims, then we would be left with two identical sounds. It would be difficult to explain how those two identical sounds could then lead to the two different meanings.

More support for the direct-access hypothesis comes from a study by Bradshaw and Nettleton (1974). They presented pairs of words that were similar in spelling but not in sound, such as MOWN–DOWN, HORSE–WORSE, and QUART–PART. When subjects pronounced the first member of the pair out loud, it took them somewhat longer to pronounce the second member—there was interference because the two words were not pronounced similarly. However, this effect did not occur in silent reading. When people read the first word silently, there was no delay in pronouncing the second word. This suggests that silent reading does not lead to a silent pronunciation of the word, because there was no evidence for any interference.

Now let us look at the evidence for the indirect-access hypothesis, which is also persuasive. Hardyck and Petrinovitch (1970), for example, noted that people often sounded out words when the material was difficult. (Incidentally, did you sound out the name *Petrinovitch* when you read it?) When people were prevented from making any lip movements, they had trouble reading difficult material. This indicates that people are translating the visual stimulus into sound.

A study by Doctor and Coltheart (1980) also supports the indirect-access hypothesis. Children saw sentences such as, "He ran threw the street," and were asked to decide whether these sentences were meaningful or not. Doctor and Coltheart found that the children were likely to judge sentences as meaningful if they *sounded* meaningful. For example, "He ran threw the street," would be pronounced just the same as the meaningful sentence, "He ran through the street." Therefore, they judged that sentence as meaningful. In contrast, they did not judge sentences as meaningful if they remained meaningless when they were pronounced, for example, "He ran sew the street."

The dual-access hypothesis which combines the direct-access and the indirect-access approaches, is becoming increasingly popular. As Mason (1978) writes, "It is apparent that both mechanisms can be and are used" (p. 568). It seems that some people favor the direct route to recognition, whereas others favor the indirect route.

Baron and Strawson (1976) identified two kinds of subjects. One kind of subject read words more quickly if they conformed to the standard spelling-sound correspondence rules (for example, SWEET) than if they violated the rules (for example, SWORD). Furthermore, in an independent test, these subjects relied heavily on spelling-sound correspondence rules. These are the people who choose the indirect access and encode the visual stimulus into sound before recognition. The other kind of subjects did not show much difference in reading speed between regular and irregular words. Also, they did not rely heavily on the spelling-sound correspondence rules. These are the direct-access readers, who directly recognize the visual stimulus.

More recently, Mason (1978) found that "mature readers"—for example, college students—were more likely to use the direct-access method. This makes sense. When children are first learning to read, they rely on sound (as the study by Doctor and Coltheart showed). As they mature, they can skip that intermediate step.

Other factors may also determine whether people select the direct-access or the indirect-access method. For example, you will recall that Hardyck and Petrinovitch found that people sounded out words when the words were difficult. Try to notice whether you are more likely to sound out unfamiliar words than ones you know well.

Furthermore, we sometimes choose the indirect-access method when we are under stress. When you are reading the questions on an essay examination, you might find yourself **subvocalizing,** sounding out the words silently. However, if you are by yourself in a quiet room, you will probably not subvocalize when you are reading the Sunday comics!

In conclusion, the dual-encoding hypothesis seems most likely. Word recognition can be either direct or indirect, depending upon the skill of the reader, the nature of the material, and other circumstances.

So far, we have considered theories of word recognition. Another important aspect of word recognition is the influence of sentence context on word recognition. In Chapter 2 we discussed the influence of word context on letter recognition. According to the word superiority effect, the context of surrounding letters in a word allows a target letter to be identified more accurately than the letter would be if it were in isolation or in a nonword. Similarly, the context of surrounding words in a sentence facilitates the recognition of a target word.

Posner and Snyder (1975) developed a theory of expectancy to explain why context helps word recognition. They reasoned that expectancy works in two different ways. First of all, it works because of spread of activation, a concept we discussed in Chapter 3. The spread of activation process occurs when information activates a memory location, thereby automatically spreading some of the activation to other related memory locations. For example, the sentence context, "In the zoo I saw a striped . . ." would spread activation to a word related to *zoo* and *striped,* namely, *zebra.* In addition to this automatic process, there is a second mechanism that requires conscious attention. This second, slower mechanism inhibits the retrieval of information from unexpected locations; it directs attention instead to the location of the expected stimulus. Stanovich and West (1981) offered experimental support for Posner and Snyder's theory, but Carr (1981) pointed out some difficulties with it; these articles from the special *Journal of Experimental Psychology: Human Perception and Performance* issue on reading can be consulted for more details.

Speed-Reading

You may have often contemplated how nice it might be to read more quickly. Wouldn't it be fantastic to read a chapter in your history of psychology textbook in, say, 20 minutes, and then recall it perfectly? You may have seen advertisements assuring you that you could read at a speed of 500 words per minute, in contrast to the usual rate of 200. Well, stop fantasizing, because speed-reading does not work. Rayner (1978) points out that the studies performed on speed-readers may record their eye movements, but they rarely measure their comprehension appropriately.

Rayner discusses the results of a few studies that have tested comprehension. Some studies show that speed-readers can change their eye movement patterns. Rather than the tiny saccades that regular readers make, speed-readers moved their eyes down the middle of the page, skipping several lines during each saccade. However, their recall of the text was incorrect and confused. In another study, speed-readers scored less than 50 percent correct on a true-false test! Furthermore, Rayner notes that most speed-readers slow down to a normal reading speed when they have been told that a comprehension test will be given.

If you are still considering paying $100 to $300 for that speed-reading course, contemplate an observation by Thomas (1962) concerning a speed-reader. Her eyes moved halfway down the center of the left-hand page, then across to the center of the right-hand page, then straight upward, and finally back across to the left-hand page. The pattern therefore resembled a square across the two pages. She never fixated on the lower third of a page. Unfortunately, writers do not confine all the facts to the upper two-thirds of the pages! Try this fixation pattern on the first two pages of the next chapter to see just how little you can comprehend using this method. As Gibson and Levin (1975) conclude, "There is no magic route to reading speedily with good comprehension" (p. 548).

SECTION SUMMARY: Reading

1. **The eyes make saccadic movements during reading. Good readers make larger saccadic movements, pause for less time, and move backward less often.**
2. **Eye movement problems are a symptom, rather than a cause, of reading difficulties.**

3. There are three different hypotheses about word recognition: the direct-access hypothesis, in which words are recognized directly; the indirect-access hypothesis, in which printed words are translated into sounds before determining their meaning; and the dual encoding hypothesis, in which word recognition can occur either directly or indirectly. The dual encoding hypothesis is most strongly supported.
4. Sentence context facilitates the recognition of individual words.
5. Speed-readers cannot maintain their high reading speeds and still score well on tests of reading comprehension.

Chapter Review Questions

1. We discussed negatives in two parts of this chapter: (a) understanding negatives (both explicit negatives and marking) and (b) remembering negatives (both verbatim memory and memory for meaning). Summarize this information.

2. Compare how we perceive language when we hear it with language perception during reading.

3. The section on context and speech perception showed how surrounding sounds and words help you figure out a segment of language. Imagine that you are interested in how people decipher sloppy handwriting. Describe what experiments you could conduct that would be similar to the context and speech perception studies and what you would expect them to show.

4. Take the first sentence of Question 3 and show how the three strategies of identifying constituents could be used to divide that sentence into its constituents.

5. Think of puns that are examples of lexical ambiguity and surface structure ambiguity. Make up several examples of underlying structure ambiguity.

6. Analyze the next conversation you overhear from the viewpoint of the social context of speech. Pay attention to (a) the Given-New Strategy; (b) conversational format; (c) speech formality; and (d) directives.

7. Ask a friend to describe an incident. Discuss how this description is similar to (or different from) the structure of stories and location descriptions.

8. Describe the constructive model of memory. How would it explain why the subjects in Sach's experiment were inaccurate for sentences with changed syntax or word arrangement? How would it explain the results in the studies on courtroom testimonies?

9. You are reading a sentence right now. Describe the processes involved as you (a) move your eyes; (b) perceive the letters; and (c) recognize the words.

10. Throughout this chapter, we emphasized the active nature of cognitive processes. Think of as many examples as possible to illustrate this point. Then use the outline for the chapter to help you think of additional examples.

New Terms

psycholinguists	parallel transmission	immediate constituents
language comprehension	invariant feature	ultimate constituents
speech perception	analysis-by-synthesis	function words
phoneme	constituent	content words

affixes
heuristics
marking
unmarked
marked
ambiguous
lexical ambiguity
surface structure ambiguity
underlying structure
   ambiguity
Given-New Strategy
directive

slips of the tongue
anticipation errors
perseverations
reversals
articulation
larynx
laryngitis
voiced sounds
voiceless sounds
prose
verbatim
syntax

constructive model of
   memory
inferences
saccadic movement
direct-access hypothesis
indirect-access hypothesis
dual encoding hypothesis
whole-word approach
phonics approach
subvocalizing

Concepts and Categories

Preview

Concepts are used to group similar items together. One example of a concept is *square objects;* another example is *vegetables.* This chapter on concepts and categories has four sections: (1) how concept formation is studied; (2) factors affecting concept formation; (3) testing hypotheses; and (4) natural categories.

The first section considers two aspects of the study of concept formation: the kinds of concept formation tasks and the ways in which concept formation can be measured. Measures of concept formation include several ways of assessing how well the subjects are performing, as well as two methods of determining which strategies they are considering.

Of the many different factors that affect concept formation, we only consider three in the second section. The number of attributes that are pictured in the stimuli has an influence on concept learning. People learn more quickly from positive examples (stimuli that represent the concept) than from negative examples (stimuli that do not represent the concept). Finally, environmental factors such as videotaping and the presence of others can inhibit learning in some conditions.

Two theories of concept formation have been suggested that both emphasize how subjects make up and test hypotheses during the experiment. Bruner's theory proposes that people proceed systematically in their hypotheses rather than making random guesses. Levine's more recent theory proposes that people have excellent memories and are able to base their responses on one main hypothesis and keep track, meanwhile, of several others.

Rosch maintains that concept formation experiments are artificial because they are very different from real-world categories. The research of Rosch and her colleagues has concentrated on these natural categories that we work with in daily life. She suggests that people decide whether an item belongs to a category by comparing the item to a prototype, which is the best example of a category. (For example, a robin is a prototype of the bird category). Furthermore, there are three different levels of categories: a general level, a basic level, and a specific level. The basic level is the most useful and important.

Concept is one of those terms that we use very often in everyday language. As a result, its meaning has drifted away from the specific use of the term in psychology. In this chapter, a **concept** refers to making the same response to a group of objects that share similar characteristics. Thus we might respond with the concept *red* to an apple, a shade of lipstick, and a Santa Claus outfit, because these objects share a similar characteristic. Thus a concept is a way of categorizing objects and demonstrating which objects are related to each other.

We use concepts whenever we group similar items together. For example, look at the books on your bookshelf. If you have more than one shelf of books, you probably made some effort to group similar items together—for example, by subject matter. If you have a record collection, think about how you have grouped together similar records. Collections of stamps, coins, matchbooks, and so on quickly become overwhelming unless you organize them according to concepts. Think about how you organize the objects in your life, such as your clothes, papers, and drawers. Notice how they reflect conceptual groupings.

Now think about alternate ways you could group a particular class of objects. For example, I had a huge envelope of warranties and instruction manuals for items I had purchased. I wanted to divide these pamphlets into two smaller envelopes, and I was impressed with the number of different ways of "cutting up" the pile into two categories. I could have put pamphlets for objects with names beginning with the letters *A* –*M* in one envelope and *N* –*Z* in the other. I could have put pamphlets for objects to be used indoors in one, outdoors in another. I could have sorted according to year of purchase, owner of the item, or price of the item. Actually, I ended up sorting the warranties and instruction manuals according to *size* of the object. (Like the children's game, there were two categories, "bigger than a bread box" and "smaller than a bread box.")

Notice, too, how you yourself can be categorized in many different ways, depending upon how you plan to cut up the population. You may be a college student, rather than a non-college student, a psychology major rather than a non-psychology major, a 20-year-old rather than a non-20-year-old, a feminist rather than a nonfeminist, a Catholic rather than a non-Catholic, a liberal rather than a conservative. There are many different ways of grouping humanity, depending upon the concept upon which you are focusing.

Johnson-Laird and Wason (1977a) observe that there are two levels of concept classification that humans use. One kind is the intuitive, relatively effortless kind of classification that we perform in daily life. The examples we have been discussing so far fall into this category. (Yes, we have to use categories in order to discuss categories.) Ordinary language falls into this category as well. When we use a word like *fruit,* we are making the same response to a group of objects that share similar characteristics; that is, we are using a concept.

The other level of concept classification is what Johnson-Laird and Wason call "cold-blooded" categorization. This kind of categorization is the systematic, formal classification device that is used in the sciences. If you have taken a biology course, you may have learned classifications for plants or for invertebrate animals. You may also have memorized some classification systems in geology or chemistry.

Some classification systems also exist in psychology, such as the classification of disorders in abnormal psychology. For example, the third edition of the *Diagnostic and Statistical Manual of Mental Disorders* (American Psychiatric Association, 1980) outlines the classification of neurotic disorders. The category of neurotic disorders can be divided into several different kinds of disorders: affective, anxiety, somatoform, dissociative, and psychosexual. Affective disorders can be further subdivided into major affective disorders, other specific affective disorders, and atypical affective disorders. The major affective disorders can be even further subdivided into bipolar disorder and major depression. Finally, each of these categories can be subdivided. Major depression, for example, is divided into single episode versus recurrent.

However, the classification system used to categorize disorders is not as formal as the systems used in biology, geology, or chemistry. For example, people frequently disagree about which classification to assign to particular patients. In general, we will not be concerned with these kinds of systematic classifications. However, if you want to pursue the topic further, read an article by Sokal (1977).

Let us leave "cold-blooded" categorization and return to intuitive, daily-life concepts and categories. Specifically, let us talk about various ways in which concepts are helpful and necessary.

1. Without concepts, each object or event would be unique, and thinking and generalization would be impossible (Johnson-Laird & Wason, 1977a). Thinking frequently requires us to treat different things as the same, and concepts allow us to relate objects and events to others that are similar. For example, without concepts, the apple that you might be about to eat would simply be a unique, lonely object, unrelated to anything you have ever experienced before. By using the concept *apple,* you relate this object to all others in the apple category. This point is nicely illustrated in a short note in *The New Yorker* magazine ("Notes and Comments," 1979):

> I was shelling peas from my garden the other afternoon, and an old saying dropped into my mind: "As like as two peas in a pod." I let it drop on through. I would be disappointed if I found only two peas in a pod, and I would be surprised if they looked exactly alike. Some peas are square, some are hexagonal, some are cone-shaped, some are disclike, some are even round, and in almost every pod there is one pea, squeezed into the middle or off at one end, that is one-tenth the size of the others. Nature—in my experience with apples and green beans and tomatoes and squash and carrots and red roses and robins and oak trees—is given to variety more than to duplication. (p. 23)

Fortunately, however, we have a concept, *pea,* that allows us to relate one miniature hexagon to another, large round object.

2. Concepts allow economy in memory (Sokal, 1977). By grouping objects together into a concept, we can remember the attributes of the concept rather than each individual object or event. For example, by saying that François Truffaut speaks *French,* we are saying that his language resembles the language of millions of other people in the category "French-speaking people." We do not need to remember all the words or sentences that Truffaut might know. Concepts let us summarize information so that this information can be stored very neatly in memory.

3. Concepts reduce the necessity of constant learning (Bruner, Goodnow, & Austin, 1956). Notice that this advantage is related to the first two. For example, we do not need to learn again at each encounter that the object we see is a tree. Instead, we have already learned the name.

4. Concepts let us know how to react to an object (Bruner et al., 1956). For example, if I see a platter of Mexican enchiladas in front of me, I know I can react by approaching. On the other hand, if I see a porcupine, I know I should react by

running. Concepts let us know in advance about the appropriate actions to be taken.

5. Concepts let us relate classes of objects and events (Bruner et al., 1956). We have classes of objects that are related to each other according to structured patterns. For example, a Red Delicious is a kind of apple, which, in turn, is a kind of fruit. Once we have categorized an object as a Red Delicious, we can go beyond this category to the higher categories.

The first three sections in this chapter are concerned with various aspects of concept formation. We begin by examining how concept formation is studied, emphasizing a theme that appears throughout the book: Cognitive processes are hidden and difficult to observe. In concept formation studies, however, psychologists have devised a variety of methods to make these hidden processes more accessible for observation. The second section investigates factors that affect concept formation. In the third section, on theories of hypothesis testing, we will emphasize the active nature of cognitive processes; humans use strategies to gather information about concepts, and they invent tentative hypotheses that require frequent revision. The last section explores natural categories, which are concepts we acquire in everyday life. Our primary concern in that section is the structure of knowledge; how do we organize the objects we see everyday, and what are the interrelationships among these objects?

How Concept Formation Is Studied

Probably the *concept* of "concept formation studies" is more clear-cut than in any other area in cognition. The studies we discussed in the memory chapter, for example, were often wildly different from each other in design. Concept formation experiments, in contrast, are somewhat standardized. In this section we will see how psychologists study concept formation. There are two basic issues: (1) the kinds of tasks and (2) how concept formation is measured.

Kinds of Concept Formation Tasks

In **concept formation** tasks, certain attributes of the stimuli are related to each other according to certain rules. *Rules,* which we will examine thoroughly later in this section, tell us how to combine attributes. An **attribute** is a characteristic that can change from one stimulus to the next. For example, a concept formation study may include stimuli that are either white or green, small or large, and triangular or square. Color, size, and shape are three attributes that are frequently studied. A study may involve learning the rules, the attributes, or both.

Attribute Discovery.   Attributes are also important in daily life. For example, when you fill out a questionnaire, you probably fill out information about your own attributes. You may not be a small green triangle, but you are perhaps a junior who is a transfer student, majoring in psychology, living on campus, and female.

In some studies, the subject is instructed to figure out which attributes are relevant. Try Demonstration 6.1, a simplified version of an attribute discovery task. In this case, there is one **relevant attribute.** When an attribute is relevant, you must say "yes" when the attribute has one value and "no" when the attribute has other values. For example, in a task in which size is the relevant attribute, you might learn that you should say "yes" to all small stimuli and "no" to all large stimuli. The **irrelevant attribute** is an attribute that is not related to this particular concept. You might sometimes say "yes" and sometimes say "no" to white stimuli, if size alone is relevant, because color is irrelevant.

Demonstration 6.1   *An Attribute Discovery Task.*

Before you begin, place a piece of paper so that it hides the correct answers on the right-hand side of the page. Looking only at the figures on the left-hand side, say "yes" if you believe that the figure is an example of the concept, and "no" if you believe that it is not. Only one attribute is relevant in this task. After judging each pair, move the paper down to see the answer. Continue until you think you know what the concept is, and then check at the end of the chapter to see whether you are correct.

Answers

1.   Yes

2.   Yes

3.   No

4.   No

5.   No

6.   Yes

7.   No

8.   Yes

Think about some examples of relevant and irrelevant attributes. At our college, for example, the only relevant attributes for the concept "qualifying for the dean's list" are (1) having at least a 3.40 grade-point average for the semester, and (2) having been enrolled for at least 15 semester hours of classes. Numerous attributes are irrelevant, however, such as (1) sex, (2) major, (3) year, (4) hair color, (5) favorite dessert—the list could go on to infinity.

Attributes vary in their **salience** (pronounced "say-lee-unse"), or the extent to which they are noticed. For example, Trabasso (1963) found that color was more salient than angle of branches in studies of concepts involving flower designs. People made almost five times as many errors when "angle of branches" was the relevant attribute, in contrast to the number of errors made when color—a very salient attribute—was the relevant attribute. Demonstration 6.1 was somewhat difficult because the relevant dimension was *eyebrows,* which is probably less salient than *smile/frown.*

It makes sense that salience influences the ease with which we learn a concept. When we approach a concept formation task, we make up hypotheses about the nature of the concept. (We will discuss these hypotheses in more detail later.) We select a salient, noticeable attribute for our initial hypotheses. Thus we might initially decide to say "yes" to all red flowers and "no" to all white flowers. If these initial hypotheses are correct, we solve the concept quickly. However, if the correct concept involves a less salient attribute, such as angle of branches, we solve the concept slowly. These less salient attributes are not examined until later in the session.

In everyday life we can have difficulty learning concepts when the relevant attributes are not very salient. Flower classification, an example of the scientific or "cold-blooded" classifications we discussed earlier, involves some low-salience attributes. One wild-flowers book I found has a fairly typical classification system (Rickett, 1966). The attributes that are relevant in deciding the group membership of a plant include the following: (1) 12 or fewer stamens versus more than 12 stamens; (2) divided versus nondivided leaves; (3) petals jointed versus petals separate; and (4) leaves in pairs versus leaves borne singly. Flowers belonging to the same family (for example, the rose family) have these kinds of attributes in common.

I recall the outcry that a group of us made as undergraduates in a class in flower classification; it seemed so unfortunate to pay attention to such relatively subtle attributes and ignore more salient attributes! Color and size, for example, are rarely relevant in determining flower classification. Roses, for example, can be white or yellow or pink or red, and they can range in size from 1 cm to about 15 cm. However, all roses resemble each other on the four characteristics mentioned above. Learning flower classifications therefore involves learning to shift your attention from the attributes you had previously regarded as important, and noticing less obvious features.

Think about the attributes of people that you consider to be most salient. Grady (1977) asked people in New York City subways to describe the person who had sold them a subway token. People always mentioned the sex of the seller. To them, sex was more salient than attributes such as race, age, hair color, weight, presence of glasses, and so on.

Rule Discovery.   **Rules,** as we said earlier, tell us how to combine attributes. In some studies the relevant attributes are identified, and the subject must discover what *rule* is being used. In one study, the concept might be *triangle*. All triangles would be considered to be positive instances of the concept, whether they are red or white, large or small. In another study, the concept might involve combined attributes, for example, *red triangles*. Only red triangles would be positive instances; white triangles and red objects that are not triangles would be negative instances. Figure 6.1 illustrates some of the most common rules, or ways in which attributes can be combined. It is worth learning these rules now because we will be referring to them throughout the chapter.

Notice that the critical words are in italics in Figure 6.1. **Conjunction** involves the word *and,* whereas **disjunction** involves *or.* The **conditional** rule, which uses *if,* specifies that all figures in one group are positive instances, but there is an additional condition placed upon another group of figures. For example, if a figure is white, then the only way it can qualify for the concept is if it is square. The **biconditional** rule, which uses *if and only if,* specifies that a figure must have both attributes present (for example, whiteness and squareness), or else neither attribute present (for example, black circles) in order to qualify.

Examples of these rules for combining attributes appear frequently in the prerequisites for certain courses on college campuses. A conjunction rule is used by one professor in order for students to enroll in his course in Psychology of Literature. Students must have completed Introductory Psychology *and* have the permission of the instructor. You cannot qualify unless you possess both of those characteristics. A disjunction rule is used for Physiological Psychology, for which you must have completed Experimental Psychology *or* have the permission of the instructor. Notice that it is easier to qualify under a disjunction rule. You qualify by

---

Figure 6.1   Rules for Combining Attributes in Concept Formation. Imagine four figures, a white square, a white triangle, a black square, and a black triangle. The following rules could be used to combine attributes. Examples of positive instances are provided.

Rule

Conjunction	All figures that are white <u>and</u> square	
Disjunction	All figures that are white <u>or</u> square, or both	
Conditional	<u>If</u> a figure is white, then it must be square to be an example; all black figures are also examples.	
Biconditional	White figures are examples <u>if and only if</u> they are square; all black circles are also examples.	

completing Experimental Psychology, by obtaining the instructor's permission, or by both methods. The only people excluded are those who have neither characteristic.

Conditional rules seldom appear in the formal prerequisites for a course, but these rules may influence the "permission of the instructor" decisions. For example, suppose that I am teaching a course for which I would like the students to have a certain amount of maturity. In particular, I might be reluctant to admit freshmen to the course. I might have a conditional rule in mind, such as, "*If a student is a freshman, then he or she must have had one previous psychology course in order to qualify. All others (sophomores, juniors, and seniors) qualify.*"

It is unlikely that course prerequisites would be worded in terms of a biconditional rule. However, there are some everyday social situations in which the biconditional rule applies. Consider, for example, the issue of wearing appropriate clothing to a party. "Appropriate clothing" can be achieved either by wearing formal clothes to a formal party or by wearing informal clothes to an informal party. We can paraphrase the verbal example for the biconditional in Figure 6.1 to describe how to wear appropriate clothing: formal clothes are examples of appropriate clothing *if and only if* the occasion is formal; informal clothes worn to an informal occasion are also examples of appropriate clothing. In contrast, formal clothes worn to an informal occasion and informal clothes worn to a formal occasion are *not* examples of appropriate clothing.

In rule discovery tasks, people are told what the relevant attributes are, and they must discover the rule for combining them. Try Demonstration 6.2 for an example of a rule discovery task. In a typical study, the series continues until the subject can classify a series of figures without making a mistake and/or can verbalize the rule or concept. (Some studies have stringent criteria, specifying no mistakes *and* verbalizing, so the conjunctive rule applies to their criteria. Others are more lenient, specifying no mistakes *or* verbalizing, with the disjunctive rule applying. Notice how you can already apply your new terms to everyday English.)

As you can imagine, some rules are easier to learn than others. Haygood and Bourne (1965) examined this issue thoroughly, studying the four basic rules listed in Figure 6.1. The setup was similar to the one you tried in Demonstration 6.2, and inexperienced subjects were tested. They found that the conjunction rule ("and") was easiest, followed by the disjunction rule ("or") and the conditional rule ("if"). The hardest rule was the biconditional rule ("if and only if").

Bourne (1974) argues that people do better on concepts that involve the conjunction rule because they are more familiar with this rule from their daily experiences. Because of these preexperimental expectations, they begin by guessing that the concept consists of two attributes being present, such as *window present* and *chimney present*. Try to recall your response to item 1 on Demonstration 6.2; did you guess "yes"? It is difficult to learn the rules other than conjunction because you expect the conjunction rule. Didn't the "yes" answer on item 2 surprise you?

Does training help subjects learn the rules? It depends upon the kind of training. Thompson, Cornell, and Kirkpatrick (1980) found that if you begin by offering people extra training on conjunction concepts, they will do even *worse* on more difficult concepts such as biconditional rules. Training on conjunction

---

Demonstration 6.2   A Rule-Discovery Task.

Before you begin, place a piece of paper so that it hides the correct answers on the right-hand side of the page. Looking only at the figures on the left-hand side, say "yes" if you believe that the figure is an example of the concept, and "no" if you believe that it is not. The attributes "presence or absence of chimney" and "presence or absence of window" are relevant. Your task is to figure out the rule for combining these attributes so that you can decide which figures are examples of the concept. After judging each item, move the paper to see the answer. Continue until you think you know what the concept is, and then check at the end of the chapter to see whether you are correct.

Answers

1.   Yes

2.   Yes

3.   No

4.   Yes

5.   Yes

6.   Yes

7.   Yes

8.   No

---

concepts strengthens even further the expectation for conjunction, and people are extremely resistant to looking for a new rule with which to combine attributes.

However, if you give people training on the less common kinds of rules, they quickly get better at solving these more difficult problems. Bourne (1970) found, for example, that people who had been previously trained on these rules performed almost perfectly after only about six problems. This was true for all kinds of rules—the difficult biconditional rule as well as the easy conjunction rule. It seems likely that when people are practicing on concept formation tasks, one skill they learn is to code the stimuli efficiently. Thus they learn to notice the status of various attributes, and an attribute such as "green color" can be coded as being either present or absent. Once the attributes are properly coded, it is relatively easy to guess the rule and master the concept.

Complete Learning.   We first discussed the kind of experiment in which people knew the rules and were instructed to discover the relevant attributes. Then we discussed the kind of experiment in which people knew which attributes were relevant and were instructed to discover which rule applied to the task. As you can imagine, it is possible to require **complete learning;** the experimenter tells people *nothing* about the task and asks them to discover both the rules and the attributes. This task is much more difficult than either attribute learning or rule learning alone. Try Demonstration 6.3 for an example of complete learning.

Demonstration 6.3   A Complete Learning Task.

Before you begin, place a piece of paper so that it hides the correct answers on the right-hand side of the page. Looking only at the figures on the left-hand side, say "yes" if you believe that the figure is an example of the concept, and "no" if you believe that it is not. Since this is a complete learning task, I will not tell you which attribute is relevant, or which rule is used to combine the attributes. After judging each item, move the paper down to see the answer. Continue until you think you know what the concept is, and then check at the end of the chapter to see whether you are correct.

Answers

1.   Yes

2.   No

3.   Yes

4.   Yes

5.   Yes

6.   No

7.   Yes

8.   Yes

Measuring Concept Formation

In this section we will look at the dependent variable in concept formation studies. As you may recall from other courses, the **dependent variable** involves the behavior of the subject. Somehow, we must measure the subject's responses. (The **independent variable,** in contrast, is the variable that the experimenter manipulates.)

Here is the problem. Subjects working on a concept formation task may indeed be forming a concept. However, one of the central themes of the book is that the cognitive processes are generally unobservable. Concept formation, too, is a **covert** (pronounced "*koe*-vurt"), or hidden process. We need to devise ways to make these thoughts **overt** (pronounced "owe-vurt"), or readily observed. Researchers in the area of concept formation have devised a wide variety of ways of making thoughts overt—perhaps a wider variety than in any other area of cognition. Therefore we will examine these methods in some detail in order to see what kinds of dependent variables can be used to "translate" those private, covert thoughts into measures that a psychologist can observe and record. We will examine performance measures, which emphasize how well a person has learned a concept, and strategy measures, which attempt to assess the strategies people use in learning the concept.

Performance Measures.   Most concept formation studies include some measure of peoples' efficiency in learning a concept. Efficiency of learning is generally measured in one of two ways: (1) the number of trials required to reach a solution or (2) the number of errors the subject makes before reaching a solution. Experimenters also sometimes measure the **latency** of the response, or the time required for the subject to make a response after the stimulus has been presented.

Although learning efficiency and latency are the two most common performance measures, another measure may also be useful: number of incorrect hypotheses. In many studies the experimenter requests the subjects to make a guess as soon as they are reasonably certain about the concept. Naturally, subjects often provide several incorrect hypotheses, or guesses, before they arrive at the correct concept. Experimenters can therefore tally up the number of incorrect hypotheses that the subject gives and use this as an additional dependent variable. Later in the chapter we will discuss an experiment in which number of incorrect hypotheses was a more sensitive measure of learning than the standard measure, the number of trials to solution. Thus the choice of dependent variables can have an important impact on the conclusions an experimenter reaches.

Strategy Measures.   So far we have discussed learning measures, latency measures, and number of incorrect hypotheses. These three kinds of dependent variables are very useful in helping us answer some questions about amount of learning, but they are nearly worthless in answering other questions. For example, none of this information will allow us to identify how the subject might have approached the problem. Many different strategies would be possible, but we cannot specify which strategy the subject actually adopted. We have no measure of what the subject was thinking during any of the trials. Let us discuss two measures that can give us some insight into subjects' strategies.

One important method of assessing strategies is called Levine's Blank Trials Procedure. Later on, we will look at Marvin Levine's (pronounced "Luh-*veen*") hypothesis-testing theory for concept formation. Now, however, we will examine a clever technique that he used to figure out what subjects were thinking as they worked on concept formation tasks. In the **Blank Trials Procedure,** people must respond on a number of trials without receiving any feedback as to whether they are right or wrong (Levine, 1966).

Try Demonstration 6.4 which illustrates the Blank Trials Procedure. The first trial in the sequence is a normal feedback trial. The suspect sees a card, which has two figures that differ with respect to four attributes: (1) black or white *color*; (2) large or small *size*; (3) X or T *shape*; and (4) left or right *position*. The subject guesses which figure is correct. As you can imagine, this is really a wild guess, since the subject has no information on which to base the judgment. Then the experimenter answers either "right" or "wrong." (Naturally, I cannot predict which one you will choose, so in Demonstration 6.4 I will simply specify which answer was correct.)

Then the experimenter presents four new cards. These are Blank Trials since the experimenter does not answer "right" or "wrong" during these four trials. The subject learns nothing during these trials since there is no feedback. The experimenter, on the other hand, learns a lot. Specifically, the experimenter can analyze the responses on those four trials and determine which attribute the subject believes to be correct.

Look over your own answers on Demonstration 6.4. Suppose after seeing pair 1, you believe that "white" is the correct answer. Then you will systematically select the white member from pairs 2−5. Since the correct response for pair 6 is consistent with the answer "white," you might continue with white selections on blank trials 7−10. On pair 11, however, you learn disappointing news: "White" cannot be right. Now if you are fortunate enough to have perfect recall of the other correct answers on pairs 1 and 6, you now know that the answer must be "right." You will therefore select the right-hand member of each pair for pairs 12−15. The answer, shown to you on pair 16, will be no surprise.

Most important, however, notice how you revealed which hypothesis you were currently considering. Consider pairs 2−5, for example. If you picked the white members of each pair, for instance, an experimenter could look at your choices and conclude that you believed that "white" was correct. Thus a person's hypothesis can be inferred from his or her consistent choices during blank trials. The Blank Trials Procedure is therefore a good way to make people's private thoughts more public. You may have guessed one problem with the method, however: It takes a long time, because four trials are necessary each time in order to assess a person's current hypothesis.

Let us now consider an alternative method for determining what people are thinking when they are forming concepts: ask them to think aloud. Dominowski (1974) asked people to do as much as possible of their thinking aloud. They were told to say what they were looking at when a card was presented and what they

Before you begin, place a piece of paper so that it hides the correct answers on the right-hand side of the page. Imagine that each of the boxes below represents a trial in a concept formation task. Circle the member of each pair that you believe to be correct. For this task, only one attribute is relevant; for example, *X* might be positive and *T* might be negative. After judging the first pair, remove the paper so that you can see the answer. The next four trials are blank, so no feedback is provided. Continue until you have finished all of the pairs.

Answers

1. The large, white T on the right is correct

2.

3.

4.

5.

6. The small, white T on the right is correct

7.

8.

9.

10.

11. The large black X on the right is correct

12.

13.

14.

15.

16. The large white T on the right is correct

thought when the correct answer was given. Dominowski notes that the subjects thought that they had given rather complete and accurate **protocols,** or verbal reports, of what they had been thinking. Thus one way to make covert ideas *overt* is simply to ask people to verbalize them.

However, there is a drawback to the thinking-aloud method. People may somehow perform the task differently if they must think aloud. Dominowski notes that it seems almost inevitable that changing the task in this way will somehow affect performance. It may be that the "think aloud" instructions encourage people to use some particular method for concept formation to a greater extent than if they learned normally (silently). On the other hand, the "think aloud" instructions may simply result in people working more *carefully* but not changing their basic strategies.

Let us examine further the possibility that we might change people's behavior by asking them to think aloud. This is a very intriguing problem: By the measurement process, we are changing the very behavior we are trying to measure! In other words, we are trying to measure people's concept formation strategies. However, if we measure them by having people think aloud, they use different strategies. We would therefore measure the wrong behavior. This problem occurs frequently in psychology. People notice the measurement process and react differently than they normally would. Consequently, we may really be measuring the reaction to our measurement. This problem is frequently discussed, particularly by experimental psychologists and social psychologists. Sometimes the measurement process can be made more subtle. Other times the problem cannot be readily resolved.

We have looked at two ways to assess subjects' strategies on concept formation tasks. Although these methods may have disadvantages, they do allow us to assess some covert thought processes that are involved when people group objects into concepts.

SECTION SUMMARY: Introduction and How Concept Formation Is Studied

1. Humans use two kinds of classifications, intuitive and formal (or "cold-blooded").
2. Concepts are helpful and necessary because: (a) otherwise each event would be unique; (b) they allow economy in memory; (c) they reduce the necessity of constant learning; (d) they let us know how to react to an object; and (e) they permit us to relate classes of objects.
3. A concept formation task can involve learning which attributes are relevant, learning which rule is being used, or learning both attributes and rule (complete learning).
4. Concepts are learned more quickly when the relevant attribute is a salient one.
5. Four rules for combining attributes are: conjunction ("and"), disjunction ("or"), conditional ("if"), and biconditional ("if and only if"). The

conjunction rule is easiest and the biconditional rule is the most difficult. Training on the more difficult rules can be helpful.

6. There are several dependent variables that measure subjects' performance, though they cannot reveal subjects' strategies: (a) learning measures, such as number of trials prior to solution and number of errors; (b) latency measures; and (c) number of incorrect hypotheses.

7. There are two techniques that can reveal subjects' strategies: (a) The Blank Trials Procedure, in which subjects respond without feedback for several "blank trials"; and (b) the thinking-aloud method, in which subjects report their thoughts as they work on concept formation tasks.

Factors Affecting Concept Formation

In the previous section we discussed how the factor "type of rule" can influence learning difficulty. The conjunction rule was the easiest to learn, and the biconditional rule was the most difficult. We also saw that learning was easiest when the relevant attribute was a salient one. Many other factors have been studied as well.

Dominowski (1974) demonstrates quite vividly how a psychologist who is interested in factors affecting concept formation could spend his or her entire career on this project. Suppose, for example, that this psychologist were to limit the factors to a modest number, seven:

1. Type of rule (simple, conjunction, or disjunction)
2. Task (attribute learning, rule learning, or complete learning)
3. Number of relevant attributes (2 or 3)
4. Number of irrelevant attributes (1, 2, 4, or 8)
5. Control of sequence (experimenters present stimuli or subjects select stimuli)
6. Categorization (subjects required to categorize stimuli when they are first seen, or not)
7. Stimulus availability (previous stimuli available for inspection, or not)

With just these seven factors, the psychologist would study about 600 different situations!

We will limit our discussion to just three factors in this section: number of attributes; positive versus negative examples; and environmental factors.

Number of Attributes

Many people have studied how the number of attributes influences learning (e.g., Laughlin, 1973). You can probably guess what these studies demonstrate. First of all, people take longer to learn a concept when there are many *relevant* attributes. The task in Demonstration 6.1, for example, had only one relevant attribute, the type of eyebrows. Imagine how much more difficult the task would have been if there had been three relevant attributes. Perhaps type of eyebrows, presence or absence of nose, and round- versus oval-shaped head could all have been relevant attributes. A positive example of the concept might be a round-shaped head with a nose and angled eyebrows. Certainly, this would be more difficult to learn than simply angled eyebrows.

The number of *irrelevant* attributes also influences concept learning. In Demonstration 6.1 you had two irrelevant attributes, eyes open versus closed and smiling versus frowning mouth. This task was more difficult than if there had been no irrelevant attributes. Imagine how easy it would be if all faces had closed eyes and smiles, and the only attribute that varied was the relevant attribute, eyebrows. However, your task was easier than if there had been seven irrelevant attributes. When the number of irrelevant attributes is increased in a concept formation task, people may pay attention to an irrelevant attribute and ignore a relevant one. Therefore they are more likely to choose a useless hypothesis.

Positive and Negative Examples

Try Demonstration 6.5, which shows you how difficult it is to learn a concept when you are provided with negative examples, rather than positive examples. Experimenters agree that **positive examples,** in which you are given examples of the concept, are more useful than **negative examples,** in which you are given examples of what the concept is *not*. This was first demonstrated by Smoke (1932), who showed that negative examples were almost useless in concept formation.

Demonstration 6.5 *Learning a Concept from Negative Examples.*

Each of the following is *not* an example of a particular concept. Cut a window in a piece of paper so that you can see only one example at a time. When you are done with the eleventh trial, guess what the concept is. (The answer is at the end of the chapter.)

1. △ △
2. ○
3. △
4. □ □
5. ▣
6. △
7. ◎◎
8. △ △
9. ○ ○
10. ▣ ▣
11. □

Why are negative examples so useless? Hovland and Weiss (1953) suggested one possible explanation: Positive examples may give the learner more information than negative examples. After all, it is more useful to know what something *is* than what it *is not!* In their experiment, Hovland and Weiss made certain that the positive and negative examples conveyed the same amount of information. Even with this provision, the subjects still learned faster with positive examples. In one condition, for instance, 100 percent of the subjects in the positive-examples condition learned the concept, in contrast to only 17 percent of the subjects in the negative-examples condition. Hovland and Weiss concluded that the negative examples are harder because people find it more difficult to *make use of* the negative information.

You may recognize that the fact about positive and negative examples is another instance of one of the themes of the book: The cognitive processes handle positive information better than negative information. We perform better on concept formation tasks if we know which items *are* examples of a concept than if we know which items *are not* examples of the concept. So far, we have seen similar tendencies in understanding and remembering language. We are better able to deal with *what is,* rather than *what is not.*

The results of another study on positive and negative examples are more hopeful. Freibergs and Tulving (1961) showed that people can learn from negative examples if they receive extensive training. People who learned concepts with only negative examples had great difficulty initially in solving those concepts. However, after working on approximately 11 different concept formation tasks, their solution times decreased impressively, to about 5 percent of the original time. In fact, a similar group of people who learned concepts with only positive examples were only a few seconds faster in learning each concept by the end of the training period.

Freibergs and Tulving remark that their experiment sheds no light on why practice is effective, particularly in the case of the negative examples. It seems likely, however, that the experiment demonstrated a general phenomenon called "learning to learn." **Learning to learn** means that experience in solving one problem influences the way we approach later problems. For example, discovering the concept underlying one set of stimuli has an influence on the way a person approaches the next concept formation task. Similarly, you may recall that Bourne (1970) found that people who had been trained on the less common kinds of concept formation rules increased their solution speeds markedly.

It is interesting to speculate about the specific changes that might occur as people "learn to learn" negative-example tasks. Do they learn to code the stimuli more effectively? Do they learn to draw implications more readily, so that the information that four green diamonds is *not* an example can readily be translated into information about the stimuli that *are* examples? Do they learn to form mental images of these absent stimuli that are examples? Do they learn to devise a formal tabulation system for keeping track of attributes? What other changes would you think might occur as people learn how to form concepts based on negative examples?

The Freibergs and Tulving study also suggests that people might be able to learn how to process other kinds of negative information more effectively. It is

Figure 6.2 *An Example of the Concept "Pedestal" and Four "Near Misses."* (After Winston, 1973.)

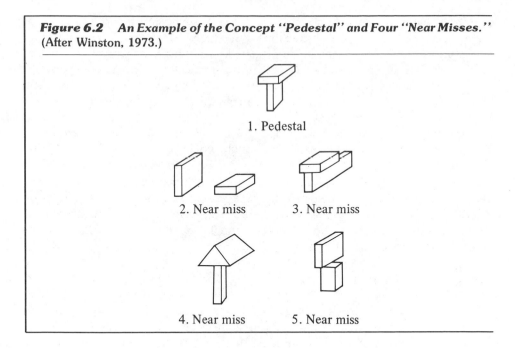

1. Pedestal

2. Near miss   3. Near miss

4. Near miss   5. Near miss

possible that people could learn to understand and remember negative sentences effectively if given sufficient practice.

Winston (1973) has pointed out that negative information can occasionally be very useful. In particular, it is sometimes useful to teach "near misses" in addition to positive examples of a concept. A **near miss** is an example that differs from the concept because of one or a few important deficiencies. Winston's paper describes a computer program in which the computer is taught how to identify toy block structures. Imagine teaching either a computer or a child the concept of a pedestal. Notice in Figure 6.2 how only the first figure is truly a pedestal. Each of the other figures is a near miss, for one reason or another. In the other figures, the base and the horizontal surface are separate, the base is too wide, the surface is not flat, or the surface is not horizontal. It is not enough to say that a pedestal consists of two blocks. You must also say what a pedestal is *not*.

Children often learn concepts by providing near misses and receiving correction from adults. Recently, for example, my daughter referred to someone's birthday, which was to be celebrated on July 10 rather than on July 13, as a "belated birthday." She had properly understood that the word "belated" indicated a discrepancy between the true date and the date of celebration. However, her use of the phrase indicated a "near miss" because it differed from the appropriate use of "belated" in one important respect. A belated birthday can only be celebrated after the true birthday, and not before.

Environmental Factors

Surprisingly few studies in concept formation have examined the importance of environmental factors in learning. Psychologists often tend to think of the concept learner alone in a relatively soundproof room, learning red triangles and black squares, without any obvious distractions. What happens to concept learning when the environment is not so simple? For example, what happens when the environment includes other people? Let us look at two studies that examine this question.

Have you ever been videotaped or watched someone being videotaped? How do you suppose that this procedure might influence performance? Laughlin, Chenoweth, Farrell, and McGrath (1972) videotaped some subjects in their experiment in order to see how people solved concepts when they were being videotaped, a situation that the authors thought would be stressful. Other subjects, in a control condition, were not videotaped. The authors used two dependent variables, number of trials to solution and number of incorrect hypotheses—that is, hypotheses that were inconsistent with the available information. The videotape-condition subjects did not differ from control subjects in terms of the number of trials to solution. However, the videotape-condition subjects did provide a greater number of incorrect hypotheses.

Notice, incidentally, that "number of incorrect hypotheses" was a more sensitive measure of performance than number of trials to solution. If the researchers had simply used the one dependent variable, number of trials to solution, they would have concluded that stress caused by videotaping had no observable influence on performance. This study clearly demonstrates the point we discussed earlier: The choice of an independent variable has an important influence on the conclusions of an experiment.

Another study showed that environmental variables can interact with other variables (Shrauger, 1972). The subjects in this study worked on a concept formation task, sometimes alone and sometimes with an "audience," a male and a

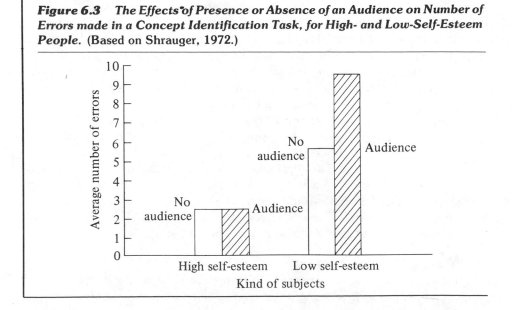

Figure 6.3   The Effects of Presence or Absence of an Audience on Number of Errors made in a Concept Identification Task, for High- and Low-Self-Esteem People. (Based on Shrauger, 1972.)

female who were said to be interested in the experiment. Shrauger also measured self-esteem for each subject. This measure was derived by asking such questions as "What percentage of people of your own age and sex have a more pleasing personal appearance than you?" Thus, we have two variables in this study: (1) presence or absence of an audience, and (2) high or low self-esteem.

Figure 6.3 shows the results of the study. Notice that people with high self-esteem generally perform more accurately than people with low self-esteem. More interesting than that result, however, is the interaction. A statistical **interaction** means that a variable has different effects under different conditions. In this case, the variable "presence or absence of audience" had a different effect upon the condition of high self-esteem than it did upon the condition of low self-esteem. People who have a high regard for themselves are not influenced by whether anyone else is watching them. However, people who have a low regard for themselves make many more errors when someone else is watching. If you are a person with low self-esteem, remember this study the next time you are working on anything that resembles concept formation. Find yourself a lonely spot where you can be certain no one can watch you!

SECTION SUMMARY: Factors Affecting Concept Formation

1. People take longer to learn a concept when there are many **relevant** attributes.
2. People take longer to learn a concept when there are many **irrelevant** attributes.
3. Positive examples are more useful than negative examples. However, people can be trained to use negative examples.
4. Examples of "near-misses" can be helpful in teaching concepts.
5. Environmental factors, such as the videotaping of performance and having an audience present, can cause slower concept learning under certain conditions.

Testing Hypotheses

Many different theories have been proposed for how people form concepts. One idea that underlies many of these theories is that people try to solve concepts by making up **hypotheses,** or tentative guesses as to the nature of the concept, and then testing them. In this section we will look at two of these hypothesis-testing theories: an early theory proposed by Bruner, Goodnow, and Austin (1956) and a more recent theory proposed by Levine (1975).

Strategies in Concept Formation (Bruner)

Bruner (pronounced "*Broo*-ner") and his colleagues wrote a book called *A Study of Thinking,* in which they argued that people actively tackle concept formation tasks. These authors observed that people typically use strategies in order to learn concepts. A **strategy** according to Bruner, is a consistent, orderly method for making decisions, rather than a disorganized, random pattern. People use strategies in order to solve the concept quickly and reliably without straining either their memories or their reasoning skills.

Try Demonstration 6.6 to understand the setup for a typical study conducted by Bruner. In his experiments Bruner presented all possible examples at once and requested people to discover the concepts by asking whether certain figures were instances of the concept. Notice that this method is different from the standard concept formation tasks in which the experimenter presents only one or two figures at the same time.

Demonstration 6.6   . *Strategies in Concept Formation.*

You will need a friend to serve as an experimenter in this demonstration. Your friend should look at this display of figures and decide upon a concept that he or she wants you to acquire—for example, three lines in the border. The friend should point to *one* instance of the concept. Now you select a figure and ask whether that figure is an example of the concept. Your friend should reply either ''yes'' or ''no.'' Continue to ask about additional figures until you are fairly certain that you have identified the concept. (From Bruner, Goodnow, and Austin, 1956.)

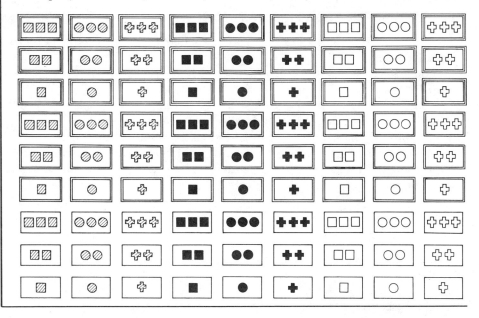

Bruner found that people did not make random guesses in order to acquire concepts. Instead, they used strategies. Let us discuss the two most common strategies, conservative focusing and focus gambling.

Conservative focusing occurs when people focus upon the figure that the experimenter chose as a positive example. In future trials they systematically select a figure that differs from the focus figure on only *one* attribute. For example, suppose that the experimenter for Demonstration 6.6 told you that the figure of one white cross with one border was an example of the concept. To use the conservative focusing strategy, you would vary only one attribute in selecting the next figure. For example, you might decide to vary number, selecting the figure of two white crosses with one border. If the experimenter says "no," you conclude that number is relevant. However, if the experimenter says "yes" to this figure, you know that number is not a relevant attribute, but shape, color, and border might be. (On later trials, you systematically test each of these attributes.) This strategy is safe, and it guarantees a solution eventually.

Focus gambling occurs when people focus upon the positive example, but on future trials they select figures that differ from the focus figure on *two* or more attributes. For example, if one white *cross* with *three borders* was an example of the concept, you might decide to vary two attributes, shape and number of borders. You might select one white *circle* with *one border*. This strategy may allow you to "get rich quick." For example, if the experimenter responds "yes" to this stimulus, you know that both number and shape are irrelevant; either color or border must be relevant. Notice that the subject does take a gamble with this method. You win the gamble if you receive a "yes" answer, but you lose if you receive a "no." You do not know which of the attributes that you changed—number or shape—is relevant.

Now return to Demonstration 6.6 and try the conservative focusing and focus gambling strategies. Conservative focusing is probably the most common strategy, as well as the easiest to use. It is less of a strain on your memory, and you will certainly solve the concept. Focus gambling, on the other hand, may pay off if there is time pressure.

Think about how you use these strategies in your daily life. For example, suppose that you slept very well last night, and you would like to determine which attributes are associated with the concept *good night's sleep*. You might decide to use the conservative focusing strategy and change just one attribute of the situation each evening. Perhaps last night you skipped your coffee at dinner, read a relaxing novel before bedtime, and slept with the window closed. With the conservative focusing strategy, you would test one hypothesis at a time. The first night, for example, you might drink coffee, but still read the novel and keep the window closed. The second night, you would test the "novel reading" hypothesis, and the third night, you would test the "window closed" hypothesis. The strategy of systematically changing one attribute at a time is the basis of the experimental research method (e.g., Matlin, 1979, pp. 12–15).

However, you may prefer a focus gambling strategy; you change all the variables at once. On the first night of your "experiment" you drink coffee, study before bedtime, and sleep with the window open. Unfortunately, if you have trouble falling asleep, you will not know which of the three factors was responsible.

Levine's Theory of Hypothesis Testing

Levine's (1975) theory of hypothesis testing has had a long history, which has been traced in his book, *A Cognitive Theory of Learning*. Many psychologists in the 19 years between Bruner's and Levine's books contributed to Levine's theory of concept formation.

Levine's theory about the nature of subjects' hypotheses is quite detailed. To a large extent, this detail is possible because his methods allowed him to know what hypotheses his subjects were considering. As you may recall, Levine's Blank Trials Procedure (see Demonstration 6.4) provided for trials without feedback. Subjects expressed their current hypothesis through their choices on these blank trials.

Levine proposed that people begin a concept formation task with a "pool" of hypotheses. In Demonstration 6.4, for example, there would be eight hypotheses in the pool: *X, T,* black, white, large, small, left, and right. From this pool each person selects a subset of hypotheses, which may be any number between one and the total number in the pool, or $1-8$ in our example. The exact number that the person selects will depend upon the difficulty of the problem, characteristics of the subjects, and so on.

From this subset, the subject selects a **working hypothesis,** which is one single hypothesis upon which the responses will be based. The feedback following the subject's response will determine what happens to the working hypothesis. For example, you might begin Demonstration 6.4 with the working hypothesis *white.* If the feedback is consistent with your working hypothesis or if you are working on blank trials (without feedback), you retain your working hypothesis. Thus, in Demonstration 6.4, you would keep the working hypothesis *white* until trial 11. After all, if your hypothesis has not been contradicted, there is no reason to change.

However, if the feedback contradicts your working hypothesis, you change to a new working hypothesis. For example, after trial 11 it would be clear that the working hypothesis *white* was not correct. Therefore you would process as much as you could remember of previous trials and shift to another working hypothesis. Levine proposes that subjects have more work to do after receiving contradicting feedback than after receiving either consistent feedback or no feedback at all. In those latter two situations, you could sit back and keep the same hypothesis. With the feedback that your working hypothesis has been incorrect, however, you know that you must shift. Unfortunately, you have to choose a new working hypothesis. This means that you must find a new hypothesis that is consistent with the current feedback, and also consistent with as much of the previous feedback as you can remember.

According to Levine, it is likely that you had several hypotheses "on the back burner" while you were using your working hypothesis. These constitute the subset of hypotheses, the ones that you selected from the whole pool of hypotheses. You responded in terms of your working hypothesis, yet you were also keeping track of these other hypotheses whenever you received feedback. For example, although your working hypothesis was *white,* you might also have been keeping track of the hypotheses *large, T,* and *right.*

Levine's research confirmed that people keep track of more than one hypothesis at a time. In one study, Levine (1966) calculated the number of trials required to solve a concept formation task if a subject had perfect memory. This imaginary subject would be able to keep track of all of the hypotheses that were consistent with the feedback. This miraculous subject would also refuse to adopt, as a working hypothesis, any hypothesis that had previously been rejected. This person, when working on a task with a total of eight possible hypotheses, should be able to figure out the concept after only three trials. In other words, after three trials, there would be only one remaining hypothesis. Levine then tested college students on the concept formation task and found that after three trials the average subject was currently considering between two and three remaining concepts. Thus, college student adults have impressive memories for the information in concept formation tasks—they are quite close to the ideal.

The strategy outlined by Levine is often called global focusing. According to the **global focusing strategy,** the subject is able to keep track of many hypotheses at the same time and reject those hypotheses that are not consistent with the feedback. Evidence from other studies supports the global focusing strategy when the subjects are intelligent adults and when the task is as simple as the one in Demonstration 6.4. When people have more limited memory skills, or when the task is more difficult, they often adopt another strategy.

SECTION SUMMARY: Testing Hypotheses

1. Many theories suggest that people try to solve concepts by making up hypotheses. Two such theories have been proposed by Bruner and his colleagues and by Levine.
2. Bruner argued that people use strategies for making decisions, rather than responding randomly.
3. Bruner found that people frequently used two different kinds of strategies: (a) conservative focusing, in which they focus upon the first positive example and change one attribute each time; (b) focus gambling, in which they change two or more attributes each time.
4. Bruner found that conservative focusing was the most popular strategy, though focus gambling may be appropriate if there is time pressure.
5. Levine's theory, based upon his Blank Trials Procedure, stated that people select a working hypothesis upon which responses are based. They change the working hypothesis if it is contradicted by the feedback.
6. According to Levine's theory, people keep track of several alternate hypotheses in addition to the working hypothesis. This strategy is called the global focusing strategy.
7. Levine's research demonstrated that college student adults have impressive memories for the information in concept formation tasks.

Natural Categories

Several psychologists have argued quite strongly that the typical concept formation experiments are very artificial. In 1973 Eleanor Rosch (pronounced "Rahsh") was among the first to make this point. She notes that the concepts learned are very arbitrary and differ from the concepts we use in everyday life. For example, the stimuli typically consist of neatly defined, discrete attributes. How often are the categories we have in "real life" really precise, so that one category consists of red squares with two borders and another consists of green circles with one border? Furthermore, Rosch complains, the categories in concept formation experiments are already well known to the subjects. American college sophomores who participate in these experiments learned the concepts *red* and *square* long ago.

In addition, Rosch points out that the experimenters can arbitrarily combine any characteristics in any way they wish in these concept formation studies. Characteristics cannot be arbitrarily combined for real-life concepts, however. Do you know anything that belongs to this arbitrary combination of categories: has fur, flies in the air, rigid, and magenta? As Rosch, Mervis, Gray, Johnson, and Boyes-Braem (1976) observe, humans do not carve up their world into arbitrary random categories. Instead, Rosch and her colleagues propose that

> [the] world is structured because real-world attributes do not occur independently of each other. Creatures with feathers are more likely also to have wings than creatures with fur, and objects with the visual appearance of chairs are more likely to have functional sit-on-ableness than objects with the appearance of cats. That is, combinations of attributes of real objects do not occur uniformly. (p. 383)

Rosch also points out that the concepts studied in experiments differ from real-life concepts because of their structure. As soon as the subjects in an experiment have learned a concept, then all of the stimuli that fit the rule are equally good examples of the concept. For example, the red square on one card is just as good an example of the concept *red square* as is the red square on any other card. That is *not* true for real-life concepts, however. Don't you think that a sparrow is a better example of the concept *bird* than a penguin is?

In short, Rosch argues that concept formation experiments are designed to answer the kind of question that requires limited, controlled stimuli. These experiments, however, do not show us the whole range of concepts that humans actually have. Therefore, Rosch, her colleagues, and others have conducted a large number of studies on real-life concepts, or **natural categories.**

Characteristics of Prototypes

Rosch and her colleagues point out that there are several ways that natural categories could be organized (Rosch, 1977). For example, each category could consist of a list of the individual members of the category. The category *bird,* for example, could be organized simply as a list of types of birds—robins, sparrows, chickens, turkeys, pheasants, scarlet ibises, blue herons, eagles, ostriches, penguins, and so on. Another possibility is that each category has a list of formal criteria or requirements that are necessary and sufficient in order to belong to that category. This **defining-features theory** of categories states that *every* item that meets the specified requirements belongs to the category; items that do not meet the requirements belong to another category. Defining features for the category *bird* might include "has feathers," "lays eggs," and "flies." According to both the member-list theory and the defining-features theory, all members of a category have equal status. A penguin belongs to the category *bird* just as much as a robin does.

Rosch and others prefer a prototype theory. According to the **prototype theory,** people decide whether an item belongs to a category by comparing that item with a **prototype** (pronounced "*proe*-toe-tipe"), or best example of the category. If the item is similar to the prototype, the item is included in the category. However, if the item is different, it is placed in another category, in which it resembles the prototype for that category more closely. Members of a category can therefore differ in their **prototypicality,** or degree to which they are prototypical. A robin and a sparrow are very prototypical, and ostriches and penguins are very low in prototypicality. In fact, ostriches and penguins could be called **non-prototypes** because they are so far removed from the prototype of a bird.

Incidentally, the term *prototype* should sound familiar, because we have discussed it in two earlier chapters. In Chapter 2, we discussed the prototype theory of pattern recognition. In Chapter 4, we mentioned prototypes in connection with the distance estimation studies of Golledge and Zannaras (1973). We will reconsider prototypes in Chapter 11 when we discuss whether some prototypes are universal.

Think about prototypes for categories you know. First of all, try to get an image of the prototypical bird. Now, if you have a dictionary that has pictures, look up the word *bird* and notice what picture they have used. It probably matches your image quite well; it is not any specific, identifiable bird, but a prototypical bird. As George A. Miller once mentioned in a lecture, that picture is BIRD (with all capital letters) rather than any one bird. Think of a prototype, or most typical member, for a particular group on campus, such as a fraternity, sorority, or other club. Also think of a nonprototype ("You mean he's a Theta Kappa? He doesn't seem at all like one!"). Think of a prototype for a professor, a fruit, and a murder weapon, and then think of nonprototypes for each category. A very young, attractive woman professor would be nonprototypical for most college students. A tomato is a nonprototypical fruit, and an icicle is a nonprototypical murder weapon.

What are the characteristics of prototypes? Rosch and her colleagues have conducted many studies in this area. They provide strong support for the argument that all members of a category are *not* equal. Instead, each category is organized in terms of a prototype, and members of the category differ in their prototypicality. We will consider six characteristics or prototypes—six ways in which prototype members of a category differ from nonprototype members.

1. *Categories based on prototypes are learned quickly.* Rosch (1973) proposed that people would learn new categories quickly if these categories were naturally structured, or organized around a prototype. In contrast, learning would be slow if the categories were "unnaturally structured," or organized around a nonprototype. Rosch examined the learning of color categories, and she needed to find a group of people who did not have a complicated color-term system. She chose members of the Dani tribe, a group of people in New Guinea who have only two color terms—roughly equivalent to *light* and *dark*—in their vocabulary.

There were many different conditions in Rosch's experiment; we will just look at two of them. In set 1, eight prototype colors were selected. Eight categories were then constructed, based on those prototypes, by selecting two additional colors for each category. Each category consisted of the prototype color plus one color on each side of the prototype color. For example, one category might consist of a pure blue color (the prototype), a blue color tending slightly toward green, and a blue color tending slightly toward purple. This category would correspond to the natural category we would call *blue*. It is naturally structured since it is based on a prototype color.

In set 2, however, Rosch began with eight colors that were not prototypes; these colors were selected from regions of the color chart that have no common name in English. Eight categories were again constructed by selecting one color on each side of these nonprototype colors. For example, one category might consist of a reddish brown (the nonprototype), a reddish brown with more red added, and reddish brown with more brown added. This category is unnaturally structured. If someone forced you, you might choose the name *reds and browns* for this category, but no one-word name would spring to your lips.

The study used the paired-associate approach that we discussed in Chapter 3. People saw the colors as stimuli and were asked to supply the same response to all the members of the same category. They kept trying until they could give the correct answer to all 24 colors. Figure 6.4 shows the number of errors they made on each of the two sets. Clearly, the items in set 1, in which the prototype colors were central, were the easiest to learn. If a category has a natural organization, learning will be relatively fast.

In a second study, Rosch (1973) extended her findings into another perceptual area, form. Once again, members of the Dani tribe were chosen as subjects because they did not have names for geometric shapes. One set of stimuli was based upon a regular, standard prototype, such as a square. Part A of Figure 6.5 shows what the members of the *square* category were. Notice how each of the six transformations can be derived from the basic, perfect square. Another set of stimuli was based upon an irregular figure that was *not* a prototype, such as a crude, hand-drawn square. The members of the *hand-drawn square* category appear in part B of Figure 6.5.

Rosch's results showed that people learned the categories that were based on regular prototypes (such as the squares in part A) more quickly than other categories. For example, they made about three times as many errors when they learned the hand-drawn categories as when they learned the basic-shape categories

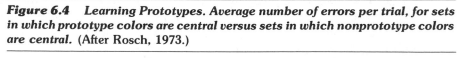

Figure 6.4   *Learning Prototypes. Average number of errors per trial, for sets in which prototype colors are central versus sets in which nonprototype colors are central.* (After Rosch, 1973.)

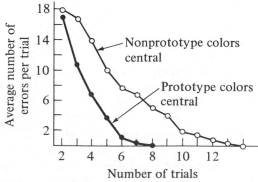

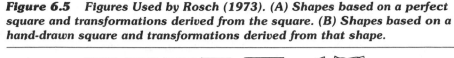

Figure 6.5 **Figures Used by Rosch (1973). (A) Shapes based on a perfect square and transformations derived from the square. (B) Shapes based on a hand-drawn square and transformations derived from that shape.**

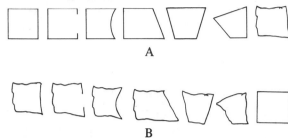

in set 1. Thus, people learn categories fastest when they are organized around natural prototypes, such as a true red or a perfect square. If categories are organized "unnaturally," so that an off-red or an imperfect square is central, learning will be more difficult.

2. *Prototypes serve as reference points.* Try Demonstration 6.7, which illustrates how prototypes serve as reference points and how other items are compared to these reference points. This demonstration is based on two studies by Rosch (1975a). In the first study, similar to part A in the demonstration, people saw pairs of numbers, colors, or lines. For the numbers, one member of each pair was a prototype—that is, a multiple of 10 that should be relevant in our decimal number system (e.g., 10, 50, or 100). The other member of the pair was a number of about the same size, but not a multiple of 10 (e.g., 11, 48, or 103). For the colors, one member of each pair was a prototype color (red, yellow, green, and blue), and the other member was a nonprototype color (e.g., purplish red). For the lines, one member was a line in a "standard" position (exactly horizontal, exactly vertical, and 45° diagonal) and the other member was a line in a position rotated 10° from the standard position. In each case, then, Rosch wanted to determine which pair member served as a reference point, the stimulus to which the other member was compared.

Her results showed quite clearly that the prototypes tended to serve as the reference points. For example, people were more likely to say "11 is essentially 10," rather than "10 is essentially 11." Check your answers in Demonstration 6.7. Did the prototypes, which are multiples of 10, occur second in the sentence, as if they were standards to which all other numbers are compared?

Rosch's second study used a different method, which was more physical than linguistic. As in part B in Demonstration 6.7, people placed pairs of items (for example, two numbers) on a surface. When the prototype served as the reference point, the other item was placed relatively close to it. However, when the nonprototype served as the reference point, the other item was placed relatively far away. Now check your own responses on this task by measuring the distance between each of the pairs of items. Is the distance between 10 and 13 shorter than the distance between 13 and 10, as Rosch would predict?

Demonstration 6.7   *Prototypes as Reference Points.*

A. Pairs of items are listed below, together with a sentence with two blanks. Choose one item to fill the first blank, and place the other item in the second blank. Take your time, try the items both ways, and choose the way in which the "sentence" seems to make the most sense.

1. (10, 11)   _____ is essentially _____
2. (103, 100)   _____ is sort of _____
3. (48, 50)   _____ is roughly _____
4. (1000, 1004)   _____ is basically _____

B. Take out four sheets of blank paper. Take the first number of each of the pairs listed below, and place it on the left-hand margin of a sheet of paper. Then draw a line to represent how far away the second number is from the first, as in the illustration below. Judge each pair in isolation from the other pairs. The same number appears more than once, but you do not need to be consistent in your judgments. Work as quickly as you can.

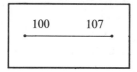

1. (14, 10)
2. (10, 13)
3. (10, 14)
4. (13, 10)

Notice what Rosch's results are saying: the distance from 10 to 13 is less than the distance from 13 to 10. This contradicts everything your third-grade teacher taught you about subtraction. The human mind does not treat these distances as equal, however, because some numbers are more important than others. These numbers serve as reference points, or landmarks, and other numbers are compared with these landmarks.

Actually, we discussed the concept of physically equal distances being judged as unequal in the chapter on imagery in the discussion of distances on mental maps. Briggs (1971) found that people gave small estimates of distance for the number of miles between a given point and a familiar location. On the other hand, they gave large estimates of distance for the number of miles between the same point and an unfamiliar location. When we use a prototype as a reference point, other items cluster in quite closely to that reference point. When we use a nonprototype—some item that is not the best example of its type—as a reference point, other items keep their distance!

3. *Prototypes have common attributes in a family resemblance category.* Before we look at common attributes and prototypes, we must discuss in some detail a new phrase: family resemblance.

The philosopher Wittgenstein (1953) was the first to discuss the family resemblance aspect of natural categories. Wittgenstein asks us to consider the kind of attributes that are shared by concepts such as *games*.

> Consider for example the proceedings that we call "games." I mean board-games, card-games, ball-games, Olympic games, and so on. What is common to them all?—Don't say, "There *must* be something common, or they would not be called 'games' "—but *look and see* whether there is anything common to all. For if you look at them you will not see something that is common to *all,* but similarities, relationships, and a whole series of them at that. (p. 31)

Think about the games you know. How is Monopoly similar to bridge? How are ball games similar to either of those? You might respond that competition is always involved, but then think about the children's game "Ring around the Rosie"—no competition there. Some games involve skill, but some depend upon luck instead. Notice how each game shares some attribute with some other game, yet there is no one attribute that is shared by all games. In fact, the members of the concept *games* have a family resemblance to each other. **Family resemblance** means that there is no single attribute that is shared by all examples of a concept, yet each example has at least one attribute in common with some other example of the concept. The term *family resemblance* is a good one. Think about your own family members and the family resemblance they share. Look at Figure 6.6, which

---

Figure 6.6　Family Resemblance. The family of Arthur and Alice White (center of picture), their five children (the woman and two men on the top left of the photo and the two men on the top right) with their spouses, and 13 grandchildren. (I am the middle of the three girls in the lower right.) There are two sets of twins in this photo, so the number of shared attributes is greater than it might be in many families.

is a picture of my father's family. Each person here looks like at least one other person in the picture. However, it is possible to locate two people who have very few characteristics in common—about as few as "Ring around the Rosie" and bridge.

Think about some other concepts that show family resemblance patterns. One concept that occurred to me as I was preparing this book was the concept *cognition*. I looked at several cognition textbooks that had been published, and I discovered that there was no single topic that was covered in all of the books. Most books covered memory, but one did not. Some books covered problem solving and concept formation, but others did not. Only two books covered decision making. As Table 6.1 shows, there is no single attribute shared by all examples of a concept, yet each example has at least one attribute in common with some other example of the concept. Clearly, authors' examples of the concept of cognition show a family resemblance to one another.

Rosch and Mervis (1975) examined the role of prototypes in family resemblances. Specifically, they proposed that the items that people judge to be most prototypical will have the greatest number of attributes in common with other members of the category. In one study, for example, they used members of categories that had previously been rated for their prototypicality; we will call these ratings **prototype ratings.** Table 6.2 shows three of the categories. For vehicle, notice that *car* was rated as the most prototypical member, whereas *elevator* was rated as least prototypical. Check over these lists to see whether they agree with your ideas of which items are the best and worst examples of each category. Rosch and Mervis asked a new group of people to list the attributes possessed by each item. For the word *dog,* for instance, they were told to list attributes like having four legs, barking, having fur, and so on.

Two judges then gathered together all the items and all the attributes for each category. From this information they calculated a number that showed the extent to which an item's attributes were also shared by other members of the same category. For example, *car* would probably share its attributes with many other members of the vehicle category. Like many other items on that list, it has wheels, moves horizontally, uses fuel, and encloses the passenger. An *elevator*, on the other hand, shares its attributes with few other members: it operates by pulleys, moves vertically, and is usually enclosed within a building.

Rosch and Mervis therefore had two measures for each category member: its

TABLE 6.1   Family Resemblance

	Memory	*Language*	*Concept Formation*	*Problem Solving*	*Decision Making*
Book A	+	+	+	+	+
Book B	−	+	−	+	−
Book C	+	+	−	−	−
Book D	+	−	−	+	+
Book E	+	+	+	−	−
Book F	+	+	+	+	−

Note: Topics covered in each of six books on cognition. No topic is covered in all six books, yet there is a family resemblance among the six examples of the concept of cognition.

TABLE 6.2   Prototype Ratings for Words in Three Categories

	Category		
Item	*Vehicle*	*Vegetable*	*Clothing*
1	Car	Peas	Pants
2	Truck	Carrots	Shirt
3	Bus	String beans	Dress
4	Motorcycle	Spinach	Skirt
5	Train	Broccoli	Jacket
6	Trolley car	Asparagus	Coat
7	Bicycle	Corn	Sweater
8	Airplane	Cauliflower	Underwear
9	Boat	Brussel sprouts	Socks
10	Tractor	Lettuce	Pajamas
11	Cart	Beets	Bathing suit
12	Wheelchair	Tomato	Shoes
13	Tank	Lima beans	Vest
14	Raft	Eggplant	Tie
15	Sled	Onion	Mittens
16	Horse	Potato	Hat
17	Blimp	Yam	Apron
18	Skates	Mushroom	Purse
19	Wheelbarrow	Pumpkin	Wristwatch
20	Elevator	Rice	Necklace

From Rosch and Mervis, 1975.

prototypicality rating and its rating of the number of common attributes. By statistical calculations, they showed that the two measures were closely related. In other words, if an item had been rated as highly prototypical (like *car*), it was also likely to be rated as having many attributes in common with other members of the category. However, if an item had been rated as low on the prototype scale (like *elevator*), it was likely to have few attributes in common.

This relationship makes sense. Think about a prototypical example of the concept *game*, for instance. To me, Monopoly is prototypical, and it shares many attributes with many other games. "Ring around the Rosie," however, is not prototypical, and it shares few other attributes with games like Ping Pong, Scrabble, and chess. See whether this relationship holds true for the following concepts: attractive person, profession, and adventure movie. In each case, it is probably difficult to find one attribute that applies to all members of the category. However, you can list several attributes that apply to several members. Furthermore, as Rosch and Mervis demonstrated, the most prototypical member of each category has the greatest number of attributes in common with the other members.

4. *Prototypes are supplied as examples of a category.* Several studies have shown that people judge some items to be "better" examples of a concept than some other items. In one study, for example, Mervis, Catlin, and Rosch (1976) looked at some category norms that had already been collected. The norms had been constructed by asking people to give examples of eight different categories, such as birds, fruit, sports, and weapons. Other people supplied prototype ratings for each of these examples. A statistical analysis showed that the items that were

rated most prototypical were the same items that people supplied most often in the category norms. For instance, for the category *bird*, people would consider *robin* to be very prototypical, and *robin* is very frequently listed as an example of this category *bird*. In contrast, people would rate *penguin* as low on the prototype scale, and *penguin* is only rarely listed as an example of the category *bird*. Thus, if someone asks you to name a member of a category, you will probably name a prototype.

Another series of studies requires people to answer "true" or "false" to certain questions, like those in Demonstration 6.8. Which set of questions did you answer more quickly, set A (the prototypical items) or set B (the nonprototypical items)? An experiment by Rips, Shoben, and Smith (1973) as well as several experiments summarized by Rosch (1977) have demonstrated that people answer more quickly when prototypes are used. For example, people respond more quickly to the sentence, "A robin is a bird" than they do to "A penguin is a bird." These studies show the same kind of pattern as the "give me an example of a bird" studies. A robin is an excellent example of a bird, and so you do not have to stop and think before answering "true" to "A robin is a bird."

Demonstration 6.8   *Answering Questions about Prototypes and Nonprototypes.*

Here are two sets of questions. Use a watch with a second hand to measure the amount of time required to answer the questions in set A. Then measure the amount of time for set B. Each question must be answered either "true" or "false."

Set A

1. A sparrow is a bird.
2. An orange is a fruit.
3. A dog is a fish.
4. A hammer is a tool.
5. A bean is a vegetable.
6. A chair is an example of furniture.
7. A shirt is an example of clothing.

Set B

1. An ostrich is a bird.
2. An tomato is a fruit.
3. A whale is a fish.
4. A crane is a tool.
5. Rice is a vegetable.
6. A telephone is an example of furniture.
7. A bat is a bird.

---

5. *Prototypes are judged more quickly after priming.* In everyday English, the term *priming* means that you prepare someone to do something or say something. In cognition research, psychologists try to determine whether **priming**, or preparing people in advance, makes people respond faster. For example, imagine that you are asked to judge pairs of colors and to respond whether they are the same or

not. On some occasions, you have primed trials, and the name of the color is shown to you before you must judge a pair of colors. Other trials are unprimed; no color name is supplied to you as a "warning." Rosch (1975b) tried this priming setup for both prototype colors (for example, a good red) and nonprototype colors (for example, a muddy red).

Priming was very helpful for prototype colors, and subjects responded more quickly after primed trials than after nonprimed trials. However, priming slowed down the judgments for nonprototype colors, even after two weeks of practice. That is, if you see the word *red* before judging two samples of a really red color, you will respond faster. However, if you see the word *red* before judging two samples of a muddy red, you will respond more slowly.

Rosch (1975c) found the same kind of results in another study with words: Priming is helpful for prototypes and harmful for nonprototypes. If you are primed by the category *bird*, your judgments will be faster for prototype birds such as sparrows. However, priming will slow down the responses for nonprototype birds such as penguins. Rosch (1977) argues that when you see a category name, like bird, you form a concrete image of a typical bird. This image resembles the good members of the bird category. When you must judge these good birds, there is a definite advantage if you have a bird image already set up. However, this image gets in the way if you must judge unlikely members of the bird category. Imagine having to judge penguins if you are already primed with an image of a typical bird. You might be startled and say to yourself, "I expected a bird, but I'm judging a penguin. OK, I guess a penguin is a kind of bird." There is an additional pause as you work to reconcile your image of a small, airborne creature with this large, waddling creature.

Incidentally, some people have produced another explanation for Rosch's findings. Loftus (1975), for example, pointed out that people might consider some of the nonprototype items to belong to another category than the one that is used as a prime. The prime would therefore be inappropriate and it might cause a conflict. For example, a screwdriver is a nonprototype murder weapon. Yes, you might imagine the hero of a macho novel using one in a pinch, but a gun is more prototypical. Thus *weapon* serves nicely as a prime for the word *gun*. However, *weapon* causes a conflict as a prime for screwdriver, which would be considered a tool instead.

6. *Prototypes can substitute for a category name in a sentence.* Rosch (1977) summarizes some studies that explored how readily prototypes and nonprototypes can be substituted for a category name in a sentence. Try Demonstration 6.9, which

---

Demonstration 6.9   *Substituting Prototypes and Nonprototypes in Sentences.*

Examine each of the sentences below and rate them as to how normal or how bizarre each one seems to you. Use this scale:

1	2	3	4	5	6	7
Normal					Bizarre	

1. Twenty birds sat on a telephone wire outside my window.
2. Twenty robins sat on a telephone wire outside my window.

3. Twenty penguins sat on a telephone wire outside my window.
4. One of my favorite desserts is fruit pie.
5. One of my favorite desserts is apple pie.
6. One of my favorite desserts is olive pie.
7. How can I go to the fair without a vehicle?
8. How can I go to the fair without a truck?
9. How can I go to the fair without an elevator?
10. The robbers had many weapons.
11. The robbers had many guns.
12. The robbers had many bricks.
13. We like to watch sports on television.
14. We like to watch baseball on television.
15. We like to watch sunbathing on television.
16. The men's wear department had a sale on clothing.
17. The men's wear department had a sale on pants.
18. The men's wear department had a sale on canes.

illustrates a typical study. In general, prototypes can substitute quite well for the category name. However, when a nonprototype is substituted, the resulting sentence is bizarre. Check over your responses in Demonstration 6.9. Did it seem more peculiar to have 20 robins or 20 penguins sitting on telephone wires? Sentences 3, 6, 9, 12, 15, and 18 involved nonprototypes and therefore probably seemed more bizarre to you.

Basic-Level Categories

You can call the wooden object upon which you are sitting by several different names: furniture, chair, or desk chair. You can refer to your pet as a dog, a spaniel, or a cocker spaniel. You can tighten the mirror on your car with a tool, a screwdriver, or a Phillips screwdriver. In other words, an object can belong to many different, related categories.

Some category levels are called **superordinate,** which means higher-level or more general. Furniture, animal, and tool are all examples of superordinate category levels. **Basic-level categories** are more specific, but not too specific. Chair, cat, and screwdriver are examples of basic-level categories. Finally, there are **subordinate** categories, which means lower-level or more specific categories. Desk chair, Siamese, and Phillips screwdriver are examples of subordinate categories. (You can remember that it is the *subordinate* categories that are lower-level by recalling the word *subway,* which is lower-level because it is below the ground.) Take a minute to make sure you know these terms. Think of examples of basic-level and subordinate categories for some superordinate terms you use often, such as musical instrument, vehicle, and clothing.

Rosch, Mervis, Gray, Johnson, and Boyes-Braem (1976) argued that objects can be classified at many different levels, but there is one level that is most basic or most important. This is the level we have called *basic level.* This is the level at which categories carry the most information and are the most different from one another. These authors discovered many characteristics of basic-level categories, which we will examine in this section.

TABLE 6.3   Examples of Items Similar to Those Used in the Experiment by Rosch and Her Colleagues (1976)

Superordinate	*Basic Level*	*Subordinate*
Fruit	Apple	McIntosh apple
Tool	Screwdriver	Phillips screwdriver
Vegetable	Tomato	Big-Boy tomato
Weapon	Knife	Hunting knife
Toy	Doll	Baby doll

1. *Members of basic-level categories have attributes in common.* Rosch and her colleagues proposed that there are natural groupings of objects, which have "bundles" of correlated features and which are obviously different from other objects. To test this idea, they set up nine categories, using each of the three levels you have learned about: superordinate, basic-level, and subordinate. Table 6.3 shows categories similar to their experiment.

People were instructed to list all of the attributes they could think of that were true for the members of the category represented by each name. For example, for *screwdriver* someone might list "metal protrusion," "ridged handle," "about 4–10 inches long," and so on.

Rosch and her colleagues then tallied up the attributes that people frequently listed for each word on the list. They found that people listed very few attributes for superordinate-level items. This makes sense—how many attributes can you think of that would hold true for all tools, for example? However, they listed a large number of attributes for basic-level items. All screwdrivers, for example, have a large number of characteristics in common, many more than are shared by all tools. People did not supply many more attributes for subordinate-level items than for basic-level items, however. Again, this makes sense. For the item, *Phillips screwdriver,* there are not many attributes we could add onto the attributes listed for *screwdriver.* (I am only aware of one additional attribute, the cross-shaped point, but maybe some of you more skilled in home repairs know of others.)

Notice that these results have some implications for everyday language. We can communicate quite effectively by using basic-level category names. When we use the word *screwdriver,* for example, people know many attributes of the object we are discussing. They wouldn't know much more if we were more specific and said "Phillips screwdriver." Furthermore, they wouldn't know much at all if we used the more general term *tool.* The basic-level term is not too specific, nor is it too general. Like the Baby Bear's porridge in "Goldilocks," the basic-level term is "just right."

2. *Members of basic-level categories have motor movements in common.* Try Demonstration 6.10, which is a variation of a second study by Rosch and her colleagues (1976). In her experiment, however, she measured the extent to which people's answers agreed with each other. Check over your answers to see what motions you make and what part of your body you use when you interact with each item. The results of Rosch's study showed that there were almost no motor movements in common for the superordinates. For example, consider the superor-

---

Demonstration 6.10   *Motor Movements for Members of Basic-Level Categories.*

Each of the following items is listed twice. Look at the first listing of the first item, *vehicle,* and picture an example of a vehicle. Think of the motor movements you make when you interact with this example. Think also about the part of your body you use in the interaction. Then repeat this task, using a different example of a vehicle. Continue the same process with each of the other pairs of items.

1. vehicle   vehicle
2. automobile   automobile
3. Volkswagen   Volkswagen
4. clothing   clothing
5. pants   pants
6. jeans   jeans
7. musical instrument   musical instrument
8. piano   piano
9. grand piano   grand piano

---

dinate *furniture.* You write on a table, turn on a lamp, and sit on a chair—you interact differently with each kind of furniture. People's answers depended greatly upon what kind of furniture they visualized. Notice how many motor movements are shared, however, by basic-level items. Rosch and her colleagues found a large number of movements in common for basic-level objects. However, subordinate-level objects did not share any more motor movements than did basic-level objects. For example, you probably had no more motor movements in common for *jeans* than you did for *pants*.

   3. *Members of basic-level categories have shapes in common.* Another study examined the extent to which members of a category have the same shape. Pictures of objects were made the same size, and their outlines were lined up in order to measure the extent of the overlap in their shapes. The overlap was greatest for members of basic-level categories. For example, the overlap in shape would not be extensive for members of the superordinate category *furniture.* A lamp and a chair have very different outlines. However, members of the basic-level category *chair* would have similar shapes; think of a desk chair and a kitchen chair. There was a little bit more overlap for subordinate-level categories than for basic-level categories. For example, "desk chairs" overlapped more than "chairs" did. In summary, then, shapes overlap to an increasingly greater extent as we move from superordinate to basic-level to subordinate categories. However, the most startling improvement in the overlap is between the superordinate and the basic-level categories.

   4. *Basic-level names are used to identify objects.* Name some of the objects that are near you right now. It is likely that you will use basic-level names for these objects. You will mention *pen,* for example, rather than the superordinate *writing instrument* or the subordinate *Bic fine-point pen.* Rosch and her colleagues (1976) asked people to look at pictures and identify the objects, and they found that people preferred to use basic-level names. It seems that a basic-level name gives enough information without being overly detailed.

Writers can often attract our attention by departing from the usual pattern of using basic-level names. I am not aware of authors who prefer the superordinate to basic-level categories, but authors often prefer subordinate names. Contrast these two passages, the first written at the subordinate level and the second written at the basic level.

> Samantha leaned back in her brocade-covered Queen Anne chair. She could feel the softness of her Pucci blouse on her body and could smell just a trace of the Je Reviens perfume that she had dabbed on her earlobes. A few bites of Beef Périgourdine and Celery Root Rémoulade lay untouched upon the gold-rimmed Limoges plate.

> The woman leaned back in her chair. She could feel the softness of her blouse on her body and could smell just a trace of the perfume that she had dabbed on her earlobes. A few bites of meat and vegetable lay untouched upon the plate.

Rosch (1978) remarks that substitution of subordinate terms for basic-level object names can create interesting effects. In some cases, it may be used for snobbery, and in other cases for satire.

5. *Basic-level names produce the priming effect.* As we saw earlier, members of the same basic-level category share the same general shape. For example, members of the category *chair* look roughly the same. We would expect, therefore, that when people hear the word *chair,* they would form a mental image that would resemble most chairs.

The reason that the mental image is relevant is that Rosch and her colleagues (1976) wanted to see whether priming with basic-level names would be helpful. Recall that in a priming study the experimenter gives the name of the object, and the subjects decide whether two pictures that follow are the same or different. For example, you might hear the word *carrot* and see a picture of two identical carrots. Presumably, priming works because the presentation of the word allows you to make a mental image of this word, which helps when you make the later decision.

At any rate, the results showed that priming with basic-level names *was* helpful—it did help to see a basic-level term like *carrot* before judging the carrots. However, priming with superordinate names (such as *vegetable*) was not helpful. Apparently, when you hear the word *vegetable,* you do not develop a mental image that is specific enough to prepare you for judging carrots. When you want to warn people that something is coming, warn them with a basic-level term—shout "Fire!" and not "Danger!"

6. *Basic-level names are central in sign language.* One interesting application of information about basic-level names concerns sign language. Newport and Bellugi (1978) studied **American Sign Language,** or ASL, which is the language used by many deaf people in the United States for everyday conversation. Some of the symbols in ASL are pantomime-like in representing objects and events, but most are not.

Newport and Bellugi decided to study ASL to determine the relationship among the superordinate, basic-level, and subordinate categories in this language. They found, first of all, that these three levels of categories are just as distinct from each other in ASL as they are in spoken English.

Most interesting, however, was their report about the signs used for basic-level and superordinate categories. Basic-level objects, such as guitar, apple, hammer, socks, and truck can be represented in ASL by a single sign. In contrast, there are relatively few commonly accepted signs for superordinate categories. For instance, there is a sign for *furniture,* but it is not commonly used. When people speaking ASL need a superordinate category term, they must often borrow the English term and spell it with their fingers. On other occasions, people construct a superordinate term by listing several basic-level objects. *Vegetables,* for example, can be expressed by using the signs for carrots, beans, and peas in rapid succession. *Sport* can be expressed by using the signs for football, basketball, and track. Figure 6.7 shows the separate signs for car, plane, and train, and how they are combined to form the sign for vehicle. In short, basic-level terms are central in sign language, just as they are in spoken English.

Natural Concepts in Animals

In Chapter 4 we examined cognitive maps in chimpanzees. In Chapter 5 we discussed whether chimpanzees could master language. Although nearly all of this

---

Figure 6.7   Signs for Basic-Level Objects and for Superordinate Objects. (A) Three Basic-Level Signs. (B) The Sign for the Superordinate, Vehicle. (Note: each of the signs used to form "vehicle" takes less time than when it is used as an isolated basic-level sign.) (From Newport and Bellugi, 1978; reprinted by permission of Lawrence Erlbaum Associates, Inc.).

(A) Three basic-level signs.

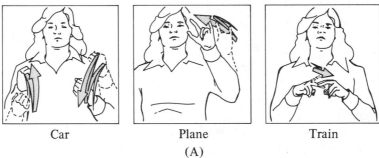

Car	Plane	Train
(A)

(B) The sign for the superordinate, *vehicle*.

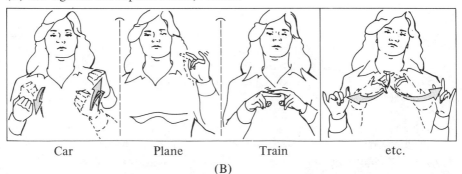

Car	Plane	Train	etc.
(B)

book is devoted to human cognition, we will now look at one more example of cognition in lower animals. In particular, we will discuss a creative study about natural. concepts in pigeons (Herrnstein, Loveland, & Cable, 1976). Natural concepts in other animals are discussed by Premack (1978).

In one experiment in this series, the pigeons saw 80 pictures. About half of them were pictures of trees, sometimes a part of a tree and sometimes one or more trees. The other half were pictures of other objects. When a picture of a tree was presented, the pigeon could peck at a key and receive food as a reward. Pecking when the other pictures were present earned no reward. After a number of training sessions a new set of pictures was presented and the pigeon's choices were recorded. The other two experiments in the series had similar procedures, except that the second experiment involved pictures of water—everything from water droplets and small puddles to an aerial view of the Atlantic Ocean. The third experiment involved 800 different pictures of a woman whom a photographer followed for a year and photographed in numerous different settings.

Impressively, the pigeons did quite well on the tasks. From the new sets of pictures, they chose pictures of trees more often than pictures of nontrees, pictures of water more often than pictures of other objects, and pictures of the woman more often than pictures of other people.

Herrnstein and his colleagues expressed surprise at the pigeons' performance, particularly since the pictures representing any one concept were so different from one another. They remark that there were no single features that were found in all the examples of a concept:

> To recognize a tree, the pigeons did not require that it be green, leafy, vertical, woody, branching, and so on. . . . Moreover, to be recognizable as a nontree, a picture did not have to omit greenness, woodiness, branchiness, verticality, and so on. Neither could we identify common elements in the other two experiments. (p. 298)

The authors suggest that the "family resemblance" idea applies for pigeons as well as humans. There was no single element found in all pictures of trees, for example, yet there was an overlap of common features. Each picture shared at least one attribute with some other example of the concept.

In a later paper, Herrnstein (1978) remarked that pigeons perform better on natural concepts, such as trees, than on artificial concepts, such as black triangles versus red squares. Furthermore, pigeons can discriminate fish from nonfish, even though they have never before seen a fish.

How do pigeons perform on caricatures, such as "Peanuts" cartoon characters? Impressively, pigeons can discriminate Charlie Brown from the other "Peanuts" characters. In a recent experiment, Charlie Brown wore sweaters, jackets, caps, snowsuits, and swim suits. He sometimes appeared lying down, sometimes standing up, and sometimes crouching, climbing, and somersaulting. Nonetheless, Cerella (1980) found that pigeons were readily able to learn the difference between Charlie Brown and the rest of the cast of characters—Linus, Marcia, Snoopy, and so on. In summary, pigeons can identify natural concepts involving trees, water, people, and even the concept of a particular cartoon character.

SECTION SUMMARY: Natural Categories

1. Some psychologists argue that concept formation experiments are artificial because real-life concepts are less precise, less well-known, and less arbitrary.
2. According to Rosch's prototype theory, people compare an object to a prototype in order to categorize it.
3. Categories based on prototypes are learned more quickly than categories based on nonprototypes.
4. Prototypes serve as reference points, and other items are compared to these reference points.
5. Family resemblance means that there is no one attribute shared by all examples of a concept, but each example shares at least one attribute with another example of the concept. Prototypes have the greatest number of attributes in common with other members of the category.
6. Prototypes are supplied more often than nonprototypes as examples of a category.
7. Prototypes are judged more quickly after priming with the category name.
8. Prototypes can substitute for a category name in a sentence, whereas nonprototypes cannot.
9. There are three category levels: superordinate (more general), basic level, and subordinate (more specific). The basic-level category is most important.
10. Members of basic-level categories have many attributes in common.
11. Members of basic-level categories have many motor movements in common.
12. Members of basic-level categories have shapes in common.
13. Basic-level names are supplied in identifying objects.
14. Basic-level names produce the priming effect; priming with superordinate names in not helpful.
15. Basic-level names are represented by a single symbol in American Sign Language. Superordinate names are either absent or formed by combining basic-level names.
16. Pigeons can be taught natural concepts such as trees, water, people, and cartoon characters.

Chapter Review Questions

1. Think about the concept *dog*, with reference to the discussion at the beginning of the chapter about the ways in which concepts are necessary. Recall as many of the five reasons as you can, and demonstrate for each reason how it is helpful to have the concept *dog*.

2. Think of the concept *friend*. What attributes are relevant, and what attributes are irrelevant? Does the concept involve the conjunction rule, the disjunction rule, the conditional rule, or the biconditional rule?

3. Imagine that you are doing an experiment with an expanded version of Demonstration 6.1. Describe the variety of dependent variables you could use in this study, with specific reference to the stimuli in that demonstration.

4. Suppose that you wanted to examine Levine's theory of hypothesis testing using the thinking-aloud method. Predict how the protocols would change as learning proceeds. Also, compare Levine's method with the thinking-aloud method.

5. Imagine that you are a first-grade teacher who is trying to teach children the concepts *triangle* and *square*. From what you know about factors affecting concept formation, what kinds of precautions should you take when you teach these concepts?

6. Think about the natural concept *household pet*. Try to describe this concept in terms of defining features and then in terms of degrees of prototypicality.

7. The first two characteristics of prototypes dealt with physical properties, such as color and number. (a) The first characteristic is that categories based on prototypes are learned quickly. Which number sequence would you expect people to learn more quickly, 10, 12, 14, or 17, 19, 21? (b) The second characteristic is that prototypes serve as reference points. Which sentence is more likely: "Blue is essentially aquamarine" or "Aquamarine is essentially blue"?

8. Think about a prototypical household pet, a dog, and contrast it with a nonprototypical household pet, a skunk. Compare these two animals with respect to: (a) the extent to which they have attributes in common with other pets (family resemblance); (b) the extent to which they would be supplied as examples of a category; (c) the extent to which they would be quickly judged after priming; and (d) the extent to which they can substitute for a category name in a sentence.

9. Consider the basic-level category, *dime,* in contrast to the superordinate, *money,* and the subordinate, *1970 dime.* Discuss how members of this basic-level category: (a) have attributes in common, and (b) have shapes in common. Discuss also how the basic-level name would be used to identify objects.

10. We defined *concept* as making the same response to a group of objects that share similar characteristics. Consider the studies on natural concepts in pigeons. In what sense are the pigeons demonstrating that they have learned concepts?

New Terms

concept
concept formation
attribute
relevant attribute
irrelevant attribute
salience
rules
conjunction
disjunction
conditional
biconditional
complete learning
dependent variable
independent variable
covert

overt
latency
Blank Trials Procedure
protocols
positive examples
negative examples
learning to learn
near miss
interaction
hypotheses
strategy
conservative focusing
focus gambling
working hypothesis
global focusing strategy

natural categories
defining-features theory
prototype theory
prototype
prototypicality
nonprototypes
family resemblance
prototype ratings
priming
superordinate
basic-level categories
subordinate
American Sign Language

Answers to the Demonstrations

6.1. The concept is: rounded, rather than sharp-angled, eyebrows.

6.2. Conditional rule: If a figure has a chimney, then it must have a window to be an example. All figures without chimneys are also examples.

6.3. Number of leaves and number of petals are relevant; flower color is irrelevant. The rule is disjunction: all figures that have three petals or one leaf or both. That is, only four-petaled, two-leafed flowers are *not* examples of the concept.

6.4. If you think that "right" is positive and "left" is negative in this example, you are correct!

6.5. A single circle with a double border is the concept.

Problem Solving and Creativity

Preview

Problem solving is necessary when we want to reach a certain goal and the goal is not readily available. We will look at four aspects of problem solving in this chapter: (1) understanding the problem; (2) solving the problem; (3) ill-defined problems; and (4) creativity.

If you understand a problem, you have, in effect, constructed an internal representation of the problem. There are many different ways of representing problems, such as lists, graphs, and visual images.

Some problem-solving strategies involve algorithms, which are methods that will always produce a solution. Random search techniques are algorithms. Heuristics, in contrast, do not always produce a solution, but they require less time. Examples of heuristics include means-ends analysis and backward search. Numerous factors affect problem-solving difficulty. For example, problems are sometimes difficult for people who have developed a habitual way of responding to objects or problems. However, problem solving can be made easier if people are provided with training.

Some problems are ill defined because aspects of the problem are not specified. In everyday life these ill-defined problems are more commonly encountered than well-defined problems.

Creativity has been defined in many different ways, but one accepted definition is that creativity involves finding a solution that is both unusual and useful. We will consider several suggestions for encouraging creativity.

Think for a moment about all the problems you solved yesterday. You may have wanted to leave a note for a professor, but you found you had no pen or pencil. Your art professor may have asked you to make a sketch using only circles. You may have planned on an interesting main course for dinner but arrived home to find the cupboards almost as bare as Mother Hubbard's. An essay exam may have asked you to compare two theories that seemed entirely unrelated to you. In spite of the fact that you spent most of the day solving problems, you may have sat down to relax late at night—and solved more problems. Perhaps you played a card game or chess or entertained yourself with a jigsaw puzzle or a Rubik's cube. Problem solving is inescapable in everyday life.

We use **problem solving** when we want to reach a certain goal, and that goal is not readily available. Thus, there is no problem to be solved regarding a writing instrument if I must leave a note for someone and I have a pen with me. Similarly, there is no problem to be solved if I know that $x = 5 + 7$. In both cases the goals are readily available. Problem solving, on the other hand, involves situations in which something is blocking our successful completion of a task.

It is useful to consider the three aspects of a problem: (1) the original state, (2) the goal state, and (3) the rules. For example, you may wish to go shopping at a store in a nearby town. The **original state,** or situation at the beginning of problem solving, might be, "I am in my room, five miles from where I want to be, with no car and no public transportation." The **goal state,** which is reached when the problem is solved, would be, "I want to be at a store five miles away." The **rules** or restrictions that must be followed in proceeding from the original state to the goal state, would be numerous. They might include the following: "I can't borrow a car from a stranger" and "I can't borrow a stick-shift car, because I can only drive an automatic." Think about the original state, goal state, and rules for a problem you have recently solved so that you are familiar with these new terms.

Throughout this chapter we will emphasize the active nature of cognitive processes in problem solving. In solving problems, people are rarely random in their approach. They seldom use a trial-and-error approach, blindly trying different options until one option finally provides a solution. Instead, they plan their attacks. We have seen that problem solving involves the attempt to reach a certain goal that is not readily available. Thus, a problem cannot be solved with a single step. The problem solver must frequently break a problem into its component steps and devise a plan for solving each of the components. In addition to plans, the problem solver also uses strategies. We will emphasize that people frequently use certain kinds of strategies that are likely to produce a solution relatively quickly. As we stressed in the introduction to this book, humans are not passive beings that absorb information from the environment. Instead, they plan their approaches to problems and choose strategies that will be likely to provide solutions to the problems.

We have four areas to cover in this chapter. The first two sections are components of problem solving: understanding the problem and solving the problem. Then we will consider the difference between ill-defined problems and well-defined problems. Finally, we will look at a particularly puzzling area of problem solving: creativity.

Understanding the Problem

What do we mean when we say that we understand a problem? According to Greeno (1977), **understanding** involves constructing an internal representation. For example, if you understand a sentence, you create some internal representation or pattern in your head so that concepts are related to each other in the same way that they are related to each other in the original sentence. In order to create this pattern in your head you must use background knowledge, such as the meaning of the various words in the sentence.

Greeno believes that understanding has three requirements: coherence, correspondence, and relationship to background knowledge. Let us look at each of these requirements in more detail.

A coherent representation is a pattern that is connected, so that all the parts make sense. For example, consider Greeno's sentence, "Tree trunks are straws for thirsty leaves and branches" (p. 44). That sentence remains at the level of complete nonsense unless you see that is is based on the similarity of tree trunks and straws in moving liquid. Once you see the analogy, the fragments of the sentence become united. Similarly, look back at Demonstration 5.9. When you originally read that paragraph, it had no coherent representation in your head because there were many unrelated fragments. However, once you had been told that the paragraph

Figure 7.1 Understanding a Problem.

Assembling Handle

Attach the "D" handle to the upper handle tube before joining the two sections of the tube (see Fig. A).

1. Remove the wing nut and bolt from the "D" handle.
2. The wire that is exposed between the two sections of the handle tube will now pass through the slot in the bottom of the "D" handle.
3. Slide the "D" handle up onto the upper handle tube.
4. Place the bolt into the "D" handle and tighten the wing nut. If the "D" handle is properly mounted, the wing nut will be on the left from the operator's point of view.
5. Form "S" shape with excess cord and stuff into handle tube (see Fig. B).
6. Slide upper handle tube into lower handle tube and line up screw holes (see Fig. B).
7. Insert the two screws into the handle tube and tighten.
8. Adjust position of "D" handle to conform to height and arm length.

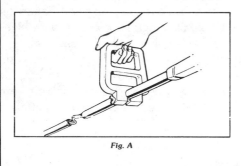

Fig. A

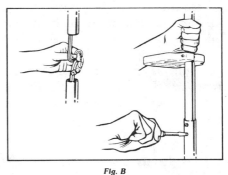

Fig. B

was about washing clothes, everything made sense. You had a coherent representation.

Greeno also proposes that understanding requires a close correspondence between the internal representation and the material that is being understood. Sometimes the internal representation is incomplete, and sometimes it is inaccurate. Important relations among the parts may be left out or mismatched. Think about an occasion when you noticed that an internal representation and the material to be understood did not correspond. I recall my mother giving her friend a recipe for yogurt, which included the sentence, "Then you put the yogurt in a warm blanket." The friend looked quite pained and asked, "But isn't it awfully messy to wash the blanket out?" The friend's internal representation unfortunately omitted the fact that the yogurt was in a container.

Greeno's third criterion for good understanding is that the material to be understood must be related to the understander's background knowledge. This point has probably occurred to you if you have ever found yourself enrolled in an advanced-level course without the proper prerequisite courses or if you have ever looked at a professional article in an area unfamiliar to you. Vocabulary and concepts must be familiar in order for material to be understood. Greeno summarizes his previous research on this topic, which involved people solving probability problems. Subjects who were told the meanings of basic concepts in probability were better at solving word problems than subjects who were only taught the formulas.

Simon and Hayes (1976a) point out that understanding is critical because of the problem of "functional illiteracy" in our society:

> A functional illiterate is someone who cannot perform the reading tasks with which his job and his daily life confront him. The illiterate cannot read and understand the directions on the medicine bottle, the do-it-yourself kit, or the soup can. He cannot understand the fine print on the traffic ticket or read his personal mail. He cannot read the instruction manual for a piece of equipment used in his job. (p. 269)

According to Simon and Hayes, functional illiteracy is basically an understanding problem instead of a reading problem. Functional illiterates can read the printed words, but they do not have the vocabulary and knowledge to interpret or understand the material. (Recall that this is Greeno's third criterion for understanding.) For example, consider a typical set of instructions, as shown in Figure 7.1. Although these instructions are no more difficult than average, functional illiterates may have trouble with them because words and phrases such as *wing nut* and *excess* may be unfamiliar. The concepts of adjusting the handle "to conform to height and arm length" and "from the operator's point of view" may not make sense. Also, it may not be clear why the excess cord is called "S shaped" in step 5.

Paying Attention

In order to understand a problem, you must pay attention to the important information in a problem. Furthermore, you must ignore the information that is irrelevant. Read over the problem in Demonstration 7.1 and decide which sentences are most important and which are least important.

Demonstration 7.1   The Five-Handed-Monster Problem.

Read over this problem and decide which sentences are most important.

1. Three five-handed extraterrestrial monsters were holding three crystal globes.
2. Because of the quantum-mechanical peculiarities of their neighborhood, both monsters and globes come in exactly three sizes with no others permitted: small, medium, and large.
3. The medium-sized monster was holding the small globe; the small monster was holding the large globe; and the large monster was holding the medium-sized globe.
4. Since this situation offended their keenly developed sense of symmetry, they proceeded to transfer globes from one monster to another so that each monster would have a globe proportionate to his own size.

5. Monster etiquette complicated the solution of the problem since it requires: that only one globe may be transferred at a time; that if a monster is holding two globes, only the larger of the two may be transferred; and that a globe may not be transferred to a·monster who is holding a larger globe.
6. By what sequence of transfers could the monsters have solved this problem? (From Simon & Hayes, 1976b, p. 168.)

Simon and Hayes (1976b) asked 20 subjects to solve this problem, thinking aloud as they worked. The authors recorded what the subjects said, and they also recorded the number of times each sentence was reread before subjects made their first move. Sentence 3 was reread a total of 23 times; this sentence describes the present situation. Sentence 4 was reread only nine times; this sentence describes the goal. Sentence 5 was reread 32 times; this sentence describes the rules. All other sentences combined were reread only five times.

What kinds of sentences did subjects pay attention to? Simon and Hayes argue that subjects will reread a sentence if (1) they believe the information in the sentence is relevant to the task and (2) they have not stored the information in memory. For instance, sentences 1 and 2 contain information that is either irrelevant (for example, that the monsters each have five hands) or repeated later (for example, the sizes of the monsters and the globes). The last part of sentence 4 is relevant to the task, but the information in that sentence—that each monster must hold a globe of a corresponding size—can easily be stored in memory. Consequently it does not deserve rereading.

Sentences 3 and 5, in contrast, are both relevant and complicated. These are the sentences that are difficult to store in memory. As a result, subjects must return to these sentences and reread them before they begin the problem. Furthermore, Simon and Hayes noticed that subjects also reread these sentences *after* they had begun to make moves. They seldom reread the other sentences once they had begun the problem.

Were your judgments about the importance of the sentences in Demonstration 7.1 similar to the rereading patterns that Simon and Hayes found? Did you tend to ignore parts of certain sentences? One subject in the Simon and Hayes study read the phrase, "Because of the quantum-mechanical peculiarities of their neighborhood . . ." and commented, "Forget that garbage!" (Hayes, 1978, p. 198). You may have had the same response.

Every day we face problems in which the major challenge is discovering what information is important and what information is irrelevant. Your statistics professor, for example, may include a problem on a test that has many details about the experimental design that are really not important for the solution of the problem. There may even be extra statistical information that you will not need in finding the answer. The challenge in the problem may be deciding what information is essential. Also, consider how this idea of discovering essential information can be applied to some riddles. Remember the St. Ives rhyme:

As I was going to St. Ives
I met a man with seven wives.
Every wife had seven sacks,

> Every sack had seven cats,
> Every cat had seven kits,
> Kits, cats, sacks, and wives,
> How many were going to St. Ives?

You may recall that finding the answer depends upon ignoring the irrelevant information about kits, cats, sacks, and wives and paying attention to the critical part of the critical sentence, "As I was going to St. Ives." In fact, only one person was going to St. Ives.

Simon and Hayes (1976a) point out that the functional illiteracy problem can be reduced by writing simple, clear instructions. They write:

> If one includes in instructions information that is not useful for interpreting the instructions, then the reader may be misled into unproductive or misleading analogies. We have seen that a vital part of the understanding process is to strip away the inessentials from the problem statement, and abstract out the elements from which the problem representation will be formed . . . (p. 283)

Simon and Hayes (1976a) suggest that if people are writing for an audience that might include functional illiterates, they should reduce the number of inessentials to be stripped away by the readers.

Methods of Representing the Problem

As soon as the problem solver has decided which information is essential and which can be disregarded, the next step is to find a good way to represent the problem. Simon and Hayes (1976b) argue that subjects regard problems like the one in Demonstration 7.1 as a "cover story" for the "real problem." Thus they must discover the abstract puzzle underneath all the details, and then they must find a good way to represent this abstract puzzle. Think about your reaction to Demonstration 7.1, for example. Did you really think it was a problem about five-handed monsters? It is more likely that you saw it as a puzzle in which certain objects were to be exchanged according to certain rules.

If people regard problems as being abstract, then a difficulty arises. After all, if something is abstract, it is difficult to keep it in your memory and perform operations on the problem. Therefore, people typically invent some method of representing the abstract problem in a concrete way—a particular concrete way that shows only the essential information.

Symbols.   Sometimes the most effective way to represent an abstract problem is by using symbols. This is what you probably learned to do in high school algebra. Try Demonstration 7.2, for example. The usual way of solving this problem is to let

---

Demonstration 7.2   *Using Symbols in Problem Solving.*

Solve the following problem: Mary is ten years younger than twice Susan's age. Five years from now, Mary will be eight years older than Susan's age at that time. How old are Mary and Susan? (The answer is found in the discussion in the text.)

---

a symbol such as *m* represent Mary's age and a symbol such as *s* represent Susan's age. We can then "translate" each sentence into a formula. The first sentence becomes:

$$m = 2s - 10$$

The second sentence becomes

$$m + 5 = s + 5 + 8$$

Now we can substitute for *m* in the second equation:

$$2s - 10 + 5 = s + 5 + 8$$

Therefore we find that

$$s = 18$$

Substituting for *s* in the first equation, we find that

$$m = 26$$

Finally, of course, we have to translate the symbols back into words; Susan is 18 and Mary is 26.

Lists.   In many other problems, however, translating words into symbols will not get us very far. The monster problem in Demonstration 7.1, for example, could be approached by making a list, as in Table 7.1. However, notice how bulky the list becomes. It is hard to keep track of which monster has which ball, so a list is not very helpful.

Matrices.   Simon and Hayes (1976b) found that more than half their subjects spontaneously made some kind of matrix to represent the problem. A **matrix** (pronounced "*may*-tricks") is a chart that shows possible combinations. In the case of the monster problem, the matrix shows which monster has which globe at different points in time, as in Table 7.2. A matrix is an excellent way to keep track of objects, particularly when the problem is a complex one.

TABLE 7.1   Representing the Monster Problem in a List

Monster Size	Globe Size
Small	Medium
Medium	Large
Large	Small
Small	Medium
Medium	—
Large	Large, Small
Small	—
Medium	Medium
Large	Large, Small

TABLE 7.2   Representing the Monster Problem in a Matrix

	Monster Size		
	Small	*Medium*	*Large*
Step 1	Medium	Large	S
2	Medium	—	Large, Small
3	—	Medium	Large, Small

Graphs. For some problems, however, symbols, lists, and **matrices** (the plural of matrix; pronounced "*may*-trih-seas") are not helpful. Consider, for example, the "Buddhist monk" problem in Demonstration 7.3. An effective way to approach this problem is by making a graph. As Figure 7.2 shows, we can use one line to show the monk going up the mountain on the first day. We use another line to show the monk coming down the mountain several days later. The point at which the lines cross tells us the spot that the monk will pass at the same time on each of the two days. I have drawn the lines so that they cross at a point 1200 feet up the mountain at 1:00 P.M. However, notice how we can vary the monk's rate (for example, so that he goes up slowly and comes down quickly), yet the two paths must always cross at some point.

Demonstration 7.3   The Buddhist Monk Problem.

Exactly at sunrise one morning, a Buddhist monk set out to climb a tall mountain. The narrow path was not more than a foot or two wide, and it wound around the mountain to a beautiful, glittering temple at the mountain peak.

The monk climbed the path at varying rates of speed. He stopped many times along the way to rest and to eat the fruit he carried with him. He reached the temple just before sunset. At the temple, he fasted and meditated for several days. Then he began his journey back along the same path, starting at sunrise and walking, as before, at variable speeds with many stops along the way. However, his average speed going down the hill was greater than his average climbing speed.

Prove that there must be a spot along the path that the monk will pass on both trips at exactly the same time of day. (The answer is found in Figure 7.2.)

Visual Images. Other people prefer to solve the Buddhist monk problem visually. Recall that in Chapter 4 we discussed the importance of visual imagery in solving problems, for example, when the chemist figured out the structure of benzene by visualizing a snake holding its tail. Koestler (1964) enjoyed tormenting his friends by presenting them with the Buddhist monk problem. One young woman without any scientific training was typical of those who chose a visual approach to the problem. She reported:

> I tried this and that, until I got fed up with the whole thing, but the image of that monk in his saffron robe walking up the hill kept persisting in my mind. Then a moment came when, superimposed on this image, I saw another, more transparent one, of the monk walking *down* the hill, and I realized in a flash that the two figures *must* meet at some point some time—regardless at what speed they walk and how often each of

Figure 7.2   A Graphic Representation of the Buddhist Monk Problem.

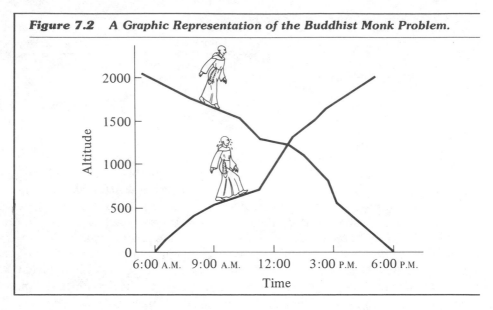

them stops. Then I reasoned out what I already knew: whether the monk descends two days or three days later comes to the same; so I was quite justified in letting him descend on the same day, in duplicate so to speak. (p. 184)

Koestler points out that a visual image has an advantage of being *irrational*. After all, how could the monk meet himself coming down the mountain? Thus, the visual image can let us escape from the boundaries of traditional representations. At the same time, however, the visual image is somewhat concrete; it is a symbol for a theory that has not yet been thoroughly developed. Incidentally, a book called *Thinking Visually* offers more details on this approach to problem solving (McKim, 1980).

Which Method is Best?   We have seen that problems can be represented by symbols, lists, matrices, graphs, and visual imagery. Naturally, some problems cannot be represented by some of the methods: The Buddhist monk problem will not fit into a matrix, for example. However, some other problems have several possible representations. Are there any methods that are more successful than others in producing solutions?

Schwartz (1971) examined this question in an article called "Modes of Representation and Problem Solving: Well Evolved is Half Solved." He gave subjects problems that involved "whodunit" types of solutions, such as the one in Demonstration 7.4. The subjects were encouraged to show all their work, so that Schwartz could observe how they represented the problem.

Demonstration 7.4   Representations of Problems.

Read the information and answer the question at the bottom of the page. (The answer is at the end of the chapter.)

Five people are in a hospital. Each one has only one disease, and each has a different disease. Each one occupies a separate room; room numbers are 101–105.

1. The person with asthma is in Room 101.
2. Mrs. Jones has heart disease.
3. Mrs. Green is in Room 105.
4. Mrs. Smith has tuberculosis.
5. The woman with mononucleosis is in Room 104.
6. Mrs. Thomas is in Room 101.
7. Mrs. Smith is in Room 102.
8. One of the patients, other than Mrs. Anderson, has gall bladder disease.

What disease does Mrs. Anderson have and in what room is she?

Schwartz found that the representation method was related to whether the subjects solved the problem. When subjects used a matrix to represent the problem, 74 percent reached the solution. Other representations produced a solution between 40 and 55 percent of the time. Subjects who did not use any particular representation method were successful only 25 percent of the time. The matrix representation was clearly the most effective.

It is important to point out, however, that Schwartz's study shows only that there is a relationship between representation method and frequency of solution. It is tempting to conclude that problem solvers could improve their accuracy by shifting to matrix representations. However, there is another possible interpretation for the data. It may be that the people who choose matrix representations are good problem solvers, and the people who choose other representations are poor problem solvers. Telling these other people about matrix representation may not aid them substantially. At present, however, we can say that people who spontaneously use matrix representations are good at solving problems. Keep in mind, also, that other kinds of problems might be solved more satisfactorily with other methods; as stated earlier, the matrix representation would not work on some problems.

SECTION SUMMARY: Understanding the Problem

1. Problem solving is necessary when we want to reach a certain goal, and that goal is not readily available.
2. Three aspects of a problem are the original state, the goal state, and the rules.
3. Understanding involves constructing an internal representation of the problem.
4. The internal representation must have coherence, correspondence, and relationship to background knowledge.
5. People pay attention to the parts of the problem that seem relevant to the task and that are not stored in memory.
6. People regard the "real problems" as being abstract puzzles, which need to be represented in a concrete way.
7. Symbols, lists, matrices, graphs, and visual images are five ways of representing problems.
8. Matrices are particularly useful in solving some kinds of problems.

Solving the Problem

Once the problem has been represented, there are many different strategies that people can use to attack the problem. Some methods are very time-consuming but they will always yield an answer—maybe immediately and maybe several years later. Other methods are less wasteful of time, but they may not produce a solution. We will consider several problem-solving strategies in this section and then look at several factors that influence problem solving.

Random Search Strategies

In **random search,** the problem solver uses trial-and-error strategies to find the answer. There are two kinds of random search, unsystematic random search and systematic random search. **Unsystematic random search** means that we try out all kinds of possible answers but make no attempt to be orderly in our search and keep no record of our previous attempts. As a consequence, we may repeat a response that has already proved to be wrong. Consider, for example, if you wanted to phone a friend who lives in the same telephone area code that you do. You pick up the phone and dial at random every seven-digit number. As you can imagine, this is an extremely inefficient method, particularly because you would dial some of the wrong numbers more than once.

In **systematic random search,** we try out all possible answers using a specified system. Assuming that we had no idea about what kinds of phone numbers are actually assigned by the phone company, we would begin with 000-0000 and move on to 000-0001 and 000-0002. This method is somewhat more efficient than unsystematic random search, but it is still impossibly time-consuming when there are many alternative answers. At times, however, this method may be appropriate. If you are solving a jigsaw puzzle, for example, and you have two similar looking pieces remaining, by all means try a systematic random search to see which of the two pieces fits into the hole. Similarly, if you are given a three-letter anagram, YBO, with instructions to unscramble it, proceed with a systematic random search: YOB, BYO, BOY—aha! However, notice how time-consuming it would be to use a systematic random search to solve a longer anagram, such as LSSTNEUIAMYOUL.

Random search techniques, whether they are unsystematic or systematic, are examples of algorithms. Algorithm is a word that cognitive psychologists use frequently, even though it may not be found in your dictionary. An **algorithm** is a method that will always produce a solution to a problem, sooner or later. Thus, a systematic random search of the possible letter orders in LSSTNEUIAMYOUL will eventually produce the word SIMULTANEOUSLY. Algorithms always work, even though they might not be efficient. Thus, a high school student faced with the algebra problem in Demonstration 7.2 on an examination could begin with $m = 0$ and $s = 0$ and try all possible values for m and s until reaching the solution $m = 26$ and $s = 18$—although the examination would certainly be over by that time.

Newell and Simon (1972) observe that the time taken to search for an answer to a problem is roughly proportional to the total size of the problem space. The **problem space** is the set, or collection, of possibilities for the solution to the problem, as the problem solver sees the situation. Thus there may be other solutions to the problem, but if the problem solver is not aware of these solutions, they are not included in the problem space. At any rate, the problem space for the anagram YBO is very small, whereas the problem space for the anagram LSSTNEUIAMYOUL is enormous.

Heuristic Search Strategies

Random search techniques are inefficient and unsophisticated. According to Newell and Simon, the effect of other, more sophisticated methods is to cut down the part of the space that must be explored in order to find a solution. The problem solver thus begins with a large space at first. However, he or she applies relevant information about the problem in order to reduce the size of the problem space, ending up with a relatively small space to examine. For example, consider a student in a botany course who is trying to discover the name of a meadow flower by using a chart. Large areas of the chart could be eliminated right at the beginning by removing from the problem space those flowers that grow in deserts, swamps, and habitats other than meadows.

We have been discussing random search as an example of an algorithm. In contrast, **heuristics** (pronounced "hyoo-*riss*-ticks") are selective searches that look at only the portions of the problem space that are most likely to produce a solution. Thus the botany student who eliminates all nonmeadow flowers is conducting a heuristic search. Heuristics are "rules of thumb" (Reitman, 1964)— that is, strategies that generally hold true.

We noted that algorithms such as random search will always produce a solution, although the process may take a long time. Heuristics, in contrast, do not guarantee a solution—they only make a solution very likely. For example, consider the botany student. A wicked fellow student may have transplanted a swamp flower into a meadow on the previous day. By using the heuristic of ignoring nonmeadow flowers, our problem solver cannot reach a solution. In summary, heuristics are less time-consuming than algorithms because the problem solver searches only a part of the problem space; this time-saving aspect is a definite "plus." However, heuristics are more risky than algorithms because they may not produce a solution; this possibility of no solution is a "minus."

Psychologists have paid more attention to how humans use heuristics than how they use algorithms. There are several reasons for this emphasis. First of all, for most problems there are no algorithms. For example, suppose that your professor tells you that you must design an experiment in cognition. There is no algorithm to tell you how to do this. A random search of the cognition literature or a random combination of concepts in cognition wouldn't solve the problem (although the search would limit the size of the problem space). Second, even if an algorithm exists for a particular problem, people are more likely to use a heuristic search. When you solve an anagram, for example, you eliminate large areas of the problem space—you would not consider letter arrangements that had more than three vowels or more than three consonants placed together. Third, algorithms are not as interesting. If you were a researcher, would you rather watch a problem solver plod through the 473rd arrangement of the letters in SIMULTANEOUSLY or watch how this person used strategies to limit the search?

Now that we have seen how heuristics differ from algorithms, let us look at some examples of heuristics as strategies in solving problems. Problem solvers can use one or more of these heuristics as they attack a problem.

Means-Ends Analysis.   Means-ends analysis is a strategy in which the problem solver divides the problem into a number of **subproblems,** or smaller problems. Each of these subproblems is solved by detecting the difference between the original state and the goal state and then reducing the difference between these two states. The name **means-ends analysis** fits the process, because it involves figuring out the "ends" you want and then figuring out what "means" you will use to reach those ends.

Every day we all solve problems by using means-ends analysis. Suppose, for example, that you are in the library at 9:37 in the morning and have just realized that you must miss an 11 o'clock class in industrial psychology because you must register for next semester's courses during that period. You know that the lecture will be important, and there will be an examination that includes that particular material during the next class session. Because of the exam, you realize that no one will lend you the notes long enough to copy them—not even your good friend Susan, who takes meticulous notes and would ordinarily be most cooperative. The original state, unfortunately, has you in the registration line at 11:00 while Susan takes notes that you may never see. The goal state would have you holding a copy of those fine notes. The problem has three subproblems: (1) discover a way for Susan to take notes for you, as well as herself; (2) discover a way to notify Susan; and (3) discover how to obtain those notes. You may solve the three subproblems separately. For example, you may realize that Rodney Wong in your 10 o'clock class passes by your industrial psych classroom and can see Susan—you have solved the second subproblem. Then it occurs to you that you can bribe a librarian for a piece of carbon paper and some sheets of paper and ask Rodney to bring them to Susan; she can make a carbon copy as she takes notes for herself. The third subproblem is the easiest; she can bring the copy of the notes to the cafeteria, where you always eat lunch together.

We use means-ends analysis so often to solve problems that we take this method for granted. For example, suppose that you must write a term paper for your course in cognition. There are several subproblems: (1) select a topic; (2) locate the literature; (3) read the literature; (4) organize the literature; (5) write the paper; and (6) retype the paper in final form. Incidentally, if you are the type of person who is overwhelmed by large projects, it might help to think of the project as a series of small, concrete, nonthreatening subproblems. Once you have identified the subproblems, you begin with the first subproblem and try to reduce the difference between your original state (for example, "no topic") and your goal state (for example, "topic appropriate for a paper").

In the next few weeks, try to notice the kinds of problems you might solve using means-ends analysis. A problem on a statistics test, for example, can be divided into subproblems of deciding upon the appropriate statistical test, figuring out what measure of variability is appropriate, deriving the critical ratio, and deciding whether the statistic is significant or not. Notice also how the difference reduction aspect of means-ends analysis can be applied to many different

---

Demonstration 7.5   The Hobbits-and-Orcs Problem.

Try solving this problem. (The answer is at the end of the chapter.)

Three Hobbits and three Orcs arrive at a river bank, and they all wish to cross onto the other side. Fortunately, there is a boat, but unfortunately, the boat can only hold two creatures at one time. Also, there is another problem. Orcs are vicious creatures, and whenever there are more Orcs than Hobbits on one side of the river, the Orcs will immediately attack the Hobbits and eat them up. Consequently, you should be certain that you never leave more Orcs than Hobbits on any river bank. How should the problem be solved? (It must be added that the Orcs, though vicious, can be trusted to bring the boat back!)

---

problems. In Demonstration 7.2, for example, difference reduction is a central part of solving the problem. Our original state at one point is an equation:

$$2s - 10 + 5 = s + 5 + 8$$

and our goal state is an equation with a single s alone on one side. We reduce the difference between the two states by adding $+5$ to each side of the equation and subtracting s from each side of the equation.

There is evidence from research that people do organize problems in terms of subproblems. Greeno (1974) used the Hobbits-and-Orcs problem in Demonstration 7.5. His study showed that subjects pause at points in the problem and plan their strategy for the next few moves. They do not move ahead at a steady pace through a long series of individual moves. Specifically, subjects took a long time before the first move and before two other critical moves. At each of these points, they were tackling a subproblem and needed to organize a group of moves.

In some cases means-ends analysis might not be the best approach. Sometimes the solution to a problem depends upon temporarily *increasing* the difference between the original state and the goal state. For example, how did you solve the Hobbits-and-Orcs problem in Demonstration 7.5? Maybe you concentrated on reducing the difference between the original state (all creatures on the right side) and the goal state (all creatures on the left side) and you therefore only moved them from right to left. If you did, you would have ignored some steps that were crucial for the solution of the problem: moving creatures *backward* across the river to the right side of the river.

In "real life," as in Hobbits-and-Orcs problems, we sometimes find that the best way to move forward is to move backward temporarily. As we are working on one of the later subproblems in a problem, we may find that our solution to an earlier subproblem was inadequate. For example, imagine that you are reading the literature in preparing a paper (subproblem 3 in our earlier analysis). You will probably learn that your solution was not complete for subproblem 2, locating the literature. You had thought you had solved that subproblem; the discrepancy between the original state (no literature) and the goal state (literature) had been reduced. Now, however, the need for more literature creates a new discrepancy, and you may have to go back to the library to find more references. Worse still, you may learn while you are reading the literature that your solution to subproblem 1, selecting a topic, was not a good one. Your topic is too broad or too narrow or too difficult or too boring. In short, in order to solve problems we must sometimes violate a strict difference reduction strategy in means-ends analysis.

Newell and Simon (1972) have examined means-ends analysis with a computer simulation approach. In **computer simulation,** a researcher writes a computer program that will perform a task the same way that a human would perform the task. For example, a researcher might try to write a computer program for the Hobbits-and-Orcs problem. The program should make some false starts, just as the human would. The program should be no better at solving the problem than a human would be, and it also should be no worse. The researcher tests the program by having it solve a problem and noting whether the steps it takes match the steps that humans would take in solving the problem.

Sometimes the computer program's performance does not match the performance of human problem solvers. This failure indicates to the researchers that their theory needs to be revised. If the researchers have created a program that does mimic human behavior, however, this success does *not* automatically imply that humans actually solve problems in this fashion. It is possible, for example, that another task could be devised for which the computer program and the human problem solver would perform differently. In psychology, we cannot "prove" that a theory is correct; we can only demonstrate that a theory is compatible or consistent with behavior. Thus, if a program does predict how humans will solve a problem, a theory can be tentatively accepted; if it does not predict problem solutions, a theory can be rejected.

What is the advantage of computer simulation? Why is it preferable to a theory stated in standard English? Many cognitive psychologists favor computer simulation because it allows them to express their theories in precise computer language. In contrast, standard English is much less explicit.

Newell and Simon developed a computer program called **General Problem Solver** or GPS, which is a program whose basic strategy is means-ends analysis. The General Problem Solver has three different methods:

1. The **transform method,** which involves (a) matching the original state (state 1) to the goal state (state 2) and finding the difference between them; (b) reducing

the difference by producing a new and different state (state 3); (c) transforming, or changing, state 3 into state 2, which is the goal state.

2. The **apply-operator method,** which involves (a) determining whether the **operator** (an action that changes the problem from one state to another) can be applied to the original state, and if so, applying it; (b) changing the original state to state 3 if the operator cannot be applied to the original state; and (c) applying the operator to state 3.

3. The **reduce method,** which involves (a) searching for an operator that would help reduce the difference; and (b) applying it to the original state to produce a new state if this operator is found.

Notice that these three methods are different ways of changing the original state into the goal state. The transform method involves creating a new, transition state; the apply-operator method involves finding a state to which the operator can be applied; and the reduce method involves a search for the right operator for the situation.

The General Problem Solver program developed by Newell and Simon has earned an excellent reputation among cognitive psychologists. It has been used to solve "transport problems" like the Hobbits-and-Orcs problem, as well as **crypto-arithmetic problems,** in which the problem solver must find appropriate numbers to substitute for letters (see Demonstration 7.6). The General Problem Solver has also been used to solve a large number of general problems, such as the grammatical analysis of sentences, proofs in logic, and trigonometry problems.

We have considered means-ends analysis in some detail because it is a strategy that people frequently use in solving problems, and it has also captured the attention of cognitive psychologists. However, there are two other heuristics that we must also consider: planning and working backwards.

Demonstration 7.6   *A Cryptoarithmetic Problem.*

```
  D O N A L D
+ G E R A L D
  ─────────────
  R O B E R T
```

There are ten different letters in this problem. Each letter stands for a different number, from 0 to 9. You will get one hint: D = 5. What are the correct numbers for the remaining nine letters? If your substitutions are correct, the arithmetic in the problem will be correct. The answer is at the end of the chapter.

The Planning Strategy.   When we use the **planning strategy,** we disregard some aspects of the problem in order to make the problem simpler. Then once we have solved this simpler problem, we tackle the more complicated problem. The planning strategy is particularly useful if the aspects that we are ignoring can easily be worked into the solution to the complicated problem.

One common kind of planning strategy is the analogy. In an **analogy** (pronounced "uh-*nal*-uh-jee") we use a solution to an earlier problem in order to help with an original problem. Think about how you use analogies in schoolwork. A test in mathematics or statistics presents problems that are analogies of problems that have been solved in class or in homework assignments. The wording may be different, with new details and different numbers, but the basic problem is the same. Remember the earlier discussion of ways of representing the problem in which we noted that people must discover the abstract puzzle underneath all the details? By peeling away the unimportant layers, we reach the core of the problem.

The analogy strategy is also very useful when we encounter problems in pronouncing new words. Imagine a first-grade girl who has just learned how to pronounce the word *though*. When she sees the word *although,* she can temporarily ignore the first two letters and solve the pronunciation of the remainder of the word by analogy. Many times, the analogy strategy will produce a correct solution.

However, the analogy strategy is a heuristic—and remember that heuristics are general rules that do not guarantee a correct solution. In English, the analogy strategy frequently produces an incorrect solution. If the girl were to solve the problem of pronouncing the word *thought* by ignoring the final *t,* she would clearly be led astray. Think about how you have been misled by analogies in the past. In fact, consider that word *misled.* Some people look at this word and think it is the past tense of a new verb called *misle.* They have incorrectly formed an analogy with a word like *tattle,* for which the past tense is *tattled.*

When we say that people use analogies to solve problems, we are really just saying that people learn from past experience. Many times when you encounter a problem, you say, "That's just like a situation that happened to me before." We will discuss this issue further when we consider analogical reasoning in Chapter 8.

Research on the analogy strategy has shown that people can often identify analogies. In some situations, however, they do not use the analogies in solving problems. Let us examine several studies.

Hinsley, Hayes, and Simon (1977) wanted to see whether people could classify various kinds of algebra word problems. They asked high school and college students who had taken courses in algebra to sort problems selected from a high school algebra textbook. They were given 76 problems and were simply told to sort the cards into piles by problem type. The phrase "problem type" was not defined, nor was the number of piles. People did categorize the word problems into clusters. Furthermore, they showed strong agreement about what the categories were.

In their research, Hinsley and his co-workers devised 18 different clusters of algebra problems. The following three examples are typical:

1. *River current.* A river steamer goes 36 miles downstream in the same amount of time that it travels 24 miles upstream. In still water, the steamer would travel at a rate that is 12 miles an hour faster than the rate of the current. What is the rate of the current?
2. *Work.* Mr. Jones takes 3 minutes less than Mr. Smith to assemble a machine when each works alone. One day, Mr. Jones spent 6 minutes assembling a machine and then left; Mr. Smith finished the machine in 4 more minutes. How long would it take Mr. Jones, working alone, to assemble a machine?

3. *Number.* In a certain number, the digit in the units place is 1 more than 3 times the digit in the tens place. If you switch the numbers around, you get a number that is 8 times the sum of the digits. What is that number?

Hinsley and his co-workers also found that people can categorize a problem very early in the presentation of the problem:

> For example, after hearing the three words, "A river steamer . . ." from a river current problem, one subject said, "It's going to be one of those river things with upstream, downstream, and still water. You are going to compare times upstream and downstream . . ." (p. 97)

People certainly do not require much information in order to grasp the analogy with other, similar problems they have encountered in the past.

Hinsley and his co-workers also found that problem categorization does not depend upon the specific words in the problem. In one clever study they substituted nonsense words in a standard problem to yield problems like this one:

> According to ferbent, the optimally fuselt grix of voipe unmolts five stens of voipe thrump 95 bines per sten. In order to embler some wuss voipe, each grix will unmolt one sten at 70 bines per sten. If the grix is to be optimally fuselt, what should the bines per sten of the rest of the voipe be? (p. 100)

A problem like this brings shudders to many people, particularly those who shudder even over problems written in standard English. Nevertheless, the subjects attacked them diligently, trying to fit them into some normal scheme or framework. One subject's **protocol** (a word-by-word record of a person's remarks during the experiment) began like this:

> There is some sort of machine, let's call it the grix. Which receives some sort of fuel, called a sten. And it produces, let's say work, out of that sten, usually whips out 90 bines per unit of sten . . . (p. 101)

Thus, people approach algebra word problems by trying to categorize them, finding similarities between these new problems and other familiar problems. They notice that the abstract representations of the problems are similar, and they can ignore the irrelevant details.

Unfortunately, however, other researchers have shown that problem solvers often ignore analogies that should prove useful. Reed (1977), for example, studied subjects' performance on two similar problems. One was the Hobbits-and-Orcs problem that you know from Demonstration 7.5. The second problem is a more difficult version of the same problem, traditionally known as the "jealous-husbands problem."

In one experiment, Reed tested whether solving one problem would produce an advantage in solving the other problem. Half of the subjects solved the Hobbits-and-Orcs problem first, and half solved the jealous-husbands problem first. To his surprise, Reed found that there was no significant transfer between the two problems. In a second experiment, subjects were told about the relationship between the two problems and were encouraged to use their solution to the first problem in attacking the second problem. Reed found that if subjects first solved the jealous-husbands problem (the more difficult one) they took less time on the

Hobbits-and-Orcs problem. However, if they first solved the Hobbits-and-Orcs problem (the easier one), there was no change in the amount of time on the jealous-husbands problem.

Reed concludes that the analogy strategy is not used as often as we might have thought. Even though two problems look similar, subjects may not show transfer between them. He proposes that analogies can be useful only if the following conditions are true: (1) subjects must notice that the present problem is analogous to the previous problem; (2) they must remember how they solved the earlier problem; (3) they must be able to translate the previous solution into steps that apply to the original problem; and (4) the time taken to retrieve, translate, and use the information in the analogy should be less than the time to discover the same information "starting from scratch."

Hayes and Simon (1977) found little transfer from one task to another in five-handed-monster problems like the one in Demonstration 7.1. They changed only a few words in each problem and asked subjects to solve both the original and the altered problems. The subjects tended to use different kinds of notations for the two versions of the problem. Furthermore, the solution to the first problem did not help as much as we might expect in solving the second problem. In summary, the analogy strategy is useful, but problem solvers do not exploit this strategy often enough.

Backward Search.   With the **backward search** heuristic, the problem solver starts at the goal state and works backward to the original state. You may have used this approach in some games. For example, if you are working on a maze puzzle, you may find that a backward search combines well with a forward search. You might start with a line from the beginning point and then leave that project for a minute while you start with another line from the goal, heading back toward the beginning point.

There are also some peg games in which the player eliminates pegs by "jumping" pegs over nearby pegs. The goal is to end up with just one peg in the center of the board. Although a major part of this game is played by a forward search, a backward search is also necessary. You must work backward from the goal of one peg in the middle in order to design a setup in which you have two pegs remaining, and one peg jumps the other in order to land in the middle hole.

We also conduct backward searches when we try to understand the punchline in jokes. Consider this joke, for example:

> A man named Rudolph and his wife were visiting Russia and they stopped at an inn for dinner. Their waiter looked out at the sky and said, "It looks like it's going to rain soon."
>
> Rudolph looked at the sky and replied that it did not look like there was any chance of rain.
>
> The wife responded, "Rudolph the red nose reindeer."

To understand this joke, we have to start with the goal of the punch line and work backward, searching for how each fragment in the punch line is related to the given information.

Backward searches are useful in academic subjects as well as for entertainment purposes. If you have ever been faced with the assignment of doing a proof in mathematics, statistics, or logic, you know that it is often helpful to work both forward and backward. In fact, this alternation—moving forward from the original state and backward from the goal state—is similar to the alternation involved in solving a maze puzzle.

Newell and Simon (1972) describe a computer simulation program called **Logic Theorist,** which is designed to conduct proofs in symbolic logic. An important feature of the Logic Theorist is that it conducts backward searches. The Logic Theorist starts with the theorem, which is the last step in a logic proof. The search will then proceed backwards in the direction of the axiom and the other assumed theorems. Newell and Simon arrived at this program after watching humans solve problems and observing that they often started at the end and worked backward. The Logic Theorist program successfully mimicked human problems; like them, it also failed to solve some of the logic problems.

When do people attack a problem by conducting a backward search? In most cases, people work forward. However, working backward is a useful strategy when the goal is relatively simple and clear-cut, but the original state is vague and cluttered with many different options. For example, a backward search would be ideal for a maze with many paths out of the beginning point yet only one path leading from the goal.

Factors Affecting Problem Solving

There are numerous factors that influence problem solving. Obviously, the total size of the problem space is an important factor, as we discussed before. The Hobbits-and-Orcs problem was challenging with just three Hobbits and three Orcs. Imagine how tricky that problem would be with ten Hobbits and ten Orcs! The characteristics we will discuss here are: (1) functional fixedness and mental set and (2) training.

Functional Fixedness and Mental Set.   Think of an occasion in the past week in which you used some object in a new way. For example, you may have stirred your coffee with a pencil (assuming that you had no spoon and were quite desperate). People typically find it difficult to use common objects in new ways because of a factor called functional fixedness. **Functional fixedness** means that the function we assign to objects tends to remain fixed or stable. If an object has one particular function for us (writing, for example), it is difficult to switch its function (to stirring, for example).

The classic study in functional fixedness, called Duncker's candle problem (Duncker, 1945), is shown in Demonstration 7.7. Weisberg and Suls (1973) summarize studies that have been conducted on this problem. When people see the setup illustrated in Demonstration 7.7, most of them either try to tack the candle to the wall or use melted wax to try to glue it up. On the other hand, if the box of tacks is empty, people are much more likely to use it as part of the solution. Weisberg and Suls conducted six experiments in which various aspects of the setup were varied, and they derived a flowchart model of subjects' performance on the task. As you may recall from the first chapter, a **flowchart** is a diagram with arrows used to connect a series of boxes, which represent different kinds of processing. A flowchart provides an overview of a computer simulation program. Thus, a person can understand the major steps in the program without requiring an understanding of the computer language.

Demonstration 7.7   Duncker's Candle Problem

Imagine that you are in an empty room that contains only a table, on which sit three items: a candle, a box of tacks, and a box of matches. You must find a way to attach the candle to the wall of the room, so that it burns properly. You may only use the three specified items in solving the problem. (The correct answer appears in the discussion of the experiment.)

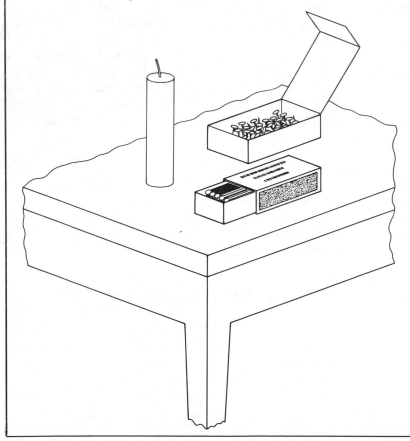

One aspect of their model, for example, is that subjects do not focus on the box at first. Instead, they consider the box only after they have found difficulties with other more direct solutions, such as tacking the candle to the wall. Weisberg and Suls recorded the protocols of subjects trying to solve the problem. Here is a typical protocol in which failures on the direct solutions lead to the correct, indirect solution:

Candle has to burn straight, so if I took a nail and put it through the candle and cardboard . . . (10 sec) . . . if I took several nails and made a row and set the candle on that. If I took the nails out of the box, nailed the box to the wall . . . . (p. 268)

The series of experiments confirmed that characteristics of the task, such as labeling the box as a separate object, makes it more likely that people will disregard functional fixedness and find new and creative uses for the box.

Functional fixedness describes a characteristic of objects in a problem-solving task. A related concept, *mental set,* describes a characteristic of people in a problem-solving task. With a **mental set,** problem solvers keep using the same solution they have used in previous problems, even though there may be easier ways of approaching the problem. In both functional fixedness and mental set, there are old ideas that persist and inhibit the development of new ideas.

The classic experiment on mental set is the Luchins water-jar problem (Luchins, 1942), which is illustrated in Demonstration 7.8.

Demonstration 7.8   Luchins' (1942) Water-Jar Problem.

Imagine that you have three jars, *A, B,* and *C.* In each of seven problems the capacity of the three jars is listed. You must use the three jars in order to obtain the amount of liquid specified in the "Goal" column. You may obtain the goal amount by adding or subtracting the quantities listed in *A, B,* and *C.* (The answers can be found in the discussion of the experiment.)

Problem	A	B	C	Goal
1	24	130	3	100
2	9	44	7	21
3	21	58	4	29
4	12	160	25	98
5	19	75	5	46
6	23	49	3	20
7	18	48	4	22

The best way to solve problem 1 is to fill up jar B and remove one jarful with jar A and two jarsful with jar C. Since problems 1–5 can all be solved in this fashion, they create a set for the problem solver. Most people will keep using this method when they reach problems 6 and 7. However, this past learning will actually be a disadvantage, because there are easier, more direct ways of solving these problems. Problem 6 can be solved by subtracting C from A, and problem 7 can be solved by adding C to A. Luchins found that almost all of the subjects to whom he gave such complex problems as 1 to 5 persisted in the same complex kind of solution on later problems. On the other hand, control subjects, who began right away with problems such as 6 and 7, almost always solved the problem in the easier fashion.

A mental set works against us in our everyday experiences, too. Consider, for example, the problem of getting to a particular location in a nearby city, a problem that resembles a maze puzzle in many respects. Have you ever worked out a long, elaborate route involving many turns—a route that you have used for years—only to find that someone else discovered a simpler, more direct route on the first try?

Functional fixedness and mental sets are two more examples of our theme that mistakes in cognitive processing can often be traced to a strategy that is basically very rational. In general, objects in our world have fixed functions. For example, we use a hammer to pound in a nail and a wrench to tighten a bolt. The strategy of using one tool for one task and another tool for another task is generally very wise; after all, each was specifically designed for its own task. Functional fixedness occurs when we apply that strategy too rigidly and fail to realize, for instance, that if all other tools are missing, a wrench could be used to pound in the nail. Similarly, it is generally a wise strategy to use the knowledge you learned in earlier problems in solving the present problem. However, in the case of mental sets, we apply the past-experience strategy too rigidly and fail to notice more efficient solutions.

Training.   Several kinds of programs have been devised to train people in problem solving. One study compared the effects of algorithmic and heuristic problem-solving training (de Leeuw, 1978). Some fifth and sixth graders were taught an algorithm that consisted of a series of decisions for students to make in order to reach the problem solution. Other students were allowed to discover relations for themselves, thus making their own sets of decisions, using the heuristic method. Immediately after the training session, students who had been given an algorithm performed best. However, several days later, the students who had used the heuristic method had the best performance. Thus, in the long run, the heuristic method was superior.

Tobias (1978) has popularized a more generalized kind of problem-solving training, which is designed to combat "math anxiety." According to Tobias, many people feel very anxious when they are faced with a mathematics problem. (How did you feel about Demonstration 7.2?) As Tobias writes,

> The first thing people remember about failing at math is that it felt like sudden death. Whether it happened while learning word problems in sixth grade, coping with equations in high school, or first confronting calculus and statistics in college, failure was sudden and very frightening. An idea or a new operation was not just difficult, it was impossible! And instead of asking questions or taking the lesson slowly, assuming that in a month or so they would be able to digest it, people remember the feeling, as certain as it was sudden, that they would *never* go any further in mathematics. (p. 44)

Tobias, who had herself avoided math courses, describes some of the training procedures used in math anxiety clinics. You may want to read her book, *Overcoming Math Anxiety,* for more details.

These math anxiety sessions start with people telling their "math autobiographies," which outline their personal experiences with math and math anxiety. The participants feel encouraged that other people have shared similar problems. The clinics try to eliminate anxiety-producing experiences, such as tests, competition, and pressure to get the right answer. The feeling of satisfaction that participants experience when they solve problems in these relaxed circumstances makes them feel more competent about tackling math problems in other settings.

Scandura (1977), in a discussion of the application of problem-solving techniques to education, made a similar point, ". . . undoubtedly the single most important ingredient of problem-solving ability is *experience*" (p. 560). He urges that the key to success is providing problems that challenge students but do not overwhelm them. Clearly, students will not learn if they are given only problems that they will fail to solve. By solving appropriate problems, however, students may—as we saw in Chapter 6—"learn to learn."

SECTION SUMMARY: Solving the Problem

1. Problem-solving strategies differ in the time they require to produce an answer and in the likelihood of producing an answer.

2. In unsystematic random search (one kind of algorithm), the problem solver uses trial-and-error strategies and may repeat a response that previously proved wrong.

3. In systematic random search (another kind of algorithm) the problem solver uses trial-and-error strategies but does not repeat any responses.

4. Heuristics—in contrast to algorithms—are selective searches that examine the parts of the problem space that are most likely to produce a solution. Heuristics do not guarantee a solution, but they are less time-consuming than algorithms.

5. Means-ends analysis is a kind of heuristic that involves dividing the problem into subproblems and then figuring out the means to reach each of the ends. The General Problem Solver is a computer program that uses means-ends analysis.

6. The planning strategy is another kind of heuristic. It involves disregarding some aspects of the problem in order to make the problem simpler, and then tackling the complicated problem. The analogy is an example of the planning strategy. People often fail to make use of analogies in solving problems.

7. The backward-search heuristic involves starting at the goal state and working backward to the original state. A computer program called the Logic Theorist is based on this strategy.

8. There are many factors that influence problem solving; two such factors are (a) functional fixedness and mental set and (b) training.

9. Some problems involve functional fixedness. Problem solution is more likely if functional fixedness can be disregarded.

10. When people have a mental set, they rely too strongly on problem-solving strategies they have used in the past, and they may avoid solving problems efficiently.

11. People can improve their problem-solving performance by training. Training can include teaching heuristic methods, reducing math anxiety, and providing experience in problem solving.

Ill-Defined Problems

Most of the problems we have considered so far could be called well defined. A **well-defined problem,** according to Reitman (1964) is a problem for which we have some systematic way to decide whether a solution is correct. For an anagram, for example, we know that we have reached a correct solution when the rearranged letters form a word. For the Hobbits-and-Orcs problem, we know we are correct if we managed to transport Hobbits and Orcs to the other side without violating any of the rules.

Reitman notes that the largest percentage of human energy is devoted to ill-defined problems, which is ironic when we consider that cognitive psychologists have primarily studied well-defined problems. An **ill-defined problem** is a problem for which we have no systematic way to tell whether a solution is correct.

Reitman discusses in detail a protocol of a musician who is composing a fugue, which is a musical form in which a theme is taken up and developed by several instruments in sequence. Obviously, this composer has no way of knowing whether he has reached the correct solution, so fugue composition qualifies as an ill-defined problem. Here are some sections of his remarks as he struggles with a portion of the fugue and wonders about using syncopation, which is a shift in the accent of a musical passage:

> Now we have a new motive, da diii (sings and plays). What shall we do with the new motive. It doesn't do anything yet (plays). Uh, some kind of syncopation, da-daa, dii (sings and plays). The rhythm has to be different from the theme, and yet hold itself as an idea, as a rhythmic idea (plays, counting). Carrying out the idea of enlarged syncopation . . . (plays). That won't work, because it's repetitive of the theme itself. . . . (erasing) I think we'll abandon the idea of the enlarged syncopation to get away from repetition of theme . . . and try to do something more pianistic. . . . (p. 291)

Notice how different this process is from the problem-solving steps you take for an algebra problem.

Simon (1973) describes another ill-defined problem, an architect designing a house. Notice, incidentally, that an architect could take a well-defined approach to the problem by selecting a standard house design and duplicating it. If the architect intends to create an original design, however, the problem is certainly ill defined. The architect could consider all kinds of structures, such as a geodesic dome, an A-frame, arches and so on. The architect would also have to consider many varieties of material, such as wood, metal, concrete, camel's hides, marble, granite, rubber, ice (as Simon notes, don't object to ice—it's been done). Furthermore, there would be many different ways of proceeding. The architect might start with floor plans, or with the design for the front of the building, or with a list of needs stipulated by the client. Very few aspects of this problem are clearly defined.

Think about some ill-defined problems you have worked on in the last week. Perhaps you wrote a paper—we considered this problem in the last section. When you were finished, you had no way of deciding whether the end result was correct. You did not have a list of features that had to be present for you to conclude that you had solved the problem. In fact, that is one of the frustrating features of writing papers—often you have no clear-cut way of knowing when to quit. Also, you may have decided to rearrange the furniture in your room. Again, there was no way of deciding whether the end result is correct.

Another characteristic of well-defined problems is that they have a clear-cut original state, goal state, and rules for transforming the original state into the goal state. In the Hobbits-and-Orcs problem, for example, all of these conditions are clearly specified. In ill-defined problems, some aspects of the original state, goal state, and rules are unclear. When you write a paper, for example, there are uncertainties for each of the subproblems. Consider the subproblem of locating the literature. Your original state is unclear: Exactly what resources are you working with? Must you confine yourself to the books and periodicals in your own campus library? The goal state is certainly vague: How many resources is enough? The rules are also ambiguous: Should you locate the literature by consulting bibliographies and references listed in textbooks, by looking in *Psychological Abstracts*, by asking the professor, by looking in the reference section of other articles, or by thumbing through some likely journals?

Reitman (1965) notes that we can also distinguish between well-defined and ill-defined problems in terms of whether people agree about the solution to the problem. If there is a high level of agreement among a group of problem solvers, the problem is well defined. For example, we all agree that the solution to the anagram LSSTNEUIAMYOUL is SIMULTANEOUSLY. If there can be disagreement, the problem is ill defined. Have you ever written a paper you considered spectacular, but the professor considered mediocre? Have you praised the architecture of a new house, only to find that your roommate thought it was an eyesore? Without a well-defined goal state, people will disagree about what constitutes an appropriate solution.

Types of Ill-defined Problems

Reitman (1964) discusses many different kinds of ill-defined problems; we'll look at several of them. Notice that they differ in the extent to which the original state, goal state, and rules are defined.

1. An example of one kind of problem is the classic impossible task of trying to convert a sow's ear into a silk purse. This problem is reasonably well specified in that we have a well-defined original state: one ear of an adult female pig. The goal state is also well-defined: one purse made out of a material made by silkworms. But notice what is *not* specified—the size of the ear, the size of the purse, whether any material can be added or subtracted, and so on.

2. An example of a second kind of problem is to invent a dispenser for glue that has one piece without a top to be removed and replaced; the mouth must be designed to open for dispensing and to close tightly after use. Now if this object has not yet been invented, the goal state is certainly not defined. Furthermore, the initial state is left entirely up to us. Many problems, such as writing a paper or composing a fugue, fit into this category.

3. According to legends, Napoleon wished to have a good dinner after he had defeated the Austrians in the battle of Marengo. His chef, because of the war, only had a chicken, some onions, mushrooms, wine, and tomatoes. Nevertheless, he created from these ingredients a delicious dish, now known as Chicken

Marengo. In this example, the original state consists of several well-defined components. However, the goal state is quite unclear.

   4. A thief has just committed a crime and is searching for an alibi. In this case, notice that the goal state—the alibi itself—is well specified. The original state, however, is entirely unspecified. There are thousands of possible explanations for what he or she might have been doing at the time of the crime.

Solving an Ill-defined Problem

If ill-defined problems lack clear-cut original states, end states, and rules, then it will be difficult to provide clear-cut methods for solving the problems. Let us consider some strategies, however, that might be useful.

   One strategy should sound familiar from the previous section of this chapter: Break the problem into several subproblems. Work on each subproblem independently, and then combine them and resolve any incompatibilities. For example, if you have to write a short story for an English class, you might block out certain sections of the story. You might first work on the opening paragraph, then write a description of the characters, then jump to the end, then fill in the middle parts. As we noted earlier, a problem is less threatening if it can be treated as several subproblems.

   A second strategy in solving ill-structured problems is to add more structure to the situation. One problem with an ill-structured problem is that there are so few constraints or limitations in the task. In order to reach a solution, we must somehow restrict the possibilities. The musician composing the fugue sometimes proposed constraints that he later rejected, such as the idea of syncopation, but on other occasions he proposed constraints that he kept, such as an idea that the work must be "pianistic." This constraint added to the structure of the problem and limited the possible solutions to the problem. Consequently, the problem was more manageable.

   A third strategy for ill-structured problems is to start work on the problem even if you do not yet understand it completely. Let us return to the example of writing a paper. You may have an area that you are interested in exploring, even if you only have a vague understanding of the field. Only by working on the project can you understand the critical questions and issues in that field. Later you might feel overwhelmed by trying to organize the literature. By writing sections of the paper, you might find similarities and structure. Sometimes you will make a mistake, but the mistake will provide useful information. Hayes (1978) has pointed out how jumping into a problem and "getting your feet wet" is a useful strategy in solving some unusual oddity problems. In a standard **oddity problem,** the problem solver must decide which member of a series is different. Try Demonstration 7.9 and "get your feet wet."

   You must work on this problem several moments before you realize that flower 1 could be the answer because it has three petals, rather than four, but flower 2 could be the answer because it has a broader leaf, and so on. In fact, flower 5 is the answer because it is the only one that has no unique attribute. Similarly, my 7-year-old daughter once noted that she and I liked corn, but her sister was an oddball because she did not like corn. On the other hand, her sister and I liked ham,

---

Demonstration 7.9   *Solving an Ill-defined Problem*.

Which of the following pictures is different from the others? (The answer is discussed in this section.)

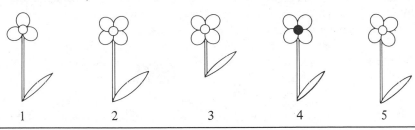

| 1 | 2 | 3 | 4 | 5 |

---

but she was an oddball because she did not like ham. Therefore, she declared me to be the oddball because I was the only one who was not an oddball!

A fourth strategy in problem solving is to stop when you have a solution, even if it may not be the best possible solution. After all, the goal state is not clear in an ill-structured problem, so how can we know when we have reached it? If an art professor gives you an assignment to draw a still-life picture, at some point you must say, "Stop, I'm finished." It may not be the best possible fruit bowl in the world, but it follows the artistic guidelines you have learned, and the apples, pears, and grapes are certainly recognizable. Yes, you could spend more time on it and perhaps improve it, but maybe if you spent more time you would come up with an inferior picture. (I remember my fifth-grade teacher looking at a disastrous picture of a sunset I had painted and remarking that I "should have left well enough alone.") In other words, the goal state is arbitrary, so we can be arbitrary about deciding that the task is finished.

The Fuzzy Boundary between Well-defined and Ill-defined Problems

Some psychologists have argued that all problems—even those that are typically considered well defined—are really somewhat ill defined. Simon (1973) suggests that the boundary between well-defined and ill-defined problems is quite vague and fluid—it cannot be formally described. He considers two examples, proving a theorem in formal logic and playing chess. Both of these problems are typically considered to be well defined. However, they both have characteristics that make them ill defined. For example, a person proving a logic theorem may not confine the search to the language of formal logic but may choose to solve the problem by using an analogy with another logic proof. Thus, the rules of formal logic proofs are ill defined. Chess playing, on the other hand, is well defined if we examine a single move in a game. However, if we consider an entire game of chess to be a problem, this problem is ill defined. After all, the game involves continually redefining what the problem is.

Greeno (1976) wrote an article titled "Indefinite Goals in Well-structured Problems," which also argues for a fuzzy boundary between ill-defined and well-defined problems. He believes that people often use indefinite subgoals even when they are faced with a well-defined problem such as a proof in geometry. In his study he asked high school students enrolled in a course in plane geometry to perform geometric proofs, for example, to prove that two triangles in a diagram are congruent. Greeno collected protocols consisting of the students' comments as they solved the problem. He then instructed raters to judge whether the protocols showed evidence of using specific goals in solving the problem.

Greeno concluded that the students seemed to use ill-defined subgoals, rather than clearly structured subgoals. For example, one student was asked whether he was thinking about specific theorems, and he replied:

> "I don't know. I was just sort of letting . . . I was just sort of letting the information . . . I shouldn't have said that I was running through all the theorems. I was just letting this stuff, the given information, sort of soak through my head, you know." (p. 483)

Perhaps it would be best to conclude that there is a continuum that runs from well-defined problems to ill-defined problems, because we cannot define a clear boundary between the two categories. Some problems fall at the well-defined end of the continuum, such as the algebra problem in Demonstration 7.2. Some problems fall way over in the ill-defined end of the continuum, such as the assignment, "Compose a fugue." Most problems, however, probably have both well-defined and ill-defined features.

Ill-defined Problems in Applied Areas

Reitman (1964) proposes that ill-defined problems are enormously important in applied areas, such as business. In business situations, there is often an ill-defined problem that must be converted into a more defined problem by adding appropriate constraints and assumptions. For example, Dill, Hilton, and Reitman (1962) have described the situation of a young executive who was assigned a problem with nothing more than the instructions to "look into" the possible opportunities that might be offered to his firm by operations research techniques. The first stages alone took four months.

Dill and his coauthors also point out that, for their sample of young executives, well-structured assignments were the exception rather than the rule. Furthermore, both individuals and organizations are limited as to the amount of information they can process as situations change. Consequently, ill-defined, unstructured problems will probably remain a significant part of the business world.

SECTION SUMMARY: Ill-defined Problems

1. With ill-defined problems we have no systematic way of judging whether a solution is correct.
2. Examples of ill-defined problems include composing a fugue and designing a house.
3. With ill-defined problems, people can disagree about the solution to the problem.
4. In ill-defined problems the original state, the goal state, and/or the rules are unspecified.

5. Strategies for solving ill-defined problems include breaking the problem into several subproblems, adding more structure to the situation, beginning work on the problem before it is completely understood, and stopping when a solution is reached—even if the solution is not ideal.
6. According to some psychologists, there is a fuzzy boundary between ill-defined and well-defined problems. Most problems have both ill-defined and well-defined features.
7. In everyday life, ill-defined, unstructured problems are more common than well-defined problems.

Creativity

It is quite possible that you breathed a sigh of relief as you finished the sections on problem solving and prepared to read a section on creativity. Problem solving sounds so routine, whereas creativity sounds inspired. People who do problem solving sit around working out their means-ends analyses, whereas people who do creative thinking sit around with light bulbs above their heads—just like cartoon characters.

Truthfully, however, creativity is an area of problem solving. Creativity, like the areas of problem solving that we have already considered, involves moving from an original state to a goal state. In fact, you can think of creativity as being the process involved in solving ill-defined problems. In situations requiring creativity, the goal state and the rules for reaching it are not clearly stated.

The area of creativity is a difficult one to summarize. There are many different definitions of creativity, as you will see, and there is no one, accepted way to measure it. We will talk about definitions and measurements and then proceed to the topic of discovering problems. We will also consider methods of encouraging creativity.

Definitions

It would be easy to write a whole chapter on the variety of definitions for creativity that have been proposed. Our discussion will be shorter, but it will still be long enough to demonstrate the wide variety of definitions that have been proposed for creativity. Before you read further, ask a friend about his or her definition of creativity.

Perhaps your friend's definition states that creativity involves coming up with a new and unusual answer to a question or problem. Certainly novelty is a necessary part of creativity, but novelty is not enough. The answer must also allow us to reach our goal—it must be practical and useful. Suppose I asked you to come up with a creative answer to the question, "How can you roast a pig?" The nineteenth-century essayist Charles Lamb observed that one way to roast a pig is to put it into a house and then burn the house down. This answer would not fulfill the usefulness requirement—though it *would* be novel. To many people, then, **creativity** involves finding a solution that is both unusual and useful; Stein (1956) and Murray (1959) were among the first to suggest this view. Let's look at some other definitions that stress other criteria for creativity.

Newell and Simon, whom we discussed in the section entitled "Solving the Problem," worked together with another colleague, Shaw, and suggested four criteria for creativity (Newell, Shaw, & Simon, 1963). One or more of these criteria must be satisfied for an answer to be considered creative:

1. The answer has novelty and usefulness, either for the individual or the society.
2. The answer demands that we reject ideas we had previously accepted.
3. The answer results from intense motivation and persistence.
4. The answer comes from clarifying a problem that was originally vague.

Taylor (1975) has an excellent discussion of the history of creativity, including its definitions. Some investigators believe that there is one kind of creativity, present to varying extents in all people. For example, some people have described creativity as simply the ability to bring something new into existence. Another view proposed by Mednick (1962), which will be considered more extensively later, is that creativity involves taking diverse associations and forming them into new combinations. In these two definitions of creativity, creativity comes in only one "flavor," but some people have more of this ability than others.

In contrast, Taylor notes that other theorists believe that there are two or more different kinds of creativity. For example, Ghiselin (1958) suggests that there are two kinds of creativity, the creativity possessed by people who devote their lives to creative works, and the creativity possessed by the rest of the population. Thus, Ghiselin and others believe that there is a qualitative difference between the two kinds of creativity—they differ in quality or type—and not just a quantitative difference, as proposed by those who believe in one kind of creativity.

Measuring Creativity

If people disagree about what creativity is, how can they possibly agree about how to measure it? As you might imagine, they do not agree at all. Furthermore, there is currently no test of creativity that has consistently predicted which people will be more creative in real-life situations. The well-known resource, *Tests in Print* (Buros, 1972) lists numerous tests of creativity. These include tests in which people make drawings, suggest possible jobs, and find faults with certain suggestions. We will consider only two of these tests, Guilford's (1967) Divergent Production tests and Mednick and Mednick's (1967) Remote Associates Test.

Guilford's test emerges from his idea that people have at least 120 different, independent kinds of mental abilities. Some of these abilities involve memory, some involve evaluating or judging, and some (in fact, 24) involve divergent production. In **divergent production,** people make a number of varied responses to each test item. Demonstration 7.10 shows some of the 24 ways in which Guilford measured divergent production.

Guilford discusses some of the support for Divergent Production tests. In one study, for example, public relations and advertising employees were judged by their superiors to be either "creative" or "less creative." All employees then took the Divergent Production tests. On five of the eight tests, the creative employees did significantly better than less creative employees. On the other hand, Guilford comments, "Correlations between DP (Divergent Production) test scores and

---

Demonstration 7.10   Divergent Production Tests.

Try the following items, which are similar to Guilford's (1967) Divergent Production tests.

1. Here is a simple, familiar form: a circle. How many pictures of real objects can you make using a circle, in a one-minute period?

2. Many words begin with an L and end with an N. List as many words as possible, in a one-minute period, that have the form L _____ N. (They can have any number of letters in between the L and the N.)
3. Suppose that people reached their final height at the age of 2, and so normal adult height was less than a meter. In a one-minute period, list as many consequences as possible that would result from this change.
4. Here is a list of names. They can be classified in many ways. For example, one classification would be in terms of the number of syllables; SALLY, LUCY, and HAROLD have two syllables, whereas BETH, GAIL, and JOHN have one syllable. Classify them in as many ways as possible, in a one-minute period.

   BETH   HAROLD   GAIL   JOHN   LUCY   SALLY

5. Here are four shapes. Combine them to make each of the following objects: a face, a lamp, a piece of playground equipment, a tree. Each shape may be used once, many times, or not at all in forming each object, and it may be expanded or shrunk to any size.

---

criteria of creativity during the years through high school have not been spectacular, to say the least" (p. 163).

The Remote Associates Test (RAT) was devised by Mednick and Mednick (1967) to measure their concept of creativity. Try Demonstration 7.11 to see several examples of the kinds of problems on the RAT. The Mednicks interpreted creativity to mean the ability to see relationships between ideas that are remote from each other. Creative people can take far-flung ideas and combine them into new associations that meet certain criteria. They quote a variety of creative artists, authors, and scientists, who comment on their own ability to combine ideas. For example, Samuel Taylor Coleridge, a nineteenth-century British poet, described his ideas: "Facts which sank at intervals out of conscious recollection drew together beneath the surface through the almost chemical affinities of common elements" (Mednick & Mednick, 1967, p. 1). The mathematician Poincaré said, "to create consists of making new combinations of associative elements which are useful. The mathematical facts worthy of being studied . . . are those which reveal to us unsuspected kinships . . ."

Demonstration 7.11   Remote Associates.

For each set of three words, try to think of a fourth word that is related to all three words. For example, the words ROUGH, RESISTANCE, and BEER suggest the word DRAFT, because of the phrases, ROUGH DRAFT, DRAFT RESISTANCE, and DRAFT BEER. (The answers are at the end of the chapter.)

1. CHARMING	STUDENT	VALIANT
2. FOOD	CATCHER	HOT
3. HEARTED	FEET	BITTER
4. DARK	SHOT	SUN
5. CANADIAN	GOLF	SANDWICH
6. TUG	GRAVY	SHOW
7. ATTORNEY	SELF	SPENDING
8. MAGIC	PITCH	POWER
9. ARM	COAL	PEACH
10. TYPE	GHOST	STORY

Using these introspections as well as similar statements about creativity from psychologists such as Freud and Binet, the Mednicks decided to measure creativity in terms of the ability to link remote associates. As Demonstration 7.11 shows, the **Remote Associates Test** items consist of three words or phrases that must be linked together with a single word.

Mednick and Mednick cite a number of studies demonstrating this relationship. For example, scientists in a chemical firm who have high RAT scores also have higher job classifications. Also, psychology graduate students who have high RAT scores tend to be rated as highly creative by their research advisors. Finally, technicians with IBM who had high RAT scores were more likely to make award-winning suggestions for improvement of the company. Unfortunately, however, other studies have found no relationship between RAT scores and measures of creativity in work situations.

A study by Andrews (1975) points out that creativity, as assessed by tests such as the RAT, may be related to real-life creativity only if all the circumstances are ideal. He located 115 scientists who had directed research projects. The scientists took the RAT, and they also answered questions about the laboratory environment in which they worked. Independent judgments were obtained on the quality of their scientific output. Andrews found no relationship between RAT measures and scientific output. However, he conducted another analysis and found that there *was* a relationship if the environmental factors were examined as well. Some of the scientists worked in a situation in which they had opportunities for innovation, made decisions about the research, felt professionally secure, and worked independently. For these scientists, high RAT scorers had greater scientific output than low RAT scorers. For the people who worked in less pleasant situations, there was no positive relationship. In other words, in ideal work settings, scores on the RAT *are* related to real-life measures of creativity.

Incidentally, you may wonder whether Divergent Production test scores are related to Remote Associates Test scores. Unfortunately, they are not, as studies using both adults (Goodman, Furcon, & Rose, 1969) and children (Ward, 1975) have demonstrated. In other words, people who make a large number of varied responses to items are not any better than average in figuring out how a variety of items might be related to each other. These two concepts of creativity therefore seem to be measuring different abilities.

Discovering Problems

Some people have argued that the real test of creativity comes not from solving problems creatively, but from discovering the right problem that needs to be solved. Mackworth (1965), for example, believes that psychologists should pay more attention to this difficult area of *problem finding*. He writes:

> First of all, problem finding is more important than problem solving. Indeed, the greatest contribution that can be made nowadays is to formulate new and testable ideas; the scientist who does not speculate is no scientist at all. (p. 52)

Mackworth also believes that problem findings are so scarce that they form a scientific bottleneck. The rate at which discoveries are made is limited by the number of people who can formulate significant research problems.

Getzels and Csikszentmihalyi (1975) also complain about the lack of attention to problem finding. They quote Albert Einstein, who said, "The formulation of a problem is often more essential than its solution . . ." (Einstein & Infeld, 1938, p. 92).

Getzels and Csikszentmihalyi report a study of artists at the School of the Art Institute of Chicago. The artists were asked to compose a still-life display, using as many objects as they wished from a table filled with items and then to draw the still life. The authors recorded three measures during this problem-finding stage: (1) the number of objects handled (scores ranged from 2−19); (2) the kinds of interactions with the objects (some people merely picked them up, whereas others smelled them, bit them, and moved their parts); (3) the uniqueness of the selected objects (many people chose a leather-bound book, whereas some objects were selected by only one person).

After all of the pictures were completed, they were rated by a panel of artists and critics. Many of the correlations were statistically significant. For example, people who had handled a large number of objects, who interacted frequently with them, and who chose unique objects produced pictures that were judged to have higher overall aesthetic value and greater originality. Furthermore, the artists were located seven years after the study had been completed. People who had received high scores on the three measures of creativity in problem finding were more likely to be successful artists, whereas people who had received low scores were likely to have left the field or to have been unsuccessful in the area. Thus an important part of the creative process occurs before the artist's charcoal has touched the paper.

Encouraging Creativity

If you turned to this section prepared to read a sure-fire way to become creative, you will be disappointed. Nonetheless, we will consider some suggestions that have been proposed in recent years for encouraging creative solutions. Other ideas are available in a book by Olson (1978).

Probably the most common group approach to encouraging creativity is Osborn's (1957) brainstorming principle. **Brainstorming** is a process conducted in a group setting in which there are four basic guidelines:

1. Evaluation of ideas must be withheld until later; thus criticism is ruled out.
2. The wilder the idea, the better. It is easier to tame an idea later than to think one up.
3. The greater the number of ideas, the better.
4. People can combine two or more ideas proposed by others.

Osborn maintains that the spirit of a brainstorm session is important. People should encourage themselves as well as encourage each other. Complete friendliness and a relaxed frame of mind are especially important.

Does brainstorming work? Barron (1969) concludes that some studies have not supported the value of brainstorming, but the majority of controlled investigations have shown an increase in both the quantity and quality of ideas when brainstorming principles are used.

Another approach to encouraging creativity is called synectics. **Synectics** is a method developed by Gordon (1961) that encourages the use of analogies in creative thinking. The method emphasizes making the strange familiar and the familiar strange through the use of four kinds of analogies:

1. The **personal analogy** encourages you to place yourself directly in the situation. For example, if you want to make a particular machine work more efficiently, imagine that you are that machine.
2. The **direct analogy** encourages you to find something else that solves the problem you are examining. Very often it is helpful to look at solutions provided by human or animal biology. Alexander Graham Bell did this when he considered how the relatively huge bones of the human ear could be moved by a relatively delicate membrane, and he invented the telephone, in which a piece of steel is moved by a membrane.
3. The **symbolic analogy** uses objective, impersonal, or poetic images to describe a problem. Gordon describes a synectics group that designed a new, smaller automobile jack by first thinking of the Indian rope trick (the one you may have seen in cartoons, in which a turbaned Indian makes a soft rope rigid enough to climb on).
4. The **fantasy analogy** frees your imagination from the boundaries of the normal world. With a fantasy analogy, it is quite reasonable to imagine yourself sprouting wings and flying five miles to a store, thus solving one of the problems we discussed at the beginning of the chapter.

Gordon describes how the synectics method has been used in industry, business, and education. For example, participants in a synectics session devoted to the government problem of science and public policy tried imagining themselves as nocturnal animals and as little fish being swallowed by big fish on the Florida Keys. The answer finally came when they formed an analogy between the government and the garment industry.

Almost every year, someone devises a new idea for encouraging creativity. However, one useful method might have occurred to you if you have recently taken a course in learning theory: Creativity can be encouraged by the use of reinforcement. Locurto and Walsh (1976) had subjects work on a repetitive association task, in which they were required to give a new word association every time they saw a word. For example, to the word *tree,* a person might respond *leaf* on one trial, *forest* on another, and *maple* on another. Some of the subjects received one point for *every* uncommon response (for example, *gingko* or *nest*) they gave, whereas other subjects in a control condition received no reinforcement. Then everyone worked on the Alternative Uses Test, in which people must list new, uncommon uses for everyday objects (such as a brick). The people who had been reinforced during the first task did better on the Alternate Uses Test than did people in the control condition.

Think of how you might apply this study to encourage creativity in your professional work. For example, if you are teaching elementary school, you could develop an exercise in which students receive reinforcement (for example, praise or a token) for unusual responses. On the basis of Locurto and Walsh's study, your students should do better in other situations requiring unusual responses. Incidentally, however, it would be wise to try a number of different training and reinforcement tasks. We could not expect a single session to have an effect that would last several years!

SECTION SUMMARY: *Creativity*

1. There are numerous definitions for creativity. One common definition is that creativity involves finding a solution that is both unusual and useful.
2. Some theorists believe that there is one kind of creativity and creative people simply have more of this creativity than others. Other theorists believe that there are two or more different kinds of creativity, with one kind being the exclusive possession of creative people.
3. Two common tests of creativity include Guilford's Divergent Production tests, in which people make up varied responses to each test item, and Mednick and Mednick's Remote Associates Test, in which different items must be linked together with a single word. Both tests have been shown to be related to some measures of creative performance, but these two measures are not related to each other.
4. Problem finding is another important aspect of creativity.
5. Suggestions for encouraging creativity include brainstorming, synectics, and reinforcement of creative responses.

Chapter Review Questions

1. Think about a well-defined problem that you are likely to encounter in your future profession. Describe the original state, the goal state, and the rules. Repeat this process with an ill-defined problem, and specify which parts of the problem are ill-defined.

2. Try to recall a problem that you found difficult to understand. Which of Greeno's three requirements for understanding (coherence, correspondence, and relationship to background knowledge) were not met?

3. Find some instructions to a game, preferably a card game or a board game. Do Simon and Hayes' conclusions regarding paying attention apply to the portions of the instructions that you would read twice? Which method of representation would you use for playing this game—symbols, lists, matrices, graphs, or visual images?

4. Think about the last time you lost something that you needed. Describe how you might have used each of the following problem-solving strategies in order to locate the object: unsystematic random search; systematic random search; means-ends analysis; and backward search.

5. Describe the planning strategy and discuss how people use (or do not use) analogies in problem solving.

6. Explain how two concepts, functional fixedness and mental set, can limit problem solving.

7. One conclusion in this chapter is that training aids problem solving. What kind of specific training have you received in college that will help you solve problems in your chosen career, and what other kind of training would be helpful?

8. Child-rearing books often warn parents that they should not issue vague commands, such as "clean up your room," to their children. In fact, these vague commands represent ill-defined problems. Discuss why this command is ill defined and how you could change it into a well-defined problem. Repeat the process with two other vague commands that you remember hearing as a child.

9. Take an example of something that you think is very creative (produced either by yourself or someone else) and see whether it fits the various definitions of creativity that were offered in this chapter. Is the creativity shown in that example a kind of creativity that everyone would possess (to varying extents) or a kind of creativity that only unusual people would have?

10. Imagine that you are a supervisor of ten employees in a small company. Describe how you would use each of the following methods to reach a creative solution to a company problem: brainstorming, synectics, and reinforcement.

New Terms

problem solving	means-ends analysis	flowchart
original state	computer simulation	mental set
goal state	General Problem Solver	well-defined problem
rules	transform method	ill-defined problem
understanding	apply-operator method	oddity problem
matrix	operator	creativity
matrices	reduce method	divergent production
random search	cryptoarithmetic problems	Remote Associates Test
unsystematic random search	planning strategy	brainstorming
systematic random search	analogy	synectics
algorithm	protocol	personal analogy
problem space	backward search	direct analogy
heuristics	Logic Theorist	symbolic analogy
subproblems	functional fixedness	fantasy analogy

Answers to the Demonstrations

7.4. In the "whodunit" problem, Mrs. Anderson has mononucleosis. She is in Room 104.

7.5. In the Hobbits-and-Orcs problem (with R representing the right bank and L representing the left bank), here are the steps in the solution:

1. Move 2 Orcs, R to L.
2. Move 1 Orc, L to R.
3. Move 2 Orcs, R to L.
4. Move 1 Orc, L to R.
5. Move 2 Hobbits, R to L.
6. Move 1 Orc, 1 Hobbit, L to R.
7. Move 2 Hobbits R to L.
8. Move 1 Orc L to R.
9. Move 2 Orcs R to L.
10. Move 1 Orc L to R.
11. Move 2 Orcs R to L.

7.6. The cryptoarithmetic problem's solution is:

$$
\begin{array}{r}
5\ 2\ 6\ 4\ 8\ 5 \\
+\ 1\ 9\ 7\ 4\ 8\ 5 \\
\hline
7\ 2\ 3\ 9\ 7\ 0
\end{array}
$$

7.11. Answers to the remote associates items: (1) PRINCE, (2) DOG, (3) COLD, (4) GLASSES, (5) CLUB, (6) BOAT, (7) DEFENSE, (8) BLACK, (9) PIT, (10) WRITER.

The remaining answers can be found elsewhere in the chapter. And, speaking of answers, have you had a chance yet to recall the list of words that you learned with the method of loci in Demonstration 4.3? Take a moment to recall the words that you associated with various familiar locations.

Reasoning

Preview

Reasoning involves drawing conclusions from several known facts, and we will be examining four different kinds of reasoning tasks in this chapter: (1) linear series problems; (2) propositional reasoning; (3) syllogisms; and (4) analogies.

An example of a linear series problem is:

If Mary likes psychology more than art,
And she likes philosophy less than art,
Which subject does she like the least?

Thus linear series problems require people to place items in order in a series. Linear series problems are relatively easy compared with the other kinds of reasoning tasks. The difficulty of these problems is influenced by factors such as the wording of the problem and prior training.

An example of propositional reasoning is:

If Mary is at this party, then she is not studying for the exam.
Mary is at this party.
Therefore, Mary is not studying for the exam.

Propositional reasoning involves relationships between conditions, typically using the phrase, "if . . ., then . . . ." People make frequent mistakes on this type of reasoning problem. Sometimes they misinterpret the sentences in the problem, and sometimes they rely too much on their everyday knowledge rather than logic. Furthermore, their strategies in approaching these problems are often inappropriate.

An example of a syllogism is:

All students are intelligent people.
Some intelligent people are pleasant.
Therefore, some students are pleasant.

Notice that syllogisms involve quantities, such as "all" and "some." Syllogism difficulty is influenced by factors such as the kind of syllogism, the wording of the problem, and the instructions that are given.

An example of an analogy is:

Night **is to** *day* **as** *moon* **is to** _____ .

An analogy has four parts; the first two parts have the same relationship to each other as the last two have to each other. We use analogies frequently in everyday life, whenever we use our previous knowledge in a new situation. Analogies are also used in problem solving, reading, and psychological testing.

Reasoning involves drawing conclusions from several known facts. For example, if you know that all of the students in experimental psychology had to complete a course in statistics prior to enrollment, and some of the courses in statistics covered the chi-square test, then you know that some of the students in experimental psychology were exposed to the chi-square test.

Courses in logic and reasoning are taught in most colleges. This observation implies that people need to be *taught* how to think logically, and that teaching this skill is so difficult that an entire term is necessary.

Throughout this chapter we will be concerned with humans' abilities on reasoning tasks. We will focus, in particular, on the kinds of errors they make, on the factors influencing reasoning, and on the theories used to explain the reasoning process. We will look at four different kinds of reasoning situations: linear series problems, propositional reasoning, syllogisms, and analogies. Although the logical operations are different for the four kinds of reasoning tasks, you should watch for similarities. Some of the same factors influence performance in several different tasks. The grammatical form of the statements, for example, is an important variable in many reasoning tasks. Furthermore, people make consistent kinds of errors, such as failing to consider all possible interpretations of the statements.

Linear Series Problems

If Susan is a worse student than Sara, and Ellen is a better student than Sara, which student is the worst? This is the kind of reasoning task known as a linear series problem. A **linear series problem** contains sentences that compare two people or objects, and it requests the solver to place the items in order within a series. Generally, the problem asks which item is highest or lowest on a particular attribute. Linear series problems are among the easiest of the reasoning problems. Nonetheless, they do require you to pause, think, and organize before responding. You may recall problems like these on intelligence tests you took when you were in elementary school. Linear series problems are frequently used as a measure of intellectual growth (Trabasso, Riley, & Wilson, 1975).

Factors Affecting Linear Series Problems

As you worked on the problem about Susan, Sara, and Ellen, it may have occurred to you that you could have solved the problem more quickly if the wording had been different. For example, this wording would be more straightforward: "If Ellen is a better student than Sara, and Sara is a better student than Susan, which student is the best?"

Clark (1969b) found that three different language factors influenced solution speeds for linear series problems. Try Demonstration 8.1, which illustrates these factors. Notice that two aspects of the **premises**, or statement sentences, are important. First of all, problems are easier if the premises are positive than if they contain the word *not*; "Mary is better than Susan" is easier than "Susan isn't as good as Mary."

Furthermore, problems are easier if the premises use *better* than if they use *worse* to compare two individuals. Words such as *better* and *good* are called unmarked adjectives in linguistics. We discussed marking in Chapter 5, but let us

---

Demonstration 8.1   *Factors Affecting the Difficulty of Linear Series Problems.*

In each of the three sets below, decide which problem is easiest.

Set I

Problem A	**Problem B**
If Mary is better than Susan,	If Joan isn't as good as Amy,
And Susan is better than Anne,	And Amy isn't as good as Beth,
Then who is best?	Then who is best?
Mary/Susan/Anne/Can't tell	Joan/Amy/Beth/Can't tell

Set II

Problem A	**Problem B**
If Herb is better than Sam,	If Ray is worse than Jeff,
And Sam is better than Roger,	And Jeff is worse than Martin,
Then who is best?	Then who is best?
Herb/Sam/Roger/Can't tell	Ray/Jeff/Martin/Can't tell

Set III

Problem A	**Problem B**
If Carol is better than Darlene,	If Dawn is better than Gail,
And Darlene is better than Kim,	And Gail is better than Linda,
Then who is best?	Then who is worst?
Carol/Darlene/Kim/Can't tell	Dawn/Gail/Linda/Can't tell

---

briefly review this concept. **Unmarked** adjectives are the more general and more neutral members of antonym pairs. You can decide which member of an antonym pair is unmarked by inserting each member into a sentence such as, "How _____ is he?" If a word makes the sentence sound general and neutral, that word is unmarked. If a word makes the sentence sound very limited, as if only one kind of response could be expected, then that word is **marked.** For example, "How *good* is the food?" sounds general and neutral. On the other hand, "How *bad* is the food?" implies that you know the food is bad already, but you need to assess the degree of badness! Similarly, "Joe is better than Sam" is more general than "Sam is worse than Joe." At any rate, Clark found that the use of unmarked adjectives, such as *better* and *good*, makes the linear series problem easier to solve.

The third factor that Clark identified was whether the question that was asked used words that matched the premises. If the premises contain the word *better*, for example, then it is easier to answer the question "Who is best?" than to answer "Who is worst?"

Clark's findings have some practical applications for writing about comparisons. The problem of describing linear series occurs frequently in psychology. If you are a school psychologist, you might want to compare a child's scores on several tests. An industrial psychologist may wish to compare three employees. A student writing a laboratory report wants to compare subjects' performance in four different experimental conditions. In each case the writer wants to convey a linear order. The writer should therefore take three precautions whenever possible: (1) avoid the word *not* in the premises; (2) use unmarked rather than marked adjectives; and (3) use words in the premises that match the aspect of the situation that you wish to stress, *worse* if you want the reader to know about the poorest performance and *better* if you wish to stress the best performance. Thus, you might write, "Subjects performed better on conjunctive concepts than on disjunctive concepts, and better on disjunctive concepts than on biconditional concepts," if you want to stress performance accuracy.

Potts (1972) found an interesting distance effect for people who had read a paragraph about a linear order that can be represented, $A > B, B > C, C > D$. (A concrete example of this order would be, "the grass is better than the sky, the sky is better than the sand, and the sand is better than the ocean.") People were more accurate when they answered questions about pairs in the series that were distant from each other, such as A and C or A and D, than they were for pairs that were next to each other, such as A and B or C and D. This finding is particularly impressive because the pairs that were next to each other had been directly presented in the paragraph, whereas the distant pairs had to be figured out from the other information. Thus, the distance by which two items are separated from each other in a linear order is more important than whether you have previously seen the two items in a direct comparison.

Incidentally, if you have a good memory for the information in the Imagery chapter, you might recall a similar distance effect for size comparisons of mental images. People are faster at comparing two mental images that are very different in size (such as a moose and a roach) than two mental images that are very similar in size (such as a moth and a roach).

Theories about Linear Series Problems
Currently there are two dominant theories of linear series problems: Clark (1969a) emphasizes verbal explanations, whereas Potts stresses the integration of information.

As we saw earlier in this section, Clark stressed that the words used in the premises and the match between the premises and the question were important factors in determining how quickly people solve these problems. Linguistic factors are centrally important in Clark's theory.

Potts (1978) emphasizes that people integrate information when they study the premises in a linear series problem. They construct an overall ordering of the items in the series, using an internal scale. When Potts examined the notes that subjects took while studying the premises, he found that 73 percent listed the items in an array, either from left to right or from top to bottom. Potts (1975) stresses that people do not store the individual sentences in memory. Instead, people store the general, integrated representation. A coherent whole is remembered, rather than the fragments. You might notice that this theory is similar to the one proposed by Bransford, Barclay, and Franks (1972), which we discussed in Chapter 5. According to Bransford and his colleagues, people do not store the individual sentences as they appear in a paragraph. Instead, they combine the information in a paragraph with the information they know from daily life, blending it all together into a single, unified idea. The whole, rather than the parts, is stored in memory.

SECTION SUMMARY: *Linear Series Problems*

1. Reasoning involves drawing conclusions from several known facts.
2. Linear series problems contain sentences that compare items, and they ask people to place the items in order within a series.
3. Linear series problems are easier to understand if they: (a) avoid the word *not* in the premises; (b) use unmarked adjectives; and (c) use a word for the question that matches the words used in the premises.
4. Items that are distant from each other in a linear order are easier to judge than items that are near each other.
5. A theory proposed by Clark states that linguistic factors are important in linear series problems.
6. A theory proposed by Potts states that people store in memory a general, integrated representation rather than the individual sentences.

Propositional Reasoning

If John gets an A on this exam, then I am the Queen of Rumania.
I am not the Queen of Rumania.
Therefore, John can't get an A on this exam.

This is an example of propositional reasoning. **Propositional reasoning** problems tell the relationship between conditions, such as the relationship between John getting an A on this exam and my being the Queen of Rumania. The kind of propositional reasoning that we will consider in this chapter is the kind that involves "if . . ., then . . ." relationships. Propositional reasoning situations occur frequently in daily life, yet they are surprisingly difficult to solve correctly. Formal principles for dealing with propositional reasoning have been devised, but people frequently contradict these principles.

The Propositional Calculus
The propositional calculus[1] is a system for categorizing the kinds of reasoning used in analyzing **propositions** or statements. There are four basic kinds of reasoning, as illustrated in Demonstration 8.2.

The word **antecedent** means the proposition that comes first; it is contained in the "if . . ." part of a sentence. The word **consequent** means the proposition that follows (is the consequence); it is contained in the "then . . ." part of a sentence. Thus, when you **affirm the antecedent,** you say that the "if . . ." part of the sentence is true. This kind of reasoning leads to a valid, or correct, conclusion.

[1]By tradition, the phrase *the propositional calculus* is used rather than *propositional calculus*.

Demonstration 8.2 **The Propositional Calculus.**

Decide which of the following conclusions are valid and which are invalid. The answers are at the end of the chapter.

1. Affirming the antecedent.

   If today is Tuesday, then I have my bowling class.
   Today is Tuesday.
   Therefore, I have my bowling class.

2. Affirming the consequent.

   If I have been at a buffet-style restaurant, then I have gained five pounds.
   I have gained five pounds.
   Therefore, I have been at a buffet-style restaurant.

3. Denying the antecedent.

   If I am a freshman, then I must register for next semester's classes today.
   I am not a freshman.
   Therefore, I must not register for next semester's classes today.

4. Denying the consequent.

   If the judge is fair, then Susan is the winner.
   Susan is not the winner.
   Therefore, the judge is not fair.

When you **affirm the consequent,** you say that the "then . . ." part of the sentence is true. This kind of reasoning leads to an incorrect conclusion. Notice, for example, that the conclusion "I have been at a buffet-style restaurant" is incorrect because there are many other ways I could have gained five pounds—eating dinner at the home of a friend who cooks like Julia Child, staying home and consuming five pounds of chocolate fudge, or whatever.

You can deny, as well as affirm. For example, you can **deny the antecedent** by saying that the "if . . ." part of the sentence is false. Denying the antecedent also leads to an incorrect conclusion. The conclusion "I must not register for next semester's classes today" is false, because it is possible that the members of *your* class, as well as freshmen, must register today.

Finally, you can **deny the consequent** by saying that the "then . . ." part of the sentence is false. This kind of reasoning leads to a correct conclusion. The four kinds of reasoning are presented in a matrix in Table 8.1. Make certain you understand these and can make up your own examples for each kind.

Try noticing how often you use the two correct kinds of reasoning. For example, a traffic sign might read, "Left turns permitted on weekends." This sign could be translated into "if . . ., then . . . " form: "*If* it is a weekend, *then* left turns are permitted." You know that it is Saturday, a weekend day. By the method of affirming the antecedent, you can conclude that "left turns are permitted."

Suppose you are watching a late-night "whodunit," which finds our hero,

TABLE 8.1   The Propositional Calculus: The Four Kinds of Reasoning

Action Taken	Portion of the Statement	
	Antecedent	*Consequent*
Affirm	Affirming the Antecedent (valid)	Affirming the Consequent (invalid)
Deny	Denying the Antecedent (invalid)	Denying the Consequent (valid)

Rock Handsome, on trial for murder. The lawyer may use the method of denying the consequent to prove Mr. Handsome's innocence: "If Mr. Handsome committed the murder, then he must have been at the Abercromby mansion at midnight on Friday." According to an eyewitness, however, Mr. Handsome was at El Sleazo Bar at midnight on Friday—he could not have been at the Abercromby mansion. "Aha!" you shout. "The eyewitness has denied the consequent, and therefore the antecedent must be false. Mr. Handsome is indeed innocent!" (The use of methods of logic in courtroom trials is discussed by Horowitz, 1974.)

　　　Also watch out for logical errors that you might be making. Think how the method of affirming the consequent might produce the wrong conclusion in the sentence, "If Mary likes me, then she will smile at me." The method of denying the antecedent also produces the wrong conclusion for the sentence, "If I get a D on this test, then I'll get a D in the course."

　　　Which kind of reasoning is the easiest? Taplin (1971) found that people were most accurate in affirming the antecedent, next best in denying the consequent, and worst in denying the antecedent and in affirming the consequent; performance was equally poor for these last two kinds of reasoning. Notice, then, that people are best at the correct kinds of reasoning. They are worst at the incorrect kinds of reasoning, which they mistakenly believe to be correct.

Factors Affecting Propositional Reasoning

Two factors that influence the number of errors made in propositional reasoning problems are the abstractness of the problem and the presence or absence of negatives.

Abstractness.　　Wason and Johnson-Laird (1972) contrast two studies to demonstrate the influence of abstractness on problem solving. One study used problems that were reasonably concrete and familiar from everyday language, such as:

> Rembrandt's work is known to every artist.
> Everyone who knows Rembrandt's work appreciates its beauty.
> John does not know Rembrandt's work.
> Therefore, (1) John does not appreciate the beauty of Rembrandt's work.
> 　　　　　(2) John is not an artist. (p. 56)

(Notice, incidentally, that the first conclusion is invalid by the method of denying the antecedent and the second conclusion is valid by the method of denying the consequent.) Other problems were shorter but more abstract, such as:

> If an object is blue, then it is rectangular.
> This object is not rectangular.
> Therefore, (1) it is not blue. (p. 56)

Wason and Johnson-Laird observed that people made far more errors with the abstract problems than they made with the "everyday language" problems.

Negation.   Many studies have demonstrated that propositional reasoning tasks are more difficult if they contain the negative *not* in the premises. (Recall that *not* also produced difficulties in linear series problems.) For instance, Evans (1972) found that people had more trouble with a problem such as

> **1. If the number is not *2* then the letter is *B*. The letter is not *B*.**

than they had with a similar problem without a negative, such as

> **2. If the number is *2,* then the letter is *B*. The letter is not *B*.**

Frequently, they read problem 1 and decided that no conclusion could be drawn.

One explanation for the difficulty with negatives, such as in problem 1, is that "double negatives" may be produced. **Double negative** sentences contain two negative words, such as two "nots," and they are very difficult to unscramble. You may recall our discussion of this issue in Chapter 5. Suppose, for example, your professor says, "I do not wish to suggest that Watson has not been influential in contemporary learning theory." You pause, combine the double negative into one positive, and might translate the sentence into your notes as "Watson is influential."

Similarly, when you try Evans' problem 1, you produce the conclusion, "It is not true that the number is not *2*." You are likely to make a mistake in translating that sentence into the correct answer, "The number is *2*." Negatives are difficult, then, because they require an additional, complicated translation. Once again, we have evidence that humans handle positive information more efficiently than negative information.

Errors in Propositional Reasoning

Unlike other areas of research on reasoning, the development of theory has not been emphasized in propositional reasoning. Instead, psychologists have been intrigued with one question: The propositional calculus is used by logicians when they work on formal reasoning problems, but is it used by "real people" when they try to solve reasoning problems? We saw that there were four categories of methods in the propositional calculus, but are these methods actually used? In general, the answer is "no." People do not use these formal methods, and their informal methods cause them to make several kinds of systematic errors. In the previous section we have seen that people tend to make errors on double negatives. They make other errors as well, including two errors in interpretation and one strategy error.

Interpretation Errors. One kind of interpretation error is referred to as "illicit conversion" (Wason & Johnson-Laird, 1972), a term that has always sounded to me like strange, exotic religious rites that are being performed illegally. However, **illicit conversion** means that you inappropriately change part of the problem into another form. Wason and Johnson-Laird point out how this works when people use the incorrect method of denying the antecedent. In this method, remember that the general form is:

> If *p*, then *q*.
> *p* is not true.
> Therefore, *q* is not true.

People use illicit conversion when they see the first statement, and they convert it—inappropriately—into:

> · If *q*, then *p*.

Then they combine that revised statement with the information that *p* is not true and they use the method of denying the consequence, which is a valid method when used appropriately. They therefore conclude that *q* is not true. Thus, some kinds of reasoning errors involve an incorrect change in the statements.

Notice that illicit conversion represents the inappropriate use of a strategy that often leads us to a correct conclusion in everyday reasoning situations. Suppose that a friend is trying to guess what the dormitory cafeteria will serve for breakfast, and she says, "If it's Tuesday, then we are having pancakes." This statement *implies* that there is a one-to-one correspondence between days of the week and breakfast menus. Thus you can reasonably conclude that the two parts of the statement can be converted to yield the statement, "If we are having pancakes, then it is Tuesday." Think of some other "if . . . , then . . ." statements in which conversions are "legal."

The conversion strategy frequently works when you make decisions in "real life," although the accuracy of your conclusion depends upon whether the implications were correct. In formal reasoning tasks, however, the conversion strategy may lead you astray. For example, if the Tuesday breakfast problem were presented as a formal reasoning task, you should note the possibility that pancakes may be served more often than once a week.

Communal knowledge is a second source of reasoning errors. **Communal knowledge** is information and assumptions that people gather from their everyday experiences (Johnson-Laird, 1975). Communal knowledge is useful in informal reasoning, but it leads us to incorrect conclusions in formal logic. For example, if we learn that John beat Tom with a stick, we draw upon our communal knowledge that beating implies wanting to hurt someone, and we conclude that John wanted to hurt Tom. Similarly, I recall an evening when a man called my friend for a date. When she replied that she was busy, he answered, "Gee, it seems that everybody is busy that night." She felt properly insulted. Drawing upon her communal knowledge, she reasoned that he must have asked several other women before her. Like other strategies, communal knowledge is often helpful in informal, everyday situations. In formal reasoning tasks, however, people make errors when they try to read between the lines and use the communal knowledge strategy inappropriately. It is incorrect to rely upon communal knowledge.

A Strategy Error.   One clear-cut conclusion of many studies is that people would much rather try to confirm a hypothesis than try to disprove it. Wason and Johnson-Laird (1972) remark that when people have arrived at a generalization, they take such pride in it that they are reluctant to try to prove it incorrect. "They may not simply want to know that a proposition is true; they feel the need to convince themselves of its truth, over and over again" (p. 241).

Try Demonstration 8.3 to see for yourself how people prefer to offer hypotheses that they believe to be true. This classic experiment was first performed by Wason (1968), who asked people to discover the rule that was followed in making the series, "2 4 6." They were told to make up hypotheses, and the experimenter would answer whether the hypotheses were correct or incorrect. They were to announce the rule only when they felt extremely confident that it was the correct rule.

Demonstration 8.3   Strategy Errors.

Ask a friend to take part in a short experiment. Then tell your "subject" that the series 2 4 6 conforms to a simple rule. The subject must discover the rule by making up series of numbers, and finding out from you whether the series is correct or incorrect. Instruct the subject to tell you what the rule is only when he or she is absolutely confident of what the correct rule is.

You will act as the experimenter. The rule is: "three numbers in ascending order." Therefore, you must say "yes" to every series of three numbers in which the second number is larger than the first and the third number is larger than the second. No other requirements are necessary for the three-number series to be correct.

If your friend was like Wason's subjects, he or she was extremely unlikely to propose any series of numbers that were *not* consistent with the hypothesis. For example, a person might propose "8 10 12," then "14 16 18," and then "20 22 24." After receiving "yes" responses from the experimenter in all cases, the person would prematurely suggest the hypothesis, "Start with an even number and add two each time to form the next number." A wiser strategy would have been to supply numbers that were inconsistent with that hypothesis. Perhaps the person might propose "9 11 13" to test whether it was necessary to begin with an even number. The series "9 13 18" might be proposed to test whether it is necessary to increase the previous number by two. Finally, the series "17 14 9" might be proposed to test whether it is necessary for the numbers to increase.

Wason (1968) also describes a later version of the task, in which people were allowed to state only one hypothesis during the experiment. If their hypothesis was wrong, they were asked, "If you were wrong, how could you find out that you were wrong?" Only two out of 16 subjects replied that they would try to make up series that were inconsistent with the hypothesis.

Try to see if you avoid disproving hypotheses in everyday life. For example, you might notice that you use a peculiar kind of "body English" when you bowl, and you are a good bowler. Do you ever test the hypothesis by trying other movement sequences and seeing whether you still bowl well? Probably you keep on trying to confirm your hypothesis rather than trying to disprove it. Mynatt, Doherty, and Tweney (1977) found that this tendency persisted for subjects in a more realistic situation than Wason's. Their setup resembled a scientific situation, and subjects were given instructions about the importance in science of disproving hypotheses. Even so, people still tried to confirm their hypotheses rather than disprove them.

Demonstration 8.4 *Avoiding Disproving Hypotheses.*

Imagine that each of the squares below represents a card. Suppose that you know from previous experience that every card has a letter on one side and a number on the other side.

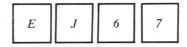

You are then given this rule about these four cards: "If a card has a vowel on one side, then it has an even number on the other side."

Your task is to decide which of these cards you would need to turn over in order to find out whether this rule is true or false. What is your answer? The answer is discussed in the text.

A classic study by Johnson-Laird and Wason (1977b) also demonstrates that people avoided disproving their hypotheses. Try Demonstration 8.4 with the warning that it is wise to try to disprove a hypothesis! People who have not been forewarned typically say that they would turn over the *E* and the *6* cards, or else just the *E* card. These strategies allow you to confirm your hypothesis. However, the correct strategy is to choose cards *E* and *7,* although only 10 percent chose that strategy.

Let's see why *E* and *7* are correct. First of all, you have to see what lies on the other side of the *E.* If there is an even number on the other side, the rule is correct. If there is an odd number on the other side, the rule is incorrect. However, you must also examine the other side of the *7,* a choice that very few people select. The information about the other side of the *7* is very valuable—just as valuable as the information about the *E.* If there is a consonant on the other side of the *7,* the rule is still correct. However, if there is a vowel on the other side, the rule is incorrect and must be rejected.

Let us examine that rule again, using the propositional calculus:

If a card has a vowel on its letter side, then it has an even number on its number side.

There are two correct kinds of reasoning. To affirm the antecedent, we check out a vowel (in this case, *E*). To deny the consequent, we must check out a number side that is *not* an even number (in this case, 7). People are eager to affirm the antecedent, but they are reluctant to deny the consequent. It is an attempt to disprove a hypothesis, and this kind of reasoning is difficult.

Now, why didn't we need to check on the J and the 6? If you look carefully, you will notice that the rule didn't say anything about consonants, such as J, so they can have odd numbers, even numbers, or giraffes on their other sides, and we wouldn't care. The rule also doesn't specify what must be on the other side of the even numbers, such as 6. Many people, however, perform an illicit conversion on the rule and read it also to mean, "If a card has an even number on its number side, then it has a vowel on its letter side." Thus, they make an error.

One further point must be made to stress the importance of disproving hypotheses, both in the "2 4 6" study and the card selection study. Once you have found negative evidence, you can throw the rule away because it cannot be true. The value of this negative evidence is sometimes shown when a person is being examined in a courtroom trial. In a recent trial in our area, a witness gave a long testimony that contained one lie. The lie was about an insignificant issue. Nonetheless, that one small piece of negative evidence was enough to have her testimony be discounted. Since she was lying on that one small point, she might be lying on other important points.

Notice how this preference for confirming a hypothesis, rather than disproving it, corresponds to one of the themes of the book. We have often seen that people perform faster and more accurately when they deal with positive information rather than negative information. We also saw in Chapter 6 that people have difficulty using negative information in a concept formation task. Here we see that, when given a choice, people would rather seek out positive information than negative information. We would rather know what something is than what it is not.

Let us discuss another variation of the card selection study that is relevant because of a fact you already know. Johnson-Laird, Legrenzi, and Sonino Legrenzi (1972) tried a more concrete variation of the task, similar to the version illustrated in Figure 8.1. They found that 92 percent of the people gave the correct answer. In contrast, only 29 percent gave the correct answer in an abstract version, which was similar to Johnson-Laird and Wason's original card selection task. With concrete tasks, people reason more accurately. With abstract tasks, they fail to use the best reasoning strategies.

Figure 8.1   Concrete Version of a Reasoning Strategy Task.

Instructions: Imagine that you are a postal worker sorting letters. Test the rule, "If a letter is sealed, then it has a 20¢ stamp on it." Which envelopes need to be turned over to see whether they violate the rule?

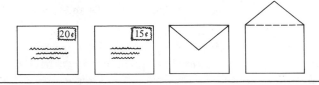

Application: The GRE Analytical Ability Measure. If you are applying to graduate school, you will probably be required to take the Graduate Record Examination (GRE). The GRE used to have only two sections: a Verbal Ability Measure and a Quantitative Ability Measure. Recently, however, a third section was added: an Analytical Ability Measure. This section consists of 70 questions that must be answered in 50 minutes.

Questions in this Analytical Ability Measure are designed to assess students' abilities to recognize logical relationships. For example, students may be asked to judge the relationship between premises and a conclusion (Conrad, Trismen, & Miller, 1977). Some of the questions involve propositional reasoning. Try Demonstration 8.5 for an example of two questions in this area.

Demonstration 8.5 *Propositional Reasoning Problems in the GRE.*

Read the six statements and then try the two problems, which involve propositional reasoning. The answers are at the end of the chapter.

(1) You cannot enter unless you have a red ticket.
(2) If you present a blue form signed by the director, you will receive a red ticket.
(3) The director will sign and give you a blue form if and only if you surrender your yellow pass·to him.
(4) If you have a green slip, you can exchange it for a yellow pass, but you can do so only if you also have a blue form signed by the director.
(5) In order to get a red ticket, a person who does not have a driver's license must have a blue form signed by the director.
(6) You can get a yellow pass on request, but you can do so only if you have never had a green slip.

1. The above procedures fail to specify
   (A) whether anything besides a red ticket is required for entrance.
   (B) whether you can exchange a green slip for a yellow pass.
   (C) the condition under which the director will sign the blue form.
   (D) how to get a red ticket if you have a yellow pass.
   (E) whether it is possible to obtain a red ticket if you do not have a driver's license.

2. Which of the following people can, under the rules given, eventually obtain a ticket?
   I.   A person who has no driver's license and who has only a green slip.
   II. A person who has no driver's license and who has only a yellow pass.
   III. A person who has both a driver's license and a blue form signed by the director.

   (A) I only   (B) II only   (C) I and II only   (D) II and III only   (E) I, II, and III

SECTION SUMMARY: *Propositional Reasoning*

1. **Propositional reasoning problems tell the relationship between conditions, such as the "if . . . , then . . ." relationship.**

2. The propositional calculus has four categories of reasoning, two valid categories (affirming the antecedent and denying the consequent) and two invalid categories (affirming the consequent and denying the antecedent).
3. Performance is most accurate for the two valid categories.
4. Concrete problems are easier than abstract problems.
5. Reasoning problems that contain negatives, such as *not,* are difficult to solve.
6. One source of errors on propositional reasoning problems is interpretation errors. People inappropriately change part of the problem into another form and inappropriately rely upon communal knowledge.
7. Another source of errors is that people would rather confirm a hypothesis than try to disprove it. People adopt a hypothesis-confirming strategy when they try to discover a rule underlying a number series and when they try to discover whether a rule is true or false. In both cases, the wiser strategy would be to show that a hypothesis was incorrect.
8. Propositional reasoning is involved in some of the questions on the Graduate Record Examination Analytical Ability Measure.

Syllogisms

A **syllogism** (pronounced "*sill*-uh-jizz-um) consists of two premises, or statements which we must assume to be true, plus a conclusion. Syllogisms involve quantities, and so they use the words *all, none, some,* or other similar terms. In propositional reasoning, we saw that statements could be represented by the letters *p* and *q*. In syllogistic reasoning, the traditional symbols are *A, B,* and *C*. Thus, an example of a syllogism using these symbols is the following:

> Some *A* are *B*.
> Some *B* are *C*.
> _____
> Therefore, some *A* are *C*.

Does that conclusion seem correct to you? At first glance, it might, and you can probably think of some concrete examples for which it would be true. However, there are some other examples for which it would not be true. For example, think about this syllogism:

> Some women are Democrats.
> Some Democrats are men.
> _____
> Therefore, some women are men.

Sometimes the conclusion to a syllogism is either true or false. However, sometimes we cannot draw a conclusion from the syllogism—it may be true for some relationships and false for others. In these cases, such as in the *A, B,* and *C* example above, we conclude, "can't say." On the surface, it looks simple to decide whether your conclusion is "true," "false," or "can't say"—after all, how hard can *some* and *all* be? However, people have difficulty solving these reasoning problems.

It is important to stress that the correctness of the conclusion does *not* depend upon the truth of the premises. I can make up some ridiculous premises, but the conclusion would be true as long as the basic form of the syllogism is true. For example, because the underlying logic is correct, the conclusion for this syllogism is true:

> **All elephants are fond of dry martinis.**
> **All those who are fond of dry martinis are bankers.**
> _____
> **Therefore, all elephants are bankers.**

So, remember that you should ignore the content of syllogisms in deciding whether the conclusions are correct.

In formal syllogisms, *all, some,* and *none* are the standard terms used to indicate quantity. In everyday language, we also have other words, such as *many, few, usually, often, certain,* and *possible* (Johnson-Laird, 1975). Frase (1978) points out how syllogisms are important in everyday communications. Usually, however, the structure of a syllogism is not as obvious as it is in the examples we have discussed. For example, the order of the sentences might be changed, with the conclusion perhaps listed first. The premises may be some distance from each other in a paragraph, with other irrelevant sentences in between. One sentence might use the word *singer,* and another sentence might substitute a synonym such as *vocalist.* Furthermore, the reader's evaluation might be required after a long delay, rather than immediately. Nonetheless, we can still decide whether the conclusion is correct or not.

One effective way to represent the information in the premises of syllogisms is in terms of Venn diagrams. A **Venn diagram** uses circles to show how two sets, called *A* and *B,* are related to each other. Figure 8.2 shows Venn diagrams for four possible relationships, or **moods,** in a syllogism. Each of the three sentences in a

---

Figure 8.2 *Venn Diagrams of Possible Interpretations of the Relationship between A and B.*

Notes:

[a]In the diagrams in which *A* and *B* are represented by a single circle, the sets *A* and *B* are identical.

[b]When logicians use the word *some,* it is different from the everyday usage, because *some* can also mean *all.* Thus, "Some *A* are *B*" can mean "All *A* are *B*."

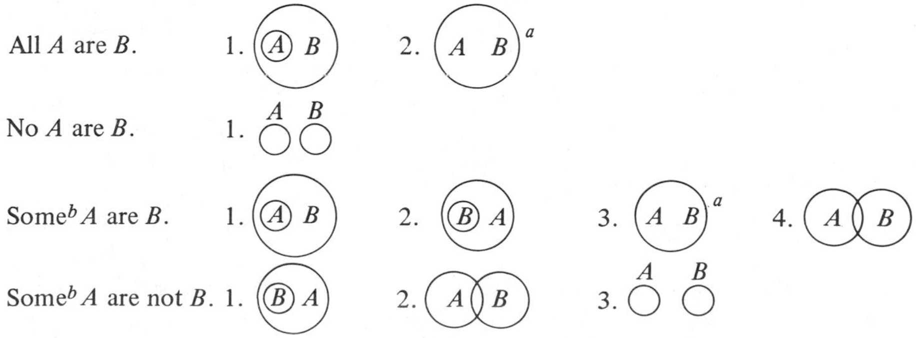

syllogism can be expressed in terms of each of these four kinds of moods: (1) all A are B, (2) no A are B, (3) some A are B, and (4) some A are not B.

Notice that there is only one way to interpret "No A are B." The other three moods, however, are ambiguous, because there are at least two ways to interpret each of them. For example, notice in diagram 1 for "All A are B" that all parts of Circle A are inside Circle B, but some parts of circle B are not inside circle A. An alternate interpretation of "All A are B" is in diagram 2; here, all parts of circle A are inside circle B, and, in addition, all parts of circle B are inside circle A.

Factors Affecting Syllogisms

We will discuss two kinds of factors that can affect syllogism difficulty: linguistic factors and instructions.

Linguistic Factors.   The linguistic form of sentences is critical in determining the difficulty of syllogisms. Lippman (1972) compared performance on active versus passive sentences and affirmative versus negative sentences. Thus, an active, affirmative syllogism would be:

> **If all gamblers lose money,**
> **And all speculators are gamblers, then . . .**

However, a passive, negative syllogism would be:

> **If money is not lost by all gamblers,**
> **And all speculators are gamblers, then . . .**

The subjects were asked to complete the sentence with the appropriate answer. It took them much longer to solve the syllogisms when they were in the passive voice and when they were negative. (I hope you guessed this already!) Furthermore, passive and negative syllogisms were rated as being more difficult. Lippman suggests that grammatical factors are important because people must recode other sentences into an active form before they can begin the reasoning process.

The practical application of Lippman's findings are clear. When you want the logic in your message to be understood, use active, affirmative sentences. This would therefore be an ideal way for an advertiser to promote a new product, Sludge toothpaste:

> **Fluoride prevents tooth decay.**
> **Sludge toothpaste contains fluoride.**
> _____
> **Therefore, Sludge toothpaste prevents tooth decay.**

In contrast, a first premise such as, "Tooth decay is not encouraged by fluoride" would take a long time to translate, and your message might be lost.

Instructions.   Some researchers have tried giving their subjects special instructions about common kinds of reasoning errors. Dickstein (1975), for example, pointed out to one group of subjects that people often make a mistake in assuming that the premise "All A are B" can also be interpreted as "All B are A." (You might remember that we called this kind of mistake *illicit conversion*.) Dickstein's subjects made far fewer errors when they had been given this warning. This is encouraging: People do not need a complete course in logic in order to improve their reasoning accuracy substantially—a simple caution is effective.

Helsabeck (1975) found that it was helpful to instruct subjects to use strategies in solving syllogisms. He gave people three kinds of instructions:

1. Spatial, in which they were shown how to make Venn diagrams.
2. Verbal-specific, in which they were told how to make up specific examples of how a syllogism could be incorrect—for example, "All dogs are animals; some animals are cats; therefore, some dogs are cats."
3. Verbal-general, in which they were told how to make up verbal descriptions of why a syllogism could be incorrect—for example, "All *A* are *B,* but not all *B* have to be *A.* The *C* could be just those *B* that are not *A.*"

The spatial and the verbal-specific instructions proved to be most useful, and they were both equally effective. The spatial instructions seem to be helpful because they encourage people to consider the general structure of the problem. The verbal-specific instructions, on the other hand, might be helpful because they discourage people from making illicit conversions. Revlin (1973), for example, found that people were less likely to make illicit conversions when they had specific, concrete premises. "All dogs are animals" was unlikely to be interpreted as "All animals are dogs." In short, people who are having trouble with an abstract syllogism involving *A, B,* and *C* should either use Venn diagrams or try to think of specific examples in which the syllogism would be false.

Helsabeck specifically suggests an application for his findings. Students who are having trouble with word problems in algebra or the logic of hypothesis testing in statistics would benefit from spatial or verbal-specific representations of the problem.

Theories about Syllogisms

In the past 20 years, several different theories about syllogisms have been proposed. We will discuss two of the most widely held theories, Erickson's (1974, 1978) set-analysis theory and Johnson-Laird and Steedman's (1978) analogical theory.

Set-Analysis Theory. Erickson's **set-analysis** theory proposes that people encounter problems at several steps in the solution of syllogisms. Erickson has suggested a three-stage model, with problems arising at each of the stages. During stage I, people interpret the premises. However, abstract premises often have several interpretations. Erickson assumes that people without training in formal logic generally consider only one possible interpretation of the premises.

During stage II the information in the first premise is combined with the information in the second premise. The problem at this stage is that people typically choose only one of the possible ways of combining the two set relationships. Each of the two premises might, for example, have two possible logical interpretations. Combining those premises, we have four possible interpretations. Unfortunately, however, a person might consider only one interpretation for each of the two premises, and this person might consider only one way of combining these two premises. Thus there might really be four possibilities to describe how the two premises are related, but an individual might be considering only one of these four.

During stage III, people make responses; they choose an answer that fits both the combined representation and the wording of the premises. If both of the two premises contain the word *some,* they typically believe that the word *some* should appear in the conclusion. *All* in the premises encourages *all* in the conclusion. Thus, a person might be working on this syllogism:

> All *A* are *B*.
> All *B* are *C*.
> _____
> Therefore, all *C* are *A*.

This person may consider only the combination of premises in which *A, B,* and *C* are represented by the same identical circle. (Draw a Venn diagram to show this relationship.) With that kind of combination and the two "alls" in the premises, the temptation is overwhelming. *Of course* the conclusion must be true! However, illustrate for yourself that the conclusion must be "Some *C* are *A*."

Erickson (1978) tested the set-analysis theory of syllogisms. The correlations between the predictions and the subjects' actual choices were very high, both for valid syllogisms and for invalid syllogisms. This theory, in which people's errors arise primarily from ignoring some of the alternate possibilities, is one view that many psychologists support.

Analogical Theory.   Johnson-Laird and Steedman (1978) found fault with other studies concerning syllogisms, so they first conducted some experiments that they believed to be relatively free of the earlier problems. They complained that earlier studies frequently allowed people to work on a syllogism without necessarily forcing them to draw their own conclusion. Also, many studies used the abstract *A, B,* and *C* format even though people are obviously much more likely to meet concrete sentence syllogisms in everyday language.

Before we discuss Johnson-Laird and Steedman's work any further, try Demonstration 8.6. For each reasoning problem, these authors presented the two premises, both concrete sentences. Then they asked people to supply the conclusion to the syllogism. (In contrast, remember, for most previous studies the experimenter supplied the conclusion and asked the subject to judge whether it was true, false, or uncertain.) More than one correct conclusion was possible for many of these syllogisms.

Demonstration 8.6   *A Simplified Version of Johnson-Laird and Steedman's (1978) Experiment.*

For each of the following syllogisms, state one conclusion. The answers are discussed in the text.

1. All of the scientists are professors.
   All of the professors are clever people.

---

2. All geologists are backpackers.
   Some nature lovers are geologists.

   _____

3. Some doctors are photographers.
   All photographers are Rotarians.

   _____

4. All ministers are gardeners.
   No gardeners are English professors.

   _____

Johnson-Laird and Steedman found that people tended to prefer some conclusions and ignore other, valid conclusions. Let us now see whether you showed the same preferences their subjects did. For syllogism 1 in Demonstration 8.6, for example, the majority of subjects gave an answer of the form, "Therefore, all of the scientists are clever people." Other valid conclusions, such as, "Therefore, some of the clever people are scientists" were almost never given. For syllogism 2 most people gave an answer such as, "Therefore, some of the nature lovers are backpackers." People avoided the other valid conclusion, "Therefore, some of the backpackers are nature lovers." The authors mention that audiences at their lectures in Chicago, New York, Scotland, England, Italy, and Holland all showed these same preferences! The most common answers for the other questions are:

3. **Some doctors are Rotarians.**
4. **No ministers are English professors.**

Notice that the study showed that people have strong preferences in the direction of their reasoning. They prefer to move in a forward direction in the syllogism (for example, from *scientists* to *clever people*), rather than moving backward through the items in the premises (for example, from *clever people* to *scientists*).

Johnson-Laird and Steedman proposed a four-stage theory to account for the data they gathered. They wanted their theory to explain both the valid and the invalid conclusions that people reached. Here are their four stages:

1. The subject interprets the meaning of the premises.
2. The subject makes an initial attempt to combine the interpretations of the premises into a representation.
3. The subject draws a conclusion based on the representation.
4. The subject tests the initial representation formed in stage 2, and this test may lead to a modification or a rejection of the conclusion.

Let us look at each of the stages in more detail. Johnson-Laird and Steedman developed a method of representing the reasoning process. Interestingly, the remarks of one subject, describing his strategy, provided the clue for this representation. This subject said, "I thought of all the little . . . artists in the room and imagined that they all had beekeeper's hats on" (p. 77). So Johnson-Laird and Steedman decided to represent the reasoning process with words or symbols to take the place of each figure that the reasoner might imagine. For example, the premise, "All of the artists are beekeepers" might be represented:

artist   artist
↓   ↓
beekeeper   beekeeper   (beekeeper)   (beekeeper)

In this kind of representation, an arrow represents the relationship between two items and can be translated "is a" or "is an." Thus, each of the first two artists is a beekeeper. There are parentheses around the other two beekeepers to indicate that there may well be some beekeepers who are *not* artists. It is important to notice, therefore, that this theory suggests that people may have more than one way of interpreting a premise's meaning during stage 1. The representation above, for example, shows that there are two possibilities: (1) All of the artists are beekeepers, and there are *some* beekeepers who are not artists, or (2) all of the artists are beekeepers, and there are *no* beekeepers who are not artists.

Notice, therefore, that Johnson-Laird and Steedman's theory is more optimistic than Erickson's about people's ability to see more than one interpretation of a premise. Also, the theory assumes that people who are solving syllogisms set up some kind of mental picture that directly corresponds to the premises. In fact, the mental picture is an analogy of the premise, because there is something in the mental picture to represent everything in the premise. Thus, Johnson-Laird and Steedman's theory is called an **analogical theory** (pronounced "an-uh-*lodge*-ih-kull") because of the way people represent the premises with mental analogies.

In stage 2, people use heuristics to combine the representations of the two premises. The most important **heuristic** or rule of thumb is to try to find a forward connection. Thus, if one premise is represented by an arrow going from $A \rightarrow B$, and another premise has an arrow from $B \rightarrow C$, people will link up these two parts. They will end up with a forward connection $A \rightarrow B \rightarrow C$. A backward connection from C to A is less likely.

For example, consider the syllogism:

All of the astronomers are baseball fans.
Some of the baseball fans are con artists.

A person might represent this symbolically as:

All A are B   *a*   *a*
                ↓   ↓
Some B are C   *b*   *b*   *(b)*   *(b)*
                ↓
                c   *(c)*   *(c)*

In stage 3, people draw their conclusion. If there is at least one positive path, they conclude "Some A are B." If there are *only* positive paths, they conclude "All A are B." If there is at least one negative path they conclude "Some A are not B." If there are *only* negative paths, they conclude "No A are B."

Notice how the heuristic of trying to find forward connections—of finding some way to get from a to c—would lead to an invalid conclusion. The person who uses the representation above would conclude, "Some of the astronomers are con artists." After all, there is at least one connection between *a* and *c,* and so there must be at least one astronomer who is a con artist. Johnson-Laird and Steedman found, in fact, that 12 out of 20 people concluded, "Some of the astronomers are con artists." This conclusion is invalid, however, because there could be some astronomers who are baseball fans but not con artists. (Draw a Venn diagram if you are not convinced!) Thus, once more, a strategy that is generally helpful can lead us to an incorrect conclusion.

In stage 4, people test their initial representation. People use logic at this stage. They try to see if the established path between *a* and *c* can be broken, without destroying the meaning of the original premises. For example, someone might try to see if a link could be established that goes from a baseball fan who is *not* an astronomer, and links up with a con artist. In the diagram, this could be represented by an arrow from (b) to (c). Once a person discovers this alternate possibility, he or she realizes that no valid conclusion can be reached. This fourth stage is necessary to explain how some people do reach the correct conclusion, even if most people reach the wrong one.

Does Johnson-Laird and Steedman's theory predict the responses of "real live people"? They conducted two experiments. In the first experiment 92 percent of the responses that subjects made were predicted by the theory. In the second experiment 95 percent were predicted. Thus the theory is strongly supported by the data.

Which theory is correct, Erickson's set theory or Johnson-Laird and Steedman's analogical theory? Both theories fit the data quite well, and it is probably too early to conclude which theory is preferable. There is another possibility: set theory might hold for some people and analogical theory might hold for others. Dominowski (1977) suggested, prior to the development of analogical theory, that people could be sorted into different "types" on the basis of the way they solved the syllogisms. Thus, it could be that some people think according to set theory, some according to analogical theory, some according to both, and some according to other theories that have not yet been developed.

SECTION SUMMARY: *Syllogisms*

1. A syllogism involves quantities and consists of two premises and a conclusion.
2. Active, affirmative syllogisms are easier to solve than syllogisms that have passive constructions or negative words.
3. Instructions that clarify the premises are useful in solving syllogisms. Strategies that require the subject to make up Venn diagrams or specific examples are also helpful.
4. Erickson's set-analysis theory proposes that people consider only one possible interpretation of the premises and only one possible combination of the premises. Furthermore, people are influenced by the wording of the premises, so they tend to use the same mood in the conclusion as was used in the premises.

5. Johnson-Laird and Steedman's analogical theory proposes that people represent the premises in terms of a mental picture. Then they try to find forward connections between the premises. They draw their conclusions and then check to see whether there might be exceptions to their conclusions.

Analogies

MITTEN : HAND : : SOCK : ?

The analogy above can be translated into a sentence, "*Mitten* is to *hand* as *sock* is to what?" An **analogy** (pronounced "un-*nal*-uh-jee") preserves the same kind of relationship between items 3 and 4 in a series that were demonstrated between items 1 and 2 in the series. Thus, the relationship between *mitten* and *hand* is that the mitten is an article of clothing that covers the hand completely. Similarly, the relationship between sock and the chosen answer must preserve that same kind of relationship. To solve the analogy you ask yourself what it is that a sock covers completely. The answer, of course, is *foot.* You may remember our previous discussions of analogies in earlier chapters. Also, you may have encountered analogies on intelligence and vocabulary tests in high school, and we will discuss the Miller Analogy Test at the end of this section.

Think about how you have used analogies recently, usually without being aware of your reasoning processes. Every time you say something such as, "That is like the time I . . ." you are using an analogy. In fact, when I ask you to think about an experience you have had in your own life that resembles the ideas I am describing, I am asking you to form analogies between principles in cognition and your everyday experiences. Analogies abound in social conversations. A person may talk about her experience with her parents, and that will remind others of similar experiences. It is almost impossible to think of something entirely new because we can typically relate it to some analogous, old experience.

Even though reasoning with analogies is extremely commonplace, there has been less research in this area than in other areas of reasoning, until quite recently. However, some theories of analogy reasoning have been developed. In this section we will cover two topics: theories about analogies and applications of analogies.

Theories about Analogies

Two competing theories have been proposed to describe people's reasoning processes when they solve analogies. They are Rumelhart and Abrahamson's spatial theory and Sternberg's componential theory.

Spatial Theory.   Rumelhart and Abrahamson (1973) complained about the lack of attention that analogies had received, and they proposed as a partial remedy their model of analogical reasoning. Their model involves a spatial representation of the four items in an analogy. We can imagine the three known items in an analogy as being arranged in some kind of psychological space, in terms of two or more dimensions. For example, the words that Rumelhart and Abrahamson used were names of animals. If you were asked to take the names of all animals and arrange them in a diagram according to, say, three important dimensions or characteristics, how would you do it? Henley (1969) used a special statistical technique to organize people's judgments into three dimensions: size, ferocity, and resemblance to humans. Her arrangement, which served as the basis for Rumelhart and Abrahamson's experiment, is illustrated in Figure 8.3.

Although it is a bit difficult to understand a three-dimensional diagram that is confined to a two-dimensional piece of paper, we will give it a try. First of all, the horizontal dimension represents size. Notice how the small animals, such as the mouse, are at the left-hand side, whereas the large animals, such as the elephant, are at the right-hand side. The vertical dimension represents humanness, with monkeys and gorillas being most like humans, and pigs and cows being least like humans. The third dimension is ferocity, and you will have to pretend that the diagram extends out toward you in order to see this dimension. The pig and the cow are least ferocious, and the tiger is the most ferocious.

Rumelhart and Abrahamson reasoned that each word in an analogy could be located in a psychological space such as the one Henley derived for animals. For example, consider the analogy:

rabbit : giraffe : : monkey : ?

Locate on Henley's diagram the rabbit, giraffe, and monkey. In order to answer that analogy, we have to find a fourth animal that has the same relationship to

Figure 8.3   *The Representation of Animals in a Three-dimensional Space.* (From Rumelhart and Abrahamson, 1973.)

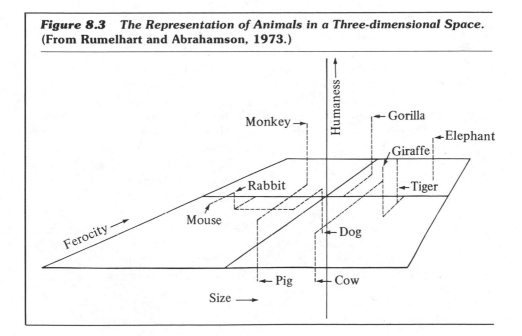

monkey as giraffe does to rabbit. Well, rabbit and giraffe are fairly similar in terms of ferocity in that both are rather meek. They are also fairly similar in terms of resemblance to humans; that is, both are somewhat more human than the average animal. They differ from each other primarily in terms of size. To go from rabbit to giraffe to Henley's diagram, we must move from a small-size animal to a large-size animal.

Now, what is the animal that we can locate by moving away from monkey, increasing in size to the same extent as we did when we moved from rabbit to giraffe? Would you choose a cow, a dog, an elephant, or a pig? The answer here is elephant, because an elephant is similar to a monkey in terms of ferocity and resemblance to humans, but it is different in size. The size relationship between rabbit and giraffe is analogous to the size relationship between monkey and elephant.

Rumelhart and Abrahamson asked people to solve analogies based on 30 animals, of which 10 were represented in Figure 8.3. They were given an analogy, together with four possible answers, such as:

rat : pig : : goat : _____
A. chimpanzee   B. cow   C. rabbit   D. sheep

They were instructed to rank the possible answers, from best to worst. How would you respond? Their subjects ranked the answers: cow, sheep, rabbit, chimpanzee.

The responses clearly supported the theory; people chose as the best answer the animal that was different from the third animal in the same dimensions and to the same degree as the first animal was different from the second animal. Rumelhart and Abrahamson propose that people solve such analogies such as $A : B : : C : ?$ by a three-step process. First, they figure out how to move from A to B. Then they move from C to some ideal answer that differs from C in the same way that B differed from A. Finally, they compare that ideal answer to each of the alternatives and select the answer that comes the closest. Thus we rely on distances and dimensions in psychological space in order to solve analogies.

Componential Theory.   Sternberg (1977) proposed a more general theory of analogies. Rumelhart and Abrahamson's spatial theory works well for some kinds of analogies, but other kinds cannot be fit into a neat cube. Sternberg's theory, like Rumelhart and Abrahamson's, has several different stages. Sternberg calls these stages *components,* and so his theory is called *the componential theory.*

Sternberg studied some verbal analogies, but he used picture stimuli as well. Demonstration 8.7 has analogies similar to the picture analogies that Sternberg asked his subjects to solve. People responded to the analogies by answering "true" or "false" rather than by selecting an answer for the fourth term in the analogy. (Also, notice that you could construct a cube to represent the three dimensions in these analogies, just as you did with Rumelhart and Abrahamson's animal problems.)

The componential theory of analogies was based on the results of Sternberg's studies. Let's look at the three major components in this theory.

1. *The first stage is attribute identification, or encoding.* During this stage, a

---

Demonstration 8.7   Analogies Based on Pictures.

Analogies can use pictures rather than words. The following analogies are similar to ones used by Sternberg (1977). Decide whether each analogy is "true" or "false," given the analogy $A : B :: C : D$. The answers are at the end of the chapter.

person translates the analogy into an internal representation. For example, suppose that you must solve this verbal analogy:

WASHINGTON : 1 : : LINCOLN : ?
Which is the correct answer?
(a) 10
(b) 5

You might encode Washington in three different ways: (1) the first president of the United States, (2) his portrait is on the $1 bill, and (3) he was a Revolutionary War Hero. The number *1* might be encoded in these ways: (1) the first number in counting, (2) the first item in a list, and (3) one unit in an amount. Lincoln could be encoded in these ways: (1) the sixteenth president of the United States, (2) his portrait is on the $5 bill, and (3) he was a Civil War hero. Finally, the two possible answers, *10* and *5* could be encoded like the number *1*. If you were encoding the pictures in Demonstration 8.7, you might encode each of the figures in terms of their size, clothing color, and sex.

2. *The next stage involves comparing attributes.* There are several parts to this stage, because there are several kinds of comparisons that must be made. If we represent an analogy with symbols—*A : B : : C : D*—the first kind of comparison that must be made is between *A* and *B*. What kind of relationship is there, for example, between Washington and 1? There are two answers: (1) Washington was the first president, and (2) Washington's portrait is on the $1 bill.

To solve an analogy, one must also make a comparison between *A* and *C*. How, for example, is Washington related to Lincoln? This comparison involves combining some of the information from the encoding stage. For Washington and Lincoln, their presidential rank orders were 1 and 16. Their portraits are on the bills whose denominations are 1 and 5.

The last part of the atribute comparison stage involves making up a rule and using that rule to find an ideal answer for *D*. It also involves evaluating the possible answers. For example, the analogy asked you to select either 10 or 5 as the answer. However, 10 doesn't match any ideal answer for *D*. The answer 5 does not match an ideal answer for *D* if we are talking about presidential rank order, but it does match the ideal answer if we are talking about money. During this part, people sometimes settle for the best answer—even if it is not perfect.

3. *The last stage involves translating the solution into a response.* In the case of the Washington and Lincoln analogy, you would choose (b) as the response. In the case of Demonstration 8.7, you would choose a response of "true" or "false" for each item.

Practical Applications of Analogies

We already discussed one application of analogies in Chapter 7. You may recall that Gordon's (1961) synectics method encourages people to use various kinds of analogies in order to arrive at creative solutions for problems. For example, you might design a new automobile jack by thinking of the Indian rope trick. The synectics method involves seeing the analogies between new situations and old.

Another application of analogies is in the area of reading, as Baron (1977) has suggested. Baron gave some nonsense words, such as KNAFE, FOCIAL, TEIGH, ROTION, and HOUGHT, to graduate and undergraduate students. He asked them to pronounce the word and to describe how they reached that conclusion. More than half of the students said that they solved the problem by making an analogy. For example, if you wonder how to pronounce the nonsense word "knafe," you might reason:

knife : pronunciation "nife" : knafe : pronunciation "nafe"

Baron also found that people were more likely to use analogies in figuring out pronunciations than they were to use the standard pronunciation rules we all learned in first and second grade. Thus, we learn some words by memorizing them, and we use these words as the basis for analogies in order to pronounce new, unfamiliar words.

Baron proposes that the analogy strategy is useful in teaching children to read. In one study, he taught four-year-olds how to read simple words such as TAX and TIN. He found that they made fewer errors on new words such as AX and IN if they had already learned the similar word TAX or TIN. Thus, children can learn the analogy strategy. Like adults, they can make use of the similarity between new words and old words.

A final application of analogies occurs in psychological testing. In particular, let us look at the Miller Analogies Test. The **Miller Analogies Test** or MAT is a difficult, 50-minute test consisting of 100 verbal analogies. Sample items appear in Demonstration 8.8. Incidentally, the source of those items is a 1974 book called *How to Prepare for the Miller Analogies Test,* prepared by the same Sternberg whose theory of analogies we examined in the previous section.

Demonstration 8.8   *Solving Analogies.*

Try the following analogies, which are similar to items on the Miller Analogies Test. The answers are at the end of the chapter.

1. PESO : MEXICO :: (*a.* ounce, *b.* pound, *c.* ruble, *d.* mark) : ENGLAND

2. WHALE : (*a.* mammal, *b.* reptile, *c.* amphibian, *d.* fish) :: LIZARD : REPTILE)

3. DEAD DUCK : GONER :: LAME DUCK : (*a.* one who serves after failing reelection, *b.* one who gives up easily, *c.* one who invests cautiously, *d.* one who complains incessantly)

4. MONOGAMY : BIGAMY :: BIPED : (*a.* unipod, *b.* pedate, *c.* millepede, *d.* quadruped)

5. METROPOLITAN MUSEUM : NEW YORK :: RIJKSMUSEUM : (*a.* Utrecht, *b.* Munich, *c.* Paris, *d.* Amsterdam)

6. EISENHOWER : REPUBLICAN :: (*a.* T. Roosevelt, *b.* Harrison, *c.* Fillmore, *d.* Wilson) : BULL MOOSE

7. CENTIGRADE : 0 :: KELVIN : (*a.* 32, *b.* 0, *c.* −100, *d.* −273)

8. JUDAISM : TORAH :: (*a.* Hinduism, *b.* Buddhism, *c.* Islam, *d.* Confucianism) : KORAN

9. FRESCO : PLASTER :: TAPESTRY : (*a.* stone, *b.* metal, *c.* cloth, *d.* wood)

10. RED SQUARE : (*a.* London, *b.* Florence, *c.* Moscow, *d.* Paris) :: TIMES SQUARE : NEW YORK

The Miller Analogies Test was developed to measure scholastic aptitude for graduate school applicants (Miller, 1960). In addition, the test is used for selection and placement in industry. Sometimes, too, it is used to determine which students should receive scholarships.

Does the Miller Analogies Test predict who will do well in graduate school? Sternberg (1977) notes that there are positive correlations between MAT scores and graduate school performance. However, the correlations are not strong. Thus a person with a high score on the MAT would be somewhat more likely to do well in graduate school than a person with a low score, but you would not want to bet much money on it!

The Miller Analogies Test has been criticized as being a test of vocabulary rather than reasoning ability. (Some of the words on the test, as you can see from Demonstration 8.8, are quite difficult.) However, Sternberg (1977) demonstrated in an experiment that the MAT measures *both* vocabulary and reasoning. The fact that the MAT does measure vocabulary suggests a precaution. The MAT should not be used to test the reasoning ability of people with poor vocabularies. Sternberg also suggests that fairly high MAT scores may be a necessary but not sufficient condition for later success. That is, a successful graduate student needs to have not only good reasoning ability, but also other qualities such as motivation and creativity.

SECTION SUMMARY: Analogies

1. **An analogy is a reasoning problem of the form $A : B :: C : ?$, such that items C and $?$ have the same relationship to each other as items A and B. We use analogies when we use our previous knowledge in a new situation.**
2. **Rumelhart and Abrahamson propose that we solve analogies by referring to the arrangement of items in psychological space. We examine the relationship between A and B, and we find a fourth item that differs from C to the same degree and in the same dimensions as B differs from A.**
3. **Sternberg proposes that we solve analogies in terms of several stages, or components. We first encode the items in the analogy and then compare the attributes. We discover a rule for the relationship and use the rule to find an ideal answer. Finally, we translate the solution into a response.**
4. **Applications of analogies include creative problem solving, learning to read, and psychological tests such as the Miller Analogies Test.**

Chapter Review Questions

1. Are human beings accurate reasoners on linear series problems and propositional reasoning problems? Explain how linguistic factors influence performance on these two kinds of tasks.

2. Give an example of each of the four kinds of reasoning tasks we have discussed in this chapter. First state the task in terms of abstract symbols, such as A, B, and C. Then think of a concrete example of each task, based on your own recent experience.

3. An ad on the back of Charmin toilet paper reads, "Charmin is measurably fluffy! And the fluffier the tissue, the gentler it feels to your skin." What kind of reasoning problem is involved in this advertisement (with a little rewording), and what kind of conclusion can be drawn?

4. How are linguistic factors relevant in reasoning problems? Imagine that you are a politician running for office, and make up examples of slogans involving linear series, propositional reasoning, and syllogisms that would be easy to understand. Then make up examples for each of the kinds of reasoning problems that are so bad that they would guarantee your losing the election!

5. CIRCLE : SPHERE : : SQUARE : ? How would Rumelhart and Abrahamson's theory explain the way you solve the analogy? Similarly, describe how Sternberg's theory would explain the solution process.

6. Imagine that you are a high school teacher. You decide that you would like to improve the reasoning skills of your students. What kinds of strategies would you teach them?

7. You and your roommate are having an argument. Your roommate's argument can be summarized:

> **Some people who are feminists are angry at men.**
> **All people who are angry at men are unhappy.**
> **Therefore, all people who are feminists are unhappy.**

Follow the steps in Erickson's set-analysis theory to show how your roommate might have reached that incorrect conclusion. Then follow the steps in Johnson-Laird and Steedman's analogical theory to show how this conclusion is incorrect.

8. In Chapter 6 we discussed the fact that negative examples were not very helpful to people trying to form a concept. List what you know about negative information from this chapter on reasoning, mentioning negative information in linguistics and negative information in propositional reasoning strategy.

9. Many reasoning errors seem to result from misunderstandings. Discuss how misunderstandings or misinterpretations cause errors on syllogisms and on propositional reasoning problems.

10. A frequent theme throughout the book has been that errors in cognitive processes arise from the inappropriate use of heuristics or strategies. Give several examples of cases in which strategies are inappropriately applied in reasoning, leading to an incorrect conclusion.

New Terms

reasoning	consequent	Venn diagram
linear series problem	affirm the antecedent	moods
premises	affirm the consequent	set-analysis theory
unmarked	deny the antecedent	analogical theory
marked	deny the consequent	heuristic
propositional reasoning	double negative	analogy
the propositional calculus	illicit conversion	Miller Analogies Test
propositions	communal knowledge	
antecedent	syllogism	

Answers to Demonstrations

8.2. 1. valid; 2. invalid; 3. invalid; 4. valid.

8.5. 1. (A); 2. (D).

8.7. 1. true; 2. false; 3. true.

8.8. 1. *b*; 2. *a*; 3. *a*; 4. *d*; 5, *d*; 6. *a*; 7. *d*; 8. *c*; 9. *c*; 10. *c*.

Decision Making

Preview

This chapter about decision making examines the choices we make about the likelihood of uncertain events. The emphasis will be on the heuristics or "rules of thumb" that we use in making choices or predictions. These heuristics generally lead us to the correct decision, but we sometimes apply them inappropriately and make an incorrect decision.

The first section of the chapter describes the representativeness heuristic. It is used when we judge a sample to be likely because it resembles the population from which it was selected and because it looks random. The representativeness heuristic is also related to other mistakes in decision making, such as failure to attend to sample size, regression toward the mean, and base rates.

A second common heuristic is the availability heuristic, which we use when we estimate frequency in terms of how easy it is to remember examples of something. Although it is generally accurate, it can lead to incorrect decisions because availability is influenced not only by objective frequency but also by search tactics, recency, familiarity, and vividness. For example, we are much more strongly influenced by a few vivid examples than by dull statistics representing large numbers of examples. The availability heuristic is also related to illusory correlations and causal scenarios.

The last section in the chapter explores four other topics. Anchoring and adjustment is a heuristic in which we guess a first approximation, which acts as an anchor, and then we make minor adjustments in the estimate. A second situation, entrapment, occurs when the decision maker spends too many resources in maintaining the current choice. The third topic concerns overconfidence, both in the decisions we make and in the accuracy with which we believe we could have predicted past events. The final topic is applications of decision making, particularly in marketing, government policy, medicine, and education.

Every day you make dozens of decisions in uncertain situations. Should you see the new movie at the Riviera that your friend raved about or the horror film that is the season's box office favorite? Should you walk past the library, where you might see Joe, or past the bookstore, where you might see Sara? Should the contestant on the game show stay with her current winnings or try for the grand prize? Should the clinical psychologist recommend that the client remain with his parents or move away to his own apartment?

Decision making involves choices concerning the likelihood of uncertain events. Decision making occurs in situations in which we make predictions about the future, select among two or more alternatives, or make estimates about frequency on the basis of scanty evidence. Reasoning, our topic in Chapter 8, is somewhat similar because it involves examining information and drawing conclusions. However, reasoning requires more certainty. The premises are either true or

---

Demonstration 9.1   *Systematic Results that Violate the Representativeness Heuristic.*

Locate a group of at least 30 people from a classroom, a dormitory, or a party. Ask each person the month and date of her or his birthday. (The year is not necessary.) After recording all dates, notice whether there are any people who share the same birthday. With a group of 30 people, the probability is about 70 percent that at least two of them will share the same birthday, and so you are reasonably likely to locate a coincidence in your sample. However, most individuals believe that coincidences are extremely unlikely because they violate the representativeness heuristic. Statistically, though, it is most likely that 28 people will have different birthdays and 2 people will share a birthday. It is less likely that all 30 will have different birthdays.

---

false, and the rules for drawing conclusions are specified. In decision making, on the other hand, the information is uncertain, rather than true or false. Much of the information may even be missing. Furthermore, there are no clear-cut rules that tell us how to proceed from the information to the conclusions. In real life the uncertainty of decision making is more common than the certainty of reasoning.

Decision making occurs frequently in our daily lives, and it has also been applied in many disciplines other than psychology. For example, decision making has been studied in medicine, economics, education, political science, engineering, geography, marketing, and management science (Slovic, Fischhoff, & Lichtenstein, 1977). A textbook called *Making Decisions* reflects the multidisciplinary approaches to the field; it was written by two psychologists, two engineers, a philosopher, a political scientist, two doctors, and an economist (Hill, Bedau, Checile, Crochetiere, Kellerman, Ounjian, Pauker, Pauker, & Rubin, 1979).

Psychologists used to approach the topic of decision making by measuring how well people performed and how closely this performance matched the way certain mathematical formulas predicted they should perform. The emphasis has now shifted, however, to an examination of the heuristics that people use in decision making (Einhorn, 1980). As you may recall from previous chapters, **heuristics** (pronounced "hyoo-*riss*-ticks") are "rules of thumb" or strategies that are most likely to produce a correct solution.

The heuristics approach to decision making has primarily been advanced by two researchers, Daniel Kahneman and Amos Tversky, whose names appear frequently throughout the chapter. They proposed that a small number of heuristics guide human decision making. Some researchers (for example, C. L. Olson, 1976) have objected to using heuristics after the fact to explain the strategies that people *probably* used in making decisions; we cannot be certain they *actually* used these heuristics. However, the heuristics approach is useful in demonstrating how the heuristics that normally guide us to correct decisions can also sometimes lead us astray.

Throughout this chapter we will discuss many studies that point out errors in decision making. These errors should not, however, lead you to conclude that humans are limited, foolish creatures. Instead, keep in mind a caution expressed by Nisbett and Ross (1980). They argue that people's decision-making strategies are

---

Demonstration 9.2   Sample Size and Representativeness.

A nearby town is served by two hospitals. About 45 babies are born each day in the larger hospital. About 15 babies are born each day in the smaller hospital. Approximately 50 percent of all babies are boys, as you know. However, the exact percentage of babies who are boys will vary from day to day. Some days it may be higher than 50 percent, some days it may be lower. For a period of one year, both the larger hospital and the smaller hospital recorded the number of days on which more than 60 percent of the babies born were boys. Which hospital do you think recorded more such days?

—The larger hospital
—The smaller hospital
—About the same (say, within 5 percent of each other)

---

well adapted to handle a wide range of problems. However, these same strategies become a liability when they are applied beyond that range. Nisbett and Ross point out that psychologists interested in decision making emphasize errors that people make, and this emphasis on what can go wrong is parallel to perception researchers' interest in illusions:

> Perception researchers have shown that in spite of, and largely because of, people's exquisite perceptual capacities, they are subject to certain perceptual illusions. No serious scientist, however, is led by such demonstrations to conclude that the perceptual system under study is inherently faulty. Similarly, we conclude from our own research that we are observing not an inherently faulty cognitive apparatus but rather, one that manifests certain explicable flaws. Indeed, in human inference as in perception, we suspect that many of people's failings will prove to be closely related to, or even an unavoidable cost of, their greatest strengths. (p. 14)

Once again, a strategy that usually leads to correct conclusions can lead us astray if it is used inappropriately.

Representativeness

One of the most common strategies that people use in making decisions is called representativeness. Let us look at an example before we consider a formal definition. Suppose that you have a normal penny and you toss it six times. Does H H H H H H seem like a typical outcome? How about H H H T T T or T H H T H T? If you are like most people, you would guess that T H H T H T would be the most likely outcome of those three possibilities. After all, you know that if a coin is tossed six times, it is likely that there will be three tails and three heads. You would be much less likely to find all heads in your sample. Furthermore, you know that coin tossing should produce heads and tails in random order, and the order T H H T H T looks much more random than H H H T T T.

A sample is called **representative** if it is similar in important characteristics to the population from which it was selected; furthermore, if the sample was selected by a random process, the sample must look random. Thus T H H T H T is a representative sample because it has an equal number of heads and tails, just like the population of all possible coin tosses. Furthermore, T H H T H T is a representative sample because it looks random rather than orderly.

Kahneman and Tversky (1972) argued that when people make decisions about the relative frequency of different samples, such as coin tosses, they often seem to be unaware of the true probabilities. For example, the *specific* sequence H H H H H H is just as likely to occur as the *specific* sequence T H H T H T. Each of these sequences occurs $1/_{64}$ of the time. Instead of using true probabilities, people use representativeness as a basis for decisions. Thus, we often use the **representativeness heuristic**; we judge a sample to be likely on the basis of similarity and randomness.

Notice that the representativeness heuristic often leads to the correct choice in everyday decisions. For example, suppose that someone asked you which of the following choices is more likely, if you were to select five people in the United States and measure their IQs: (1) 100, 100, 100, 100, 100, or (2) 140, 140, 140, 140, 140. You would appropriately select the first option because it is similar in important characteristics to the population from which it was selected; namely, both the sample and the population have a mean of 100. Furthermore, there are more IQs of 100 than IQs of 140 in the population. Representativeness is generally a useful heuristic that leads us to the correct decision. When we overuse it, however, we can make incorrect decisions.

Examples of the Representativeness Heuristic

According to the representativeness heuristic, we believe that random-looking outcomes are more likely than orderly-looking outcomes. Have you ever added up a sum of numbers and found an answer that looked *too* orderly, such as 999? You might even check your arithmetic again, because addition is a process that should yield a random-looking outcome. You'd be less likely to check your answer if it were 927 because that random-looking outcome is a more representative kind of answer.

Kahneman and Tversky (1972) discuss how the representativeness heuristic operated during World War II. London was intensively bombed during this war. A few sections of the city were hit several times, whereas other sections were not hit at all. People therefore generally believed that there must have been a systematic plan guiding the bombing; they did not believe that a random plan could have produced such an orderly bombing pattern. However, a statistical analysis demonstrated that the pattern was in fact consistent with random bombing. People find it difficult to believe that a random process can produce occasional orderly patterns. Try Demonstration 9.1 to illustrate the likelihood of people sharing the same birthday, another situation in which the results are more systematic than we might expect on the basis of the representativeness heuristic.

Nisbett and Ross (1980) point out how we rely on a more general form of the representativeness heuristic when we try to analyze the causes for certain events. Just as we expect a sample to resemble the random process by which the sample was produced, we expect a cause to resemble its effects. Thus, if a baby is born with a birth defect called a harelip, people used to suspect that the baby's mother had

TABLE 9.1   Two Distributions of 20 Marbles

Distribution 1		*Distribution 2*	
Beth	4	Beth	4
Sally	4	Sally	4
Jerome	4	Jerome	3
Darlene	4	Darlene	4
Pedro	4	Pedro	5

been startled by a rabbit during her pregnancy. Furthermore, people are skeptical if a proposed cause does *not* resemble the effects. Nisbett and Ross point out that early in the twentieth century, a Washington newspaper complained that the government was wasting its money on some ridiculous proposed explanations for yellow fever. They were particularly critical of an explanation proposed by a scientist named Walter Reed, who had suggested that yellow fever might be caused by a mosquito. The resemblance between the proposed cause (a mosquito) and the effect (yellow fever) was minimal, and so the newspaper rejected the causal link. Presumably, they would have been happier if Reed had proposed overconsumption of mustard as a cause of yellow fever.

So far, we have considered anecdotal support for the operation of the representativeness heuristic in decision making. Kahneman and Tversky (1972) conducted several experiments that emphasize the importance of representativeness. In one study, for example, they asked people to make judgments about families with six children. People judged the sequence G B B G B G to be more likely than the sequence B B B G G G. People base their decisions on representativeness, rather than true probability.

Kahneman and Tversky also asked people to imagine that five children were playing a game involving the random distribution of 20 marbles. They were asked to guess which of two possible distributions would be more likely to occur; the distributions were similar to those in Table 9.1. Actually, the uniformity in distribution 1 is statistically more likely than the nonuniformity in distribution 2. (Distributions *similar* to distribution 2 are likely, but that exact distribution is unlikely.) However, distribution 2 is more representative. This distribution is basically equal, with just enough deviation from equality to look random. People therefore judge distribution 2 to be more likely.

Sample Size and Representativeness

Representativeness is such a compelling heuristic in decision making that people often ignore other important information, such as sample size. How did you respond to Demonstration 9.2? Kahneman and Tversky (1972) asked college students this question, and most of them responded "about the same." Apparently it seems equally likely for a hospital to report having at least 60 percent baby boys born on a given day, whether the hospital is large or small. Thus sample size was ignored by the college students surveyed.

In reality, however, sample size is an important characteristic that should be considered whenever you make decisions. If an advertisement claims that four out of five doctors recommend Zowee vitamins, you should trust the statement more if it is based on a sample of 500 doctors (400 of whom recommend Zowee vitamins) than if it is based on a sample of five doctors (four of whom recommend Zowee vitamins). A large sample is more reliable than a small sample.

Similarly, a large sample is more likely than a small sample to reflect the true proportions in a population. For example, if about 50 percent of all babies are boys in a population, then a large sample is likely to have close to 50 percent boy babies. For example, it is unlikely that 40 of the 45 babies in the large hospital—about 90 percent—would be boys. It is much more likely for about 90 percent of the babies in the small hospital to be boys; 13 out of 15 boy babies would not be an unusual outcome. However, people are usually unaware of the relationship between sample size and deviance from a population proportion. Representativeness guides their decisions, and deviations from representativeness—such as more than 60 percent boy babies—seem equally likely whether the sample is large or small.

Tversky and Kahneman (1971) point out that we should believe in the **law of large numbers,** which states that large samples will be representative of the population from which they are selected. However, we mistakenly also believe in the **law of small numbers,** which states that small samples will be representative of the population from which they are selected. The law of large numbers is a correct law. The law of small numbers is an incorrect law, but we believe it anyway. It applies not only in relatively abstract statistics problems but also in social situations. For example, we may draw conclusions about a group of people on the basis of only a few group members (Quattrone & Jones, 1980).

Kahneman and Tversky (1972) had tested college students without statistical training on the babies-in-the-hospital question in Demonstration 9.2. Courses in statistics emphasize the importance of sample size in making statistical decisions. Would students who have had at least one course in statistics also ignore sample size? Kahneman and Tversky found that students with a statistics background also based their decisions on representativeness; sample size was relatively unimportant to them. Even more amazing, Tversky and Kahneman (1971) tested professional mathematical psychologists. These "experts" also paid too much attention to representativeness and too little attention to sample size.

Regression toward the Mean and Representativeness

Suppose that you get the highest score on the first test of the semester. However, you take the second test and, to your disappointment, there are five people who scored higher than you. Should you scold yourself for not having studied harder on the second test? Not necessarily, because it is likely that your performance merely demonstrated regression toward the mean. The **mean** in a distribution of scores is an average, which can be calculated by adding together all the scores and dividing by the number of scores. **Regression toward the mean** occurs when two measures are **correlated,** or statistically related, to each other; if a score on one measure is extreme, the score on the other measure is likely to be closer to the mean of the distribution. For example, the scores for members of your class on the two tests are likely to be correlated. That is, people who do well on one test will generally do well on the other test, and people who do poorly on one test will do poorly on the other test. However, the correlation is less than perfect, and so regression toward the mean will occur. The person who receives the top score on the first test should expect to do better than average on the second test. However, for statistical reasons, the score on the second test should be less outstanding; the score should be closer to the class average.

We all occasionally forget about regression toward the mean. When I first began teaching, I used to make comments on the students' second tests, based on my comparison of the first and second tests. "Much better! Keep it up," I would write enthusiastically on the test of a student who had previously received a D and now scored a C−. "What happened? See me if I can help," I would lament for a student who sank from an A to a B. In fact, their shifts probably represented regression toward the mean.

As Kahneman and Tversky (1973) write,

> Regression effects are all about us. In our experience, most outstanding fathers have somewhat disappointing sons, brilliant wives have duller husbands, the ill-adjusted tend to adjust and the fortunate are eventually striken by ill luck. (pp. 249−250)

Let's consider why regression toward the mean is related to representativeness before we look at some other examples. Kahneman and Tversky argue that when people make a prediction about the future, their prediction is similar to—or representative of—the measure upon which they are making the prediction. Thus, if a student has an outstanding score on a first test, I predict a similarly outstanding score on the second test. After all, an outstanding score is representative of the outstanding past performance. A more accurate prediction might be "fifth score from the top," but I might be likely to reject this prediction because it is not representative. Erroneously, I would be relying too heavily on representativeness. Similarly, if you are very tall, you might erroneously predict that your children will be very tall. A better prediction would be that your children will be tall, but not as tall as you are. In summary, people rely too heavily upon representativeness, and they fail to take account of regression toward the mean.

Kahneman and Tversky note that people are extremely confident about their predictions, even when this confidence is unjustified. In reality, the measure upon which the prediction is based often has low predictive validity. If a measure has high **predictive validity,** the measure can be used to make an accurate prediction about future behavior. Low predictive validity, in contrast, means that the measure has little relationship to future behavior. However, people have an **illusion of validity**; they mistakenly believe that a measure can accurately predict future behavior.

The illusion of validity in prediction tasks is so strong that people often trust their predictions as firmly as they trust their evaluations. For example, Kahneman and Tversky provided people with a description of a male college freshman, who was described by a counselor as being intelligent, self-confident, well-read, and hardworking. One group of people were asked to evaluate the student by estimating the percentage of students who would receive higher evaluations than this student. A second group of people were asked to make predictions. Specifically, they were asked to predict the student's class standing at the end of his freshman year. Now these predictions *should* show regression toward the mean; a student who receives an outstanding evaluation should receive a prediction that is closer in toward the mean. After all, the correlation between a description of a student and that student's performance many months later is far from perfect. However, people's predictions agreed quite closely with the evaluations. After all, people rely on representativeness, and if someone receives an outstanding evaluation, the representative prediction is "outstanding" rather than "good."

    Now that you know about the perils of representativeness and the importance of regression toward the mean, try Demonstration 9.3 and see whether you can apply your knowledge. Also, think about how you can apply information about regression toward the mean when you make predictions. First of all, try to assess the predictive validity of the information on which you are basing your judgment. If the predictive validity is very high, then the representativeness heuristic *will* be useful; a person with an outstanding score on one measure will receive an outstanding score on the second measure. If the predictive validity is somewhat lower, your prediction should be closer in toward the mean. If the predictive validity is close to zero—so that there is no relationship between the two measures—then your best prediction on the second measure will be the group mean.

Demonstration 9.3   *Regression toward the Mean.*

The instructors in a flight school adopted a policy of consistent positive reinforcement recommended by psychologists. They verbally reinforced each successful execution of a flight maneuver. After some experience with this training approach, the instructors claimed that contrary to psychological doctrine, high praise for good execution of complex maneuvers typically results in a decrement of performance on the next try (Kahneman and Tversky, 1973).

    What should the psychologist say in response?

    For example, suppose that someone asks you to predict how well a student will do in high school on the basis of her sense of humor in second grade. The predictive validity of second-grade sense of humor in determining high school performance is probably close to zero. Therefore, you would be reasonably safe in guessing "average" for the high school performance, whether the second-grade sense of humor was outstanding, average, or poor.

Base Rates and Representativeness

So far we have seen that representativeness is such a compelling heuristic that people ignore other useful information—such as sample size and knowledge of regression toward the mean—when they make predictions. People also ignore the **base rate,** or the proportion in the population. Try Demonstration 9.4 before we proceed. In several studies, Kahneman and Tversky (1973) demonstrated that people use representativeness when they are asked to judge category membership. They ignore the relative proportions of the categories in the population, and they focus on the extent to which a description is representative of members of each category.

Demonstration 9.4 **Base Rates and Representativeness.**

Imagine that some psychologists have administered personality tests to 30 engineers and 70 lawyers, all people who are successful in their fields. Brief descriptions were written for each of the 30 engineers and the 70 lawyers. A sample description follows. Judge that description by indicating the probability that the person described is an engineer. Use a scale from 0 to 100.

Jack is a 45-year-old man. He is married and has four children. He is generally conservative, careful, and ambitious. He shows no interest in political and social issues and spends most of his free time on his many hobbies which include home carpentry, sailing and mathematical puzzles.

The probability that this man is one of the 30 engineers in the sample of 100 is _____ %. (Kahneman and Tversky, 1973, p. 241).

In one study, people were presented with a personality sketch of an imaginary person named Steve. Steve was described in the following words:

Steve is very shy and withdrawn, invariably helpful, but with little interest in people, or in the world of reality. A meek and tidy soul, he has a need for order and structure, and a passion for detail. (Tversky & Kahneman, 1974, p. 1124)

After reading the passage, people were asked to judge Steve's occupation. A list of possibilities—such as farmer, salesperson, airline pilot, librarian, and physician— were supplied. If people pay attention to base rates, they should select a profession that has a high base rate in the population, such as farmer or salesperson. However, people used the representativeness heuristic, and they tended to guess that Steve was a librarian. The description of Steve was highly similar to (that is, representative of) the stereotype of a librarian.

You might argue, however, that the experiment with Steve was unfair. After all, Tversky and Kahneman did not make the base rates of the various professions at all prominent in the problem. People may not have considered the fact that salespeople are more common than librarians. Well, the base rate was made very clear in Demonstration 9.4; you were told that the base rate was 30 engineers and 70 lawyers in the population. Did you make use of this base rate and guess that Jack was highly likely to be a lawyer? Most people ignored this base rate information and judged on the basis of representativeness. In fact, this description is highly representative of our stereotype for engineers, and so people guess a high percentage for the answer to the question.

Kahneman and Tversky (1973) point out how their studies are related to Bayes' rule. **Bayes' rule** (also called Bayes' theorem) states that judgments should be influenced by two factors, base rate and the likelihood ratio. The **likelihood ratio** is the ratio of the probability that the description came from population *A,* in comparison to the probability that the description came from population *B.* For example, in the engineer-versus-lawyer decision, let us say that engineers represent population *A* and lawyers represent population *B.* Now the description in Demonstration 9.4 is probably much more representative of a typical engineer than of a typical lawyer. Thus, the likelihood ratio is very high, because the likelihood ratio is the probability that the passage describes an engineer in comparison to the probability that the passage describes a lawyer. We seem to base our decision only on this likelihood ratio, and we ignore base rates. However, Bayes' rule says that we must also pay attention to base rates. Because people ignore base rates, they are not obeying Bayes' rule.

In some cases, however, the base rate can be made more concrete, and people will pay attention to base rate information. A social psychology study by Manis, Dovalina, Avis, and Cardoze (1980) manipulated base rate in terms of feedback regarding the beliefs of individual people. In more detail, these researchers asked college student subjects to make predictions about the attitudes of other college students toward the legalization of marijuana. The subjects were asked to look at a yearbook photograph and judge whether the person in the photograph favored the legalization of marijuana. Some subjects received no feedback about whether their judgment had been accurate, and they simply proceeded to the next photograph. A second group of subjects received feedback that indicated that most of the people in the photographs favored marijuana legalization. After 80 percent of the judgments, they were told that the person in the photograph was prolegalization; 20 percent of the time the person was described as antilegalization. In a third group of people, the ratios were reversed; 20 percent of the people were described as prolegalization and 80 percent of the people were described as antilegalization.

Manis and his colleagues continued to ask for guesses during five blocks of ten trials each. If people do pay attention to base rates, we would expect to see their guesses drifting in the direction of the base rates. Figure 9.1 shows the results. Notice that the 80 percent base rate group does drift upward in their estimate of the

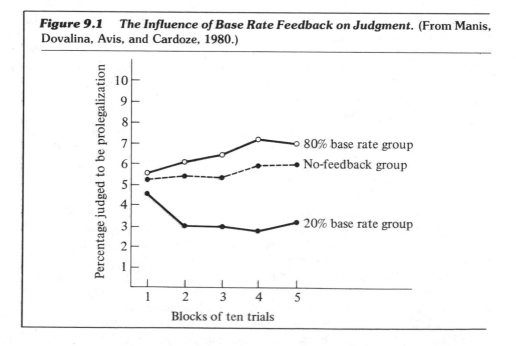

Figure 9.1   The Influence of Base Rate Feedback on Judgment. (From Manis, Dovalina, Avis, and Cardoze, 1980.)

number who favor legalization. On the other hand, the 20 percent base rate group drifts downward. Nisbett and Ross (1980) argue that people paid attention to base rate information in this particular study because the base rate information is not simply a dull, one-shot statistic. Instead, it is concrete and vivid; information about base rates is also provided continuously throughout the experiment. (We will return to the issue of concrete, vivid information later in the chapter.) Thus people may normally ignore base rate information, but they pay attention to it when the circumstances are right.

Bayes' rule is a popular research topic for decision makers, and our treatment of the topic in this chapter is very brief. An article by Slovic and Lichtenstein (1971) provides an extensive overview of the area, concluding that people do not base their probability judgments on Bayes' rule. Other studies are more optimistic. Although people may not initially operate according to Bayes' rule, they can learn to do so (Donnell & DuCharme, 1975; Messick & Campos, 1972). Beach (1975) reviews how Bayes' rule can be useful in several areas of applied decision making, such as medicine, business, and weather forecasting. Bayesian decision making has even been studied in connection with people's attitudes toward conspiracy theories for the assassination of presidents (McCauley & Jacques, 1979).

SECTION SUMMARY: Representativeness

1. Decision making involves choices about the likelihood of uncertain events.
2. The major emphasis in psychological decision making has been upon heuristics, which are rule-of-thumb strategies that are likely to produce correct solutions.
3. Errors in decision making are primarily due to an overuse of heuristics, beyond the range for which they were intended.
4. According to one common heuristic, the representativeness heuristic, we judge a sample to be likely if it is similar to the population from which it was selected and if it looks random.
5. In experiments, people consider a sample to be likely if the alternatives are approximately equally represented and if it looks random.
6. People tend to ignore sample size in decision making; they make decisions on the basis of representativeness rather than the number of items in the sample.
7. According to regression toward the mean, if a score on one measure is extreme, the score on a correlated measure will be closer to the mean. However, people ignore regression toward the mean in favor of choices that are representative.
8. People have an illusion of validity; they mistakenly believe that measures can accurately predict future behavior when they really have low validity.
9. People ignore base rate, or proportions in the population, when they make decisions; they pay much more attention to whether information is representative. In other words, they tend to ignore Bayes' rule, which states that both base rate and likelihood ratio must be considered.

Availability

Another important heuristic that people use in making decisions is availability. You use the **availability heuristic** whenever you estimate frequency or probability in terms of how easy it is to think of examples of something (Tversky & Kahneman, 1973). In other words, people judge frequency by assessing whether relevant examples can be easily retrieved from memory or whether this memory retrieval requires great effort. For example, suppose that someone asked you whether there were more psychology majors or more Spanish majors at your college. You have probably not memorized the enrollment statistics, so you would be likely to answer the question in terms of the relative availability of examples of psychology majors and Spanish majors. It is easy to retrieve names of psychology majors ("Karl, Lucia, Peter, . . .") because your memory has stored the names of dozens of people you know in psychology. However, it is difficult to retrieve names of Spanish majors. Since examples of psychology majors were easy to retrieve, you conclude that there are more psychology majors at your college. Now try Demonstration 9.5 before you read further.

Demonstration 9.5   *Availability and Letter Estimates.*

Some experts studied the frequency of appearance of various letters in the English language. They selected a typical passage in English and recorded the relative frequency with which various letters of the alphabet appeared in the first and the third positions in words. For example, in the word *language*, L appears in the first position and N appears in the third position. In this study, words with less than three letters were not examined. Consider the letter K. Do you think that the letter K is more likely to appear in the first position or the third position? Now estimate the ratio for the number of times it appeared in the first position in comparison to the number of times it appeared in the third position. For example, if you guess 2:1, this means that it appeared in the first position twice as often as in the third position; if you guess 1:2, this means that it appeared in the third position twice as often as in the first position.

Recall that a heuristic is a rule of thumb that is generally accurate. The availability heuristic *is* generally accurate—there probably are more psychology majors than Spanish majors at your college. Thus the availability heuristic is useful in judgment, insofar as availability is correlated with true, objective frequency. However, the availability heuristic can lead to errors. As we will see in this section, there are other factors that influence memory retrieval but are *not* correlated with objective frequency. These factors distort availability and therefore decrease the accuracy of our judgments. We will see that recency, familiarity, and vividness—all factors that influence memory—can influence availability.

The availability heuristic makes sense, even though it can lead to errors. We know from our everyday experience that things we see frequently are easier to recall than things we see seldom. For instance, you have seen the names Kahneman and Tversky frequently in this chapter, and so you can remember the names easily. The names McCauley and Jacques were mentioned only once, and these names would probably be more difficult to remember. We know that frequency produces better memory, and so we turn the rule around when we are asked to judge frequency. We assume that if we have better memory for an item, than that item must have greater frequency. (If your memory for Chapter 8, on reasoning, is good, you may recall that this kind of reasoning error is called "affirming the consequent.") The problem arises, as mentioned previously, because factors other than frequency also produce better memory.

Kahneman and Tversky (1972) point out how availability differs from representativeness. When we use the representativeness heuristic, we are given a specific example (such as T H T T H H). We then make judgments about whether the specific example is similar to the general process by which the example could have been produced. When we use the availability heuristic, however, we must *supply* the specific examples (such as examples of psychology majors). We make judgments on the basis of the ease with which these specific examples come to mind. We focus on the general process in representativeness and on the specific examples in availability.

Examples of the Availability Heuristic

What was your response to Demonstration 9.5, which concerned the number of words with K in the first versus the third position? Most people guess that the ratio of first-position K's to the third-position K's is about 2:1—that is, about twice as many K's in the first position as in the third position (Tversky & Kahneman, 1973). However, in reality there are about twice as many K's in the third position as in the first position. Why do we overestimate the frequency of first-position K's? Well, consider how you approached the question in Demonstration 9.5. You probably tried to think of how easy it would be to recall examples of words beginning with K (kitty, koala, kitchen, kind, . . .) versus examples of words with K in the third position (like, . . .). It is much easier to search for words in terms of their first letter than in terms of their third letter, and we make judgments on the basis of the ease of search. Consequently, we erroneously judge first-letter K's to be more common.

We said that factors such as recency, familiarity, and vividness can influence availability and lead to a distortion in frequency estimation. Let us now examine recency and familiarity; vividness deserves a separate section because of the abundance of material on that topic.

As we saw in Chapter 3, memory for items generally declines with the passage of time, and thus more recently experienced items are recalled better. As a result, availability is greater for recent items. For example, if you had been asked to estimate the incidence of assassination attempts in the spring of 1981, your estimate would probably have been very high. Your estimate would have been influenced by the recent attempts to assassinate Pope John Paul II and Ronald Reagan. In the relatively peaceful spring of 1980, your estimate would probably have been lower. Recency also influences judgments about natural hazards. Slovic, Kunreuther, and White (1974) note that people rush to purchase earthquake insurance immediately after an earthquake. The purchase rate drops steadily thereafter, as the earthquake ceases to be a recent event.

Familiarity of the examples also leads to a distortion in frequency estimation. Slovic, Fischhoff, and Lichtenstein (1976) point out that media reporters overexpose us to some events and underexpose us to others. As a result, we may be inappropriately familiar with some events that actually occur with low frequency. Slovic and his coauthors summarize part of their research:

> The frequencies of accidents, cancer, botulism, and tornadoes, all of which get heavy media coverage, were greatly overestimated; asthma and diabetes are among the events whose frequencies were most underestimated. Both of these events are relatively common in their nonfatal form and deaths are rarely attributed to them by the media. Similarly, the spectacular event, fire, which often takes multiple victims and which gets much media coverage, was perceived as considerably more frequent than the less spectacular, single-victim event, drowning, although both are about equal in terms of actual frequency. (p. 172)

Similarly, Nisbett and Ross (1980) note that protesters in the huge antiwar marches of the Vietnam era resented the media's distortion of antiwar and prowar sympathizers. The media would often devote almost as much film to several dozen counterprotesters as they devoted to the 100,000 protesters. The protesters were understandably concerned that the media made both protesters and counterprotesters equally available to television viewers. Viewers might therefore reach inaccurate conclusions about the sizes of the two groups. Notice whether you can spot the same tendency in current news broadcasts.

Now try Demonstration 9.6, a modification of a study by Tversky and Kahneman (1973). Did your friends respond according to the familiarity of the examples, rather than true frequency? Tversky and Kahneman presented people with lists of 39 names. A typical list might contain 19 names of famous women and 20 names of less famous men. After hearing the list, they were asked to judge whether the list contained more men's names or more women's names. About 80 percent of the subjects erroneously guessed that the group with the most famous, familiar names was the more frequent, even though it was objectively less frequent.

Demonstration 9.6   *Familiarity and Availability.*

Read this list of names to several friends. After you have finished the entire list, ask your friends to estimate whether there were more men or women listed. Do not allow them to answer "about the same." (In reality, there are 14 women's names and 15 men's names.)

Louisa May Alcott	Pearl Buck
John Dickson Carr	Amy Lowell
Emily Dickinson	Robert Lovett
Thomas Hughes	Edna St. Vincent Millay
Laura Ingalls Wilder	George Nathan
Jack Lindsay	Allan Nevins
Edward George Lytton	Jane Austen
Margaret Mitchell	Henry Crabb Robinson
Michael Drayton	Joseph Lincoln
Edith Wharton	Emily Bronte
Henry Vaughan	Arthur Hutchinson
Kate Millett	James Hunt
Eudora Welty	Erica Jong
Richard Watson Gilder	Brian Hooker
	Harriet Beecher Stowe

Vividness and Availability

Vividness influences availability, according to extensive evidence summarized in a book by Nisbett and Ross (1980), who argue that vivid, concrete information is given too much weight in decision making. In contrast, pale, dull statistics—usually a more accurate reflection of the truth—may be ignored. For example, consider some passages from a flier from Amnesty International, a group that campaigns for human rights and opposes torture of political prisoners:

> [according to one Guatemalan soldier] ". . . before my very eyes they killed three people: they strangled them. The way they killed them was with a piece of rope, a kind of noose, which they put round the neck and then used a stick to tighten it like a tourniquet from behind—handcuffed, and with their heads held down in the trough. Then they came out, their eyes were open; they'd already turned purple. It took at most three minutes in the water. . . . They just showed me the other six bodies and said the same thing would happen to me if I tried to lie to them." (Amnesty International/USA, 1981, pp. 1–2)

Contrast the impact of that passage with a passage from a newspaper article about Amnesty International receiving the Nobel Peace Prize. The passage remarks that Amnesty International's chairperson said that the money

> . . . will be used to strengthen the outfit in countries where it is not strong and where there is a need. Such as Indonesia where there are reckoned to be 50,000 prisoners of conscience; up to 5,000 in Chile and maybe 2,000 in Malawi. Not to mention an estimated 10,000 in Russia. (Cunningham, 1977, p. 11)

Which information haunts you more, the vivid description of the conditions in Guatemala or the 50,000 political prisoners in Indonesia? If you had been asked which country had more serious human rights problems, would you guess Guatemala? According to the viewpoint of Nisbett and Ross, you would probably respond "Guatemala" on the basis of the vividness of the information.

Vivid information has played an important part in persuasion throughout history. According to Nisbett and Ross, Abraham Lincoln once met Harriet Beecher Stowe, whose *Uncle Tom's Cabin* vividly described the miserable condition of slaves on plantations. He commented to her that he was "happy to meet the little lady who started the Civil War." Similarly, Upton Sinclair's examples of exploitation of immigrants in the Chicago stockyards led to stricter supervision in the meat-processing industry.

Nisbett and Ross argue that vivid information has a greater influence than less vivid information because it is more likely to be stored and remembered. Perhaps you could have guessed at a possible mechanism for the operation of vividness on the basis of your knowledge of imagery in Chapter 4. Vivid information is certainly higher in imagery than pallid information. You can picture the Guatemalan prisoners, but the information about the 50,000 Indonesian prisoners is too abstract. High-imagery material is remembered better than low-imagery material. Judgments of frequency are based on availability, or the ease with which you remember the examples. It is simply easier to remember the Guatemalan examples than the Indonesian examples.

Think about some occasions on which you paid more attention to vivid information than to pallid statistics. For example, try Demonstration 9.7, based on an example from the Nisbett and Ross book. Notice that if you are a rational decision maker, you would calmly conclude from the cocktail party information that the number of Volvo owners from whom you have information has increased beyond the several hundred in *Consumer Reports* to several hundred and one. The frequency-of-repair record for the several hundred and one Volvos must also be increased by a tiny amount to accommodate this new information. However, every one of us would probably react much more violently to this new information. In fact, we might find ourselves returning to *Consumer Reports* to recheck the statistics on the Saab.

Demonstration 9.7   *Vividness and Availability.*

Imagine that you want to buy a new car. After much contemplation, you decide to purchase either a Volvo or a Saab. Being a sensible person, you consult *Consumer Reports*. You learn that the magazine's experts reached a consensus that the Volvo is mechanically superior. Furthermore, the consensus of the readership is that the Volvo requires fewer repairs. With this information in mind, you decide to buy a Volvo before the week is through. Meanwhile, however, you go to a cocktail party and you announce your intentions to a friend. He reacts with dismay, "A Volvo! You've got to be kidding. My brother-in-law had a Volvo. First that fancy fuel injection computer thing went out. 250 bucks. Next he started having trouble with the rear end. Had to replace it. Then the transmission and the clutch. Finally sold it in three years for junk" (Nisbett, Borgida, Crandall, & Reed, 1976, p. 129).

How do you respond to your friend? Does this information influence your decision to buy a Volvo? (Be honest!)

Perhaps your college has a systematic evaluation of professors, published in the campus newspaper or some other public forum. If so, do you trust these statistics more than you trust the information from a student who took the course last semester? This issue was examined by Borgida and Nisbett (1977) at University of Michigan. Psychology majors either examined course ratings, based on evaluations from at least 30 students, or listened to comments from students who had taken the courses. Then they were asked to indicate which courses they would like to take in future semesters. The results showed that the face-to-face comments had a much greater impact on course choices than did the course evaluations.

Think about other applications of the relationship between vividness and availability, such as in the courtroom. Reyes, Thompson, and Bower (1980) designed a study involving mock jury decisions. People were asked to make judgments about a court case involving drunken driving. The case involved a defendant who was driving home from a Christmas party and collided with a garbage truck. The summary of the evidence was presented in either a vivid or a pallid version. For example, one part of the evidence implied that the defendant, named Sanders, was drunk shortly before leaving the party. The pallid version read, "On his way out the door, Sanders staggered against a serving table, knocking a bowl to the floor" (p. 4). The vivid version read, "On his way out the door, Sanders staggered against a serving table, knocking a bowl of guacamole dip to the floor and splattering guacamole on the white shag carpet" (p. 4). After reading one of the versions, people made an immediate judgment of Sanders' apparent guilt. They also returned two days later to provide a delayed judgment.

The·results showed that the immediate judgments of apparent guilt were only slightly influenced by vividness. As Reyes and his coauthors suggest, most of the arguments are still available, whether the information was vivid or pallid. However, vividness clearly affected the delayed judgments. People were much more likely to judge Sanders to be guilty if they read a vivid description. Can't you visualize the thick, green avocado paste seeping down through the expensive, plush fibers of the white carpet? That information is much more available than the abstract information about a bowl falling to the floor.

The relationship between vividness and availability also has applications in other areas of psychology, such as social psychology. For example, Ross and Sicoly (1979) found that people overestimate their own contributions to a joint project. Information about their own contributions is probably more vivid than information about others. Therefore, judgments will be more influenced by this vivid self-related information. Furthermore, Rothbart, Fulero, Jensen, Howard, and Birrell (1978) show how vividness and availability may influence the formation of stereotypes. Members of a group who create a particularly vivid impression will be easily recalled as examples of the group. In contrast, "mild" individuals who belong to the group will not be recalled. As a consequence, our impressions of a group will be influenced by the abundance of vivid group members in our memory.

Illusory Correlation and Availability

Another error in human judgment is called *illusory correlation.* We mentioned the term *correlation* before; it means a statistical relationship between two variables. *Illusory* (pronounced "ill-*loo*-serr-ee") is a term derived from *illusion*; it means deceptive or unreal. Therefore, an **illusory correlation** occurs when people believe that a statistical relationship exists between two variables, yet there is no real evidence for this relationship. In particular, people often believe that two kinds of events tend to occur together, when an honest tabulation would show that these two kinds of events occur together at just a chance level.

Hirschberg (1977) provides an example of an illusory correlation. Some research, such as a study by Berscheid and Walster (1974), has shown that a person who is physically attractive is also perceived to be blessed with other desirable characteristics. For example, we believe that attractive people are also intelligent, witty, and imaginative. It may be that there is some real relationship between attractiveness and these other good characteristics. However, we probably distort the relationship, so that it appears stronger than it really is.

Think of other examples of illusory correlations that you find in everyday life—illusory correlations that either have no basis in fact or much less basis than is commonly believed. For instance, fat people are jolly, if you wash your car it will rain soon afterwards, people who eat spinach are strong, and so forth.

The first systematic investigation of illusory correlation was performed by the Chapmans (Chapman & Chapman, 1967, 1969), who approached the problem from a clinical psychology framework. They were concerned that clinicians consistently reported associations between responses on projective tests and certain clinical symptoms. However, many studies have demonstrated that there is no true relationship between the responses and the symptom. How could intelligent people, well educated in scientific methods, maintain these illusory correlations? For example, one projective test is called the Draw-a-Person test. The test assumes that people project their emotions and motivations onto the figure they draw. Careful studies have demonstrated that the responses on this test are really unrelated to clinical symptoms. Nevertheless, many clinical psychologists believe that the Draw-a-Person test is useful. For example, they claim that paranoid or suspicious patients typically exaggerate the eyes, whereas dependent patients (who like to be cared for and fed) typically exaggerate the mouth.

Chapman and Chapman (1967) asked patients in a state hospital to take the Draw-a-Person test. These drawings were then paired *completely at random* with six symptoms, such as suspiciousness and dependence. College students then examined these drawings, paired together with the symptoms of the people who had presumably drawn them. Afterwards, they were asked to report what features of the drawings were most often paired with each symptom. Remember, now, that the stimuli had been arranged so that there was indeed no systematic relationship between the drawings and the symptoms. Nonetheless, the college students reported the same kind of associations that clinical psychologists report. College students who have had no experience in a clinical setting reported, for example, that drawings with exaggerated eyes had been done by the paranoid people, whereas drawings with exaggerated mouths had been done by dependent people. Chapman and Chapman (1969) also extended their findings to reports of homosexuality on the Rorschach test.

Notice, then, that the Chapmans' subjects reported a correlation that did not really exist. How did this illusory correlation arise? Tversky and Kahneman (1974) point out that availability provides a reasonable explanation for the illusory-correlation effect. When people judge the frequency with which exaggerated eyes and paranoid symptoms occur together, they may make judgments in terms of the associative bond between these two events. In everyday life, we associate suspiciousness with the eyes more than with any other part of the body; this association is therefore particularly strong. Thus, our judgment about how often

TABLE 9.2 A Matrix Representing Four Kinds of Information

	Number in Each Category	
	Spinach Eaters (+)	*Non−Spinach Eaters* (−)
People who are strong (+)	9	15
People who are not strong (−)	3	5
Totals	12	20

events occur together is heavily influenced by our previous ideas rather than by the actual events.

An additional explanation of the illusory-correlation effect emphasizes attention rather than memory (for example, Slovic, Kunreuther, and White, 1974). It seems likely that both memory (availability) and attention contribute to illusory correlations. When we try to determine whether two variables are related to each other, we really ought to consider four kinds of information. For example, suppose that we want to determine whether people who eat spinach are strong. As Table 9.2 shows, we should pay attention to the frequency of the four possible combinations: spinach eaters who are strong, spinach eaters who are not strong, non−spinach eaters who are strong, and non−spinach eaters who are not strong. Our decision should be based on a comparison of two ratios:

$$\frac{\text{spinach eaters who are strong}}{\text{total number of spinach eaters}} \quad \text{versus} \quad \frac{\text{non−spinach eaters who are strong}}{\text{total number of non−spinach eaters}}$$

Using the data from Table 9.2, for example, we find that 9 out of the 12 spinach eaters (or 75 percent) are strong, and 15 out of the 20 non−spinach eaters (also 75 percent) are strong. We should conclude that there is no relationship between spinach consumption and strength. However, people frequently pay attention to only one cell, the cell in which both of the attributes are positive. In this example, for instance, we notice only the spinach eaters (+) who are strong (+). We ignore the three other cells that represent the three other combinations: (1) +−; (2) −+; and (3) −−.

We pay attention to the purely positive cell and we ignore the cells that contain any information involving negatives. Does that sound familiar? Recall that in the language chapter we saw that people have difficulty understanding and remembering negative, as opposed to affirmative, sentences. Furthermore, remember that in the reasoning chapter we discussed the difficulty people face when negatives appear in reasoning problems. We also saw in that chapter that people would rather try to confirm a hypothesis than try to disprove it. It seems, then, that cognitive processes are designed to handle positive information in preference to negative information: We can deal with what *is* better than we can deal with what *isn't*.

By now, you may have grown disgusted with the apparent inadequacy of human decision-making capabilities. However, McArthur (1980) points out a bright side to our tendency to believe in illusory correlations. Yes, humans tend to be overly anxious to believe that a relationship exists when in fact there is no relationship. As a consequence, we may mistakenly believe in some illusions. However, in the long run it might be wiser to make errors in the direction of being *too* anxious to detect relationships, rather than not anxious enough. For example, it is biologically adaptive to overdetect the correlations between particular foods and illnesses. We are more likely to survive if we remove a particular food dye from the market once we suspect that there is a relationship between this dye and cancer.

Similarly, McArthur argues that it is adaptive to overdetect associations between scowling or fearful faces and aversive, unpleasant stimuli. Overdetection may cause us to mistakenly avoid some innocent people, but we may also protect ourselves from serious harm.

Furthermore, Einhorn and Hogarth (1981) point out the risk involved in trying to determine whether a correlation is real or illusory. Think about a waiter in a busy restaurant who thinks that he can predict which customers will leave generous tips, and he gives special attention to these customers. Now the waiter could perform a proper experiment by giving poor service to those people whom he predicts will leave good tips and good service to those people whom he predicts will leave poor tips. Notice, however, that the waiter must risk the possible loss of income in the short run in order to determine whether customer's characteristics are really correlated with the size of the tips they leave. Thus we often have the opportunity to learn that a correlation may be illusory. However, we frequently decide that it is not worth the risk in order to discover the correct information.

Causal Scenarios and Availability

So far we have discussed decisions that can be made by thinking of examples and judging the relative frequency of these examples. The correct answer to these decisions could be obtained by counting an unbiased list of the examples. For example, the problem about first-letter versus third-letter K's could be answered by counting letters in a passage of text.

In real life, however, probabilities are often judged in situations that cannot be evaluated by simply counting the list of examples. For example, what is the probability that Bill and Jane will get divorced? What is the probability that the operation on Jim's leg will be a success? Each marriage and each leg is unique, so we cannot provide an answer by counting examples of other people's marriages and legs. Nonetheless, we use the availability heuristic to judge the likelihood of various outcomes. In particular, we may make judgments by trying to construct causal scenarios (Tversky & Kahneman, 1973). A **causal scenario** is a story in which one event causes another, leading from the original situation to the end result. We then make a judgment about the likelihood of the end result on the basis of the ease with which the causal scanario came to mind. Thus causal scenarios are similar to the availability heuristic, in which judgments are based on the ease with which examples come to mind.

For example, suppose that you want to judge the likelihood of your becoming a clinical psychologist. You might construct a causal scenario in which you do extremely well in your coursework, receive a high score on the graduate records, receive complimentary letters of recommendation from your professors, graduate at the top of your class, get accepted into the graduate school of your choice, do well in graduate school, complete your dissertation in good time, receive your Ph.D., complete your internship, and set up your practice. If you have no difficulty imagining each of the events in this scenario, then you may judge the entire scenario as being likely. On the other hand, constructing a causal scenario for your becoming the president of the United States may be more difficult, and so you would judge the scenario as being unlikely.

We saw that the inappropriate use of the availability heuristic could lead to errors. Similarly, the causal scenario heuristic can lead to errors. In particular, a sequence of events often occurs even though the causal scenario is difficult to imagine. Try Demonstration 9.8 to see whether the causal scenarios for decisions about career choices, marriage partners, and geographic locations are believable. Some will certainly seem plausible, yet others may seem highly unlikely. For example, McCall (1981) describes how Mavis Hetherington, the editor of the prestigious journal *Child Development,* decided to abandon her career in English and pursue psychology because her college English department did not offer a course on Chaucer in 1947.

Demonstration 9.8 *Causal Scenarios.*

Locate several married adults who are currently employed. Ask them three questions: (1) How did you end up in your current occupation? (2) How did you meet your spouse? (3) How did you end up in your current geographic location? Notice in each case whether the causal scenario is one that would come readily to mind.

Abelson (1976; Schank & Abelson, 1977) uses the term *script* to describe a concept related to causal scenarios. A **script** is a coherent chain of events that a person expects to happen. We will use the terms *causal scenario* and *script* interchangeably. Abelson (1976) describes how scripts operate in decision making. When people must make a decision, they call forth a script based on a similar past situation. For example, imagine that a committee in charge of graduate admissions is reviewing a set of applicants. The committee opens a folder describing John Kolodny. They begin with the information in this folder and construct scripts leading to either a successful or unsuccessful outcome for this student. A committee member may be reminded of another similar student in the past and think ''Mr. Kolodny reminds me very much of Paul Pippik, who hung around for eight years never writing his dissertation. Let's not get into that again'' (p. 37).

Notice, incidentally, that scripts involve both representativeness and availability. Representativeness is relevant because a person assumes that similarities on some attributes implies similarity on other dimensions. (Don't you assume that someone who has the same first name as you will be like you in other, important ways?) Availability is relevant because we base our judgment on the ease with which a script comes to mind. In the case of poor Mr. Kolodny, the Paul Pippik script came to mind more readily than a script involving a successful outcome.

SECTION SUMMARY: *Availability*

1. People use the availability heuristic when they estimate frequency in terms of how easy it is to remember examples of something.
2. The availability heuristic is generally accurate, but it can lead to errors because factors other than objective frequency can influence memory.
3. Search tactics, recency, and familiarity influence availability, so they influence frequency estimates.
4. In determining availability, vivid, concrete information has a stronger

influence than concrete, dull statistics. As a consequence, a few vivid examples have more impact on decisions than statistics based on a large sample.

5. Evidence for the relationship between vividness and availability comes from studies on course enrollment, mock jury trials, and social psychology.
6. An illusory correlation occurs when people believe that two variables are related to each other even when there is really no statistical relationship.
7. In a study with implications for clinical psychology, people judged certain drawing features to be frequently paired with clinical symptoms even though they really occurred together at a chance level.
8. Illusory correlations occur because the associative bond between two events may be strong and because we pay more attention to positive instances of two events than to combinations involving negative instances.
9. To figure out the likelihood of a certain outcome, we can construct causal scenarios or scripts that lead us from the original situation to the outcome. We judge the outcome to be likely if the causal scenario comes to mind readily.

Additional Topics in Decision Making

So far we have explored two topics in the area of decision making: representativeness and availability. These two heuristics have been widely researched. Furthermore, we saw that many other biases in decision making can be traced to the inappropriate use of either representativeness or availability. However, psychologists who are interested in decision making have examined many other areas. For example, some psychologists have studied an area that is also important for economists, the relationship between value and choice. When people must choose between two financial alternatives, are their decisions rational? This area will not be covered here, but if you want to know more about this interdisciplinary topic, consult a book called *Making Decisions* (Hill et al., 1979) or an article by Kahneman and Tversky (1979).

The four topics we will consider in this part of the chapter include another heuristic called anchoring and adjustment. We will also examine a situation called entrapment, in which people decide to maintain a position because they have already invested too many resources to quit. The third topic is overconfidence in decision making. Finally, applications of decision making will be summarized.

Anchoring and Adjustment

A heuristic that we often use when we make estimates is called anchoring and adjustment. In the **anchoring and adjustment heuristic,** we begin by guessing a first approximation—an anchor—and then we make adjustments in that number on the basis of additional information (Slovic, Kunreuther, & White, 1974). This heuristic often leads to a reasonable answer. (Recall that representativeness and availability also often lead to reasonable answers.) However, people typically rely too heavily on the anchor, and their adjustments are too small.

In one study, Tversky & Kahneman (1974) asked people to estimate various quantities. For example, a typical question might ask them to estimate the percentage of African countries in the United Nations. Before requesting the reply, the experimenters spun a wheel of fortune while the subjects looked on. The wheel of fortune selected, purely at random, a number between 0 and 100. The subjects were asked to indicate whether the answer to the question was higher or lower than the selected number, and to reply to the question by moving upward or downward from that selected number.

Tversky and Kahneman found that the arbitrarily selected number acted as an anchor for the estimates. For example, if the wheel of fortune had stopped on 10, people estimated 25 as the percentage of African countries in the United Nations. If the wheel had stopped on 65, people estimated 45. In other words, an arbitrary number that had no real relationship to the question acted as an anchor for the response. People made adjustments from this number, based on information related to the question. However, these adjustments were often far too conservative.

Tversky and Kahneman found that the anchoring effect was not reduced when people received money for more accurate guesses. Anchoring is such a trusted heuristic that we fail to abandon it even when we are promised modest wealth! Furthermore, Lichtenstein and Slovic (1973) found an anchoring bias among gamblers on the floor of a Las Vegas casino.

We use anchoring and adjustment when we estimate a single number. We also use this heuristic when we estimate **confidence intervals,** or ranges within which we expect a number to fall a certain percentage of the time. (For example, you might guess that the 98 percent confidence interval for the population of a particular town is 2000−7000, meaning that you think that there is a 98 percent chance that the population is between 2000 and 7000.)

Try Demonstration 9.9 to see how accurate your estimates are for various

---

Demonstration 9.9 *Anchoring and Adjustment.*

For each of the following questions, answer in terms of a range, rather than a single number. Specifically, supply a 98 percent confidence interval, or a range within which you expect the correct answer will almost certainly fall. For example, if you supply a 98 percent confidence interval that is 2000−7000, this means that you think there is only a 2 percent chance that the real answer is either more than 7000 or less than 2000. All questions apply to U.S. statistics, unless otherwise noted. (*The World Almanac & Book of Facts,* 1981.)

1. What was the per capita income of residents of South Dakota in 1979?
2. What was the average salary of male bakers in 1978?
3. How many commemorative and regular postage stamps were issued in 1980?
4. How many women were arrested for embezzlement in 1978?
5. How many active M.D.s were there in the state of New York in 1978?
6. How many Americans had high blood pressure in 1979?
7. What was the total expenditure of the Defense Department in 1979?
8. How many dollar bills were printed in 1979?
9. How many registered autos, trucks, and buses were there in California in 1980?
10. How many bushels of wheat were produced in the United States in 1979?

kinds of almanac information. The answers can be found at the end of this section. Slovic, Kunreuther, and White (1974) point out how a typical decision maker might respond to a question asking for an estimate of the number of foreign cars imported into the United States in 1968:

> I think there were about 180 million people in the U.S. in 1968; there is about one car for every three people; thus there would have been about 60 million cars; the lifetime of a car is about 10 years, this suggests that there should be about 6 million new cars in a year but since the population and the number of cars is increasing let's make that 9 million for 1968; foreign cars make up about 10% of the U. S. market, thus there were probably about 900,000 foreign imports; to set my 98% confidence band, I'll add and subtract a few hundred thousand cars from my estimate of 900,000. (p. 195)

Check to see how many of your confidence interval estimates included the correct answer. If a large number of people were to answer a large number of questions, we would expect their confidence intervals to include the correct answer about 98 percent of the time, assuming that their estimation techniques are correct. However, studies have demonstrated that the confidence intervals actually include the correct answer only 50 to 70 percent of the time (Slovic, Kunreuther, & White, 1974; Tversky & Kahneman, 1974). In other words, the confidence intervals that we estimate are too narrow.

Tversky and Kahneman (1974) point out how anchoring and adjustment are relevant when we make confidence interval estimates. We arrive at a best estimate and use this figure as an anchor. We make adjustments upward and downward from this anchor in order to construct the confidence interval estimate. However, our adjustments are much too small. Look back over the quotation on the foreign car estimates and notice the number of times when a large estimation error could have occurred. Errors could have occurred in estimating the U.S. population, the ratio of cars to people, the lifetime of each car, and the percentage of cars that are foreign. Given the enormous potential for large errors, an adjustment of just a few hundred thousand is much too small. Again, we establish our anchor and we do not wander far from it in the adjustment process.

Think about applications of the anchoring and adjustment heuristic. Suppose that you are trying to guess how much you will make in tips in your summer job. You will probably make a first guess and then make adjustments in this figure. However, your final answer will depend too heavily on that first guess (which may not have been carefully chosen), and the adjustments will not adequately reflect all the additional factors that you consider after you made your first guess.

Nisbett and Ross (1980) summarize the anchoring and adjustment problem: ". . . once subjects have made a first pass at a problem, the initial judgment may prove remarkably resistant to further information, alternative modes of reasoning, and even logical or evidential challenges" (p. 41). Thus, we are amazingly "conservative." We are loyal to the original estimate, and we shut our eyes to new evidence.

Incidentally, the answers to Demonstration 9.9 are: 1. $7455; 2. $15,683; 3. 22; 4. 83,087; 5. 45,570; 6. 33,740,000; 7. $117,921,453,000; 8. 757,813,744; 9. 15,973,000; 10. 2,141,732,000.

Entrapment

You call Blatz Airlines and a recording answers: "All lines at Blatz Airlines are temporarily busy. The calls are being handled automatically, and your call will be given to the next available sales representative." You wait anxiously, seconds and minutes speeding by on your watch. You are tempted to hang up, yet you have already invested so much time, and those minutes would be wasted if you hung up now. So you wait for a much longer time than you had originally intended. Your decision to continue waiting, rather than to hang up, is an example of a special kind of escalation called entrapment. **Escalation** means an increase in the size of a conflict. **Entrapment** is a kind of escalation in which the decision maker spends more resources—such as time, energy, and money—in the conflict than appropriate (Hill et al., 1979).

We can all think of examples of entrapment. You have just spent $500 repairing your car's transmission, and then the brakes go, and you need new tires. You may find yourself spending more on repairs than the car was worth. Similarly, you may find yourself in a love relationship that is not personally satisfying, yet it is difficult to ignore the years you have invested so far. A friend may be about to graduate from college and enter a career that no longer seems interesting, but it appears too late to back out. On a more trivial level, you have watched one hour of a poorly made Western on the Late Show. It's a painfully bad movie, yet you have invested too much to quit.

Too Much Invested to Quit is the title of a book by Teger (1979), an interesting investigation of the entrapment phenomenon. According to Teger, one of the best examples of entrapment was the involvement of the United States in the Vietnam War:

> We invested lives, money, and prestige for a goal which was measured in terms of political and military influence, long range economic gains, etc. In such a situation, it is much more difficult to make an objective comparison between the value of the investments and the value of the outcome. It is difficult, therefore, to determine whether or not the situation has reached the level at which quitting is warranted. . . . While some [members of Congress] took the position that any amount of lives and money was justified in order to obtain victory, others saw limitations to the amount of investments that would be warranted—but differed in where to draw the line. Some took the position that one more investment was acceptable since it was sure to be the last, while others noted that we had said the same thing before concerning other "last" investments. There were some who said that the war was not worth it any more but that we had to continue so that our "dead shall not have died in vain," so that our investments in money and raw materials would not be wasted, and so that our prestige and honor would be upheld. This last postion amounts to a statement that we had "too much invested to quit" for it justified current investments in terms of past investments. The longer the war continued, the more difficult it was to justify the additional investments in terms of the value of possible victory. On the other hand, the longer the war continued the more difficult it became to write off the tremendous losses without having anything to show for them. Justifications for past investments, then, became the reason for continuing the war. We were fighting the war because of the war—it had become a self-perpetuating system. (p. 4)

Try Demonstration 9.10, a modification of the dollar auction method used in Teger's studies. Teger tried this technique about 40 times, with undergraduates, graduates, and faculty members in groups of 10 to 300 people. The bidding always exceeded $1.00 and occasionally went as high as $20.00. A typical game might end with the loser paying $4.25 to the auctioneer and the "winner" (who won by bidding $5.00 but wins $1.00 in the auction) paying a net sum of $4.00 to the auctioneer. The same pattern was also found in laboratory studies involving variations of the dollar auction.

Demonstration 9.10   *Entrapment.*

Try this demonstration in an informal setting with about ten friends. Announce that you are going to hold an auction and that you will auction something off to the highest bidder. Use a variation of this statement: "I'm going to auction off a dollar bill." (Hold up the dollar bill to the audience.) "It is a real dollar bill. Now you are familiar with the way an auction works. Anyone can make a bid, and people keep on making bids until only one bidder remains. That person is the highest bidder and pays the last bid to the auctioneer. That person gets the prize—in this case, it's the dollar bill.

"However, there is one difference between this auction and the typical auction. In this auction, the highest bidder pays the last bid and gets the dollar bill, but the second highest bidder also pays his or her last bid. This second highest bidder therefore also pays but gets nothing in return. Here's an example. Suppose that when the bidding stops, someone has bid 20 cents, someone else has bid 30 cents and someone else has bid 40 cents. What happens is that the person who bid 40 cents wins the bid, pays me 40 cents and gets the dollar. The person who bid 30 cents pays me 30 cents and gets nothing. The person who bid 20 cents pays nothing."

Then let the auction begin. Notice the extent to which entrapment occurs. (If the bidding has reached excessive proportions, you may decide not to collect on the bids.)

Why do we find ourselves in entrapment situations? As Hill et al. (1979) summarize the reasons, there are three pressures that drive the decision maker to remain in the present situation rather than quit: (1) the reward that is associated with reaching the goal; (2) the perceived increase in the nearness of the goal—often referred to as the "light at the end of the tunnel"; and (3) the cost associated with giving up what has been previously invested.

Teger suggests that the next time we meet a potential problem situation, we should ask ourselves as soon as possible if the problem is one of the "too much invested to quit" situations. We should set a limit on the future investments and not be afraid to quit because of past investments. Furthermore, we should resist blaming our actions on the situation and on the other participants in the decision.

Overconfidence in Decisions

We have already seen some evidence that people are too confident in the decisions they make. At the beginning of the chapter we saw that people were too confident in their predictions, failing to consider regression toward the mean. In the section on illusory correlations we saw that people are confident that relationships between variables are strong when in fact they are weak or nonexistent. In the discussion of anchoring and adjustment, we discussed how people are so confident in their estimation ability that they supply very narrow ranges for their estimates. In many other areas we have seen that people make incorrect decisions, and therefore extreme confidence in decisions is unjustified.

Dawes (1976) discussed how people trust their own judgment in decisions, in preference to statistical predictions. For example, studies in clinical psychology have overwhelmingly demonstrated that statistical methods are preferable to clinical judgments when several kinds of information about clients must be integrated. The implications are clear: Clinicians should give various tests and then combine this information by inserting the scores into a statistical formula. However, as Dawes says,

> The belief that clinicians somehow can do better than a statistical model, can integrate the information from such diverse sources into a reasonable picture of their clients, persists despite lack of supporting evidence. (p. 5)

Another area in which people trust their judgment more than statistical formulas is decision making for admission to graduate school. In many schools, students are selected unscientifically. Faculty members may spend 15 minutes looking at an applicant's transcript and reading letters of recommendation. Then they form a decision, taking into account—in some unspecified way—the grade-point average and the scores on the Graduate Record Examination. Nonetheless, people trust their judgments more than they would trust a decision based on a formula that statistically combines information about GPA, GRE, and ratings of letters of recommendation. In fact, many people are outraged at the option of using a "dehumanizing" selection device such as a statistical formula.

Why are we so confident that we can do a better job than a formula in decision making? Dawes (1979) suggests that we persist in our confidence because of several factors. For example, the availability of examples of successful clinical predictions is high. We can easily call to mind several examples of people who were exceptions to a formula but were "saved" because of someone's clinical judgment: a student who did poorly in high school and is now a star scholar in college, for instance. Furthermore, you already know that people trust a single, vivid example more than pale statistics.

A third reason for our confidence in our decisions is due to a self-fulfilling effect discussed by Einhorn and Hogarth (1978, 1981). For example, admissions officers who judge that a candidate is particularly qualified for admission may feel that their judgment is supported when their candidate does well. However, the candidate's success may be primarily due to the positive effects of the program itself. Even the people who were rejected might have become successful if they had been allowed to participate in the program. Finally, we are confident in our decisions because the statistical methods—even though they may be the best prediction methods we have—are far from perfect. We usually have information about the predictive validity of our statistical formula, but we do not have information about the predictive validity of less formal human judgments. We therefore maintain an illusion that these human judgments can be quite accurate, when they really are less accurate than the statistical formula.

Not only do we exaggerate our decision-making abilities; we also overestimate the accuracy of our hindsight. Specifically, people have a **hindsight bias:** They overestimate the accuracy with which they could have predicted past events if they had been asked to do so, and they overestimate the extent to which others should have been able to predict past events (Slovic, Fischhoff, & Lichtenstein, 1977).

Fischhoff (1975) provides an example of a hindsight bias. In 1974 a prisoner named Cletus Bowles, who had been previously convicted of murder and bank robbery, was allowed to leave the penitentiary on a four-hour social pass. He promptly fled and later allegedly murdered two people. The public demanded the resignation of the prison warden who had issued the pass. In retrospect, perhaps we could have predicted the escape. However, the prison warden may well have made a good decision, given the information he had at the time. Bowles had in fact been a model prisoner before he left the penitentiary. Unfortunately, however, good decisions can have bad outcomes. Notice why a hindsight bias is operating here. As you were reading about Cletus Bowles, weren't you tempted to conclude that the prison warden had been a fool? You in fact probably overestimated the extent to which the warden should have been able to predict that Bowles would harm someone.

Experimental evidence for the hindsight bias comes from several studies (Fischhoff, 1977; Slovic & Fischhoff, 1977; and Wood, 1978). Demonstration 9.11 is based on a study by Slovic and Fischhoff called "On the Psychology of Experimental Surprises." Perhaps you have had this experience. You are reading about an experiment in a textbook and then you say to yourself that the results were not at all surprising. In fact, you "knew it all along." In reality, the hindsight bias may have led you to overestimate your confidence.

Demonstration 9.11   The Hindsight Bias.

Find two friends who can spare a few minutes for an experiment. They should be tested separately, one friend hearing version A and one friend hearing version B. In each case, announce that you will read a paragraph and then ask a question.

Version A (foresight)

A goose egg was placed in a soundproof, heated box from time of laying to time of cracking. Approximately two days before it cracked, the experimenter began intermittently to play sounds of ducks quacking into the box. On the day after birth, the gosling was placed on a smooth floor equidistant from a duck and a goose, each of which was in a wire cage. The gosling was observed for two minutes. The possible outcomes were (a) the gosling approached the caged duck or (b) the gosling approached the caged goose (Slovic & Fischhoff, 1977, p. 546). If the gosling does approach the caged duck, what is the probability that in a replication of this experiment with ten additional goslings,

a. all will approach the duck? _____
b. some will approach the duck? _____
c. none will approach the duck? _____

Note that these must sum to 100%.

Version B (hindsight)

Read the same story as in version A up to the Slovic and Fischhoff reference. Then read this ending:

The initial gosling that was tested in this experiment approached the caged duck. Suppose that a replication of the experiment was performed with ten additional goslings. What is the probability that in this replication,

a. all will approach the duck? _____
b. some will approach the duck? _____
c. none will approach the duck? _____

Note that these must sum to 100%.

After you have tested your two subjects (or better still, five on each version), compare the percentages. Were people in the hindsight condition more likely to guess that all of the goslings would approach the duck?

Slovic and Fischhoff (1977) asked people to make judgments about either a foresight version (such as version A) or a hindsight version (such as version B). The people in the foresight version were not told which outcome occurred, whereas the people in the hindsight condition were told the results. The results showed that people assigned much higher probabilities to the stated outcome if they were in the hindsight condition. For instance, combining three of the examples, the average probability of the initial outcome always being replicated was .38 for those who read the foresight version and .55 for those who read the hindsight version. (Think about your hindsight on this hindsight study. Did you "know it all along" that hindsight is better than foresight?)

Applications of Decision Making

We have discussed some applications of decision making throughout this chapter. A sample of these applications includes the following areas: education (course selection, college admission, and training pilots), law (mock jury decisions), history (London bombing, entrapment in Vietnam), medicine (yellow fever causes), natural hazards (flood predictions), and media (availability of vivid information).

Numerous articles have been written about other applications of decision making. For example, an article by Russo, Krieser, and Miyashita (1975) demonstrated that people were more likely to make use of unit price information in deciding which product to buy if the comparison information was listed on a single sheet, rather than displayed on separated shelf tags. If you have ever tried to decide which dishwashing liquid was cheapest by looking at the tiny tags under each of the brands, you can certainly appreciate the recommendation that stores shift over to lists with unit price information. Other applications of decision making in marketing are discussed by Bonoma (1977).

Government policy is another area in which decision making has many applications. For example, Wainer, Zill, and Gruvaeus (1973) discuss senatorial decision making. Tetlock (1979) examines groupthink, the tendency toward uniformity in political decision making that is caused by group pressures. The public's reaction to the risks and benefits of nuclear power has also been examined (Fischhoff, Slovic & Lichtenstein, 1979; Slovic, Fischhoff, and Lichtenstein, 1979).

Decision making is a critical part of medicine. A patient complains of a sore throat. Is this a major problem or a minor problem? Does it require medication? If so, what kind, how much, and how long? Even though decision making represents a major part of medical practice, few physicians have had any formal training in this area (Hill et al., 1979). Knafl and Burkett (1975) discuss how orthopedic surgeons acquire decision-making skills informally. Other research focuses on the development of heuristics to guide doctors in their decision making. For example, an article by Pantell, Naber, Lamar, and Dias (1980) offers a rule of thumb regarding fevers in young infants: fevers above 38.3°C (101°F) are likely to be associated with diseases such as meningitis and respiratory infection, whereas fevers below that temperature are seldom associated with serious illnesses.

Some psychologists have suggested that an important way to apply our knowledge about decision making is in educational programs, designed to improve people's strategies. As we have seen in this chapter, the heuristics that often help us reach correct decisions can also lead us to the wrong solutions. For example, Nisbett and Ross (1980) advise programs for as wide a public as possible. They suggest that a first step is to convince people that they are prone to certain, predictable kinds of decision errors. A potential problem at this stage in the education process is that some students may become so convinced of their inabilities in decision making that they may doubt whether they can even master the appropriate techniques.

Nisbett and Ross suggest that statistics courses offered in college should be geared more toward the everyday problems of informal decision making and judgment. Ideally, some aspects of decision making could also be taught in elementary school or high school. Nisbett and Ross stress that any educational program should take advantage of the relationship between vividness and availability. In particular, a program should offer vivid examples rather than pallid statistics, in order to convince people. Anecdotes particularly geared to the audience will be more effective than abstract information.

Nisbett and Ross also suggest that social scientists should try to invent proverbs and slogans that capture some of the more common kinds of reasoning errors. They admit that some of their suggestions lack the polish of a Madison Avenue advertising agent. However, here are some possibilities: "Okay, what do the other three cells look like?" (to attempt to untangle an illusory correlation); "Methinks I detect the availability (or representativeness) heuristic at work"; "That's a vivid example all right, but I'll still consult the base rates, thank you"; and "Before considering a fancy causal explanation, how about considering simple regression" (p. 285). Furthermore, familiar proverbs could be modified to reflect appropriate decision-making strategies. For example, two proverbs that fail to take into account the concept of regression toward the mean could be reworded "As ye sow, so shall ye reap . . . but generally less so" and "As the twig is bent . . . so the tree is slightly and occasionally inclined" (p. 285).

SECTION SUMMARY: Additional Topics in Decision Making

1. In the anchoring and adjustment heuristic we begin with an anchor or first approximation to an answer and then make adjustments based on other information.
2. People typically rely too heavily on the anchor, and their adjustments are too small.
3. We use the anchoring and adjustment heuristic when we make estimates of single numbers or confidence intervals.
4. Entrapment is a kind of increasing conflict that occurs when the decision maker spends more resources in the conflict than seem appropriate.
5. Entrapment occurs because of the reward associated with the goal, the perceived increase in the nearness of the goal, and the cost associated with giving up previous investments.
6. We are often overconfident about the decisions we make.
7. People are talented at choosing the variables that need to be considered in reaching a decision, but statistical formulas are better than human decision makers in combining the information about the variables.
8. People have a hindsight bias; they overestimate the accuracy with which they or others would have been able to predict past events.
9. In addition to applications of decision making that were considered earlier in the chapter, other applications appear in the areas of marketing, government policy, and medicine.
10. Some psychologists have proposed educational programs designed to improve decision-making strategies. These programs should use vivid anecdotes and proverbs invented to capture appropriate strategies.

Chapter Review Questions

1. In the following examples of some everyday errors in decision making, decide which heuristic each one demonstrates: (a) you decide that you have many things in common with someone because you both like mushrooms, a certain country and western song, and movies starring Katharine Hepburn; (b) someone asks you whether cardinals or robins are more common and you respond on the basis of the number of birds of each kind you have seen this winter; (c) your younger sister's class has two children named Scott and three named Jennifer, which seems too coincidental to be due to chance alone; (d) you estimate the number of bottles of soda you will need for the Fourth of July picnic based on the Christmas party consumption, taking into account the fact that the weather will be warmer.

2. You have taken a quiz that has six true-false questions on it, and you look over your answers. Explain how the representativeness heuristic is related to your examination of the pattern in your responses (for example, T T T F F F).

3. You read about two surveys on people's attitudes toward capital punishment. One survey is based on 100 interviews, and the other is based on

1000 interviews. Which survey do you trust most? What part of the chapter is this question related to?

4. What information do we ignore in decision making in situations in which we pay too much attention to representativeness? Describe and give an example of each of three kinds of information.

5. How is representativeness related to the idea of prototype, as discussed in the chapter on concepts and categories?

6. We saw that the availability heuristic can lead to errors. Explain how the anchoring and adjustment heuristic could be used to supplement the availability heuristic and produce more accurate decisions (assuming that your adjustment is not too conservative). How can the anchoring and adjustment heuristic be used to correct our tendency to ignore regression toward the mean? Show how it could be used when the predictive validity of your information is zero, low, medium, and high.

7. Pick your favorite political issue and figure out an effective advertising campaign for that issue, taking advantage of the kinds of errors people make in decision making.

8. Many proverbs may in fact represent illusory correlations. Explain why the following proverbs and sayings may represent too much attention to the + + cell and too little attention to the remaining three cells in the matrix representing the two variables: (a) The early bird catches the worm. (b) The moss grows on the north side of the tree. (c) Every cloud has a silver lining.

9. Often in hindsight we realize that we have been in an entrapment situation. Think of examples illustrating that statement and explain the concepts of hindsight and entrapment.

10. At the end of the chapter we mentioned a public education project designed to improve decision-making strategies. Go through the chapter and note 15–20 sentence-long suggestions that should be included in such a program.

New Terms

decision making	correlated	causal scenario
heuristics	predictive validity	script
representative	illusion of validity	anchoring and adjustment
representativeness heuristic	base rate	heuristic
law of large numbers	Bayes' rule	confidence intervals
law of small numbers	likelihood ratio	escalation
mean	availability heuristic	entrapment
regression toward the mean	illusory correlation	hindsight bias

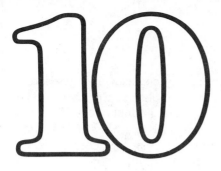

Cognitive Development

Preview

In this chapter, we examine the development of cognition in three areas: memory; language; and concept formation and problem solving. Some skills show an improvement as children approach young adulthood and then a decline as adults reach old age. However, other skills show less change than had been previously believed. Our fourth topic in this chapter is an introduction to Piaget's developmental theory.

Research on infant memory has shown that even young babies have developed memories. Children's recognition memory is surprisingly accurate, but their recall memory is substantially lower than that of adults. Their use of memory strategies and their knowledge about memory both improve as they grow older. Elderly people show a decline in semantic long-term memory when it is measured by recall, but other kinds of memory show little change during the aging process.

The development of language is one of the most impressive human accomplishments. Recent research has shown that infants are able to distinguish between similar sounds. Children's production of language lags behind their understanding and is characterized by overextensions and telegraph-style utterances. They understand some of the rules about the appropriate social use of language, but they need to be coached about other rules.

In the section on the development of concept formation and problem solving, we will see that young children prefer basic-level categories, just as adults do. As children grow older, they begin to appreciate that the boundaries between natural concepts are not well defined. We will look at recommendations for teaching concepts in the schools and will discover how children's question strategies change as they grow older. The performance of elderly people often shows a decline, but a self-instructional strategy has been devised to aid in problem solving.

The last section of this chapter is an overview of the developmental theory proposed by Jean Piaget. His theory focuses on the process through which our thoughts respond to the environment. There are four stages in his theory, progressing from an early stage in which thought is represented in actions to a stage in which thought can be abstract.

Most of the studies we have examined in the book have used young adults as subjects. Usually the participant in a cognition study is a college student who fulfills a requirement for an introductory psychology course by taking part in an experiment. Furthermore, most of the theories that we have discussed attempt to describe cognitive functioning in young or middle-aged adults. Our purpose in this chapter is to examine how cognitive functioning changes with age. Do infants and young children process information in the same way that an adult does? Furthermore, does the performance of elderly people differ from the performance of younger adults?

A number of years ago, psychologists would have described infants and young children as being relatively incompetent. It was thought that infants had only the most primitive of perceptual skills and that their memory and language skills were nonexistent. Even the preschooler was seen as remarkably inept (Gelman, 1978). Recently, however, the view has changed. The increasing sophistication of research equipment and research designs has allowed psychologists to discover that infants and young children are quite impressive. Humans are quite competent, even before they reach school age. We will see many areas in which children's performance and strategies are clearly below adult levels. However, as Gelman (1979) stresses: "The time has come for us to turn our attention to what young children can do as well as to what they cannot do" (p. 904).

Similarly, psychologists used to be very pessimistic about the abilities of elderly people. Memory and problem-solving skills were supposed to fade as we grow older, leaving us quite incompetent by the time we reach our seventieth birthday. Fortunately, this view has also changed. First of all, psychologists realized that there were methodological problems in many of the studies that demonstrated poorer performances in the elderly than in younger people. For example, many experiments compared the performance of young, healthy college students with the performance of elderly people whose health, intelligence, and education were relatively poor. Any of these factors, rather than age, might have been responsible for the difference in performance. As we will see throughout this chapter, studies that adequately control these irrelevant variables often show that elderly people perform just as well as younger adults.

Furthermore, psychologists now acknowledge that many experimental tasks provide insufficient motivation for the elderly participants. As Whitbourne and Weinstock (1979) note, the tasks often involve meaningless information that elderly people are not interested in learning. Elderly people may also be extremely anxious in a testing situation. A study by Langer, Rodin, Beck, Weinman, and Spitzer (1979) demonstrated that elderly people could be motivated to attend to and remember material by having experimenters reveal some personal facts about their own lives. It is clear that some cognitive abilities do decline as we grow older, but well-controlled studies that consider motivational factors offer optimism. Many cognitive skills remain at a high level throughout adulthood. Thus, we will see evidence for some developmental changes in cognitive abilities. However, the infant and the young child are not helpless, and elderly people are quite competent.

We will look at the development of three cognitive areas: (1) memory; (2) language; and (3) concept formation and problem solving. Then we will examine a comprehensive theory of development proposed by Piaget.

The Development of Memory

A major part of this textbook has focused on memory. In addition to Chapter 3, we looked at sensory memory in Chapter 2, imagery and memory in Chapter 4, and memory for language in Chapter 6. Now we will examine the development of memory, with special attention to the ways in which memory strategies change as children develop into adults and as adults approach old age.

Memory in Children

In this section we will consider three topics: memory performance, memory strategies, and metamemory, or knowledge about memory. Thus we will move from a consideration of the amount of material remembered, to ways of increasing the amount remembered, to knowledge about the amount remembered.

Memory Performance.   We'll first look at infant memory, before we examine the topic of memory in older children. Ashmead and Perlmutter (1979) share an entry from a diary that describes a 9-month-old baby's use of memory:

> One day her brother changed the bows and ribbons to a different drawer. When she went to the chest, she opened the former bow drawer and found it without ribbons and bows. She went through the other drawers until she found what she wanted, threw them on the floor and went about her business. Today she crawled to the chest and went right to the new bow drawer. (p. 1)

Although people often assume that babies have no memories, the example of the baby and the bow drawer clearly contradicts that viewpoint. Many other kinds of infant behavior show evidence of infant memory. For example, babies can imitate a model. To repeat a sound, a gesture, or some other activity the baby must store information about a model's action. Furthermore, babies develop attachment to other people. In order to establish an emotional bond to a person, the baby must be able to recognize that person consistently. Other indirect evidence for infant memory is discussed by Cohen and Gelber (1975) and by Olson (1976).

Most of the studies that directly examine infant memory are concerned with recognition memory, rather than recall. After all, traditional recall tests rely on verbal responses, and so they are useful only for people who have developed language. One way to test recognition in infants is to use a habituation procedure. In the **habituation-dishabituation procedure,** a stimulus is presented many times until the baby stops responding to it; then a new stimulus is introduced, and the experimenters notice whether the baby responds to the new stimulus. There is evidence of memory if the baby stops responding to the first stimulus but responds to the new one.

What is the youngest age at which babies demonstrate memory? According to a review of the literature (Werner & Perlmutter, 1979), the infants in some studies do not respond differently to old and new stimuli until they are at least 2 months of age. However, other studies make more impressive claims about infant memory. For example, Werner and Perlmutter summarize several studies that demonstrate memory in newborn infants who are just a few days old. More impressive still, Werner and Siqueland (1978) found that even premature babies could distinguish between old and new stimuli. Thus, babies seem to have memory even prior to the normal age of birth.

Another impressive aspect of infant memory is the amount of time for which information can be retained. Fagan (1973), for example, discovered that 5-month-old babies remembered some information about faces after a two-week delay. It is likely that infant memory is even more impressive than we currently believe, but our current measurement techniques are too crude to assess it properly. Furthermore, it is likely that infants have many different kinds of memory skills, beyond the visual memory that is typically assessed. For example, Gottfried and Rose (1980) found that infants could recognize the shapes of objects by touch alone.

When we examine memory in older children, we can assess the components of memory with more confidence. For example, the availability of verbal responses allows us to investigate sensory memory—that brief, accurate recording of information from the senses. In general, adults and children have similar kinds of sensory memory. Furthermore, the capacity and decay rates for both iconic (visual) and echoic (auditory) memory are similar for adults and for 5-year-old children (Kail & Siegel, 1977).

Memory span tests which measure the number of items that can be correctly recalled in order immediately after presentation, have often been included in children's intelligence tests. These tests have established that memory span improves with age (P. L. Harris, 1978). Thus the number of items that can be stored and retrieved in short-term memory increases as children grow older.

What is the pattern in the development of long-term memory, the retention of material for longer periods of time? Developmental psychologists have often distinguished between recognition memory and recall memory. In general, young children have excellent recognition memory but poor recall memory. The literature on recognition memory has been summarized by Kail (1979). Naturally, children's performance is more remarkable when the familiar and unfamiliar items on the recognition test are quite different from each other. For example, in a study by Brown and Scott (1971), 4-year-old children were 75 percent accurate in their recognition of pictures that had been shown one week earlier.

Given the impressive accuracy of children's recognition, it might seem that there is little room for improvement. This may be true for the recognition of simple objects. However, children's recognition for complex scenes improves markedly as they grow older, according to Kail. Furthermore, their pattern of recognition changes as they grow older. Meyer (1978) found that young children base their recognition mainly on the central figure in a scene, whereas older children use both the central figure and the background.

In general, however, it is the recall measures that reveal the major differences between children's memory and adult's memory. For example, Myers and Perlmutter (1978) performed studies similar to those in Demonstration 10.1. Their subjects were 2- and 4-year-old children. To test recognition, they showed children 18 unrelated objects. Then they presented 36 items, including 18 old objects and 18 new objects. As you can see in Figure 10.1, children of both ages were quite accurate.

Demonstration 10.1 *Age Differences in Recall and Recognition.*

In this experiment you will test a college-age person and a preschool child for their recall and recognition of objects. First, assemble 20 common objects. Some ideas are: pen, pencil, piece of paper, leaf, stick, rock, book, key, apple, and so on. Place the objects in a box or cover them with a cloth.

You will use the same testing procedure for your two subjects, although the preschool child will require more extensive explanation. Remove ten objects in all, one at a time. Show each object for about 5 seconds and then hide it again. After all ten objects have been shown, ask your subject to recall as many of the objects as possible. Do not provide feedback about the correctness of the responses. After recall is complete, test for recognition. Remove one object at a time, randomly presenting the old objects mixed in sequence with new objects. In each case, ask whether the object had been seen before.

Count the number of correct recalls and the number of correct recognitions for each subject. You should find that both of your subjects show a similar high level of performance on the *recognition* measures. However, the older subject will *recall* far more than the younger subject.

Myers and Perlmutter also tested recall in a different group of children. These children saw nine unrelated objects from the recognition task. After the experimenter presented each item and named it, the children were told that they could keep all the objects that they correctly recalled. Despite the tempting incentive, recall was poor, as shown in Figure 10.1. Myers and Perlmutter discuss many reasons for children's superior performance on recognition tests in contrast to recall tests. For example, recall—but not recognition—may require more active rehearsal strategies and more thorough searches of memory.

Although there is some disagreement (for example, Huttenlocher & Burke,

Figure 10.1   Recognition and Recall for 2- and 4-year-olds.

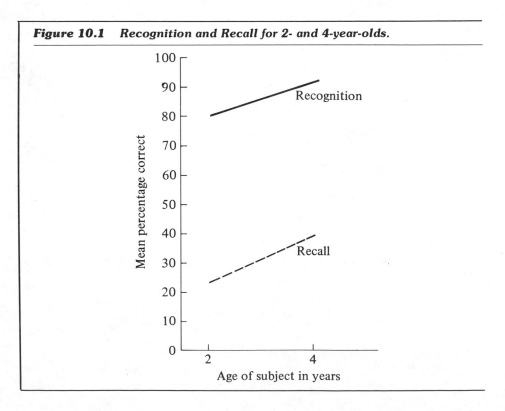

1976), most researchers who have examined children's memory agree that younger children recall fewer items than older children because they make less effective use of memory strategies. Let us now examine the development of these memory strategies.

Memory Strategies.   **Memory strategies** are deliberate, purposeful activities that we use to improve our memories. Memory strategies show clear changes as children grow older. As several researchers in the area of children's memory have concluded, the reason that older children remember more information than younger children is not because they have an inferior memory capacity. Instead, the difference arises because older children improve their performance by making more use of mnemonic strategies (Brown, 1975; Hagen & Stanovich, 1977; P. L. Harris, 1978). We will survey four kinds of memory strategies: rehearsal, organization, imagery, and retrieval.

Rehearsal, or merely repeating items over and over, is not a particularly effective strategy. You may recall from Chapter 3 that some researchers are skeptical about whether mere rehearsal really aids long-term memory. Nonetheless, it is useful in maintaining items in short-term memory. In a classic study on children's rehearsal patterns, Flavell, Beach, and Chinsky (1966) asked 5-, 7-, and 10-year-olds to watch as the experimenter pointed to several objects in sequence. The children were told that they themselves would later have to point to the same objects in the same order. During the delay prior to recall, a trained lip-reader carefully noted any spontaneous lip movements that would indicate rehearsal. The results showed that the older children were much more likely to rehearse the items during the delay period.

Other aspects of the development and use of rehearsal in children's memory have been discussed by Flavell (1977) and Garrity (1975). For example, it seems that younger children benefit from rehearsal strategies, but they do not always use these strategies spontaneously.

Organization strategies, such as grouping and categorization, are frequently used by adults, as we saw in Chapter 3. However, young children do not group similar items together in order to aid memorization. Try Demonstration 10.2 to illustrate children's reluctance to adopt organization strategies.

It is not surprising that young children avoid this rather sophisticated memory strategy. After all, their semantic development is far from complete. As Moely (1977) points out, younger children differ from older children in (1) the tendency to process semantic, or meaning, features of items; (2) the number of known concept categories; and (3) the nature of features used to group items, assuming that they can process semantic features. For example, a child may respond to the shape of pictures rather than their meaning. Furthermore, there may not be an established category for some objects (e.g., vehicles). Finally, even if children do pay attention to objects' meaning, they may group items in the same category if they occur together rather than if they are similar. Thus, a coat may be grouped with a car if the child typically wears a coat to go for a ride in a car.

Another reason that young children do not use organizational strategies is that there is a lag between the development of semantic abilities and the use of

---

Demonstration 10.2   *Organizational Strategies in Children.*

Make a photocopy of the pictures on this page and use scissors to cut them apart (or, alternatively, cut pictures out of magazines that belong to four different categories). In this experiment you will test a child between the ages of 4 and 8; ideally, it would be interesting to test children of several different ages. Arrange these pictures in random order in a circle facing your subject. Instruct the child to study the pictures so that they can be remembered later. Mention that the pictures can be rearranged in any order. After a two-minute study period, remove the pictures and ask the child to list as many items as possible. Notice two things in this demonstration: (1) Does the child rearrange the items at all during the study period? (2) Does the child show clustering during recall, with similar items appearing together?

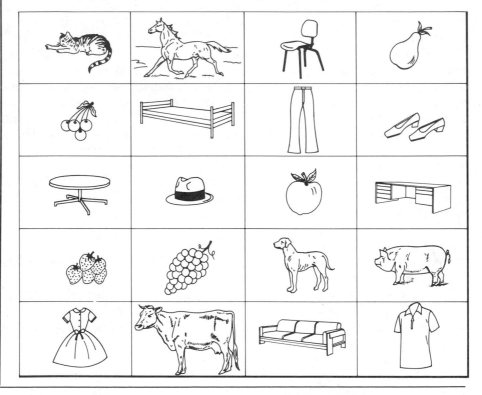

---

these abilities in organizational strategies. For example, Moely, Olson, Halwes, and Flavell (1969) asked children to study pictures from four categories: animals, clothing, furniture, and vehicles. During the two-minute study period, they were told that they could rearrange the pictures in any order they wished. Younger children rarely moved the pictures next to other similar pictures, but older children frequently organized the pictures in terms of categories. Other groups of children were specifically urged to organize the pictures. This training procedure encouraged even the younger children to adopt an organizational strategy, and this strategy increased their recall. Thus, children often have the ability to organize, though they are not aware that organization will be helpful. As Moely concludes:

> Given such a lack of awareness of the usefulness of organization, young children appear to be unable to interpret the instructions to "remember these items" as a suggestion to engage in organizing activity. (p. 218)

Imagery, the topic of Chapter 4, is an extremely useful device for improving memory in adults. Although imagery is also useful for older children, there is some evidence that it may not be as useful for younger children (for example, Reese, 1977). However, Kosslyn (1976) found that children as young as 6 spontaneously used mental images in various tasks. Furthermore, Yuille and Catchpole (1977) found that first graders' memories improved after they had been trained to form interactive images. Specifically, these authors displayed pairs of objects, one at a time, and asked children to imagine the two objects playing together. After five minutes of this kind of training, one group of children was given 20 pairs of objects. Other children received no special training. Recall was measured both immediately and after a one-week delay. In both cases, training aided recall substantially. Thus, just five minutes of training can lead to a long-lasting improvement in learning. Yuille and Catchpole suggest that educators should offer more instruction on how to learn. In particular, young children can benefit from training designed to improve their memory.

In addition to strategies involving rehearsal, organization, and imagery, adults have also developed retrieval strategies. When there is a cue that might help them retrieve a memory, they use it spontaneously. Kobasigawa (1977) reviewed numerous studies on the development of the use of retrieval cues. In one experiment, for example, Kobasigawa (1974) showed pictures of items together with a retrieval cue. For instance, a child might see a bear, a lion, and a monkey together with the retrieval cue of a picture of a zoo. One group of children then tried to recall the names without using the cues; their recall was quite low. Another group of children were handed the cue cards—for example, the zoo picture—and were instructed to supply the items that had been associated with each card. Children of all ages were uniformly accurate in this condition.

The most interesting results came from a third group, who were given the cue cards, face down, and told to use them if they thought that the cards would be helpful. The youngest children in that group (first graders) seldom spontaneously used the cue cards, and when they did, they typically recalled only one item for each card. The oldest children (sixth graders), on the other hand, made good use of the cue cards, and their recall was about twice that of the youngest children. In short, all children benefited when they were required to use retrieval cues. However, only the older children spontaneously used the retrieval cues.

Metamemory. **Metamemory** (pronounced "*meh*-tah-*meh*-muh-ree") is knowledge of and awareness of memory (Flavell & Wellman, 1977). Whenever you think about your memory, you are using metamemory. Examples of metamemory include the following: (1) knowing that your memory is better in the middle of the morning than late at night; (2) knowing that you can remember people's faces better than their names; and (3) knowing that you remember material better if you study a little on five different days rather than "cramming" the night before an examination. Try Demonstration 10.3 to compare metamemory in a child and in an adult.

Demonstration 10.3   Metamemory in Adults and Children.

Ask the following questions to an adult and to a child (ideally, several children of different ages). Compare the accuracy and/or the completeness of the answers. Note that some questions should be adapted to a level appropriate for your subject.

1. A child will be going to a party tomorrow, and she wants to remember to bring her skates. What kinds of things can she do to help her remember them?
2. Suppose that I were to read you a list of words. How many words do you think you could recall in the correct order? (Then read the following list and count the number of words correctly recalled. Use only part of the list for the child: *cat   rug   chair   leaf   sky   book   apple   pencil   house   teacher*)
3. Two children want to learn the names of some rocks. One child learned the names last month but forgot them. The other child never learned the names. Who will have an easier time in learning the names?
4. Suppose that you memorize sombody's address. Will you remember it better after two minutes have passed or after two days have passed?
5. Suppose that you are memorizing two kinds of words. One kind of word is abstract (refers to things you cannot see or touch, such as *idea* or *religion*) and the other kind is concrete (refers to things that you can see and touch, such as *notebook* or *zebra*). Which kind of word will you learn better?

One of the primary researchers in metamemory is John Flavell (pronounced "*flay*-vuhl"). He points out that metamemory is one variety of metacognition (Flavell, 1979). **Metacognition** is knowledge of and awareness of cognitive processes. Thus, metacognition includes all the thoughts you have had about your own thought processes as you have read the chapters in this book. Like metamemory, metacognition is quite limited in young children; they do relatively little monitoring of the way they use language or the way they form concepts, solve problems, and make decisions.

Dozens of studies on metamemory have been performed in recent years, and they have been summarized elsewhere (Flavell, 1977; Kreutzer, Leonard, & Flavell, 1975). Let us examine a representative study by Yussen and Levy (1975), who studied preschool children (mean age of 4.6 years), third graders (mean age of 8.9), and college students (mean age of 20.2). Each person was first asked to estimate the number of picture names that he or she could recall in correct order. Notice that this question measures metamemory because it asks people to think about their memory abilities. Next, Yussen and Levy measured everyone's true memory span on this task. They first presented a single picture and asked for recall, then two pictures and then three. Testing continued with increasingly longer lists until subjects made errors in recall.

Figure 10.2 shows both memory estimates and actual memory spans for the three age groups. Notice that the preschoolers are wildly optimistic in their memory estimates. As people grow older, however, their estimates become more modest at the same time as their actual memory spans increase. Consequently, college students are quite realistic in their estimates.

Figure 10.2   *Estimated versus Actual Memory Span, as a Function of Age.*

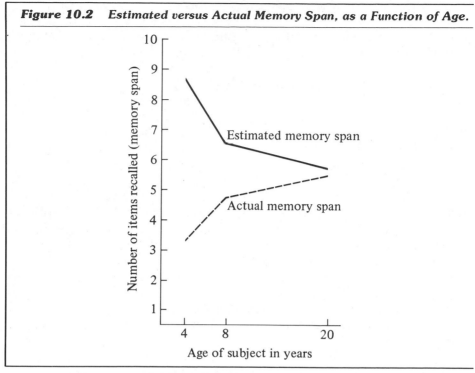

How are metamemory skills acquired? Flavell and Wellman speculate that most of children's knowledge about memory is gained from feedback from their own experiences. Children can notice the relationships between their own storage and retrieval activities and the amount of the material that is successfully retrieved. They can see that the activities they performed on the material are related to the amount that is remembered.

Chevalier (1981) points out, however, that our schools should be more concerned with teaching students to think about the learning process. Thus educators should teach metacognitive and metamemory skills in addition to the direct content instruction that is customarily their only concern. Specifically, children should be told how to use mnemonic devices, such as the ones we discussed in Chapter 3. However, they should also be explicitly taught how, when, and where the skills should be employed. They must also be told why these mnemonic devices will help them to learn how to learn. In contrast, **blind training** results if students are simply trained in a technique but not informed about why the technique will aid their learning.

Furthermore, students must be encouraged to become active, knowledge-able participants in the process of learning how to think. Chevalier notes that students who are allowed to have some control and active participation in their learning program are more likely to transfer their knowledge to other tasks. Transfer to other tasks is particularly critical; what use does a training program serve if children fail to use the techniques in their regular schoolwork? Chevalier recommends that students should be told why various learning strategies are being taught.

They should be encouraged to frequently ask themselves questions such as "What have I learned so far?" "What do I remember?" "What else do I need to know?" and "Is this strategy working for me?" Thus, the encouragement of metamemory skills will lead to an improvement in children's memory.

Memory in Elderly People

We often have a stereotype of forgetful elderly people. According to this stereotype, they cannot remember where they put their glasses, they forget what they are saying in the middle of a sentence, and they are unable to remember the name of their granddaughter's best friend. In this section we will see that memory does decline in some areas as people grow older. However, some kinds of memory show very little change with age.

Baltes, Reese, and Lipsitt (1980) summarize their review of memory in the elderly, ". . . memory changes in old age may reflect *difference* rather than *deficit*" (p. 85). They point out that most of the experiments on memory involve deliberate memorizing. As you may recall from Chapter 3, subjects in a typical memory experiment see a list of words, memorize it in a short period of time, and then recall it. This kind of memory task is quite similar to many of the memory tasks we encounter in school. Furthermore, both the memory experiment and the school testing setting prohibit the use of external memory aids, such as the use of notes during testing. Thus children and young adults are familiar with the kinds of memorizing strategies that would be useful in a memory experiment.

In contrast, elderly people are seldom required to memorize material in their everyday life, and so they probably develop other kinds of strategies to deal with the kinds of memory tasks they encounter every day. For example, they may make more use of external memory aids, such as shopping lists. Consequently, elderly people may have memory skills that are *different* from those of younger people, but these skills are not necessarily *deficient* when we consider how their memories function in everyday life.

This discussion of memory in elderly people is divided into two sections. First we will discuss memory performance and then memory strategies.

Memory Performance.   First of all, are there age-related differences in sensory memory? Crowder (1980) reports that there has been no systematic examination of echoic, or auditory, memory in elderly people. Iconic, or visual, memory has been investigated in several studies. In general, these studies show only a slight decline in iconic memory as people grow older (Craik, 1977). For example, an experiment by Walsh and Thompson (1978) found that iconic memory lasted for an average of 289 milliseconds when they tested their younger subjects, whose average age was 21. It lasted an average of 248 milliseconds when they tested their older subjects, whose average age was 67. A 41-millisecond difference is probably not crucial. As Craik concludes, the basic cause of memory difficulties in the elderly does not lie in sensory memory but in the more advanced stages of memory processing.

Similarly, short-term memory seems to show little change as people grow older. Welford (1980), for example, concludes that memory span declines little, if at all, until people are at least in their sixties. Thus, a 55-year-old and a 20-year-old should not differ in their ability to recall a telephone number several seconds after they hear it.

Elderly people do differ from younger people in terms of some kinds of long-term memory tasks. For example, Gordon and Clark (1974) compared the memory performance of a group of older people, with an average age of 71, and younger people, whose average age was 25. They selected their samples very carefully, so that they would be equivalent in terms of factors related to memory, such as number of years of education and verbal intelligence. Earlier we discussed how it would be unfair to compare a group of young people who are college students with a group of unselected older people. Gordon and Clark's younger group consisted of graduate students, and their older group consisted of members of the Institute for Retired Professionals, so their study was well controlled. People in both groups read a paragraph and then attempted to recall the material. The younger group was somewhat more accurate in terms of immediate recall, but they were much more accurate when they were asked to recall the material one week later. In this delayed recall task, younger people recalled an average of 10.7 items, whereas older people recalled an average of only 4.4 items.

It is unclear whether there are substantial age differences when long-term memory is measured in terms of recognition rather than recall. A classic study by Schonfield and Robertson (1966), for example, showed a significant drop in *recall* for older people, but no change in *recognition.* A recent study by Perlmutter (1979) also demonstrated that 20-year-olds did not differ from 60-year-olds in terms of recognition accuracy. However, Craik (1977) summarizes several studies that show that older people do have problems with recognition memory.

It is probably safe to conclude that, in comparison to recall memory, recognition memory shows less decline as people grow older. Thus, a young person may be much better than an old person on a recall memory task. However, the two people may not differ much on a task in which they must state whether or not they have previously encountered an item.

Lachman and Lachman (1980) offer some optimistic news regarding long-term memory for world knowledge. World knowledge includes information about facts and relationships in the real world. World knowledge is therefore one kind of semantic memory, or organized knowledge about words and symbols, in contrast to episodic memory, or information about when events happened.

Lachman and Lachman studied groups of people who ranged between 27 and 61 years of age. They asked general information questions about a wide range of topics, including current events, movies, history, and geography. A typical question was, "What was the previous name of Muhammed Ali?" Then they applied a correction factor to the results in order to find a measure of recall efficiency. They argued that the amount of information in memory should be taken into account when measuring memory. Retrieving one fact when there are 40 relevant facts in memory is not as impressive as retrieving one fact when there are 100 facts in memory. Recall efficiency, a measure which corrected for the number of facts in memory, showed that age had no effect on memory. Thus, although episodic memory may suffer as we grow older, there is evidence that some kinds of semantic memory do not change.

In summary, sensory memory, short-term memory, recognition memory, and semantic memory show little, if any, decline as people grow older. However, long-term memory that is measured by recall (rather than recognition) and is episodic in nature (rather than semantic) is substantially poorer for elderly people.

Memory Strategies.   There is some evidence that memory strategies differ for young and old people. For example, Smith (1980) measured subjective organization that people used in learning a 60-word list. As you may recall from Chapter 3, subjective organization is a person's own individual organization of words on a list. Notice in Figure 10.3, that each of the groups showed an increasing amount of subjective organization as learning progressed. However, the increase is most dramatic for the younger subjects. Younger subjects are therefore more likely to relate words in a list to each other in a consistent fashion.

Elderly people also seem to differ from young people with regard to their use of visual imagery. Several studies have shown that the elderly are less likely to use visual imagery spontaneously when they are learning material (Hulicka & Grossman, 1967; Weinstein, Duffy, Underwood, & MacDonald, 1979). Other studies, summarized by Smith (1980), demonstrate that elderly people are less likely than younger people to benefit from instructions that suggest the use of visual images. Nonetheless, imagery mnemonics typically do improve recall, even if the improvement is not as startling as it might be with younger subjects. Poon, Walsh-Sweeney, and Fozard (1980) located 17 studies in which elderly people were encouraged to use imagery, and 14 of the 17 studies showed that imagery helped.

Winograd and Simon (1980) suggest that there probably are large individual

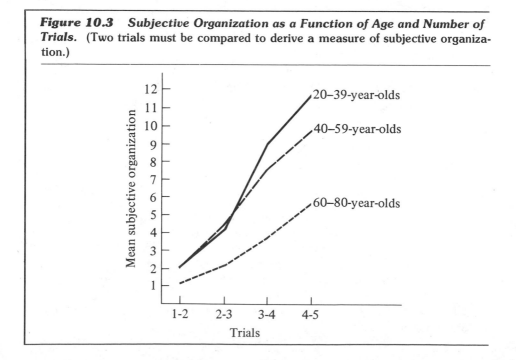

Figure 10.3   Subjective Organization as a Function of Age and Number of Trials. (Two trials must be compared to derive a measure of subjective organization.)

differences in memory strategies among elderly people. Individual differences must be kept in mind when designing programs to aid memory. Some people will benefit from imagery instructions, whereas others will benefit more from instructions that encourage certain verbal rehearsal strategies. Poon and his coauthors suggest that the learner should be involved in the development of his or her own individualized program for memory training. Participation in the development is likely to lead to more appropriate material and to increased practice on the materials.

The improvement of memory is important for many people, but it is particularly important for one group of elderly people: the blind. Robertson-Tchabo (1980) reports that about 5 percent of Americans over the age of 65 have a severe visual handicap. As a consequence, they cannot use external memory aids such as lists and schedules. Furthermore, memory is especially important for them because a blind person must commit to memory thousands of details about everyday activities. Blind people must memorize the order of pill bottles in the medicine cabinet and the number of steps in a flight of stairs. Thus an accurate memory is critical for the health and safety of a substantial number of elderly people.

Why are the memory strategies of older people different from the memory strategies of younger people? Some studies show that memory for pictures declines faster than memory for words (Winograd & Simon, 1980), and so visual imagery may be more difficult for the elderly. Furthermore, it is possible that some strategies, such as organization, are encouraged in formal education. However, once we are finished with school, we no longer practice these active learning strategies (Smith, 1980). As suggested at the beginning of this section, deliberate memorizing is not essential in most of the everyday experiences of elderly people.

SECTION SUMMARY: The Development of Memory

1. Psychologists used to think that infants and children were relatively incompetent; however, psychologists now emphasize their abilities.
2. Psychologists used to think that cognitive skills declined markedly in old age; however, carefully controlled studies have shown that elderly people perform just as well as younger adults.
3. Evidence for infant memory includes imitation, attachment, and habituation-dishabituation. Even premature babies have memories, and 5-month-olds remember information after a two-week delay.
4. The capacity and decay rates of sensory memory are similar in adults and children.
5. The amount of material that children recall from short-term memory is relatively limited.
6. Children's recognition memory is closer to the adult level than is their recall memory.
7. Children make increasing use of memory strategies—such as rehearsal, organization, imagery, and retrieval—as they grow older.
8. Young children typically do not use memory strategies spontaneously, but they can be trained to adopt strategies and consequently improve their memory performance.

9. Metamemory is knowledge of and awareness of memory. Children's metamemory skills improve as they grow older.
10. School programs should include the training of metamemory skills.
11. Memory experiments are similar to the everyday experiences of young adults, whereas elderly people are seldom required to memorize material in everyday life.
12. Iconic memory, short-term memory, recognition memory, and semantic memory show little change as people grow older. Episodic long-term memory measured by recall does decline.
13. Elderly people use subjective organization strategies less, and imagery strategies seem to be less helpful.

The Development of Language

"Mama!" (8 months old)

"Wash hair." (1 year, 4 months old)

"Don't tickle my tummy, Mommy!" (1 year, 11 months old)

"My Grandma gave me this dolly, Cara. My Grandma is my Mommy's Mommy. I have another Grandma, too. She's my Daddy's Mommy. And Aunt Elli is my Daddy's sister." (2 years, 9 months old)

These selections from the early language of my daughter Sally are typical of the remarkable accomplishment involved in language acquisition. Within a period of two to three years, all normal children progress from one-word utterances to complex descriptions of relationships. Language acquisition is often said to be the most spectacular of human accomplishments. Carey (1978) estimated that 6-year-old children have some mastery of about 14,000 words. To acquire this many words, children must learn approximately nine new words each day from the time they start speaking until their sixth birthday (Gelman, 1979). If 14,000 words does not seem impressive, think of the effort adults must make to acquire 1000 words in a foreign language—and these spectacular language learners are only waist high! Furthermore, they combine these words into phrases that have never been heard before, such as "My dolly dreamed about toys" (2 years, 2 months).

Our discussion of language development will be confined to children, since language development in the elderly has not been a popular research topic. We will examine two of the topics that were covered in Chapter 5, understanding language and producing language. Summaries of studies on remembering language are available in Flavell (1977) and Paris and Lindauer (1977).

Understanding Language

If you have recently seen a baby who is less than 6 months old, you might have been tempted to conclude that the baby's mastery of language was roughly equivalent to that of a tennis shoe. Until the early 1970s, psychologists were not much more optimistic. However, experiments have demonstrated that an infant's speech perception is surprisingly advanced. They can make very subtle distinctions among many sounds, an important early stage in the understanding of language.

Eimas, Siqueland, Jusczyk, and Vigorito (1971) were among the first to discover infants' capacity for speech perception. They used a method called **nonnutritive sucking,** in which babies suck on nipples in order to produce a particular sound. No liquid is delivered through the nipple, but the infant is required to suck at least two times each second in order to maintain the sound. Typically, babies begin each session by sucking frequently in order to keep the sound on. However, they then show habituation. Remember that habituation occurs when a stimulus is presented frequently, and the response rate decreases. Presumably, the sound is now too boring, and it is not worth the hard work of frequent sucking.

How can the nonnutritive sucking technique be used to provide insight into speech perception? Eimas and his colleagues shifted the speech sound after the 1- to 4-month-old infants had habituated to the first sound. For example, an infant who had shown habituation to *bah* was suddenly presented with a highly similar sound, *pah*. These infants show dishabituation. That is, when *pah* was presented, they suddenly started sucking vigorously once more. The infants showed more modest dishabituation to other sounds that were more similar to each other than *bah* and *pah*. However, there was no dishabituation when infants continued to hear the same *bah* sound; their response rate continued to decrease. Thus, the nonnutritive sucking technique revealed that infants respond at different rates to different sounds, and so they can perceive the difference between them.

Other research, summarized by Eimas and Tartter (1979), demonstrated that 2-month-old infants can distinguish between the syllables *bad* and *bag*. Their chapter also lists other, similar speech perception accomplishments.

Even newborn babies seem to have impressive speech perception abilities. A study by Condon and Sander (1974) examined synchrony. **Synchrony** literally means "moving together," such as the synchrony between what you say and your body movements as you speak. Previous research had established that adults show synchrony with their own speech, called **self-synchrony,** and that they also show **interactional synchrony;** that is, their body movements are coordinated with the speech of other people. Try Demonstration 10.4 to see if you can notice self-synchrony and interactional synchrony. Amazingly, however, Condon and Sander found interactional synchrony in newborns!

Demonstration 10.4   Self-Synchrony and Interactional Synchrony.

First, try to observe self-synchrony. The easiest way to do this may be to watch a professor who is lecturing to a large audience. Let us say that Dr. John Jones is teaching Introductory Psychology to 300 students this semester. Does his hand fall rapidly at the end of a sentence? Does he look up at the audience and then down at the floor at the end of a phrase? Notice also any pacing patterns, leaning forward on the lecturn, and turning of the body. In other words, does Dr. Jones synchronize his body movements with his words?

Interactional synchrony is more difficult to observe. However, notice couples talking to each other. Do the listener's movements correspond to the speaker's words?

Condon and Sander located 16 babies, all younger than 2 weeks of age, and took movies of the infants' movements as they listened to the speech of an adult. The movies were later analyzed to detect whether the infants' body movements were related to the individual sounds of the speaker. The correspondence was impressive. For example, consider a typical newborn's movements when the adult said the word "come." During the k sound of the word, the left elbow extends slightly, but the speed is much faster at the end of the word. The big toe of the left foot moves during the k sound but stops at the end of the word. The left hip extends slightly during the k sound but rotates at the end of the word. Thus, newborns move in rhythm with adult speech; the speed of movement and type of movement changes as the speaker's speech sounds change. This movement indicates that they can locate the boundaries between sounds and words.

Babies begin to understand the meaning of words toward the end of their first year of life. They often understand more than they can say—as we will discuss later in the chapter—and they respond appropriately to words before they can produce language (Clark & Clark, 1977). Often it is the adult's voice tone and gestures that convey the meaning, rather than the words themselves. For example, if a father quickly raises his arms and loudly shouts, "Don't do that!" the baby will probably stop the activity. However, the baby would probably also stop if he used the same tone and gestures to shout, "Interactional synchrony!" (We should also note that adults are sensitive to voice tone. Try yelling "Interactional synchrony!" at your roommate.)

Furthermore, children's understanding of the meaning of some words is often quite different from the adult meaning. Clark and Clark cite an example of a mother who had told her young child to close the screen door so that flies wouldn't come in, because flies bring germs into the house with them. When the child was later asked what germs are, she replied that germs were something that the flies play with!

Children must determine a word's meaning from the context in which it is used, but the context often permits many different interpretations. After hearing words in many different contexts, children's interpretations coincide more closely with adult's interpretations. Naturally, it is difficult to recall how we acquired the meanings of the thousands of words we use every day. Demonstration 10.5 is an attempt to recreate the acquisition of meaning for one such word. More details on the acquisition of meaning are available in books or chapters by Clark and Clark (1977), deVilliers and deVilliers (1978), Keil (1979), and Nelson (1978). (Incidentally, you'll discover what a *miggum* is in the next section.

Demonstration 10.5   *Acquiring the Meaning of a Word.*

Take a sheet of paper and cover up the numbered sentences. The object of this demonstration is to learn the meaning of the word *miggum*. Move the paper down to expose the first sentence. Think about what *miggum* could mean. Keep moving the paper down until you are reasonably certain you know what a *miggum* is. Check the answer at the end of the section, if you need to.

1. Please pass the *miggums*.
2. Jane hates green *miggums*.

3. The green *miggums* sometimes have a red stuffing.
4. Most people I know feel very passionate about either their love or their hatred of *miggums*.
5. Italians and Greeks use a lot of *miggum* oil in their cooking.
6. *Miggums* come in sizes with incredible names like "colossal" and "jumbo."
7. Black *miggums* sometimes come with pits and sometimes without.
8. You can make a good sandwich with cream cheese and chopped black *miggums*.

Producing Language

Children's production of language lags behind their understanding of language. Understanding requires the listener to take in a statement, analyze it, interpret it, and respond appropriately. Production requires the speaker to plan the message, choose the right words and the right format, and to produce the words. As Clark and Clark (1977) point out, adults' production of language also lags behind their understanding. You yourself understand the meaning of hundreds of words that you would not use. Furthermore, you can easily understand people who speak very different dialects, such as southern, British, or Caribbean English. However, you probably couldn't successfully produce these dialects.

Children can often identify errors in words that they are not yet mature enough to pronounce. Berko and Brown (1960) described what has since been labeled the "fis" phenomenon:

> One of us, for instance, spoke to a child who called his inflated plastic fish a *fis*. In imitation of the child's pronunciation, the observer said: "This is your *fis*?" "No," said the child, "my *fis*." He continued to reject the adult's imitation until he was told, "That is your fish." "Yes," he said, "my *fis*." (p. 531)

Furthermore, children can understand words that they cannot yet spontaneously produce. Try Demonstration 10.6 to illustrate the discrepancy between understanding and production.

Demonstration 10.6   *The Discrepancy between Understanding and Production.*

Turn back to the pictures in Demonstration 10.2. Locate a child who is between the ages of 18 months and 36 months. Point to each item in Demonstration 10.2 and ask the child to tell you what it is. Record the number of items that are correctly identified; this is a measure of production. Now ask the child to point to items as you say their names, for example, "Where is the apple?" Record the number of correct responses; this is a measure of understanding. Does understanding exceed production?

Psychologists used to explain children's mastery of language production in terms of learning theory. Concepts such as stimulus, response, reinforcement, and imitation were assumed to be sufficient. For example, a child might learn the word *cookie* by seeing a cookie (the stimulus), saying the word *cookie* (the response), and receiving the cookie to eat (reinforcement). However, there is litttle evidence that children really learn language in that fashion.

The precise mechanisms of language acquisition are still controversial, but most psychologists now view the child as an active language learner, rather than the passive learner implied by learning theory. As Moskowitz (1978) remarks:

> The picture that is emerging from the more sophisticated investigations reveals the child as an active language learner, continually analyzing what she hears and proceeding in a methodical, predictable way to put together the jigsaw puzzle of language. Different children learn language in similar ways. It is not known how many processes are involved in language learning, but the few that have been observed appear repeatedly, from child to child and from language to language. (p. 94)

The first attempts at intentional communicating occur at about 9 months of age. As Bates (1979) notes, children communicate before this point by crying or reaching toward a goal until an adult intervenes. However, **intentional communication** differs from this more primitive kind of communication because it involves the expectation that the adult will help in reaching the goal. For example, suppose that the child in Figure 10.4 wants the ball. Prior to 9 months, the child will reach out to the ball and fuss. A child who uses intentional communication, however, will alternate eye contact between the ball and the parent while fussing. At about 9 months, then, the child apparently sees some relationship among the goal, the adult, and the communication signal.

What are children's first words? According to Nelson (1973), the first ten words are likely to refer to toys, food, and animals. By the time the children are about 18 months old and have a vocabulary of about 50 words, the words describe toys, food, animals, body parts, clothing, people, household items, and vehicles. Overextensions occur frequently during language acquisition. An **overextension** is the use of a word to refer to other objects in addition to the appropriate object.

Figure 10.4   Primitive Communication versus Intentional Communication (see text for explanation).

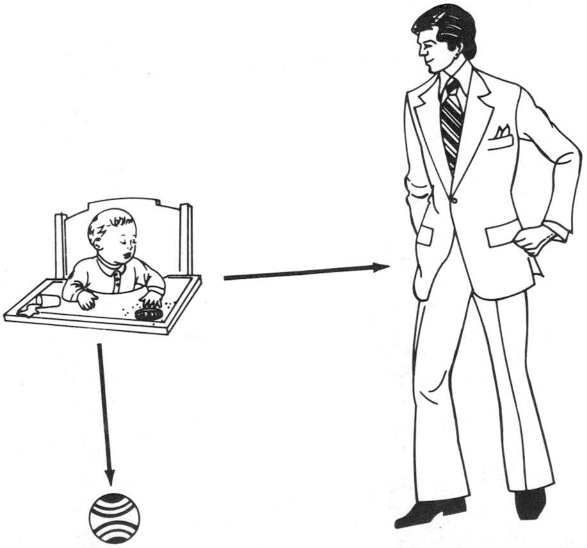

Clark (1975) describes the overextensions a child used for a unique word, *gumene*. Initially, *gumene* was applied to a coat button, but it was later used to refer to a collar stud, a door handle, a light switch, and other small round items. My daughter Beth used the word *baish* to refer initially to her blanket, and then the term was later applied to a diaper, a diaper pin, and a vitamin pill. Often, an object's shape is important in determining overextensions, but sometimes (as in the case of the vitamin pill), overextensions defy adult explanation. Incidentally, they frequently occur for properly pronounced English words as well as children's own invented words. You've probably heard of children who call every adult male—including the milkman—"Daddy."

Soon after children produce one-word utterances, they begin to string them together into two-word utterances. These two-word utterances express many different kinds of relationships, such as possessor-possessed ("Daddy pants"), actor-action ("Baby sleeping"), action-object ("Eat cookie"), and action-place ("Sit chair"). Clark and Clark (1977) describe the structure of two-word utterances and emphasize the variety of different relation relationships that children choose to express.

Children learning all languages—not just English—use telegraphic speech (deVilliers & deVilliers, 1978; Slobin, 1979). **Telegraphic speech** is speech that includes content words, such as nouns and verbs, but omits the extra words that only serve a grammatical function, such as prepositions and articles. The name *telegraphic speech* is appropriate because when adults need to conserve words (for example, when sending a telegram or placing an advertisement in a newspaper), they also omit the extra words. Thus, "I lost a lady's wristwatch with a gold band at the concert at Kilbourne Hall on Saturday, June 20," becomes: "Lost: Lady's wristwatch, gold band at concert Kilbourne Hall June 20." Similarly, a child who wants to convey, "The puppy is sitting on my blanket," will say "Puppy blanket."

After children have reached the two-word stage, they begin to fill in the missing words and word endings and to master the complexities of word order. "Baby cry" becomes "The baby is crying," for example. These more sophisticated developments in children's language are discussed in Chapter 9 of Clark and Clark's book.

In addition to knowing how to pronounce words, understand their meanings, select the correct word endings, and combine them in the proper order, children must also know *when* to use language, or the pragmatics of language. **Pragmatics** (pronounced "prag-*maa*-ticks") means the appropriate social use of language. A 2-year-old I knew once told a woman that her husband looked like a monkey. The child's description was stunningly accurate, yet both the child's mother and the woman reacted more strongly to the fact that the child had broken a pragmatic rule than to the fact that the child had produced a grammatically perfect and factually accurate sentence.

Gleason and Weintraub (1976) examined the use of pragmatic rules in Halloween trick-or-treat routines, certainly a novel setting for a language study. Think about the pragmatic rules that would govern behavior on Halloween if you were a 10-year-old child. When the door opens, you say "Trick or treat." Greetings that would be appropriate on other nights, such as "Good evening" would clearly break an unspoken pragmatic rule. After the adult puts candy in your bag, you say "Thank you." As you leave, you say "Goodbye." Gleason and Weintraub mounted tape recorders near the doors of two suburban Boston homes and recorded each trick-or-treat conversation. Then they stopped the children and asked them their ages. (Incidentally, Gleason and Weintraub mention that children replied with hostility to this question—apparently in this case the adults had broken the pragmatic rules of Halloween!)

The youngest children, 2- and 3-year-olds, typically said nothing at all during the entire sequence. The 4- and 5-year-olds typically said only "Trick or treat." Somewhat older children added a "Thank you," but only the children over 10 produced the whole routine of "Trick or treat, thank you, goodbye." Gleason and Weintraub found that adults accompanying the children often explicitly coached the children in the three segments of the routine. Try checking with your parents to see if they, too, specifically trained you in the pragmatic rules of Halloween.

Children also learn how to adapt their language to the listener. Until recently, psychologists had believed that children's language tended to ignore the level of understanding of the listener. However, Shatz and Gelman (1973) found that 4-year-olds modified their speech substantially when the listener was a 2-year-old rather than a peer or an adult. Specifically, the 4-year-olds described a toy to their 2-year-old listener using short, simple utterances. When describing the toy to another 4-year-old or an adult, their utterances were much longer and more complex. Thus children understand some of the social aspects of language, such as the need to modify speech for younger listeners, even if they need training in other areas, such as the pragmatics of language. (By the way, a miggum is an olive.)

SECTION SUMMARY: The Development of Language

1. Language development is a remarkable accomplishment; children master thousands of words in two to three years.
2. Studies using the nonnutritive sucking method show that babies can distinguish between sounds such as *bah* and *pah*.
3. Newborns show interactional synchrony, which indicates that they can locate the boundaries between sounds and words.
4. Children acquire word meaning through context.
5. Children's production of language lags behind their understanding of language.
6. Learning theory is no longer accepted as the explanation of language acquisition; children are now viewed as active—rather than passive—language learners.
7. Intentional communication develops at about 9 months of age.
8. Overextensions occur frequently in children's early language.
9. Children's two-word utterances are telegraphic.
10. Pragmatics means the appropriate social use of language. Some pragmatic rules must be taught, but even young children understand that the level of language must be geared to the listener.

The Development of Concept Formation and Problem Solving

Many of the "higher mental processes" have received inadequate attention from developmental psychologists. We do not have much information about reasoning, and we know even less about decision making. Concept formation and problem solving have been somewhat more popular topics, however, and we will combine these two areas into a single section. We will also discuss some educational implications of these topics, specifically guidelines in teaching concept formation to children and training programs to aid problem solving in the elderly.

Concept Formation and Problem Solving in Children

Several aspects of children's concept formation have been extensively researched. One popular area of research in children's concept formation is the relationship among different levels of a concept hierarchy. Young children have difficulty, for example, if they see ten pictures of animals, of which six are dogs and four are cats. Older children and adults understand that these pictures can be organized in a hierarchy, so that the upper-level category *animals* includes two lower-level categories, *dogs* and *cats*. However, younger children have difficulty constructing hierarchies.

Even when children are successful in constructing a hierarchy, they may fail to understand the relationship among the different levels. For example, they may not understand that the category *animal* consists of all the dogs plus all the cats. When asked, "Are there more animals or more dogs?" the child may reply that there are more dogs. **Class inclusion** is a term that designates the relationship among the different levels in a hierarchy. Aspects of the development of class inclusion have been described by Ginsburg and Opper (1969) and by Markman and Seibert (1976).

Let us look at two other aspects of children's concept formation in more detail: natural concepts and concept formation in school settings. Then we will examine the topic of problem solving.

Natural Concepts.   Rosch, Mervis, Gray, Johnson, and Boyes-Braem (1976) conducted many studies on basic-level categories, as you may recall from Chapter 6. Remember that basic-level categories are neither too specific or too general. On the other hand, superordinate categories are of higher level and more general and subordinate categories are of lower level and more specific. For example, *animal* is a superordinate category, *cat* is a basic-level category, and *Siamese* is a subordinate category. Rosch and her colleagues found, as we discussed in Chapter 6, that adults use basic-level names to identify objects. Their research also demonstrated that children prefer basic-level categories.

In one study, for example, Rosch and her colleagues studied children between the ages of 3 and 10, as well as college-age adults. They used color photographs of animals (cats, dogs, butterflies, and fish) and vehicles (cars, trains, motorcycles, and airplanes). Children were shown three pictures and were instructed to select the two pictures that were alike. There were two different kinds of sets similar to those in Figure 10.5. Set 1, for example, shows a Siamese cat, a a sportscar, and Persian cat. The correct response for this set would be to form a basic-level category *cat* and select the two cats as being alike. Set 2, on the other hand, shows a Siamese cat, a German shepherd dog, and a sportscar. The correct response for this set would be to form a superordinate-level category *animal* and select the cat and the dog as being alike.

The results showed that even the youngest children found it extremely easy to form basic-level categories. For items such as those in set 1, even the 3-year-olds had virtually perfect scores. However, the youngest children had difficulty in forming superordinate-level categories. For items such as those in set 2, the 3-year-olds responded correctly only about half the time. By the age of 4, however, children were quite accurate. People who were 5 and older had nearly perfect scores on both basic-level category tasks and superordinate-level category tasks. Rosch and her colleagues concluded that an understanding of basic-level categories is mastered early in development, prior to an understanding of superordinate-level categories. Thus, young children prefer the basic level of categories, the same kind of preference that Rosch's other research had established in adults.

Finally, you may recall that we discussed the imprecision of natural categories. For example, a category such as *game* does not have a single attribute that is shared by all examples of the concept (Wittgenstein, 1953). Other researchers, such as Labov (1973), have stressed that the boundaries between categories are often vague. For example, consider the boundary between *cup* and *glass.* Think of examples of objects that are: (1) clearly *cups,* (2) clearly *glasses,* or (3) sometimes called *cups* and sometimes called *glasses.* Notice, too, that a paper drinking vessel is usually called a *cup,* even though it lacks the handle that is typical of most cups. The boundary between a cup and a glass is certainly fuzzy.

Andersen (1975) examined how children acquire knowledge about the

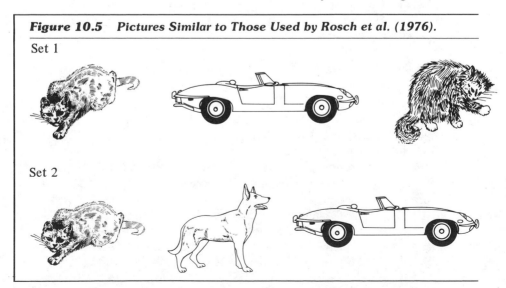

Figure 10.5   Pictures Similar to Those Used by Rosch et al. (1976).

Set 1

Set 2

vague boundaries between cups and glasses. She assembled 25 assorted drinking vessels and asked children between the ages of 3 and 12 to name each object. Then the children were asked to sort all the objects into two groups, cups and glasses. Next, the children provided definitions for the words *cup* and *glass*. Finally, they selected the best example of each concept.

Andersen's results showed that there was a clear developmental sequence in learning about boundaries. First, the younger children showed overextension of the word *cup.* They used *cup* to refer to objects that no older child or adult would call a *cup,* such as a clear wine glass without a handle. During the next stage, children pay attention to certain physical attributes of the objects, such as size, shape, and material. At this stage, children draw the boundaries too sharply on the basis of whether or not a particular physical attribute is present. For example, a child might call any object made of glass or china a *glass,* whether or not it had a handle or other important features.

During the last stage, which is comparable to adult usage, children made decisions in terms of how the objects are used, rather than how they look. Their decisions no longer depend upon the presence or absence of particular physical attributes. Thus the boundaries between the categories become fuzzier and more realistic. These older children's definitions reflect the fuzziness of boundaries. For example, a cup was defined as *sometimes* having a handle. In summary, the development of natural concepts progresses from an overextension of some concepts, to a rigid dependence on physical attributes, to an appreciation of the fuzziness of boundaries.

Concept Formation in School Settings. Hudgins (1977) discusses how the research on children's concept formation can be translated into suggestions for teaching. Imagine, for example, that you are teaching a course in introductory psychology to high school seniors and you want your students to understand the concept of a perceptual illusion. Hudgins suggests several steps that should be used in teaching the concept.

1. The students should be told that they are expected to learn a concept. They should also be told how their understanding of the concept will help master a larger field of knowledge.
2. The presentation should be geared to the students' existing knowledge.
3. The teacher should provide clear, positive examples of the concept. Any irrelevant features should either be absent or should vary. For example, a student might think that an illusion must be visual unless you present examples of musical illusions, taste illusions, and so forth.
4. If possible, all examples should be accessible at the same time, to reduce the memory load and allow comparison.
5. Prototypical examples should be provided first, with less clear examples provided later. In teaching the concept *illusion,* for example, prototypical illusions such as line-length illusions should be mentioned before more "exotic" illusions.
6. Negative examples should sometimes be introduced later in learning, particu-

larly if two different concepts might be mistaken for each other. For example, a teacher discussing illusions should point out the difference between a perceptual illusion (a psychological phenomenon) and a mirage (a physical phenomenon).
7. Important superordinate concepts that are necessary for understanding an entire area should be practiced frequently until they are mastered. Less important concepts can be communicated by a definition and one or two examples.

Concept formation is clearly a major part of the educational process. A second grader must master the concept of subtraction. A fifth grader learns abstract terms such as *government* and *legislature* in an elementary civics course. High school students must acquire dozens of complex concepts, such as *cell, democracy,* and *iambic pentameter.* If you plan to be a teacher, Hudgins' points are important to remember.

Problem Solving.   Experimental psychologists have not studied children's problem solving as extensively as they have studied children's concept formation. Nonetheless, let us examine one classic study that illustrates how problem-solving strategies can change as children grow older. Demonstration 10.7 is a variation of a study by Mosher and Hornsby (1966). Like the game called Twenty Questions, children were instructed to find out which one of the objects the experimenter had in mind, using as few questions as possible. The children, aged 6 to 11, were first asked to identify each of the pictures in the display of 42 pictures. (Notice that this identification step was necessary in order to establish that the younger children were not at a disadvantage with respect to labels for the pictures.) They then tried to discover the critical object, asking only questions that could be answered "yes" or "no."

Demonstration 10.7   The Twenty-Questions Game.

Turn back to the pictures in Demonstration 10.2. Locate a child between the ages of 6 and 11. Ideally, several children of different ages should be tested. If you have no access to children, test a friend. Tell the subject that you are thinking of one of the pictures in the display, and the subject must ask questions that can be answered either "yes" or "no." The object of the game is to ask as few questions as possible in order to identify the picture that you are thinking of. Notice what kind of questions your subject asks. Are they primarily constraint-seeking questions or hypothesis-scanning questions?

The experimenters recorded all of the questions and classified them into two categories:

1. **Constraint-seeking questions,** which were questions that were general enough to refer to two or more pictures. For example, "Is it alive?" would be a constraint question in Demonstration 10.7. This strategy is usually the more efficient one.
2. **Hypothesis-scanning questions,** which were very specific and referred to only one picture. For example, "Is it a doll?" is a hypothesis-scanning question. "Wild guesses" would qualify as hypothesis-scanning questions.

Children's strategies changed dramatically between the ages of 6 and 11. Nearly all of the 6-year-olds' questions showed the hypothesis-scanning strategy. However, constraint-seeking questions rose sharply; these questions formed the majority of the 11-year-olds' questions. Thus, children learn to use a more efficient strategy as they grow older. Rather than guessing impulsively, they ask questions that systematically eliminate a large proportion of the possibilities.

In this section on concept formation and problem solving, we mentioned children's difficulty in understanding class inclusion. Next we examined some research on natural concepts, such as children's ease in learning basic-level categories and their gradual appreciation of the fuzziness of boundaries. Then we looked at some suggestions on teaching concepts to children. Finally, we saw how children's problem-solving skills change as they grow older. Now let us see how elderly people form concepts and solve problems.

Concept Formation and Problem Solving in Elderly People

As Rabbitt (1977) observed, information on concept formation and problem solving in elderly people—as opposed to college students or children—is scanty. However, reviews of the literature (Meichenbaum, 1974; Rabbitt, 1977) frequently show an age-related decline in both skills.

One factor that probably contributes to this decline in performance is that many of these tasks, particularly concept formation tasks, rely heavily on memory. In a typical concept formation task, for example, you must remember from trial 1 that a black X on the left is a positive instance of a concept, whereas a small white T on the right is a negative instance. On trial 2, a large black T on the right is a positive instance, whereas a small white X on the left is a negative instance, and so forth. As you may recall, elderly people perform well on a variety of memory tasks, but they have difficulty when the tasks involve episodic long-term memory. This is precisely the kind of memory that concept formation tasks require. In solving problems, elderly people often ask for information to be repeated, another indication of memory difficulties (Meichenbaum, 1974). Furthermore, Rabbitt reported that elderly people may have difficulty following instructions in the experiment, such as pressing a key to stop a timer, another problem related to memory difficulties.

However, memory difficulties may not be entirely responsible for the decline in concept formation and problem solving. To some extent, elderly people may differ from younger people in their organizational strategies. Training the elderly to organize information efficiently has sometimes led to improved performance. Rabbitt (1977) proposed two alternate interpretations for this improvement. It is possible that the elderly do not discover any organizational strategies, and so they improve when a useful strategy is demonstrated to them. Alternately, it is possible that the elderly do spontaneously use organizational strategies. However, these strategies may be complex, and they may be unsuitable for the task that is currently being performed. Elderly people may be reluctant to abandon these strategies in favor of other, more appropriate strategies unless they are specifically trained to use a particular strategy.

We have seen that memory problems and lack of organizational strategies may contribute to the difficulties that elderly people experience on problem-solving tasks. Hoyer, Rebok, and Sved (1979) identified another factor: irrelevant information. In their study, young, middle-aged, and elderly people solved problems that required them to match geometric stimuli. Elderly people were particularly likely to make a large number of errors when there was too much irrelevant information. For example, elderly people made errors about 70 percent of the time when number was the relevant dimension and three irrelevant dimensions (color, shape, and position) were also varied. In contrast, young and middle-aged people made errors only about 20 percent of the time in that condition. A practical application of this study is obvious. Elderly people can be helped in their solution of everyday problems if efforts are made to remove irrelevant, unimportant information.

Although the majority of studies show a decline in performance with an increase in age, some studies have found no age differences. For example, Kesler, Denney, and Whitely (1976) tested groups of middle-aged (30−50 years) and elderly (65−81 years) people on three problem-solving tasks. One of the tasks involved solving written problems, such as those in Demonstration 10.8. The second task was a Twenty-Questions task similar to the one used by Mosher and Hornsby (1966) that we discussed in the previous section on children's problem solving. The third problem involved the use of an efficient heuristic to locate a switch that controlled one of 16 lights.

Demonstration 10.8   *Solving Written Problems.*

Try each of the following written problems, which are reworded versions of the problems used in the study by Kesler, Denney, and Whitely (1976). The answers are at the end of the section.

1. A man wants to send a pair of ski poles by mail. He learns, however, that the postal rules forbid shipping any article whose greatest dimension is more than 1 yard. The ski poles are each 4 feet long. How does he solve the problem?
2. A man bought a horse for $60 and then sold it later for $70. The next day, he bought the horse back for $80 and sold it for $90. How much profit did he make?
3. Suppose that an empty cocktail shaker with some ice at the bottom of it is in your sink. Suppose that you want to retrieve the ice. However, the shaker is too cold to handle and there is nothing around which can be used to tip it over. Furthermore, the neck is too small to put your hands in, and there is nothing around to help you fish the ice out. How do you solve the problem?
4. A woman has four pieces of chain, each of which is made up of three links. She wants to join the pieces into a single, closed ring of chain. It costs 2 cents to open a link and it costs 3 cents to close a link. She performs the task in a way that costs 15 cents. How did she do it?

An examination of the raw performance scores for the three tasks showed that the middle-aged people performed substantially better than the elderly people. However, Kesler and her colleagues also obtained measures of their subjects' education, occupation, and intelligence. When these measures were included in the statistical analysis, age was no longer related to problem-solving performance. Instead, education and intelligence scores were the important determinants of problem-solving ability.

Keep in mind that this study does *not* demonstrate that age is of no importance on problem-solving tasks. Instead, it means that there were no age effects above and beyond the effects accounted for by education and intelligence. Thus, if you found 100 middle-aged people and 100 elderly people who were matched in terms of the number of years of education they had received and matched in terms of intelligence, those two groups would be equivalent in their ability to solve problems.

Other psychologists have examined applications of the concept formation and problem-solving research. In particular, they have devised training programs to aid performance in the elderly. Baltes and Schaie (1974), for example, report a study focusing on the slower response speed of elderly people. They trained people 65 to 80 years of age to increase their speed on a simple letter-canceling task. When these people took various intelligence tests, many of which stressed problem solving, they received higher scores than other people who had received no training.

Meichenbaum (1974) designed a training program that emphasized a self-instructional strategy. This strategy mainly involved talking to oneself while performing the task. In more detail, Meichenbaum first performed the task while talking aloud to himself while the subjects observed. Thus the experimenter served as a model of appropriate problem-solving behavior. Then the subjects performed the task while the experimenter instructed them. During the next phases the subjects learned to perform the task themselves while talking aloud and then while whispering to themselves. Finally they performed silently without moving their lips.

Meichenbaum argues that the self-instructional strategy is successful for several reasons. First of all, verbalizing during task performance helps to organize information in the problem. Secondly, verbalization helps people evaluate the feedback. Third, active rehearsal of the alternate hypotheses helps to reduce the memory load of the task. Finally, the self-instructional strategy may help people develop a more positive attitude toward the task and provide methods of coping with failure. Meichenbaum also notes that similar kinds of training programs have been used successfully with groups as diverse as normal first graders, geriatric patients, children with Attention Deficit Disorder, and schizophrenics.

Incidentally, the answers to Demonstration 10.8 are: (1) He places the poles diagonally in a box that measures 3 feet on each side. (2) The man made $20, $10 on the first transaction and $10 on the second transaction. (3) You fill the shaker with cold water, and the ice will float to the top. (4) She cuts all three links from one piece of chain apart; then she uses each cut link to hook two other chains together. The three openings and three closings cost 15 cents.

SECTION SUMMARY: *The Development of Concept Formation and Problem Solving*

1. **Children have difficulty constructing hierarchies and answering questions on class inclusion tasks.**
2. **Young children acquire basic-level categories prior to superordinate-level categories.**
3. **The development of natural concepts progresses from overextension, to a**

rigid dependence on physical attributes, to an appreciation of the fuzziness of boundaries.

4. The research on children's concept formation has been adapted to recommendations for education.

5. Young children show hypothesis scanning on the Twenty-Questions game; their questions refer to only one picture. Older children ask constraint-seeking questions, which are general enough to refer to two or more pictures.

6. Elderly people frequently show a decline in concept formation and problem solving.

7. The decline may be due to memory difficulties, inappropriate organizational strategies, and the effects of irrelevant information.

8. In some studies, elderly people do not differ from younger people when other factors are controlled.

9. Meichenbaum's self-instructional strategy, which involves talking to oneself while performing, has aided problem solving in the elderly.

Piaget's Developmental Theory

A chapter on cognitive development would be incomplete without some discussion of the contributions of Piaget. Jean Piaget (pronounced "Zhawn Pea-ah-*zhay*") was a Swiss psychologist and theoretician who lived from 1896 to 1980. Many psychologists and educators consider Piaget to have been the foremost contributor to the study of cognitive development. In fact, Ginsburg and Koslowski (1976) credit Piaget's work as being one of the major forces that contributed to the decreasing influence of behaviorism on developmental psychology. Since developmental psychologists no longer felt compelled to examine overt behaviors, they began to emphasize children's cognitive processes.

Our emphasis throughout the book as well as in the previous part of this chapter has been on information processing approaches to cognition. In general, these approaches describe thought processes in adults. With few exceptions (for example, Klahr & Wallace, 1976), information processing approaches have not attempted to describe how cognition changes with development. In contrast, Piaget has developed a comprehensive theory with a specified set of principles that can account for cognitive change.

A summary of Piaget's theory and research in a few pages cannot capture the scope and the complexity of his work. More complete summaries can be found in books by Piaget (1970), Flavell (1963, 1977), and Ginsburg and Opper (1969). The discussion in this section is based largely on those resources. Incidentally, the adjective **Piagetian** (pronounced "pea-ah-*zhet*-ee-an") applies to research and theory based on Piaget's approach to psychology. Our examination of Piagetian theory begins with some basic concepts and proceeds through the stages in the life span.

Basic Concepts of Piagetian Theory

One of the most important concepts in Piagetian theory is **adaptation,** or the process through which our thoughts respond to the environment. Adaptation consists of two mechanisms called assimilation and accommodation. **Assimilation** means that we deal with the environment in terms of our current thought structures. Thus stimulation from the environment must be modified and molded until it matches what we currently know about. For example, a child seeing a little pony for the first time might call it *doggie,* because *doggie* is a concept that the child currently knows. Notice then that overextensions, which we discussed in the language section, represent a form of assimilation. Another example of assimilation is a child who customarily puts objects into her mouth. When she is handed a rattle—an object in the environment that is really intended for shaking—she shows assimilation by putting the rattle into her mouth.

Accommodation is the mirror image of assimilation. In assimilation the object in the environment is changed until it fits our thought structures, but in **accommodation,** our thought structures change to fit the stimulation in the environment. For example, the previous concept *doggie*, previously used to refer to medium-sized, hairy, four-legged creatures, might now be broken into two categories, *doggie* and *horsie.* Furthermore, a child who had previously responded to the rattle as "something to put in my mouth" shows accommodation if she now responds to the rattle as "something to shake and produce interesting noises."

Adaptation requires a balance between assimilation and accommodation, the two complementary processes. Think about how assimilation and accommodation are involved in adult learning. For example, consider how you learned about the prototype theory of pattern recognition in Chapter 2. You had already learned about the template theory, so you had a thought structure for template theory. Then you learned that prototype theory was similar in some ways to template theory, so you could *assimilate* prototype theory into your concept of template theory. However, you then learned that prototype theory was different from template theory because it was more flexible. Now you had to *accommodate* in order to make a distinction between the two types of theories. Much of education combines assimilation and accommodation as we notice the similarity between old information and new information and then we notice the differences.

Another important concept in Piagetian theory is the scheme. A **scheme** is an internal representation of an activity. A scheme is one of the earliest kinds of mental activity that a young infant develops. One example of a scheme is the sucking scheme, in which the child consistently shows certain kinds of activities in response to certain kinds of stimulations, such as the insertion of objects into the mouth. Babies also develop schemes of grasping, hitting, pushing, kicking, and so forth (Flavell, 1977). Schemes show orderliness and organization.

A final important concept in Piaget's theory is egocentrism. When we use the word *egocentrism* in everyday speech, we imply selfishness. Piaget's use of the term is different. **Egocentrism,** in Piagetian theory, means that a person sees the world from only one point of view—his or her own. The person is unaware of the existence of other viewpoints or perspectives. For example, a 3-year-old boy may tell a teacher an elaborate story about Mary, but fail to acknowledge that the teacher does not share his set of experiences and consequently has no idea who Mary is. Furthermore, children are not aware of their own egocentrism. Piaget argues that children cannot take the listener's point of view into account. (Recall, however, that the study by Shatz and Gelman discussed in the language section demonstrated impressive lack of egocentrism among 4-year-olds, who used simpler language when speaking to a 2-year-old than when speaking to another 4-year-old or an adult.)

Let us now briefly consider the developmental sequence in Piaget's theory of cognitive development.

The Stages of Piagetian Theory

Piaget proposed four stages in human development:

1. The sensorimotor period (birth to about 2 years)
2. The preoperational period (2 to 7 years)
3. The concrete operational period (7 to 11 years)
4. The formal operational period (11 to 15+ years)

We will discuss each of these stages as well as the performance on Piagetian tasks in old age.

The **sensorimotor period** is the first stage of cognitive development, during which the major cognitive projects are sensory activities (such as seeing, hearing, touching, smelling, and tasting) and motor activities (such as sucking, kicking, and reaching). Language and symbols are not yet available to the child, but actions are available. Piaget believes that these actions constitute the very first forms of intelligence. In the first few weeks of life, reflexes, such as the sucking reflex, are most important. Newborns do not understand that their actions can produce reactions in the environment, and they do not understand that an object still exists even if it is temporarily out of sight. By the end of the sensorimotor period, however, babies actively experiment with objects in the environment to determine how their actions can produce different sounds and sights. Furthermore, these older babies have developed a more sophisticated concept of objects, and they realize that objects continue to exist even when they have been hidden.

The **preoperational period** begins at about 2 or slightly younger, when the child has developed language. The child can therefore use symbols and words, rather than physical actions, to represent thought. Language provides an enormous advantage to children; they can now refer to objects that are not physically present.

Two topics in the preoperational period have received the most attention: classification and conservation. We briefly discussed classification in the section on concept formation when we noted that young children have difficulty with class inclusion tasks. **Conservation** means an awareness that the quantity of a substance remains the same in spite of changes in that substance's appearance. Young children in the preoperational period fail to conserve, and they believe, for example, that you can change the amount of water by pouring it from a short wide container into a tall, narrow one. Try Demonstration 10.9 to illustrate several examples of children's difficulty with conservation.

Conservation has been a particularly popular topic for American researchers. Most of these research projects have attempted to teach conservation to preoperational children. Murray (1977) estimated that there were about 140 such research studies between 1961 and 1976. Piaget noted that Americans are preoccupied with

---

Demonstration 10.9   Testing Conservation.

Locate a child who is between the ages of 4 and 9. First, take two lumps of a substance such as clay or dough. Ask the child whether they are equal in quantity and ask him or her to adjust the amounts if they are not. Then flatten one lump and ask the child whether there is still the same amount. Ask for an explanation for the answer.

Now take two glasses of equal size and fill them with the same amount of water. Again, ask the child whether they are equal, and ask for an adjustment if they are not. Then pour the contents of one glass into a third glass that is different in shape (either wider or narrower). Ask whether there is still the same amount of water and request an explanation.

Finally, take 18 pennies and arrange them into two rows of 9 pennies each. Ask the child whether they are equal, and ask for an adjustment if they are not. Then take one of the rows and spread it apart so that it is about twice as long as the other row. Ask whether there is still the same number in each row and request an explanation.

---

accomplishing things in the least possible time. If children do not ordinarily acquire conservation until they are 7, for example, Americans are determined to teach it to 5-year-olds! Kuhn (1974) points out the results of these studies have generally been ambiguous and inconclusive. It appears to be difficult to produce a complete restructuring of the thought process by means of brief training sessions. Although interest in teaching Piagetian concepts to young children has generally declined, some schools still base their programs on attempts to apply Piaget to the classroom (see, for example, Furth & Wachs, 1975, and Lawton & Hooper, 1978).

During the **concrete operations period,** which lasts from about 7 to 11 years of age, children have mastered classification tasks that involve class inclusion, and they can demonstrate conservation. They are able to argue, for example, that there is the same amount of clay in the flattened ball as there was in the round ball because the clay could be reshaped to its original form. However, as the term *concrete* implies, these classification and conservation tasks can be understood only if the concrete, physical objects are present. If the objects are absent, children have difficulty with the abstract tasks.

The **formal operations period** begins about the age of 11 and becomes consolidated during adolescence; young people in the formal operations period can think abstractly. They can solve reasoning problems and perform classification and conservation tasks "in their heads" without the physical presence of objects. The abstract kinds of problems we discussed in the problem-solving and reasoning chapters, for example, can now be attempted. Many factors, such as aptitude and educational opportunity, influence the age at which people reach the formal operations period.

Whitbourne and Weinstock (1979) summarized the Piagetian research that has been performed on adults and elderly people. Some psychologists have suggested that as people grow older they lose their mental abilities and return to their earlier difficulties on Piagetian tasks; this hypothesis has been called the **regression hypothesis.** Thus an elderly individual would be expected to return to the level of a preoperational child. Whitbourne and Weinstock find little evidence for the regression hypothesis. Elderly people sometimes have difficulty on Piagetian tasks, but this difficulty can often be traced to factors such as motivation. For example, elderly people may be insulted if the study uses a setup that would be more appropriate for young children.

Tesch, Whitbourne, and Nehrke (1978) examined spatial egocentrism for evidence of the regression hypothesis. **Spatial egocentrism** means the inability to take another person's spatial point of view. Young children show spatial egocentrism, for example, when they say "See my new shoes" to someone in another room. They are unaware that someone in another location does not have the same view of objects in space that they have. In the experiment by Tesch and her colleagues, people were asked to arrange checkers on a checkerboard so that they would have a certain configuration if someone seated directly across were looking at them. Male volunteers from a Veterans Administration center, who were between the ages of 33 and 83, were tested on this task. The results showed that age had no significant influence on peformance. Thus, there was no evidence for regression on a task assessing spatial egocentrism. Piaget had proposed that the formal operations level is maintained throughout the life span, and the results of this study are consistent with that viewpoint.

SECTION SUMMARY: Piaget's Developmental Theory

1. Jean Piaget, a Swiss psychologist, developed an influential theory of cognitive development, which includes basic concepts and stages of cognitive development.
2. Adaptation is the process through which our thoughts respond to the environment; it requires a balance of assimilation and accommodation.
3. Assimilation means that we deal with stimulation from the environment in terms of our current thought structures.
4. Accommodation means that our thought structures change to fit the stimulation in the environment.
5. A scheme is an internal representation of an activity.
6. Egocentrism means that a person sees the world from only his or her own point of view.
7. The sensorimotor period, which is the first stage of cognitive development, involves sensory activities and motor activities.
8. The preoperational period begins when the child develops language. Preoperational children have difficulty with class inclusion tasks and conservation tasks.
9. During the concrete operations period, children can perform class inclusion and conservation tasks when the objects are physically present.
10. In the formal operations period, class inclusion and conservation tasks as well as other complex problems can be solved abstractly.
11. Some psychologists have suggested that elderly people regress to their earlier performance levels on cognitive tasks, but research has shown no change in spatial egocentrism as people grow older.

Chapter Review Questions

1. Recall Gelman's (1979) quotation that we must turn our attention to what young children *can* do. If you wanted to impress someone with children's cognitive abilities, what would you mention about their memory, language, and concept formation?

2. Part of the difficulty with infant research is designing experiments that reveal the infants' true competence. Describe how experimental procedures have been applied to memory and language in order to uncover information about infants' ability.

3. Compare children, young adults, and elderly people with respect to their sensory memory, short-term memory, recognition memory, and recall memory.

4. Your mother complains that her elderly father has a very sharp memory for events that occurred long ago but has poor recall for events from several seconds ago. Do the data support that report as being typical of elderly people?

5. Suppose that you decide to teach third grade. What kind of memory strategies would you teach children, and how would you encourage their metamemory skills? Select a concept and show how Hudgins' suggestions could be applied in teaching that concept.

6. A friend has a 13-month-old child who is just beginning to talk. Summarize what she can expect to find in her child's understanding and production of language during the next few years.

7. What are pragmatic rules in language? Why are they relevant to the Piagetian concept of egocentrism? Describe some research that argues against egocentrism in young children. Discuss the research that shows that elderly people do not show increasing egocentrism.

8. What are overextensions and how are they relevant in language acquisition, concept formation, and Piaget's theory?

9. In light of our discussion of problem solving in the elderly, what recommendations would you make for revising problems so that they could be more readily solved by elderly people?

10. Name each of the four stages in Piagetian theory, list the typical age span for each stage, and describe the important skills that are acquired during that period.

New Terms

habituation-dishabituation procedure
memory strategies
metamemory
metacognition
blind training
nonnutritive sucking
synchrony
self-synchrony
interactional synchrony
intentional communication

overextension
telegraphic speech
pragmatics
class inclusion
constraint-seeking questions
hypothesis-scanning questions
Piagetian
adaptation
assimilation
accommodation

scheme
egocentrism
sensorimotor period
preoperational period
conservation
concrete operations period
formal operations period
regression hypothesis
spatial egocentrism

Individual Differences in Cognition

Preview

In the preceding chapter we examined the extent to which age makes a difference in three areas: (1) memory, (2) language, and (3) concept formation and problem solving. In this chapter, we will examine individual differences in these three areas, and we will also consider a topic called cognitive styles.

In the section on memory, we see that people in other cultures sometimes remember more material than Americans, and sometimes remember less. Other studies show that people in other cultures remember different kinds of material. Sex differences in memory are not large, but females sometimes remember more than males if the material is verbal or social. We will also examine differences in ability, such as retardation and organizational strategies, and their influence on memory.

The language section begins with an examination of linguistic universals, which are features shared by most languages. This section also examines sex differences in language, which are somewhat more consistent than other kinds of cognitive sex differences. Females acquire language faster than males and they receive higher scores on various tests of verbal abilities; however, the differences are relatively small. Our final topic is Black English, which is a language system that is separate from Standard English and has its own rules; it is *not* a deficient form of Standard English.

The section on concept formation and problem solving focuses on object classification, which seems to be highly influenced by education, and on the Whorfian Hypothesis. According to the Whorfian Hypothesis, the words we use influence the way we organize our thoughts; evidence is mixed on this topic. Sex differences in concept formation and problem solving are minimal.

Finally, we examine cognitive styles, which are consistent differences in the way people organize and process information. We emphasize two kinds of cognitive styles, field dependence-independence and reflection-impulsivity. If you are the kind of person who easily solves hidden-figure problems, quickly locating the 10 pictures of fruits that are carefully concealed in a woodland scene, you are probably field independent, and your strategies differ from those of a field dependent person. If you are the kind of person who carefully considers all the possible answers on a multiple-choice test, rather than quickly circling the answer that looks best, you are probably reflective, rather than impulsive.

In most of our discussion so far we have examined the cognitive processes of college students. In Chapter 10 we extended our investigation to children and elderly people. Still, our inspection was generally limited to middle-class, white, English-speaking people living in the United States—a small proportion of the world's population. In this chapter we will look at some studies of cognitive processes in people of other cultures. Our conclusion in these cross-cultural studies will be that culture generally does *not* make an enormous difference in the way people remember, speak, form concepts, and solve problems. Thus the cognitive processes we have discussed in the preceding ten chapters apply to some extent to all humans, not just Americans.

Most of the studies we have examined in this book have included both male and female participants. Does sex make a difference in cognitive functioning? Do males process information one way, whereas females operate according to completely different strategies? In general, we will conclude that sex has very little influence on cognitive processes. As Sherman (1978) observed,

> Grasping the limited extent of the cognitive differences between the sexes, one is struck by their inconsequential nature at least in terms of any kind of evidence that would warrant advising boys and girls to pursue . . . careers on the basis of sex differentials in ability. (p. 66)

In fact, Sherman concludes that the amount of variability in people's cognitive performance that can be attributed to sex is *at most* 5 percent. Fortunately, then, you won't have to read two books, one entitled *Cognition in Females* and the other, *Cognition in Males*.

We will compare people of different cultures and sexes with respect to three important areas: memory, language, and concept formation/problem solving. Several other factors that could influence these cognitive processes will also be considered. Our final topic will be individual differences in cognitive tasks, rather than their level of performance.

Individual Differences in Memory

A certain Russian man, typically known only by his initial, S., had an astounding memory. As described by Luria (1968), S. could remember a list of 70 items perfectly, after only one presentation. Furthermore, he was equally able to recall the list backwards. S. was also adept at recalling symbols. He was once shown a lengthy mathematical formula, about 5 percent of which looked like this:

$$N \cdot \sqrt{d^2 \cdot \frac{85}{x \ vx}} \cdot \sqrt{\frac{276^2 \cdot 86x}{n^2 v \cdot \pi 264}}$$

He looked at the formula for about five minutes and coded it into a story. He recalled it perfectly half an hour later. Even more impressive, he recalled it perfectly 15 years later!

Clearly there are individual differences in memory, even among people who have more ordinary memory spans. In this part of the chapter we will examine three aspects of individual differences. The first two sections focus on cross-cultural differences and sex differences in memory. The last section examines the relationship between memory and various other abilities, such as general intelligence, verbal intelligence, and ability in organizational strategies. Other kinds of individual differences that influence cognition are discussed elsewhere, including extraversion-introversion (Eysenck, 1976b); race and social class (Flynn, 1980; Jensen, 1974, 1980; Kamin, 1975; and Yando & Zigler, 1979); deaf versus hearing individuals (Liben & Drury, 1977); and schizophrenic versus normal individuals (Larsen & Fromholt, 1976).

Cross-cultural Differences in Memory

In the late nineteenth century there was a widespread belief that "primitive people" had unusually impressive memories (Deregowski, 1978). As we will see in this section, some current research demonstrates that people in other cultures sometimes do have memory capabilities that are superior to the capabilities of Americans. However, other research finds evidence for more limited performance, both in terms of amount and in terms of strategies. Perhaps the most interesting research, though, shows different *patterns* of abilities rather than different *levels* of abilities.

A study by Ross and Millsom (1970) is representative of the studies that demonstrate superior recall by people in other cultures. College students in the African nation Ghana and in New York City heard one of three stories. One story appears in Demonstration 11.1; try this demonstration before you read further. Recall was requested 40 minutes after hearing the story and also several weeks later. The students from Ghana generally had superior recall, both in terms of the number of themes recalled and the number of words recalled. Dube (cited in Neisser, 1978) also found that children in Botswana had story recall that was far more accurate than the recall of American schoolchildren.

Demonstration 11.1   Recall for a Story.

Read the following story:

The Son Who Tried to Outwit His Father

> A son said to his father one day: 'I will hide, and you will not be able to find me.' The father replied: 'Hide wherever you like,' and he went into his house to rest. The son saw a three-kernel peanut, and changed himself into one of the kernels; a fowl coming along picked up the peanut and swallowed it; and a wild bush-cat caught and ate the fowl, and a dog met and caught and ate the bush-cat. After a little time the dog was swallowed by a python, that, having eaten its meal, went to the river and a was snared in a fish-trap. The father searched for his son and, not seeing him, went to look at the fish-trap. On pulling it to the river-side he found a large python in it. He opened it, and saw a dog inside, in which he found a bush-cat, and on opening that he discovered a fowl, from which he took a peanut, and breaking the shell, he then revealed his son. The son was so dumbfounded that he never again tried to outwit his father. (Ross & Millsom, 1970, p. 176)

Forty minutes from now, write down as much of the story as you can recall. Aim for verbatim recall whenever possible. Then count the number of words that you correctly recalled. Ross and Millsom (1970) found that the Ghana students recalled an average of 161 words, in contrast to 127 words for the New York City students.

A different pattern emerges in other studies involving the memorization of lists of words. (It is not clear whether the nature of the material is responsible for the difference or whether it is simply a coincidence.) Cole and Scribner (1974) describe the extensive research that they and their colleagues conducted with the Kpelle people of Liberia, Africa. They found that as American children grow older, their recall increased substantially. In contrast, older Kpelle children recalled only slightly more than the younger Kpelle children. Furthermore, the American children— particularly the older ones—showed much more clustering of similar items in their recall. Thus the two groups differed not only in the amount of recall, but also in the strategies for recall. Cole and Scribner conclude that the Kpelle do not spontaneously reorganize material as an aid to memory.

Still other research emphasizes the difference in the pattern of abilities. For example, Wagner (1978) remarks that mnemonic strategies are culture-specific. People growing up in urban societies with formal school experience may develop certain kinds of rehearsal strategies. People growing up in other cultures may use other strategies. For example, Kpelle informants reported that their recall was aided by singing and dancing.

Meacham (1975) found different patterns of recall for American and Guatemalan children. The participants in his study included children from an isolated agricultural village near Guatemala City and middle-class children from Buffalo, New York. He presented small objects, such as a plastic dog and a small wooden chair, paired together with various locations, such as a flower garden and a house. During recall, some children were given the objects and were asked to supply the locations (for example, "Where did we hide the dog?"). Other children were given the locations and were asked to supply the objects (for example, "What did we hide in the house?").

As you can see in Figure 11.1, the Guatemalan children did better when they

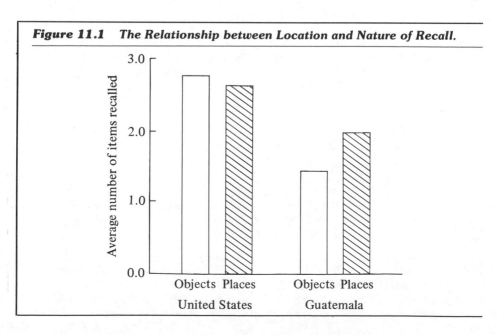

Figure 11.1   The Relationship between Location and Nature of Recall.

were asked to recall the locations than when they were asked to recall the objects. However, the American children performed equally well on both tasks. Meacham concludes that environment and culture contribute to differences in the development of various memory abilities. Thus the culture we live in can influence the types of memory strategies we use and the kind of information we remember. We should also note that experiences in a particular culture obviously makes people familiar with certain objects and concepts. For example, did it seem to you that the ideas in Demonstration 11.1 would be more familiar to a student in Ghana than to a student in New York City? In any event, it seems that we do not have any compelling evidence for cross-cultural differences in memory ability.

Sex Differences in Memory

One of the most important reviews of the literature on sex differences was written by Maccoby and Jacklin (1974). They divide the studies on memory into four categories: (1) memory for verbal content; (2) memory for objects and numbers; (3) memory for a combination of verbal and nonverbal material; and (4) social memory.

Of the 22 studies involving verbal content, 12 studies showed no difference in the performance of males and females, and 10 studies showed that females recalled more than males. Sex differences were particularly likely to be found after about the age of 7. Maccoby and Jacklin conclude that females show somewhat better memory for verbal content, perhaps because their verbal skills are also somewhat better—a topic we will consider shortly.

In the other categories of memory material, Maccoby and Jacklin conclude that there were no systematic differences related to sex. Thus, males and females performed approximately the same when they had to remember objects, numbers, and social material (for example, characters in a fairy tale). Other recent research suggests, however, that there might be a difference in men's and women's recall of social material. For example, Bahrick, Bahrick, and Wittlinger (1975) found that women generally remembered more of their high school classmates' names and faces years after graduation. Thus a sex difference may exist in this area when the social information refers to one's own friends, but it does not apply to all kinds of people-related material.

Maccoby and Jacklin conclude that males and females probably do not differ in their memory capacity or in the skills involved in storing and retrieving information. Furthermore, males and females probably do not differ in their choice of memory strategies. In some cases, however, the nature of the content can influence recall. Specifically, females probably perform better when the content is verbal, and females possibly perform better when the content is social.

Ability Differences in Memory

A large number of studies have attempted to discover whether there is a relationship between general abilities—such as intelligence—and memory. Other studies have focused upon the identification of more specific factors that underlie performance on memory tasks.

A representative study on the relationship between intelligence and memory was conducted by Cohen and Sandberg (1977). They examined children whose IQ scores ranged between about 75 and 125. They found that the children with higher IQs performed better on a test of short-term memory, particularly on the most recent items.

Other studies have focused on the memory abilities of retarded individuals, which are clearly different from the memory abilities of people with normal intelligence. Brown (1974) suggested that the primary reason for the difference is that retarded people have not developed appropriate memory strategies. You will recall that we saw in Chapter 10 that children develop more effective memory strategies as they grow older. Similarly, retarded people seem to be developmentally immature with respect to the strategies used to memorize material. Studies have demonstrated that retarded children do not spontaneously rehearse the material that they must remember. For example, they do not show enhanced memory for the first few items in a list, a characteristic of normal memory that is attributed to rehearsing the first items more thoroughly than later items.

Although retarded people do not spontaneously rehearse, they can be trained to adopt a rehearsal strategy. Brown, Campione, Bray, and Wilcox (1973) trained one group of retarded people to try to recall previous items by saying them out loud. Another group of retarded people received no such training. The results showed that the people who had received rehearsal strategy training performed substantially better than the control people.

In a second experiment, Brown and her colleagues tested two groups of normal junior high students. One group served as a control, but the second group was prevented from rehearsing cumulatively. That is, they were required to repeat the current item as often as possible, which prevented their rehearsal of the earlier items. The results showed that the performance of the children who had been allowed to rehearse was similar to the performance of the retarded children who had been trained in rehearsal strategies. In contrast, the performance of the normal children who had not been allowed to rehearse was similar to the performance of the untrained retarded children. Thus, rehearsal aids memory. However, if people do not spontaneously rehearse or if rehearsal is prevented, memory performance suffers.

Research on metamemory (or knowledge about memory) has also been applied to the training of retarded children. Campione and Brown (1978) developed a training program for children whose IQ scores were about 70. The training program particularly stressed self-testing, or a "stop-check-and-study" routine. That is, children were asked to study the material, assess their knowledge, and study more until they had mastered the items. The children's memories improved substantially with this program. More important, the effects of training were still present a year later. The program had clearly changed their learning strategies.

Other studies have attempted to develop specific measures of memory abilities. Unfortunately, however, these attempts have not always been successful. Erickson and Scott (1977) review the field of memory testing in clinical settings. They note that laboratory research on learning and memory has been abundant, but little attention has been directed to preparing tests for measuring memory functioning in clinical settings. For example, the Wechsler Memory Scale (1945) is a widely used test that was developed to detect memory deficits among people suffering from brain injuries. However, comparatively little research has been conducted to establish whether the test really measures what it claims to measure. Erickson and Scott urge the development of carefully constructed new batteries that yield several measures, rather than a single score.

Earl Hunt and his colleagues have conducted several studies on the relationship of verbal intelligence to memory skills (e.g., Hunt, 1978). For example, Hunt, Lunneborg, and Lewis (1975) studied students at University of Washington who had taken a test of verbal ability called the Washington Pre-College Test. They compared students who had scored in the top 25 percent ("high verbal" students) with students who had scored in the bottom 25 percent ("low verbal" students). They found that the high verbal students performed better than the low verbal students on a large number of tests of memory ability. For example

1. High verbal students were better at accessing overlearned material. In a task similar to one described in Chapter 3, high verbal students could identify very rapidly that two different physical stimuli, such as *A* and *a*, represented the same letter.
2. High verbal students were superior on a test similar to the Peterson and Peterson (1959) technique for measuring short-term memory. They were highly accurate in their recall of letters after a short delay.
3. High verbal students showed more release from proactive inhibition. That is, they showed greater improvement in recall when the material was shifted from one category to another.

Ozier examined another factor that might be responsible for differences in memory ability: organizational strategies. Her extensive research (for example, Ozier, 1980) has contrasted people with high and low subjective organization scores. As you may recall from Chapter 3, subjective organization is the tendency to impose one's own, individual organization on a list of words that does not otherwise have any obvious organization. Ozier found that people who showed high subjective organization consistently performed better on free-recall tests, serial learning, and paired-associate learning. These people were also superior on several memory tasks involving recognition. Ozier speculates that high-subjective-organization people may establish better quality traces than low-subjective-organization subjects. These high quality traces are relatively easy to discriminate from one another. Incidentally, if you have very high quality traces for the material in Chapter 3, you may recall that Craik (1979) proposed a similar concept called distinctiveness, which described the extent to which a stimulus is different from the other memory traces in the system.

SECTION SUMMARY: *Individual Differences in Memory*

1. In general, culture and sex do not have a strong influence on cognition.
2. People used to believe that "primitive people" had memory abilities beyond our own.

3. Some studies show that people in other cultures are superior in their recall of stories.
4. Other studies show that people in other cultures are inferior in their memorization of lists of words and in their organizational strategies.
5. Still other studies show that people in other cultures differ in the kind of information they remember.
6. Females sometimes recall more than males if the content of the material is verbal, and it is also possible that they recall more if the content is social.
7. There are no sex differences when the content of the material is objects or numbers.
8. The major reason that retarded people do not recall as much as people of normal intelligence is that they have not developed appropriate memory strategies; their memory is enhanced by training programs.
9. High verbal students differ from low verbal students on a variety of tests of memory ability.
10. People who show high subjective organization consistently perform better on several kinds of memory tasks.

Individual Differences in Language

We will consider three topics in this chapter. First, we will look at **linguistic universals,** or features shared by all (or most) languages. Then we will briefly examine sex differences in language ability. Our final topic is Black English; we will mention applications to education in this section. Other aspects of individual differences in language are discussed in a book by Fillmore, Kempler, and Wang (1979).

Linguistic Universals

This section could have been labeled "Cross-Cultural Differences in Language," parallel with similar sections on memory and concept formation/problem solving. Such a section could have covered the obvious cross-cultural differences in vocabulary, syntax, and complexity. However, the similarities among languages are far more interesting. Different languages do not demonstrate infinite variations; instead, the variations are limited. As Clark and Clark (1977) remark, the limits on the variation that occurs in language tell us something about the nature of language:

. . . every human language must be susceptible of:

(1) Being learned by children.
(2) Being spoken and understood by adults easily and efficiently.
(3) Embodying the ideas people normally want to convey.
(4) Functioning as a communication system in a social and cultural setting.

Consider English and Navaho. One might well be surprised to discover that they have features in common. They are historically unrelated and until recently have not been in contact with each other. The features they have in common, if not accidental, must therefore be there because it is a requirement of a human language that they be there. They are just the features that fulfill the four conditions placed on human language. Thus, if we knew what is common to all languages, it might be possible to characterize what is inherent in the human capacity to speak, understand, and acquire language. (pp. 516–517)

Let us now consider some of these linguistic universals. We will examine four characteristics that are shared by most or all languages.

1. *Complex ideas tend to be expressed in complex language* (Clark & Clark, 1977; Greenberg, 1966). For example, the plural form of a concept is a more complex idea than the singular form, and the plural word is more complex than the singular word—*apples* is more complex than *apple*. Other contrasts between complex and simple concepts are expressed in the following word pairs, all of which require extra letters or words to express the more complex concept:

complex	simple
have walked	walk
grandmother	mother
pale yellow	yellow
interestingly	interest
Golden Delicious apple	apple
undo	do

Similarly, other languages also use extra letters and words to express more complex concepts.

2. *Some word orders are more common than other word orders.* There are six possible orders in which the subject, verb, and object can be arranged in a sentence. In English, we use a subject-verb-object (SVO) order, as in the sentence, *The woman made a statue.* Greenberg (1963) reported that almost all languages confine themselves to one of three basic orders, SVO, SOV, and VSO. Notice, then, that the object of the sentence is typically not allowed to precede the subject. As Slobin (1979) remarks, action seems to flow from subject to object.

3. *Modifiers are placed near the words they modify.* For example, we customarily say, *We quickly devoured the magnificent cheesecake,* rather than *We devoured magnificent the quickly cheesecake.* From an information processing perspective, it is simpler to understand language that places words near each other when they belong together conceptually.

4. *Pleasant words have higher frequencies than unpleasant words.* In connection with the Pollyanna Principle mentioned in Chapter 3, I examined the frequency of pleasant and unpleasant words in various languages (Matlin & Stang, 1978). In every sample obtained, pleasant words were used more frequently than unpleasant words. This was true in English, French, German, Spanish, Chinese, Russian, and Urdu (a language spoken in India and Pakistan). For example, Urdu newspapers used the word *good* three times as often as *bad* and *success* appeared twice as often as *failure*. People in a wide variety of languages speak in terms of the pleasant, rather than the unpleasant.

In our examination of linguistic universals we have seen that there are certain consistencies that appear in different languages. Uniformities in our cognitive processes are mirrored in these linguistic universals.

Sex Differences in Language

In this section we will look at differences in language ability. The question of whether males and females differ in the style of their language is discussed elsewhere (for example, Henley, 1977; Orasanu, Slater, & Adler, 1979).

As Maccoby and Jacklin (1974) point out, "Female superiority on verbal tasks has been one of the more solidly established generalizations in the field of sex differences" (p. 75). However, the differences are rarely large, and many studies report equal performance from males and females. A survey by L. J. Harris (1977) of language development shows some areas in which young boys and girls differ. For example, at 2½ years of age, girls have mastered a greater number of different sounds than boys. Also, the average girl says her first word at 11.4 months, whereas the average boy says his first word at 12 months. Young girls acquire additional words at a faster rate, too. Nelson (1973) reported that, on the average, girls acquire their first 50 words by 22.1 months. In her sample, nearly all of the boys were slower than the slowest girl. Girls also excel in the precision of their pronunciation and in their comprehensibility.

Sex differences also occur in the language of older males and females. For example, females receive higher scores than males on tests of verbal fluency similar to Demonstration 11.2. Maccoby and Jacklin reviewed 26 comparisons of male and female performance on various kinds of verbal ability. The females scored higher than males on 22 of these comparisons. Males scored higher on the other 4 comparisons, all based on samples of British children. At least in the United States, then, females typically excel in language skills. It should be stressed once more, however, that the differences among individuals are so great that there will almost always be an overlap in the scores of males and females.

Demonstration 11.2   Verbal Fluency.

For each of the sequences of letters below, construct a four-word sentence so that each word begins with the specified letter. For example, S _____ a _____ b _____ h _____ could be answered, "Send all boats home." Count the number of items for which you can construct a sentence in a two-minute period.

1.   B _____   i _____   n _____   n _____ .

2   M _____   t _____   w _____   s _____ .

3.   T _____   f _____   g   t _____ .

4.   H _____   l _____   r _____   c _____ .

5.   S _____   h _____   h _____   p _____ .

6.   L _____   i _____   v _____   a _____ .

7.	A	_____	a	_____	b.	_____	b	_____ .
8.	J	_____	i	_____	f	_____	m	_____ .
9	R	_____	c	_____	b	_____	d	_____ .
10.	D	_____	m	_____	s	_____	a	_____ .

Black English

In this section, we will examine Black English, comparing it with Standard English and noting implications for education. If you are interested in a careful examination of one kind of Black English, you should read Folb's (1980) study of black teenagers in south central Los Angeles. Other, theoretical issues concerning Black English are discussed by Harrison & Trabasso (1976).

Black English is a dialect that is spoken by about 80 percent of Black Americans (Dillard, 1972). Many scholars believe that Black English has its origins in the language that developed in the southern plantations. As speakers began to have increased contact with whites, Black English was influenced by Standard English. Thus, Black English has its own separate historical basis (Foss & Hakes, 1978).

In earlier years, a deficiency interpretation of Black English was popular. According to Labov (1970), educational psychologists who supported the **deficiency interpretation of Black English** believed that black children from the ghetto area received little verbal stimulation. This interpretation also maintained that black children heard very little well-formed language. Consequently, black children were viewed as impoverished in their ability to communicate verbally. It was argued that black children could not speak complete sentences, lacked the names for common objects, could not form concepts, and could not convey logical thoughts.

Labov's influential papers presented a very different view of Black English:

> The concept of verbal deprivation has no basis in social reality. In fact, Negro children in the urban ghettos receive a great deal of verbal stimulation, hear more well-formed sentences than middle-class children, and participate fully in a highly verbal culture. They have the same basic vocabulary, possess the same capacity for conceptual learning, and use the same logic as anyone else who learns to speak and understand English. (pp. 154–155)

Labov stresses that linguists, in contrast to psychologists and educators, are more likely to believe that nonstandard dialects are highly structured systems. According to linguists, a dialect is not merely errors caused by the failure to master Standard English. Instead, they believe that Black English is a separate system that differs from Standard English in certain systematic patterns.

Baratz (1970) has outlined some of the differences. You may notice that many of the differences arise because, in Black English, words in a sentence do not always have to agree with each other.

1. When you have a number such as 2, 9, 75, and so on, you do not need to have a plural noun. Thus "50 cent" is correct.
2. The possessive is indicated by two words near each other rather than the Standard English construction 's. "John cousin" is used rather than "John's cousin."
3. The -s is dropped from some verb forms. "She work here" is the correct Black English version of "She works here."
4. Certain verb agreements are different, allowing sentences such as "She have a bike," and "They was going."
5. Some verb parts (which you might have called "helping verbs" when you were taught grammar) can be omitted, producing acceptable sentences such as "I going," and "He a bad boy."
6. The double negative form is used, so that the Standard English sentence, "I don't have any," becomes "I don' got none." If you have studied French or Spanish, you know that double negatives are used in these languages, too. Thus, Standard English is unusual in its rejection of double negatives.
7. The word "be" is used to express habitual action, as in the sentence, "He be working *every* day." A single action, occurring right now, does not use "be"—for example, "He working right now."

The pronunciation of individual words in Black English also differs from Standard English. For example, the "sk" sound is often reversed to "ks," so that the Standard English word "ask" becomes "aks" in Black English. The letter *t* is frequently dropped from the end of the word, as in "nex'," "ain'," and "isn'." Other letters, such as *l,* may be dropped from the middle of a word, as in "hep" for the Standard English word "help."

Educators who acknowledge that Black English is a separate system, just as legitimate as Standard English, still face a dilemma. If they teach Black children using Black English, these children may not learn Standard English. Consequently, they may be at a disadvantage later in life, since they will face considerable discrimination in academic and business settings in which Standard English is often the only acceptable speech form.

Some educators have suggested a **bidialectical approach**, with instruction both in Black English and in Standard English (Adler, 1979). Adler feels that the bidialectical approach shows respect for a child's culture and language, yet also provides exposure to an "establishment" dialect.

Gibson and Levin (1975) also point out that teachers are more likely to influence the scholastic achievement among black children if they have high expectations for the success of their students, if they avoid direct questioning, and if they do not misinterpret certain behaviors. For example, black children may talk and move when someone else is speaking. In the black community, this behavior would be interpreted as paying attention, whereas a white teacher may interpret it as inattention.

SECTION SUMMARY: *Individual Differences in Language*

1. Linguistic universals are features shared by most languages.
2. Some linguistic universals are: complex ideas are expressed in complex language; certain orders of subject, verb, and object are likely, whereas others are avoided; modifiers are placed near the words they describe; and pleasant words are used more often than unpleasant words.
3. Young girls are generally superior to young boys in language acquisition measures such as pronunciation and vocabulary.
4. Older females are generally superior to males on various tests of verbal ability.
5. The deficiency interpretation of Black English proposed that black ghetto children received little verbal stimulation.
6. The deficiency interpretation has little support now, because linguists believe that Black English is a separate system with its own rules.
7. Educators have suggested bidialectical instruction, in both Standard English and Black English; they have also proposed that teachers have high expectation for their students' success, avoid direct questioning, and avoid misinterpreting certain behaviors.

Individual Differences in Concept Formation and Problem Solving

In this section on concept formation and problem solving, we will examine two factors that could potentially influence performance. First, we will look at cross-cultural studies to determine whether culture and language influence categorization. Then we will see whether females and males perform differently on problem-solving and creativity tasks.

Cross-cultural Differences in Concept Formation and Problem Solving

As Cole and Scribner (1974) remark, both scientists and laypeople agreed for many years that people in other cultures were deficient in their higher mental processes. They might have admitted that these so-called primitive people could have excellent memories or complex languages. However, it was generally assumed that they could not think systematically. Cole and Scribner cite a respected early anthropologist, who wrote:

> Between our clearness of separation of what is in the mind from what is out of it, and the mental confusion of the lowest savage of our own day, there is a vast interval. (Tylor, 1929, p. 125)

The present view of the thought processes in other cultures is certainly more flattering than the "mental confusion" conclusion that Tylor proposed. However, as Deregowski (1978) notes, there is an interesting pattern in cross-cultural research. There are many studies available on purely perceptual processes, fewer studies available on memory processes, and even fewer available on the higher cognitive processes. Thus, more sophisticated thinking skills are rarely investigated. For example, the topics of planning and creativity are relatively neglected. However, Deregowski offers evidence of the outstanding planning ability shown by the inhabitants of Micronesia. These navigators journeyed from one small island to another, equipped only with their knowledge of the ocean. Clearly, the planning involved in these adventures was substantial.

Regrettably, then, we will not be able to discuss how Nigerians or Laotians or Eskimos perform on the Hobbits-and-Orcs problem or the water-jar problem. Concept formation and categorization have been more thoroughy explored, and so we will examine these topics. We will first examine whether people in different cultures classify objects in different ways, and then we will discuss whether language influences the way we form our categories. Incidentally, if you are interested in cross-cultural performance on Piagetian tasks, consult a book edited by Dasen (1977).

Classification of Objects.   In a typical classification task an experimenter presents a group of objects and asks people to place the objects together that are similar in some way. One such study by Sharp and Cole is summarized by Cole and Scribner (1974). Try Demonstration 11.3, which is a variation of their study. They

---

Demonstration 11.3   *Classifying Objects.*

For this study, you will need to locate a first- to sixth-grade child. Photocopy the figures below and cut out the cards. Ask the child to sort the cards into piles so that the piles are alike in some way. Notice the number of piles and the consistency of sorting. Notice in Table 11.1 that 17 percent of first graders and 84 percent of sixth graders in Yucatan were successful on this first sorting task.

If the child was successful on this task, ask him or her if there is a different way to form groups of cards that are similar in some way. Ask the child to demonstrate this different way.

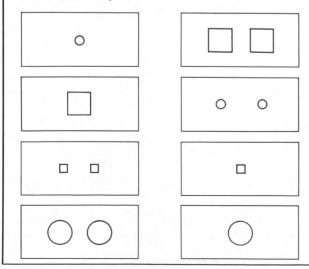

worked in Yucatan, Mexico, with people of various ages and educational backgrounds. In each case they arranged the cards in a random arrangement and asked people to arrange piles so that the piles were alike in some way.

In most cases, people sorted the cards into two piles. Some people used a consistent rule—for example, color—to sort all of the cards. However, many people sorted inconsistently. For example, a person might sort some of the cards according to color and some of the cards according to form. The left-hand column in Table 11.1 shows the percentage of each group that showed a consistent sorting rule. If you look at the first three age groups, it appears that children become increasingly consistent as they grow older. Notice, though, that the low performance level of the teenage groups contradicts that trend. These teenagers had attended no more than three years of school, and their performance was below that of the third graders.

The people who had successfully sorted the pictures the first time were asked whether they could find a different way to form groups of cards that were similar in some way. The right-hand column in Table 11.1 shows the percentage of each group that showed a new, consistent sorting rule. Notice the same pattern: number of years of education seems to be more important than chronological age.

As Pick (1980) observed, education seems to reduce many differences in object classification that might initially appear to be traceable to differences in culture. Cole and Scribner review several cross-cultural studies on classification, and they note that people who attend Western-type schools are often more likely to use a different classification style. There are four ways in which Western-educated people differ from those who have not been formally educated in that system:

1. They are more likely to classify on the basis of superordinate categories, rather than lower-level categories.
2. Western schooling seems to encourage a different approach to the task. Specifically, Western-educated people search for a rule that can be consistently applied to categorize all items.
3. Western education promotes an awareness that alternative rules are possible. For example, children realize that there is more than one way to classify the cards in Demonstration 11.3.
4. Schooling helps people explain their own mental operations. Studies demonstrated that children who had been trained in Western schools were much more

TABLE 11.1   Performance on a Classification Task as a Function of Age and Years of Education

Type of Subject	Consistent First Sorting, Percent	New, Consistent Second Sorting, Percent
First grader	17	3
Third grader	47	44
Sixth grader	84	60
Teenager (0−1 years of education	25	8
Teenager (2−3 years of education)	52	28

Based on data from Cole and Scribner, 1974.

likely to be able to provide reasons for their groupings, in contrast to untrained children.

However, the situation is not that simple. Children growing up in Western cultures or children who have been exposed to Western-style education are often more advanced in their categorization, but there are exceptions. For example, Okonji (1971) found that Nigerian children between the ages of 11 and 12 were more advanced than Scottish children of the same ages in their sorting of familiar African objects. Furthermore, uneducated Liberian adults showed more advanced sortings of bowls of rice than American college students did. The Liberians sorted in terms of features such as cleanliness, polish, and type of grain, whereas the Americans sorted in terms of a more "primitive" feature, quantity (Irwin & McLaughlin, 1970). Thus, familiarity and non-Western kinds of education can provide advantages when the tasks are appropriate. Far from showing the "mental confusion" that Tylor described, people in other cultures are capable of impressive sophistication in their classifications.

Does Language Influence Categorization?   The question of whether language influences categorization has a fairly long history. In recent years, it has been linked with Eleanor Rosch's notion of prototypes, which we discussed in Chapter 6. The issue began with an idea about the relationship between language and cognition known as the Whorfian hypothesis (Whorf, 1956). Whorf wrote:

> We dissect nature along lines laid down by our native languages. The categories and types that we isolate from the world of phenomena we do not find there because they stare every observer in the face; on the contrary, the world is presented in a kaleidoscopic flux of impressions which has to be organized by our minds—and this means largely by the linguistic systems in our minds. We cut nature up, organize it into concepts, and ascribe significances as we do, largely because we are parties to an agreement to organize it in this way—an agreement that holds throughout our speech community and is codified in the patterns of our language. (p. 213)

According to the **Whorfian hypothesis,** the words that people use will determine how they organize those categories in their heads. That is, the structure of language determines the structure of thought. Furthermore, people who speak different languages have different terms for the members of a category, and therefore their thought structures are different from one another. For example, the Eskimos have four different words for snow, such as wet snow and hard-packed snow. Because they have different language structures, argued Whorf, their organization of objects in the world will be different from the organization used by speakers of American English.

The first experimental support for the Whorfian hypothesis came from an experiment by Brown and Lenneberg (1954). The purpose of this experiment was to show that language influences thought; it did not attempt to test whether speakers of different languages had different thought structures. Brown and Lenneberg showed that language is related to cognition in the categories used for color. They asked English-speaking people to provide names for 24 colors. From these names, they derived measures of **codability,** or the ease with which a color could be named. As the measure to be used for further study they selected

interpersonal agreement, in this case, the extent to which different subjects agreed upon a name for a color. Thus, the interpersonal agreement might be high for a bright, true red, because many people would give the name "red" to this color. In contrast, interpersonal agreement would probably be low for the brownish-green color like the inside of an avocado that has been exposed to the air for a day; people would supply many different names for this color. Codability, as measured by interpersonal agreement, was therefore the measure of language that Brown and Lenneberg chose to use.

Since the Whorfian hypothesis stated that there was a relationship between language and thought, Brown and Lenneberg needed a measure of thought. They chose a recognition task. Subjects saw a color, waited, and then tried to recognize which color they had seen, out of 120 different alternatives. The results showed that the colors that were most codable were also the easiest to recognize. Thus, a true red could be recognized more easily than old-avocado-insides-green. If a color has a nice, readily available name that people agree upon, that color will be easier to remember. Language, as measured by codability, influences thought, as measured by recognition.

The Brown and Lenneberg study assumed, as Brown (1976) has pointed out, that English divides the color space into arbitrary categories and that there are other, non-English-speaking communities that divide up the color space in different ways. In some other community, for instance, red might be a low-codable color and old-avocado-insides-green might be a highly codable color.

However, other studies have demonstrated that the color space is not divided into arbitrary categories. Berlin and Kay (1969) looked at 20 very different languages, such as Arabic, Thai, and Hungarian. They asked native speakers of these languages to give names for certain color samples and to select the best example of each color on a color chart. Berlin and Kay found that the best examples of colors in the various languages seemed to be located in similar positions. For example, the best example of our color red might be very similar to the best example that the speakers of Arabic selected for one of their basic colors. Color names are assigned rather consistently in many different cultures; they do not demonstrate an arbitrary division of the color space. The "best examples" or prototypes for color terms seem to be reasonably universal. (As you will recall, we used the word *prototype* to refer to these "best examples" in Chapter 6.)

Before we examine the universality of prototypes any further, let me emphasize that some prototypes are universal, but others may not be. Prototypes for categories in the color space may be universal, for example, but many other prototypes are probably not universal. For example, your prototype for the concept "bird" is probably quite different from the prototype that residents of tropical South America might have. As Rosch (1978) comments, the context can be extremely important in determining judgments. The prototype bird in South America might be somewhat larger and much more colorful. Basic, perceptual categories such as color (and possibly shape) might have universal prototypes. It is likely that our basic equipment for color vision forces all humans to use these categories. Semantic categories, which emphasize more complex relationships among the examples of a concept, probably do not have universal prototypes.

Let us now return to research on the Whorfian hypothesis. Eleanor Heider (the same person as Eleanor Rosch) questioned Brown and Lenneberg's research on codability because she suspected that color systems were universal. Heider (1972) chose 8 colors considered to be prototypes by English speakers, and 13 colors considered to be nonprototypes by English speakers. In one study, her subjects were 23 speakers of 23 languages other than English. She found that prototype colors were *more codable* than nonprototype colors across all langauges. Thus, true red might be highly codable in all languages, but old-avocado-insides-green might be low-codable.

Furthermore, Heider (1972) conducted some studies on the Dani people of New Guinea, who have only two color names, roughly equivalent to "dark" and "light." They recognized prototype colors better than nonprototype colors.

Heider's experiments are important because they demonstrate that certain colors that we consider basic are also basic to people in other cultures. These basic, prototypical colors are "best examples," even for speakers of languages that are very different from English. People choose the same prototypes and they recognize these prototypes easily, whether they have many different names for the color space—as English does—or only two—as the Dani language does. Categorization and thought do not always depend upon language, as the Whorfian hypothesis had claimed.

Furthermore, Heider's results imply that the reason that Brown and Lenneberg had found the relationship between language (codability) and cognition (recognition) was that the highly codable words happened to be prototypes—that is, basic colors with names that people would agree upon. Prototypes, as we saw in Chapter 6, are remembered better than nonprototypes. Certain colors are remembered better, then, because they are prototypes, and not because they are more codable. Thus the current answer to the question "Does language influence categorization?" is "Probably not."

Sex Differences in Concept Formation and Problem Solving

Several studies conducted in the 1940s and 1950s, which are summarized by Maccoby and Jacklin (1974), showed males to be superior in solving problems such as the water-jar problem and the two-string problem. (As you may recall, the water-jar problem requires people to break a set and shift their strategy away from a familiar, complicated formula for obtaining a certain amount of water. The two-string problem requires people to break a set and swing one of the strings in order to tie the two strings together.) Thus there was some evidence in these early studies that males were superior on nonverbal tasks that required breaking a set. However, Sherman (1978) notes that any conclusions would be premature until well-designed studies have been conducted using contemporary subjects.

Anagram tasks also require set breaking, but they are verbal in nature rather than nonverbal. Maccoby and Jacklin summarize ten studies conducted in the 1960s and 1970s on anagram-solving ability. Of these ten studies, six show no sex difference and four show that females were superior. Thus there is some evidence that females are better on verbal set-breaking tasks.

You may recall the extensive study that Kesler, Denney, and Whitely (1976) conducted on problem solving in elderly people, which we discussed in Chapter 10. This study also examined sex differences on three kinds of tasks, written problems (such as those in Demonstration 10.6), a Twenty-Questions task, and a problem requiring the development of an efficient heuristic. An examination of the raw performance scores for the three tasks showed that the males were superior to females. However, in another analysis Kesler and her colleagues included measures of subjects' education, occupation, and nonverbal intelligence. When these measures were included, sex was no longer related to problem-solving ability.

Demonstration 11.4   *A Creativity Test Assessing Figural Creativity.* (Based on Guilford, 1967).

Cut 17 narrow strips of paper, about 5 cm by 1 cm. Arrange them in the configuration shown below. How can you remove four pieces of paper and leave three squares—no more and no less? The answer is at the end of the section.

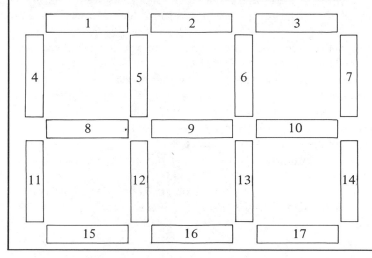

Are there sex differences in that special kind of problem-solving ability called creativity? Maccoby and Jacklin divide the numerous studies on creativity into two categories: verbal and nonverbal measures of creativity. It seems that there are no sex differences in verbal creativity at the preschool or early school level. However, after about the age of 7, females show an advantage in a majority of verbal-creativity studies. There is no consistent sex difference on the nonverbal measures of creativity at any age; seven studies found no sex difference, eight studies found females to be superior to males, and eight studies found males to be superior to females.

Alpaugh and Birren (1975) examined sex differences in creativity across the adult life span. Participants in this extensive study took a battery of seven creativity tests. Males and females performed equally well on six of the creativity tests, and males were superior on a creativity test that assessed figural abilities. (Demonstration 11.4 is a variation of this creativity test.)

In summary, any sex differences in creativity are minimal. However, there is some evidence that females may perform better when verbal creativity is emphasized, and males may perform better when figural creativity is emphasized.

Incidentally, the solution to Demonstration 11.4 is to remove strips 6, 9, 10, and 13, leaving two small squares on the left and one large square on the right, or else to remove strips 5, 8, 9, and 12, leaving two small squares on the right and a large square on the left.

SECTION SUMMARY: Individual Differences in Concept Formation and Problem Solving

1. People used to believe that "primitive people" were deficient in their higher mental processes, this view is no longer accepted.
2. Education seems to reduce many differences in object classification that might initially appear to be traceable to differences in culture.
3. Western-educated people are more likely to classify on the basis of superordinate categories, more likely to search for a consistent rule, more aware of the possibility of alternate rules, and more likely to explain their operations.
4. Familiarity and non-Western kinds of education can provide advantages on appropriate categorization tasks.
5. According to the Whorfian hypothesis, language determines how people organize their thoughts.
6. A study by Brown and Lenneberg demonstrated that language, as measured by codability, influences thought, as measured by recognition; however, Heider provided an alternate interpretation.
7. Other studies showed that the color space is not divided into arbitrary categories; color systems seem to be universal.
8. Sex differences in concept formation and problem solving are minimal.
9. There is some evidence that females excel in verbal creativity and males excel in figural creativity.

Cognitive Styles

An important area in the study of individual differences in cognition is called cognitive styles. **Cognitive styles** are consistent individual differences in the preferred ways of organizing and processing information (Messick, 1976). It is important to stress that cognitive styles do *not* emphasize the content of cognition or the level of skill shown on a cognitive task. Instead, cognitive styles represent attitudes, preferences, or strategies that a person uses in thinking.

In the previous sections of this chapter we stressed individual differences in ability. When we talk about abilities, it is clearly better to have high ability than low ability. When we talk about cognitive styles, however, one kind of cognitive style is not necessarily preferable to the opposite kind of cognitive style. The two styles are different, but one is not consistently better than the other. For example, we will see that a field-independent person excels on hidden-figure puzzles, whereas a field-dependent person excels in interpersonal relations.

Numerous different kinds of cognitive styles have been investigated. Some of the more common cognitive styles include the following:

1. **Breadth of categorization** involves consistent preferences for broad versus

narrow ranges for categories. Thus, one person might interpret the category *furniture* very broadly, so that a rug, a lamp, and a typewriter mat are all included in the category. Another person might interpret *furniture* in a narrow sense, so that only tables, chairs, and a few other items would be included.

2. **Conceptualizing styles** reflect consistent patterns in using stimulus properties as a basis for forming concepts. For example, suppose that people are instructed to sort a large number of items into whatever categories they wish. Some people may sort in terms of class membership (for example, fruits versus animals versus clothing), whereas other people may sort in terms of attributes (for example, red color versus brown color).

3. **Risk taking versus cautiousness** refers to consistent preferences for situations with uncertain outcomes versus situations where the outcome is known.

We will discuss two of the most frequently mentioned cognitive styles, field dependence-independence and reflection-impulsivity. If you are interested in other cognitive styles, Messick (1976) includes a useful dictionary of 19 different cognitive styles. Kogan (1976) discusses four cognitive styles in infancy and early childhood. Goldstein and Blackman (1978) emphasize cognitive styles related to personality differences, and Smith (1979) discusses many different cognitive styles in law school students and professors.

Field Dependence-Independence

Field dependence-independence has been the most extensively studied of all the cognitive styles (Witkin, Moore, Goodenough, & Cox, 1977). **Field-dependent** people tend to experience events globally; they have difficulty separating an object from its background. In contrast, **field-independent** people can analyze and restructure experiences in new ways; they can easily separate an object from its background. Although Witkin and his colleagues originally used the concept of field dependence-independence in connection with individual differences in perceiving objects, the concept has been broadened to include social interactions and cognitive tasks.

Perhaps the best way to clarify field dependence-independence is to describe how it is measured. Demonstration 11.5 includes tasks similar to those on the **Embedded Figures Test,** which requires a person to locate a simple figure that is hidden in a more complex figure. A person who is field-dependent will require a long time to find the hidden figure, if he or she finds it at all, because field-dependent people have difficulty separating an object from its background. However, a field-independent person can locate a hidden figure quickly and accurately. The second method of measuring field dependence-independence is the **rod-and-frame test,** in which a person in a darkened room must orient a luminous rod so that it is perfectly upright, even though the luminous square frame that surrounds it is tilted. A person who is field dependent selects a position that is somewhat tilted, corresponding to the tilted background, whereas a field-independent person selects a true upright position. Other methods of measuring field dependence-independence in infants and young children are discussed by Kogan (1976).

Demonstration 11.5   Embedded Figures.

Below are three embedded-figures problems. First, study the figure on the left. Then cover it up and try to find where it is hidden in the figure on the right. Follow this procedure with each of the three problems. (Note: The orientation of the left-hand figure may need to be shifted in order to locate it in the right-hand figure.)

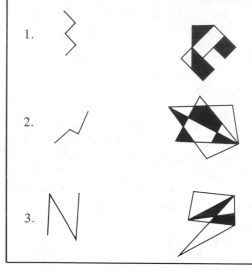

Witkin (1976) stresses that the concept of cognitive style does *not* imply that there are two distinct groups of people—either field-dependent or field-independent. Instead, the scores form a continuous distribution between the two extremes. Thus, many people have scores that are somewhere in between—for example, slightly more field-dependent than field-independent.

Witkin (1976) has found that performance on the field dependence-independence test is related to other kinds of behavior. For example, field-dependent people are more likely to be influenced by authority figures or peer groups. They also spend more time looking at the faces of the people with whom they interact. These people, in general, have more highly developed social skills.

Goodenough (1976) related field dependence-independence to performance on other cognitive tasks. In a review of many studies, he reached the following conclusions:

1. Field-dependent people are dominated by the salient (or most noticeable) attributes in concept formation tasks, whereas field-independent people sample more widely from the less salient attributes. For example, a field-dependent person might base hypotheses on a salient attribute such as color, whereas a field-independent person might also pay attention to less noticeable attributes such as thin versus thick borders.
2. Field-dependent people are more passive in their approaches to learning, whereas field-independent people are more active; they are more likely to use mediation and to restructure the learning situation.

3. Field-dependent people are more likely to remember socially relevant material, such as photographs of faces.
4. Both kinds of people respond equally well to positive reinforcement, such as praise (contrary to expectations), but field-dependent people are more influenced by criticism.

It is clear that field dependence-independence has potential applications in education. For example, Goodenough's fourth point suggests that a field-independent child would be relatively insensitive to a teacher's criticism. Other applications of field dependence-independence are discussed extensively by Chickering (1976), Witkin (1976), and Witkin et al. (1977).

Witkin and his coauthors (1977) point out other applications for education, in connection with characteristics of the teachers. For example, teachers who are field-dependent believe that discussion is more important than lectures, whereas teachers who are field-independent emphasize the importance of lectures. Furthermore, teachers and students like each other better if their styles are compatible. For example, a field-independent teacher and a field-independent student view each other positively, but each person is more negative toward a field-dependent person. By now, you have probably placed yourself informally in some position along the field-dependence-independence continuum. Think about the kind of professors you prefer. Is your preference pattern consistent with the conclusions of Witkin and his colleagues? You can consult Witkin's article for other applications to education, such as career choice and career success.

Reflection-Impulsivity

Reflection-impulsivity involves the speed and accuracy with which people consider alternative hypotheses in solving problems (Messick, 1976). Reflection-impulsivity is also called **conceptual tempo.** A **reflective** person is a person who reflects, or considers carefully the various alternative hypotheses. The reflective person takes a long time to respond and is more accurate than the impulsive person. An **impulsive** person responds quickly and makes many errors. Typically, reflection-impulsivity is measured in terms of both response time and errors (Messer, 1976).

The instrument that is most often used to measure reflection-impulsivity is the **Matching Familiar Figures Test** (MFFT), devised by Kagan, Rosman, Day, Albert, and Phillips (1964). Demonstration 11.6 shows an item similar to the problems on the MFFT. Notice that the figure on top is identical to only one of the six figures on the bottom. The other five figures differ in one or more details. A reflective person would take a long time comparing the various figures and would be more accurate than an impulsive person, who would quickly select one of the figures without careful inspection of the details. Young children are typically impulsive. As they grow older, they become more reflective. They take longer to respond, and they also become more accurate (Messer, 1976).

What other variables are related to reflection-impulsivity? There is a relationship between reflection-impulsivity and field dependence-independence. According to Messer's review of the literature, people who are field-independent (as

---

Demonstration 11.6   Matching Figures.

The figure at the top is exactly the same as only one of the figures below. Select the correct answer.

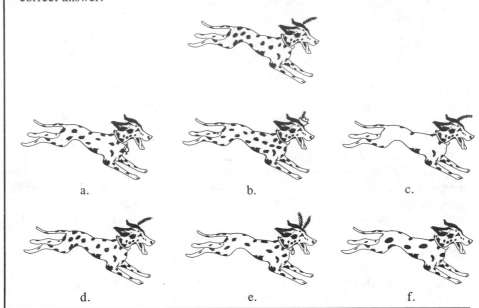

measured by the Embedded Figures Test) tend to be more reflective. The two kinds of tests are somewhat similar, after all; both tests involve response uncertainty, and both tests require a person to scan and analyze a visual field. Also, as you may have guessed, reflective children tend to have higher IQs, although the relationship is not strong.

Reflective and impulsive people perform differently on several kinds of cognitive tasks that we have discussed throughout the book. For example, reflective people are more likely to answer analogies correctly. If people are asked to complete the analogy, "Five is to number as black is to ————," impulsive people may answer in terms of a familiar—but incorrect—association such as "white." In contrast, reflective people pause, reflect, and answer "color" (Achenbach, 1969). Also, in the Twenty-Questions game, reflective children are more likely to use constraint-seeking questions (those that eliminate many possibilities at once), whereas impulsive children are more likely to use hypothesis-scanning questions (those that refer to only one possible figure). Furthermore, on a problem-solving task, reflective children verbalized more mature kinds of problem-solving strategies than impulsive children.

According to Kogan (1976), there is some evidence that impulsive children are more likely to fail in school. However, almost all of the information about reflection-impulsivity and academic performance has been gathered from elementary school children. In elementary school, it may be the best strategy to carefully consider all the various options before responding. It is possible, however, that an extremely reflective cognitive style might work to a student's disadvantage in other academic settings. For example, imagine how extremely reflective students might perform in graduate school when they must write a thesis or dissertation. They might endlessly ponder each of several dozen options at each step in the preparation and never complete the writing. Somewhat more impulsive people (though certainly not extremely impulsive) would probably respond more capably, because they would be willing to move ahead when they were reasonably confident that they had selected the best alternative.

SECTION SUMMARY: Cognitive Styles

1. Cognitive styles are consistent individual differences in the way people organize and process information.
2. Breadth of categorization involves preferences for broad versus narrow ranges for categories.
3. Conceptualizing styles involve differences in the way stimulus properties are used to form concepts.
4. Risk taking versus cautiousness involves preferences for situations with uncertain versus certain outcomes.
5. Field-dependent people have difficulty separating an object from its background, whereas field-independent people can analyze experiences in new ways.
6. Field-dependent people are more influenced by other people, and they are more interested and skilled in social situations.
7. Field-dependent and field-independent people differ in their learning styles.
8. Reflection-impulsivity involves the speed and accuracy with which people make decisions among several alternatives.
9. As children grow older, they become more reflective.
10. Reflective people are more likely to be field-independent, and they tend to have higher IQs.
11. Reflective people perform better in elementary school.

Chapter Review Questions

1. Some people have suggested that females, who generally excel on verbal tasks, should receive one kind of instruction in school, whereas males, who generally excel on spatial tasks, should receive a different kind of instruction. How would you respond to this suggestion?

2. Summarize the major findings of the studies on cross-cultural differences in memory. Relate the findings on school experience to similar findings in the section of concept formation and problem solving.

3. In general, as mentioned in Question 1, females excel on verbal tasks and males excel on spatial tasks. There is some evidence, too, that females are superior on some social tasks, such as guessing emotions from facial expressions. How could these kinds of sex differences explain the sex differences we discussed in memory, language, concept formation, problem solving, and creativity.

4. Explain how each of the following is related to memory ability and memory strategies: retardation, high and low verbal ability, and subjective organization ability.

5. What are linguistic universals, and how are they relevant to language and to the information on the Whorfian hypothesis?

6. Explain the origins of Black English, specify how its grammatical rules differ from the rules of Standard English, and describe the current status of the deficiency interpretation of Black English.

7. From what you know about cognitive styles, predict how each style would be related to tasks mentioned elsewhere in the book: (a) breadth of categorization and classification of objects; (b) conceptualizing styles and concept formation; (c) breadth of categorization and confidence intervals in decision making; (d) field dependence-independence and problem solving; (e) field dependence-independence and creativity; (f) reflection-impulsivity and depth of processing.

8. In general, what would you conclude about the size and the consistency of individual differences due to culture and sex?

New Terms

linguistic universals
deficiency interpretation of
   Black English
bidialectical approach
Whorfian hypothesis
codability
interpersonal agreement
cognitive styles

breadth of categorization
conceptualizing styles
risk taking versus
   cautiousness
field-dependent
field-independent
Embedded Figures Test
rod-and-frame test

reflection-impulsivity
conceptual tempo
reflective
impulsive
Matching Familiar Figures
   Test

Bibliography

Abelson, R. P. Script processing in attitude formation and decision making. In J. S. Carroll & J. W. Payne (Eds.), *Cognition and social behavior.* Hillsdale, N.J.: Erlbaum, 1976.

Achenbach, T. M. Cue learning, associative responding, and school performance in children. *Developmental Psychology,* 1969, *1,* 717–725.

Adler, S. *Poverty children and their language: Implications for teaching and treating.* New York: Grune & Stratton, 1979.

Alpaugh, P. K., & Birren, J. E. Are there sex differences in creativity across the adult life span? *Human Development,* 1975, *18,* 461–465.

American Psychiatric Association. *Diagnostic and statistical manual of mental disorders* (3d ed.). Washington, D.C.: American Psychiatric Association, 1980.

American Psychological Association. *Publication manual of the American Psychological Association* (2d ed.). Washington, D.C.: American Psychological Association, 1974.

Amnesty International/USA. Information letter, May 1981.

Andersen, E. S. Cups and glasses: Learning that boundaries are vague. *Journal of Child Language,* 1975, *2,* 79–103.

Anderson, J. R. *Language, memory and thought.* Hillsdale, N.J.: Erlbaum, 1976.

Anderson, J. R., & Bower, G. H. *Human associative memory.* Washington, D.C.: Winston, 1973.

Andrews, F. M. Social and psychological factors which influence the creative process. In I. A. Taylor & J. W. Getzels (Eds.), *Perspectives in creativity.* Chicago: Aldine, 1975.

Anisfeld, M., & Klenbort, I. On the functions of structural paraphrase: The view from the passive voice. *Psychological Bulletin,* 1973, *79,* 117–126.

Are those apes really talking? *Time,* March 10, 1980, p. 50.

Ashmead, D. H., & Perlmutter, M. *Infant memory in everyday life.* Paper presented at the meeting of the American Psychological Association, New York, 1979.

Atkinson, R. C., & Raugh, M. R. An application of the mnemonic keyword method to the acquisition of a Russian vocabulary. *Journal of Experimental Psychology: Human Learning and Memory,* 1975, *104,* 126–133.

Atkinson, R. C., & Shiffrin, R. M. Human memory: A proposed system and its control processes. In K. W. Spence & J. T. Spence (Eds.), *The psychology of learning and motivation: Advances in research and theory* (Vol. 2). New York: Academic Press, 1968.

Averbach, E., & Coriell, A. S. Short-term memory in vision. *Bell System Technical Journal,* 1961, *40,* 309–328.

Baddeley, A. D. *The psychology of memory.* New York: Basic Books, 1976.

Baddeley, A. D. The trouble with levels: A reexamination of Craik and Lockhart's framework for memory research. *Psychological Review,* 1978, *85,* 139–152.

Baddeley, A. D., & Hitch, G. Working memory. In G. H. Bower (Ed.), *The psychology of learning and motivation* (Vol. 8). New York: Academic Press, 1974.

Bahrick, H. P., Bahrick, P. O., & Wittlinger, R. P. Fifty years of memory for names and faces: A cross-sectional approach. *Journal of Experimental Psychology: General,* 1975, *104,* 54–75.

Baird, J. C., Merrill, A. A., & Tannenbaum, J. Studies of the cognitive representation of spatial relations: II. A familiar environment. *Journal of Experimental Psychology: General,* 1979, *108,* 92–98.

Baltes, P. B., Reese, H. W., & Lipsitt, L. P. Life-span developmental psychology. *Annual Review of Psychology,* 1980, *31,* 65–110.

Baltes, P. B., & Schaie, K. W. The myth of the twilight years. *Psychology Today,* March 1974, pp. 35–39.

Banks, W. P., & Barber, G. Color information in iconic memory. *Psychological Review,* 1977, *84,* 536–546.

Baratz, J. C. Teaching reading in an urban Negro school system. In F. Williams (Ed.), *Language and poverty: Perspectives on a theme.* Chicago: Markham, 1970.

Baron, J. What we might know about orthographic rules. In S. Dornic (Ed.), *Attention and Performance VI.* Hillsdale, N.J.: Erlbaum, 1977.

Baron, J., & Strawson, C. Use of orthographic and word-specific knowledge in reading words aloud. *Journal of Experimental Psychology: Human Perception and Performance,* 1976, *2,* 386–393.

Barron, F. *Creative person and creative process.* New York: Holt, Rinehart and Winston, 1969.

Bartlett, F. C. *Remembering.* Cambridge, England: University Press, 1932.

Bates, E. *The emergence of symbols: Cognition and communication in infancy.* New York: Academic Press, 1979.

Beach, B. H. Expert judgment about uncertainty: Bayesian decision making in realistic settings. *Organization Behavior and Human Performance,* 1975, *14,* 10–59.

Berko, J., & Brown, R. Psycholinguistic research methods. In P. H. Mussen (Ed.), *Handbook of research methods in child development.* New York: Wiley, 1960, 517–557.

Berlin, B., & Kay, K. *Basic color terms: Their universality and evolution.* Berkeley and Los Angeles: University of California Press, 1969.

Berscheid, E., & Walster, E. Physical attractiveness. In L. Berkowitz (Ed.), *Advances in experimental social psychology.* New York: Academic Press, 1974.

Biederman, I. Perceiving real-world scenes. *Science,* 1972, *177,* 77–80.

Bjork, R. A. The updating of human memory. In G. H. Bower (Ed.), *The psychology of learning and motivation* (Vol. 12). New York: Academic Press, 1978.

Bolles, R. C. Learning, motivation, and cognition. In W. K. Estes (Ed.), *Handbook of learning and cognitive processes* (Vol. 1). Hillsdale, N.J.: Erlbaum, 1975.

Bonoma, T. V. Business decision making: Marketing implementations. In M. F. Kaplan & S. Schwartz (Eds.), *Human judgment and decision processes in applied settings.* New York: Academic Press, 1977.

Borgida, E., & Nisbett, R. E. The differential impact of abstract vs. concrete information on decisions. *Journal of Applied Social Psychology,* 1977, 7, 258–271.

Boring, E. G. *A history of experimental psychology* (2d ed.). New York: Appleton, 1950.

Bourne, L. E., Jr. Knowing and using concepts. *Psychological Review,* 1970, 77, 546–556.

Bourne, L. E.,Jr. An inference model of conceptual rule learning. In R. Solso (Ed.), *Theories in cognitive psychology.* Hillsdale, N.J.: Erlbaum, 1974.

Bousfield, W. A. The occurrence of clustering in the recall of randomly arranged associates. *Journal of General Psychology,* 1953, *49,* 229–240.

Bower, G. H. Analysis of a mnemonic device. *American Scientist,* 1970, *58,* 496–510.

Bower, G. H. Mental imagery and associative learning. In L. Gregg (Ed.), *Cognition in learning and memory.* New York: Wiley, 1972.

Bower, G. H. Experiments on story understanding and recall. *Quarterly Journal of Experimental Psychology,* 1976, *28,* 511–534.

Bower, G. H., & Clark, M. C. Narrative stories as mediators for serial learning. *Psychonomic Science,* 1969, *14,* 181–182.

Bower, G. H., Clark, M. C., Lesgold, A. M., & Winzenz, D. Hierarchical retrieval schemes in recall of categorized word lists. *Journal of Verbal Learning and Verbal Behavior,* 1969, *8,* 323–343.

Bower, G. H., & Springston, F. Pauses as recoding points in letter series. *Journal of Experimental Psychology,* 1970, *83,* 421–430.

Bower, G. H., & Winzenz, D. Group structure, coding and memory for digit series. *Journal of Experimental Psychology Monograph Supplement,* 1969, *80,* 1–17.

Bower, G. H., & Winzenz, D. Comparison of associative learning strategies. *Psychonomic Science,* 1970, *20,* 2, 119–120.

Bradshaw, J. L. Three interrelated problems in reading: A review. *Memory & Cognition,* 1975, *3,* 123–134.

Bradshaw, J. L., & Nettleton, N. C. Articulatory interference and the MOWN-DOWN heterophone effect. *Journal of Experimental Psychology,* 1974, *102,* 88–94.

Bransford, J. D., Barclay, J. R., & Franks, J. J. Sentence memory: A constructive versus interpretive approach. *Cognitive Psychology,* 1972, *3,* 193–209.

Bransford, J. D., & Franks, J. J. Abstraction of linguistic ideas. *Cognitive Psychology,* 1971, *2,* 331–350.

Bransford, J. D., Franks, J. J., Morris, C. D., & Stein, B. S. Some general constraints on learning and memory research. In L. S. Cermak & F. I. M. Craik (Eds.), *Levels of processing in human memory.* Hillsdale, N.J.: Erlbaum, 1979.

Bransford, J. D., & Johnson, M. K. Contextual prerequisites for understanding: Some investigations of comprehension and recall. *Journal of Verbal Learning and Verbal Behavior,* 1972, *11,* 717–726.

Briggs, R. *Urban cognitive distances.* Unpublished doctoral dissertation, Ohio State University, 1971.

Broadbent, D. E. *Perception and communication.* New York: Pergamon, 1958.

Broadbent, D. E. The magic number seven after fifteen years. In A. Kennedy & A. Wilkes (Eds.), *Studies in long term memory.* London: Wiley, 1975.

Brooks, L. R. Spatial and verbal components of the act of recall. *Canadian Journal of Psychology,* 1968, *22,* 349–368.

Brown, A. L. The role of strategic behavior in retardate memory. In N. R. Ellis (Ed.), *International review of research in mental retardation* (Vol. 7). New York: Academic Press, 1974.

Brown, A. L. The development of memory: Knowing about knowing, and knowing how to know. In H. W. Reese (Ed.), *Advances in child development and behavior* (Vol. 10). New York: Academic Press, 1975.

Brown, A. L., Campione, J. C., Bray, N. W., & Wilcox, B. L. Keeping track of changing variables: Effects of rehearsal training and rehearsal prevention in normal and retarded adolescents. *Journal of Experimental Psychology,* 1973, *101,* 1, 123–131.

Brown, A. L., & Scott, M. S. Recognition memory for pictures in preschool children. *Journal of Experimental Child Psychology,* 1971, *11,* 401–412.

Brown, J. A. Some tests of the decay theory of immediate memory. *Quarterly Journal of Experimental Psychology,* 1958, *10,* 12–21.

Brown, J. A. (Ed.). *Recall and recognition.* London: Wiley, 1976.

Brown, P., & Fraser, C. Speech as a marker of situation. In K. R. Scherer & H. Giles (Eds.), *Social markers in speech.* Cambridge: Cambridge University Press, 1979.

Brown, R. Reference: In memorial tribute to Eric Lenneberg. *Cognition,* 1976, *4,* 125–153.

Brown, R., & Kulik, J. Flashbulb memories. *Cognition,* 1977, *5,* 73–99.

Brown, R., & Lenneberg, E. H. A study in language and cognition. *Journal of Abnormal and Social Psychology,* 1954, *49,* 454–462.

Brown, R., & McNeill, D. The "tip of the tongue" phenomenon. *Journal of Verbal Learning and Verbal Behavior,* 1966, *5,* 325–377.

Bruner, J. S., Goodnow, J. J., & Austin, G. A. *A study of thinking.* New York: Wiley, 1956.

Bull, B. L., & Wittrock, M. C. Imagery in the learning of verbal definitions. *British Journal of Educational Psychology,* 1973, *43,* 289–293.

Burns, D. D., & Beck, A. T. Cognitive behavior modification of mood disorders. In J. P. Foreyt & D. P. Rathjen (Eds.), *Cognitive behavior therapy.* New York: Plenum, 1978.

Buros, O. K. *Tests in print: II.* Highland Park, N.J.: Gryphon Press, 1972.

Cairns, H. S., & Kamerman, J. Lexical information processing during sentence comprehension. *Journal of Verbal Learning and Verbal Behavior,* 1975, *14,* 170–179.

Campione, J. C., & Brown, A. L. Training general metacognitive skills in retarded children. In M. M. Gruneberg, P. E. Morris, & R. N. Sykes (Eds.), *Practical aspects of memory.* London: Academic Press, 1978.

Canter, D., & Tagg, S. Distance estimation in cities. *Environment and Behavior,* 1975, *7,* 59–80.

Carey, S. The child as word learner. In M. Halle, J. Bresnan, & G. A. Miller (Eds.), *Linguistic theory and psychological reality.* Cambridge, Mass.: MIT Press, 1978.

Carpenter, P. A. On the comprehension, storage, retrieval of comparative sentences. *Journal of Verbal Learning and Verbal Behavior,* 1974, *13,* 401–411.

Carpenter, P. A., & Eisenberg, P. Mental rotation and the frame of reference in blind and sighted individuals. *Perception & Psychophysics,* 1978, *23,* 117–124.

Carr, T. H. Research on reading: Meaning, context effects, and comprehension. *Journal of Experimental Psychology: Human Perception and Performance,* 1981, *7,* 592–603.

Cautela, J. R. Covert conditioning: Assumptions and procedures. *Journal of Mental Imagery,* 1977, *1,* 53–64.

Cautela, J. R. Imagine you're better. (Review of *In the mind's eye: The power of imagery for personal enrichment* by A. Lazarus). *Contemporary Psychology,* 1979, *24,* 649–650.

Cerella, J. The pigeon's analysis of pictures. *Pattern Recognition,* 1980, *12,* 1–6.

Cermak, L. S. *Improving your memory.* New York: McGraw-Hill, 1976.

Chapman, L. J., & Chapman, J. P. Genesis of popular but erroneous psychodiagnostic observations. *Journal of Abnormal Psychology,* 1967, *72,* 193–204.

Chapman, L. J., & Chapman, J. P. Illusory correlations as an obstacle to the use of valid psychodiagnostic signs. *Journal of Abnormal Psychology,* 1969, *74,* 271–280.

Cherry, C. Some experiments on the recognition of speech with one and with two ears. *Journal of the Acoustical Society of America,* 1953, *25,* 975–979.

Chevalier, Z. W. *Can thinking be debugged?* Unpublished manuscript, Geneseo, N.Y., 1981.

Chickering, A. W. The double bind of field dependence/independence in program alternatives for educational development. In S. Messick & associates (Eds.), *Individuality in learning.* San Francisco: Jossey-Bass, 1976.

Chomsky, N. *Syntactic structures.* The Hague: Mouton, 1957.

Clark, E. V. Knowledge, context, and strategy in the acquisition of meaning. In D. P. Dato (Ed.), *Georgetown University Round Table on Languages and Linguistics 1975.* Washington, D.C.: Georgetown University Press, 1975.

Clark, H. H. Linguistic processes in deductive reasoning. *Psychological Review,* 1969, *76,* 387–404. (a)

Clark, H. H. Influence of language in solving three-term series problems. *Journal of Experimental Psychology,* 1969, *82,* 205–215. (b)

Clark, H. H., & Chase, W. G. On the process of comparing sentences against pictures. *Cognitive Psychology,* 1972, *3,* 472–517.

Clark, H. H., & Clark, E. V. *Psychology and language: An introduction to psycholinguistics.* New York: Harcourt Brace Jovanovich, 1977.

Cohen, L. B., & Gelber, E. R. Infant visual memory. In L. B. Cohen & P. Salapatek (Eds.), *Infant perception: From sensation to cognition.* New York: Academic Press, 1975.

Cohen, R. L., & Sandberg, T. Relation between intelligence and short-term memory. *Cognitive Psychology,* 1977, *9,* 534–554.

Cole, M., & Scribner, S. *Culture and thought.* New York: Wiley, 1974.

Cole, R. A. Listening for mispronunciations: A measure of what we hear during speech. *Perception & Psychophysics,* 1973, *14,* 153–156.

Cole, R. A., & Jakimik, J. A model of speech perception. In R. A. Cole (Ed.), *Perception and production of fluent speech.* Hillsdale, N.J.: Erlbaum, 1980.

Cole, R. A., & Scott, B. Toward a theory of speech perception. *Psychological Review,* 1974, *81,* 348–374.

Collins, A. M., & Loftus, E. F. A spreading-activation theory of semantic memory. *Psychological Review,* 1975, *82,* 407–428.

Collins, A. M., & Quillian, M. R. Retrieval time from semantic memory. *Journal of Verbal Learning and Verbal Behavior,* 1969, *8,* 240–248.

Condon, W. S., & Sander, L. W. Synchrony demonstrated between movements of the neonate and adult speech. *Child Development,* 1974, *45,* 456–462.

Conners, C. K. *Food additives and hyperactive children.* New York: Plenum, 1980.

Conrad, L., Trismen, D., & Miller, R. *Graduate Record Examinations technical manual.* Princeton, N.J.: Educational Testing Service, 1977.

Conrad, R. Acoustic confusions in immediate memory. *British Journal of Psychology,* 1964, *55,* 75–84.

Cooper, L. A., & Shepard, R. N. Chronometric studies of the rotation of mental images. In W. G. Chase (Ed.), *Visual information processing.* New York: Academic Press, 1973.

Corteen, R. S., & Wood, B. Autonomic responses to shock-associated words in an unattended channel. *Journal of Experimental Psychology,* 1972, *94,* 308–313.

Craik, F. I. M. Age differences in human memory. In J. E. Birren & K. W. Schaie (Eds.), *Handbook of the psychology of aging.* New York: Van Nostrand Reinhold, 1977.

Craik, F. I. M. Levels of processing: Overview and closing comments. In L. S. Cermak & F. I. M. Craik (Eds.), *Levels of processing in human memory.* Hillsdale, N.J.: Erlbaum, 1979.

Craik, F. I. M., & Levy, B. A. The concept of primary memory. In W. K. Estes (Ed.), *Handbook of learning and cognitive processes* (Vol. 4). Hillsdale, N.J.: Erlbaum, 1976.

Craik, F. I. M., & Lockhart, R. S. Levels of processing: A framework for memory research. *Journal of Verbal Learning and Verbal Behavior,* 1972, *11,* 671–684.

Craik, F. I. M., & Tulving, E. Depth of processing and the retention of words in episodic memory. *Journal of Experimental Psychology: General,* 1975, *104,* 268–294.

Craik, F. I. M., & Watkins, M. J. The role of rehearsal in short-term memory. *Journal of Verbal Learning and Verbal Behavior,* 1973, *12,* 599–607.

Crowder, R. G. Sensory memory systems. In E. C. Carterette & M. P. Friedman (Eds.), *Handbook of Perception* (Vol. 8). New York: Academic Press, 1978.

Crowder, R. G. Echoic memory and the study of aging memory systems. In L. W. Poon, J. L. Fozard, L. S. Cermak, D. Arenberg, & L. W. Thompson (Eds.), *New directions in memory and aging.* Hillsdale, N.J.: Erlbaum, 1980.

Cunningham, J. Nobel Prize for diplomatic clout. *Manchester Guardian,* October 11, 1977, p. 11.

Darwin, C. J. The perception of speech. In E. C. Carterette & M. P. Friedman (Eds.), *Handbook of perception* (Vol. 7). New York: Academic Press, 1976.

Darwin, C. J., Turvey, M. T., & Crowder, R. G. An auditory analogue of the Sperling partial report procedure: Evidence for brief auditory storage. *Cognitive Psychology,* 1972, *3,* 255–267.

Dasen, P. R. *Piagetian psychology: Cross-cultural contributions.* New York: Gardner, 1977.

Dawes, R. M. Shallow psychology. In J. S. Carroll & J. W. Payne (Eds.), *Cognition and social behavior.* Hillsdale, N.J.: Erlbaum, 1976.

Dawes, R. M. The robust beauty of improper linear models in decision making. *American Psychologist,* 1979, *34,* 571–582.

Deese, J. Cognitive structure and affect in language. In P. Pliner et al. (Eds.), *Communication and affect: Language and thought.* New York: Academic Press, 1973.

de Leeuw, L. Teaching problem solving: The effect of algorithmic and heuristic problem-solving training in relation to task complexity and relevant aptitudes. In A. M. Lesgold, J. W. Pellegrino, S. D. Fokkema, & R. Glaser (Eds.), *Cognitive psychology and instruction.* New York: Plenum, 1978.

Dember, W. N., & Warm, J. S. *Psychology of perception* (2nd ed.). New York: Holt, Rinehart and Winston, 1979.

Deregowski, J. B. In search of a wider perspective: Cross-cultural studies. In A. Burton & J. Radford (Eds.), *Thinking in perspective.* London: Methuen, 1978.

Deutsch, J. A., & Deutsch, D. Attention: Some theoretical considerations. *Psychological Review,* 1963, *70,* 80–90.

deVilliers, J. G., & deVilliers, P. A. *Language acquisition.* Cambridge, Mass.: Harvard University Press, 1978.

Dickstein, L. S. Effects of instructions and premise order on errors in syllogistic reasoning. *Journal of Experimental Psychology: Human Learning and Memory,* 1975, *1,* 376–384.

Dill, W. R., Hilton, T. L., & Reitman, W. R. *The new managers.* Englewood Cliffs, N.J.: Prentice-Hall, 1962.

Dillard, J. L. *Black English: Its history and usage in the United States.* New York: Random House, 1972.

Doctor, E. A., & Coltheart, M. Children's use of phonological encoding when reading for meaning. *Memory & Cognition,* 1980, *8,* 195–209.

Dominowski, R. L. How do people discover concepts? In R. L. Solso (Ed.), *Theories in cognitive psychology: The Loyola Symposium.* Hillsdale, N.J.: Erlbaum, 1974.

Dominowski, R. L. Reasoning. *Interamerican Journal of Psychology,* 1977, *11,* 68–77.

Donnell, M. L., & DuCharme, W. M. The effect of Bayesian feedback on learning in an odds estimation task. *Organizational Behavior and Human Performance,* 1975, *14,* 305–313.

Dooling, D. J., & Christiaansen, R. E. Levels of encoding and retention of prose. In G. H. Bower (Ed.), *The psychology of learning and motivation: Advances in research and theory* (Vol. 11). New York: Academic Press, 1977.

Downs, R. M., & Stea, D. *Maps in minds: Reflections on cognitive mapping.* New York: Harper & Row, 1977.

Duncker, K. On problem solving. *Psychological Monographs,* 1945, *58* (Whole No. 270).

Eimas, P. D., Siqueland, E. R., Jusczyk, P., & Vigorito, J. Speech perception in infants. *Science,* 1971, *171,* 303–306.

Eimas, P. D., & Tartter, V. C. On the development of speech perception: Mechanisms and analogies. In H. W. Reese & L. P. Lipsitt (Eds.), *Advances in child development and behavior.* New York: Academic Press, 1979.

Einhorn, H. J. Learning from experience and suboptimal rules in decision making. In T. S. Wallsten (Ed.), *Cognitive processes in choice and decision behavior.* Hillsdale, N.J.: Erlbaum, 1980.

Einhorn, H. J., & Hogarth, R. M. Confidence in judgment: Persistence of the illusion of validity. *Psychological Review,* 1978, *85,* 395–416.

Einhorn, H. J., & Hogarth, R. M. Behavioral decision theory: Processes of judgment and choice. *Annual Review of Psychology,* 1981, *32,* 53–88.

Einstein, A., & Infeld, L. *The evolution of physics.* New York: Simon and Schuster, 1938.

Engen, T., & Ross, B. M. Long-term memory of odors with and without verbal descriptions. *Journal of Experimental Psychology,* 1973, *100,* 221–227.

Erickson, J. R. A set analysis of behavior in formal syllogistic reasoning tasks. In R. L. Solso (Ed.), *Theories in cognitive psychology: The Loyola Symposium.* Hillsdale, N.J.: Erlbaum, 1974.

Erickson, J. R. Research on syllogistic reasoning. In R. Revlin & R. E. Mayer (Eds.), *Human reasoning.* Washington, D.C.: V. H. Winston & Sons, 1978.

Erickson, R. C., & Scott, M. L. Clinical memory testing: A review. *Psychological Bulletin,* 1977, *84,* 1130–1149.

Ervin-Tripp, S. On sociolinguistic rules: Alternation and co-occurrence. In J. J. Gumperz & D. Hymes (Eds.), *Directions in sociolinguistics.* New York: Holt, Rinehart and Winston, 1972.

Ervin-Tripp, S. Is Sybil there? The structure of some American English directives. *Language in Society,* 1976, *5,* 25–66.

Estes, W. K. Perceptual processing in letter recognition and reading. In E. C. Carterette & M. P. Friedman (Eds.), *Handbook of perception* (Vol. 9). New York: Academic Press, 1978.

Evans, J. St. B. T. Reasoning with negatives. *British Journal of Psychology,* 1972, *63,* 213–219.

Eysenck, M. W. Arousal, learning, and memory. *Psychological Bulletin,* 1976, *83,* 389–404. (a)

Eysenck, M. W. Extraversion, verbal learning, and memory. *Psychological Bulletin,* 1976, *83,* 75–90. (b)

Fagan, J. F. Infants' delayed recognition memory and forgetting. *Journal of Experimental Child Psychology,* 1973, *16,* 424–450.

Feingold, B. Food additives and child development. *Hospital Practice,* 1973, *8,* 10.

File, S. E., & Jew, A. Syntax and the recall of instructions in a realistic situation. *British Journal of Psychology,* 1973, *64,* 65–70.

Fillmore, C. J., Kempler, D., & Wang, W. S-Y. *Individual differences in language ability and language behavior.* New York: Academic Press, 1979.

Fischhoff, B. The silly certainty of hindsight. *Psychology Today,* April 1975, *8,* 71–72, 76.

Fischhoff, B. Perceived informativeness of facts. *Journal of Experimental Psychology: Human Perception and Performance,* 1977, *3,* 349–358.

Fischhoff, B., Slovic, P., & Lichtenstein, S. Weighing the risks. *Environment,* 1979, *21,* 17–38.

Fisher, D. F. In the beginning was the word: Basic processes in reading. *Journal of Experimental Psychology: Human Perception and Performance,* 1981, *7,* 489–494.

Flagg, P. W., Potts, G. R., & Reynolds, A. G. Instructions and response strategies in recognition memory for sentences. *Journal of Experimental Psychology: Human Learning and Memory,* 1975, *1,* 592–598.

Flavell, J. H. *The developmental psychology of Jean Piaget.* Princeton, N.J.: Van Nostrand, 1963.

Flavell, J. H. *Cognitive development.* Englewood Cliffs, N.J.: Prentice-Hall, 1977.

Flavell, J. H. Metacognition and cognitive monitoring. *American Psychologist,* 1979, *34,* 906–911.

Flavell, J. H., Beach, D. R., & Chinsky, J. M. Spontaneous verbal rehearsal in a memory task as a function of age. *Child Development,* 1966, *37,* 283–299.

Flavell, J. H., & Wellman, H. M. Metamemory. In R. V. Kail, Jr., & J. W. Hagen (Eds.), *Perspectives on the development of memory and cognition.* Hillsdale, N.J.: Erlbaum, 1977.

Flexser, A. J., & Tulving, E. Retrieval independence in recognition and recall. *Psychological Review,* 1978, *85,* 153–171.

Flynn, J. R. *Race, IQ, and Jensen.* London: Routledge, 1980.

Fodor, J. A., Bever, T. G., & Garrett, M. F. *The psychology of language: An introduction to psycholinguistics and generative grammar.* New York: McGraw-Hill, 1974.

Folb, E. A. *Runnin' down some lines: The language and culture of black teenagers.* Cambridge, Mass.: Harvard University Press, 1980.

Forgus, R., & Shulman, B. H. *Personality: A cognitive view.* Englewood Cliffs, N.J.: Prentice-Hall, 1979.

Foss, D. J. Some effects of ambiguity upon sentence comprehension. *Journal of Verbal Learning and Verbal Behavior,* 1970, *9,* 699–706.

Foss, D. J., & Hakes, D. T. *Psycholinguistics: An introduction to the psychology of language.* Englewood Cliffs, N.J.: Prentice-Hall, 1978.

Franks, J. J., & Bransford, J. D. Abstraction of visual patterns. *Journal of Experimental Psychology,* 1971, *90,* 65–74.

Frase, L. T. Inference and reading. In R. Revlin & R. E. Mayer (Eds.), *Human reasoning.* Washington, D.C.: V. H. Winston & Sons, 1978.

Freibergs, V., & Tulving, E. The effect of practice on utilization of information from positive and negative instances in concept identification. *Canadian Journal of Psychology,* 1961, *15,* 101–106.

Friedman, M. Every author's perfect dream comes true. *San Francisco Sunday Examiner & Chronicle,* August 7, 1977, p. 3 of *Scene.*

Furth, H. G., & Wachs, H. *Thinking goes to school: Piaget's theory in practice.* New York: Oxford University Press, 1975.

Gardner, B. T., & Gardner, R. A. Evidence for sentence constitutents in the early utterances of child and chimpanzee. *Journal of Experimental Psychology: General,* 1975, *104,* 244–267.

Garner, W. R. Letter discrimination and identification. In A. D. Pick (Ed.), *Perception and its development: A tribute to Eleanor J. Gibson.* Hillsdale, N.J.: Erlbaum, 1979.

Garrett, M. F. The analysis of sentence production. In G. H. Bower (Ed.), *The psychology of learning and motivation* (Vol. 9). New York: Academic Press, 1975.

Garrity, L. I. An electromyographical study of subvocal speech and recall in preschool children. *Developmental Psychology,* 1975, *11,* 274–281.

Gelman, R. Cognitive development. *Annual Review of Psychology,* 1978, *29,* 297–332.

Gelman, R. Preschool thought. *American Psychologist,* 1979, *34,* 900–905.

Getzels, J., & Csikszentmihalyi, M. From problem solving to problem finding. In I. Taylor & J. Getzels (Eds.), *Perspectives in creativity.* Chicago: Aldine, 1975.

Ghiselin, B. *The creative process.* New York: Mentor, 1952.

Ghiselin, B. Ultimate criteria for two levels of creativity. In C. Taylor (Ed.), *The Second (1957) University of Utah Research Conference on the Identification of Creative Scientific Talent.* Salt Lake City: University of Utah Press, 1958.

Gibson, E. J. *Principles of perceptual learning and development.* New York: Prentice-Hall, 1969.

Gibson, E. J., & Levin, H. *The psychology of reading.* Cambridge, Mass.: MIT Press, 1975.

Ginsburg, H., & Koslowski, B. Cognitive development. *Annual Review of Psychology,* 1976, *27,* 29–61.

Ginsburg, H., & Opper, S. *Piaget's theory of intellectual development: An introduction.* Englewood Cliffs, N.J.: Prentice-Hall, 1969.

Gittelman-Klein, R., Klein, D. F., Abikoff, H., Katz, S., Gloisten, A. C., & Kates, W. Relative efficacy of methylphenidate and behavior modification in hyperkinetic children: An interim report. *Journal of Abnormal Child Psychology,* 1976, *4,* 361–379.

Gleason, J. B., & Weintraub, S. The acquisition of routines in child language. *Language in Society,* 1976, *5,* 129–136.

Glenberg, A., Smith, S. M., & Green, C. Type I rehearsal: Maintenance and more. *Journal of Verbal Learning and Verbal Behavior,* 1977, *16,* 339–352.

Goldstein, E. B. *Sensation and perception.* Belmont, Calif.: Wadsworth, 1980.

Goldstein, K. M., & Blackman, S. *Cognitive style: Five approaches and relevant research.* New York: Wiley, 1978.

Golledge, R. G., & Zannaras, G. Cognitive approaches to the analysis of human spatial behavior. In W. H. Ittelson (Ed.), *Environment and cognition.* New York: Seminar Press, 1973, 59–94.

Goodenough, D. R. The role of individual differences in field dependence as a factor in learning and memory. *Psychological Bulletin,* 1976, *83,* 675–694.

Goodman, P., Furcon, J., & Rose, J. Examination of some measures of creative ability by the multimethod matrix. *Journal of Applied Psychology,* 1969, *5,* 240–243.

Gordon, R. A very private world. In P. W. Sheehan (Ed.), *The function and nature of imagery.* New York: Academic Press, 1972.

Gordon, S. K., & Clark, W. C. Application of signal detection theory analysis to prose recall and recognition in aged and young adults. *Journal of Gerontology,* 1974, *29,* 64–72.

Gordon, W. J. J. *Synectics: The development of creative capacity.* New York: Harper & Row, 1961.

Gottfried, A. W., & Rose, S. A. Tactile recognition memory in infants. *Child Development,* 1980, *51,* 69–74.

Grady, K. E. *The belief in sex differences.* Paper presented at the meeting of the Eastern Psychological Association, Boston, April 1977.

Greenberg, J. H. Some universals of grammar with particular reference to the order of meaningful elements. In J. H. Greenberg (Ed.), *Universals of language.* Cambridge, Mass.: MIT Press, 1963.

Greenberg, J. H. *Language universals.* The Hague: Mouton, 1966.

Greeno, J. G. Hobbits and Orcs: Acquisition of a sequential concept. *Cognitive Psychology,* 1974, *6,* 270–292.

Greeno, J. G. Indefinite goals in well-structured problems. *Psychological Review,* 1976, *83,* 479–491.

Greeno, J. G. Process of understanding in problem solving. In N. J. Castellan, Jr., D. B. Pisoni, & G. R. Potts (Eds.), *Cognitive theory* (Vol. 2). Hillsdale, N.J.: Erlbaum, 1977.

Groninger, L. D. Mnemonic imagery and forgetting. *Psychonomic Science,* 1971, *23,* 161–163.

Gruneberg, M. M. The feeling of knowing, memory blocks and memory aids. In M. M. Greenberg & P. Morris (Eds.), *Aspects of memory.* London: Methuen, 1978.

Guilford, J. P. *The nature of human intelligence.* New York: McGraw-Hill, 1967.

Haber, R. N., & Hershenson, M. *The psychology of visual perception* (2d ed.). New York: Holt, Rinehart and Winston, 1980.

Hagen, J. W., & Stanovich, K. G. Memory: Strategies of acquisition. In R. V. Kail, Jr. & J. W. Hagen (Eds.), *Perspectives on the development of memory and cognition.* Hillsdale, N.J.: Erlbaum, 1977.

Halle, M., & Stevens, K. N. Speech recognition: A model and a program for research. In J. A. Fodor & J. J. Katz (Eds.), *The structure of language: Readings in the philosophy of language.* Englewood Cliffs, N.J.: Prentice-Hall, 1964.

Hardyck, C. D., & Petrinovitch, L. R. Subvocal speech and comprehension level as a function of the difficulty level of reading material. *Journal of Verbal Learning and Verbal Behavior,* 1970, *9,* 647–652.

Harris, J. E. External memory aids. In M. M. Gruneberg, P. E. Morris, & R. N. Sykes (Eds.), *Practical aspects of memory.* London: Academic Press, 1978.

Harris, L. J. Sex differences in the growth and use of language. In E. Donelson & J. Gullahorn (Eds.), *Women: A psychological perspective.* New York: Wiley, 1977.

Harris, P. L. Developmental aspects of memory: A review. In M. M. Gruneberg, P. E. Morris, & R. N. Sykes (Eds.), *Practical aspects of memory.* London: Academic Press, 1978.

Harris, R. J. Comprehension of pragmatic implications in advertising. *Journal of Applied Psychology,* 1977, *62,* 603–608.

Harris, R. J., & Monaco, G. E. The psychology of pragmatic implication: Information processing between the lines. *Journal of Experimental Psychology: General,* 1978, *107,* 1–22.

Harris, R. J., Teske, R. R., & Ginns, M. J. Memory for pragmatic implications from courtroom testimony. *Bulletin of the Psychonomic Society,* 1975, *6,* 494–496.

Harrison, D. S., & Trabasso, T. *Black English: A seminar.* New York: Wiley, 1976.

Haviland, S. E., & Clark, H. H. What's new? Acquiring new information as a process in comprehension. *Journal of Verbal Learning and Verbal Behavior,* 1974, *13,* 512–521.

Hayes, C. *The ape in our house.* New York: Harper & Row, 1951.

Hayes, J. R. *Cognitive psychology: Thinking and creating.* Homewood, Ill.: Dorsey Press, 1978.

Hayes, J. R., & Simon, H. A. Psychological differences among problem solving isomorphs. In N. Castellan, Jr., D. Pisoni, & G. Potts (Eds.), *Cognitive theory* (Vol. 2). Hillsdale, N.J.: Erlbaum, 1977.

Haygood, R. C., & Bourne, L. E., Jr. Attribute and rule learning aspects of conceptual behavior. *Psychological Review,* 1965, *72,* 175–195.

Hearst, E. One hundred years: Themes and perspectives. In E. Hearst (Ed.), *The first century of experimental psychology.* Hillsdale, N.J.: Erlbaum, 1979.

Heider, E. R. Universals in color naming and memory. *Journal of Experimental Psychology,* 1972, *93,* 10–20.

Helsabeck, F., Jr. Syllogistic reasoning: Generation of counterexamples. *Journal of Educa-*

tional Psychology, 1975, *67,* 102–108.

Hendrick, C. (Ed.). *Perspectives on social psychology.* Hillsdale, N.J.: Erlbaum, 1977.

Henley, N. M. A psychological study of the semantics of animal terms. *Journal of Verbal Learning and Verbal Behavior,* 1969, *8,* 176–184.

Henley, N. M. *Body politics: Power, sex, and nonverbal communication.* Englewood Cliffs, N.J.: Prentice-Hall, 1977.

Hermnstein, R. J. *Natural concepts in pigeons.* Paper presented at S.U.N.Y. Geneseo, 1978.

Hermnstein, R. J., Loveland, D. H., & Cable, D. Natural concepts in pigeons. *Journal of Experimental Psychology: Animal Behavior Processes,* 1976, *2,* 285–302.

Higbee, K. L. *Your memory: How it works and how to improve it.* Englewood Cliffs, N.J.: Prentice-Hall, 1977.

Higbee, K. L. Some pseudo-limitations of mnemonics. In M. M. Gruneberg, P. E. Morris, & R. N. Sykes (Eds.), *Practical aspects of memory.* London: Academic Press, 1978.

Hilgard, E. R. Consciousness in contemporary psychology. *Annual Review of Psychology,* 1980, *31,* 1–26.

Hill, J. W., & Bliss, J. C. Modeling a tactile sensory register. *Perception & Psychophysics,* 1968, *4,* 91–101.

Hill, P., Bedau, H., Checile, R., Crochetiere, W., Kellerman, B., Ounjian, D., Pauker, S., Pauker, S., & Rubin, J. *Making decisions: A multidisciplinary introduction.* Reading, Mass.: Addison-Wesley, 1979.

Hinsley, D., Hayes, J. R., & Simon, H. A. From words to equations: Meaning and representation in algebra word problems. In P. Carpenter & M. Just (Eds.), *Cognitive processes in comprehension.* Hillsdale, N.J.: Erlbaum, 1977.

Hirschberg, N. W. Predicting performance in graduate school. Human judgment and decision processes in applied settings. In M. F. Kaplan & S. Schwartz (Eds.), *Human judgment and decision processes in applied settings.* New York: Academic Press, 1977.

Holton, G. On trying to understand scientific genius. *American Scholar,* 1972, *41,* 95–110.

Hooper, D. *A pedestrian's view of New York, London and Paris.* Unpublished manuscript, Harvard University, 1966. Cited in S. Milgram, The experience of living in cities. *Science,* 1970, *167,* 1468.

Hornby, P. A. Surface structure and presupposition. *Journal of Verbal Learning and Verbal Behavior,* 1974, *13,* 530–538.

Horowitz, L. M. *Elements of statistics for psychology and education.* New York: McGraw-Hill, 1974.

Hovland, C. I., & Weiss, W. Transmission of information concerning concepts through positive and negative instances. *Journal of Experimental Psychology,* 1953, *43,* 175–182.

Hoyer, W. J., Rebok, G. W., & Sved, S. M. Effects of varying irrelevant information on adult age differences in problem solving. *Journal of Gerontology,* 1979, *34,* 553–560.

Hubel, D. H., & Wiesel, T. N. Receptive fields and functional architecture of monkey striate cortex. *Journal of Psychology,* 1968, *195,* 215–243.

Hudgins, B. B. *Learning and thinking: A primer for teachers.* Itasca, Ill.: Peacock, 1977.

Hulicka, I. M., & Grossman, J. L. Age-group comparison for the use of mediators in paired-associate learning. *Journal of Gerontology,* 1967, *22,* 46–57.

Hulse, S. H., Fowler, H., & Honig, W. K. *Cognitive processes in animal behavior.* Hillsdale, N.J.: Erlbaum, 1978.

Hunt, E. Mechanics of verbal ability. *Psychological Review,* 1978, *85,* 109–130.

Hunt, E., Lunneborg, C., & Lewis, J. What does it mean to be high verbal? *Cognitive Psychology,* 1975, *7,* 194–227.

Hunter, I. M. L. Imagery comprehension and mnemonics. *Journal of Mental Imagery,* 1977, *1,* 65–72.

Huttenlocher, J., & Burke, D. Why does memory span increase with age? *Cognitive Psychology,* 1976, *8,* 1–31.

Irwin, M. H., & McLaughlin, D. H. Ability and preference in category sorting by Mano school children and adults. *Journal of Social Psychology,* 1970, *82,* 15−24.

James, W. *The principles of psychology.* New York: Henry Holt, 1890.

Jarvella, R. J. Syntactic processing of connected speech. *Journal of Verbal Learning and Verbal Behavior,* 1971, *10,* 409−416.

Jaynes, J. *The origin of consciousness in the breakdown of the bicameral mind.* Boston: Houghton Mifflin, 1976.

Jenkins, J. J. Remember that old theory of memory? Well, forget it. *American Psychologist,* 1974, *29,* 785−795.

Jensen, A. R. Interaction of level I and level II abilities with race and socioeconomic status. *Journal of Educational Psychology,* 1974, *66,* 99−111.

Jensen, A. R. *Bias in mental testing.* New York: Free Press, 1980.

Johnson-Laird, P. N. Models of deduction. In R. J. Falmagne (Ed.), *Reasoning: Representation and process in children and adults.* Hillsdale, N.J.: Erlbaum, 1975.

Johnson-Laird, P. N., Legrenzi, P., & Sonino Legrenzi, M. Reasoning and a sense of reality. *British Journal of Psychology,* 1972, *63,* 395−400.

Johnson-Laird, P. N., & Steedman, M. The psychology of syllogisms. *Cognitive Psychology,* 1978, *10,* 64−99.

Johnson-Laird, P. N., & Wason, P. C. Introduction to conceptual thinking. In P. N. Johnson-Laird & P. C. Wason (Eds.), *Thinking: Readings in cognitive science.* Cambridge: Cambridge University Press, 1977. (a)

Johnson-Laird, P. N., & Wason, P. C. A theoretical analysis of insight into a reasoning task, and postscript. In P. N. Johnson-Laird & P. C. Wason (Eds.), *Thinking: Readings in cognitive science.* Cambridge: Cambridge University Press, 1977. (b)

Jonides, J., Kahn, R., & Rozin, P. Imagery instructions improve memory in blind subjects. *Bulletin of the Psychonomic Society,* 1975, *5,* 424−426.

Kagan, J., Rosman, B. L., Day, D., Albert, J., & Phillips, W. Information processing in the child: Significance of analytic and reflective attitudes. *Psychological Monographs,* 1964, *78* (1, Whole No. 578).

Kahneman, D. *Attention and effort.* Englewood Cliffs, N.J.: Prentice-Hall, 1973.

Kahneman, D., & Tversky, A. Subjective probability: A judgment of representativeness. *Cognitive Psychology,* 1972, *3,* 430−454.

Kahneman, D., & Tversky, A. On the psychology of prediction. *Psychological Review,* 1973, *80,* 237−251.

Kahneman, D., & Tversky, A. Prospect theory: An analysis of decision under risk. *Econometrica,* 1979, *47,* 263−291.

Kail, R. V., Jr. *The development of memory in children.* San Francisco: Freeman, 1979.

Kail, R. V., Jr., & Siegel, A. W. The development of mnemonic encoding in children: From perception to abstraction. In R. V. Kail, Jr., & J. W. Hagen (Eds.), *Perspectives on the development of memory and cognition.* Hillsdale, N.J.: Erlbaum, 1977.

Kamin, L. *The science and politics of IQ.* Hillsdale, N.J.: Erlbaum, 1975.

Keil, F. C. *Semantic and conceptual development: An ontological perspective.* Cambridge, Mass.: Harvard University Press, 1979.

Kemper, S., & Thissen, D. *Dimensions of requests.* Manuscript submitted for publication, 1980.

Kesler, M. S., Denney, N. W., & Whitely, S. E. Factors influencing problem solving in middle-aged and elderly adults. *Human Development,* 1976, *19,* 310−320.

Kimball, J. P. Seven principles of surface structure parsing in natural language. *Cognition,* 1973, *2,* 15−47.

Kintsch, W. Recognition and free recall of organized lists. *Journal of Experimental Psychology,* 1968, *78,* 481−487.

Kintsch, W., & Bates, E. Recognition memory for statements from a classroom lecture. *Journal of Experimental Psychology: Human Learning and Memory,* 1977, *3,* 150−159.

Kintsch, W., & Buschke, H. Homophones and synonyms in short-term memory. *Journal of*

Experimental Psychology, 1969, *80,* 403−407.

Klahr, D., & Wallace, J. G. *Cognitive development: An information-processing view.* Hillsdale, N.J.: Erlbaum, 1976.

Klatzky, R. L. *Human memory: Structures and processes* (2d ed.). San Francisco: Freeman, 1980.

Knafl, K., & Burkett, G. Professional socialization in a surgical specialty: Acquiring medical judgment. *Social Science and Medicine,* 1975, *9,* 397−404.

Kobasigawa, A. Utilization of retrieval cues by children in recall. *Child Development,* 1974, *45,* 127−134.

Kobasigawa, A. Retrieval strategies in the developmment of memory. In R. V. Kail, Jr., & J. W. Hagen (Eds.), *Perspectives on the development of memory and cognition.* Hillsdale: N.J.: Erlbaum, 1977.

Koestler, A. *The act of creation.* London: Hutchinson, 1964.

Kogan, N. *Cognitive styles in infancy and early childhood.* Hillsdale, N.J.: Erlbaum, 1976.

Kopell, S. Testing the attentional deficit notion. *Journal of Learning Disabilities,* 1979, *12,* 52−57.

Kosslyn, S. M. Information representation in visual images. *Cognitive Psychology,* 1975, *7,* 341−370.

Kosslyn, S. M. Using imagery to retrieve semantic information: A developmental study. *Child Development,* 1976, *47,* 433−444.

Kosslyn, S. M. *Image and mind.* Cambridge, Mass.: Harvard University Press, 1980.

Kosslyn, S. M., & Pomerantz, J. R. Imagery, propositions and the form of internal representations. *Cognitive Psychology,* 1977, *9,* 52−76.

Kosslyn, S. M., & Shwartz, S. P. A simulation of visual imagery. *Cognitive Science,* 1977, *1,* 265−295.

Kozlowski, L. T., & Bryant, K. J. Sense of direction, spatial orientation, and cognitive maps. *Journal of Experimental Psychology: Human Perception and Performance,* 1977, *3,* 590−598.

Kreutzer, M. A., Leonard, C., & Flavell, J. H. An interview study of children's knowledge about memory. *Monographs of the Society for Research in Child Development,* 1975, *40*(1, Serial No. 159).

Kubovy, M., & Howard, F. P. Persistence of a pitch-segregating echoic memory. *Journal of Experimental Psychology: Human Perception and Performance,* 1976, *2,* 531−537.

Kuhn, D. Inducing development experimentally: Comments on a research paradigm. *Developmental Psychology,* 1974, *10,* 590−600.

LaBerge, D., & Samuels, S. J. Toward a theory of automatic information processing in reading. *Cognitive Psychology,* 1974, *6,* 293−323.

LaBerge, D., & Samuels, S. J. *Basic processes in reading: Perception and comprehension.* Hillsdale, N.J.: Erlbaum, 1977.

Labov, W. The logic of nonstandard English. In F. Williams (Ed.), *Language and poverty: Perspectives on a theme.* Chicago: Markham, 1970.

Labov, W. The boundaries of words and their meanings. In C.-J. N. Bailey & R. W. Shuy (Eds.), *New ways of analyzing variation in English.* Washington, D.C.: Georgetown University Press, 1973.

Lachman, J. L., & Lachman, R. Age and the actualization of world knowledge. In L. W. Poon, J. L. Fozard, L. S. Cermak, D. Arenberg, & L. W. Thompson (Eds.), *New directions in memory and aging.* Hillsdale, N.J.: Erlbaum, 1980.

Lachman, R., Lachman, J. L., & Butterfield, E. C. *Cognitive psychology and information processing: An introduction.* Hillsdale, N.J.: Erlbaum, 1979.

Langer, E. J., Rodin, J., Beck, P., Weinman, C., & Spitzer, L. Environmental determinants of memory improvement in late adulthood. *Journal of Personality and Social Psychology,* 1979, *37,* 2003−2013.

Larsen, S. F., & Fromholt, P. Mnemonic organization and free recall in schizophrenia. *Journal of Abnormal Psychology,* 1976, *85,* 61−65.

Laughlin, P. R. Focusing strategy in concept attainment as a function of instructions and task complexity. *Journal of Experimental Psychology,* 1973, *98,* 320–327.

Laughlin, P. R., Chenoweth, R. E., Farrell, B. B., & McGrath, J. E. Concept attainment as a function of motivation and task complexity. *Journal of Experimental Psychology,* 1972, *96,* 54–59.

Lawrence, D. M., & Banks, W. P. Accuracy of recognition memory for common sounds. *Bulletin of the Psychonomic Society,* 1973, *1,* 298–300.

Lawton, J. T., & Hooper, F. H. Piagetian theory and early childhood education: A critical analysis. In L. S. Siegel & C. J. Brainerd (Eds.), *Alternatives to Piaget.* New York: Academic Press, 1978.

Lazarus, A. *In the mind's eye: The power of imagery for personal enrichment.* New York: Rawson, 1978.

L'Estrange, R. *Fables of Aesop.* New York: Dover, 1692/1967.

Levine, M. A. Hypothesis behavior by humans during discrimination learning. *Journal of Experimental Psychology,* 1966, *71,* 331–338.

Levine, M. A. *A cognitive theory of learning.* Hillsdale, N.J.: Erlbaum, 1975.

Lewis, D. J. Psychobiology of active and inactive memory. *Psychological Bulletin,* 1979, *86,* 1054–1083.

Liben, L. S., & Drury, A. M. Short-term memory in deaf and hearing children in relation to stimulus characteristics. *Journal of Experimental Child Psychology,* 1977, *24,* 60–73.

Liberman, A. M. The grammars of language and speech. *Cognitive Psychology,* 1970, *1,* 301–323.

Lichtenstein, S., & Slovic, P. Response-induced reversals of preference in gambling: An extended replication in Las Vegas. *Journal of Experimental Psychology,* 1973, *101,* 16–20.

Linde, C., & Labov, W. Spatial networks as a site for the study of language and thought. *Language,* 1975, *51,* 924–939.

Lindsley, J. R. Producing simple utterances: How far ahead do we plan? *Cognitive Psychology,* 1975, *7,* 1–19.

Lippman, M. F. The influence of grammatical transform in a syllogistic reasoning task. *Journal of Verbal Learning and Verbal Behavior,* 1972, *11,* 424–430.

Locurto, C. M., & Walsh, J. F. Reinforcement and self-reinforcement: Their effects on originality. *American Journal of Psychology,* 1976, *89,* 281–291.

Loftus, E. F. Spreading activation within semantic categories: Comments on Rosch's "Cognitive representations of semantic categories." *Journal of Experimental Psychology,* 1975, *104,* 234–240.

Loftus, E. F. *Eyewitness testimony.* Cambridge, Mass.: Harvard University Press, 1979.

Loftus, E. F., & Loftus, G. R. On the permanence of stored information in the human brain. *American Psychologist,* 1980, 409–420.

Loftus, E. F., Miller, D. G., & Burns, H. J. Semantic integration of verbal information into a visual memory. *Journal of Experimental Psychology: Human Learning and Memory,* 1978, *4,* 19–31.

Loudon, D. L., & Della Bitta, A. J. *Consumer behavior: Concepts and applications.* New York: McGraw-Hill, 1979.

Luchins, A. S. Mechanization in problem solving. *Psychological Monographs,* 1942, 54 (Whole No. 248).

Luria, A. R. *The mind of a mnemonist: A little book about a vast memory.* New York: Basic Books, 1968.

Lynch, K. *The image of the city.* Cambridge, Mass.: MIT Press, 1960.

Maccoby, E. E., & Jacklin, C. N. *The psychology of sex differences.* Stanford, Calif.: Stanford University Press, 1974.

Mackworth, N. Originality. *American Psychologist,* 1965, *20,* 51–66.

Mackay, H., & Osgood, C. E. Hesitation phenomena in spontaneous English speech. *Word,* 1959, *15,* 19–44.

MacNeilage, P., & Ladefoged, P. The production of speech and language. In E. C. Carterette & M. P. Friedman (Eds.), *Handbook of perception* (Vol. 7). New York: Academic Press, 1976.

Maier, N. R. F. Reasoning in humans: II. The solution of a problem and its appearance in consciousness. *Journal of Comparative Psychology,* 1931, *12,* 181–194.

Mandler, G. Organization and repetition: Organizational principles with special reference to rote learning. In L. G. Nilsson (Ed.), *Perspectives on memory research: Essays in honor of Uppsala University's 500th Anniversary.* Hillsdale, N.J.: Erlbaum, 1979.

Manis, M., Dovalina, I., Avis, N. E., & Cardoze, S. Base rates can affect individual predictions. *Journal of Personality and Social Psychology,* 1980, *38,* 231–248.

Markman, E. M., & Seibert, J. Classes and collections: Internal organization and resulting holistic properties. *Cognitive Psychology,* 1976, *8,* 561–577.

Marks, D. F. Imagery and consciousness: A theoretical review from an individual differences perspective. *Journal of Mental Imagery,* 1977, *1,* 275–290.

Martin, E. Toward an analysis of subjective phrase structure. *Psychological Bulletin,* 1970, *74,* 153–166.

Martin, M. Speech recoding in silent reading. *Memory & Cognition,* 1978, *6,* 108–114.

Marx, J. L. Ape-language controversy flares up. *Science,* 1980, *207,* 1330–1333.

Mason, M. From print to sound in mature readers as a function of reader ability and two forms of orthographic regularity. *Memory & Cognition,* 1978, *6,* 568–581.

Massaro, D. W. Preperceptual auditory images. *Journal of Experimental Psychology,* 1970, *85,* 411–417.

Matlin, M. W. *Human experimental psychology.* Monterey, Calif.: Brooks/Cole, 1979.

Matlin, M. W. *Perception.* Boston: Allyn & Bacon, in press.

Matlin, M. W., & Stang, D. J. *The Pollyanna Principle: Selectivity in language, memory, and thought.* Cambridge, Mass.: Schenkman, 1978.

Matlin, M. W., Stang, D. J., Gawron, V. J., Freedman, A., & Derby, P. L. Evaluative meaning as a determinant of spew position. *Journal of General Psychology,* 1979, *100,* 3–11.

McArthur, L. Z. Illusory causation and illusory correlation: Two epistemological accounts. *Personality and Social Psychology Bulletin,* 1980, *6,* 507–519.

McCall, R. Mavis Hetherington: Tracking children through the changing family. *APA Monitor,* May 1981, *12,* 4–5.

McCauley, C., & Jacques, S. The popularity of conspiracy theories of presidential assassination: A Bayesian analysis. *Journal of Personality and Social Psychology,* 1979, *37,* 637–644.

McConnell, J. V. *Understanding human behavior* (3d ed.). New York: Holt, Rinehart and Winston, 1980.

McKellar, P. Imagery from the standpoint of introspection. In P. W. Sheehan (Ed.), *The function and nature of imagery.* New York: Academic Press, 1972.

McKim, R. H. Thinking visually: A strategy manual for problem solving. Belmont, Calif.: Wadsworth, 1980.

Meacham, J. A. Patterns of memory abilities in two cultures. *Developmental Psychology,* 1975, *11,* 50–53.

Mednick, S. A. The associative basis of the creative process. *Psychological Review,* 1962, *69,* 220–232.

Mednick, S. A., & Mednick, M. T. *Examiner's manual, Remote Associates Test.* Boston, Mass.: Houghton Mifflin, 1967.

Mehler, J. Some effects of grammatical transformation on the recall of English sentences. *Journal of Verbal Learning and Verbal Behavior,* 1963, *2,* 346–351.

Meichenbaum, D. Self-instructional strategy training: A cognitive prothesis for the aged. *Human Development,* 1974, *17,* 273–280.

Menzel, E. W. Chimpanzee spatial memory organization. *Science,* 1973, *182,* 943–945.

Mervis, C. B., Catlin, J., & Rosch, E. Relationships among goodness-of-example, category norms, and word frequency. *Bulletin of the Psychonomic Society,* 1976, *7,* 283–284.

Messer, S. B. Reflection-impulsivity: A review. *Psychological Bulletin,* 1976, *83,* 1026–1052.

Messick, D. M., & Campos, F. T. Training and conservatism in subjective probability revision. *Journal of Experimental Psychology,* 1972, *94,* 335–337.

Messick, S. Personality consistencies in cognition and creativity. In S. Messick & Associates (Eds.), *Individuality in learning.* San Francisco: Jossey-Bass, 1976.

Meyer, D. E. On the representation and retrieval of stored semantic information. *Cognitive Psychology,* 1970, *1,* 242–300.

Meyer, J. S. Visual and verbal processes involved in the development of picture-recognition skills. *Child Development,* 1978, *49,* 178–187.

Miller, G. A. The magical number seven, plus or minus two: Some limits on our capacity for processing information. *Psychological Review,* 1956, *63,* 81–97.

Miller, G. A. *Psychology: The science of mental life.* New York: Harper & Row, 1962.

Miller, W. S. *Manual of the Miller Analogies Test.* New York: The Psychological Corporation, 1960.

Mistler-Lachman, J. L. Queer sentences, ambiguity, and levels of processing. *Memory & Cognition,* 1975, *3,* 395–400.

Moely, B. E. Organizational factors in the development of memory. In R. V. Kail, Jr., & J. W. Hagen (Eds.), *Perspectives on the development of memory and cognition.* Hillsdale, N.J.: Erlbaum, 1977.

Moely, B. E., Olson, F. A., Halwes, T. G., & Flavell, J. H. Production deficiency in young children's clustered recall. *Developmental Psychology,* 1969, *1,* 26–34.

Moray, N. Attention in dichotic listening: Affective cues and the influence of instructions. *Quarterly Journal of Experimental Psychology,* 1959, *11,* 56–60.

Moray, N. *Listening and attention.* Baltimore: Penguin Books, 1969.

Morris, P. E. Sense and nonsense in traditional mnemonics. In M. M. Gruneberg, P. E. Morris, & R. N. Sykes (Eds.), *Practical aspects of memory.* London: Academic Press, 1978.

Morrison, J. K. Successful grieving: Changing personal constructs through mental imagery. *Journal of Mental Imagery,* 1978, *2,* 63–68.

Moscovitch, M., & Craik, F. I. M. Depth of processing, retrieval cues, and uniqueness of encoding as factors in recall. *Journal of Verbal Learning and Verbal Behavior,* 1976, *15,* 447–458.

Mosher, F. A., & Hornsby, J. R. On asking questions. In J. S. Bruner, R. R. Oliver, & P. M. Greenfield (Eds.), *Studies in cognitive growth.* New York: Wiley, 1966.

Moskowitz, B. A. The acquisition of language. *Scientific American,* 1978, *239,* 92–108.

Moyer, R. S. Comparing objects in memory: Evidence suggesting an internal psychophysics. *Perception & Psychophysics,* 1973, *13,* 180–184.

Moyer, R. S., & Dumais, S. T. Mental comparisons. In G. H. Bower (Ed.), *The psychology of learning and motivation* (Vol. 12). New York: Academic Press, 1978.

Murray, F. B. Teaching strategies and conservation training. In A. M. Lesgold, J. W. Pellegrino, S. D. Fokkema, & R. Glaser (Eds.), *Cognitive psychology and instruction.* New York: Plenum, 1977.

Murray, H. A. Vicissitudes of creativity. In H. H. Anderson (Ed.), *Creativity and its cultivation.* New York: Harper & Row, 1959.

Myers, N. A., & Perlmutter, M. Memory in the years from two to five. In P. A. Ornstein (Ed.), *Memory development in children.* Hillsdale, N.J.: Erlbaum, 1978.

Mynatt, C. R., Doherty, M. E., & Tweney, R. D. Confirmation bias in a simulated research environment: An experimental study of scientific inference. In P. N. Johnson-Laird & P. C. Wason (Eds.), *Thinking: Readings in cognitive science.* New York: Cambridge University Press, 1977.

Neisser, U. *Cognitive psychology.* New York: Appleton, 1967.

Neisser, U. *Cognition and reality.* San Francisco: Freeman, 1976.

Neisser, U. Memory: What are the important questions? In M. M. Gruneberg, P. E. Morris, & R. N. Sykes (Eds.), *Practical aspects of memory.* London: Academic Press, 1978.

Neisser, U., & Becklen, R. Selective looking: Attending to visually significant events. *Cognitive Psychology,* 1975, *7,* 480–494.

Nelson, K. Structure and strategy in learning to talk. *Monographs of the Society for Research in Child Development,* 1973, *38* (Serial No. 149).

Nelson, K. Semantic development and the development of semantic memory. In K. E. Nelson (Ed.), *Children's language* (Vol. 1). New York: Gardner, 1978.

Newell, A., Shaw, J. C., & Simon, H. A. The process of creative thinking. In H. E. Gruber, G. Terrell, & M. Wertheimer (Eds.), *Contemporary approaches to creative thinking.* New York: Atherton, 1963.

Newell, A., & Simon, H. A. *Human problem solving.* Englewood Cliffs, N.J.: Prentice-Hall, 1972.

Newport, E. L., & Bellugi, U. Linguistic expression of category levels in a visual-gestural language: A flower is a flower is a flower. In E. Rosch & B. Lloyd (Eds.), *Cognition and categorization.* Hillsdale, N.J.: Erlbaum, 1978.

Nisbett, R. E., Borgida, E., Crandall, R., & Reed, H. Popular induction: Information is not always informative. In J. S. Carroll & J. W. Payne (Eds.), *Cognition and social behavior.* Hillsdale, N.J.: Erlbaum, 1976.

Nisbett, R. E., & Ross, L. *Human inference: Strategies and shortcomings of social judgment.* Englewood Cliffs, N.J.: Prentice-Hall, 1980.

Nisbett, R. E., & Wilson, T. D. Telling more than we can know. Verbal reports on mental processes. *Psychological Review,* 1977, *84,* 231–259. (a)

Nisbett, R. E., & Wilson, T. D. The halo effect: Evidence for unconscious alteration of judgments. *Journal of Personality and Social Psychology,* 1977, *35,* 250–256. (b)

Norman, D. A., & Bobrow, D. G. On data-limited and resource-limited processes. *Cognitive Psychology,* 1975, *7,* 44–64.

Norman, D. A., & Rumelhart, D. E. *Explorations in cognition.* San Francisco: Freeman, 1975.

Notes and Comments. *The New Yorker,* August 6, 1979, p. 23.

Novaco, R. W. Anger and coping with stress: Cognitive behavioral interventions. In J. P. Foreyt & D. P. Rathjen (Eds.), *Cognitive behavior therapy.* New York: Plenum, 1978.

Okonji, M. O. A cross-cultural study of the effects of familiarity on classificatory behavior. *Journal of Cross-Cultural Psychology,* 1971, *2,* 39–49.

Olson, C. L. Some apparent violations of the representativeness heuristic. *Journal of Experimental Psychology: Human Perception and Performance,* 1976, *2,* 599–608.

Olson, G. M. An information processing analysis of visual memory and habituation in infants. In T. Tighe & R. Leaton (Eds.), *Habituation: Perspectives from child development, animal behavior, and neurophysiology.* Hillsdale, N.J.: Erlbaum, 1976.

Olson, R. W. *The art of creative thinking: A practical guide.* New York: Harper & Row, 1978.

Orasanu, J., Slater, M. K., & Adler, L. L. *Language, sex, and gender: Does "la différence" make a difference? Annals of the New York Academy of Sciences,* Vol. 327. New York: Academy of Sciences, 1979.

Orwell, G. Politics and the English language. In G. Orwell (Ed.), *Shooting an elephant and other essays.* New York: Harcourt, 1945.

Osborn, A. *Applied imagination.* New York: Charles Scribner's Sons, 1957.

Ozier, M. Individual differences in free recall: When some people remember better than others. In G. H. Bower (Ed.), *The psychology of learning and motivation* (Vol. 14). New York: Academic Press, 1980.

Paap, K. R., & Ogden, W. C. Letter encoding is an obligatory but capacity-demanding operation. *Journal of Experimental Psychology: Human Perception and Performance,* 1981, *7,* 518–527.

Paivio, A. Abstractness, imagery, and meaningfulness in paired-associate learning. *Journal of Verbal Learning and Verbal Behavior,* 1965, *4,* 32–38.

Paivio, A. A factor-analytic study of word attributes and verbal learning. *Journal of Verbal Learning and Verbal Behavior,* 1968, *7,* 41–49.

Paivio, A. Mental imagery in associative learning and memory. *Psychological Review,* 1969, *76,* 241–263.

Paivio, A. On exploring visual knowledge. In B. S. Randhawa and W. E. Coffman (Eds.), *Visual learning, thinking, and communication,* New York: Academic Press, 1978. (a)

Paivio, A. Comparisons of mental clocks. *Journal of Experimental Psychology: Human Perception and Performance,* 1978, *4,* 61−71. (b)

Paivio, A. *Imagery and verbal processes.* Hillsdale, N.J.: Erlbaum, 1979.

Palmer, S. E. Visual perception and world knowledge: Notes on a model of sensory-cognitive interaction. In D. A. Norman & D. E. Rumelhart (Eds.), *Explorations in cognition.* San Francisco: Freeman, 1975. (a)

Palmer, S. E. The effects of contextual scenes on the identification of objects. *Memory & Cognition,* 1975, *3,* 519−526. (b)

Pantell, R. H., Naber, M., Lamar, R., & Dias, J. K. Fever in the first six months of life. *Clinical Pediatrics,* 1980, *19,* 77−82.

Paris, S. G., & Lindauer, B. K. Constructive aspects of children's comprehension and memory. In R. V. Kail, Jr. & J. W. Hagen (Eds.), *Perspectives on the development of memory and cognition.* Hillsdale, N.J.: Erlbaum, 1977.

Patten, B. M. The ancient art of memory. *CMD,* 1972, *39,* 547−554.

Penfield, W. Consciousness, memory, and man's conditioned reflexes. In K. Pribram (Ed.), *On the biology of learning.* New York: Harcourt, 1969.

Perlmutter, M. Age differences in adults' free recall, cued recall, and recognition. *Journal of Gerontology,* 1979, *34,* 533−539.

Peterson, L. R. Verbal learning and memory. *Annual Review of Psychology,* 1977, *28,* 393−415.

Peterson, L. R., & Peterson, M. J. Short-term retention of individual verbal items. *Journal of Experimental Psychology,* 1959, *58,* 193−198.

Piaget, J. Piaget's theory. In P. H. Mussen (Ed.), *Carmichael's manual of child psychology* (Vol. 1). New York: Wiley, 1970.

Pick, A. D. Cognition: Psychological perspectives. In H. C. Triandis & W. Lonner (Eds.), *Handbook of cross-cultural psychology* (Vol. 3). Boston: Allyn and Bacon, 1980.

Pisoni, D. B. Speech perception. In W. K. Estes (Ed.), *Handbook of learning and cognitive processes.* Hillsdale, N.J.: Erlbaum, 1978.

Poon, L. W., Walsh-Sweeney, L., & Fozard, J. L. Memory skill training for the elderly: Salient issues on the use of imagery mnemonics. In L. W. Poon, J. L. Fozard, L. S. Cermak, D. Arenberg, & L. W. Thompson (Eds.), *New directions in memory and aging.* Hillsdale, N.J.: Erlbaum, 1980.

Posner, M. I., Goldsmith, R., & Welton, K. E., Jr. Perceived distance and the classification of distorted patterns. *Journal of Experimental Psychology,* 1967, *73,* 28−38.

Posner, M. I., & Keele, S. W. Decay of visual information from a single letter. *Science,* 1967, *158,* 137−139.

Posner, M. I., & Snyder, C. R. R. Attention and cognitive control. In R. Solso (Ed.), *Information processing and cognition: The Loyola Symposium.* Hillsdale, N.J.: Erlbaum, 1975.

Postman, L. Verbal learning and memory. *Annual Review of Psychology,* 1975, *26,* 291−335.

Postman, L., & Underwood, B. J. Critical issues in interference theory. *Memory & Cognition,* 1973, *1,* 19−40.

Potts, G. R. Information processing strategies used in the encoding of linear orderings. *Journal of Verbal Learning and Verbal Behavior,* 1972, *11,* 727−740.

Potts, G. R. Bringing order to cognitive structures. In F. Restle, R. M. Shiffrin, N. J. Castellan, H. R. Lindman, & D. B. Pisoni (Eds.), *Cognitive theory* (Vol. 1). Hillsdale, N.J.: Erlbaum, 1975.

Potts, G. R. The role of inference in memory for real and artificial information. In R. Revlin & R. E. Mayer (Eds.), *Human reasoning.* Washington, D.C.: V. H. Winston & Sons, 1978.

Premack, D. On the abstractness of human concepts: Why it would be difficult to talk to a pigeon. In S. H. Hulse, H. Fowler, & W. K. Honig (Eds.), *Cognitive processes in animal behavior,* Hillsdale, N.J.: Erlbaum, 1978.

Prytulak, L. S. Natural language mediation. *Cognitive Psychology,* 1971, *2,* 1−56.

Pylyshyn, Z. W. What the mind's eye tells the mind's brain: A critique of mental imagery. *Psychological Bulletin,* 1973, *80,* 1–24.

Pylyshyn, Z. W. Imagery and artificial intelligence. In C. W. Savage (Ed.), *Perception and cognition issues in the foundations of psychology* (Minnesota studies in the philosophy of science, Vol. 9). Minneapolis: University of Minnesota Press, 1978.

Quattrone, G. A., & Jones, E. E. The perception of variability within in-groups and out-groups: Implications for the law of small numbers. *Journal of Personality and Social Psychology,* 1980, *38,* 141–152.

Rabbitt, P. Changes in problem solving ability in old age. In J. E. Birren & K. W. Schaie (Eds.), *Handbook of the psychology of aging.* New York: Van Nostrand Reinhold, 1977.

Rabinowitz, J. C., Mandler, G., & Patterson, K. E. Determinants of recognition and recall: Accessibility and generation. *Journal of Experimental Psychology: General,* 1977, *106,* 302–329.

Rayner, K. Eye movements in reading and information processing. *Psychological Bulletin,* 1978, *85,* 618–660.

Reed, S. K. Pattern recognition and categorization. *Cognitive Psychology,* 1972, *3,* 383–407.

Reed, S. K. Structural descriptions and the limitations of visual images. *Memory & Cognition,* 1974, *2,* 329–336.

Reed, S. K. Facilitation of problem solving. In N. J. Castellan, Jr., D. B. Pisoni, & G. R. Potts (Eds.), *Cognitive theory* (Vol. 2). Hillsdale, N.J.: Erlbaum, 1977.

Reed, S. K., & Johnsen, J. A. Detection of parts in patterns and images. *Memory & Cognition,* 1975, *3,* 569–575.

Reese, H. W. Imagery and associative memory. In R. V. Kail & J. W. Hagen (Eds.), *Perspectives on the development of memory and cognition.* Hillsdale, N.J.: Erlbaum, 1977.

Reicher, G. M. Perceptual recognition as a function of meaningfulness of stimuli material. *Journal of Experimental Psychology,* 1969, *81,* 275–280.

Reid, D. K., & Hrensko, W. P. *A cognitive approach to learning disabilities.* New York: McGraw-Hill, 1981.

Reitman, J. S. Without surreptitious rehearsal, information in short-term memory decays. *Journal of Verbal Learning and Verbal Behavior,* 1974, *13,* 365–377.

Reitman, W. R. Heuristic decision procedures, open constraints, and the structure of ill-defined problems. In M. W. Shelley & G. L. Bryan (Eds.), *Human judgments and optimality.* New York: Wiley, 1964.

Reitman, W. R. *Cognition and thought: An information processing approach.* New York: Wiley, 1965.

Resnick, L. B., & Weaver, P. A. *Theory and practice of early reading* (Vols. 1, 2, and 3). Hillsdale, N.J.: Erlbaum, 1979.

Revlin, R. *Representation and set size in syllogistic reasoning.* Paper presented at the annual meeting of the Psychonomic Society, 1973.

Reyes, R. M., Thompson, W. C., & Bower, G. H. Judgmental biases resulting from differing availabilities of arguments. *Journal of Personality and Social Psychology,* 1980, *39,* 2–12.

Richardson, J. T. E. Reported mediators and individual differences in mental imagery. *Memory & Cognition,* 1978, *6,* 376–378.

Richardson, J. T. E. *Mental imagery and human memory.* London: Macmillan, 1980.

Rickett, M. W. *Wild flowers of the United States.* New York: McGraw-Hill, 1966.

Rips, L. J., Shoben, E. J., & Smith, E. E. Semantic distance and the verification of semantic relations. *Journal of Verbal Learning and Verbal Behavior,* 1973, *12,* 1–20.

Robertson-Tchabo, E. A. Cognitive-skill training for the elderly: Why should "old dogs" acquire new tricks? In L. W. Poon, J. L. Fozard, L. S. Cermak, D. Arenberg, & L. W. Thompson (Eds.), *New directions in memory and aging.* Hillsdale, N.J.: Erlbaum, 1980.

Rock, M. A. Keyboard symbols enable retarded children to "speak." *Smithsonian,* 1979, *10,* 90–96.

Roediger, H. L., III. Levels of processing: Criticism and development. (Review of *Levels of processing in human memory*, L. S. Cermak & F. I. M. Craik, Eds.). *Contemporary Psychology*, 1980, *25*, 20−21.

Rogers, T. B., Kuiper, N. A., & Kirker, W. S. Self-reference and the encoding of personal information. *Journal of Personality and Social Psychology*, 1977, *35*, 677−688.

Rosch, E. Principles of categorization. In E. Rosch & B. Lloyd (Eds.), *Cognition and categorization*. Hillsdale, N.J.: Erlbaum, 1978.

Rosch, E. H. Natural categories. *Cognitive Psychology*, 1973, *4*, 328−350.

Rosch, E. H. Cognitive reference points. *Cognitive Psychology*, 1975, *7*, 532−547. (a)

Rosch, E. H. The nature of mental codes for color categories. *Journal of Experimental Psychology: Human Perception and Performance*, 1975, *1*, 303−322. (b)

Rosch, E. H. Cognitive representations of semantic categories. *Journal of Experimental Psychology: General*, 1975, *104*, 192−233. (c)

Rosch, E. H. Human categorization. In N. Warren (Ed.), *Advances in cross-cultural psychology* (Vol. 1). London: Academic Press, 1977.

Rosch, E. H., & Mervis, C. B. Family resemblances: Studies in the internal structure of categories. *Cognitive Psychology*, 1975, *7*, 573−605.

Rosch, E. H., Mervis, C. B., Gray, W. D., Johnson, D. M., & Boyes-Braem, P. Basic objects in natural categories. *Cognitive Psychology*, 1976, *8*, 382−439.

Ross, B. M., & Millsom, C. Repeated memory of oral prose in Ghana and New York. *International Journal of Psychology*, 1970, *5*, 173−181.

Ross, M., & Sicoly, F. Egocentric biases in availability and attribution. *Journal of Personality and Social Psychology*, 1979, *37*, 322−336.

Rothbart, M., Fulero, S., Jensen, C., Howard, J., & Birrell, B. From individual to group impressions: Availability heuristics in stereotype formation. *Journal of Experimental Social Psychology*, 1978, *14*, 237−255.

Rubin, D. C. Very long-term memory for prose and verse. *Journal of Verbal Learning and Verbal Behavior*, 1977, *16*, 611−621.

Rubin, D. C., & Olson, M. J. Recall of semantic domains. *Memory & Cognition*, 1980, *8*, 354−366.

Rumelhart, D. E. Notes on a schema for stories. In D. G. Bobrow & A. Collins (Eds.), *Representation and understanding: Studies in cognitive science*. New York: Academic Press, 1975.

Rumelhart, D. E., & Abrahamson, A. A. A model for analogical reasoning. *Cognitive Psychology*, 1973, *5*, 1−28.

Rundus, D., & Atkinson, R. C. Rehearsal processes in free recall: A procedure for direct observation. *Journal of Verbal Learning and Verbal Behavior*, 1970, *9*, 99−105.

Russo, J. E., Krieser, G., & Miyashita, S. An effective display of unit price information. *Journal of Marketing*, 1975, *39*, 11−19.

Saarinen, T. F. The use of projective techniques in geographic research. In W. H. Ittelson (Ed.), *Environment and cognition*. New York: Seminar Press, 1973.

Sachs, J. Recognition memory for syntactic and semantic aspects of a connected discourse. *Perception & Psychophysics*, 1967, *2*, 437−442.

Safire, W. "I led the pigeons to the flag." *The New York Times Magazine*, May 27, 1979, 9−10.

Sakitt, B. Iconic memory. *Psychological Review*, 1976, *83*, 257−276.

Sampson, E. E. Cognitive psychology as ideology. *American Psychologist*, 1981, *36*, 730−743.

Scandura, J. M. *Problem solving: A structural/process approach with instructional implications*. New York: Academic Press, 1977.

Schank, R., & Abelson, R. *Scripts, plans, goals, and understanding*. Hillsdale, N.J.: Erlbaum, 1977.

Schegloff, E. A. Sequencing in conversational openings. *American Anthropologist*, 1968, *70*, 1075−1095.

Schneider, W., & Shiffrin, R. M. Controlled and automatic human information processing: I. Detection, search, and attention. *Psychological Review*, 1977, *84*, 1−66.

Schonfield, D., & Robertson, B. A. Memory storage and aging. *Canadian Journal of Psychology,* 1966, *20,* 228–236.

Schwartz, S. H. Modes of representation and problem solving: Well evolved is half solved. *Journal of Experimental Psychology,* 1971, *91,* 347–350.

Segal, S. J., & Fusella, V. Influence of imaged pictures and sounds on detection of visual and auditory signals. *Journal of Experimental Psychology,* 1970, *83,* 458–464.

Shaffer, L. H. Multiple attention in continuous verbal tasks. In P. M. Rabbitt & S. Dornic (Eds.), *Attention and performance* (Vol. 5). London: Academic Press, 1975.

Shatz, M., & Gelman, R. The development of communication skills: Modifications in the speech of young children as a function of listener. *Monographs of the Society for Research in Child Development,* 1973, *38*(2, Serial No. 152).

Shepard, R. N. Recognition memory for words, sentences and pictures. *Journal of Verbal Learning and Verbal Behavior,* 1967, *6,* 156–163.

Shepard, R. N. Externalization of mental images and the act of creation. In B. S. Randhawa & W. E. Coffman (Eds.), *Visual learning, thinking, and communication.* New York: Academic Press, 1978.

Shepard, R. N., & Chipman, S. Second-order isomorphism of internal representations: Shapes of states. *Cognitive Psychology,* 1970, *1,* 1–17.

Shepard, R. N., & Metzler, J. Mental rotation of three-dimensional objects. *Science,* 1971, *171,* 701–703.

Sherman, J. A. *Sex-related cognitive differences.* Springfield, Ill.: Charles C Thomas, 1978.

Sherman, M. A. Adjectival negation and the comprehension of multiply negated sentences. *Journal of Verbal Learning and Verbal Behavior,* 1976, *15,* 143–157.

Shrauger, J. S. Self-esteem and reactions to being observed by others. *Journal of Personality and Social Psychology,* 1972, *23,* 192–200.

Shulman, H. G. Similarity effects in short-term memory. *Psychological Bulletin,* 1971, *75,* 399–415.

Shulman, H. G. Semantic confusion errors in short-term memory. *Journal of Verbal Learning and Verbal Behavior,* 1972, *11,* 221–227.

Simon, H. The structure of ill-structured problems. *Artificial Intelligence,* 1973, *4,* 181–201.

Simon, H. How big is a chunk? *Science,* 1974, *183,* 482–488.

Simon, H. A., & Hayes, J. R. Understanding complex task instructions. In D. Klahr (Ed.), *Cognition and instruction.* Hillsdale, N.J.: Erlbaum, 1976. (a)

Simon, H. A., & Hayes, J. R. The understanding process: Problem isomorphs. *Cognitive Psychology,* 1976, *8,* 165–190. (b)

Slobin, D. I. *Psycholinguistics* (2d ed.). Glenview, Ill.: Scott, Foresman, 1979.

Slovic, P., & Fischhoff, B. On the psychology of experimental surprises. *Journal of Experimental Psychology: Human Perception and Performance,* 1977, *3,* 544–551.

Slovic, P., Fischhoff, B., & Lichtenstein, S. Cognitive processes and societal risk taking. In J. S. Carroll & J. W. Payne (Eds.), *Cognition and social behavior.* Hillsdale, N.J.: Erlbaum, 1976.

Slovic, P., Fischhoff, B., & Lichtenstein, S. Behavioral decision theory. *Annual Review of Psychology,* 1977, *28,* 1–39.

Slovic, P., Fischhoff, B., & Lichtenstein, S. Rating the risks. *Environment,* 1979, *21,* 14–39.

Slovic, P., Kunreuther, H., & White, G. F. Decision processes, rationality and adjustment to natural hazards. In G. F. White (Ed.), *Natural hazards, local, national and global.* New York: Oxford University Press, 1974.

Slovic, P., & Lichtenstein, S. Comparison of Bayesian and regression approaches to the study of information processing in judgment. *Journal of Organizational Behavior and Human Performance,* 1971, *6,* 649–744.

Smith, A. D. Age differences in encoding, storage, and retrieval. In L. W. Poon, J. L. Fozard, L. S. Cermak, D. Arenberg, & L. W. Thompson (Eds.), *New directions in memory and aging.* Hillsdale, N.J.: Erlbaum, 1980.

Smith, A. G. *Cognitive styles in law schools.* Austin: University of Texas Press, 1979.

Smith, E. E. Theories of semantic memory. In W. K. Estes (Ed.), *Handbook of learning and cognitive processes* (Vol. 6). Hillsdale, N.J.: Erlbaum, 1978.

Smith, E. E., Shoben, E. J., & Rips, L. J. Structure and process in semantic memory: A featural model for semantic decisions. *Psychological Review,* 1974, *81,* 214–241.

Smith, E. R., & Miller, F. D. Limits on perception of cognitive processes: A reply to Nisbett and Wilson. *Psychological Review,* 1978, *85,* 355–362.

Smith, F. *Understanding reading.* New York: Holt, Rinehart and Winston, 1971.

Smith, S. M., Glenberg, A., & Bjork, R. A. Environmental context and human memory. *Memory & Cognition,* 1978, *6,* 342–353.

Smoke, K. L. An objective study of concept formation. *Psychological Monographs,* 1932, *42*(4, Whole No. 191).

Sokal, R. R. Classification: Purposes, principles, progress, prospects. In P. N. Johnson-Laird & P. C. Wason (Eds.), *Thinking: Readings in cognitive science.* Cambridge: Cambridge University Press, 1977.

Solman, R. T., May, J. G., & Schwartz, B. D. The word superiority effect: A study using parts of letters. *Journal of Experimental Psychology: Human Perception and Performance,* 1981, *7,* 552–559.

Sommer, R. *The mind's eye: Imagery in everyday life.* New York: Delacorte. 1978.

Spelke, E., Hirst, W., & Neisser, U. Skills of divided attention. *Cognition,* 1976, *4,* 215–230.

Sperling, G. The information available in brief visual presentations. *Psychological Monographs,* 1960, *74,* 1–29.

Standing, L. Learning 10,000 pictures. *Quarterly Journal of Experimental Psychology,* 1973, *25,* 207–222.

Standing, L., Conezio, J., & Haber, R. N. Perception and memory for pictures: Single-trial learning of 2560 visual stimuli. *Psychonomic Science,* 1970, 19, 73–74.

Stanovich, K. E., & West, R. F. The effect of sentence context on ongoing word recognition: Tests of a two-process theory. *Journal of Experimental Psychology: Human Perception and Performance,* 1981. *7,* 658–672.

Steger, J. C. Cognitive behavioral strategies in the treatment of sexual problems. In J. P. Foreyt & D. P. Rathjen (Eds.), *Cognitive behavior therapy.* New York: Plenum, 1978.

Stein, M. I. A transactional approach to creativity. In C. W. Taylor (Ed.), *The 1955 University of Utah Research Conference on the Identification of Creative Scientific Talent.* Salt Lake City: University of Utah Press, 1956.

Sternberg, R. J. *How to prepare for the Miller Analogies Test.* Woodbury, N.Y.: Barron's Educational Series, 1974.

Sternberg, R. J. *Intelligence, information processing, and analogical reasoning.* Hillsdale, N.J.: Erlbaum, 1977.

Svartik, J. *On voice in the English verb.* The Hague: Mouton, 1966.

Taplin, J. E. Reasoning with conditional sentences. *Journal of Verbal Learning and Verbal Behavior,* 1971, *10,* 219–225.

Taylor, I. A. A retrospective view of creativity investigation. In I. A. Taylor & J. W. Getzels (Eds.), *Perspectives in creativity.* Chicago: Aldine, 1975.

Teger, A. I. *Too much invested to quit: The psychology of the escalation of conflict.* New York: Pergamon, 1979.

Terrace, H. *Nim: A chimpanzee who learned sign language.* New York: Knopf, 1979.

Tesch, S., Whitbourne, S. K., & Nehrke, M. F. Cognitive egocentrism in institutionalized adult males. *Journal of Gerontology,* 1978, *33,* 546–552.

Tetlock, P. E. Identifying victims of groupthink from public statements of decision makers. *Journal of Personality and Social Psychology,* 1979, *37,* 1314–1324.

Thomas, E. L. Eye movements in speed reading. In R. G. Stauffer (Ed.), *Speed reading: Practices and procedures* (Vol. 10). Newark, Del.: University of Delaware, Reading Study Center, 1962, 104–114.

Thomas, E. L., & Robinson, H. A. *Improving reading in every class: A sourcebook for teachers.* Boston: Allyn and Bacon, 1972.

Thompson, J. G., Cornell, J. H., & Kirkpatrick, C. The role of pre-experimental set in adult concept formation. *Journal of General Psychology,* 1980, *102,* 167–174.

Tobias, S. *Overcoming math anxiety.* New York: Norton, 1978.

Trabasso, T. R. Stimulus emphasis and all-or-none learning in concept identification. *Journal of Experimental Psychology,* 1963, *65,* 398–406.

Trabasso, T. R., Riley, C. A., & Wilson, E. G. The representation of linear order and spatial strategies in reasoning: A developmental study. In R. J. Falmagne (Ed.), *Reasoning: Representation and process in children and adults.* Hillsdale, N.J.: Erlbaum, 1975.

Treisman, A. M. Contextual cues in selective listening. *Quarterly Journal of Experimental Psychology,* 1960, *12,* 242–248.

Treisman, A. M. Monitoring and storage of irrelevant messages and selective attention. *Journal of Verbal Learning and Verbal Behavior,* 1964, *3,* 449–459.

Trillin, C. *Runestruck.* Boston: Little, Brown, 1977.

Trillin, C. *Alice, let's eat: Further adventures of a happy eater.* New York: Random House, 1978.

Tulving, E. Subjective organization in free-recall of "unrelated" words. *Psychological Review,* 1962, *69,* 344–354.

Tulving, E. Episodic and semantic memory. In E. Tulving & W. Donaldson (Eds.), *Organization of memory.* New York: Academic Press, 1972.

Tulving, E., & Pearlstone, Z. Availability versus accessibility of information in memory for words. *Journal of Verbal Learning and Verbal Behavior,* 1966, *5,* 381–391.

Tulving, E., & Thomson, D. M. Encoding specificity and retrieval processes in episodic memory. *Psychological Review,* 1973, *80,* 352–373.

Tversky, A., & Kahneman, D. Belief in the law of small numbers. *Psychological Bulletin,* 1971, *76,* 105–110.

Tversky, A., & Kahneman, D. Availability: A heuristic for judging frequency and probability. *Cognitive Psychology,* 1973, *5,* 207–232.

Tversky, A., & Kahneman, D. Judgments under uncertainty: Heuristics and biases. *Science,* 1974, *185,* 1124–1131.

Tylor, E. B. *Primitive culture* (Vol. 1). Reprinted 1971. London: J. Murray, 1929.

Underwood, B. J., Boruch, R. F., & Malmi, R. A. Composition of episodic memory. *Journal of Experimental Psychology: General,* 1978, *107,* 393–419.

Wagner, D. A. Culture and mnemonics. In N. M. Gruneberg, P. E. Morris, & R. N. Sykes (Eds.), *Practical aspects of memory.* London: Academic Press, 1978.

Wainer, H., Zill, N., & Gruvaeus, G. Senatorial decision making: II. Prediction. *Behavioral Science,* 1973, *18,* 20–26.

Walsh, D. A., & Thompson, L. W. Age differences in visual sensory memory. *Journal of Gerontology,* 1978, *33,* 383–387.

Ward, W. C. Convergent and divergent measurement of creativity in children. *Educational Psychology Measurement,* 1975, *35,* 87–95.

Wardlaw, K. A., & Kroll, N. E. A. Autonomic responses to shock-associated words in a non-attended message: A failure to replicate. *Journal of Experimental Psychology: Human Perception and Performance,* 1976, *2,* 357–360.

Warren, R. M. Perceptual restoration of missing speech sounds. *Science,* 1970, *167,* 392–393.

Warren, R. M., & Warren, R. P. Auditory illusions and confusions. *Scientific American,* 1970, *223,* 30–36.

Wason, P. C. On the failure to eliminate hypotheses—A second look. In P. C. Wason & P. N. Johnson-Laird (Eds.), *Thinking and reasoning.* Baltimore: Penguin Books, 1968.

Wason, P. C., & Johnson-Laird, P. N. *Psychology of reasoning: Structure and content.* Cambridge, Mass.: Harvard University Press, 1972.

Watson, J. B. *Behaviorism.* Chicago: University of Chicago Press, 1924.

Webber, S. M., & Marshall, P. H. Bizarreness effects in imagery as a function of processing level and delay. *Journal of Mental Imagery,* 1978, *2,* 291–300.

Wechsler, D. A standardized memory scale for clinical use. *Journal of Psychology,* 1945, *19,* 87–95.

Weinstein, C. E., Duffy, M., Underwood, V. L., & MacDonald, J. E. *Whose learning strategies deficit . . . the elderly's or the researcher's?* Paper presented at the annual meeting of the American Psychological Association, New York, 1979.

Weisberg, R., & Suls, J. M. An information-processing model of Duncker's candle problem.

Cognitive Psychology, 1973, *4,* 255–276.

Weisstein, N., & Harris, C. S. Visual detection of line segments: An object-superiority effect. *Science,* 1974, *186,* 752–755.

Weizenbaum, J. ELIZA—A computer program for the study of natural language communication between man and machine. *Communications of the Association for Computing Machinery,* 1966, *9,* 36–43.

Welford, A. T. Memory and age: A perspective view. In L. W. Poon, J. L. Fozard, L. S. Cermak, D. Arenberg, & L. W. Thompson (Eds.), *New directions in memory and aging.* Hillsdale, N.J.: Erlbaum, 1980.

Werner, J. S., & Perlmutter, M. Development of visual memory in infants. In H. W. Reese & L. P. Lipsitt (Eds.), *Advances in child development and behavior* (Vol. 14). New York: Academic Press, 1979.

Werner, J. S., & Siqueland, E. R. Visual recognition memory in the preterm infant. *Infant Behavior and Development,* 1978, *1,* 79–94.

Wheeler, D. Processes in word recognition. *Cognitive Psychology,* 1970, *1,* 59–85.

Whitbourne, S. K., & Weinstock, C. S. *Adult development: The differentiation of experience.* New York: Holt, Rinehart and Winston, 1979.

Whorf, B. L. Science and linguistics. In J. B. Carroll (Ed.), *Language, thought and reality: Selected writings of Benjamin Lee Whorf.* Cambridge, Mass.: MIT Press, 1956.

Wickelgren, W. A. Acoustic similarity and intrusion errors in short-term memory. *Journal of Experimental Psychology,* 1965, *70,* 102–108.

Wickelgren, W. A. The long and the short of memory. *Psychological Bulletin,* 1973, *80,* 425–438.

Wickens, D. D., Dalezman, R. E., & Eggemeier, F. T. Multiple encoding of word attributes in memory. *Memory & Cognition,* 1976, *4,* 307–310.

Williams, A., & Weisstein, N. Line segments are perceived better in a coherent context than alone: On object-line effect in visual perception. *Memory & Cognition,* 1978, *62,* 85–90.

Williams, J. I., Cram, D. M., Tausig, F. T., & Webster, E. Relative effects of drugs and diet on hyperactive behaviors: An experimental study. *Pediatrics,* 1978, *61,* 811–934.

Wilson, T. D., & Nisbett, R. E. The accuracy of verbal reports about the effects of stimuli on evaluations and behavior. *Social Psychology,* 1978, *41,* 118–131.

Winograd, E., & Simon, E. W. Visual memory and imagery in the aged. In L. W. Poon, J. L. Fozard, L. S. Cermak, D. Arenberg, & L. W. Thompson (Eds.), *New directions in memory and aging.* Hillsdale, N.J.: Erlbaum, 1980.

Winston, P. Learning to identify toy block structures. In R. L. Solso (Ed.), *Contemporary issues in cognitive psychology: The Loyola Symposium.* Washington, D.C.: V. H. Winston & Sons, 1973.

Witkin, H. A. Cognitive style in academic performance and in teacher-student relations. In S. Messick et al. (Eds.), *Individuality in learning.* San Francisco: Jossey-Bass, 1976.

Witkin, H. A., Moore, C. A., Goodenough, D. R., & Cox, P. W. Field-dependent and field-independent cognitive styles and their educational implications. *Review of Educational Research,* 1977, *47,* 1–64.

Wittgenstein, L. *Philosophical investigations.* New York: Macmillan, 1953.

Wittrock, M. C. Learning as a generative process. *Eduvational Psychologist,* 1974, *11,* 87–95.

Wollen, K. A., Weber, A., & Lowry, D. H. Bizarreness versus interaction of mental images as determinants of learning. *Cognitive Psychology,* 1972, *2,* 518–523.

Wood, G. The knew-it-all-along effect. *Journal of Experimental Psychology: Human Perception and Performance,* 1978, *4,* 345–353.

Woodward, A. E., Bjork, R. A., & Jongeward, R. H. Recall and recognition as a function of primary rehearsal. *Journal of Verbal Learning and Verbal Behavior,* 1973, *12,* 608–617.

World almanac & book of facts, 1981. New York: Newspaper Enterprise Association, 1981.

Yando, R., & Zigler, E. *Intellectual and personality characteristics of children.* New York: Halsted Press, 1979.

Yarmey, D. A. *The psychology of eyewitness testimony.* New York: Free Press, 1979.

Yavuz, H. S., & Bousfield, W. A. Recall of connotative meaning. *Psychological Reports,* 1959, 319–320.

Young, M. N., & Gibson, W. B. *How to develop an exceptional memory.* North Hollywood, Calif.: Wilshire, 1974.

Yuille, J. C., & Catchpole, M. J. Imagery and children's associative learning. In A. M. Lesgold, J. W. Pellegrino, S. D. Fokkema, & R. Glaser (Eds.), *Cognitive psychology and instruction.* New York: Plenum, 1977.

Yussen, S. R., & Levy, V. M. Developmental changes in predicting one's own span of short-term memory. *Journal of Experimental Child Psychology,* 1975, *19,* 502–508.

Zajonc, R. B. Feeling and thinking: Preferences need no inferences. *American Psychologist,* 1980, *35,* 151–175.

Name Index

Subject Index

Note: This subject index includes all bold-faced terms.